Packaging the Presidency

Packaging the Presidency

A HISTORY AND CRITICISM OF PRESIDENTIAL CAMPAIGN ADVERTISING

Kathleen Hall Jamieson

New York   Oxford
OXFORD UNIVERSITY PRESS
1984

Copyright © 1984 by Kathleen Hall Jamieson

Library of Congress Cataloging in Publication Data

Jamieson, Kathleen Hall.
  Campaign advertising.

  Bibliography: p.
  Includes index.
  1. Presidents—United States—Election. 2. Adver-
tising, Political—United States. 3. United States—
Politics and government—1945–   . I. Title.
JK524.J36 1984   324.973′092   84-7134
ISBN 0-19-503504-6

Printing (last digit): 9 8 7 6 5 4 3 2 1

Printed in the United States of America

To my parents
Wayne and Katherine Hall

Preface

In 1968 Richard Nixon's media advisers allowed a relatively unknown journalist with little prior inside campaign experience to follow them around, see their reports, and write a best-selling and highly controversial book about their role in the presidential race. Both because the Nixon media people were the first to expose themselves so openly to reportorial scrutiny, and because the reporter himself was so unfamiliar with the inner workings of American campaigns, the book, *The Selling of the President,* tended to create the impression that what its author had found in the Nixon campaign was new to American politics or unique to the campaign he had examined. Neither was the case.

It was, of course, easy to elevate public concern about the power of political advertising. If there is one area of our lives in which we would like to believe that "what you see is what you get," it is in political elections, a fact reflected in a 1983 Harris Poll that reported that 84% of the American public favored a limit on the amount that could be spent on political ads, 82% condemned political ads as "too negative," and 79% worried that political ads were offering the electorate "packaged" candidates.

What an historical analysis reveals, however, is that from the country's first contested election, strategists have offered voters advertising that venerated their candidate and vilified his opponents. If one side did not offer the public a cultivated image of its candidate, the other side's caricatures would shape a voter's decision. So advertising provided the means of reaching a mass audience with the "truth" as the campaign saw it and with rebuttals of "untruths" by the other side. The advent of nonpartisan newspapers and then of broadcast news added a second reason for a means of communication controlled by the candidates. Only by use of advertising could candidates guarantee that their messages would be communicated in their most persuasive form to the electorate.

Underlying this book is the assumption that presidential campaigns can be viewed productively through the lens provided by their print, radio, and television advertising. Were the book to focus only on ads that aired, it would overlook such intriguing spots as the one scripted but unproduced promising that Reagan would negotiate arms limitations with the Soviets within his first 100 days as president. The book would bypass as well an ad that in 1964 allied Goldwater with the Ku Klux Klan and one that in 1956 magnified fears about a Nixon presidency. Both were scrapped after reaching final production. Were the book to limit itself to television spot advertising, it would have to ignore the most influential ad of 1960, Kennedy's repeatedly aired speech to the Houston ministers, as well as Nixon's decisive Checkers speech. If the book focused solely on television, it could not explain how JFK used print and radio to rally black voters in 1960 or how in 1976 Ford capitalized on Carter's revelation that he had "lusted in his heart." Were it to limit itself to national ads, it could not explain how Carter mobilized the South in 1976.

The book starts from the assumption that, like the rest of us, media consultants are persons of good will and human failings and as such are neither as innocent as their mothers believe nor as invidious as their doubters aver.

Because media strategists, like the rest of us, suffer from selective recall, the book tests their claims against those of their colleagues, and against the campaign memos they wrote in the heat of battle.

Although political advertising is the act that dares not speak its name in presidential memoirs, this book also draws evidence from the candidates' own recollections of how they came to win and lose. Finally, the book shamelessly mines the campaign reports of such fine journalists as Jules Witcover, Martin Schram, Elizabeth Drew, Theodore White, and Robert MacNeil.

Out of this sifting and winnowing comes a chronicle of the schemes and strategies presidential candidates and their ad executives have employed to sway the hearts and ballots of sometimes unsuspecting voters. Focusing on each presidential election from 1952 through 1980, it explains how presidential advertising came to be and what it has become, how candidates have shaped it and been shaped by it, what it has contributed, and the ways in which it has contaminated the political process.

The book reveals how one presidential contender counterfeited an image . . . how another bankrolled his own advertising while contending publicly that he was funded by small donors . . . how corporate America almost closed one party out of Madison Avenue . . . how a candidate's confidence in his own skills as an adman and campaign manager may have spelled his downfall . . . how an ad team was pressured to violate professional ethics . . . how one candidate's ads succeeded in part because they were dull while another's failed because the candidate could not master televised communication.

Interlaced throughout is an examination of the role that campaign finance and the changing laws that govern it have played in presidential campaigns. The book also asks what the advertising revealed and concealed about the persons who would be president. Finally, by setting contemporary presidential advertising in an historical context, dating from the country's first contested election, the book shows how the ways in which the presidency is packaged have changed and how they have remained the same.

Hyattsville, Maryland   K.H.J.
June 1984

Acknowledgments

For help in securing photos and facts about them I wish to thank Patricia A. Vance of *Broadcasting,* Mark Renovitch of the Franklin D. Roosevelt Library, Catharine Heinz of the Broadcast Pioneers Library and Herbert R. Collins, William L. Bird, Edith P. Mayo, and Joyce M. Goulait of the Smithsonian as well as Mary Ison of the Library of Congress. Herbert Collins, William Bird, and Murray Edelman also provided helpful readings of chapters. Jules Grieten of Bara Photographic Inc., made a copy of a rare photo; Mark E. Neely, Jr., director of the Louis A. Warren Lincoln Library and Museum provided a copy of the Cooper Union photo; and Dr. Edmund Sullivan assisted in tracking down an important handbill. Linda and Jim Cherry provided access to their collection of political memorabilia as did Claude and Sharon Rankin. Dwight Hall Sullivan and Rodney R. Lushwell tried valiantly to capture television's elusive images for this book. Irving Linkow developed many of the photos. My thanks to the three of them. Additionally, Robert Jamieson, John Wright, and David Harriman provided cabbages and kings.

The research assistants who sweated and swore in service of this book are Lynn Derbyshire, Maura Clancy, Dwight Sullivan, Rod Schwartz, Phil Wilbur, Lars Hafner, and Craig James. Seamus Neary carried the largest burden. For his unfailing competence and tenacity, omnipresent index cards, and good humor, I am especially grateful.

The staffs of the Truman, Eisenhower, JFK, LBJ, and Ford presidential libraries as well as of the Wisconsin and Minnesota Historical Societies and of the Denove collection at UCLA have provided service beyond the call of duty as have the reference librarians at the University of Maryland and at the Library of Congress. Anyone who writes about presidential advertising owes a special debt to Victoria Schuck who had the foresight to collect and preserve television's early presidential advertising.

Without the cooperation of the people listed on page xiii I could not have written this book. Thank you to them for sharing with me the story of their involvement in these campaigns.

I am grateful to Robert Cathcart, professor at Queens College and Sam Schoenbaum, professor at the University of Maryland for guiding *Packaging the Presidency* to Oxford and to Susan Rabiner, my editor, who championed the book, leashed its tangents, and excised its excesses. I would thank Rosemary Wellner, manuscript editor, at the length her sensitive and sensible editing deserves but were I to do so she would excise the praise on the grounds that this book already is too long.

For fourteen years the students in my classes in Television and Politics, Political Broadcasting, and Political Communication at the University of Maryland have contributed ideas and inspiration. I am indebted to them as I am to my colleagues Vicki Freimuth, Andy Wolvin, Charles Kauffman, Larry Lichty, Gene Weiss, and L. John Martin for their selflessness and sanity through it all.

Through bad times and better, Jane Blankenship at the University of Massachusetts, Rod Hart at the University of Texas, and Herb Simons at Temple University have been the sort of colleagues academics covet as has Karlyn Kohrs Campbell at the University of Kansas who red-lined non sequiturs and Latinisms and added information and insight to the work in progress and Tony Schwartz, a teacher's teacher and friend.

The University of Maryland generously provided research and writing time in the form of a Distinguished Scholar Teacher Award in 1981–82 and a Provost's Research Leave in fall 1983. I owe a great deal to Dean Robert Shoenberg, Provost Shirley Kenny, and my former department chair Thomas Aylward for making possible that much needed support.

Patrick and Robert Jamieson provided bicycle service to the copying center, supervision of the computer's printer, retrieval and return of library books, and peanut butter and jelly or tuna salad sandwiches; they were as quiet and thoughtful during "work hours" as any mother could reasonably ask; they limited to once a day their posing of the questions "Are you done yet?" and "Will you put our names in the book?" So, to Pat and Robert, "Yes," "Yes," and thank you. Thank you too to my sister Rita Hall for typing and care-taking and to my parents, to whom this book is dedicated, for providing the kind of support over the years that makes it possible for daughters also to be authors.

Any contribution this book makes to our understanding of presidential advertising reflects the collective wisdom of my sources, students, colleagues, editors and friends. For its flaws I alone am to blame.

I wish to acknowledge gratefully the assistance of the following individuals in the preparation of this book. Unless otherwise indicated, the persons listed were interviewed or responded to written queries between

January 1983 and February 1984. An * indicates that the statements attributed to them were made during presentations at a debriefing seminar at the University of Maryland. These seminars occurred in November 1972, 1976, and 1980 and in Fall 1983.

Roger Ailes
Maxwell Arnold
Earl Ashe
Doug Bailey
George Ball
Reggie Shuebel Ballard
Gabriel Bayz
William McCormick Blair, Jr.
Ken Boehm
*Vincent Breglio
Sam Brightman
Muriel Humphrey Brown
Richard Cheney
Elliott Curson
Peter Dailey
*Terry Dolan
Maxwell Dane
Richard Denove
Robert Finch
Clayton Fritchey
Frank Gannon
Cyrus Gardner
Leonard Garment
*Bob Goodman
Charles Guggenheim
Bernard Haber
Becky Hendrix
Beverly Ingram
Don Irwin
Michael Kaye
Denison Kitchel
Gene Kummel
Morris Leibman
Charles Lichenstein
Frank Mankiewicz
Edward McCabe
Eugene McCarthy
Joe McGinniss
George McGovern

Carl McGowan
Louis Martin
Bill Moyers
*Roger Mudd
Joseph Napolitan
Carroll Newton
William Novelli
Larry O'Brien
Vincent O'Brien
*Brad O'Leary
*Richard T. O'Reilly
Don Oberdorfer
William Oldacker
Jeno Paulucci
Ray Price
Gerald Rafshoon
Estelle Ramey
Leonard Reinsch
Ted Rogers
*Greg Schneiders
Reenah Schwartz
Tony Schwartz
Donald Segretti
Frank Shakespeare
Craig Shirley
Bob Shrum
Ted Sorensen
Tim Smith
Philip Stern
Bob Squier
Bill Taylor
Roger Tubby
Jack Valenti
*Paul Wilson
William Wilson
Willard Wirtz
Bob Woodward
Lloyd Wright

112326

Contents

Packaging the Presidency

Chapter One

Broadsides to Broadcasts

In 1888, Scottish scholar and statesman James Bryce observed that during election campaigns in the U.S. "For three months, processions, usually with brass bands, flags, badges, crowds of cheering spectators, are the order of the day and night from end to end of the country." Such business, Bryce continued, "pleases the participants by making them believe they are effecting something; it impresses the spectators by showing them that other people are in earnest, it strikes the imagination of those who in country hamlets read of the doings in the great city. In short, it keeps up the 'boom,' and an American election is held to be, truly or falsely, largely a matter of booming."[1]

The "booming" Bryce described is as alien to modern Americans as it was to Bryce. Most of us now experience presidential campaigns in the privacy of our living rooms, and little more than half the population emerges from them on election day to vote. But substitute "political advertising" as the subject of Bryce's observation, change the idiom to modern English, and David Broder could comfortably open a column with the resulting claims: "For three months political advertising is the order of the day and night from coast to coast. These ads please those who have conceived and produced them by making them believe they are effecting something; they impress the public by showing their candidates to be earnest people; they strike the imagination of those in country towns who vicariously meet the candidates and experience the campaign through the excitement of the advertising. This advertising creates the 'boom,' and an American election is held to be, correctly or not, largely a matter of booming."

This was not the plan of the founders of the Republic, who would have been shocked both by the booming of Bryce's processions, bands, and banners and by the political advertising campaigns that are their heirs. Additionally, our founders would have been surprised by our almost universal right to vote, the active and insistent role of political parties in our selection of presidential candidates, the audacity of presidential candidates in taking their case directly to the American people, and especially by technology that enables packaged images of candidates to be presented to mass audiences so effortlessly. Because political advertising* as we know it presupposes a large electorate, contested elections, campaigning candidates, as well as the existence of the mass media, this chapter will chronicle briefly how each came to be.

In the country's infancy, the number of eligible voters was severely restricted by the conviction that sex, race, and property and not nationality or residence qualified a person to vote. Early guardians of the ballot-box also demanded evidence of interest in the community, which often meant evidence of likemindedness. So, for example, an act passed in South Carolina in 1716 imposed a strict property test as well as a religious test on would-be voters and specifically excluded Jews and free Negroes.[2] In Rhode Island voters had to own property carrying a minimal value of forty pounds; Catholics were excluded from the polls.

At the time of the American Revolution, seven of the thirteen original colonies restricted the vote to property owners. In Virginia the prospective voter had to own at least fifty acres of undeveloped land or twenty-five acres of developed land occupied by a house at least twelve feet square.[3] The impact of these restrictions on voting was severe. In the first quarter century of the nation's existence "not more than 6 percent of the adult population was eligible to vote."[4]

The tide shifted in the last decade of the eighteenth century when states permitting "full manhood suffrage" began to enter the Union. Vermont, for example, required only a year's residence and "quiet and peaceable behavior." The requirement that voters own property collapsed rapidly. After 1824 only two states, Virginia and Rhode Island, qualified voters by property tests.[5]

Previously disenfranchised persons swelled voter rolls during the nineteenth and twentieth centuries when suffrage for Negro males was added to the Constitution, when women were granted the vote, and when those 18 to 21 were enfranchised. Through this period, waves of immigrants continued to expand the size of the electorate, particularly after 1900.†

High voter turnout in presidential elections—between 75 and 85 per-

---

*I am using the phrase political advertising to mean those messages controlled by candidates who pay to transmit them to large audiences. In this book I focus primarily on advertising appearing in newspapers and on radio and television, including 30 and 60 second spot ads, and 5 minute, half hour, hour, and two hour paid programming.

†The universal enfranchisement of blacks was short-lived. After 1900, poll taxes and literacy tests substantially diminished voting by Southern blacks.

cent throughout the last half of the nineteenth century—also magnified the size of the vote. By contrast, in our most recent national election only 55.1 percent of the eligible voters cast a ballot.[6]

The creators of our government envisioned the electoral process as a staid, dignified activity—"a few respected electors, state by state, sifting the merits of the worthiest eligibles. Something like a church council naming a new pastor, or a faculty bestowing a professorship."[7] Alexander Hamilton argued in the 68th *Federalist* letter that these men would "be most likely to possess the information and discernment requisite to such complicated investigations." They would, he reasoned, analyze "the qualities adapted to the station," and act "under circumstances favourable to deliberation."

The ideal unraveled rapidly. Only George Washington was chosen in a manner approximating that glorified by Hamilton. The father of the country's Farewell Address precipitated the nation's first contested election, a contest manifest in "newspaper polemics, pamphlets, and political rallies"[8] that venerated and vilified the leading candidates. Republican handbills praised Jefferson as a Republican and pilloried Adams as a monarchist. The Federalist press termed Jefferson an atheist, a freethinker, and an enemy of the Constitution. In Massachusetts "[h]andbills denouncing Adams as an aristocrat and monarchist were nailed to gateposts, doors of houses, and posts . . . and men were hired to ride through the state, their saddlebags stuffed with Anti-Federal broadsides."[9] Throughout this free-for-all, Jefferson and Adams remained aloof and silent.

The homage and hostility of the handbills had as their end persuading the voters to select electors favorable to one candidate or the other. A broadside distributed in Pennsylvania listed the slate of Republican electors and urged citizens to vote for the person who had advocated equal rights and against the "panegyrist of the British monarchial form of government."[10] Sample ballots listing the names of Republican electors were scattered throughout Pennsylvania.

By the election of 1828, electors favorable to either Jackson or John Quincy Adams were clearly and publicly identified throughout the states. Newspapers and handbills were the prime means of associating specific electors with a specific candidate.

Eighteen twenty-eight is a watershed year in presidential campaigns for the number of participating voters more than tripled that year. This was also the first time most votes cast were for electors committed to particular candidates. So, by 1828, a mass audience of voters existed who were able to determine directly who would win the presidency. Not surprisingly, we see calculated efforts to popularize the legend of "Old Hickory."

Although the enemies of earlier presidents had lampooned them with unflattering nicknames, Jackson was the first identified by an affectionate one. The name "Hickory" was originally bestowed on him by his troops in 1813 "in testimony to his toughness"[11] when, after his troops were stranded by his superiors, Jackson gave up his horse, borrowed funds on his own note to procure rations, and escorted his sick and fever-ridden Tennessee militia home from Natchez. Consequently, the name "Old Hickory" implied "not only the sense of fraternity but the suggestion that here was a man who would act for justice untrammeled by forms."[12]

As attested to by Michael Chevalier, a visitor to the U.S. on a mission for the French government, hickory branches and hickory poles were powerful symbols in Jackson's campaigns: "I stopped involuntarily at the sight of the gigantic hickory poles which made their solemn entry on eight wheels for the purpose of being planted by the democracy on the eve of the election. I remember one of these poles, its top still crowned with green foliage, which came on to the sound of fifes and drums and was preceded by ranks of Democrats, bearing no other badge than a twig of the sacred tree in their hats. . . . Astride the tree itself were a dozen Jackson men of the first water, waving flags with an air of anticipated triumph and shouting, *Hurrah for Jackson!*"[13]

Throughout the campaign of 1828, Jackson's supporters painted him as "The Modern Cincinnatus," "The Farmer of Tennessee," "The Second Washington," and "The Hero of Two Wars." Portraits of Jackson in general's uniform astride a horse were carried in processions alongside portraits of him in the clothing of a Tennessee farmer, hickory cane in hand. By contrast, John Quincy Adams was portrayed in one of Jackson's handbills as "driving off with a horsewhip a crippled old soldier who dared to speak to him, to ask an alms."[14]

The image of Jackson as soldier-farmer was reinforced by the claim that he now farmed the land he had once defended from a foreign foe. These images were underscored in his 1824 campaign biography, the first published in the history of the presidency.

Jackson's opponents sneered that unlike his two-time opponent, John Quincy Adams, Jackson was unschooled, uncultured, and inexperienced in affairs of state; he was not even the farmer at his own plow as his propagandists proclaimed, but instead a plantation owner and slaveholder who had never worked the land with his own hand. As for Jackson's service in two wars, Adams' supporters noted that he was only 13 years old in 1780.

To counter the legend of "Old Hickory" Jackson's opponents distributed "coffin handbills" indicting him for executing six soldiers, one of them a Baptist minister who deserted after the Battle of New Orleans.

The men had served their three-month tour, noted the handbills, and thought they were entitled to return home. A handbill printed in Boston in July 1828 reduced their "Mournful Tragedy" to verse. "We thought our time of service out/ Thought it our right to go;/ We meant to violate no law;/ Nor wish'd to shun the foe." But Jackson was obdurate. "He order'd Harris out to die,/ And five poor fellows more!/ Young gallant men in prime of life,/ To welter in their gore!!" Another handbill, which should give pause to those inclined to see recent political advertising as more negative than that of the past, charged Jackson with ordering other executions, massacring Indians, stabbing a Samuel Jackson in the back, murdering one soldier who disobeyed his commands, and hanging three Indians.

Jackson's supporters responded with a handbill that mimicked the form of the originals. Six coffins dominate the message which, like that of the originals, is penned by a self-proclaimed "eyewitness." But this "eye-witness" account reduces the original to absurdity. In the parody, which like the coffin handbills survives in the Library of Congress, the "monster Jackson" not only ordered the soldiers executed but "swallowed them whole, coffins and all, without the slightest attempt at mastication!!!!!!" Make him president, says the handbill, and, should a governor incur his displeasure, Jackson will "muster an army and march to the metropolis of that State, hang up the Governor 'without trial.' " Moreover, should he "happen to have one of his anthropophagian fits on him" he and his army may "devour" the Governor and the legislators before leaving the city.[15]

The campaign organization created on Jackson's behalf presaged those that would dominate future campaigns. In addition to planning meetings and devising and distributing campaign materials to newspapers and voters, Jackson's organizers created a precursor of the Democratic and Republican National Committees by establishing a Washington-based central correspondence committee. These organizers also "collected funds, compiled lists of voters, and made arrangements for printing ballots. They founded newspapers, increasing in number as the campaign progressed; they issued pamphlets, broadsides and biographies."[16]

Political Parties

The 1828 election also gave rise to national political parties, a phenomenon portended by the clashes of the Federalists and anti-Federalists of Jefferson's days. National parties altered the nature of presidential campaigns by limiting the number of serious contenders for the presidency, magnifying the contest among them, and facilitating the expansion of campaign organizations.

Although Jackson had been elected without the backing of a national political party, the electors who had pledged themselves to him set the groundwork for a political party by claiming political appointment as the spoils of victory. Jackson responded in his first presidential message by identifying "rotation," for which we should read displacement, of past appointees "a first principle in the Republican creed." Although we tend to view it disapprovingly, and refer to it as the "spoils system," Jackson's commitment to rotation-in-office was intended to reform a corrupt bureaucracy. But more important for our purpose was the spoils system's ability to solidify support for Jackson and his annointed successor and to subvent political parties.[17]

The existence of a party label not only helped voters to identify candidates but also ensured that certain functions would be performed including "nominating candidates and campaigning in the electoral arena, and readiness to undertake management or the general conduct of public business in the governmental arena."[18] But in a democracy, as political scientist Clinton Rossiter argues, the primary function of political parties is "to control and direct the struggle for power."[19]

Despite the prophecies of such founders as Washington who condemned "the demon of party spirit"[20] and Jefferson, who noted that "If I could not go to heaven but with a party, I would not go there at all,"[21] political parties invigorated the political system. Elections were systematically contested; voter interest and voter participation increased.[22] During the transitional stage between conception and birth of national parties, "Where opposing parties had been formed to contest the election, the vote was large, but where no parties, or only one, took the field, the vote was low."[23]

National parties did not emerge overnight. By the second Jackson election in 1832, a two party system existed in barely half of the states. Not until 1840 were viable parties organized throughout the states. But, as Bryce observed, by the last decade of the nineteenth century, their influence would be decisive: candidates and candidacies were controlled by parties and electoral victories won by "the cohesion and docility of the troops."[24]

The landmark election of 1840 occurred in a climate ripe for political advertising: a mass of voters eager to decide which candidate should lead the country, a contested election in which the incumbent—Martin Van Buren—was supported by the current beneficiaries of Jackson's spoils and the challenger—William Henry Harrison, who also had been the challenger in '36 against Van Buren—was advanced by a hungry party out of power that coveted the spoils of victory.

Like Jackson before him, Harrison lay claim to being a military hero.

But unlike Jackson's decisive Battle of New Orleans, Harrison's glory rested on an indecisive battle against the Shawnee Indians at Tippecanoe in 1811. After repelling an Indian attack, Harrison's forces razed the Indian village. Although Harrison subsequently retreated, the power of the Shawnees had been broken. The name of the battle replaced that of the general in the alliterative slogan of 1840, "Tippecanoe and Tyler Too."

In 1840, the presidency's first full-blown campaign functioned as a form of national jamboree replete with orchestrated parades, banners, torches, transparencies, and flags, omnipresent log cabins and hard cider, and coonskin caps. William Henry Harrison's 1840 campaign produced a series of firsts in the history of political advertising, including the first systematic and widespread use of what today would be called image advertising as well was the first songster.

Prior to 1840, campaign artwork evoked the story of the nation. But in 1840, these glorifications of country in the form of the Constitution, Lady Liberty, the ship of state, and the eagle gave way to highly personalized symbols associated with the particular candidate. Commenting on the transformation, Philip Hone, a New York Whig, observed in his diary "on all their banners and transparencies the temple of Liberty is transformed into a hovel of unhewn logs; the military garb of the general into the frock and shirtsleeves of a laboring farmer. The American eagle has taken his flight, which is supplied [supplanted] by a cider barrel, and the long-established emblem of the ship has given place to the plow. 'Hurrah for Tippecanoe!' is heard more frequently than 'Hurrah for the Constitution!' "[25]

Once such symbols were established and linked to the candidates, they seemed to have a life of their own, as Van Buren's supporters discovered to their chagrin. Disparaging Harrison's fitness for the White House, *The Baltimore Republican* contended that he would be content in a log cabin with a jug of cider and a military pension. Harrison's supporters appropriated the log cabin and cider to transform the wealthy son of a governor into a farmer and backwoodsman. The symbol of the log cabin was a potent one for it identified Harrison with the pioneers who cut the country from the wilderness and with rural voters still residing in log cabins. Hone gleefully concludes that "Never did the friends of Mr. Van Buren make so great a mistake as when, by their sneers, they furnished the Whigs those powerful weapons, 'log cabin' and 'hard cider'; they work as the hickory poles did for Jackson. It makes a personal hurrah for Harrison which cannot in any way be gotten up for Van Buren."[26]

By describing his lush two thousand acre estate farmed by tenant

1840 lithograph. (Courtesy Library of Congress)

farmers, the Democratic press tried to undercut the crafted rustic image. But the voters would have none of it. Enveloped by propaganda picturing a log-cabin-dwelling farmer, they clung tenaciously to the fabricated image.

The symbol did have some grounding in fact. Although it scarcely resembled the humble cabin depicted in the banners, Harrison did own a log cabin in North Bend Ohio that he had built for his bride near the turn of the century (hence his designation as "the farmer of North Bend"). But Harrison had been born not in a log cabin but in a fine two story brick home at Berkeley on the James River in Virginia and at the time of the campaign owned a palatial Georgian mansion in Vincennes, Indiana.

Still, log cabins were carried in parades; log cabins were pictured on kerchiefs, bandannas, and banners; log cabin pins, songs, and badges served as the outward signs of inward political convictions. Hard cider was dispensed to converts and the curious alike. The cabins, cider, and coonskin caps enabled voters vicariously to experience the supposedly hardy, healthy, heroic life of their candidate.

So while revealing little of his past and less of his future, and while misrepresenting himself as a cider-loving, log-cabin farmer, Tippecanoe

Berkeley, Charles City Co., Virginia. Home built by Harrison family. The photograph was taken about 1934 or 1935. Since then the house has been renovated to represent the period of about 1800; the most noticeable difference is the removal of the peristyle (the series of columns surrounding the house). (Courtesy Library of Congress)

won the election but died soon after the ink reporting his inauguration had dried, thereby winning an almost full term for "Tyler Too."

In an age of television, the counterfeit image would likely have been exposed by Roger Mudd or Dan Rather live from the Georgian mansion. Doctors' records mysteriously would have found their way within camera range of investigative journalists. But in 1840 claims about Harrison's considerable wealth and failing health could be discounted by partisans unwilling and to some extent unable to confirm them.

The Harrison campaign's visual symbol of the log cabin presages what has come to be called "image" advertising in politics. As Washburn argues, "Its modern-day equivalent would be the 30-second television spot commercial, which ignores issues, ignores party label, and concentrates on some aspect of the candidate's personality, usually one that links him closely with the ordinary voter."[27] In its contemporary incarnation, such advertising rhapsodizes over candidates reading to their children, fishing in a rushing stream, or pausing to inspect peanuts in a warehouse bin. In its modern visage, Harrison in farmer's overhalls is Jimmy Carter in a work shirt and blue jeans addressing voters from his home in Plains or Ronald Reagan splitting firewood or riding horseback on his ranch.

By 1860 image advertising had become a staple of political campaigns. So, for example, a rail presumably split by Lincoln in his youth was carried into the Republican convention affixed to a banner rich in the raw stuff of which myth is made:

ABRAHAM LINCOLN
The Rail Candidate
For President in 1860
Two rails from a lot of 3000 made in 1830 by
John Hanks and Abe Lincoln, whose father
was the first pioneer of Macon County.[28]

Image advertising reappeared in such forms as the teddy bears of Theodore Roosevelt's campaigns, and the "hole in the shoe" in Stevenson's '52 campaign.

The songster and image advertising are not the only legacies of the 1840 Harrison campaign. That campaign also transformed the role of the candidate from of the contest but not in the contest to both in and of the contest. Only after candidates and the public had abandoned the notion that the office sought the person and not the person the office could direct appeals by the candidate become part of political advertising. By speaking publicly on his own behalf and in his own defense, Harrison in 1840 set the stage for this change in the presidential candidate's role.

The wave of advertising that washed across the 1840 campaign has obscured the fact that in 1836 Harrison made what would now be called campaign tours "to counteract the opinion, which has been industriously circulated, that *I was an old broken down feeble man.*"[29]

During the tour of 1836, Harrison had delivered ostensibly apolitical speeches extolling the country's past and, in Philadelphia, glorifying the Declaration of Independence, which his father had signed. At each stop on his 1836 trip through Pennsylvania, New Jersey, Maryland, and Ohio, a Harrison committee choreographed "welcoming citizens on horseback, carriage processions, brass bands, bonfires, torchlights, clanging church bells, booming cannon, young ladies with flowers. . . . Old soldiers with tears in their eyes crowded forward. 'Hurrah for Harrison!' 'Hail Columbia' was played in every village and town."[30]

Still behind its apolitical veneer, Harrison's political message had been plain. If elected president, he not only would defend constitutional principles but draw policy from the venerated past. And most important, and most deceptive, Old Tip was healthy enough to faithfully execute the demands of the office he sought.

By the 1840 campaign, both candidates were ready to hit the campaign trail, but it was Harrison who would finally deliver the first overtly partisan presidential campaign speech on his own behalf. Under the pretense of a journey from Washington D.C. to his birthplace in Kinderhook, New York, President Van Buren mounted a comparable though less enthusiastically received tour than the one Harrison had undertaken in 1836. Where Harrison had gone round the circle to silence rumors that he was mentally and physically enfeebled, Van Buren mingled with the crowds to quiet Whig claims that he was a corrupt, venal aristocrat.

But Harrison would go one step further when, in the preliminary jousting of the 1840 campaign, the Democratic press branded him a "superannuated and pitiable dotard"[31] (a suspicion magnified when a committee of correspondence rather than Harrison himself answered Harrison's political mail). When charges of military incompetence were added to claims that Old Tippecanoe was senile, Harrison could take it no more. Wounded by the personal attack, he took to the stump to avenge his impugned reputation. "I am here," he told a crowd in Chillicothe, "because . . . I have been slandered by reckless opponents . . . [who claim] that I am devoid of every qualification, physical, mental and moral, for the high place to which at least a respectable portion of my fellow-citizens have nominated me."[32]

In ringing, forceful speeches, Harrison attempted to refute the charges of infirmity, while defending his military career, decrying the activities of abolitionists, opposing two terms for presidents, objecting to casual uses of the presidential veto, and championing such controversial causes as prudent use of the monies of the treasury and the right of the people to govern. Although attack had been present in American political rhetoric at least since Washington was charged with monarchical aspirations, Harrison's apologia demonstrated that a candidate could respond publicly to attack without sacrificing the presidency.

The speeches also provided a forum for Harrison to underscore the image capsulized in the broadsides and songs. So, for example, he interrupted a speech at Fort Meigs to beckon an old soldier from the crowd to stand with him on the platform; elsewhere in the speech he paused to drink hard cider.[33]

In the rhetoric of the presidency's first active campaigner we hear the studied humility that will become a stock in trade of political advertising and campaign speaking: "I am not a professional speaker, nor a studied orator, but I am an old soldier and a farmer, and as my sole object is to speak what I think, you will excuse me if I do it in my own way."[34]

And like many who would follow, Harrison also fell victim to a desire to please all of the people all of the time, and in the process fooled opposition editors none of the time. "There is not a single question of magnitude," complained one, "on which his opinions have not been cited by the advocates of contradictory creeds and theories."[35]

In a campaign packed with log cabins, cider, and coonskin hats, the pseudo-event flourished. To ally himself with "the new coonskin Whiggery, [Daniel] Webster camped with Green Mountain boys in a pine wood before an open fire, ate meals from shingles, paid tribute to log cabins, and challenged at fisticuffs anyone who dared call him an aristocrat."[36] The pseudo-event then is not the child of television but the stepchild of image making itself.

Beginning with Harrison's self-defense turned self-advancement, the first break is made in the long-standing taboo against partisan political stumping by presidential candidates. But in the next three presidential elections, only one nonincumbent candidate for president would even address voters directly. In 1852, General Winfield Scott, the Whig candidate, claiming that "I do not intend to speak to you on political topics"[37] toured the country selecting sites for homes for infirm soldiers. Scott was defeated by the person whose supporters had chanted "We Polked you in 1844; we shall Pierce you in 1852." And indeed, Franklin Pierce, who had engaged in no personal campaigning, won in a landslide.

Eight years later, in the famous 1860 campaign, the proscription against active presidential campaigning on one's own behalf weighed heavily with both Lincoln and Douglas but ultimately was rejected by Douglas. According to Helen Nicolay, the daughter of Lincoln's secretary, "Being a presidential candidate made astonishingly little difference in Mr. Lincoln's daily habits. . . . Lincoln wrote no public letters, and

Photo of Abraham Lincoln taken by Mathew Brady in New York on February 27, 1860, the day of Lincoln's famous address at the Cooper Institute. (Courtesy Library of Congress)

made no set or impromptu speeches, with the exception of speaking a word of greeting once or twice to passing street parades."[38] Meanwhile, of course, Lincoln's supporters campaigned on his behalf. These efforts included widespread distribution of copies of Mathew Brady's photo of Lincoln at the Cooper Institute, efforts designed to counter the cartoons and caricatures of Lincoln circulated by his opponents. Throughout the campaign, Lincoln tended his law practice in Springfield, ignoring the political campaigning of the man he had debated two years earlier in a sectional contest. Indeed, only under pressure from his supporters did Lincoln even cast a ballot in 1860 and only when persuaded by his law partner that the state candidates might need his vote. Even then Lincoln clipped "the list of presidential electors from the ballot and [voted] for the rest of the Republican ticket."[39]

That this proscription against campaigning was not a shield for timid or tiresome orators to hide behind but was instead a tradition rooted in conviction and convention is illustrated by the fact that so great an orator as Lincoln felt bound to observe it. So too, for example, had "Old Man Eloquent," Whig Party founder Henry Clay, who also had remained silent during his own campaigns. Still it is no accident that the three major party candidates to break most decisively with this ivy-encrusted tradition—Douglas, William Jennings Bryan, and Woodrow Wilson— were also eloquent and forceful orators, men whose rhetorical skill had served them well in the past.

While in 1860 Abraham Lincoln referred those who inquired about his views on slavery to his debates with Douglas in the senatorial campaign of 1858, Stephen Douglas took to the stump on behalf of his own candidacy. Douglas predicated his active candidacy on the urgency of the issues of slavery and the impending disunion.

The tradition that restrained Lincoln from campaigning for the presidency on his own behalf applied solely to the presidency and soley to the candidate's own campaign. Lincoln, for example, had no qualms about speaking out in the 1858 senatorial race, expressing himself forcefully on a number of issues in the Lincoln-Douglas debates. Likewise, he had made speeches in 1856 in support of John C. Frémont. Ironically, it was the visibility gained in the Frémont campaign and his unsuccessful 1858 senatorial bid, that influenced the Republican party in 1860 to make him its nominee. The 1896 presidential nominee William McKinley, who rocked on his front porch waiting for votes to come to him, had delivered dozens of speeches in 1892 on behalf of presidential candidate Benjamin Harrison, William Henry Harrison's grandson.

Though the contrast between the presidential campaigns of the mid-nineteenth century—when even discussion of issues in public by a presidential candidate was taboo—and those of the mid-twentieth, when candidates regularly are faulted for failing to discuss issues, is marked, the transformation occurred gradually. Once parties began writing platforms in the mid-nineteenth century, it became acceptable for the party's candidate to indicate publicly his views on the platform. After being notified by a delegation that he was the party's nominee, the candidate typically delivered a speech of thanks and set about drafting a formal letter of acceptance that endorsed the planks of the platform on which the candidate would stand. After releasing the letter to the press, the candidate, with few exceptions, fell silent on political matters until notified of the election results.

In 1892 Cleveland inched from behind the confines of the taboo when before a crowd of 18,000 he publicly accepted the nomination and indicated his opposition to the GOP tariff. Still, Cleveland did not take to the stump to press the issue.

William Jennings Bryan delivering a speech on behalf of his presidential candidacy. Note the glamorized campaign poster. (Courtesy Library of Congress)

But in 1896 William Jennings Bryan did. Having won the nomination with his impassioned Cross of Gold Speech, the "Boy Orator of the Platte" pioneered the modern campaign. Bryan launched that campaign with a speech delivered at his notification ceremony in Madison Square Garden. In the process Bryan learned the hazards of adapting to the media's audience at the expense of the immediate audience. Because Bryan viewed the newspaper readers as his primary audience, he chained himself to his text. The result was a hobbled speech, the oratorical low point of the campaign. From there Bryan traversed the country speaking with ease and greater effect to hugh crowds.

William Jennings Bryan's campaign of 1896 marked the beginning of the end of torchlight parades and campaign songs. By campaigning vigorously for the presidency, by taking the eloquence that had enthralled the Chautauqua audiences onto the stump on behalf of a political cause,Bryan overshadowed such surrogate message carriers as the banner and the song.

Mark Hanna, William McKinley's political godfather, responded to the Bryan campaign by enlisting the aid of the GOP-leaning railroad moguls, who offered excursion passes to those journeying to McKinley's front porch in Canton, Ohio. Once there, a representative delivered a speech to McKinley, providing an opportunity for McKinley to respond. McKinley's actions further established the right of a candidate for president to respond on his own behalf. But could a candidate leave the front porch, pursue the votes, and win?

In 1912 Woodrow Wilson underscored the affirmative answer provided by Harrison in 1840. This candidate, who conceived of himself as an orator, and who viewed the president as the spokesman for the nation, followed in the footsteps of his two stumping Democratic predecessors, Bryan and Douglas; unlike either, Wilson won the election.

So by 1912 the presidential candidate was accepted as an active campaigner and advocate of his own cause. Once the technology was available, this newly conceived role would make it possible for candidates to speak directly to the mass of voters.

William McKinley making his nomination acceptance speech from the front porch of his Canton, Ohio, home. Immediately behind the candidate, with his hand resting on a cane, is Mark Hanna, McKinley's campaign manager. (Courtesy Smithsonian Institution, Photo No. 50571, Division of Political History)

Woodrow Wilson, campaigning for president. (Courtesy Smithsonian Institution, Photo 76-15373, Division of Political History)

Transporting Political Advertising into Living Rooms, Bedrooms, and Theaters: Radio, Film, and Television

In the days in which radio was still a controversial new gadget, Elihu Root, diplomat and Senator from New York, exclaimed to a person setting a microphone before him: "Take that away. I can talk to a Democrat, but I cannot speak into a dead thing."[40] By 1928 the dead thing had transformed political communication. Radio audiences of a size unimaginable in an era of stump oratory were now available in an instant. In 1924 there were three million radios in America; by 1935 ten times that number existed.

Instead of gathering in town halls or town squares or in open fields, thousands and later millions of radio listeners assembled in twos and threes in parlors and living rooms and later in cars as well. By giving that "vast body to be persuaded" the opportunity to "know its persuaders," radio bridged the separation between the people and their leaders that Woodrow Wilson had decried.[41] Over the course of 100 days in the campaign of 1896 William Jennings Bryan, by his own account, had made 600 speeches in 27 states and had traveled over 18,000 miles to reach 5,000,000 people.[42] In a single fireside chat delivered while seated in his parlor, Franklin Delano Roosevelt reached twelve times that number.

Its early advocates argued that radio would preserve the presidents' health. After Harding's death, the National Broadcasters' Association reminded his successor, Calvin Coolidge, that Woodrow Wilson's health had been broken by his tour on behalf of the League of Nations and that the strain of a similar trip had contributed to Harding's death![43]

Radio also transformed the content, audience, and delivery of political messages. No longer did candidates have to travel from town to town to convey their message personally to the voters. At the same time, radio created a national audience. The message delivered in the North was also heard in the South. The message heard by farmers was also heard by city dwellers. As the *New York Times* observed in 1928, "Radio 'hook-up' has destroyed the old-time politicians' game of promising in each locality the things which that locality wishes. They can no longer promise the Western farmer higher prices for wheat without arousing the Eastern factory population against higher bread prices."[44]

In its youth, radio was eulogized for removing the voter from the frenzy of the maddening crowd to the quiet of the living room. "In the olden days," FDR recalled in a radio address on July 30, 1932, "campaigns were conducted amid surroundings of brass bands and red lights. Oratory was an appeal primarily to the emotions and sometimes to the passions. . . . [W]ith the spread of education, with the wider reading of newspapers and especially with the advent of the radio, mere oratory and mere emotion are having less to do with the determination of public questions under our representative system of Government. Today, common sense plays the greater part and final opinions are arrived at in the quiet of the home."[45]

But radio did not fulfill a *New York Times* writer's prophecy that cunning politicians would vanish under its influence.[46] Nor did they disappear in the wake of television. After his defeat in 1952 Stevenson complained about the "the all-things-to-all-men demogoguery" and the "clamor of political salesmanship" that pervade political campaigns and observed that "the people might be better served if a party purchased a half hour of radio and TV silence during which the audience would be asked to think quietly for themselves."[47]

Radio did change the standards for effective political oratorical style. By shouting into the microphone, for instance, Frank Knox, unsuccessful Republican candidate for vice-president in 1936, violated the intimacy of the parlor, abrading the sensibilities of the audience he was trying to woo.

By 1928, the first year in which the Republicans earmarked the majority of their publicity monies for radio, critics and audiences had developed expectations about the sort of delivery appropriate to the new medium and politicians were tested by those expectations. "Governor Smith is a success over the radio," wrote a reporter for the *New York Times,* "in spite of certain faults carried over from a long platform career. He has a tendency to walk up and down and a habit of turning from the audience to address those behind him on the platform."[48] Critics also chided Smith for giving "first" his own Lower East Side pronunciation "foist" and Hoover for affecting the English pronunciation "speciality."[49]

Those habituated to the norms of stump oratory foundered in the presence of a medium whose more effective mode was intimate conversation. "The easy conversational tones, with the instinctive sentence accents and cadences, which the radio makes it possible to convey, are quite beyond the conception or practice of many who make use of it" noted the *New York Times* in 1936.[50]

Politicians participated in the process of schooling the electorate in the expectations of the new medium. In his final radio address of the 1928 campaign, for example, Al Smith observed: "Tonight I am not surrounded by thousands of people in a great hall and I am going to take this opportunity to talk intimately to my radio audience alone, as though I were sitting with you in your own home and personally discussing with you the decision that you are to make tomorrow."[51]

As radio made necessary a new set of skills, so too, in time, did television. The realization that radio listeners and television viewers adjudged the first Kennedy-Nixon debate differently, with listeners giving the debate to Nixon and viewers to Kennedy, reminded us that television is not simply radio made visual but a medium with its own stylistic requirements and communicative facilities. Some politicians, such as FDR and Nixon, were uniquely skilled in communicating with radio's listeners.

During FDR's presidency, a talent for intimate communication, temperament, the times, and the technology of radio fused to provide calming reassurance to a country traumatized by depression. Stump oratory, well suited to the delivery of impassioned appeals, is ill suited to conveying quiet reassurance. In his "Fireside Chats," which at their peak reached upwards of 60 million listeners, Roosevelt capitalized on this previously unappreciated strength of the new medium.

In addition to favoring some messengers and foiling others, radio circumscribed the content and length of the political messages it carried. By transmitting messages from antagonistic candidates and opposing parties, radio broke the partisan hold that party newspapers had on their constituents' attention. "Tune out of one political speech," wrote John Calvin Brown for the *New York Times* in 1928, "and you tune into

FDR delivering "Fireside Chat." (Courtesy *Broadcasting* magazine)

another one and you finally settle down and listen to the wrangle until
you find yourself getting in a far more independent frame of mind than
was possible in yesterday's politics."[52] National radio and the national
television that would follow signaled the end of the days in which "Democrats read Democratic papers and went to Democratic meetings and
avoided exposure to Republican influences and arguments."[53]

From the infancy of the presidency, newspapers were identified with
specific causes and politicians. The shift from being organs of a politician
or party to being ostensibly independent of either occurred gradually.
The 1850 census classified a mere 5 percent of the newspapers as "neutral
and independent" rather than political, scientific, or literary.[54] In the
early decades of this century, controversy raged over whether a Democratic paper should accept Democratic advertising and vice versa. By
1940, 48 percent of the newspapers labeled themselves independent with
another 24 percent identifying themselves as Independent Democratic or
Republican and only 28 percent calling themselves either Democratic or
Republican.[55] Newspapers gradually shifted from partisan propagandizing
for one side or the other to nonpartisan reporting of the messages and
moves of both sides. Where in Jefferson's time newspapers had been a
form of advertising, in our time newspapers both carry political advertising and report on it.

As late as 1948 a major newspaper refused to carry a candidate's ad,
and in the process underscored an issue incubating during the campaign.

On the eve of the election the New York *World-Telegram* refused to print a Truman ad indicting Dewey's fiscal management of New York as governor. After failing to goad the *New York Times* into rejecting the ad as well, Democrats responded by distributing 700,000 reprints of the ad under the heading "The ad the *World-Telegram* refused to print."[56] Truman used the spurned ad and the networks' habit of cutting his speeches from the air when they ran overtime as evidence of big Republican-dominated corporations' hostility toward his cause.

Radio fenced political messages into predictable time boundaries. Those who did not carefully time their speeches found themselves either abruptly severed from their audience or liable for a bill for the next half hour of radio time. This rule was skillfully managed by Truman's press agents in 1948. When applause absorbed an unexpected amount of Truman's time and the campaign lacked the funds to pay for the next half hour, Truman's staff loudly announced within hearing range of reporters that the networks would not let the president finish his speech.[57]

The medium's rigid time boundaries coupled with the listener's ability to switch channels or silence the radio receiver entirely tended to replace stylistic embellishment with stylistic economy.

But in one respect the bargain that gave the politician access to millions of voters was a Faustian one, for access to the masses from the silence of the studio sacrificed the inspiration the crowd provides a skilled orator. Gone was the ability to adapt the message to the cheers, scowls, and silences of palpable individuals.

To compensate for the inability to gauge personally the responses of an invisible audience, the politician increasingly relied on audience measures to determine who and how many had listened, and on polls to chart audience predispositions and responses. With polling came the danger that politicians would carve their own identities out of the hopes and fears of the mass audience.

In addition to intuiting audience responses by such indirect means as ratings and polls, politicians offered the electronic audience a new identity as eavesdropper on speeches personally delivered to crowds. In this new role, the audience at home ideally would conceive of itself as an extension of the cheering multitude of partisans and would be cued to comparable levels of enthusiasm. But in the shadows of this new role resided the possibility that instead of being participants in elections, audience members would become mere observers.

Although radio precipitated some important changes in political communication, during its early years it served in many respects as a powerful conserver of campaign forms of the past. In its infancy, for instance, radio simply carried the dominant verbal form of the campaign—the campaign speech—to a larger audience. The recognition of radio as an advertising medium capable of selling candidates as it had sold soap did not come until later.

Political use of radio escalated rapidly. In 1919 Woodrow Wilson delivered the first broadcast presidential speech to a handful of listeners. His successor's campaign train was equipped with its own radio transmitter. But Coolidge, who assumed the presidency at Harding's death, brought about a dramatic change in the political role radio would play. On December 6, 1923, in a conversational but nasalized tone, Coolidge delivered the first broadcast State of the Union address. So clear was the transmission that when a radio station in St. Louis called the Capitol to ask "What's that grating noise?," experts responded "That's the rustling of the paper as he turns the pages of his message."[58]

Because radio and television have become, like cake mixes and jet planes, presupposed parts of our lives, we have trouble imagining the sensation Coolidge's broadcast speech created. Groups gathered in the private offices and homes of those owning radios; stores selling receiving sets amplified the speeches for the benefit of those gathered on sidewalks to hear "the words of their President, not as embalmed text, but as living things while he was in the very act of speaking them."[59] Presidential aspirant Senator Hiram Johnson of California also reportedly sat glued to his receiving set. Recognizing an effective vehicle when he saw it, silent Cal staked out his claim to the nomination of his party in a series of radio broadcasts begun five months before the convention and ending the week before it.

In 1924, political conventions were broadcast for the first time. In the same year the Republicans broadcast from their own stations each day from October 21 to election day.

Use of radio in the campaign of 1924 was limited by the "spotty geographic distribution" of existing stations and the difficulty in linking a national network.[60] Still in that year when a single hour of coast-to-coast broadcast time cost $4,000, the Republican National Committee spent $120,000 on radio and the Democrats $40,000.[61]

Since the Columbia Broadcasting System and the National Broadcasting Company did not yet exist, there was no "regular, systematic network broadcasting, no regularly scheduled programs, and a maze of negotiations to be gone through everytime a hookup was needed."[62] By 1928 both CBS and NBC had taken their place alongside the Radio Corporation of America, making national radio broadcasts a political fact of life.

Still, because of the extra expense of "leasing the wires of outside service companies,"[63] the cost of a national hookup was expensive. Politicians developed two methods of circumventing this expense: individual speakers at individual stations used their own material or local speakers were supplied with " 'canned' speeches, so that the same speeches could be delivered throughout the country upon the same day."[64]

As the size of radio's audience multiplied, use of the medium by politicians increased. In 1924, Coolidge spoke an average of 9000 words per month by radio.[65] On March 4, 1925, Coolidge's inaugural address was transmitted by 27 stations to about 15 million listeners. In Coolidge's judgment, the existence of radio had eliminated the need for speaking from "rear platforms." "It is so often that the President is on the air," he wrote in his autobiography, "that almost any one who wishes has ample opportunity to hear his voice."[66] During his tenure in office more Americans heard Coolidge than had heard all of his predecessors combined.

The *New York Times* summarized the importance of radio in the 1928 campaign in a headline that read: "The New Instrument of Democracy Has Brought the Candidates into the Home, Enabled Them to Reach All of the People, and Radically Changed the Traditional Form of Political Appeal."[67] Additionally, as broadcasting historian and theorist Samuel Becker has argued persuasively, broadcasting "pushed the President further up the pole of political power, relative to the Congress."[68] Prior to radio, citizens had ongoing personal contact with their congressional representatives but not with the president. Their congressional representatives could communicate directly to them when they returned to the home district; the president's words were filtered through the newspapers. Before radio the Congressman or postmaster—not the president—symbolized the government for most citizens. So radio and its offspring television personalized our concept of the presidency and shifted the locus of perceived political power from Congress to the President.

By 1928 political proselytizing guised as entertainment had overflowed from the parades onto the airwaves. The Democrats, for example, created "radio entertainment in its best vein"[69] with their "all-star dramatization of Governor Smith's life." The program, which included stage and concert stars, opened and closed with a few bars from "East Side. West Side"—Smith's signature music. The Republicans adapted radio to the interests of the local communities by scripting five-minute speeches to be delivered by "Minute Men" over 174 stations.[70]

By 1928, politicians were expected to pay for air time. To entice them into using it, the broadcasters aired conventions and acceptance speeches without charge. From the close of that speech to election day, candidates were charged the standard commercial rate, the rate at which department stores or manufacturers were billed. By today's standards, the cost was low—a coast-to-coast hookup cost no more than $10,000 an hour.

In 1936 FDR circumvented the fee schedule by claiming until the final weeks of the campaign that he was speaking not as a candidate but as president and, as such, he persuasively argued, he was entitled to free coverage. This was a valuable move since only in 1936 had the Democrats paid off their radio debts from the previous campaign and in that four-year interval the networks had decided to demand cash in advance.

In the judgment of Roosevelt's "political manager" James Farley, "the influence of the radio in determining the outcome of the 1936 election can hardly be overestimated."[71] Radio enabled Roosevelt to overcome the "false impression created by the tons of written propaganda put out by foes of the New Deal." "[N]o matter what was written or what was charged, the harmful effect was largely washed away as soon as the reassuring voice of the President of the United States started coming through the ether into the family living-room,"[72] Farley explained.

As the size of the listening audience increased, so too did the cost of air time. At the same time, however, radio's novelty began to wane. Audiences no longer granted the medium their uncritical attention. Consequently, to minimize cost and magnify audience attention, other means of audience enticement including music, song, and testimony from supporters were added to unadorned speeches. Campaigning politicians also turned from long messages to shorter ones. In 1928 the usual time purchased by candidates was one hour. In 1980 the typical political message was thirty seconds long.

Politicians moved from the unadorned speech to forms characterized by greater variety. So, for example, in 1944 Norman Corwin produced an ad whose use of personal testimony sidestepped CBS and NBC's faltering ban on dramatization and whose skillful use of music and editing created a sense of urgency about voting for FDR. The ad opened with short statements from "a soldier and a sailor returning from action; a TVA farmer; several union members; a World War I veteran who had sold apples in the Depression; a housewife; an industrialist; a small businessman; a prominent Republican for Roosevelt; an old man who had voted in fourteen elections; a young girl about to vote in her first election—who would introduce the President."[73] Toward its end, the pace quickened. Musically backed choral sounds simulated the locomotive rhythm of a train as a long list of famous people including Lucille Ball, Tallulah Bankhead, Irving Berlin, Mrs. Berlin, and philosopher John Dewey added their eight-to-ten-word endorsements to the "Roosevelt Special." Chairman of the Democratic National Committee Paul Porter informed Corwin that some in the party credited his ad with a million votes.[74]

When the comedian Jimmy Durante canceled from the "Roosevelt

Special" at the last minute, the program was forced to end a few minutes early. Ponderous organ music was substituted for the absent comedian, creating the sense that programming had ended for the evening. Roosevelt's radio adviser Leonard Reinsch recalls:

> I was with Roosevelt at Hyde Park because he appeared at the close of the broadcast. The deadly organ music ran from 10:55 to 11:00. When the Republicans came on, the audience carry-over was practically zero. Roosevelt thought we'd planned it that way. The Republicans said they didn't want entertainment, they just wanted to talk facts. About then, Fala who was sitting at the president's feet fell asleep. Roosevelt said, "They've even put my dog to sleep."[75]

Producers of political radio realized both the engaging power of humor and radio's utility in reaching subsections of the voting population. Consequently, in 1948 Don Gibbs of the Warwick & Legler staff produced a classic series of comedic Democratic programs aimed at a listening audience of women in the middle of the afternoon. Borrowing blatantly from the conventions of hit radio shows of the time, the programs ricocheted with snide one liners. Each program opened and ended with a cut from "The Missouri Waltz," Truman's signature music. In one, after a brief introduction, the announcer played Eddie Cantor's "Now's the Time to Fall in Love." In the fashion of a hit show of the time, at the point when Cantor sang "Tomatoes are cheaper, potatoes are cheaper" the announcer shouted "Stop the music!" A litany of prices that had increased under Republican inflation followed. Next a woman blamed inflation on the Republicans who dropped price controls. The telephone rang. A voice asked for the Democratic record. The announcer complied by playing "Every Day I Love You a Little Bit More." A booby prize was then awarded to the Republican senator who "knocked out" meat controls. The prize: a tour of a butcher shop guided by Senator Taft. Next, listeners were asked to identify a mystery song. It turned out to be "Why Was I Born." This title, noted the announcer, asked a question formerly asked by those born during the Republican depression. Democratic spokeswoman India Edwards then was introduced to say a few kind words about the Truman family whom "you'd like for next door neighbors." Following more music, the wailing of a ghost was heard. He couldn't sleep because of the cries of the hungry and homeless victims of the Republican Congress. Vote Democratic, he urged the audience so that he can sleep peacefully.

Contests varied from program to program. One asked the audience to identify the candidate; the clue was a period of dead silence. The answer? Governor Dewey "who says nothing on any issue." Local party organizations ran print ads to promote listenership.[76]

Before they made their debut on the national stage, many influential politicians such as Huey Long and FDR refined their radio style at the state level. In 1924, for instance, Huey Long concluded his unsuccessful campaign for the governorship of Louisiana with a radio speech. In 1935, as a U.S. senator, Long made an unprecedented number of radio speeches over the National Broadcasting Company network—three in a two week period. NBC gave Long free time because he attracted listeners and because the airing of his radical proposals demonstrated that radio was not censored.[77]

Like Long, FDR carried to the national level lessons he had learned in his state-wide use of radio while governor. Before entering the presidency he wrote: "Time after time, in meeting legislative opposition in my own state . . . I have taken an issue directly to the voters by radio, and invariably I have met a most heartening response."[78]

As the number of sets and the amount and quality of programming multiplied so too did radio's audience, a fact dramatically illustrated by the tenfold increase in audience in the six year period 1936 to 1942—from 6,300,000 listeners to FDR's speech delivered June 10, 1936, to the 61,365,000 who tuned in to the speech of February 23, 1942.[79]

Once radio was recognized as a powerful political tool and a precedent was set for sale of advertising time to candidates, broadcasters and politicians asked what restrictions, if any, should govern the content and cost of such ads? In the 1924 campaign the Democrats charged that they had enjoyed neither equal access to nor equal charges for radio time. Coolidge's supporters were more often invited onto the air, they said. Others noted that the Republicans had outspent the Democrats in purchase of radio time three to one in 1924. Weighing into the controversy, Section 18 of the Federal Radio Act of 1927, which became Section 315 of the Communications Act of 1934, forbade the censorship of political broadcasts and noted that although a station had no obligation to permit candidates to use the station's facilities, equal opportunities must be provided to all bona fide candidates for public office. So censorship was outlawed and favoritism banned. To the alarm of station owners in 1932 the Supreme Court held that although the station could not censor material broadcast by a candidate, it remained liable for defamatory statements broadcast by such candidates. That decision was reversed in 1959.

In 1940 the Hatch Act was amended to limit the spending by any single political committee to $3,000,000. Instead of curbing campaign spending, the law produced a proliferation of political committees, thus decreasing the candidates' control over the advertising produced on their behalf. In 1952 Section 315 was changed to bar stations from charging more for political broadcasts than for comparable use of the station for other purposes.

In 1936 NBC and CBS made an ill-fated attempt to circumscribe political broadcast content with their decision not to permit dramatized political argument. With that guideline in place, would CBS permit a U.S. senator to debate replayed promises of a presidential candidate?

The controversy spawned by the Republican-National-Committee-sponsored Vandenberg broadcast reveals radio in the process of defining itself. Vandenberg had smuggled into the radio station a recording of segments from speeches by FDR. He planned to play a promise by Roosevelt, such as his pledge to balance the budget, then to demonstrate that the promise had been broken. In short, Vandenberg was going to contrast FDR's promise and performance. When some of the CBS stations realized what was happening they shut off the broadcast. The CBS network refunded the Republican's money. The Democrats charged the Republicans with unfair campaign practices. The FCC investigated. Editorials criticized Vandenberg for sneaking the recording into the studio; others castigated the stations for cutting the broadcast.[80]

The ban on dramatized content had little impact because, first, as in the Vandenberg case, it was not uniformly applied and, second, because stations with unpurchased time eagerly sold it to air such dramatizations as the Republican's "Liberty at the Crossroads"[81] which drew lessons from homey little vignettes. In one, a marriage license clerk asked a young couple what they plan to do about the national debt. They would, he reminded them, "shoulder a debt of $1017.26—and it's growing every day." After recalling that they had thought they didn't "owe anybody in the world," they reconsidered whether they should get married. The prospective groom concluded "Somebody is giving us a dirty deal." The Voice of Doom interjected "And the debts, like the sins of the fathers, shall be visited upon the children, aye even unto the third and fourth generations!" Music swelled.[82]

Newsreels and Film

Side by side with radio, a major type of filmed entertainment developed—newsreels. Introduced into the U.S. in 1911, newsreels at their height reached forty million theater patrons a week. For most of the current century, moviegoers saw a newsreel with every feature movie they attended. In 1927, when sound was added, audiences were able to reexperience sections of speeches they had heard earlier on radio or read in newspapers. So, for example, movie patrons came to applaud or hiss the newsreels of Roosevelt's Fireside Chats. Finally in 1967 the last surviving newsreel company—Hearst's News of the Day—went out of business, the victim of the Justice Department's breakup of the American film monopolies and of television's ability to transmit more timely visual recaps of the news.

Partisan films distributed through newsreel's channels and newsreels about political figures presaged televised political advertising. Their use in the campaign against Upton Sinclair, in both the Truman and Dewey campaigns of 1948, and in campaigns for New York Mayor Fiorella La-Guardia and against Louisiana Senator Huey Long is particularly noteworthy, for in all five instances the films are recognizably akin to contemporary televised political ads.

The creative talents of Hollywood and the distribution network in place to dispatch movies were both mobilized against Socialist California gubernatorial candidate Upton Sinclair in 1934. Newsreels attacking Sinclair were distributed to every movie house in the state. In the newsreels, actors playing the parts of ordinary citizens expressed concern, shock, and outrage at the prospect of Sinclair's election. So fearful of Sinclair were the owners of the motion picture industry that they threatened to relocate their studios in other states should he emerge victorious.

In April 1935, a "March of Time" newsreel, made with the unwary cooperation of Louisiana Senator Huey Long, demonstrated how a candidate and his supporters can become strong indictments of themselves and their cause. By so doing, the attack on Long prefigured attack ads that remind audiences of the opposition's self-damaging statements or actions. These ads include reminders of the unfulfilled promises of incumbents as did the National Conservative Political Action Committee's (NCPAC's) '80 replaying of footage from the Ford-Carter debates of '76 in which Carter promised lower inflation, lower unemployment, a lower deficit, and a balanced budget; McGovern's reminders in '72 that Nixon had promised in '68 to end the war in Vietnam; and Kefauver's evocations in '56 of the televised promise Ike made about lowering inflation when "Answering America" in '52. They also include ads that replay an opponent's gaffes as Ford's ads did in '76 when they recalled Carter's promise to increase taxes for those above the median income, as Carter's ads did in '80 when they reminded voters that Reagan had blamed most air pollution on trees, as Humphrey's ads did in '68 by repeating Agnew's statement that "if you've seen one slum you've seen 'em all." But in none of these instances did the indicted candidate cooperate in making the damning ad. In 1935 Huey Long made political history by poisoning the arrow that would be used to shoot him.

Unaware that the newsreel would ridicule him, Long permitted "March of Time" to film a reenacted phone call is which he asked the Senate leadership for more space to accommodate the huge quantities of mail he was receiving. To those scenes the "March of Time" added an impersonator's reenactments of "some of Long's more obnoxious behavior, including an unbelievably crude affront to the commander of the

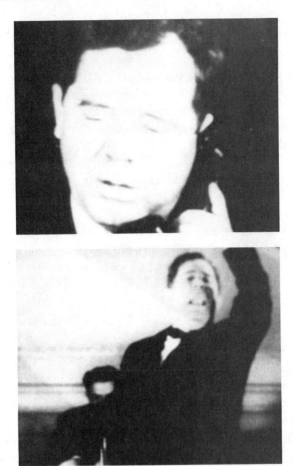

Stills from the "March of Time" newsreel about Huey Long. (Courtesy of SFM Media Productions, by permission of Stan Moger)

visiting German cruiser *Emden,* whom Long received in his hotel room, dressed in pajamas" and a brawl in the men's room of a private club.[83] The narration accompanying the incidents in the film was condemnatory: "To run his state, dictator Long puts in O.K. Allen, his good-natured henchman—new puppet governor of Louisiana. To his new friends in Washington, Huey boasts that back in Louisiana he has the best legislature money can buy."[84]

At the time the newsreel was shown, Long was a politically powerful senator who, as we noted earlier, commanded free network radio time, and who was touted by some as a successor to the man whom he had once supported and then bitterly opposed—FDR. The film's conclusion can be interpreted as a reminder that Long coveted FDR's job. In it "several newsreel shots of Huey Long giving a speech appear optically superimposed over each other, the very image of a modern demagogue, uttering what emerged on the sound track as gibberish. This, in turn, was followed by a brief but dignified statement by President Roosevelt."[85]

So incensed was Long at the newsreel that he introduced legislation into the Louisiana legislature authorizing censorship of movies and news-reels. The bill passed. Mysteriously but not surprisingly, although the film was distributed before passage of the censorship provision, it was not aired as scheduled in New Orleans.

Although campaign-sponsored films had been created on behalf of presidential candidates in earlier campaigns (e.g., Landon in 1936), in 1948 a film may have provided Truman with his razor-thin margin of victory.

Documentary films created for Truman and Dewey in the 1948 election and distributed to movie theaters prophesy the form and content of televised political campaign documentaries. Truman's film opens with his swearing the presidential oath, then telescopes his life and career, from his Missouri birthplace, to his service in World War I, through segments from key presidential speeches on civil rights, foreign affairs, housing, and Taft-Hartley, to enunciation of the Marshall Plan and the Truman Doctrine. The film culminates in footage of the 1948 Democratic convention and closes with the proclamation " 'Soldier . . . statesman . . . farmer . . . humanitarian . . . Harry S. Truman . . . President of the United States!' As the band played 'The Star-Spangled Banner,' the shot of the President faded into the streaming folds of the American flag."[86]

Where Truman's low-budget film was assembled from existing foot-age, Dewey's was specially produced. Where Truman's film stressed his stands on issues, Dewey's stressed his personality. The support cast in the Truman film included world leaders such as Stalin, Churchill, and Atlee whose presence placed Truman on a footing as an international leader and statesman. By contrast, Dewey marshaled Senator Arthur Vandenberg, whose testimony about Dewey's character and temperament seemed to have been extracted under duress.

In the newsreels' outtakes, the Democratic National Committee staff found an exchange between Truman and a March of Dimes poster child that underscored Truman's humanity and implicitly heightened the contrast between his candidacy and that of the person who Alice Roosevelt Longworth called the man on top of the wedding cake. "The child was looking stilted throughout the picture-taking," recalls Sam Brightman a Democratic National Committee staff member who worked on the film. "After it was all over, Truman smiles at her. She smiles at him and just reaches out and hugs him. You couldn't have actors do that. You couldn't get that kind of reality."[87]

Ironically, the Truman film, which would not have existed had the Republican's not distributed the Dewey film, benefited from its last minute low budget character. The use of existing footage gave the film a documentary, newsreel-like texture consistent with the theatergoers' experience of newsreels. The assembled footage made effective use of Truman's incumbency and by so doing heightened voter awareness of Dewey's comparative inexperience in national and international affairs. Because it was assembled late in the campaign, the Truman film was aired in the campaign's last week, a more opportune time in a close election than Dewey's earlier airings. The Director of Public Relations for the Democratic National Committee, Jack Redding, claims that "during the last six days of the campaign no one could go to the movies anywhere in the United States without seeing the story of the President" and concludes: "It was probably the most important and most successful publicity break in the entire campaign."

Redding reasoned that the weekly audience of the nation's 20,000 theaters was approximately 65,000,000 people who constituted "a 'captive' audience, for they paid to sit in the theatre and were not going to get up and leave when our film came on the screen. Nearly as important was the fact that we'd be reaching people of all political persuasions, not just Democrats."[88]

As noteworthy as the large captive bipartisan audience is the role the film industry played in producing the Truman film. Under threat that the Senate would investigate the production of the Dewey film and the theaters showing the Dewey film would be picketed, a representative of the film industry, Universal Newsreels, produced the Truman biography. Industry sources then printed and distributed it at no charge, an in-kind contribution worth at least $30,000.

Sam Brightman, who joined the Democratic National Committee's communications staff in 1947, explains the process by which the film industry came to produce the film this way:

> The movie people said "You make the film; we'll distribute it." We said, "We don't have money to make a film. We thought the newsreel industry would want to do a nice film about Truman." They seemed reluctant. Jack [Redding] remarked that no matter how the election came out the Democrats were sure to control the Senate and he knew some Senators who sure would want to hold hearings. They would be very curious to know how the arrangements were made to show the Dewey film. So the newsreel companies drew lots. The loser handled the hunt for footage and the other handled putting it together.[89]

So in 1948 over 50,000,000 people paid to view a political ad produced and distributed by the film industry at no cost to the Democratic party or the Truman campaign. "Newsreels were much more important to us than TV," concludes Brightman.

Television

In 1939 at the World's Fair in New York, FDR became the first incumbent president to deliver an address to a television audience. Although it reached less than 100,000 viewers, in 1940 television covered its first political conventions. By 1948 politicians were factoring television coverage into their political equations. In that year both conventions were scheduled in Philadelphia on the co-axial cable linking New York and Washington D.C., putting their messages within viewing range of voters who would decide 168 electoral votes.[90]

By 1948 political hopefuls had come to understand the visual nature of this new medium. Truman, for example, delivered his convention speech in a white suit and dark tie, which a reporter for the *New York Times* termed "the best masculine garb for the video cameras."[91] Another speaker, India Edwards, dramatized high prices by waving a piece of meat at the cameras. When the Publicity Director of the Democratic National Committee learned that she planned to use such visual aids he insisted that her speech be scheduled for prime time.[92]

The 1948 election was the first in which presidential candidates purchased television time to influence voters. Although Dewey would also purchase television time before the campaign ended, the first paid television appearance by a presidential candidate occurred on October 5, 1948, when Truman delivered a televised speech from Jersey City, New Jersey. In the aftermath of his narrow victory, Truman concluded that "television had been important in the areas where it was available" but regretted that "it did not cover more of the country."[93]*

By the end of Truman's presidency, coast-to-coast TV was a reality. In September 1951 Truman's address before the Japanese peace treaty conference in San Fransisco inaugurated the new transcontinental microwave video network.[94]

Once radio and television made mass audiences available, it was only

---

*Whether in 1948 the Truman campaign sponsored the first televised political spot ad remains, for me at least, an open question. A short clip of film in which he delivers a nonpartisan message urging voting does survive in the Schuck Collection at the John F. Kennedy Library. Since none of the Democrats who worked on media for Truman, including Leonard Reinsch, Roger Tubby, and Sam Brightman, recall such an ad, it may have been produced and aired locally in New York, may have been produced but not aired, or may have been part of a newsreel. Professor Victoria Schuck, who preserved the material as part of the collection given to her by the Democratic National Committee, does not know whether the material was created as a TV spot or a newsreel or whether it ever aired.

a question of time before a new political powerbroker emerged, the person who would ultimately come to create the candidates' broadcast and print advertising and shape the strategy of the campaign as well. In 1952, the media consultant, for the most part, was a technician who lifted quotes from speeches, as Rosser Reeves did, located citizens to ask questions, filmed both the question and the answer, edited them together, and added an announcer. Essentially, media consultants were technicians who purchased the air time, checked the lighting, supervised the make-up, arranged the set, and timed the speech. They played little role in the planning of the campaign. Often they did no more than produce live televised speeches. In 1952 the one media adviser whose role prefigured that of the media consultant of today was BBD&O's Ben Duffy whose long-standing relationship with the Republican party elevated his status. It was Duffy who determined that Ike should not debate Stevenson in 1952.

The first generation of television advisers learned politics on the job. Some like Nixon's Ted Rogers, Stevenson's Lou Cowan and William Wilson, and Kennedy's Jack Denove were live television producers; others such as Eisenhower's Carroll Newton and Rosser Reeves and the Democrat's Joseph Katz were professional admen; Charles Guggenheim was a film producer.

By 1964 the adteams had come to stand on an equal footing with the political operatives in the campaign. Veto power, however, still resided with what one of the admen called "the political types." In 1964 those responsible for political advertising begin to speak of themselves and the candidate in the intimacy of the royal "we." "What we were saying is . . ." "What we stood for was . . ." "We won a close election."

Although others in the campaign often produced or brought in producers of advertising apart from those retained by the agency, until 1960 a separate agency had never been spawned simply to create a campaign. What had occurred as the Democrats sought and failed to secure a large Madison Avenue agency in 1952, 1956, and 1960 was that the middle-sized agencies the Party retained supplemented their small staffs with sympathizers borrowed from larger agencies. In 1972, however, Nixon asked Carroll Newton to form an ad hoc agency, one independent of any existing ones, that would come together solely for the duration of the campaign. Newton did. That pattern gave rise to Nixon's November Group in 1972 and Reagan's "Campaign 80" in 1980.

In 1968, for the first time, the advertising supervisor managed an almost autonomous operation. Humphrey's campaign manager, Larry O'Brien, turned advertising over to his old friend Joe Napolitan. Napolitan had O'Brien's trust. O'Brien had Humphrey's trust. Napolitan pretty much did what he wanted.

By 1972 the person creating the Democratic advertising had the kind of access to McGovern that O'Brien had had to Humphrey. Charles Guggenheim had worked in McGovern's races for the Senate and created his media in the primaries and most of the general election with a free hand.

In 1976 after a few Ford intimates wrestled control of advertising away from one advertiser, who then resigned, and had three embarrassing ads produced by his replacement, the campaign learned its lesson. In the general election, a newly engaged firm, Bailey/Deardourff, was given wide latitude within which to work.

Carter sought the presidency in 1976 backed by the media created by the person who had produced the advertising for his winning run for the governorship of Georgia. Like Guggenheim in 1972, Gerald Rafshoon was an insider who participated in strategy decisions and produced what he thought would work. For a brief period during the Carter presidency, Rafshoon became the first media adviser to move from advertising in the general election campaign to a position in the White House.

In 1980 Rafshoon again created Carter's advertising while Reagan formed a group like Nixon's November Group headed by that group's former head, Peter Dailey.

The role of media adviser evolved from one of technical adviser unwelcome in the strategy sessions that governed the campaign to campaign insider responsible for the strategy for all the campaign's advertising and, often, for its communication strategy, as well. In this evolution the power of the media consultant and that person's autonomy progressively increased. Concurrently, in a story that requires another book, polling and media production moved from a passing acquaintance to an intimate liaison.

Midway through this evolutionary process, political media consulting became a profession. By the sixties, firms specializing in it emerged. Guggenheim opened his own firm as did Humphrey's live TV producer Robert Squier. The firm now called Bailey/Deardourff was founded in 1967. Humphrey's media director, Joe Napolitan, who had been a consultant since the late fifties, founded The American Association of Political Consultants (AAPC) in 1969. In 1957 Alexander Heard identified 41 public relations firms that offered campaign services. None focused solely on these services. In 1972, Rosenbloom identified about 60 firms that did the "bulk of their business in political campaigns" and at least 200 others "offering professional campaign management services as part of their business."[95]

With the publication of Joe McGinniss' *The Selling of the President:*

1968 in 1969, the focus of press and public on consultants and their product increased. Prior to the late sixties, an ad would garner media coverage only if it had been aired on behalf of a major contender and was controversial as were Goldwater's "Choice" and Johnson's "Daisy" ad.

As their presence became publicly known, media advisers stepped out of the shadows to hold press conferences screening their ads in the hopes of obtaining free exposure for their message. Candidates also held press conferences to announce which adviser they had retained. In 1970 CBS' Mike Wallace devoted a half hour program to political advertising and admen. When a media consultant resigned or was fired, news reporters wrote explanatory stories.

Since the following chapters will view the campaigns through the optic provided by their advertising, one might well ask what factors govern the sorts of ads a media adviser will create. Six seem to play a role of varying importance:

1. The strengths and weaknesses of the candidate and the opponent.
2. What has worked in the past.
3. Finances.
4. Circumstances such as the public's need for certain types of assurances.
5. The nature of the news coverage of the campaign.
6. The aesthetic inclinations of the media adviser.

In addition to examining the factors shaping the advertising strategies in each of the campaigns from 1952 to 1980, the following chapters will note how advertising was used to define the campaign. Kennedy, for example, wanted the electorate to view the 1960 campaign through the optic of domestic policy and the question who can better get this country moving again. On the other hand, Nixon wanted voters to ask who better understands what peace demands. In the process of seeing the candidate's preferred definition of the election through its advertising we will observe that advertising reveals well when a campaign is foundering in search of an overarching theme as Humphrey's was in September 1968 and Carter's throughout the general election of 1980. We will see candidates impaled on their own definitions as Carter's "Leadership for a Change" in 1976 confronts Reagan's "The Time is Now For Leadership" in 1980. We will also observe candidates caught in dilemmas as Ford was when he wanted to base his campaign on "I'm feeling good about America" but by so doing reminded voters that he pardoned Nixon in the name of putting Watergate behind us.

We will observe advertising setting expectations by which the victor's presidency will be assessed. These expectations•are the product both of candidate's claims about the future and of their opponent's prophesies about them.

In addition to telling us how the candidates define the election and what expectations will govern the presidency of the victor, the ads reveal the electoral significance of various voting groups, the relevance the candidates attach to various issues, and the extent to which past presidents have lived up to the images they and their opponents have created for them in their campaigns.

Chapter Two

1952: The Election
of a Popular Hero

In June 1950, the first armed confrontation of the Cold War began as North Korean troops crossed the thirty-eighth parallel dividing North and South Korea. The UN condemned the move and called on its members to help South Korea. Although an international contingent of troops was assembled under U.S. command, the majority of those sent came from the United States. As 1950 moved into '51 and '52, and the Korean War, with its attendant cost in American lives, showed little prospect of ending soon, the mood of the nation soured.

Things at home were not going smoothly for the Truman Administration either. Wisconsin Republican Senator Joseph McCarthy was engaged in his own little war, a well-publicized search for Communists in government, and a Senate investigation into activities of the Reconstruction Finance Corporation revealed that members of the corporation had submitted to pressures from Democratic politicians in making loans. "Korea, Communism, and Corruption" were the millstones the Republicans were prepared to hang around Harry S. Truman's neck in the primaries and general election of 1952, were he to run for a second complete term of office.

Truman's lack of popularity even within his own party was soon made manifest. In early March, in the first test of the season, Senator Estes Kefauver of Tennessee defeated the incumbent president in the New Hampshire primary. Less than thirty days later, on March 29, 1952, Truman surprised Democrats and Republicans alike by announcing that he would not be a candidate for reelection. Truman favored reformist Illinois Governor Adlai Stevenson as his successor, but Stevenson, who was then running for the Illinois governorship, repeatedly declared that he would accept the nomination for one office only, the one for which he was presently running.

The Democrats prepared for the '52 presidential convention with no clear front-runner in view. Stevenson's name was still the one most frequently cited but the man on whom the Democrats were about to place their trust seemed less than eager to accept it. Further, Stevenson was a divorced man and up to that time neither of the two national parties had ever had a divorced individual as their candidate. Nonetheless, when the Illinois governor's welcoming address approached William Jennings Bryan's "Cross of Gold" speech in dramatic effect, the Democratic nomination was his. On the third ballot, it was official.

In his acceptance speech, Stevenson "hoped" and "prayed" that "we, Democrats, win or lose, can campaign not as a crusade to exterminate the opposing party as our opponents seem to prefer, but as a great opportunity to educate and elevate a people." As his running mate, Stevenson chose Alabama Senator John Sparkman, who had served in the House of Representatives and as a delegate to the UN before entering the Senate. Although liberal by Southern standards, Sparkman brought regional and ideological balance to the Democratic ticket, being both a Southerner and a segregationist.

If the Republicans were prepared to focus on the very mixed Democratic record of Harry Truman's past four years in office, the Democrats saw their best chance for victory in reminding voters of Democratic achievements over the past twenty. But to understand the single most important factor in the 1952 campaign, the one the Democrats would have to counter to win, one must first know the background and promise of the man who would receive the Republican nod.

The Republican nominee in 1952, Dwight Eisenhower, would have been a difficult candidate for any politician to challenge. A career military officer who had been rapidly advanced from the lower ranks during the wartime emergency to become Supreme Commander of all Allied Expeditionary Forces,* Eisenhower emerged from the war the sort of popular hero of which kingmaker's dreams are made. Less than a month and a half after V-E Day, on June 27, 1945, the man who had coordinated the D-Day landings on Normandy was approached by reporters, who asked the obvious: did he have any plans to enter politics?

Eisenhower responded, "I'm a soldier and I'm positive no one thinks of me as a politician." This statement was more prescient than even Eisenhower could have imagined. But then he added, with less prescience, "In the strongest language you can command, you can state that I have no political ambitions at all. Make it even stronger than that if you can. I'd like to go even further than Sherman in expressing myself on the subject."

---

*In March 1941, Eisenhower had just attained the rank of colonel. By 1944 he had been moved through five ranks to become a five star general.

Nonetheless, in 1948 liberal Republicans still tried to lure this very model of a major modern general into the Republican primaries; likewise, the Americans for Democratic Action and such liberals as Florida Democrat Claude Pepper urged Ike to seek the Democratic nomination. He rejected these overtures and retired from the army to accept the presidency of Columbia University. Two years later, in 1950, Truman appointed Eisenhower "Supreme Commander, Europe" of the North Atlantic Treaty Organization.

In the spring of 1951, as Democrats and Republicans began to think about the upcoming election, Eisenhower's name remained prominent; in fact, a Gallup poll concluded that Republicans favored Ike over all other Republican hopefuls, including conservative Senator Robert Taft, New York Governor Thomas Dewey, and California Governor Earl Warren. Even more surprising, Democrats preferred him 40% to 20% over incumbent President Truman. When Massachusetts Senator Henry Cabot Lodge and New Hampshire Governor Sherman Adams entered Eisenhower's name in the New Hampshire primary, Ike won handily. His candidacy was endorsed by the *New York Times* as well as by other major newspapers.

A March 1952 Roper poll found that Eisenhower was the most admired of all living Americans, a popularity that translated readily into victories in the Republican primaries following New Hampshire. Eisenhower received twice Taft's vote in the primaries in which they faced each other directly. By convention week, the outcome was all but decided; the nomination was Eisenhower's at the end of the first ballot.

As his running mate, Eisenhower named California Senator Richard Nixon, a lawyer who had previously served in the House of Representatives. Nixon too was a ticket balancer, being more conservative than Eisenhower and coming from a key Western state. Best known as a tireless crusader against "the Communist conspiracy," Nixon had achieved national recognition by playing a prominent role in securing the perjury conviction of Alger Hiss. Hiss, a former State Department official, had been accused of turning classified material over to the Russians and had then denied ever having had contact with his accuser, former Communist party member Whittaker Chambers.

If ever a candidate entered the race for the presidency an untainted popular hero, Eisenhower was the candidate. His apolitical past insulated him at the same time as his military past prophesied that he would be uniquely able to end the stalemate in Korea honorably. Precisely because few thought of him as a politician or ascribed political ambition to him, Dwight D. Eisenhower appealed to political Independents and Democrats as well as traditional Republicans. Though other issues would take center stage in the '52 campaign from time to time, underneath it all lay the enormous appeal of this one man. What Eleanor Roosevelt would say of Stevenson's loss in '56 would be true of his loss in '52 as well—"the love affair between President Eisenhower and the American people is too acute at present for any changes evidently to occur."[1]

Selection of Advertising Agency

In a deal by which Michigan's delegates swung from Taft to Eisenhower at the Republican convention, Arthur Summerfield, chairman of the Michigan delegation, was named head of the Republican National Committee for the 1952 election. Summerfield's neighbor, Harlow Curtis, head of the Buick Division of General Motors, suggested that for their advertising the Republicans use the Kudner agency, which handled the Buick advertising account. On Labor Day, in Denver, Colorado, John Ellis, head of Kudner, made a presentation to Ike and his advisers.

Following the Republican defeat in 1948, Ellis had detailed for the strategy committee of the Republican National Committee what he viewed as the reasons for the loss. Subsequently, Ellis created advertising for Robert Taft's 1950 senatorial campaign and for his presidential bid in 1952.

As it turned out, Ellis's presentation to Ike and his advisers was judged inadequate and the Kudner agency was given responsibility for accounting only. The substantive responsibilities for the overall advertising plan were given once again to Ben Duffy at Batten, Barton, Durstine and Osborne (BBD&O), the firm that had handled Dewey's unsuccessful run in 1948. Working with him was BBD&O executive Carroll Newton.

In the general election as in the primaries, Young and Rubicam handled advertising for the Citizens for Eisenhower Committee, a group set up to permit those who would not contribute money to the Republican party to contribute nonetheless to Eisenhower's election. The Citizens Committee produced both live television and spots. In cooperation with the Disney studio, they produced an animated musical cartoon showing various animals parading with banners for Ike. Testimonials from senators such as James Duff and congressman such as Walter Judd also were aired.

No formal liaison between BBD&O and Young and Rubicam was established. The materials prepared by both were reviewed by Ike and his staff as were the general election spots prepared by campaign volunteer Rosser Reeves, then of the Ted Bates agency.

Joseph Katz, head of a medium-sized agency in Baltimore, had persuaded the Democratic National Committee of the advantages of hiring his agency, which, he pointed out, was located near Washington and could devote most of its energies to the Democratic account. The Baltimore office of the Katz agency had produced the advertising for the Democrat's senatorial campaigns in Maryland in previous years, while Katz' New York office had created the materials for the Democratic party in New York state.

In their relationships with their advertising agencies, Eisenhower forecast the future of politics while Stevenson was a throwback to the past. When Frank Stanton, president of CBS, suggested that Ike debate Stevenson on television, Ike asked whether Stanton had checked the idea out with Ben Duffy of BBD&O, Ike's main media adviser. Halberstam reports that "Stanton said he had. 'And what did he say?' asked Eisenhower. 'No,' said Stanton. 'Well, that's my answer,' said Ike."[2] By contrast, Joseph Katz functioned for Stevenson more as a technician than an adviser. He made sure that there were signs and balloons at the convention and supervised the purchase of time. Stevenson's perception of the status of television consultants was revealed clearly when one morning at 1 A.M. during the Democratic Convention in 1956, Stevenson summoned William Wilson, who had produced his live political broadcasts in the primaries. "I'm having terrible trouble with my television set," said Stevenson, "—the reception is very bad, and I wonder if you could drop down and fix it."[3] Wilson refused.

Estimates vary on how much the Republicans spent to air their spots. Republicans claimed one and a half million dollars but that estimate was scaled back later to $800,000. Whatever the figure, the amount substantially exceeded the sparse $77,000 spent by the Democrats. The nature of the spots differed as well. The Republican spots featured Ike. With a single exception, Stevenson was nowhere to be seen in the Democratic spots.

Where the Republicans outspent the Democrats in spot time, the reverse was true in time purchased for the delivery of speeches. Since Stevenson was a better public speaker than Ike this choice is understandable. Stevenson's lack of name recognition also accounts for the choice. As Robert Bendiner noted at the time,[4] television "enabled Adlai Stevenson, until the eve of the Democratic convention virtually the Great Unknown of American politics, to establish himself in three months as a figure of authentic stature."

Both parties made extensive use of broadcast endorsement speeches in 1952. Eleanor Roosevelt spoke repeatedly for Stevenson as did President Harry Truman. In an endorsement speech that probably did Ike more harm than good, Senator Joe McCarthy repeatedly called Adlai "Alger." Both Eisenhower and Nixon delivered televised speeches on behalf of the Republican ticket, as did Stevenson for the Democrats.

The Republicans' broadcasts reached a larger audience than did those of the Democrats' with Ike reaching an average TV audience of 4,120,000 to Stevenson's average audience of 3,620,000. Similarly, the Republicans reached an average radio audience of 1,868,000 to the Democrats' 1,514,000.[5] The difference was the function of a fateful decision by Joseph Katz to buy time for the Democrats sufficiently early to avoid paying preemption charges and to buy 10:30–11 P.M. rather than the more widely watched earlier hours of prime time.

A preemption charge is a fee over and above that charged for the purchase of time that reimburses the producers of a program for the money spent on a segment of a program or a program produced but displaced by a political ad. If enough notice is given, the producer can simply produce a shorter program for that date, a move that obviates the need for a preemption charge.

In an effort to regain the Democratic account in 1955, Katz would defend this decision by arguing that he had saved the Democrats $360,000. This was a small saving at the cost of a large loss in average audience. By paying preemption charges, the Republicans increased their short-term cost but gained a larger audience. Audiences did not know in advance that their favorite program would be replaced by a Republican political message but had ample warning of Democratic scheduled broadcasts and so could more readily choose to avoid them.

By replacing top-rated shows rather than less popular and less expensive shows, the Republicans intended to minimize the liklihood that the viewer or listener would find acceptable alternative entertainment on a competing channel. The Republican buying strategy backfired once in 1952, however, when viewers flooded the network with telegrams protesting the preemption of top-rated "I Love Lucy." "I like Ike" said the telegrams but "I Love Lucy." Newton notes that the lesson was quickly learned. The Republicans did not again preempt the most popular show.

All totaled, the Republicans outspent the Democrats on radio and television by about three to two, 3.4 million dollars to 2.6 million.[6] Unlike the Republicans, the Democrats were not always confident that they would have the money to air the broadcasts they had scheduled. Stevenson aide Carl McGowan recalls that a number of times the campaign was unsure of whether the money would be raised to pay for the half hour broadcasts. "In Baltimore we came within an hour of not having the money."[7]

In 1952 for the last time in the twentieth century, the amount spent on radio ($3,111,050) exceeded that spent on television ($2,951,328). Yet there is no reason to believe that if the Democratic and Republican totals had been reversed the Democrats could have won the election.

As the campaign got underway, public perception of the two candidates revealed in surveys showed that Stevenson's appeal exceeded Ike's in only three categories: he was perceived to have more direct political experience, be more educated, and to be a better speaker.[8] Ike was perceived to have a better family life, to be more likable, sincere, religious, and inspiring, to have a greater sense of duty, more integrity, independence, and strength, to be more decisive, a better administrator and leader, to have a better record in Europe, more military experience, and generally to be a good, capable, experienced man. The difference in public perception of the two would translate into 33,824,351 votes for Ike, the largest number given to any candidate in the history of the country to that time.

Defense of and Attack on Ike as Soldier-Statesman

Ike was the sixth general to translate military victories into election to the presidency. He followed in a tradition that included George Washington, Andrew Jackson, William Henry Harrison, Zachary Taylor, and Ulysses S. Grant. Significantly, these six generals won in high turnout elections in which a "surge" of interest in a "popular hero" drew previously apathetic citizens to the ballotbox in record numbers.[9] Indeed, "the capacity to draw transcendent popular support seems, across 44 American presidential elections, the particular domain of the military hero."[10]

Victorious generals who have led national armies in popular wars are strong presidential contenders because the role of general mimics that of president without entailing the encumbrances of a legislative past. But Eisenhower was more than just a great military figure. In his role as Supreme Commander in World War II, he had also functioned as the symbolic equal and occasionally the symbolic superior of great national leaders, such as Winston Churchill and Charles de Gaulle.*

In his dealings with these national leaders, Eisenhower had held his ground. For example, when he and Churchill clashed over the advisability of "Anvil," later named "Dragoon"—a plan that involved seizing the port cities of Marseilles and Toulon—Ike's view had triumphed.[11] Similarly, when de Gaulle threatened to remove the French soldiers from Eisenhower's command, Ike reminded the French leader that unless the French troops remained under the Supreme Allied Commander they

---

*Of course, in this regard, the one person who could have rivaled Ike in 1952 was the person with whom he had shared the role of leader of the allied forces, Franklin D. Roosevelt, who had died in 1945. Ike's ads would evidence a subtle awareness of this fact by describing Eisenhower as the one who "knows more about how to defeat Communism at home and abroad than any other living man."

would receive no food or ammunition. De Gaulle backed down.[12] Such actions rehearse a role we would like our president to play, that of first among equals. By applauding Eisenhower's personification of our aspirations in World War II and in NATO, by approving the way in which he vanquished the evil of Hitler in our name, by acknowledging his finesse in leading such leaders as Churchill and de Gaulle, leaders who would figure prominently on the world stage in the fifties, we viscerally experienced a dress rehearsal of the Eisenhower presidency. As the polls attested, his out-of-town tryout for the job was a smashing success.

While Eisenhower's speeches and advertising underscored the claim that his military past was sound preparation for the presidency, they were also careful to dispel any suggestion that here was a person whose military past caused him to favor war as a solution to international problems. "A soldier all my life, I have enlisted in the greatest cause of my life—the cause of peace,"[13] Ike noted. Though Republican ads continued to adopt military idiom, such as when they urged the election of Republican senators and members of Congress on the grounds that we should "Give a Good General a Good Army," Eisenhower's televised appearances communicated that his image in World War II had been that of the "GI General"—understanding, knowledgeable, sympathetic; in short, a wise father.[14] Those who both saw Ike on television and voted for him would later claim that he was "good-natured, sincere, honest, cheerful, and clear-headed." "Television," as Chester concludes, "humanized the General, making him more than just a military figure to the public."[15]

In their valient attempts to establish that the accomplishments of a professional soldier did not qualify one for the presidency, Democrats were confounded by "a lack of subjective barriers or compartments in the respondents' minds between the world of the military and civil politics." After a study of the political rise of both de Gaulle and Eisenhower, political scientists Philip Converse and Georges Dupeux concluded that "the past military splendor of the conquering hero diffuses through a wide variety of references which make up these images—patriotism, past record, leadership, capacities in dealing with foreign problems, etc."[16] Thus any attempt to disqualify Ike based on his military past would simply not be understood.

The Case for the Soldier-Statesman

Like Nixon's in 1968, Ike's campaign was strengthened by the Democrat's inability to extricate the country from a victoryless, costly, casuality-ridden war. As Gallup indicated in his analysis of the 1952 election results, the issue of Korea "played heavily into Eisenhower's hands." A September 7 Gallup poll found that 67% of the voters believed that Ike could better handle the Korean situation while only 9% thought Stevenson could.

Making the most of Ike's ability to capitalize on this Democratic weakness, and of the widespread public perception that the Republican party was better able to secure and maintain peace, a Republican print ad asked: "Is your boy America's only answer to Korea?" "Take a look at your boy." "The way things are going he's 'draft age' no matter how young he is. As a parent, wouldn't you be *ashamed* to turn your family problems over to him because you weren't bright enough to solve them?" Although we are the world's wealthiest nation, supposedly "long on brains," we are "booby-trapped" in Korea—"booby-trapped by our own futile, fumbling, blustering, retreating, hot-and-cold-running leadership in Washington."[17]

But did not Adlai Stevenson also offer a fresh chance of ending the conflict? The primal premise underlying the Republican attack on Stevenson was that he simply offered a continuation of the failed policies of Truman. So the ad says "Tuesday we vote to keep that leadership, under a new alias, or to scrap it forever and put America's brains back to work." Why Ike? the reader might ask. "The man who led us to victory in Europe, the man who put NATO together, is the man to release us from futility . . . not the man whose only counsel is 'patience' and whose only hope is 'wait.' " So, the ad concluded, "Take another look at your boy. Think about him when you vote Tuesday."

In a play on Truman's "The Buck Stops Here," the ad urged "Don't vote to pass the buck to him." Tying Korea into the mess in Washington, and playing on the fact that Stevenson was Truman's choice as his successor, the ad then notes "Don't vote to reshuffle the mess. Vote to *end* it. Vote for Dwight D. Eisenhower."

Republicans succeeded in their efforts to increase the importance of Korea as an issue. When asked to name major issues, one-quarter of those polled in January 1952 named Korea. By September that figure had increased to one-third. In late October it exceeded one-half.[18]

The Republicans also appear to have succeeded in their second maneuver regarding the Korean War—that is, in allaying any fears the public might have that the professional soldier in Ike might secretly relish waging and winning wars, a proclivity clearly dangerous in a person who would be president. A series of carefully written ads communicate the message that Eisenhower has clearly made the shift from military leader to civilian-statesman; that even out of uniform he commands the respect of international figures; that he can "persuade" as successfully as he could command; and, most important, that what he carries over from his

This still of General Dwight Eisenhower is taken from an ad called "The Man from Abilene" aired in the general election campaign of the Republican nominee in 1952.

military days are leadership qualities, not a love of war.* Yet, interestingly, the single most important sentence uttered in the 1952 campaign came out of an Eisenhower broadcast speech, not one of those carefully crafted print or spot ads.

On October 24, 1952, "a date late enough in the campaign to assure a high level of popular attention, yet not so late as to invite criticism as a last-minute device, slyly delayed as to escape rebuttal,"[19] Eisenhower

---

*One of Eisenhower's TV ads, patterned on the "March of Time" newsreels, transformed a soldier-statesman into a civilian-statesman who was the beneficiary of lessons learned in his military past. The spot juxtaposed scenes from V-E Day, 1945, with a card reading "Nov. 4, 1952, ELECTION DAY" as an announcer intoned "V-E Day. Now, another crucial hour in our history." The announcer then previewed "the big question." On screen a middle-aged man asked, "General, if war comes is this country really ready?" Looking steadily into the camera, Eisenhower responded "It is not. The administration has spent billions for national defense. Yet today we haven't enough tanks for the fighting in Korea." Ike then added the campaign's slogan: "It's time for a change." On screen a gun implacement appeared as the announcer said "The nation, haunted by the stalemate in Korea, looks to Eisenhower." A picture of Eisenhower along with British and Russian generals, appears as the announcer claimed "Eisenhower knows how to deal with the Russians." A picture of Ike strolling with Churchill followed. "He has met Europe's leaders, has got them working with us." In the last scene Ike now in civilian clothes was shown accepting the Republican nomination. As the civilian clothes certify, the transformation from soldier-statesman to civilian-statesman is now complete. "Elect the number one man for the number one job of our time" says the announcer. "November 4, vote for peace."

declared: "I shall go to Korea." If uttered by an Illinois governor, the pledge would have seemed contrived. Indeed, Stevenson had rejected the idea earlier in the campaign. But coming from a bona fide military hero, the pledge was political gold.

In that speech Ike argued that Korea "has been a symbol—a telling symbol—of the foreign policy of our nation." Having hung Truman, and by implication Stevenson, with this symbol, Ike refashioned it as a bold, decisive reminder that that his past qualified him to end that conflict. Democrats cried that Ike had not revealed what he would do once he arrived in Korea but the newsreels' fusion of Eisenhower and V-E Day, rehearsed repeatedly in Ike's ads, smothered such questions. The associative magic of television advertising had fused stalemate to Truman and victory to Eisenhower. Once the Republicans successfully linked Stevenson to Truman and the Democrats failed to bond Eisenhower to the Great Depression, Stevenson's prospects plummeted.

The Democratic Attack on the Soldier-Statesman

Stevenson's ads assaulted the link between soldier and statesman that Ike's ads had forged and in the process defined the job of president in a way that disqualified Ike from holding it. But if the Democratic contention that Ike lacked the experience to govern succeeded in underscoring the public perception that Stevenson had more positive political experience, it did not dent the public perception that generally Ike was more capable and more experienced, a better leader, better able to handle people, a better administrator, stronger, and more decisive. But most damaging to the Democratic conjurings of Ike dominated by Senators Taft, Jenner, and company was the public perception that Ike was more independent that Stevenson.[20] In short, the climate was more ripe to link Stevenson to "the mess in Washington" than to link Ike to Jenner and McCarthy.

Responding to the *New York Times'* endorsement of Eisenhower, an ad taken out in the *Times* by Stevenson's supporters attempted to rebut the claim that Ike is "our best hope of peace" by arguing that Eisenhower's past as a professional soldier has left him ignorant of domestic affairs and correlatively that nothing in his military past qualifies him to lead the nation. Here the ad drew strength from Ike's poor performance as a platform speaker and the vague and sometimes inconsistent positions he had taken in the campaign. The ad rehearsed such Eisenhower blunders as his claim that "the Soviet threat is no more to be feared than a pollywog swimming down a muddy creek." But, it noted that Ike "has devoted much time to stressing the fact that he is the best qualified man to deal with the ominous threat of world communism he likened to a pollywog."

The ad suggests that Ike's blunders were the byproduct of a hurried political education. Still, says the ad, he now has "loud, firm, and frequently inconsistent opinions on almost every subject under the sun."

Then, in a political reconstruction of Pascal's famous wager, the ad urges "If you must gamble with flat statement and unsupported opinion, wouldn't it be a better gamble to say that the general is emphatically disqualified?" Shifting to the second line of attack, the ad then asks since he is "innocent of background," "Who will advise him later? . . . Taft? McCarthy? Jenner? Revercomb?" He has after all endorsed them. And what of the danger of electing a professional soldier "accustomed to provide only *military* solutions to problems?" Certainly Ike is respected worldwide, the ad concedes, "but is a general in the White House our best "hope of peace?"

The Democratic ad then reminds its readers that "General Hindenberg, the professional soldier and national hero, also ignorant of domestic and political affairs," was "cajoled from the role of soldier to that of statesman. . . . He too had advisors. The net result was his appointment of Adolf Hitler as Chancellor and then World War II."*

Having planted the analogy, the ad then disclaims it, but only after having enumerated all the points of comparison—professional soldier, national hero, ignorant of domestic affairs, symbol of national unity, cajoled into role of statesman, . . . advisers. Of course, stress the ad's authors, they are not predicting that Ike would appoint an American Hitler. "But isn't it a better 'hope of peace' to keep the military subordinate to a civilian president?" Indeed from Eisenhower himself comes evidence that it is. The ad reminds us that in 1948 Ike wrote: "The necessary and wise subordination of military to civil power will best be sustained . . . when lifelong professional soldiers . . . abstain from seeking high political office."[21]

A print ad sponsored by "Ex-GI's for Adlai" took a different approach in its argument that we need civilian leadership. "We've had the military. We remember waste, bungling, red tape, bureaucratic confusion. We remember segregation, regimentation, the 'West Point Protective Association,' favoritism and cronyism. We don't think that's what this country needs. We want a President who knows the facts of civilian

---

*Although it may seem surprising to modern readers, both parties summoned the trauma of Hitler's conquest of Germany and Europe in support of their claims. Reminding voters that Democrats have controlled the White House for 20 years, a Republican ad (*New York Times*, October 28, p. 24) asks readers to "Remember—ONE PARTY RULE MADE SLAVES OUT OF THE GERMAN PEOPLE UNTIL HITLER WAS CONQUERED BY IKE."

government. High Brass has its place, but we want a civilian in the White House."[22] Above the copy is a Bill Mauldin cartoon showing a sign on the White House lawn. The sign reads "Off limits to enlisted men." It is signed "Gen. Taft, Gen. McCarthy, Gen. Jenner," and at the bottom of the list "Lt. Eisenhower."

A series of "open letters from Ike's fellow veterans" amplified these claims in such newspapers as the Washington *Star*. These ads argued that by treating them as he had his military assignments, Ike had bungled his only two civilian jobs, head of Columbia University and presidential candidate. "Academic amenities were dispensed with." Instead faculty and heads of departments were told when to rendezvous at the general's residence, instructed on the expected procedure, told what points the general would make and that he would accept questions. Then they would proceed out. In the environment the general created "Political opinion on the part of the faculty was considered 'out of bounds.' "

The ad recalled that one of the three hundred faculty members at Columbia who had signed an ad endorsing Stevenson told the *New York Times* that we need a president in the White House who "can exercise independent judgment under pressure and not be dependent upon a system of military briefing." Instead of "civilianizing" himself at Columbia, the ad argued, Ike had started "militarizing" the university.

Citizens for Eisenhower TV ads responded by arguing that only one who appreciated the horror of war could share Ike's dedication to peace and by noting that great generals had made great presidents in the past.

The Battle Over Whether as President Ike Would Give or Take Orders

The prophesy that Eisenhower's inexperience as a civilian officeholder would translate into a White House in which the politically naive Eisenhower would take orders from conservative Robert Taft, Joseph McCarthy, William Jenner, and associates was widespread in the Democratic advertising of 1952. The theme emerged when Ike made peace with his Republican rival and primary opponent, Bob Taft.

Taft, who had won both the Wisconsin and Illinois primaries, received 500 votes on the first convention ballot. As the candidate of the conservative wing of the Republican party, Taft, son of a president, in themes that prefigured the campaigns of Barry Goldwater in 1964 and Ronald Reagan in 1976 and 1980 campaigned against "creeping control of government encroaching upon the people."

To solidify his support from the conservatives, Ike had met with Taft at Ike's residence in Morningside Heights in New York. There Ike assured Taft of his support for conservative policies and promised Taft his share of party patronage. After the meeting Taft announced that the two were in fundamental agreement on the issues and declared that he would campaign for Ike's election.

Stevenson observed that the meeting at Morningside Heights had transformed the "Great Crusade" that Ike had promised in his acceptance speech into a "Great Surrender." "Taft lost the nomination but won the nominee," Stevenson observed. Stevenson's televised advertising argued that if Ike were elected, "Bob Taft would give the orders," indicted the General's "unconditional surrender" to Taft, and appropriated some of the lyrics and the tune of a popular song to sing that Ike "would look sweet upon the seat of a White House that's built for two."

Ike's battle against Taft in the primaries had raised two questions that we will address both here and in subsequent analysis of other campaigns: how does a presidential nominee's advertising in the general election reflect the need to regain support lost to opponents in the primaries, and what use does advertising in the general election make of the rhetoric of those who lost in the primaries?

Under a principle comparable to "my enemy's enemy is my friend," opponents mine the intra-party rhetoric from their opponent's primary battles. Accordingly, Nixon's print ads in 1960 recall reservations expressed by Truman, Johnson, and others about JFK; statements by Romney, Scranton, and Rockefeller are resurrected in Democratic ads against Goldwater in 1964; and Bush's assault on Reagan's "voodoo economics" is quoted in Carter's ads in 1980.

Under the rules of this game, the vanquished candidate whose rhetoric is being resurrected must demonstrate that his uniform is now that of his party's victor. In the process he must praise the former foe and fire upon the opposing nominee. The vanquished endorse their party's victor in broadcast and print ads with the apparent intent of ensuring that their supporters will not bolt to the opposing party and of muting the impact of the other party's use of their fratricidal rhetoric from the primaries. Such ostensible selflessness is the price of political survival; such endorsements immunize them from charges of being "sore losers," "bad sports," and, most important, of being unworthy of the elusive nomination in the future. So although Ford's election in 1976 might have squashed Reagan's chances of ever reaching the Oval Office, Reagan's taped ads urged the election of the man who had beaten him for the Republican nomination. Similarly in radio spots taped for the general election of 1960 Hubert Humphrey reversed a position he had taken during the primaries and argued that the election of Kennedy would benefit the farmer.

To unify a party wounded by divisive infighting during the primaries, the runner-up may be offered the second spot on the ticket. So Rockefeller is asked to be Nixon's vice-presidential candidate in 1960; Johnson becomes Kennedy's, Bush becomes Reagan's, and Ford, who retained a following from his razor-thin loss to Carter in 1976, is offered the vice-presidency by Reagan in 1980. Alternatively, an ideological cousin of the prominent loser is added to the ticket. Accordingly, Carter's choice of Mondale soothed Udall's liberal supporters, Ford's choice of Dole was a bone thrown to Reagan's constituency, and Ike's selection of Nixon placated Taft's followers.

As a general rule, when the losing candidates from the primaries stand ideologically to the center of the nominee, as Rockefeller did in '64, the winning candidate fears that disappointed voters will cross over the party line to vote for the opposing party's nominee. When the losing candidates are to the right or left of the victor, as Reagan was to Ford's right in 76, Taft to Ike's right in '52, Udall to Carter's left in '76, and Kennedy to Carter's left in 80, the fear is that, faced with two ideologically unsatisfactory choices, the losers' supporters either will not vote at all, a choice made by many Reagan supporters in '76, or will switch to third party candidates. Get-out-the-vote advertising courting these potential supporters is generally a prominent feature of such races.

Ike's accommodation of Taft and his conservative supporters was not the only one of Ike's gestures of intra-party harmony exploited in Stevenson's ads. When Ike endorsed the election and reelection of other Republicans, the claim that Taft would run the White House was extended to forecast that isolationist, red-baiting, Republican senators would also influence White House policy making.

Underlying this strategy is the assumption that these Republicans were either disreputable, dangerous, or both. Evidence for such claims was laid out in an ad that declared that the General had urged the "re-election of the rabidly isolationist Senators—men who as a group fought to cripple rearmament, aid to Korea, NATO, the UN, the Point Four Program, and almost every other measure to keep strong against the Soviet threat."[23] The senators labeled "reckless, often unscrupulous, consistently evil force[s] in American politics" were Joe McCarthy, William Jenner, Harry Cain, James Kem, John Bricker, Arthur Watkins, Zales Ecton, and George Malone.

Transporting the conventions of the radio-play to television, one of Stevenson's TV ads pitted a male Stevenson supporter in an argument with a male Eisenhower supporter in an elevator stalled during what the female elevator operator presumes may be an air raid. In the course of the argument, as the female worries about her hair and her boyfriend, the Democrat identifies McCarthy, Jenner, and the like as the members of Eisenhower's "team," a word that echoed Ike's recurrent use of it. The ad also rehearses the "team's" foreign policy votes, and recalls that although McCarthy called General Marshall a "traitor," Eisenhower failed to repudiate the Wisconsin senator. This attack challenged Ike on his refusal to read McCarthy out of the party but also on his decision during a campaign tour through the junior Senator's home state of Wisconsin not to deliver an already scripted paragraph praising Marshall and condemning his attackers.

Pictures of McCarthy that appear in Stevenson's televised ads uniformly resemble the mug-shots on post office "wanted" posters. Capitalizing on the visual potential of the infant medium, the tele-play also vilifies Jenner, Kem, and company with roguelike photos.

The Democratic ads that claim Ike wants to see McCarthy and company in power are making a more cogent argument than those that indict him for inviting them to join his team. In the first case, their candidacies are endorsed despite their positions; in the second they are invited to embrace Ike's principles, principles that the Democratic ad tacitly endorses when it indicts Ike for embracing those whose principles differ from his own.

The attack on the isolationism and abridgment of civil liberties championed by the vilified senators reveals the intended audience of the Jenner-McCarthy claims. Eisenhower's political "innocence," as one ad called it, had in 1948 led liberal Republicans and liberal Democrats alike to read onto his tabula rasa their own political convictions. Not surprisingly, as the campaign drew to a close, polls were registering substantial support for Ike within traditional Democratic households. The ties to Jenner and McCarthy among others are an attempt to draw traditional Democrats, particularly Democratic liberals, out of Ike's embrace.

An attempt to impale Ike's candidacy on his own military metaphors characterized the Democratic print ads. In the world envisioned in Mauldin's cartoon, McCarthy and company would give Ike orders. Evidence prophesying this eventuality was drawn from Eisenhower's meeting with Taft at Morningside Heights. As the tele-play notes, "If you have any doubts about who would run the White House, read Taft's statement after Eisenhower's surrender."

The final attempt to turn both the military metaphor and Ike's military past against the Republicans occurred in a series of ads patterned on Ben Shahn's anti-Eisenhower poster "The Man on the White Horse." The print ads that analogized the maligned senators to the soldiers inside the Trojan horse ran daily in the *New York Times* from October 27 through November 3. Each carried the warning "Watch Out for the Man on a White Horse." Then under the horse the appeal "Better Vote for Stevenson."

Watch out for The Man on a White Horse!

—better vote for Stevenson

"Man on the White Horse" print ad from the 1952 Stevenson campaign. (Reprinted with the permission of Adlai Stevenson III)

In the first ad the Trojan horse is on a platform on wheels. Nixon, Taft, McCarthy, Kem, and Jenner, briefcases in hand, are shown entering the belly of the horse through a door in its side. A larger-than-life-size grinning caricature of Eisenhower is perched on its back, sword upraised in a mock heroic posture. In the second, Ike is again perched on the horse. This time he is fiercely ordering it to go. The horse stands motionless as Nixon and his cronies peer from its belly. In the third, the size of the horse has increased and the size of Ike decreased, but the message is the same. The fourth shows a puppet horse with the Senators and Nixon carrying it and constituting its legs. Ike, astride the horse, is carrying a sign that reads "Me Too." The fifth shows a militaristic Eisenhower grinning maniacally and brandishing a sword. The lifeless horse contains the Senators peering from the hole in its side. In the sixth, the Senators are in Grecian military attire. Nixon, with a microphone in hand, holds the wooden horse's reins as the Senators enter its side. Ike, with a bewildered look straddles the horse. In the seventh ad, the wooden horse has given way to a horse balloon tied by strings to the Senators who are guiding its journey. Again Nixon holds the microphone. In the final ad the horse has been mechanized. Taft is behind it winding it up as Nixon and McCarthy watch from a side panel. Eisenhower, sword in hand, seems to believe that he is directing the horse. He cannot see that the prime mover is Taft. This reconstruction is one of the most famous ancient legends offers an historically resonant optic for viewing Ike's candidacy. What you see, the ads imply, is not what you get.

The attack on the reactionary Republicans was a strategic response to the most vexing question confronting the Democrats in both 1952 and 1956: Without discrediting oneself in the process, how does one discredit a person who is loved and respected? These ads do not appeal directly for a vote against Ike but for a vote against the vilified team one supposedly embraces by embracing Ike.

This appeal is plausible only if we assume the mistaken but widespread public belief that the House and Senate are controlled by the party whose nominee sits in the White House or if we believe that Americans in 1952 are likely to vote a straight party ticket. Under either scenario, electing Ike will carry Republicans into office. And with them comes their advice to the political neophyte. So electing them and him, goes the reasoning, might well mean that the conservatives or worse, the reactionaries, will run the White House.

But Americans were well able to divorce their support for Ike from their support for other Republicans. Three out of five of those who voted for Ike in 1952 failed to support the rest of the ticket. Consequently, of the Republicans who in the Democratic construction of reality would run the Eisenhower White House, half lost their seats in 1952. Malone, Jenner, Bricker, and McCarthy were winners; Ecton, Kem, Revercomb, and Cain losers. Taft, reelected in 1950, was not on the ballot in 1952.

Ads Directed to Times Readers

When, on October 23, the *New York Times* endorsed Eisenhower, it dealt the presumed candidate of the intellectuals a severe blow. Capitalizing on this coup, the Republicans bought ad space in the *Times*[24] to reprint the endorsement. Two of Stevenson's supporters countered with two strongly worded ads urging the *New York Times* to switch its endorsement to Stevenson.

The day after the *Times* endorsed Ike, Stevenson's supporters argued in an ad that Ike had embraced candidates whose policies "the *Times* has always courageously fought."[25] A second Stevenson ad noted that the *Times' had "regretted" Eisenhower's endorsement of some of the Republican senators.*[26] The *Times* stuck by its endorsement.

Perhaps fearful that the endorsement and the surrounding controversy would damage its credibility with the so-called "eggheads" who both supported Stevenson and read the *New York Times,* the *Times* ran an ad of its own that included a memo to reporters and news editors articulating the *Times' policy "for covering this year's campaign." The memo said, in part: The Times* is supporting General Eisenhower on its editorial page. It goes without saying, of course, that the news columns should offer no clue to this position. The editorial page is no concern of *Times* reporters and news editors."[27]

The Truman Factor

To Stevenson fell the task of establishing that he was better qualified than Ike to deal with economic problems, Korea, and corruption. Here Truman's nationally broadcast speeches on October 22, 24, and 30, and his presence along with that of vice-president Alben Barkley on Stevenson's election eve broadcast did more harm than good, for they linked Stevenson with the Truman record when the issues that led the opinion polls—Korea, taxes, costs, and corruption—indicted the status quo. Moreover, they allied the Democratic candidate with an unpopular president. On November 12, a Gallup Poll reported that 55% disapproved of Truman's handling of the presidency while only 32% approved.

"For many of the wrong reasons Truman was very unpopular," recalls Carl McGowan who served on Stevenson's gubernatorial and 1952 campaign staffs. "The last thing a Democratic candidate needed was to be Truman's hand picked candidate."[28] Moreover, in his whistlestop tour and in his televised addresses Truman focused on his own record and the

Democrat's twenty year record in the presidency rather than on Stevenson's unique merits. His vice-president did the same. So, for example, in his speech in the election eve telecast Barkley defined the election as one in which the American people would "render a decision on a twenty year record of the Democratic Party." With sentiment for change running high, this contention framed the election in terms damaging to the Democratic nominee.

Why then did the Democratic nominee and the Democratic National Committee permit an unpopular president to play such a central role in the 1952 campaign? Willard Wirtz, a central member in Stevenson's research and writing group known as the Elks' Club, explains it in simple political terms. Truman commanded the loyalty of party regulars—the precinct captains who would turn out the traditional Democratic vote; Stevenson did not.[29] Another aide adds that Stevenson did not want to be disrespectful and "didn't want to seem churlish. If the man wanted to make a speech for him, let him." I suspect an additional factor was operating as well. Once before, the polls had predicted that a Truman campaign would end in defeat; once before Truman had proven the pollsters wrong. So in 1952, using the same whistlestop technique that had worked in 1948, Truman tried a second time to pull the rabbit out of the hat. How could Stevenson's supporters deny him that opportunity when it ostensibly had saved the White House for the party against all predictions in '48? The difficulty in '52 was that the hat was empty.

The Democratic election eve telecast crystallized the dilemma that Truman's campaigning foisted on Stevenson. Where in the second speech of the evening Truman offers a ringing defense of his administration's handling of "the danger of Communist imperialism," in the final speech of the program, Stevenson indicts "the miserable stalemate" in Korea and urges that the war and the stalemate "must be freshly reviewed by fresh minds." No one in the Stevenson campaign had seen a copy of Barkley's or Truman's speech before their delivery. But if they had it is doubtful that any would have asked the president to abandon the defense he had mounted so forcefully throughout his whistlestop tour of the country and in his earlier televised speeches.

The Old Order Passes: Stevenson and the Televised Campaign Speech

Stevenson first came to public notice and at the same time recognized his potential as a political candidate when his introductions of guest speakers at the Chicago Council on Foreign Relations were better received than the featured speech. Indeed as special assistant to Secretary of the Navy Knox, he wrote his speeches.

Stevenson's comfort with the speech as a rhetorical form and his manifest discomfort with both the spot announcement and with television symbolize the passing of the old order.

In his moving eulogy of Adlai Stevenson, Judge Carl McGowan described him as "of a generation of Princeton students who thrilled to the saga of Woodrow Wilson—that figure in our history in whom the contrasting worlds of the university and the precinct have had their most dramatic conjunction." And, speaking in the Washington National Cathedral in which Wilson is buried, he added "the youthful admirer has completed the course with honor, and is at rest with the admired."[30]

In the comparison resides an important insight into the political successes and failures of both Stevenson and Wilson. Central to the conception both held of the presidency was a belief that the president was a spokesman; both viewed the word as the expression of the person, a means by which a candidate could be judged. Both shared the conviction that if they talked sense to the American people, their cause would triumph.

Once the broadcast media became mass media, they propelled candidates toward reliance on speechwriters as national radio and TV audiences demanded original discourse, not reruns. In an earlier age, a candidate could deliver the same speech over and over for years without reaching the entire nation. So, for example, William Jennings Bryan delivered "The Prince of Peace" hundreds of times. In such an environment, Stevenson's desire to perfect a text would not have taxed his candidacy. The existence of mass audiences in campaigns, in which the principle paid form of message was the speech, rendered Stevenson's vision of the presidential candidate obsolete.

At the same time, the insistence of television and radio that broadcasts segment themselves into pre-set time blocks—such as thirty minutes—grated against his sense that the content of his speeches was paramount and sacrosanct. In the age in which the stump speech was the candidate's main means of reaching audiences, length was dictated not by a stopwatch but by content and by the forbearance of the audience. Ironically, had Stevenson been transplanted into a presidential campaign in the eighties, the wonders of videotape editing could have camouflaged his tendency to speak beyond the prescribed time limits by compressing his speeches to the required length.

Additionally, television's preference for a direct, intimate style demanded that Stevenson adapt to the teleprompter; he engaged it in a victoryless war. Finally, Stevenson was foiled by the broadcast media's simultaneous embrace by the most as well as the least educated members of society. To this audience, Stevenson offered complex, highly nuanced ideas expressed in the language of the university, not the middle school.

Not only were the style and tone of Stevenson's broadcast speeches dissonant with the broadcast media's standard fare but they were unlike the
rhetoric of his opponent as well. The audience able to appreciate Stevenson's eloquence was a small segment of the larger whole—a segment too
small to elect him in either '52 or '56.

Words as Monstrances

The importance Stevenson attached to the written word is evident in his
autobiographical statements as well as his actions. In his election eve
telecast in 1952 he placed "writing" at the head of the list of his activities,
followed by "travelling, speaking almost incessantly, yes, and listening to
countless thousands of American people."[31] His advisers reinforced this
tendency by contrasting it to Eisenhower's willingness to be made over by
his managers. Stevenson "wants the campaign to be his own and to express his real personality. . . . The General," Stevenson's aides say, "is
being pushed by his advisors into talking and acting differently from his
instincts."[32] The half hour documentary televised by the Stevenson campaign on his behalf also highlighted the candidate's writing of his own
speeches.

Stevenson's agonized choice of the best from among the available
means of persuasion altered the character and the press' perception of his
campaign. By agonizing over the choice of one word rather than another,
Stevenson raised speculation in the press that he was indecisive. Mary
McGrory writes "The running argument in the press bus was that the
campaign, like war, reveals the man. It followed as the night the day that
a candidate who could not choose between words could not choose between courses of action in the White House."[33] To this McGowan responds: "he may have taken a lot of time but he usually found the right
word."

But Roger Tubby, who in 1956 coordinated press coverage for Stevenson, shared McCrory's reservations. "As the campaign wore on,"
Tubby recalls, "I really began to wonder if he had to make a critical
decision would he worry over it. I'd come from working for Harry Truman who was very thoughtful but didn't worry and fret endlessly. This
was or seemed to be a real weakness." Tubby overcame these doubts by
recalling instances in which Stevenson had acted decisively as governor of
Illinois.[34]

Reliance on the speech as the major form of political mass communication hobbled the 1952 Stevenson campaign. By the standards of the
contemporary political campaign, in both '52 and '56 the Republicans' use
of television was more versatile than the Democrats'. The Republicans'

broadcasts also demonstrated their understanding of television as essentially a medium of entertainment. Whenever a choice was possible, Stevenson choose the speech as a form while, by contrast, the Republicans often chose more visually interesting, attention-holding vehicles. "Campaigning with Stevenson," a half hour telecast, is little more than clips of campaign speeches edited together. Similarly, in their election eve telecasts of 1952 both parties used simulcasts enabling them to reach radio and television audiences at the same time, but where the Democrats broadcast speeches by Truman's vice-president Alben Barkley, Truman himself, John Sparkman, Stevenson's running mate and Stevenson himself, the Republicans broadcast a fast-paced, multivisual half hour that included both questions and statements of support from persons around the country.

For Stevenson, sentences were monstrances displaying ideas, not motors driving actions. Guiding his introspective 1952 election eve telecast was the premise that assumed that a decisive test of a presidential candidate was the clarity with which he expressed his vision for the country. At the same time he conceded that he was not "wholly content" that he had "said or said well" what was in his heart and that he was not sure that he had made his views "on all of our concerns clear and precise." The clarity with which the vision is expressed was then at least as important as the vision itself.

Stevenson's obsession with writing and rewriting often minimized his effectiveness as a communicator. Charles Guggenheim, who directed Stevenson's televised speeches in the general election of 1956, recalls that Stevenson wrote and rewrote one speech to the extent that he could not read his text. In his description of his activities in the 1952 campaign,[35] Stevenson acknowledged that his obsessive revising minimized his ability to deliver his message. You must, he said, "bounce gaily, confidently, masterfully, into great howling halls, shaved and made up for television with the right color shirt and tie—I always forgot that—and a manuscript so defaced with chicken tracks and last minute jottings that you couldn't follow it even if the spotlights weren't blinding and even if still photographers didn't shoot you in the eye every time you looked at them."[36]

The consequences of Stevenson's rewriting are memorialized in dozens of anecdotes. Stevenson insistently revised one speech to the very last minute as the staff frantically conveyed new page after new page to be reset on the teleprompter. As a result of Stevenson's last minute rewriting, the section of the speech with which he was most displeased but which he rewrote last arrived too late to be put on the teleprompter. When Stevenson realized that the peroration appearing on the teleprompter was the one he had earlier rejected, he was visibly displeased.

"I thought he was going to pick up and walk out," Wirtz recalls. But Stevenson stayed and delivered the conclusion offered him by the teleprompter.[37]

The experience was more typical than not. "The Governor was so busy working on the speeches themselves until the last minute that Lou Cowan [Stevenson's TV advisor and producer in 1952] never really had the chance to have him rehearse. . . . As a professional Cowan was used to having elaborate rehearsals of important television performances. He really was in despair that he was not even able to approach the kind of rehearsal that he would have expected by CBS' standards" recalls McGowan. "The Governor regarded the content of the speeches as more important than anything else." The same difficulty plagued Stevenson's television producer in 1956. Charles Guggenheim estimates that because of Stevenson's rewriting until the last minute, he typically delivered only about two-thirds of his speech on the air.

"Adlai's insistence upon working on his speeches to the last minute has become part of the legend," wrote George Ball. "We used to tell him that 'he would rather write than be President.' On more than one occasion he completely missed press coverage by withholding his speeches for further polishing until after it was too late to make the morning newspapers."[38] Stevenson's insistence on drafting and redrafting also taxed his energies "as he stayed up late into the night to the despair of the staff when he was under heavy physical pressures anyway."[39]

Stevenson also believed that audiences were entitled to new speeches specifically tailored to them. "On the first whistlestop from San Fransisco to Los Angeles, he would see the familiar faces of the press. So in the first four speeches he gave a different speech each time. Then Scotty Reston and a couple of others asked to see him. They said 'Governor, don't feel that you have to deliver a separate speech each time for us. You'll kill yourself if you keep this up.' "[40]

Rebellion Against Pre-set Time Limits for Speeches

Stevenson also resisted Procrustean efforts to cut the length of his speeches to the ordained time limits of the telecast. His aides employed every form of clock to forewarn him that his time was about to end. Only in the mid-term elections of 1954 did they obtain some measure of success when William McCormick Blair responded to Stevenson's inquiries about the number of words in a thirty minute speech with a deflated estimate. The success of this approach was short-lived. "Not once in the 1956 campaign did Stevenson finish a nationally broadcast speech on time," recalls Guggenheim. "We'd fade out as he was still talking."

So, although historians quote the eloquent peroration of Stevenson's 1952 election eve speech as if it had in fact been delivered to the nation,[41] the producer had faded to the disclaimer long before Stevenson stated "Tomorrow you will make your choice. . . . If your decision is General Eisenhower and the Republican party, I shall ask everyone who voted for me to accept the verdict with traditional American sportsmanship. If you select me, I shall ask the same of the Republicans—and I shall ask Our Lord to make me an instrument of His peace." Frantically, Stevenson's aides scrambled to buy time later in the evening to broadcast the peroration. Stevenson's rate of delivery varied from speech to speech and within a speech itself, so one designed to be delivered in a half hour might still take longer.

Stevenson seemed to compulsively extend his speeches beyond television's ordained time. His running mate in 1952, John Sparkman, recalled that Stevenson read and timed his speech before the election eve program. Adequate time was allotted for the speech at the end of the telecast. "Somehow, however, he seemed to read very slowly as he was 'cut off.' "[42]

Kinescopes of Stevenson's televised speeches in 1952 and 1956 confirm that his inability to finish speeches within pre-set times was often a function of extemporaneous additions to the introductions of speeches. Such was the case with his 1952 election eve speech. Only after engaging the members of the immediate audience (in this case his two sons and his running mate) in small talk did Stevenson turn to his prepared remarks. Today the adaptive warm-up would wind up on the editing room floor; live broadcasts afforded Stevenson no such luxury.

Stevenson's loathing of abbreviation translated as well into dislike of spot announcements. In Wirtz' judgment, Stevenson's view of spot announcements coincided with Woodrow Wilson's of whistlestops. Each afforded the opportunity to commit only a compound fracture of an idea.

A Difference in Creation of the Ads

Although Stevenson agonized over every word of his broadcast speeches, he delivered scripts for ads as written. He apparently responded to the task of filming them as he had to the job of delivering a speech attacking Nixon, which we discuss further in the next chapter, by holding his nose, gritting his teeth, and getting the job done. As a result, his delivery in the spots is more wooden than that of the broadcast speeches which in turn were delivered more haltingly than his extemporaneous remarks.

Stevenson also balked at the intrusions of Madison Avenue. After winning the nomination in 1956 he seemed relieved to turn responsibility for television over to the firm hired by the Democratic National Committee, Norman, Craig and Kummel. The relief was transformed into regret when a brash adman on the account attempted to revamp Stevenson's delivery and resculpt his image. Stevenson responded by reconscripting Charles Guggenheim, a young filmmaker from St. Louis who on the advice of Louis Cowan, Stevenson's '52 media adviser, had produced some of Stevenson's ads in the 1956 primaries. Subsequently, Guggenheim directed the broadcast speeches of the general election and the Man from Libertyville spots.

Stevenson's reluctance to recast himself in the image desired by media advisers marked him as the last of a kind. "He was offended by the idea that he might be required to put on a sentiment or an important emotion," says William Wilson, who produced live television for Stevenson in '56 and worked in three subsequent presidential campaigns. "After that, candidates said 'What do you want me to do?' 'Where do you want me to stand?' Stevenson was the last one who said 'I can't be phony.' "[43]

The Battle with the Teleprompter

What Wirtz calls the "contrivances" of television also plagued Stevenson, who intensely disliked the teleprompter. He thought, recalls Wirtz, "that the devil him or herself had a personal copyright on the teleprompter. He had an obsessive dislike of contrivances." The teleprompter intruded between him and his audience; additionally, the reflection of the lights on it made it difficult for him to read his speech, a factor contributing to his faulty delivery of the important opening speech of the 1956 campaign. And when teleprompters were set to each side and before the center of the podium, as they were in that speech, "it was" according to Ball, "an absolute disaster because he kept turning from left to right as though he were in a Ping Pong match." That crucial speech, carried on all three networks, was in the judgment of Stevenson's aides a "catastrophe." So frustrated were a group of miners watching Stevenson's bout with the teleprompter that Roger Tubby remembers them shouting "Adlai, don't pay any attention to that God damned thing. Talk to us straight."

Prompted by a friendship spawned by their attacks on and by Joe McCarthy, Edward R. Murrow tried to increase Stevenson's comfort with and aptitude for televised speech. Murrow's interview with Stevenson on "Person to Person" in 1954 revealed a warm, intimate side of the once and future Democratic nominee, unconstrained by text or teleprompter. Before the 1956 race, George Ball invited Murrow to give Stevenson two or three lessons in televised delivery. The studio time was paid for by the Stevenson campaign. "Murrow was trying to get him to speak with

In 1952 the Democratic nominee relied primarily on half hour speeches to carry his message to the American people.

greater ease on television," Ball recalls, "and to adopt a uniform speaking pace." Murrow addressed other problems as well. "Stevenson had the habit of smiling on television in a way that resembled a facial tic. It was a quick smile that looked artificial. He was aware that he had a bald head and that when he read a speech he would look down at it and the audience would principally see his bald head. On the other hand he was never patient enough to learn to use the teleprompter." Stevenson proved immune to the teaching of even Murrow. The delivery of his scripted television speeches was in 1956 as stilted as it had been in 1952.

The furor over columnist and commentator George Wills' role in preparing Ronald Reagan for his 1980 debate with Carter points out the extent to which the ethics of the profession of journalism have changed over the years. Apparently, neither Murrow nor Ball considered Murrow's coaching of Stevenson a potential conflict of interest. "I think you could make that claim," says Ball. "[At the time] it never occurred to me." Nor did CBS reporter David Schoenbrun, who provided comparable advice to Eisenhower, apparently consider that role problematic. Ironically, Ike's and Stevenson's advisers shared a concern addressed by Murrow and Schoenbrun respectively that when tilting their heads to read their speeches over television, the candidates' hairless scalps were elongated, suggesting giant eggs.

The Reluctant Candidate in '52 and the Language of Reservation

The man with the hole in his shoe* seemed to harken to an age in which the office sought the man, not the man the office. Although he jokingly promised to shoot himself if nominated, Stevenson reluctantly accepted his party's nomination in 1952. "I accept your nomination—and your program," he said in his acceptance speech at the Democratic Convention in Chicago on July 26, 1952. "I should have preferred to hear those words uttered by a stronger, a wiser, a better man than myself. . . . I have not sought the honor you have done me. . . . I have asked the Merciful Father—the Father of us all—to let this cup pass from me. But from such dread responsibility one does not shrink in fear, in self-interest, or in false-humility. You have summoned me," he declared, "to the highest mission within the gift of any people." The rhetoric is that of the nineteenth century's acceptance speeches delivered on porches by nominees just formally notified of their party's call. Throughout the campaign of 1952 he played out the nineteenth century role of the reluctant candidate sought by the office.

Consistent with this sense of political reserve, Stevenson seemed uncomfortable asking audiences for their votes for him, a discomfort reflected in his anti-climactic perorations. "He was allergic to a big emotional build-up at the end of a speech," Tubby notes. "It was out of character for him to be a tub thumper. He was more professorial. His talks were essays, thoughtful and broad ranged." For example, in a speech to the AFL-CIO so central to the '52 campaign that an excerpt from it was aired as a TV spot and also included in the half hour televised documentary "Campaigning with Stevenson," Stevenson concludes: "a nation's best wishes go with you of labor as you set out now on your united and stronger pursuit of, I hope, these high promises. Good Luck!" The ability to deliver an appeal for support was also muted in '52, at least, by speeches that advocated views contrary to those of his audience.

There is also in Stevenson's spoken prose a level of reservation uncharacteristic of political rhetoric in general and the rhetoric of Madison Avenue in particular. In 1952 Stevenson seemed to recoil from hyperbole. So where in the election eve broadcast of 1952 Truman claimed that "We have brought this country the greatest prosperity and the greatest

---

*Stevenson had been photographed from below the stage with a hole showing in the sole of his shoe.

standard of living in history," Stevenson claimed instead that the "Democratic Party over the long sweep of its history and of our history has performed a great mission as a mechanism for the expression of political opinion, the development of policy and the attainment of a truly Democratic society in which the people are sovereign."

Stevenson also differed from the political norm in his willingness to acknowledge that he was not uniquely a repository of wisdom. He "makes it clear that he does not know all the answers, that nobody really can or does."[44] Of U.S. involvement in South Korea, Stevenson told a group of Marines: "It is fighting which might, conceivably, have been avoided on that particular battlefield had we acted otherwise than we did—though as to that, no man can surely say."[45]

Speaking in an Alien Tongue

In his acceptance speech in '52 he declared: "Let's talk sense to the American people." But the speech went on to demonstrate that in important respects it was a task for which Stevenson was ill suited. In the next sentence he assumed the posture of moral superior that would plague his candidacy when he said "Let's tell them the truth. . . ." The posture is Platonic. "I have tried to educate," he declared in his election eve broadcast. Stevenson's Platonic view permitted small latitude for the belief that the people are the repository of wisdom. Where Ike noted in late August that I "now resume my education,"[46] on election eve Stevenson declared that if he had not succeeded altogether in educating the people, "I have certainly educated myself about these questions," a statement that casts him as the source of his own education.

The speech promising that Stevenson would talk sense was itself long on syntactic complexity and short on simplicity, one begging to be read not heard. It is a speech surfeited with such words as "citadel," "acumen," "imprecations." "Let's tell them," Stevenson proclaimed, "that the victory to be won in the twentieth century, this portal to the Golden Age, mocks the pretensions of individual acumen and ingenuity. For it is a citadel guarded by thick walls of ignorance and of mistrust which do not fall before the trumpets' blast or the politicians' imprecations or even a general's baton." When Stevenson asked Truman "What am I doing wrong?" Truman "walked over to the window of their hotel and pointed to a man standing in the entrance of a hotel across the street. 'The thing you have got to do is to learn how to reach that man.' "[47] Truman's daughter concludes: "Unfortunately for him and the Democratic party, Mr. Stevenson never mastered this difficult art."

Stevenson's view of the word as an end in itself and his reluctance to

rally the support of audiences for his candidacy rather than his cause were
summed up well when in 1960 in California, he introduced John Kennedy
by saying "Do you remember that in classical times when Cicero had
finished speaking, the people said, 'How well he spoke,' but when De-
mosthenes had finished speaking, they said, 'Let us march'?"[48]

The Case for Stevenson the Reformist Governor

Corruption was the first C in the Republican formula for victory: K_1 (one
part Korea), C_2 (Corruption and Communism). In the process of dealing
with these issues, Stevenson made a major strategic error when he argued
that he was more qualified than Ike to clean up the mess in Washington.
The error was repeated in a print ad claiming that Stevenson was better
able "to root out corruption in Washington."[49] By conceding the existence of corruption, Stevenson legitimized a powerful Republican indictment of the Truman administration, an administration to which Truman
repeatedly tied the governor of Illinois.

The contention should have been couched not as an admission of the
existence of corruption but rather as a claim that if corruption existed, be
it among Republicans or Democrats, Stevenson's record demonstrated an
ability to rid the polity of it. This was the approach used in testimonial
TV ads by the man who would run as Stevenson's vice-presidential candidate in '56, Chairman of the Senate Crime Investigating Committee,
Estes Kefauver. Kefauver noted that as chair of that committee, he "had
occasion to compliment and highly commend Governor Stevenson upon
his work against the cartel of crime and corruption in the State of Illinois"
and forecast that Stevenson would "ferret out and expose any corruption
that may be found in our Federal government."

Democratic ads based their conclusion that Stevenson would eradicate corruption on both his record as governor and his actions as candidate. Broadcast and print ads touted Stevenson's record as a reform
governor. Seated before an oversized ballot marked for Stevenson, Illinois Senator Paul Douglas argued, for example, that "Stevenson inherited a very bad situation in Illinois but he has cleaned it up and he has
done so with integrity and ability."

Stevenson's record as a reform governor was impressive. He had, as
his print ads contended, "tightened administrative practices, lopped off
useless political jobs, exercised sound economy, eliminated special privilege in awarding contracts, struck a powerful blow against illicit gambling
and organized crime."[50] By contrast, the ad argues, Ike, who has no
history of civilian administration, would simply take orders from the "unsavory" elements in his own party. Additionally, Ike's treatment of

Nixon's "slush fund" indicated that the Republicans didn't know corruption when they saw it.

The ads also perceived candidate Stevenson's actions as evidence that he was the captive of no one but the American people. Here Stevenson's promise to "talk sense to the American people" was taken to mean that he told audiences truths they did not want to hear. "There's a man with real courage," declared one TV ad. "When I think of what he believes and what he has the backbone to say. Well, for example, he said that he'd resist any special privileges for pressure groups and he told that to labor unions in Detroit and another time he said he wouldn't stand for special privilege for any special interests including veterans and he told that to the American Legion. . . . He hasn't sold out."

The Democratic nominee closed his campaign on the same theme. In his election eve speech he recalled: "I remember the night in Dallas when I spoke to Texans of my views of tidelands oil. I remember the crowd in Detroit on Labor Day when I said I would be the captive of all of the American people and no one else. I remember the evening in the railroad station in New Haven when I identified a powerful Democratic leader as not my kind of a Democrat. . . . I have done my best frankly and forthrightly."

In the election eve speech Stevenson argued that he had kept faith with the pledge he had made in accepting the nomination: "Better we lose the election than mislead the people." The implication was clear. Ike has purchased popularity by pandering to his audiences. Stevenson was more worthy than Eisenhower because only he risked losing the election by telling his audiences things they did not want to hear; Stevenson offered what he hoped would function as evidence that he could be trusted to rebuff the special interests and eliminate corruption.

Corruption: Nixon and the "Secret" Fund

For a week in September 1952 it appeared that the issue of corruption might be transformed into a bonanza for the Democrats. Then a decisive speech by the Republican vice-presidential candidate vanquished that possibility.

On September 18, 1952, a headline on the front page of the New York *Post* proclaimed: "Secret Rich Men's Trust Fund Keeps Nixon in Style Far Beyond His Salary." The story that followed claimed that Nixon's rich friends in such fields as banking, oil, real estate, railroads, and manufacturing had maintained a fund for his use. The fund was administered by corporate attorney Dana Smith who explained that it existed to help Nixon sell "the American people" on "private enterprise and integrity in government." The group that financed the fund hoped that Nixon's efforts would compensate for the effects of the New Deal and Fair Deal, which Smith characterized as "full of Commies, men who believe in big government and those who have a backward looking philosophy. They are the real reactionaries."

The public disclosure that Nixon had drawn on this fund to pay expenses created a question: was the candidate who had so forcefully indicted the mess in Washington corrupt? The Democrats eagerly exploited the issue. At a stop in Eugene, Oregon,[51] Nixon was greeted with signs saying "No mink coats for Nixon—just cold cash," "Shhh, anyone who mentions $16,000 is a Communist," and "Will the veep's salary be enough, Dick?" As Nixon's train departed, the crowd converged on one of the sign carriers to tear his sign to bits. The sign carrier responded by making a citizen's arrest of one of those who had assaulted him. In Portland, banner carriers wearing dark glasses and carrying tin cups hoisted signs pleading for "Nickels for Nixon."

The existence of the fund raised an issue whose centrality was a function of the role Eisenhower had defined for Nixon. It was Nixon's belief that Ike wanted him on the ticket because as "an upstanding young man and a good speaker I should be able not only to flail the Democrats on the corruption issue but also to personify the remedy for it."[52] Nixon who had indicted the Democrats for their "scandal a day" administration was now himself the cause of scandal. As Ike recalled, leaders of Stevenson's party "writhing under the Republican attack, could make no plausible reply. But now, with the charges about the mysterious Nixon fund to fill the papers and divert attention, they saw their main chance."[53]

The reports of the fund created a test of Eisenhower's leadership. And in the absence of decisive action from Nixon, Ike was damned regardless of the course he chose. "I have come to the conclusion," Eisenhower told Nixon, "that you are the one who has to decide what to do. After all, you've got a big following in this country, and if the impression got around that you got off the ticket because I forced you off, it is going to be very bad. On the other hand, if I issue a statement now backing you up, in effect people will accuse me of condoning wrongdoing."[54]

The Washington *Post* and the New York *Herald Tribune* called for Nixon's resignation from the ticket. As Nixon approached the most important speech of his career, his wires and Ike's were running 3–1 against his staying on the ticket.[55]

Although various commercial sponsors offered to pay to air the broadcast, Nixon's aides refused. To defend oneself from charges of being bought and paid for in a broadcast bought and paid for by a large corporation would have been suicidal. The $75,000 required to purchase a half hour of television time was put up by the Republican National Committee and the Senatorial and Congressional Campaign Committees. In his announcement that the time for the speech had been purchased Republican National Committee Chairman Arthur E. Summerfield stated that "Sen. Nixon has devoted a great part of his life to fighting Communism and exposing traitors. Now a smear of him has been intimated by men who have promoted Communism, supported traitors and never fought so much as one day for their country."[56]

Because network television could only originate from New York, Chicago, or Los Angeles, Nixon flew from Portland to Los Angeles to deliver the speech. The address was aired nationally at 6:30 P.M., Pacific Daylight Time.

Since the highest rated show on Tuesday night was the "Milton Berle Show," Ted Rogers, who produced the Fund Speech, recommended that time be purchased "as close to Berle" as possible. Nixon's program employed what Rogers called "preventive TV," which meant that no matter what Nixon did, Rogers could "get a picture." "I had a large shallow oval of a white line painted on the floor downstage of the library set (between Richard Nixon and the TV cameras and hardware)," Rogers recalls,[57] "and when Richard Nixon came in, we told him that, as long as he didn't cross that white line, we would get a picture and a good one." The program was directed by John Claar, the regular director on the "Eve Arden Show," and produced by Rogers, Nixon's media consultant, who had worked as a CBS producer, director, and writer in Hollywood as well as as the Head of Broadcast Production for Dancer, Fitzgerald, Sample Inc.

Expecting a detailed financial statement from Price Waterhouse, the firm hired to audit Nixon's records and the "fund," Rogers and Nixon were prepared to illustrate Nixon's income and expenditures with large lettered visual aids. When a summary statement was all that arrived, Nixon substituted his own account of his finances. The plans to use visual aids were scrapped. On the assumption that an office setting in a telecast from California would look artificial, Nixon and Rogers agreed to a library setting for the program.

On Tuesday, September 23, following Milton Berle, Richard Nixon entered America's living rooms fighting for his political life. Within the following half hour, in the most remembered and most widely watched paid political television of the 1952 campaign, the cocker-spaniel Checkers took his place beside FDR's Fala in history. Nixon's "Checkers Speech" reached 48.9% of the possible television audience[58] and saved his spot on the Republican ticket.

The speech implied that those raising "smears" about Nixon were

Nixon delivering the Checkers speech. (From the Washington *Star's* Washingtoni-
ana collection in the Martin Luther King, Jr. Library, Washington, D.C.)

Communist sympathizers; (some of the columnists attacking him were are
the same ones who had opposed him in "the dark days of the Hiss case";
the "purpose of the smears" was "to silence" Nixon).

Without reporting the names of those who gave him the money and
exactly how it was spent, the Republican vice-presidential candidate
created the illusion that the speech was brimming with self-disclosure. He
claimed, for instance, that he was "baring his soul." Yet, some of his
disclosures conflicted with others. The amount he owed on the house in
Whittier, for example, shifted mysteriously from $3,000 to 10,000. This
was, Nixon's press secretary would later explain "a verbal error that
could occur in any extemporaneous talk."[59] Other disclosures raised questions. A young woman whose monthly income was $85 sent him a check
for $10 ("it's one that I will never cash") and a pledge of confidence in

him and General Eisenhower. By establishing a normative standard of living, his report of her monthly income undercut his claim that his $41,000 home bespoke a modest life-style.

The level of personal detail in the speech served to cloud the actual questions before him. He revealed that he and Pat experienced difficulties of an unspecified but presumably financial nature when first married: "We had a rather difficult time after we were married, like so many of the young couples who may be listening to us." Though no one had described the family dog as an improper gift, he revealed that the children had wanted a dog, got one by crate from a Texan, picked it up at Union Station in Baltimore, and named it Checkers. "And you know the kids love the dog and I just want to say this right now, that regardless of what they say about it, we're gonna keep it." He referred to the fact that his wife, who is called Pat (that isn't really her name), was born on St. Patrick's Day (she wasn't). In the event that the audience was now identifying him with the free deep freezers and mink coats that had come to symbolize corruption in the Truman administration, he revealed that "Pat doesn't have a mink coat. But she does have a respectable Republican cloth coat. And I always tell her that she'd look good in anything." To discount the possibility that he had feathered his own nest from the fund, Nixon catalogued what "we have" and "what we owe." After the war, he and Pat had savings totaling $10,000, he noted, "every cent of that, incidentally, was in government bonds." For four years they lived in an $80-a-month apartment in Alexandria, Virginia. He has $4,000 in life insurance. They owe his parents $3,500 and pay interest on that loan "regularly" "because it's part of the savings they made through the years they were working so hard." They have "a house in Washington which cost $41,000 and on which they owe $20,000."

Through all of this Pat Nixon sat frozen at the edge of the set, separated from her husband by the small bare table. At one point when the camera panned over to her it caught her only at the edge of the screen and focused for a moment in bewildered anxiety on the small empty table. So Checkers and Pat's respectable Republican cloth coat that later came to symbolize maudlin, self-serving humility served that night as an important diversion.

Incubating in the Checkers speech are patterns of thought and habits of expression that later would etch themselves into the public portrait of President Nixon. There in embryonic form is "Let me make one thing perfectly clear" ("I want to make this particularly clear"), Nixon's legacy to Rich Little. When making an emotional appeal, the folksy, down home diction appeared, with its gonna's and wanna's. Nixon's tendency to dramatize was also plain ("I was just there when the bombs were falling").

So too he rehearsed the "modest circumstances" of his childhood, a feature of the rhetoric of his subsequent campaigns.

The speech also disassociated the speaker from the Senator Nixon under attack. "I say that it was morally wrong if any of that $18,000 went to Senator Nixon for my personal use." Instead, he noted, the fund financed "the necessary political expenses of getting my message to the American people and the speeches I made, the speeches that I had printed, for the most part, concerned this one message—of exposing this Administration, the communism in it, the corruption in it—the only way I could do that was to accept the aid which people in my home state of California who contributed to my campaign and who continued to make these contributions after my election were glad to make." "And let me say," he added, "I am proud of the fact that not one of them has ever asked me for a special favor."

But, most important, the speech turned the tables on both Eisenhower and Stevenson. In his discussion of whether the fund was ethical, Nixon had implied that ethical questions could properly be raised if one put one's wife on his staff payroll. He had not, he noted, but Sparkman, Stevenson's vice-presidential running mate had. He also suggested that if his were a secret fund, it would be suspect. Stevenson's fund was secret, he notes. His was not. Yet the evidence he marshaled to support the claim that his fund was not secret is instead evidence that when asked about the existence of the fund by a reporter he acknowledged it. In addition to offering a standard of propriety that he reportedly met and Stevenson and Sparkman did not, Nixon, by equating owning up when caught red-handed with prior disclosure, set a standard of disclosure for the Democratic ticket that he had not himself met.

Nixon succeeded in shifting the public spotlight from his fund to Stevenson's. Following the speech on the fund, the nation's newspapers juxtaposed stories of Ike's embrace of Nixon with headlines stalking Stevenson for a disclosure comparable to Nixon's. "Nixon Flies East, Says 'Fight Has Just Begun' " declared a headline on the same front page of the *Herald Express* that contained the headline "Stevenson Rejects Nixon Request to Explain his Fund." "Ike Keeps Vindicated Nixon on Ticket" declared a front page headline of the Los Angeles *Times*,[60] as another announced "Stevenson Won't Say Who Got Paid." The *Washington Post*'s front page noted "Eisenhower 'Renominates' Sen. Nixon, Declares Him 'Completely Vindicated.' " Beneath that statement on the front page was the headline "Stevenson Won't Name Fund Donors: Adlai Also Refuses To List Recipients or Use of Money."

Although Stevenson had revealed the existence of his fund in a public speech several years before, John Bartlow Martin, Stevenson's speechwriter and biographer, recalls that "in the Nixon context, the national press treated Stevenson's fund as a scandal and demanded explanation." The size of Stevenson's fund, finally reported at $84,000, dwarfed Nixon's $18,000 fund.

The day after Nixon's speech, Stevenson told a group of his volunteers that the fund had been used to supplement the low salaries of those he wanted to recruit into government service. From it Stevenson also drew money to finance presents for his staff and to contribute to charities. A final accounting by his aides concluded that the fund also had been used to underwrite the campaigns of other Democratic candidates. His aides could not account for the dispersement of over $13,000.

Like Nixon, Stevenson engaged in the rhetoric of distraction. Like Nixon he failed to disclose either the precise sources of the money or the exact expenditures from the fund. Instead he released his tax returns from recent years and a summary of the expenditures financed by the fund. "While Stevenson's statement and accompanying exhibits amounted to less than a full disclosure," noted Martin, "they satisfied most of the press. . . . his disclosure of his income overshadowed the fund, and Stevenson was home free."[61]

Stevenson was not the only object of Nixon's maneuvering. Nixon also boxed Ike into a level of financial disclosure the general neither sought nor desired and took the decision about whether he should remain on the ticket effectively out of Ike's hands. Nixon's unprecedented financial disclosures had been Ike's idea; by stating that only those who have something to hide would refuse to do likewise, Nixon trapped not only Stevenson and Sparkman into releasing financial data but Eisenhower as well. And as Garry Wills wrote in *Nixon Agonistes,*[62] "There were reasons why it was inconvenient for Eisenhower to make his books public— e.g., the special tax decision on earnings of his *Crusade in Europe*. Besides, as Alsop delicately puts it, 'the military rarely get into the habit of making charitable contributions. . . .' More important, Nixon was turning the tables on Ike. Eisenhower had brought him to this revelation. Nixon would force the same hard medicine down his mentor's throat."

Nixon also skillfully circumscribed Eisenhower's ability to remove him from the ticket, for he suspected that the New York *Herald Tribune*'s call for his resignation may have been a message from Ike,[63] a message reinforced when in a last-minute call Dewey, representing himself as expressing Ike's wishes, urged Nixon to offer his resignation in the broadcast.[64]

In defiance of this recommendation, in the final moments of the broadcast Nixon situated the decision where legally it belonged, in the hands of the Republican National Committee, a group staffed by party

regulars likely to be loyal to Nixon. Unsurprisingly, in response to Summerfield's request that they wire him their personal decision immediately,
the members of the Republican National Committee voted 107–0 in
Nixon's favor.[65] In reporting the results to Ike, Summerfield praised
Nixon as one who "walked unafraid through the valley of despair and
emerged unscathed and unbowed."

By appealing to the public to send its sentiments to the Republican
National Committee, Nixon also invited tangible public evidence of his
popularity, an invitation freighted with advantages for him and disadvantages for those who favored jettisoning him from the ticket. By appealing
directly to those strongly committed partisans who are disproportionately
likely to respond to any form of partisan political communication, Nixon
charted for himself a much safer course. The speech skillfully reminded
those like Dana Smith and Arthur Summerfield who viewed him as their
champion against communism that here was their chance to ratify their
own ideological convictions.

Nixon's fierce anti-Communism had propelled him into the Senate.
In his race against Helen Douglas in 1950 Nixon had linked Douglas'
voting record to that of "the notorious Communist party-liner, Congressman Vito Marcantonio of New York." Nixon's now famous "pink lady
sheets," so called because they were printed on pink paper, charged
Douglas with seeing eye to eye with the New Yorker on "Un-American
Activities and Internal Security." By contrast, Congressman Nixon "has
voted exactly opposite to the Douglas-Marcantonio Axis." One of the
"pink lady sheets" concluded: "After studying the voting comparison
between Mrs. Douglas and Marcantonio, is it any wonder that the Communist line newspaper, the *Daily People's World,* in its lead editorial on
January 31, 1950, labeled Congressman Nixon as "The Man To Beat" in
this Senate race and the Communist newspaper, the *New York Daily
Worker,* in the issue of July 28, 1947, selected Mrs. Douglas along with
Marcantonio as "One of the Heroes of the 80th Congress." "Remember!" the ad entreated, "The United States Senate votes on ratifying
international treaties and confirming presidential appointments. Would
California send Marcantonio to the United States Senate?"

Meanwhile, Nixon's 1950 radio and televised ads appealed for votes
under such slogans as "Fight the Red fear with a fearless man—Dick
Nixon," "Old Glory Forever—Red Glory Never," "If you want to work
for Uncle Sam instead of Slave for Uncle Joe, vote for Dick Nixon."
"Don't be left, be right, with Nixon," "Be an American, Be for Nixon,"
"Don't vote the Red Ticket, vote the Red, White and Blue Ticket. Vote
for Dick Nixon."[66]

By reminding viewers that he had used the fund to battle communism and corruption and by pledging to continue that fight whether on or off the ticket, Nixon cast his cause in terms dear to his natural constituency.* The Checkers speech's strategy was effective. The estimated two million telegrams, letters, and phone calls sent to the Republican National Committee registered support for Nixon 350 to 1.[67] Western Union offices reported being deluged.[68] From Washington, an Ap wirephoto transmitted to the nation a picture of Wayne Hood of the GOP National Committee peering from behind a mountain of mail.

As would be expected, the newspapers' assessments of the speech generally mirrored their political preference. Those endorsing or favoring Eisenhower labeled the speech "magnificent" (New York *Journal American*), "extraordinary" (New York *World-Telegram*); those favoring Stevenson as did the New York *Post,* which had originally broken the story of the secret fund, branded the speech "a soap opera."[69]

A number of newspapers urged their readers to send supportive telegrams and letters. *The Los Angeles Evening Herald Express,* a Hearst newspaper, stated in a front page editorial: "Senator Richard M. Nixon spoke to America from his heart last night in an eloquent and manly explanation of his financial affairs down to the last detail of what he and his wife have earned, what they own and what they owe." After a long positive assessment of the speech, the editorial noted that Nixon "left the verdict to his party and to the American people" and asked "What is your answer, America?"[71]

The genius of the speech is that it successfully defined the test that would determine whether Nixon would stay on the ticket and then fashioned an appeal that would ensure that the test was met. Neither could be accomplished in a pre-broadcast age, for both required a national audience able to respond to an appeal such as the one Nixon made.

The close of the speech is equally ingenious. Since the Republican National Committee would not force a decision down an unwilling general's throat, Nixon moved to close Ike's options by concluding with his earnest plea to "remember folks, Eisenhower is a great man. Believe me. He's a great man. And a vote for Eisenhower is a vote for what's good for America." Despite its transparency, the appeal cleverly set up Ike as turning his back on a loyal subordinate if he chose to spurn a man who spent what might be his dying political breath touting the general's greatness. At the same time it offered an olive branch to the head of the ticket whose role in deciding Nixon's fate had just been substantially diminished.

---

*Of the total telegrams and letters, approximately one-fifth were from California. The majority of the letters and telegrams were sent by persons of high socioeconomic status.[70]

When Rogers had asked Nixon to tell him how he would end the speech Nixon replied "I don't know but you'll know when I'm finished." Pressed by Rogers, Rogers recalls that Nixon repeated that "he didn't know what he would say or do at the closing, and that I'd simply have to feel it, but he felt certain I would know when he was finished."

In the last ten minutes of the program, Rogers, crouching next to the pedestal of the number one camera gave Nixon his "ten minute," "five minute," "thirty seconds," and "cut" signals. "At the close," Rogers remembers, "Nixon is standing, his hands outstretched, making his appeal for mail reaction. The picture takes a slow iris-down fade to black and that's it. We had to do that, because even though I saw his head nod on the "cut" signal he did not stop talking." So emotionally involved was he in the speech that, apparently unaware that he was off the air, Nixon continued speaking as he walked steadily toward the "head-on" camera. "He walked physically smack into the camera hitting his shoulder," Rogers remembers. "He was in a complete emotional daze, and the number one cameraman, tears streaming down his own face, jumped around and steadied Nixon. Nixon said, "I'm sorry, Ted. I loused it up." He then "turned and went to the up stage drapes and buried his head in them."

The public reaction was immediate. That same night as Eisenhower entered the Cleveland Public Auditorium where he had been scheduled to speak, he was greeted with chants of "We want Nixon" from the 13,000 people in the audience who had just watched the Checkers speech. Discarding his prepared text on inflation, Ike declared "I have seen brave men in tough situations. I have never seen anyone come through in better fashion than Senator Nixon did tonight." The crowd roared its agreement. The vice-presidential nominee had won his gamble.

Ike's judgment of the speech was that "the underdog had come up off the floor to win a fight; his popularity was more firmly based than ever."[72]

On that night in September, a campaign and a political career hung in a balance tipped by a single paid broadcast. The broadcast had an important impact on future campaigns as well, for it set a norm of financial disclosure unprecedented in the history of the presidency. As a result of Nixon's challenge, all four candidates representing the major parties on the two national tickets "laid open their private financial records to public inspection for the first time in American history."[73] Moreover, the smashing success of the speech created in Nixon a false sense of what a speech could accomplish; during Watergate he repeatedly tried and failed to deliver another Checkers speech.

The salvific effect of Checkers also magnified Nixon's estimate of his own abilities as a speaker, an overestimation that probably played in his decision both to debate Kennedy and to spend little time preparing for that decisively catastrophic first debate. At the same time, Nixon concluded that the print reporters, to whom he had catered, were comparatively inconsequential. His relations with print reporters chilled. To aides he contemptuously derided their importance. If they were not there when the campaign bus was scheduled to depart, he'd say "Fuck 'em. We don't need 'em."[74]

The Checkers speech took its place next to Nixon's victory over Alger Hiss in the public mind. They would later be joined by the debate with Khrushchev in the kitchen of a model home in Moscow in 1959; the ghostly grey image of Nixon in the first Kennedy-Nixon debate; Nixon at the Great Wall of China; and Nixon announcing his resignation. These snapshots of the career of Richard Nixon define the memories of many Americans only marginally interested in politics long after his other triumphs and tragedies have faded from mind.

But this speech deeded an added legacy to the public, press, and future president. There were doubts about the speech later. David Halberstam comments:[75] "It was as if somehow in saving himself Nixon had paid too high a price. He had made himself even more the issue—not just his politics but *himself*. There was a growing feeling among the political and journalistic taste makers of the country that Nixon was not quite acceptable for very high office."

The Checkers speech is historically important for salvaging Nixon's place on a winning ticket. "If it hadn't been for that broadcast," he contended, "I would never have been around to run for the presidency."[76] It is also significant for creating a filter through which he, the public, and the press would interpret such important events as the first debate of 1960, the Watergate charges, and Richard Nixon's responses to them.

During the week that Nixon's and then Stevenson's "funds" drew the political spotlight, the issue of corruption assumed a new face. At the same time, other issues were sidelighted or shoved into the shadows. As the "funds" exhausted their welcome on the front pages, attention returned to Democratic attempts to lodge and Republican attempts to dislodge a venerable issue benefiting the Democrats and burning the Republicans.

The Spectre of Another Depression

The Great Depression was manna in the desert for the Democratic party for it made a permanent Democratic majority of what had been a Republican majority. Not surprisingly, the prospect of another depression is a weapon the Democrats have wielded deftly against the Republicans ever since Democratic publicist Charles Michelson transformed huts into "Hoovervilles." The Democratic slogans "You've Never Had It So Good" and "In '52 Remember '32" evoked memories of the depression while Democratic spot ads compared the state of the economy in 1932 with 1952. "They'll promise you the sky. They'll promise you the earth. But what's a Republican promise worth?" asks one ad. Underscoring the same theme, a female singer declares: "We'd rather have a man with a hole in his shoe than with a hole in everything that he says." She also professed an ardor stronger than that of those who "like Ike" by singing "we love the guv."

The spot ads used homey illustrations to contrast the Democratic and Republican records. "The Democratic Party took apples off the streets and put apple pie on the table" claims one. After asking a passerby to "open your pocketbook," another TV ad reassuringly catalogues its contents for him: pictures of a happy well-fed family, a bank deposit book, and a Social Security card. Old MacDonald and his farm animals appear in a TV ad that consists of still framed line drawings. To the melody of "Old MacDonald," singers recall that the farmer lost his farm in '31, regained it under the Democrats, and would keep it under Stevenson. The same notion reappeared in an ad that observed that the farmer was making money and hay now. In the election eve broadcast, President Truman reduced this ocean of images to the single claim that "This election may decide whether we shall go ahead and expand prosperity here at home or slide back onto a depression."

Print ads reinforced the message. "Don't forget the last Republican president" implored one. "Don't forget the Hoovervilles, breadlines, foreclosed mortgages, busted banks. Don't forget the 15 million desperate unemployed! Don't forget 1932! Is that the party you want to trust your security to?"

Since twenty years out of office might be seen as a long period of penance for the sin of the depression, the ad argues that the Republicans have not repented the philosophy that produced and prolonged the depression. "The Republicans vote against Social Security, against high minimum wages, against fair prices for farmers, against full employment. The Republican Party is *against* a better life for you and yours. They voted against you every chance they got!"[77]

Raising the spectre of depression carried definite advantages for the Democrats. Americans indicated in mid-summer that the best argument to vote Democratic heard at the Democratic Convention was "The Democratic Party had brought full employment and prosperity, so why change." In 1952 voters made pro-Democratic references to prosperity

These stills are taken from one of the ads in the "Eisenhower Answers America" series created by Rosser Reeves of the Ted Bates agency for the general election campaign of the Republican nominee in 1952.

and depression more than 13 times more often than pro-Republican ones. The Democrats were also widely held to be the party of "the common people, working people, the laboring man, Negroes, farmers" while the Republicans were viewed as the party of "big businessmen, the upper class, the well-to-do."[78] Stevenson's running mate underscored this finding by reminding viewers on election eve that they consistently told pollsters that the Democratic Party best serves the interests of the people. This was political territory the Republicans would not concede to the Democrats without a fight.

Ike's Apolitical Past as a Buffer Against "a New Depression"

In his spots, Ike's expressed concern about taxes, costs, corruption, communism, and Korea seemed genuine; his quick factual descriptions suggested that he understood the problems that would confront a new president. And his promise of change, unlike any similar promise uttered by a major presidential candidate in modern memory, was set against a backdrop of success untainted by failure. There was no political past by which his promised performance could be assessed.

What this meant in practical terms was that the once apolitical general could not readily be blamed for the Great Depression. Since both parties had sought him as their nominee, he could not easily be cast as the architect of a new depression. So Eisenhower was immune to the print ads' evocation of the breadlines, soup kitchens and apple-sellers of 1932.

Where another Republican with a political past might have been mortally wounded by the spot that recalled that "the Republican party was in power back in 1932 . . . thirteen million were unemployed . . . bank doors shut in your face," the ad barely scratched the apolitical Eisenhower.

The Democrats argued from Stevenson's successes as governor, rehearsed the material benefits attained by individuals under the Democrats, and, while prophesying another depression if the Republican was elected, attempted to link Ike to unsavory elements in his party who would supposedly dominate the political novice.

Problems in Making the Case Against Ike Stick

The difficulty of Stevenson's task was compounded by Eisenhower's use of television to underscore his competence and trustworthiness. In the closing weeks of the election, Eisenhower's presence in his televised spots and speeches provided the people with direct experience consistent with their beliefs about him and counter to the claims about him made by actors (in the tele-play) and by unknown Stevenson supporters in the print ads.

Ike's Televised Image as Visual Rebuttal

Carroll Newton, who with Ben Duffy and John Elliot of BBD&O supervised the campaign's advertising, explains that the advertising was intended to "show Ike to people for what he was, an intelligent, experienced, thoroughly decent man, the kind people would like to identify with." The amiable, reassuring, paternal Eisenhower who "Answered America" in the spots did not seem like or sound like "high brass." At the same time, his strong assertive answers underscored his image as leader and immunized audiences from the charge that he would simply take orders from others in his party. The ads visually reinforced his posture as leader by having the questioners, tourists recruited at Radio City Music Hall, look up as they ask their questions. In responding, Ike, whose responses were filmed separately and then edited into the film of the questioners, gazes down from the superior position.

Before describing the content and form of the Eisenhower Answers America spots that inaugurated televised general election spot advertising in presidential campaigns, let's pause, for a moment to explain their origin.

According to legend, during a golf game three wealthy Republicans were bemoaning the power of Truman's claim "You never had it so good." After failing to concoct an equally effective Republican slogan, they called adman Rosser Reeves, a partner in the ad firm of Ted Bates and Company. Reeves argued that a spot campaign should be used to counter the Democrat's slogan. By 1952 the number of households owning sets justified a TV spot campaign. By the conventions in the summer of 1952 over 18 million American homes—about 39% of the total—owned television sets.[79]

The businessmen agreed to raise the money to put the campaign on the air; Reeves agreed to create the spots. A market analysis was drawn up. It showed that the Republicans could win by capturing forty-nine usually Democratic counties in twelve key states. Spot advertising was concentrated in these states. In eleven states, including New York, New Jersey, Illinois, Massachusetts, Michigan, Maryland, Indiana, California, Pennsylvania, Texas, and Connecticut, the spots were broadcast at a saturation level. A voter would see an Eisenhower spot four or five times a day in these states. Production cost $60,000. Air time cost between $800,000 and 1.5 million dollars.[80]

Three arguments were used to justify the spot campaign: "the low cost per thousand homes reached; the fact that spots, unlike full-length programs, would reach people not already prejudiced in favor of the candidate; and the opportunity to concentrate fire in the relatively few critical states which could not certainly be counted in either candidate's column."[81]

Reeves wrote the radio and TV spots. Most of the TV spots were 20 seconds long. Three one minute spots included newsreel footage of Eisenhower's past and scenes from Korea. In the second week of September, Ike filmed 40 spots for broadcast in 40 of the 48 states during the closing weeks of the campaign.

The format of the Eisenhower Answers America spots was consistent throughout. An announcer intoned "Eisenhower Answers America." Individuals or couples looking off camera then asked a question to which Eisenhower responded. Ike's answers underscored the problems of taxes, high costs, corruption, communism, and involvement in Korea and then promised a solution.

The questioners also built the case that it's time for a change. One woman holding a bag of groceries said, for example, "I paid twenty-four dollars for these groceries—look, for this little." Ike responds "A few years ago, those same groceries cost you ten dollars, now twenty-four, next year thirty. That's what will happen unless we have a change." A young black male asked "Food prices, clothing prices, income taxes, won't they ever go down?" Ike responded "Not with an eighty-five billion dollar budget eating away on your grocery bill, your clothing, your food, your income. Yet the Democrats say, "You never had it so good!"

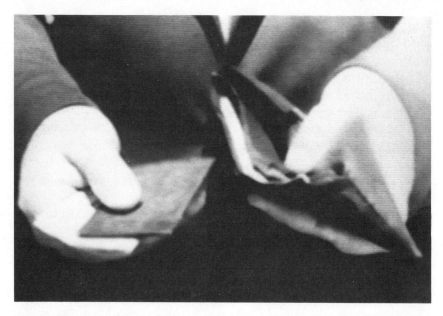

This still is drawn from a spot in a series created by the Joseph Katz agency for airing on behalf of the Democratic nominee in the general election of 1952. The ads in this series stressed that the Democrats had saved the country from the "Republican" depression and subsequently preserved prosperity.

On cue Ike played either Santa or Scrooge. He appeared as all things to all people. In a move comparable to that of Carter in '76 and Reagan in '80, the general promised to increase services and decrease taxes by cutting out fraud, waste, and corruption. He pledged to "put the lid on government spending" in one ad but promised "expanded Social Security and more real benefits" in another, more tanks and planes for Korea in a third, and a cut in taxes in a fourth. Democratic ads highlighted Ike's "promise them anything" posture by stating that Stevenson "is too honest to promise drastic cuts and adequate preparedness at the same time."[82]

There was unintended humor in one of the spots where Ike declared "[M]y Mamie gets after me about the high cost of living. It's another reason why I say, it's time for a change." One would hope for Ike's sake that Mamie did not interpret the spot as calling for a change in her.

Reeves' spots are not the masterpieces folklore has fabricated them to be.[83] Mixed metaphors sabotage meaning. Americans will "be even deeper [in debt] unless you help put the lid on Washington waste and extravagance." "[T]he Democrats are sinking deeper into a bottomless sea of debt and demanding more taxes to keep their confused heads above water. Let's put out a sturdy lifeboat in November." A lifeboat for Democrats? Hyperbolic conjecture strains credibility as well. A middle-aged white male says "General, this suit costs sixty dollars. I used to buy the same for thirty dollars." Ike responds, "You paid one-hundred and one taxes on that suit. And next year you may pay two hundred unless you vote for a change so that we may clean things up in Washington."

The spots' purpose was articulated by Michael Levin who prepared the preliminary market analysis for Reeves. "The spots themselves would be the height of simplicity. . . . People from each of the 49 areas would each ask the General a question . . . The General's answer would be his complete comprehension of the problem and his determination to do something about it when elected. Thus he inspires loyalty without prematurely committing himself to any strait-jacketing answer."[84] Not only do the ads not commit Ike to a strait-jacketing answer, they rarely commit him to any answer at all. Throughout, the ads are vague about precisely what the general will do about the problems. "We're going to put an end to these national scandals." "[I]f I'm president," he says in another, "I'll give you older folks action not just sympathy." Throughout, Ike attacks the Democratic record rather than any specific Democrat. Unmentioned is Stevenson's record in Illinois. A visitor from Pluto who surmised the identity of the candidates from the broadcast ads would assume that Eisenhower was running against Truman and Stevenson against Hoover.

With the rise of paid media consultants some would ask if advertising changes the candidate or falsifies the candidate's image. In the Eisenhower campaign the answer was yes. In ads Ike bordered on making promises he earlier had foresworn. During the campaign Eisenhower had told aides: "I'll talk about the burden of taxes and their danger to a people's initiative, but let me tell you—I'll be darned if anyone is going to talk me into making any idiotic promises or hints about elect-me-and-I-will-cut-your-taxes-by-such-and -such-a-date. If it takes that kind of foolishness to get elected, let them find someone else for the job."[85] In the second week of September 1952 in the Transfilm studios in Manhattan, adman Rosser Reeves handed Eisenhower a script that had him respond to the question: "Mr. Eisenhower, can you bring taxes down?" with the answer "Yes. We will work to cut billions in Washington spending and bring your taxes down."

Between takes of the spots, Eisenhower shook his head and muttered "To think that an old soldier should come to this." But come to it he had.

Madison Avenue affected other changes in Ike as well. The Eisenhower who answered America appeared without glasses, a feat that required the construction of giant hand-lettered cue cards. Despite their mixed metaphors and ambiguous constructions, Ike's statements in the spots are simpler and clearer than his extemporaneous speech which, according to one reporter, was "apt at any moment to sink down in a bog of sticky syntax."[86] Madison Avenue had made its political presidential debut in national television.

Still, apart from the existence of the spot ads themselves and Ike's glasses-free gaze into the camera in them, Reeves deserves little of the blame or credit for sculpting Ike's image. If there was counterfeiting, it had been done earlier and elsewhere, for Reeves' researchers drew most of the material for the spot ads directly from Eisenhower's already delivered speeches.

Reeves' contribution lies in the focus he provided for the Republican campaign. From the smorgasbord of issues being addressed in the speeches Reeves highlighted those that pollster George Gallup had discovered were most important to the American people. Consequently, Reeves' spot ads focused on the Korean War, corruption in Washington, taxes, and the high cost of living.

Communism was not a major concern of the electorate and Ike's ads made no effort to make it one. So, not surprisingly, the Michigan researchers would find that "the issue of domestic Communism was little mentioned by the public in 1952."[87]

The Democratic Counter-assault

Before the ads were aired, Sam Brightman, a veteran of the Democratic National Committee, managed to secure a copy of "all of the scripts and the inter-office memos from the Ted Bates-Rosser Reeves spots."[88] He recalls:

> The person who handed over the material thought as I did that that ad campaign set a dreadful precedent. It was very easy to determine that this was authentic material and not a plant. We thought that there had been an effort to plant some stuff on us in that campaign. George Ball then criticized the Republican campaign. History has vindicated him.
>
> There wasn't a lot of cops and robbers about it. I don't remember anything like debategate [in which a congressional investigation followed press reports that in 1980 Reagan's advisers obtained copies of Carter's planning materials for the Carter-Reagan debate].
>
> They had all of this money and bought all of this time and clobbered us. Some of our [state-level] polls showed that the only time there was any movement for Stevenson was before these spots were aired. The spots used a hammer to kill a fly but they worked and they set a horrible precedent.

Stevenson's aide George Ball responded to this evidence that the Republicans were about to launch a massive spot advertising campaign with a strongly worded attack on Eisenhower's "cornflakes campaign."

"In the sale of soap and toothpastes," Ball argued, "the saturation of the mind by contrived gimmicks and ear-dinning repetition has become an accepted though painful part of everyday American life. But in the sale of political candidates and ideologies it has its obvious—and proven— dangers."

Ball went on to note that "The tyrant, Commodus, in his vanity, ordered the heads chopped off every statue of Hercules in Rome and a reproduction of his own head substituted. Even the most ignorant Romans were not fooled, of course. Hercules ultimately got his head back; Commodus lost his. I do not mean to liken the General to Commodus; but I do suggest that even Batten, Barton, Durstine and Osborne will not be able to make him look like Hercules."[89]

Why then did the Democrats in 1952 air spots—although comparatively few of them? "It was," notes Ball, "a feeble effort to compete on their own ground. Stevenson was very much opposed to the whole idea." The spots gave the Democrats "something to put on the air besides the half hour programs because we couldn't afford too many of the half hour programs." "We were attacking them for the blitz quality . . . the saturation [of their spot campaign]. It numbed people rather than persuading them." The Stevenson campaign used spots to conserve funds, says Ball. By contrast, "they [the Republicans] had ample funds. I think they thought that a very brief exposure of Eisenhower was better than a sustained 30 minute speech."

Sooner or later, Ball bitterly but presciently predicted, "presidential campaigns would have professional actors as candidates."[90]

The Election Eve Broadcasts

The telecast election eve "report" to Pat and Dick, Mamie and Ike brought the question-and-answer format of the spots full circle. In the half hour extravaganza that included 81 changes from filmed to live broadcast from around the country, individuals affirmed their support of Ike. But first he answered another series of questions. So the election eve broadcast synopsized the form of the spots and then dramatized Ike's success, as persons from different occupations, of different ages, and from different regions pledged him their vote. At the program's close, Ike and Dick Nixon "urged all citizens to vote" and conveyed their "grateful thanks to all the people who had participated in this renewal of America's great quadrennial competition."[91] Like the earlier radio election eve bandwagon broadcasts, this was designed to evince the inevitability of Ike's election. It was also the first time that state of the art techniques of television were employed in a full length political broadcast.

By contrast, the Democrats simply offered viewers and listeners talking heads. First from St. Louis: Alben Barkley, clutching the desk in front of him as if trying to levitate it; then from Kansas City; Harry Truman, preoccupied with the manuscript in front of him; finally from Chicago: the nominee and his running mate. When their turn came in a conversation both strained and strange, Stevenson observed that he hasn't seen Sparkman in a while and asked what he'd been up to. Sparkman dutifully reported that he had been working hard. Then after frittering away valuable time with awkward extemporaneous comments while toying with what appeared to be a pen holder, Stevenson launched into a speech that was still in progress when the announcer broke in to end the program on the half hour.

In an exchange with his young son during the broadcast, Stevenson offers the most descriptive and revealing remark of the evening. In answer to his father's question about his impression, the child says: "Well, I like watching television better than being on it." To which Stevenson adds "I guess that goes for all of us, doesn't it."

Slogans

As Harrison's log cabin and "Tippecanoe and Tyler Too" attest, the meaning of campaigns can be distilled into visual as well as verbal symbols. Because such symbols telegraph meaning quickly they are powerful political weapons. Consequently, the other side predictably attempts to overthrow or better still transform the symbol from a positive to a perjorative one. So, for example, in 1936 when the Republicans symbolized Alf Landon's campaign with the Kansas state flower of Kansas, the sunflower the Democrats countered with a bumper sticker that read "Sunflowers die in November."

Co-opting slogans is another favorite political game. Accordingly, Democrats responded to the anti-Roosevelt "No Third Term" buttons with buttons proclaiming "Two good terms deserves another." Not to be outdone, the Republicans countered with buttons that said "Two good terms deserves a rest."

In 1952 the picture of Adlai Stevenson with a hole in his shoe served as a powerful means of allying him with the people. The Republicans countered with a button showing a shoe with a hole in it. But this button playfully appropriated what is usually Democratic rhetoric to warn "Don't let this happen to *you!* Vote for Ike."

Just as advertising digests the central messages of campaigns into memorable units, so too its slogans capsulize the messages of the advertising campaign. Consequently, they can function as an optic through which

the campaign can be viewed. In the 1952 campaign, the Democratic slogan "You Never Had It So Good" clashed with the Republican's "It's
Time for a Change."

In the battle of the slogans, the Republicans had an advantage for
their slogan was drawn from the public vocabulary. A Gallup survey in
July 1952 found that the third most often mentioned argument "to get
people to vote Republican" was "The Democratic party has been in
power too long and it's time for a change." (Ironically, that was a sentiment Stevenson privately shared. While resisting efforts to draft him in
1952, he told Carl McGowan, "I really can't deal with this argument that
it's time for a change. It is time for a change." After the 1948 election,
the Republicans in Congress, Stevenson argued, were becoming "increasingly irresponsible" in foreign affairs. Stevenson believed, recalls McGowan, that if a Democrat were elected in 1952, they would be "absolutely
impossible." "What the country needs most is to get the Republicans
back in power.")

To controvert the other's slogan, the Democrats conjectured about
the changes the Republicans would produce and urged change for the
better, not the worse. "You do not want to change to unemployment, to
job hunting, to idle factories, to apple selling, bread lines and soup kitchens," said one Democratic ad. Other ads portrayed the change as one in
which undesirables would dominate the politically inexperienced general.
The Republicans countered in the Eisenhower Answers America spots
with testimony from voters who reflected on the increase in taxes, costs,
corruption and on the seemingly endless war in Korea and concluded that
the Democratic slogan was an empty one. The title of Ike's memoirs,
Mandate for Change, reveals which slogan was more resonant.

CHAPTER THREE

1956: The Reelection of a Popular Hero

By the end of Eisenhower's first term, K_1, C_2 had been eliminated as potential issues. The war in Korea was over. Eisenhower's cabinet, staff, associates, and administration were untarnished by scandal. And thirty-six days of televised hearings had discredited the Red-baiter, Joseph McCarthy, who had offended many civil libertarians.

The biggest national trauma of Eisenhower's first term was his heart attack on September 24, 1955. Many speculated that he would not seek a second term, but on February 29, 1956, Eisenhower announced that he would run again. Again Richard Nixon was his running mate. In his acceptance speech, Eisenhower reminded the nation of the peace, prosperity, and progress it had enjoyed under his leadership; he promised to be guided in his second term as he had in his first by long-range principles, not short-range expediency.

Unlike 1952, in 1956 Stevenson aggressively sought his party's nomination. His chief rival was Tennessee Senator Estes Kefauver. Stevenson unexpectedly lost to Kefauver in the Minnesota primary but squeaked by him in Florida and decisively defeated him in California. After the California primary, Kefauver withdrew from the race. The convention nominated Stevenson. When Stevenson threw the vice-presidential spot open, Kefauver and Massachusetts Senator John F. Kennedy contested for it, a fight resulting in a narrow victory for Kefauver.

Estes Kefauver was a well-known senator who had gained national exposure in 1951 by holding televised hearings on organized crime. As chair of the Senate Crime Investigating Committee, Kefauver had held such hearings in various large cities throughout the country. His audience was estimated to have included between 20 and 30 million people.[1]

In his acceptance address, Stevenson promised a "New America where freedom is made real for all without regard to race or belief or economic condition," a call suggesting that the Republican's prosperity had benefited the rich but not the rest.

10 REASONS WHY WE SHOULD RE-ELECT

EISENHOWER•NIXON

1. Korean War ended—America has kept out of war.

2. The nation has an effective foreign policy, backed up by a powerful defense force.

3. Conversion from war to peace achieved with the greatest prosperity the American people have ever known.

4. Crook-and-crony government replaced by restoring honesty, integrity and saneness to our national government.

5. The trend toward socialism stopped by turning to the initiative and ability of the American people rather than government regimentation.

6. Republicans made possible the biggest tax cut in American history by cutting government spending and waste.

7. Budget balanced and fiscal integrity achieved. Cost of living stabilized, inflation halted and the value of the dollar preserved.

8. Welfare and security programs increased by promoting the well being of Americans without regimentation and centralization.

9. This Republican Administration is liberal in dealing with people and conservative in dealing with peoples' money.

10. This is an Administration for all Americans—regardless of political affiliation, race, creed, color, or economic background.

FOR PEACE ★ PROSPERITY ★ PROGRESS

VOTE REPUBLICAN NOV. 6th

ISSUED BY
Republican National Committee
Leonard W. Hall, Chairman
1625 EYE STREET, NORTHWEST   WASHINGTON 6, D.C.

1956 campaign handbill for Eisenhower. (Courtesy Smithsonian Institution, Photo No. 54462, Division of Political History)

Not only do the fates torture us by whispering "what might have been" but mercifully or mercilessly they also occasionally deal us a second chance in the form of a new hand against an old opponent. Sometimes, as for William Henry Harrison in 1840, both the candidate's hand and his skill at the game improve. At other times, fate is not so kind; for Adlai Stevenson in 1956 the redealt hand was surely worse and the odds longer.

Differences Between '52 and '56

Gone in '56 was the advantage Stevenson held in '52 as the more politically experienced candidate. Gone was his ability to conjure visions of Ike as either despot or dupe. At the same time, four years of Republican prosperity "destroyed most of the 14–1 margin" the Democrats formerly registered in voters' responses about prosperity and depression, a finding that signaled the futility of trying to hang the threat of another Great Depression around the Republican candidate's neck. Additionally, with the Korean War confined to scrapbooks and with peace at hand, voters by a ratio of more than 35 to 1 identified the Republican party as the one most likely to maintain the peace.[2] Meanwhile, press coverage of the actions by Stevenson's former wife, including her public announcement that she did not support her former husband for president and her dramatic arrival at the bedside of their son, who had been injured in an auto accident, heightened public awareness and disapproval of his divorce.

These factors, combined with Ike's immense personal popularity, armored the incumbent president against the knuckles and knives of political attack. To appreciate the difficulties Stevenson faced, one need only recall that in May 1955 almost six of ten Democrats surveyed by Gallup said that if the Republicans did not nominate Ike in '56, the Democrats should. Indeed, at no time in the surveys of '55 or '56 did Stevenson defeat Ike in the pollsters' national trial heats.

The Ad Agencies and the Campaign

The 1956 campaign pitted the agency with the third highest billings against the agency with the 25th; it was the battle of a giant against a gnome. The Republican National Committee returned to its firm from 1952: BBDO; as in 1952 Young and Rubicam handled the account of Citizens for Eisenhower. Although the Joseph Katz agency of Baltimore was again willing to handle the Democrat's account, Democratic National Committee Chairman Paul Butler sought to set the Democrats on an equal footing with the Republicans by hiring a firm of comparable size and reputation, a "glamorous big time agency."[3] "He had an absolute obsession with Madison Avenue" recalls a staff member. "Butler had never been involved in national politics until he got the [DNC] job. He had been involved in local politics," recalls Clayton Fritchey who in 1956 headed the Democratic National Committee's Public Affairs Division. "I think he was personally dazzled by those big name agencies. [In this search] he went off on his own and didn't consult anyone at the committee that I know of."[4]

Under Butler's leadership the committee tried and failed to secure a commitment from the leading agencies in New York. When it finally succeeded in hiring a firm there was no talk of a separate agency for the candidate's committee. Scarce funds simply did not permit such a luxury.

So, like it or not, the candidate was bound to the agency selected half a year before the nomination by the Democratic National Committee.

The process by which that selection was made was complicated but revealing. The Democrats were repeatedly rebuffed by firms that feared the wrath of their large Republican corporate clients, saw no merit in siding with what they foresaw to be a losing campaign, and viewed the Democrat's projected budget as wishful thinking.

Consequently, Butler wrote to wealthy Democrats not for money but rather for an entré into the agencies that handled their companies' advertising. "I tell you in confidence," he wrote one such Democrat, "that I have contacted fifteen or twenty of the top agencies in New York. The reluctance of all of them to take on our account boils down to the fact that they have big business clients who would not approve of their agency being responsible for the advertising and promotion of the Democratic Party."[5]

One agency executive explained his dilemma this way: "If a big agency took on the Democrats' account and the Democrats won, it would simply enrage Republican clients and drive them away. On the other hand, if it took them on and the Democrats lost, it wouldn't look too good for its selling ability."[6]

Fearful that the refusal of the top agencies to take the account would look bad for the advertising industry, a committee of top ad executives operating under the rubric of the American Association of Advertising Agencies offered to search for a firm willing to take the account. Butler rejected their offer on the grounds that he did not want his party to be the object of charity. Quietly and behind the scenes the ad executives nonetheless prodded firms to apply for the account.

Whether on their own or in response to encouragement from the four A's, a group of small and medium-sized agencies, many with no previous political experience, expressed interest in the account. Butler finally offered the often spurned account to Norman, Craig and Kummel, a medium-sized agency that then borrowed talent from large agencies. The president of the four A's called on the giant agencies to cooperate. Many did. SSC&B contributed a creative director and a copywriter and J. Walter Thompson supplied a writer.

The professionals at the Democratic National Committee were taken aback by the agency's lack of political experience. "We discovered they knew nothing about politics," Fritchey recalls. "We had to break them in at the level of two plus two makes four." In a story that may be apocryphal, another staff member recalls an agency representative gleefully producing a storyboard claiming that under Eisenhower, inflation had increased 37%. Astonished, the staffer asked how the figure had been calculated. "I added the rate of inflation for food to that for housing and transportation," the novice replied. Out of the need to marry political and communication skills, the professional political communication consultant was born.

The Democrat's agency was the first to produce a large number of what I call televised production spots—ads that do not require the presence of the candidate. Stevenson's television adviser William Wilson explains them not as the product of design but of desperation:

> The contest was between doing something decent on television and the demands of the candidate's schedule. Because we [Guggenheim and I] were part of the campaign we could get more time than the agency. The agency could not get the time it needed. So they started making issue or concept spots which did not require the presence of the candidate. That kind of spot, which I consider a cheat and a lie and bad for America, was born of not having access to the candidate. Concept spots are not representative of the candidate or the campaign but an abstract thought of what some outsider thinks the campaign is about.[7]

Cost

The Report of the Senate Subcommittee on Privileges and Elections indicates that the Republicans reported outspending the Democrats almost 2 to 1, $20.69 million to $11 million. Labor gave the Democrats $2.6 million while large corporations donated $2.6 million to the Republicans. From a dozen wealthy families alone, the Republicans received more than $1 million. The subcommittee's survey of TV networks and stations indicated that in purchase of TV time for presidential ads and programs the Democrats were outspent two to one.

This formidable difference in the amount of televised communication prompted calls for reform. In an introduction to a collection of Stevenson's 1956 campaign speeches, Seymour Harris and Arthur Schlesinger, Jr., wrote:

> The transmission of political speeches by presidential candidates through television has come to be almost indispensable to the operations of our democracy. The overriding public interest would therefore seem to lie in devising some system by which a limited amount of free television time would be made available to the parties in the interests of providing the flow of information and the equality of debate necessary for a democracy. Why, for example, should not every party which polled over 10 per cent of the vote in the previous election be granted an assured minimum of free television time—say ninety minutes a week—during the last eight weeks of the campaign?[8]

For cash Stevenson substituted castigation. Intertwined in the lining of Stevenson's speeches are indictments of the Republicans for relying on

Madison Avenue, for merchandising their programs, and for confusing advertising with governing. "Very early in this administration a high administration official, C. D. Jackson, said: 'We're going to merchandise the living hell out of the Eisenhower administration.' " Stevenson told an audience of journalists in Pittsburgh in April: "They have merchandised the American people—tried to sell them a bill of goods, to put it in language the advertising business can understand."[9] "Drift cannot lead us to" the New America, Stevenson told an audience in September, "nor smug complacency, nor fear of change, nor slick slogans and advertising arts, nor pious homilies and campaign promises."[10] "Mr. Nixon's advertisers call him 'adaptable,' " said Stevenson in Los Angeles in October. "Well, that's just the trouble. For what 'adaptable' means here is that this man has no standard of truth but convenience and no standard of morality except what will serve his interest in an election."[11] The spine of Stevenson's attack was exposed in his acceptance speech when he warned:

> The men who run the Eisenhower administration evidently believe that the minds of Americans can be manipulated by shows, slogans and the arts of advertising. And that conviction will, I dare say, be backed up by the greatest torrent of money ever poured out to influence an American election—poured out by men who fear nothing so much as change and who want everything to stay as it is—only more so.
>
> This idea that you can merchandise candidates for high office like breakfast cereal—that you can gather votes like box tops—is, I think, the ultimate indignity to the democratic process.[12]

This posture would have been more credible had Stevenson spurned the strained scripts of the Man from Libertyville ads and relied instead on nationally broadcast confrontations with actual questioners or on speeches. Stevenson's uncomfortable concession to political pragmatism revealed the perceived power of advertising.

By 1956 politicians had concluded that the presence of advertising for a candidate legitimized the candidacy and the absence of advertising undercut it. Indeed, the Democratic National Committee OK'd production of ads without the money to air them in the hope that local committees would finance the purchase of time and that the display of the advertising at press previews would communicate to party members the seriousness of Stevenson's candidacy. In both 1952 and 1956, publicity director Sam Brightman recalls, "we produced spots and had press previews even though we didn't have enough money to make the slightest bit of difference with them. It was worth doing to keep our troops from quitting completely."[13]

Even after becoming convinced that their candidate would lose, committee staffers argued that election eve advertising was necessary to save Democrats in congressional, state, and local races. "A few days before the end of the 1956 campaign, Democratic National Committee Treasurer Matt McCloskey decided that it was a waste of money to spend any more on the presidential race so he issued an order to cancel all network television," Brightman remembers. "There was panic until the order was undone. Win or lose, unless you have the traditional election eve assorted advertising and the rallies, party workers all over the country are going to go to bed and not bother to get up to work on election day."

In 1952 the Democrats had learned that certain types of ad buys secured more news coverage than others. The quantity and quality of the news coverage of Stevenson's speeches was a function of whether the speech was billed as a network broadcast. "DuPont was the worst and the cheapest," says Brightman, "but it was a national network so we bought it to improve the bites we got on TV and radio news and the coverage we got in the newspapers."

Just as the amount of available money penalized the Democratic candidate so too did the time at which the money was available. While the Republicans approached the general election with over 5 million dollars in the bank, the Democrats had amassed a mere $100,000.[14] So while raising money was a preoccupation of the Democrats, it was an afterthought for the Republicans.

In both 1952 and 1956, Stevenson was the victim of a phenomenon that also would haunt Hubert Humphrey in 1968. When the candidate was far behind in the polls and his political anemia required the infusion of funds to secure the advertising that would revive his chances, big contributors hid. When for a fleeting moment Ike's ill health bolstered Stevenson's prospects, money was available. But in mid-October, when it was clear that he was a very long shot, money dried up. As a result the final wave of already produced one minute ads was not aired. These were the ads that summarized Stevenson's vision of the New America.

Two forces propelled the Democrats toward use of five minute spots in 1956. "We couldn't afford too many thirty minute programs," says Ball, "and the politicians were convinced that no one listened to thirty minute speeches anyway."[15] While hardly supporting the conclusion that "no one" would listen to a thirty minute speech, the viewing data from 1956 do suggest that five minute spots consistently reached larger audiences than half hour political telecasts.

The '56 campaign also gave lie to the assumption that viewing a political broadcast signaled either support or the inclination to support the candidate on whose behalf it was aired. Speeches by those on the Democratic national ticket outdrew those by the Republican nominees.

Interestingly, the spot drawing the highest number of viewers was a five minute defense of Republican principles by Herbert Hoover broadcast on October 29. Were it not for Hoover's ability to attract a sizeable television audience to a thirty minute speech he delivered in 1952, the large audience in 1956 might easily be dismissed as the luck of the buy. It is difficult to divine whether the popularity of Hoover's telecasts was an indication that the depression no longer held the Republican party in a stranglehold or a sign of viewer curiosity. In 1956 Hoover's spot was paid for not by the Republican National Committee or by Citizens for Eisenhower but as in 1952 by the Republican National Senatorial Committee.[16]

If exposure did indeed predispose an audience to embrace a speaker, then the effect of the Republican's two to one advantage on television in 1956 would certainly have been substantial. Yet an intriguing finding in a Pulse Inc. survey of 1000 television set owners in the New York City area suggests that Nixon's appearance may have hurt rather than helped Eisenhower. When asked whether after exposure to the candidate on TV they liked him more, less, or about the same, Eisenhower was liked less by only 3.4% while 36.4% liked him more. Stevenson and Kefauver were each liked more by a bit more than twice the percent that liked them less. But Nixon was liked more by only 21.3% and liked less by 24.8%.[17] During the campaign Nixon delivered three half hour televised speeches, one October 4, another October 17, the third November 2, and was featured in a five minute spot aired October 20, and on another broadcast on November 1. He also appeared with Ike on all three networks in the one hour election eve special. Nixon's speeches occasionally outdrew Eisenhower's, suggesting either that the data gathered by Pulse Inc. were faulty or that Nixon was the politician audiences loved to hate.

The major innovation of the '56 campaign was its increasing reliance on the five minute spot. In 1952, network political broadcasts were primarily a half hour or fifteen minutes long, requiring the preemption of scheduled programming. By 1956, in an innovation noted by both Republican and Democratic media consultants, the preemption problem was solved by the use of the five minute spot, a use made possible by the cooperation of the major networks. Wherever possible, producers of the network programming simply shortened scheduled programs so that the commercials did not appear to cut into viewer time. When the program was filmed, the film was simply edited. Live programs were pretimed to be shortened. The political sponsor paid the cost of editing the shows.

This strategy did not always succeed. One Stevenson five minute ad cut the end from "Name That Tune" just as viewers were seeing films of the wedding of the young couple who had just won $20,000. CBS was deluged with protesting letters, calls, and telegrams. Stevenson responded with a telegram that was read over the air the following week. It said "I'm sorry that Name That Tune last week switched abruptly to Name That Candidate. . . . I particularly regret that we cut off Mr. and Mrs. Keil who constitute the happy combination of being Kansans, farmers, newlyweds and Democrats. There are not enough Democratic voices being heard on radio and television these days; we of all people should not be interrupting one another. But I am certain that the Kiels' voices will be heard with the rest of the country on November 6th."[18]

The Keils responded that Stevenson could cut into their time any time. "He's our boy" they said in an unintended paraphrase of Eisenhower's blessing of Nixon after Checkers.

Democratic time buyer Reggie Schuebel and Republican media executive Carroll Newton saved both political parties $20,000 per five minute spot by negotiating a change in the way in which preemption charges were calculated. In 1956 network rate cards were based on an hourly rate. Consequently, a full hour cost 100% of the hourly rate; a half hour 60%; fifteen minutes 40%. No standard rate existed for five minute programs. So the networks simply manufactured a rate. Using an hourly rate as their rate card standard, the networks planned to charge 30% of the hour rate for such preemption. Under pressure from Newton and Schuebel, that rate was altered to one-sixth of the half hour rate with the original sponsor paying five-sixths.[19]

In her efforts to secure an equitable five minute rate from CBS, Schuebel bargained with unusual leverage. "During the war CBS radio had a news program from 7:55 to 8:00 P.M.," she explains. "I had a program on for one of my clients from 7:30 to 8:00. When they preempted the last five minutes of our time, they paid 1/6 of the cost of the 30 minutes. Since everybody in '56 said the half hour speeches were too long and we didn't have the money to afford many anyway, I went to CBS and told them I'd give them the same rate for five minute spots that they had given me and assured them that we'd only buy programs that could be shortened by five minutes."[20] Schuebel also pioneered the policy by which candidates paid the agency in advance for time.

The Democratic professionals who worked with her in 1956 and 1960 universally praise her genius. But not until the final days of the campaigns did they recognize that her shrewd shepherding of their media monies had protected them from cash flow crises. "I never told the Democrats the truth about cost," Schuebel now admits. "If I needed $10,000, I said I needed $12,000 or $15,000. Consequently I had reserves when they ran short and wanted me to square it with the networks. We could make it because I had been saving the extra money."[21]

Ike's Health as an Issue in the Campaign

Two factors tantalized the Democrats with hopes of victory. First, during his first term, Eisenhower had suffered a heart attack and a bout with ileitis, medical crises raising the prospect initially that he would not seek the nomination, later that he would not live through his second term. The heart attack occurred on September 23, 1955; the surgery for ileitis on June 8, 1956.

When word of Ike's heart attack had been released, prominent Democrats, the public, and the press assumed that he would not seek a second term. For example, almost 9 out of 10 of the Washington correspondents told a pollster that Ike would not seek renomination.[22] The public concurred. An October Gallup poll found 62% of the American people convinced that Ike would not be a candidate. Still, both in August before the heart attack and in December—after it—3 out of 4 Americans approved of Ike's work as president.

The Attack on Ike as Part-time President

The Democrats knew that their strongest issue, indeed their only bankable issue against this immensely popular, immensely successful president was his ill health. They would allude to it, directly and indirectly, in a number of campaign attacks. First and foremost was Stevenson's charge that Ike was a part-time president. "Maybe I was fishing that day," Stevenson reported Ike as having said in answer to the question: why didn't the president know about the House resolution expressing sympathy for the satellite nations? In a speech in Los Angeles, Stevenson juxtaposed Ike's vacation schedule with major world events:

> On February 12 the *New York Times* reported that Senate leaders "alarmed by fears of possible U.S. involvement in the Indochina war" had called high members of the Administration to an urgent secret conference. On the same day The *Times* also reported that President Eisenhower had gone South for hunting with Secretary Humphrey and had bagged his limit of quail.
>
> Two days later the alarm had deepened in Washington and the papers reported that President Eisenhower was leaving for a six-day vacation in California. On Feb. 19, Secretary Dulles returned from the critical four-power conference in Berlin. He couldn't report to the president. The *New York Times* said "it was golf again today for President Eisenhower" at Palm Springs.[23]

An extended litany followed. Dulles explored military action in Indochina; Ike was golfing in Georgia. Nixon said the U.S. might intervene with military force; the president golfed in Atlanta. The last outposts around Dienbienphu fell; Ike began a golfing holiday. Dulles called the defeat in Indochina a victory; when asked his opinion, Ike stated that he hadn't read the article. The illustrations plodded on through a page and a half of printed single spaced speech text. "The list could go on endlessly," noted Stevenson. Indeed it seemed that it had. "I have left out of the list every case where the President's absence from Washington or his ignorance of crucial facts could be traced to his illnesses."

In the closing days of the campaign, Democratic ads called on voters to "Defeat part-time EISENHOWER and full-time NIXON,"[24] an appeal that underscored the claim that during Ike's convalescence, Nixon and others had run the country and a reminder that Ike had, on doctor's orders, delegated an increasing number of tasks to others. The Democrats assumed that the audience would carry to the ad the truckload of evidence about Ike's vacations and would add corroborating evidence of their own from recollections of his illnesses.

But three flaws, each more fatal than either of Ike's illnesses, marred this strategy. First the "part-time" indictment had little attitudinal ground in which to root. A Gallup survey in January 1956 found that by a vote of 57 to 22% the electorate favored turning some of the president's jobs over to others. Second, the public was satisfied with Ike's performance. During his tenure in the White House, the U.S. had not gone to hell either in a golf-cart or a wheelchair.

The third difficulty encountered by Stevenson's pirouettes on the theme of the part-time president was that the indictment cast him in the role of school master assigning demerits to the kid playing hookey—a move likely to beckon the Tom Sawyer in each of us. The moral superiority presupposed in indicting "the part-time president" fueled a smoldering public sense that Stevenson thought he was better than both the American people and their personifier, the amiable general.

The print ads for Ike subtly magnified the insult latent in Stevenson's posture. "Think of a leader who scorns the slick device of dividing a great people for political profit . . . who regards *all* his countrymen as equals in the quest of liberty and happiness," suggests one. "That man is Eisenhower."[25] The breath of the "l" in "the slick device" whispered the difference between slick and sick; Stevenson was being accused obliquely of one and even more obliquely of the other, a move that phonically turned the issue of health against the Democrat.

The ad also put a downward spin on the public perception that Stevenson was an egghead—a characterization that yolked the soft-boiled Democratic nominee to the worst puns cracked in the scrambled history of presidential campaigns. By assuming a posture of moral and intellectual superiority, Stevenson invested the Republican claim that he thought he was "too good" for the American people with credibility otherwise denied it.

Having heightened the audience's awareness of the distance Stevenson implied between it and himself, the Republicans extended the claim to appeal to the so-called "eggheads" on the grounds that Stevenson was taking them for granted. "We tried the 'eggheads' once. Besides, where else can they go?" a Republican ad quoted Stevenson's campaign managers as saying. The Republicans of course were ready with an answer. Under the banner "The 'Eggheads' are Going for Eisenhower,"[26] a testimonial ad signed by artists, educators, entertainers, writers, musicians, and scientists argued that Ike had provided the peace, prosperity, and encouragement for individual enterprise conducive to culture, art, science, and education. The signatories were members of CASE, the committee of the Arts and Sciences for Eisenhower, a group organized in July 1956.

Republicans Reconsider the Heir Apparent

In the lull before Ike's February 29, 1956, announcement that, were it offered, he would accept renomination, pollsters tested the strength of other Republican hopefuls. The polls reflected the Democrats' second reason for optimism. Although Ike was overwhelmingly popular, his constitutionally ordained successor was not.

Initially, by a narrow margin, Nixon had led the pack of Republicans favored by their party. In early October, for example, he had led Earl Warren 28% to 24%. By late October, his lead over Warren had increased to 11% among Republican voters. But concurrent trial heats pairing Stevenson and Nixon showed Nixon losing. That fact prophesied a change in the Republican rankings. By mid-December, Warren was beating Nixon in the polls of Republicans 27% to 24% and among Independents 28% to 18%. And in trial heats Stevenson's lead over Nixon was increasing. By January the gap among Independents widened. Thirty-seven percent of them now preferred Warren, while only 13% favored Nixon.

According to Nixon's *Memoirs*, Ike counseled him on December 26, 1955, to accept a cabinet post rather than run again as vice-president, but left the final decision to Nixon. "He said that he was disappointed," Nixon recalls, "that other suitable candidates for the presidency had not emerged from the party during the last few years and he referred to some of Gallup's trial heats in which Stevenson beat me by a fairly wide margin. He said it was too bad that my popularity had not grown more during the last three years."[27] Nixon opted nonetheless to stay on.

Subsequently, the story of the tête-à-tête leaked to *Newsweek*. When asked about it in a press conference on March 7, a week after he had publicly announced that he would run again, Ike responded: "I have not presumed to tell the vice president what he should do with his own future. . . . The only thing I have asked him to do is to chart out his own course, and tell me what he would like to do. I have never gone beyond that."[28]

In Nixon's judgment, the press read Ike's comment "to indicate varying degrees of indifference toward me, or even an attempt to put some distance between us."[29] Still after 23,000 voters in the New Hampshire primary of March 13 penned Nixon onto their ballots, a tribute to the backstage organizational skills of a handful of party regulars,[30] Ike narrowed the distance by saying at a press conference "there are lots of people in New Hampshire that agree with what I have told you about Dick Nixon" and announced "I would be happy to be on any political ticket in which I was a candidate with him."[31]

Nonetheless, scheming continued by those who wanted to dump Nixon from the ticket. In July, for instance, Harold Stassen told Ike of a private poll that demonstrated that Nixon would lose more votes for Ike than other possible running mates.[32]

Democratic Attacks on the Heir Apparent

Since as far as the public knew, President Eisenhower had not been mesmerized by any Svengalis, only in a scenario in which Ike was required to delegate additional authority to the vice-president or to turn the reins of government over to him could the Democrats exploit the political vulnerability of Richard Nixon. Here Ike's coronary and ileitis gave the Democrats their opening. But before they could use it, they had to find a way to circumvent the powerful political taboo that defines attacks on someone's health as unfair and as a self-indictment of the sensibilities of the attacker.

Evidence of this taboo is easy to marshal. Partisan attack on Gerald Ford ceased when his wife entered the hospital for breast cancer surgery; attacks on Teddy Kennedy were muted when his son faced cancer; a moratorium was called on political assaults on Reagan and Reaganomics when the president was shot. Unsurprisingly, then, in late July 1956 a Gallup Poll revealed that 65% of those surveyed thought that Ike's health should not be made an issue. Only 28% thought it should.

Yet had this taboo not existed or not been as strong, the Democrats were still taking a risk in adopting this approach since the need to predicate Nixon's ascent on Ike's disability meant that the Democrats, in effect, would have to confront the electorate with the mortality of a popular hero, the person who purportedly saved the country in World War II, the person who pulled the nation out of the quagmire of Korea, the person who promised and delivered prosperity. By magnifying the mortality of the popular hero, these attacks also situated the Grim Reaper at the dining room table of voters, who saw their own mortality reflected in Ike's. Confronted with such unpleasantries, some undoubtedly either avoided messages prophesying Ike's death or denied their truth.

At the same time, such attacks risked igniting the primitive belief lingering from our genetic infancy that saying is willing. Since Stevenson would benefit politically from Ike's death, he could not predict it without seeming himself to be brandishing a bloody dagger. Moreover by pivoting the case against the Republicans on Ike's impending demise, the Democrats in effect granted that if Ike were healthy, he should be reelected.

In summary, intra-party jockeying and speculative polling revealed Nixon as the Achilles heel of the Republican ticket. Unable to argue as they had in '52 that Nixon would manipulate Ike, Democratic ads shifted in '56 to the claim that Nixon "is all set to take over,"[33] a claim shy of asserting that Nixon in fact would ascend to the presidency upon Ike's death during his second term.

In late October the claim edged into daylight. "Can America Take a Chance with Nixon Becoming the First Man of the Nation?" a print ad asked in late October[34] in a synopsis that bespeaks a world as yet untouched by women's rights rhetoric. He would of course become "first man" only in the event of Ike's incapacitation or death.

As Halloween arrived with Ike still ahead in the polls, the rhetoric escalated. A Roman bust of Nixon is shown before a Roman colonnade. Although it does not say so explicitly, in this print ad[35] Nixon will play either Brutus or Cassius to Eisenhower's Caesar. "No matter whom you like," the ad reads, recalling the slogan "I like Ike" from the 1952 campaign, "the Republican Party is firmly controlled by the young and ambitious Richard Nixon and [Chairman of the Republican National Committee] Leonard Hall." What is implied is that the ailing Eisenhower will not be strong enough to stave off such lean and hungry men.

The story behind these anti-Nixon ads, which usually were locally produced and sponsored, is revealing. Stevenson's researcher and speechwriter Willard Wirtz recalls that Stevenson believed that such attack "seemed wrong in principle."[36] Aides such as Roger Tubby report that they disagreed with the candidate's assessment, arguing that "attacking Richard Nixon might draw from him a counter-attack that would boomerang" and contending as well that since Nixon was "a pretty evil guy" Stevenson should go on the record opposing him.[37] A debate among members of Stevenson's campaign staff resulted in the conclusion that the

only hope of election lay in direct attack by Stevenson on Nixon. Reluctantly, Stevenson agreed to deliver an extended attack. But as Wirtz now
recalls, Stevenson's delivery betrayed his discomfort:

> In 1956 in Flint Michigan, Stevenson gave the only speech in which he
> took out an indictment point by point of Richard Nixon. That speech
> had been worked on quite assiduously. He hated the idea and refused to
> give the speech. Finally close to the end of the campaign he was pre-
> vailed upon to give it. He delivered it exactly as written—the only time
> he followed a text exactly. He decided to hold his nose and give that
> speech. He read it as if he were reading a telephone directory.[38]

Nonetheless, subsequent attacks on Nixon were produced as broadcast spot ads. These ads each carried the same verbal message: "Nervous
about Nixon? President Nixon? Vote Democratic—the Party for you, not
just the few." In one, a still of Nixon underscored the opening claims, in
another a line drawing of Nixon dwarfed by a presidential chair, in a
third, a picture of the U.S. Capitol. Here, as in the majority of the
anti-Nixon print ads, the evidence warranting nervousness about Nixon is
unstated. The rationale for this strategy is explained in a memo from the
Democratic National Committee's ad agency "Norman, Craig and Kummel Inc." to the Stevenson campaign staff:

> Everyone, we believe, is in agreement that the possibility of Vice Presi-
> dent Nixon succeeding to the Presidency is an important issue in the
> 1956 campaign. As with the issue of the President's health, the principal
> problem in connection with the Nixon issue is how it should be handled.
>
> It is our opinion that we can inflict a great deal more damage by an
> indirect attack on Nixon than by a frontal assault. It is peculiarly diffi-
> cult to pin down specific charges against Nixon. On the other hand, we
> are fortunate in the fact that an amazingly large segment of the popula-
> tion, and even of his own party, seems to dislike and mistrust him
> instinctively.
>
> Having experimented with both the direct and indirect methods of han-
> dling the Nixon issue, we have come to the conclusion that it is best to
> start with the assumption that Nixon as President of the United States is
> an extremely distasteful idea to millions of Americans, and that our best
> tactic is to proceed from this assumption without wasting valuable time
> in establishing his undesirability.[39]

In short, the "Nervous about Nixon" ads were undisguised ad hominem
attacks. They were not aired, explains Stevenson's director of public relations George Ball, because Stevenson opposed the idea of purely negative
advertising and because the staff concluded that they "put Nixon in too
important a position."[40]

Also scripted was an anti-Nixon half hour take off on "This Is Your
Life," a popular prime time program that honored famous persons by

resurrecting former teachers, playmates, and the like to testify to the winning ways of the celebrities before they received public acclaim. Philip Stern, then on the staff of the Democratic National Committee, recalls that the telecast was to include "storekeepers from Whittier telling that they were told that if they didn't display Nixon's poster in their window they would be evicted and people from the American Legion who would testify that at the legion's convention they had heard Nixon say [horrible things] about Truman." The script was not produced because the staff concluded that "it would look like desperation. Ike was the issue not Nixon. It would have looked like we were grasping at straws."[41]

Nonetheless, Nixon drew sustained attack from Democratic print ads in both '52 and '56. Still, he served an important function for the Republicans for as Carroll Newton, an executive on the Republican advertising team in '52, '56, and '60, notes, he "drummed up the Republican party faithful, stirred up the campaign workers, and provided help with fundraising."[42]

Specific Use of Ike's Health as an Issue

On November 1, the Democratic assault on Ike's health took a new, more direct tact. A print ad signed by such notables as Henry Steele Commager, Allan Nevins, Van Wycke Brooks, Harold Lasswell, and Carl Sandburg addressed "An open letter to Governor Stevenson on THE PRESIDENT'S HEALTH."

The ad was drawn line for line, word for word from the Democratic National Committee's *Fact Book,* a 110-page document mailed to 100,000 state and county Democratic leaders in late August. Designed to provide ammunition for Democratic speakers, the *Fact Book* had been modeled on digests of facts that the committee had been providing to congressional staffers. Its author, Philip Stern, explains that its form was that of a legal brief. The italicized declarative sentences tell the story. All else amplifies these key sentences.[43]

Revealed in the *Fact Book* is the communication strategy of the campaign. In the world it projects, Ike had been a part-time president even before his coronary and attack of ileitis; his aides had kept and would continue to keep the tough problems from him; his illnesses would reduce his capacity to function as president and open the way to a Nixon White House; his successor, Nixon, was not a statesman but a scoundrel.

To locate evidence, for example, that the combination of ileitis and a heart attack made a person uninsurable and disqualified him for some corporate jobs, Stern tapped the expertise of doctors and insurance experts inside and out of the federal government. When he found the army regulation that indicated that a person with Eisenhower's health history would be denied an Army commission, he "freaked out with glee."

The "open letter" ad drawn from the *Fact Book* opened by quoting Ike's statement of February 29, 1956, that "I am determined that every American shall have all available facts concerning my personal condition." So Ike's own words are used to legitimize the health issue. Consequently, the ad urges Stevenson "to reconsider your decision that you 'will not make an issue of the President's health.' "

Under the guise of reporting the facts as Ike had instructed and with the ostensible purpose of convincing Stevenson that he ought properly to make Ike's health an issue, the signers of the ad insinuate that a person with Ike's medical history in a high stress job is a medical risk. So, for example, the ad argues that "most men with heart trouble are not insurable"; that "most healthy men over 65 retire from full-time work"; that "most major corporations retire executives at age 65"; that "the army will not commission men with heart trouble or ileitis," and that "the mortality rate on ileitis victims is three times above normal." The tone of the ad is scholarly; its form betrays its legal ancestry; its quantity of detail betokens persuasion guised as education.

Unburdened of its weighty evidence, the ad asked "Shall Vice-President Nixon assume presidential powers?" The answer is not immediately given. Instead concern is expressed about the Constitutional crisis that will occur if Ike is stricken again because "there is no provision or precedent for the delegation of Presidential powers during a President's disablement." The ad then raises the fear that "the powers of the president may pass to Vice-President Nixon." The reasons for the fear are unspecified; instead, in an act of enthymematic complicity, the audience is expected to dress the ad with them.

The ad closes with a quote from Walter Lippmann, whose misspelled name had prompted a recall of the *Fact Book* and the addition of a truant "n." But the framers of the ad were the guardians of an uncorrected copy. Consequently, in the ad "Lippman" termed probing Ike's health "a horrid duty" imposed by Ike's decision to seek a second term "despite his age and his serious illnesses." To refrain from such discussion, "Lippman" declared, "would be to engage in a sentimental conspiracy of silence."

The genius of this ad is that it solved the dilemma the press had isolated when the *Fact Book* first announced that the president's health was going to be an issue in the campaign. "[M]any Democrats," wrote a reporter for the *New York Times,* "think the medical facts make the President's health a perfectly fair political issue—and their best hope for victory this year—but . . . have no idea how to use it without causing a backfire of sympathy for him."[44]

Under the guise of urging Stevenson to make it an issue, the ad provided a way. After raising the health issue and supplying medical evidence to back its claims, the ad concluded, in effect, that Ike was not long for this world. It accomplished this without lodging responsibility for those claims and any subsequent backlash with Stevenson.

Ike's Age as an Issue

In the process of underscoring its claims about Ike's health, this ad also played on powerful age stereotypes. In its stress on mandatory retirement of executives, the ad reinforced the mistaken assumption that increasing age signals decreasing competence. Here Ike was vulnerable, for only 1% of the electorate viewed 65 and over as "the ideal age for a man to be elected President."[45] But neither Republicans nor Democrats considered Ike, who would turn 66 in 1956, beyond the "maximum" age at which a candidate should run. While Democratic voters put that age at 68, Republicans set it at 70.

To enwrap the age issue in a more personal context, the Republicans decided to celebrate Ike's sixty-sixth birthday on national television. Using a format similar to that of "This is Your Life," the program reminisces about Ike's childhood, his life as a cadet, and his service to the country as general and president. The show was both personal and patriotic. When a picture of Cadet Eisenhower appeared on the screen, for example, the Fred Waring Glee Club sang West Point's alma mater.

The audience was explicitly invited to see itself as part of Ike's extended family, particularly when the president's granddaughter introduces a cherubic little boy who carries a large piece of cake to the president. Hollywood stars sang the president's favorite songs and cut the cake, baked from Mamie's favorite recipe.

The extended family with which we are expected to identify is a fine, honorable one. The child who carries the cake has the sort of angelic countenance parents dream of. The celebrants, such as James Stewart, the M.C., and Helen Hayes and Irene Dunne, who cut the cake, transport into the TV special the residues of wholesome and heroic roles they have played on stage and screen.

The extended family embraced thousands who assembled at Republican-sponsored gatherings around the country to watch the television show, sing happy birthday to Ike, and eat birthday cakes, also baked from Mamie's recipe.

These familial gatherings organized around Mamie's cake forced those who held Ike's age against him into the role of ungracious guests who would sing Happy Birthday to Grandfather and eat the cake that

Grandma had made in his honor, while planning to stab Grandpa with the crumb-crusted knife. Although Ike seemed uncomfortable with this public spectacle, it transformed a traditional family celebration into a televised communal event the divorced Stevenson could not replicate.

"The divorce issue was brought up a lot in '56," recalls William P. Wilson, who produced Stevenson's live local television. "None of us knew what to do with it."[46]

Stevenson's divorce figured in his campaign's decision to originate the election eve telecast in Boston, where Stevenson's grandchild had just been born, rather than in the home he had once shared with his wife in Libertyville. "We had to find a family situation for him," notes Wilson. By contrast, Ike and Mamie and Dick and Pat hosted an election eve report reminiscent of the one with which they had closed the 1952 campaign.

Posters, such as the one shown here, also underscored a family image providing they did not prompt the question of whom Stevenson was smiling at. To buffer himself from the implication that divorce meant he was not "a good family man," Stevenson's sister and children traveled with him on campaign trips and his family was prominently displayed in a series of five minute ads shot at his farm. In one of the Man from Libertyville ads, Stevenson, his daughter-in-law Nancy, and his oldest son, Adlai III, sift through the morning mail as Stevenson explains his notion of the New America to them. In another, two of his sons and his daughter-in-law listen as he and Kefauver discuss the significance of the vice-presidency. In a third, Stevenson and his daughter-in-law do the family's marketing as he discusses his plans to curb the increases in the cost of living.

"The idea [for the Man from Libertyville spots] originally sprang from the campaign in 1952," recalls the DNC's public affairs director Clayton Fritchey. "To keep our distance without offending Truman, Stevenson ran from his own state capitol of Springfield, Illinois—Abe Lincoln territory. We were spreading the idea 'the man from Springfield.' It was an easy jump from there in '56 to 'the Man from Libertyville.' If we'd wanted to name a town for Stevenson, 'Libertyville' could not have been better named. Since he was no longer governor, we couldn't use 'man from Springfield' anymore."

The difficulty with the Man from Libertyville spots was not their strategy but Stevenson's discomfort with their artificial dialogue and the deadening frequency with which they were aired. Repeated airing bored viewers and focused attention on the ad's technical flaws. "All of us—including the agency—were such neophytes at this new form of campaigning that none of us were sure of our ground," comments Fritchey. "Now there are political agencies that aren't regular advertising agencies but

1956 Stevenson poster. (Courtesy Smithsonian Institution, Photo No. 75-469, Division of Political History)

which practice political psychology. Then there wasn't that kind of expertise around. Everyone was feeling their way."

Despite the efforts of Stevenson's spot ads, posters, and election eve
program to mute the divorce issue, in the judgement of his staff it hurt his
candidacy in both '52 and '56, particularly among Catholic voters who
defected from the Democratic party in record numbers. "There was still a
strong feeling," recalls McGowan, "not only among Catholics that a man
who has been married ought to still be married."

Although Newton says that Mamie's prominence in the election eve
telecast is not a deliberate attempt to contrast Eisenhower's family life
with Stevenson's, the program had that effect. Mamie's presence had
other advantages as well, for as Newton explains "whenever she was with
Ike his appearance of warmth increased."

Use of Television to Persuade the Public That Ike Was Healthy

Just as in 1952 Ike's paternal reassurances in televised speeches and spots
muted the Democratic claims that he was inexperienced, dangerous, and
likely to be dominated by unsavory elements in his own party, so too in
1956 television's visual verification of Ike's health muffled the Democrat's
claims that he was likely to be incapacitated or die during his second
term. Early in 1956 Ike gave a televised press conference "not so much to
answer questions as to show the country he looked fit."[47] After his ab-
dominal surgery for ileitis, another televised press conference "gave reassuring evidence of his fitness."[48] "Ike looked fine and vigorous," Newton
recalls. Consequently, Democratic attacks on his health sounded like
"sour grapes to the average voter who could see the President's picture
on television."

But two reasons dictated that TV appearances alone would not eradicate the health issue. First, overreliance on television would have raised
questions about Ike's "ability to meet the physical demands of his
office."[49] As important, as Allen Drury of the *New York Times*
reported,[50] "the ruddy glow that is so characteristic [of Ike] simply did not
come across in black and white. The only sure answer to this was fewer
sermons from the White House and more face-to-face contact with the
voters." Ike's need to demonstrate to the voting public that he in fact was
healthy dictated that, contrary to his advisers' early plans, his campaigning would not be limited to five or six televised speeches but would
instead take the candidate before live audiences on the stump. So, although the Republicans budgeted $1.5 million for television and the
Democrats $1.3,[51] each nominee campaigned vigorously.

Both campaigns were conscious that television's image of a candidate was a major factor in the public's diagnosis of his fitness for office. Before the Democrats had selected a candidate, the Democratic National Committee staff and the staff of its ad agency had agreed that the candidate should not make live appearances in five minute spots. The minutes of a meeting on February 15, 1956, explain that "candidate during the course of the campaign is under tremendous physical strain and this strain would show up in his physical appearance."[52]

Ike's claim that he was healthy enough to handle the job of president for another term was blessed by the public's perception that he was trustworthy and honest. Indeed in December 1955 Ike led Gallup's list of the most admired men in any part of the world. Winston Churchill was in second place. Adlai Stevenson in tenth. In a climate in which favorable mentions of Ike's integrity and ideals outnumbered those about Stevenson by over 4 to 1[53], Ike's claim to health, underscored by his televised and personal appearances, was more credible than Stevenson's prognosis.

The public's confidence in Ike was solid. In October 1955, one out of two thought that even if his doctors said it was all right, President Eisenhower should not run again; yet 56% stated that if he did run they would vote for him. Public confidence in the truth of Ike's claims about his health was justified when late in the campaign he handled the Suez crisis without a relapse.

Additionally, the Democrat's 1952 claims about Ike had proven false, fomenting public suspicions that here was a party prone to cry wolf. In his second term, however, Ike did suffer a minor but not incapacitating stroke.

International Crises as Issues in '56

On October 27, a Gallup poll reported that voters considered "war, threat of war, Suez, foreign policy" the most important problem facing the country today. By 48–13% it led the "high cost of living," a pro-Democratic issue.

Foreign policy emerged as a major issue when Egypt recognized Communist "Red" China and purchased arms from Czechoslovakia. In response, the U.S. both canceled support for the Aswan Dam project and persuaded some of her allies to do the same. Egyptian President Abdul Gamel Nasser retaliated by seizing from the British control of the Suez Canal, a vital passage through which most of Western Europe's oil was transported. Britain and France considered going to war. Fearful of aggression and concerned that Egypt might bar her from the Canal, Israel sent troops into Egypt's Sinai Peninsula. France and England joined Israel despite Eisenhower's warning that foreign policy crises cannot be resolved by war. When the United States voted for a cease-fire in the UN and made clear that it would not support its usual allies, France and England were forced to withdraw.

Eisenhower's handling of the Suez Crisis established that even the coalition of the country's traditional allies and one of the most powerful lobbying groups in the U.S., the American Jewish community, could not drag him into a war he had cautioned against. When France and England went ahead with military action, despite Eisenhower's warning that if they did they could not count on U.S. support, he refused to support them militarily even though such action might have been politically expedient. Although there were more people in the U.S. whose interests coincided with those of Israel, France, and England than with Egypt's or with abstract principles of foreign conduct, Eisenhower resisted political pressures and by so doing confirmed that he would resist such pressures even at the expense of his own popularity. By acting forcefully but without military force, Eisenhower gained an important political victory.

As the nation's attention focused on the prospect and then the fact of war in the Middle East, a second international crisis erupted. On October 23, an anti-Communist uprising occurred in Budapest, Hungary. A newly formed coalition government declared Hungary a neutral nation and announced that it was withdrawing from the Warsaw Treaty Organization. The new government appealed to the UN and to the free world for help. Opponents of the new government formed a countergovernment and requested Soviet assistance to topple the coalition.

Although Russian tanks crushed the revolt as the U.S. ignored the protestors' pleas for assistance, the crisis in Hungary and in the Suez were godsends for the incumbent president. Not only does the country rally behind its elected leader in times of international crisis but Ike's perceived strength was foreign affairs. He was also the beneficiary of the public's gratitude for ending the Korean War and subsequently keeping the peace.

Democrats Attack Ike's Handling of Suez and Hungary

Stevenson argued that the crisis in the Middle East manifested the failure of Ike's foreign policy. In a nationally broadcast speech from Madison Square Garden, he declared that "had the Eisenhower administration taken a firm stand in the Middle East, had it aided Israel with arms and territorial guarantees, we might, I believe, have been able to prevent the present outbreak of hostilities. And if this government of ours had not alternately appeased and provoked Egypt, I think we would command more influence and respect, not only there, but throughout the Arab world today." Stevenson also charged in the closing days of the campaign that the Eisenhower administration had repeatedly been caught off guard by such world events as the death of Stalin, the uprisings in East Berlin and Poznan, and the revolts in Poland and Hungary. Eisenhower had failed, argued Stevenson, to exploit the weaknesses in the Soviet ranks.[54]

Apparently recognizing that Stevenson's attacks on Ike's handling of Suez and Hungary were being muffled by perceptions that his postures were spawned by self-interest, the Democrats turned to a spokesperson perceived both to be selfless and Ike's equal. That task fell to Eleanor Roosevelt, widow of the only person who when matched in 1955 by Gallup in a hypothetical race with Ike would win 52–43%.

An ad with a letter from Roosevelt had a second advantage for its primary audience was women, an important contingent for Stevenson since by giving Ike 58% of their votes in 1952 women had contributed "heavily" to his victory. Roosevelt urged women to beg their friends and neighbors to change this leadership.* She asked "Do we have to side with the Kremlin and the Dictator of Egypt?"[55] The ad underscores the anxiety at the goings on in the Middle East and then notes that only a week before Ike had assured us that the news from that part of the world was good.

From there the ad reminds readers that the U.S. resolution on the Middle East presented to the Security Council of the UN had been vetoed "by the two most important allies of the U.S.—Great Britain and France." Was it possible that our relationships with them had deteriorated so far that we were unaware of their plans to veto? If we felt that their position was wrong and told them so, why didn't they listen to us? It could not be possible, speculates Roosevelt, that we would present such a resolution knowing that it would pit us against France, Britain, and "the only Democratic country in the Near East," Israel, and pair us with the Soviet Union and the Dictator of Egypt. Roosevelt is implying that under the Republican administration our relationships with our allies have deteriorated badly.

She set this implication against Nixon's claim that in this crucial time we need a "tried and true general as our leader." How could we have worse leadership than we currently have, she asks.

Piling indictment on indictment, Roosevelt then observed that what Ike did not say in his nationally broadcast speech was that the Soviets had succeeded in dividing the West and we are thereby weakened. Under the

---

*Print ads headed "For Women Only" solicited the support of women directly. In a public letter to business and professional women, Stevenson proclaimed his commitment to equal pay for equal work, strong schools, and the presence of women in policy-making positions at all levels of government (*New York Times*, November 2, 1956).

Democrats we would not find ourselves unexpectedly confronting such situations, she argues.

Roosevelt's ad simply repeated claims found in Stevenson's October 31 speech in Pittsburgh and his nationally broadcast response to Eisenhower's report on Hungary and Suez. The claims also paralleled those made by Truman in a press conference October 31. But neither Truman nor Stevenson could throw the popularity of the most revered Democratic president of the century against that of the most popular Republican. And neither could reach female voters, traditionally more likely to vote for "peace" candidates, more directly than Roosevelt.

The Republican's in-house polls revealed that the Democratic attack on Suez "completely backfired," recalls Newton. By asking each of its 10 to 12 offices to randomly call 100 people over a weekend, BBD&O in 1952, 1954, 1956 and 1958 conducted its own polls to isolate issues of importance to voters. These polls not only helped determine what topics Ike should address in broadcast speeches but also monitored the impact of Democratic assaults. What the polls showed in 1956 was that about half of the potential voters were aware of Stevenson's charges and that most who were aware—whether Republicans or Democrats—were convinced that in the event of war they would prefer Eisenhower in the White House.

Stevenson's biographer concludes that "Suez turned a certain victory for Eisenhower into a landslide." Stevenson reportedly believed that the Suez cost him four million votes.[56] Of course, there has to be some question about this since Ike's failure to support Israel surely risked offending the vocal and influential, albeit traditionally Democratic, Jewish vote.

The Conflict over Response Time

Emphasizing that he was speaking not as candidate but as president, on October 31, Ike calmly reassured the country over national radio and television that the situations in Hungary and the Middle East were being closely monitored and that the U.S. was behaving prudently and intelligently in both.

Acting on Stevenson's behalf, Ball, who reports that he was "way out of his milieu" and "didn't know a damned thing about the television business," spent an entire night trying to persuade the network presidents that Stevenson deserved equal time.[57] When the networks denied the request, Stevenson's staff appealed to the FCC. The FCC stated that it lacked sufficient time to deal with such a complicated case. Fearful lest they violate the equal time law, the networks gave Stevenson time on

November 1. On the day before the election the FCC ruled that when the president reports to the nation on an international crisis, Congress did not intend Section 315 to grant equal time to all presidential candidates. In response to the ruling, the networks offered Ike equal time to respond to Stevenson. The Eisenhower campaign wisely declined the offer. As Newton notes, "To go on the air and talk about Stevenson's speech would merely have advertised Stevenson."

The Republicans' rejection of the network's offer of equal time underscored the "presidential" strategy underlying their paid broadcasts. Between mid-September and mid-October they aired one half hour television program per week. In mid-October these increased to three a week with four aired the final week of the campaign. On October 16 the Republicans began a series of thirty-three five minute televised statements. These newslike reports to the nation featured Ike, Nixon, or members of the cabinet touting the administration's achievements and making the case for a Republican Congress.*

The Suez crisis and the uprising in Hungary also hurt Stevenson's candidacy by undercutting two of the issues on which he was running in '56: suspending H-bomb testing and instituting a volunteer army. In a climate thick with international tension, the Republicans quickly transmuted those positions into evidence that Stevenson did not believe in a strong defense.

The international crises increased the vulnerability of Stevenson's proposals that the draft be ended and H-bomb testing banned. A Republican print ad capitalized on this vulnerability by claiming[58] "President Eisenhower says 'Weakness invites aggression . . . strength stops it.' The Democrat candidate says that America must have stronger defense . . . and in the same speech he recommends that America suspend H-bomb tests and terminate the draft! A change in the Presidency now would amount to trading a proven leader for a speechmaker who contradicts himself."

The ad subtly allies Ike to his conquest of Hitler by quoting him as saying "It is not enough that their elders promise 'peace in our time'; it must be peace in their time, too, and in their children's time. Indeed, there is only one real peace, and that is peace for all time." Although the tautology in the final sentence weakens its impact, the ad recalls Cham-

---

*Reports to the nation by members of the cabinet were the natural extension of an earlier use of television also orchestrated by Batten, Barton, Durstine, and Osborn. In June 1953, key members of the cabinet had joined Ike in a carefully rehearsed roundtable discussion of the problems facing the country and the solutions the administration was implementing. The next year television brought the nation a full dress cabinet meeting, complete with memorized lines and cues.

berlain's ill-fated promise after what would come to be called "the sell-out at Munich." By controverting "peace in our time" Ike reminds us that he dealt successfully with the consequences of Chamberlain's blunder and implies that in advocating a ban on H-bomb testing and ending the draft Stevenson is another Chamberlain. If true, then Stevenson could unwittingly lead the country into war. So the ad closes with the appeal "Vote for Ike and Peace."

The crises in Suez and Hungary quashed public sympathy for proposals to end the draft and stop H-bomb testing. But even in the absence of such international tension Stevenson's presentation of the proposal to end the testing of the nuclear bomb was self-detonating. As George Ball argues persuasively, Stevenson never made clear precisely what he was advocating:

> In his original speech to the American Society of Newspaper Editors, he had, in the final draft, dropped out any reference to a prior agreement with the Soviet Union for a cessation of bomb testing, proposing instead that the United States act on its own and resume tests only if the Soviets continued to test. . . . Then in his speech to the American Legion in Los Angeles on September 5, after the campaign had started, he spoke about his "proposal asking to halt further testing of large nuclear devices, conditioned upon adherence by the other atomic powers to a similar policy." Later, on September 29, he referred to it as "a moratorium on the testing of more super H-bombs. If the Russians don't go along—well, at least the world will know we tried. And we will know if they don't because we can detect H-bomb explosions without inspections."[59]

Similarly, Eisenhower concluded that Stevenson's "arguments would do his cause little good, particularly since he confused his hearers by apparently advocating initially a unilateral suspension of American tests, in the hope others would follow and then shifting to the view that we should 'take the lead in promoting curtailment' of such tests."[60]

When Stevenson's stress shifted from cessation of testing of nuclear bombs to the argument that the Strontium 90 in fallout was endangering American health, Ball enlisted Dr. Benjamin Spock to "announce that increasing Strontium 90 in the atmosphere could prove fatal for infants" and also collected testimony from chemists and physicists underscoring Stevenson's claim.

Eleanor Roosevelt also endorsed Stevenson's proposal at a press conference that was subsequently rebroadcast by the Democrats as a radio ad. But, like Stevenson's initial formulation of his proposal, Roosevelt's statement bristled with problems for it betrayed her own fears that the risk, although worth taking, was high. Indeed an uncritical listener might well infer that the purpose of her statement was to argue that Stevenson's proposal was risky. "There was worry about 'risk, risk, risk," Roger Tubby recalls, "but the fact that she endorsed Stevenson's idea certainly helped."

Meanwhile, Ike was offering the public the reassurances of the National Academy of Sciences that the existing level of testing did not endanger health. He also was affirming we would accept a test ban only if the Soviets would agree to stop testing and would make that pledge in an agreement we could trust.

Which Party Has Done More for the People?

Parenthetically but purposively, the Democratic ads allied the Republicans with the rich and the Democrats with the rest. The claim that the Republicans favored the rich resonated with voters in 1956 as it had in 1952.[61]

In late September in a speech in Cleveland, Ike seemed to play into Stevenson's hands with his suggestion that "one issue of the election should be whether the Republican party or the Democratic party had done most for the people."[62] Stevenson accepted the challenge in a nationally televised speech from Pittsburgh that stressed the high cost of living and the plight of farmers.

Goaded by Stevenson's claim that the Republican party was the party of General Motors, Republicans attempted to "make a fool of the Democratic charge that the President is the captive of big business"[63] in a half hour telecast brimming with garment workers, shopkeepers, union workers, and farmers. This visual rebuttal employed a split screen and remote pickups to enable "ordinary citizens" to ask supposedly spontaneous questions of the president. Although the president could actually see these "ordinary people" only on his television monitor, their presence on the screen with Ike visually countered the Democratic claim that where the Democrats saw people, the Republicans saw only statistics. The format had the additional advantage of familiarity for it was the logical technological extension of the Eisenhower Answers America spots of 1952. Some of the five minute broadcasts employed by the Republicans in the closing weeks of the campaign elaborated on the same theme. In one, enthusiastic citizens representing various professions testified to their devotion to Ike and the Republicans. In another, individual Democrats explained why they planned to vote Republican.[64]

A campaign film titled "These Peaceful and Prosperous Years" also immunized Ike from the image as a president for the rich. This film, created by the Republican Congressional Campaign Committee for use by Republican candidates in House and Senate races, demonstrated what an average family of four is able to do with the earning power gained under the Republicans. The narrator reminded the smiling family of their blessings:

> A peaceful way of life—first and foremost, that is what these peaceful, prosperous years have meant.
>
> No more casuality lists. They ended with the Korean war. No more telegrams—'The War Department regrets—'
>
> Yes; Mr. and Mrs. America you can be truly thankful . . . there has been no new war under the republicans. No new police action. Only years of peace and prosperity . . . everything has been booming in America for the last four years . . . everything except the guns.[65]

Pinning the label "party of the rich" on the Republicans was much easier than pinning it on Ike. Still, the Democratic appeals did not go unheard. Despite a last minute blitz of spots showing Ike with congressional and senatorial candidates, the election of a Democratic House and Senate confirmed that Ike's coattails were barely as long as those on the Eisenhower jacket.

Promise vs. Performance

In every presidential election in which a challenger faces an incumbent, advertising in some form argues that the promises on which the incumbent was elected have not been met by performance. The 1956 campaign was no exception. In a series of TV and radio ads titled "How's That Again, General?" the Democrats juxtaposed footage of Eisenhower making promises in 1952 with claims by vice-presidential candidate Kefauver that those promises had not been kept. The series was designed to enable local candidates to cut in with their own message in the final ten seconds of the ads. Because Eisenhower had carried over the format of the Eisenhower Answers America ads into his 1956 campaign, Democratic replaying of the actual 1952 spots was effective. The following storyboards[66] are representative of the form and content of this series of ads:

DEMOCRATIC NATIONAL COMMITTEE TELEVISION
ANNOUNCEMENT—FILM "HOW'S THAT AGAIN GENERAL?"
60 SECONDS—CORRUPTION

VIDEO

1. OPEN POP ON WORD BY WORD LEGEND "HOW'S THAT AGAIN, GENERAL?" HOLD IN LIMBO. FADE OUT SLOWLY AND FADE IN.

AUDIO

ANNOUNCER: (*voice over*)
How's that again, General?

---

2. FROZEN FIRST FRAME NEWS-
REEL WITH EISENHOWER TALK-
ING. SUPER "1952"

ANNOUNCER:
During the 1952 campaign, General Eisenhower promised a "great crusade."

SET IN MOTION

EISENHOWER: (*lip sync*)
When it comes to casting out the crooks
and cronies . . . I can promise you that
we won't wait for Congressional prodding, and investigation . . .

FREEZE FRAME

ANNOUNCER: (*voice over*)
How's that again, General?

RUN AGAIN

EISENHOWER: When it comes to casting
out crooks and cronies . . . I can
promise . . .

3. DISS TO VP CANDIDATE
STANDING BEFORE PHOTO-
GRAPHS OF VARIOUS MEN BE-
HIND HIM. HE INDICATES THEM,
AND ADDRESSES CAMERA

VP CANDIDATE: (*lip sync*) This is
(*name*). Let's see what happened to that
promise.

HE POINTS TO WESLEY ROBERTS

Wesley Roberts, Republican National
Chairman, sold Kansas a building it already owned for $11,000! He got a
silver tray from the General!

HE SKIPS OVER A COUPLE,
POINTS TO HAROLD TALBOTT

VP CANDIDATE   (*continues*)
Harold Talbott persuaded defense
plants to employ a firm which paid him
$130,000 while he was Air Force Secre-
tary. He received the General's warm
wishes for success.

HE SHRUGS AT ENTIRE DISPLAY
OF PHOTOS.

Despite case after case of wrongdoing—
nobody was fired or punished. Think it
through on November 6!

4. FAMILY EMBLEM

ANNOUNCER: (*voice over*)*
Vote Democratic—the party for you—
not JUST THE few.

5. STEVENSON AND NAME SU-
PERED. SUPER SMALL LEGEND
LOWER SCREEN: "A PAID DEMO-
CRATIC PARTY ANNOUNCE-
MENT."

Elect Stevenson president.

*local cut in here if desired.

August 9, 1956

DEMOCRATIC NATIONAL COMMITTEE TELEVISION
ANNOUNCEMENT—FILM "HOW'S THAT AGAIN, GENERAL?"
60 SECONDS—COST OF LIVING

VIDEO

AUDIO

1. OPEN POP ON WORD BY WORD LEGEND "HOW'S THAT AGAIN, GENERAL?" HOLD IN LIMBO. FADE OUT SLOWLY AND FADE IN.

ANNOUNCER: (*voice over*)
How's that again, General?

2. TELEVISION SET SCREEN, NEARLY FULL SCREEN. FROZEN FRAME. STILL OF EISENHOWER FROM "TIME FOR A CHANGE SERIES." SUPER "1952"

In the 1952 campaign, the General complained about the cost of living. He promised his television audience . . .

3. IN MOTION FULL SCREEN. DROP "1952" TO LOWER SCREEN.

EISENHOWER: (*lip sync*)
". . . people today can afford less butter, less fruit, less bread, less milk. Yes, it's time for a change."

FREEZE FRAME

ANNOUNCER: (*voice over*)
How's that again, General?

SET IN MOTION

EISENHOWER:
Yes, it's time for a change.

4. DSS TO VP CANDIDATE ON CAMERA. HE ADDRESSES IT DIRECTLY.

VP CANDIDATE: (*lip sync*)
This is (*name*). The General's promise to bring down prices was another broken promise. Today, the housewife gets less butter, less fruit, less bread, less milk for the money than she got in 1952. Since the Republicans took office, the cost of living has reached its highest point in history. The General promised a change for the better . . . and we got short-changed for the worse. Think it through!

5. FAMILY EMBLEM

ANNOUNCER: (*voice over*)*
Vote Democratic—the party for you, not just the few.

6. STEVENSON WITH NAME SUPERED. SUPER SMALL LEGEND: "A PAID DEMOCRATIC PARTY ANNOUNCEMENT."

Elect Stevenson president.

August 9, 1956

*local cut-in here if desired.

The problem these spots confronted was the same general problem the Democrats faced throughout the campaign: voters approved of Eisenhower's record.

Slogans

In 1956 "Peace, Prosperity, and Progress" battled for votes against the "New America." If the Republican's claim to peace and prosperity was accepted, then there was no need for a new America—the old one was working well. As we noted in the introduction to this chapter, peace and prosperity were seemingly at hand.

Added to these was popular affection for Eisenhower. More than any other statement, "I like Ike" and "I still Like Ike," sported on buttons, banners, and bumper stickers, explained the election's outcome. In 1956, a likeable, popular, trusted, national hero was reelected.

CHAPTER FOUR

1960: Competence, Catholicity, and the Candidates

This chapter is the story of how a millionaire senator from Massachusetts with an undistinguished record in the Congress effectively neutralized his opponent's eight years of experience as vice-president and in the process established that he too understood what peace demanded. This chapter describes the campaign in which Catholicity was removed from the list of characteristics disqualifying one to serve as president of the U.S. Finally, it is the tale of how, until it was too late, Richard Nixon cast his own campaign in the image of Eisenhower's past campaigns while failing to invite Ike to perform the role that might have ensured a Republican victory in 1960.

Say the word "president" and each of us conjures up an image. Until 1960, conventional wisdom had it that a president was tall, middle-aged, heterosexual, Caucasian, Protestant, and male. So, for example, labor informed Alben Barkley in 1952 that at 74 he was "too old"; Shirley Chisholm learned in 1972 that "The Presidency is for white males."[1]

The press safeguards these implicit criteria by taking note only when a candidate appears to violate one of them. The height of candidates is not mentioned, for example, unless a candidate seems to fall outside the expected range as Howard Baker did in 1980. Similarly, Al Smith's status as the first Catholic nominee and Jimmy Carter's as the first born again Baptist were noted because both challenged the mainstream Protestantism that has been the norm for American presidents. Most recently, Ronald Reagan's age became an issue in 1980, for his election promised to produce the first president over the age of seventy to begin a term in the White House. In the 1960 Kennedy-Nixon campaign, both age and religion became national issues, for if Kennedy won, he not only would be the country's first Catholic president but also would assume the presidency at the age of 43, the youngest age ever for an elected president. Teddy Roosevelt served at a younger age but only by acceding to the presidency upon the death of William McKinley.

It came as no surprise to anyone involved in politics that Richard Nixon was given the nod in 1960. Dwight Eisenhower's heart attack, bout of ileitis, and mild stroke had given the nation a chance to try on the prospect of a Nixon presidency. Then, as in the "kitchen debate" with Nikita Khruschev at the opening of the American exhibit in Moscow, Nixon had held his own on the national stage. Unopposed in the primaries, Nixon skillfully headed off the only serious threat to a unified party. Learning that New York Governor Nelson Rockefeller was prepared to contest certain parts of the party platform, Nixon agreed to meet Rockefeller to work out a compromise. Nixon was nominated on the first ballot and in his acceptance speech he called for "an offensive for peace and freedom" that would obviate the need for war.

As his running mate, Nixon named Henry Cabot Lodge, the man Kennedy had defeated for the Senate in 1952. After leaving the Senate, Lodge retained public attention in his role as ambassador to the UN where he berated the Russians for their invasion of Hungary and condemned them for planting bugging devices in U.S. embassies.

The Democratic candidate, John F. Kennedy, had been relatively unknown just four years earlier. But at the 1956 Democratic convention, Kennedy had taken what, in retrospect, would be viewed as the first step toward winning the presidency in 1960. Despite his relative obscurity and a lackluster congressional record, he scrambled to win the vice-presidential nomination that had been thrown open to the convention by Adlai Stevenson. Although Kennedy lost the spot to Estes Kefauver, he gained incalculable national exposure in the attempt. Just how much he gained was apparent to Kennedy. "With only about four hours of work and a handful of supporters," Kennedy told an aide, "I came within thirty-three and a half votes of winning the Vice-Presidential nomination. . . . If I work hard for four years, I ought to be able to pick up all the marbles."[2] Kennedy later noted that if he had won the nomination in 1956, he might never have been in a position to capture his party's nomination in 1960, for presumably Stevenson would have been defeated and Kennedy's Catholicity would perhaps have absorbed a share of the blame.

A three-term congressman and two-term senator from Massachusetts, John Fitzgerald Kennedy seemed to have been born to politics. His father had served as FDR's controversial ambassador to Great Britain. His maternal grandfather, "Honey Fitz," had been the colorful mayor of Boston. But while Kennedy brought many tangible assets to the presidential race, he also came with three potentially serious liabilities: he was young, he was wealthy, and he was Catholic. By the campaign's end, two of the three had become assets and the third had proven insufficiently troublesome to deny him the presidency.

After defeating his chief rival, liberal Minnesota Senator Hubert Humphrey, in the two key primaries and derailing a last-minute Truman-backed bid by Texas Senator Lyndon Johnson and Missouri Senator Stuart Symington, Kennedy won the Democratic nomination on the first ballot.

As his running mate, Kennedy selected his previous rival, Texas Senator Lyndon Baines Johnson, a former school teacher, who was his party's majority leader in the Senate and a prime mover behind passage of the bipartisan Eisenhower foreign policy. Johnson was given the task of carrying the South in general and Texas in particular.

In his acceptance speech, Kennedy forecast a theme that would reverberate throughout his campaign and his presidency: "We stand today on the edge of a New Frontier—the frontier of the 1960's—a frontier of unknown opportunities and perils—a frontier of unfulfilled hopes and threats." It was a frontier he envisioned not as a set of promises but as a set of challenges.

Should Catholicism Disqualify a Candidate for President?

In an internal campaign memo dated August 15, 1960, Theodore Sorenson, Kennedy's speechwriter and aide, wrote: "Given the normal Democratic majority, and assuming that his personal appeal, hard work and political organization produce as before, Senator Kennedy *will* win in November *unless* defeated by the religious issue. This makes *neutralization* of this issue the key to the election."[3]

Kennedy's religion was a different sort of issue from his experience or lack of it, for although there are various levels of experience between innocence and incumbency, one either is or is not a Catholic. If Catholicity disqualified Kennedy, then the disqualification was absolute. Kennedy's job would be to show that it did not have to be this way, that a Catholic candidate could win his party's nomination, the presidency, and perform competently in that job.

When the spectre of Al Smith and his 1928 defeat were evoked early in the primaries, Kennedy and his aides exorcised them deftly. "1960 is not 1928," Ted Sorensen told an audience in February 1960. "Al Smith bore the handicaps of being from Tammany Hall and the east side of New York, of being a Wet in a Dry year, and, above all, of being a Democrat in a Republican year. As a Catholic he faced a country far less urbanized, far less educated and far less sophisticated and tolerant than the country today. Yet he lost only one state—North Carolina—which was not carried by the Republicans against his two predecesors or Adlai Stevenson. Of course his religion was a factor—but every poll, every recent election, shows that factor's importance has diminished sharply—that today it is more of a conversational novelty, particularly among politicians, than it is a mass issue."[4]

Simultaneously, without mentioning the religion issue directly, Kennedy's advertising made the point that his "stunning victories" in his Senate races proved that he was a winner. Unstated in the ads was the fact that these victories had been gained in the state with the highest percentage of Catholics in the nation and that fate and the Kennedy family fortune had facilitated even these early wins. By remarkable coincidence, for example, Kennedy's father had loaned the publisher of the *Boston Post* $500,000 and the paper unexpectedly endorsed Kennedy in his successful bid for the Senate in 1952.[5]

Of course, in tackling the issue of religion, Kennedy could have argued, with some justification, that his baptism as a Catholic was an accident of birth and that he was well grounded neither in his Church's history nor in its doctrine and hence unlikely to be shackled by either. But Kennedy would not make these arguments. Early on in the campaign, the staff had defined drawing back the Catholic Democrats who had bolted to Ike in 1956 as a necessary part of winning. If he were to do so, Kennedy could not begin by spurning the Catholic religion he and they shared.

The idea that the Catholic vote might turn out to be crucial to the 1960 election had its roots in a memo written in 1956. During Kennedy's unsuccessful dash for the vice-presidential nomination his advocates circulated a memo arguing both the existence and importance of the Catholic vote and how this vote could be safeguarded by a Catholic nominee. By the calculations in that memo—prepared by Ted Sorensen but credited to Connecticut party chief John Bailey—fourteen key states had a sufficiently large Catholic population to decisively shape the outcome of a close election. These states included New York with an estimated Catholic population of 40%, Illinois with 30%, and Massachusetts with 50%.[6] In 1960, estimates placed the percent of Catholics in the U.S. at somewhere between 20 and 30%. Still, the concerns of Protestant voters did have to be addressed and the first test of Kennedy's ability to do so came in the West Virginia primary.

In a brilliantly executed transformation, Kennedy recast questions of religion as ones of tolerance. A vote for Kennedy became a sign of open-mindedness, a vote against him a potential sign of bigotry. As Theodore White wrote of the clash between Hubert Humphrey and John Kennedy in the West Virginia primary, "once the issue could be made one of tolerance or intolerance, Hubert Humphrey was hung. No one could prove to his own conscience that by voting for Humphrey he was displaying tolerance. Yet any man, indecisive in mind on the Presidency, could prove that he was at least tolerant by voting for Jack Kennedy."[7]

Kennedy began this transformation in a volley of speeches, ads, and broadcasts in the West Virginia primary, a primary, in what reporters called a Protestant state, where he engaged a Protestant opponent whose campaign song was sung to the tune of "Give Me That Ol Time Religion."

By addressing the issue of religion in question-and-answer sessions, first with voters in televised five and one minute ads, then by answering queries from FDR's namesake Franklin Roosevelt Jr. in a televised half hour exchange, Kennedy demonstrated that he did not need to clear his statements with either Cardinal Cushing or the pope and also showed that he could withstand the pressure of scrutiny by skeptics and their stand-in FDR Jr. The tension of the encounters rivetted attention and invited identification with Kennedy as the candidate under seige and as the champion of such American virtues as fairness, tolerance, equal opportunity, freedom of religion, and separation of church and state.*

The heir of the most popular Democratic president of this century publicly endorsed Kennedy's answers as well. The endorsement was a potent one for, as Larry O'Brien writes, "President Roosevelt was still regarded as a savior in West Virginia. I was in many homes where the only pictures on the walls were of FDR and John L. Lewis, the former leader of the mine workers."[9]

Using questions prepared for him by Kennedy's staff, FDR Jr. asked the candidate: Would Kennedy's church influence him in the White House? Would the pope tell him what to do? What was Kennedy's attitude toward restriction of the rights of Protestants in such countries as Spain and Italy? Would he as president have difficulty attending a funeral service in a Protestant church? Is Kennedy bound by the declarations of popes and bishops that differ from those he espouses? Between questions, FDR Jr. summarized and then blessed Kennedy's answers. He concluded that there wasn't anything else Kennedy could say to convince reasonable persons that he would formulate public policy with complete

---

*Kennedy's counterassault on claims that his religion disqualified him was synopsized in a TV ad broadcast in the West Virginia primary. "There is no article of my faith," he declared in response to a questioner, "that would in any way inhibit—I think it encourages the meeting of my oath of office. And whether you vote for me or not, because of my competence to be president, I am sure that here in this state of West Virginia that no one believes that I would be a candidate for the presidency if I didn't think I could meet my oath of office." A portion of that ad reappeared in the half hour documentary on Kennedy broadcast by the Democrats in the general election. In that form the confrontation reminded the audience that after scutinizing the "religion question" the voters of West Virginia had dispatched it.[8]

independence. Kennedy had shown, testified Roosevelt, that his place of worship did not minimize his allegiance either to the country or to its Constitution.

In effect, Roosevelt argued that he and Kennedy were both heirs of the New Deal. If they were not brothers, they were at least political cousins. "His father and mine were this close," Roosevelt told West Virginians as he held up interlocked fingers. Those old enough to recall the fissure that had existed between the New Deal President and his Ambassador to England might have divined in the crossed fingers the irony of either double cross or betrayal but the young Roosevelt's fervent pleading on Kennedy's behalf gave lie to either interpretation.

Entitled by name and family resemblance to pass the legacy of the New Deal to the next generation, Roosevelt's familial embrace of JFK granted him a legitimacy within the party withheld both by Truman, who favored Symington, and by Stevenson, who retained hopes of again heading the Democratic ticket. In passing the torch to Kennedy, Roosevelt bypassed the wishes of the party's titular heads as well as those of Eleanor Roosevelt, the queen mother, who no longer held the power to elevate her chosen candidate to the status of heir apparent. They were Democrats but he alone was FDR's namesake and son by birth. To attest to this argument from ancestry, letters from Roosevelt to all West Virginia voters were shipped to Hyde Park to be postmarked (Roosevelt resided in Washington).[10] The role of enwrapping Kennedy in the mantle both of Democratic and Protestant approval was one FDR Jr. was splendidly equipped to play.

In the general election, Nixon, to his credit, steadfastly refused to make religion an issue and instructed his campaigners to do likewise. A statement to that effect was distributed within the campaign and Campaign Director Robert Finch repeated the instruction as he moved from city to city. "Nixon was dead serious about it," Finch recalls. "There were many in the South who wanted some kind of tacit approval to use it [the issue of religion] and I made a number of calls" to ensure that that didn't happen.[11] Investigations by reporters and by the Fair Campaign Practices Committee failed to find any evidence that the venomous attacks on Kennedy's faith were Republican sponsored or sanctioned.

The closest the Republican's advertising came to raising the religion issue even indirectly was a print ad in which "Al Smith's Daughter Looks at the Record and Casts Her Vote for Richard M. Nixon." But rather than an attack on Kennedy's religion, the ad is a not-so-subtle reminder to Catholics that one ought not vote for Kennedy simply because he is Catholic. After noting that no one should vote for or against a candidate because of religion, an appeal implicitly grounded in her father's experi-

ence, Mrs. Emily Smith Warner concluded that were her father alive, he
would have opposed Kennedy as too young in years and immature in
thought. Her father also would have disapproved of a candidate who
makes promises he could not keep, she declared. The ad concluded with
the reminder that "No man ever had better training for the Presidency
than Mr. Nixon."[12] That ad as well as many other Republican print ads
that appeared in metropolitan dailies were created at the state level and
not submitted for approval by the national campaign. Neither were radio
programs aired throughout Texas by Texans for Nixon. These ads quoted
editorials that argued that Kennedy's Catholic friends had given him the
nomination and that Kennedy would feel bound to implement papal policies. The group was headed by Carr P. Collins Sr., a leader in the Southern Baptist Convention.[13]

In the general election, as in the primaries, the religious attack came
from conservative Protestant ministers allied with some long-lived pur-
veyors of hate such as Gerald Smith, who flooded the country with print
messages, some of which had been used against Al Smith, arguing that a
vote for a Catholic was a vote for the pope, that to circumvent oaths to
which they could not in good conscience swear, Catholics appended secret reservations that invalidated the oaths, that Kennedy would institute
Catholicism as a state religion, and—more extreme still—that, if Kennedy
were elected, Protestants would be robbed of their property, disenfranchised, and slaughtered.

An undated Democratic campaign memo summarized the conten-
tions this way:

> A Roman Catholic president, as a faithful member of his church,
> would tend to follow and put into practice the views of his church
> that run counter to democracy.
>
> The Roman Catholic Church does not believe in full religious liberty
> for all persons or for other faiths.
>
> The Roman Catholic Church seeks preferential treatment, state assis-
> tance, and support in every country where its members are in the
> majority.
>
> The Roman Catholic Church seeks to influence and dominate public
> officials for its own advantage.[14]

Still the Kennedy organization was quick to capitalize on any association, no matter how weak, between Republicans and anti-Kennedy claims
about religion. So, for example, on September 15 the Citizens for Kennedy in Omaha issued a press release stating:

> Anti-Catholic jokes by a professional entertainer warmed up the crowd awaiting Vice-President Richard Nixon's plane at the Omaha airport early Friday morning.
>
> Jimmy Edmondson of Houston Tex., a comedian known for his portrayal of "Professor Backwards" on the Ed Sullivan television show, had the crowd of 900 faithful Republicans roaring over his jokes about Senator John F. Kennedy and the pope.

> Said Edmonston: "When this election is over, Kennedy will send just one wire, and that to the pope. The message will be simply, 'Unpack.' And then Senator Kennedy will go into the business of selling POPEsickles."[15]

The press release then quoted the Lutheran head of "Citizens for Kennedy" in Nebraska as "deploring the attack" and noted further that the "Republicans have not as yet repudiated the statement by Dr. Norman Vincent Peale and other leading Republican Protestant. . . [questioning] whether a Roman Catholic president would be able to withstand the efforts of his church to breach the wall of separation of church and state."

It was in part to mute this statement, made on September 7, 1960, by the widely read and well-respected Protestant minister that Kennedy accepted the invitation of the Greater Houston Ministerial Association to respond to its questions on September 12. Peale had suggested that a Catholic president would be under "extreme pressure from the Catholic hierarchy to publicly embrace and implement church policies."*

At the Ministerial Association, as in the primary in West Virginia, Kennedy used broadcast messages to combat messages conveyed in the main by print. In the process, he personally assumed the burden of rebuttal, enabling audiences to assess the sincerity and conviction with which he expressed his belief in the separation of church and state.

Answer by answer, Kennedy sidestepped the mines the ministers had

---

*Attempting to turn the issue of religion to Kennedy's advantage, a UAW pamphlet included as a supplement in the September 26 issue of the union's paper instead fueled the debate. Its cover paired a Klansman with the Statue of Liberty and asked: "Which do You choose? Liberty or Bigotry?" Over a million of the pamplets were circulated to union members (*New York Times,* October 18, 1960. p. 26).

Eisenhower attacked the pamphlet indirectly in a speech decrying "false or extreme propaganda." When asked about the pamphlet in a news conference, Kennedy who said he had not seen it, repudiated "the support of any group taking such a line." Walter Reuther, head of the UAW, expressed regret that the pamphlet had been published.

That expression of regret also was embedded in a union-sponsored ad that argued for Kennedy's candidacy and then stated "As a victim of hate group propaganda, we are deeply distressed and regret most sincerely that a recent publication issued by the UAW to counteract some of this poisonous hate material was misinterpreted. The implications that some have read into this publication were not intended. As its text makes clear, the purpose of the publication was to emphasize that religion is NOT a proper issue in the campaign and that bigotry is being used to obscure the real issues" (*New York Times,* October 25, 1960, p. 19).

laid with their questions. So, for example, he skirted the dangers inherent in the request that he ask Cardinal Cushing "Mr. Kennedy's own hierarchical superior in Boston, to present to the Vatican Senator Kennedy's statement relative to the separation of church and state in the United States and religious freedom as separated in the Constitution of the United States, in order that the Vatican may officially authorize such a belief for all Roman Catholics in the United States." If he acceded to the request, Kennedy would establish that he did indeed submit his views to the Catholic hierarchy and that he and Catholics were bound by any statements their Church might make on such matters. Instead, Kennedy contended that "I do not accept the right" of any "ecclesiastical official to tell me what I shall do in the sphere of my public responsibility as an elected official" and "I do not propose also to ask Cardinal Cushing to ask the Vatican to take some action."[16] The skill in rebuttal Kennedy demonstrated in the exchange with the ministers should have caused Richard Nixon to reassess his view of Kennedy's mental agility in debate.

But the centerpiece of the session was not Kennedy's skilled maneuvers around the ministers' loaded questions but his eloquent opening statement.

Kennedy's masterful apologia before the Greater Houston Ministerial Association is, in my judgment, the most eloquent speech he made either as candidate or president. It was, according to Halberstam, "an example of his mastery of a great new skill in televised politics: deliberately allowing someone else to rig something against you that is, in fact, rigged for you. . . . Kennedy appeared calm and cool, with a fine sense of himself, and he had dealt with these questions a thousand times; by contrast, the ministers posing the questions not only were highly emotional but laboring under the impression that Kennedy had never dealt with these issues before. . . . The Houston audience was, much to its own surprise, a prop audience."[17]

"I am grateful for your generous invitation to state my views" Kennedy said, establishing that they not he had raised the issue of religion. While acknowledging the need to address this issue, Kennedy then signalled his concern for the nation's major political constituencies—young and old, urban and rural—in a way that reminded them of the solutions he had offered elsewhere—a higher minimum wage, medical care for the aged, federal aid for education. At the same time he undercut the perceived Republican strength in foreign affairs by recalling the Communist influence in Cuba and our loss to the Russians in the space race. All of this in a single paragraph that affirmed that "we have far more critical issues in the 1960 election: the spread of Communist influence, until it now festers only ninety miles off the coast of Florida—the humiliating

Senator John F. Kennedy, Democratic nominee for the presidency, addresses the Houston ministers, September 12, 1960. (Used by permission of the Houston *Chronicle*)

treatment of our President and Vice-President by those who no longer respect our power—the hungry children I saw in West Virginia, the old people who cannot pay their doctor's bills, the families forced to give up their farms—an America with too many slums, with too few schools, and too late to the moon and outer space."

Then, after exempting the members of his immediate audience from the accusation, Kennedy questioned the motivation of those who raised the issue of religion, accusing some of deliberately using it to obscure the real issues. "But because I am a Catholic, and no Catholic has ever been elected President, the real issues in this campaign have been obscured— perhaps deliberately in some quarters less responsible than this."

Without invoking the golden rule, Kennedy argues from it. "For while this year it may be a Catholic against whom the finger of suspicion is pointed, in other years it has been, and may someday be again, a Jew— or a Quaker—or a Unitarian—or a Baptist." Addition of "a Quaker" is a reminder that Nixon too is a member of a faith that is not part of main-stream Protestantism. Conclusion of the list with the "Baptist," however, reveals the religious group of most concern to Kennedy. His use of his-torical illustration underscored this conclusion. "It was Virginia's harassment of Baptist preachers, for example, that led to Jefferson's statute of religious freedom."

Having marshaled in defense of religious equality, cherished American principles such as separation of church and state, basic cultural truisms such as fair play and the golden rule, a revered founding father, and a powerful historical illustration, Kennedy now turns to embrace specific Constitutional guarantees. "I would not look with favor upon a President working to subvert the First Amendment's guarantees of religious liberty (nor would our system of checks and balances permit him to do so). And neither do I look with favor upon those who would work to subvert Article VI of the Constitution by requiring a religious test—even by indirection—for if they disagree with that safeguard, they should be openly working to repeal it."

Fair play and consistency are again invoked against such a religious test—but here the invocation assumes a powerful personal form that has been repeatedly underscored in Kennedy ad accounts of PT 109. "This is the kind of America I believe in—and this is the kind of America I fought for in the South Pacific and the kind my brother died for in Europe. No one suggested then that we might have a 'divided loyalty,' that we did 'not believe in liberty' or that we belonged to a disloyal group that threatened 'the freedoms for which our forefathers died.' "

"And in fact this is the kind of America for which our forefathers did die when they fled here to escape religious test oaths, that denied office to members of less favored churches, when they fought for the Constitution, the Bill of Rights, the Virginia Statute of Religious Freedom—and when they fought at the shrine I visited today—the Alamo. For side by side with Bowie and Crockett died Fuentes and McCafferty and Bailey and Bedillio and Carey—but no one knows whether they were Catholics or not. For there was no religious test there."

Declaring that he will disavow neither his views nor his church to win the election, Kennedy returns to the theme of fair play, adding: "If I should lose on the real issues, I shall return to my seat in the Senate, satisfied that I tried my best and was fairly judged."

Again, Kennedy dramatizes the meaning of judging him on alternative, unfair, religious grounds. "But if this election is decided on the basis that 40,000,000 Americans lost their chance of being President on the day they were baptized, then it is the whole nation that will be the loser in the eyes of Catholics and non-Catholics around the world, in the eyes of history, and in the eyes of our own people."

The audience is then invited to witness Kennedy's rehearsal of the taking of the presidential oath, an act that is the natural extension of the speech itself, for if Kennedy is bound by his God, then he will not profane that relationship by swearing falsely that he will "faithfully execute the office of President of the United States and will do the best of my ability preserve, protect and defend the Constitution, so help me God."

Playing a trump card, Kennedy states: "without reservation, I can, and I quote, 'solemnly swear that I will faithfully execute . . . .' " The candidate who was invited to state his views to a hostile audience has, before them, concluded with an act that none take lightly—swearing before God. In the process he has tried on the presidency before their eyes and before the eyes of millions in the states in which the speech and subsequent question-and-answer period were aired. And the fit was good.

Subsequent Use of the Houston Session

The idea of taping and replaying the Houston session is the child of a thousand parents. "It was the most significant media event of the campaign," Bill Wilson, Kennedy's live television producer, says. "I wanted to tape it. The staff said 'Why tape it, it's going to be terrible?' I said, 'But what if it's good?' "[18] "We had a video truck," recalls Richard Denove—brother and partner of Kennedy's filmmaker, Jack Denove, "and took the Ministers' speech off the air. We must have made 300 or 400 prints of it. We deluged America. The UAW alone ordered 100 prints."[19] "A friend of mine managing the station in Houston called me and said that it was the greatest speech he's ever heard," recalls time buyer Reggie Schuebel. "After hearing it I called Bobby [Kennedy] and recommended that we get it on the air right away. Jack recommended instead that it be aired prior to his arrival at key cities in the campaign tour. That's what I did."[20] "One of the most important factors in the campaign was the playing of the tape of the Baptist conference in Texas in which Kennedy won over a very difficult audience by his direct answers," says Kennedy's TV adviser Leonard Reinsch. "We played that in a lot of Baptist communities."[21] With a bit of nipping and tucking, the accounts can be stitched into a consistent report.

Kennedy's exchange with the Houston ministers was originally aired live throughout Texas. Subsequently, the master was dubbed and one minute and five minute ads were cut from it for selective broadcast. A half hour of the exchange also was widely aired.

A key contention of the campaign, first raised by Hubert Humphrey*

---

*If Humphrey's suspicions were true, they were far more serious than the charges raised about the Houston tape. In his autobiography, Humphrey recalled that during the Wisconsin primary he learned of the "anonymous mailing of anti-Catholic, Protestant fundamentalist tracts to Catholic households which angered the Catholics" and "solidified any latent identification they had with Kennedy" (p. 209).

and then by Nixon's supporters and denied to this day by Kennedy's staff
was that ads, in general, and the half hour program and the ads lifted
from it in particular were distributed disproportionately in areas in which
a Catholic vote could be mobilized. If this were so, the purpose of running the ads was not so much to allay Protestant concerns about how a
Catholic president might act, but rather to inflame Catholic voters over
the fact that a candidate of their religion had been subjected to aggressive
interrogation about his own faith, an ordeal Protestant candidates had not
been obliged to endure.

In general, the anti-Kennedy charges were more accurate than the
Kennedy campaign's denial. While *the spots* lifted from the confrontation
were aired in the last two weeks of the general election primarily in states
in which Protestant objection to Kennedy was palpable, *the half hour
program drawn from the confrontation was aired disproportionally often in
the fourteen states that the Bailey-Sorensen memo of 1956 had identified as
states that could be swung into the Democratic column by Catholic voters.*
This list indicates the number of airings of the half hour program in each
of the fourteen states:

New York: 10

Pennsylvania: 8

Illinois: 7

New Jersey: 0 (there is spillover from New York media markets into
N.J.)

Massachusetts: 0 (no need to air the ad in the state from which
Kennedy had overwhelmingly been elected in 1958)

Connecticut: 0 (spillover from New York)

Rhode Island: 0

California: 7

Michigan: 8

Minnesota: 8

Ohio: 7

Wisconsin: 7

Maryland: 1

Montana: 4[22]

The thirty minute tape of the exchange at the Ministers' conference
was aired in 39 states and the District of Columbia. Of the 39 states, 24
were outside the South. These included California, Colorado, Idaho,
Illinois, Indiana, Iowa, Kansas, Maryland, Michigan, Minnesota, Mon-

tana, Nebraska, Nevada, New Mexico, North Dakota, New York, Ohio, Oregon, Pennsylvania, South Dakota, Vermont, Washington, Wisconsin, and Wyoming. Of its 213 airings, over half, 115, were outside the South. The Ministers' session was aired most often in Texas where it was broadcast live on 19 stations and subsequently aired on two more for a total of 21 airings. But the state that follows in the rankings is New York, the state first on the list in the Bailey-Sorenson memo, a state with 40% Catholics. In New York the half hour broadcast was aired 10 times. In North Carolina and Florida it was broadcast 9 times. In Michigan, Minnesota, and Pennsylvania 8 times. At 7 broadcasts the program appeared as often in Illinois, Wisconsin, Ohio, and California as it did in Louisiana and Missouri. And the 6 broadcasts in Iowa and Oregon equalled the 6 in Georgia.*

Not only was Kennedy's counterassault on the issue of religion heavily aired outside the South but it was aired in largely Catholic cities that had defected to the Republicans in 1956. A post-1956 election memo in the files at the Kennedy Library confirmed "a steady trend of Catholic voters away from the Democratic party".[23] "Such Catholic, and previously Democratic, strongholds as Chicago (estimated 49% Catholic), Hudson County, New Jersey (estimated 53%), Milwaukee (estimated 41%), and Baltimore (estimated 31%) went Republican after years of heavy Democratic majorities. New York City (estimated 38%), Boston (estimated 55%), Pittsburgh (estimated 46%), and Philadelphia (estimated 42%) very nearly went Republican. Rhode Island (60% Catholic), Massachusetts (50%), New Jersey (39%), and Connecticut (49%), including such cities as Hartford, New Haven, and Bridgeport, all went Republican, as did all other states with large Catholic populations, including even Louisiana (34%) and New Mexico (46%)." It seems safe to assume that the half hour exchange with the ministers was aired 7 times in Louisiana and 3 times in New Mexico to draw their large Catholic populations back to the Democratic fold. That factor also could explain the airing in Baltimore, the 2 airings in New York City, airings in Pittsburg, Philadelphia, Chicago, and Milwaukee and the broadcasts from adjacent media markets that reached New Jersey and Connecticut.

Ted Sorensen still denies that the broadcast was used to bring out the Catholic vote, saying "I wouldn't think that for a minute. My understanding is that it aired in markets where polls showed that objections to Kennedy on religious grounds remained at a very high level. High Cath-

*The importance of this pattern is evident when we realize that, as Asher notes, "Kennedy's Catholicism cost him 16.5 percent of the two party vote in the heavily Protestant South while it resulted in a 1.6 percent gain outside the South, hurting Kennedy in the popular vote but helping him in the electoral vote, which he won 303–219" (p. 153).

olic areas are also sometimes areas in which there is anti-Catholic feeling. I wish the Baptists were our only opponents on religious grounds." Sorensen also questions the existence of a Catholic vote. "If there is such a thing as a Catholic vote," he says, "it split in the sixty election. Places like Cincinnati would indicate that a large number of Catholics voted against Kennedy because they were Republicans."[24]

That conclusion is corroborated by political scientist Philip Converse who found that in 1960 "Protestant Democrats were more likely to behave as Democrats than as Protestants, and Catholic Republicans were more likely to behave as Republicans than as Catholics."[25]

If judged by the quantity of printed material attacking Kennedy on the issue and the amount of television and radio time purchased to respond, Kennedy's religion was indeed the major issue of the 1960 campaign. The distributors of the anti-Catholic print material and the Fair Campaign Practices Committee placed the number of pieces in the tens of millions at a cost of hundreds of thousands of dollars.[26] Leonard Reinsch, Kennedy's TV and radio adviser, confirms that more total time was purchased to rebroadcast Kennedy's September 12 performance in Houston than any other single piece of campaign propaganda.[27]

By drawing the issue of religion into daylight and exposing its dark undersides to public scrutiny Kennedy forced voters to examine their own religious tolerance, a move that required an explanation of why a vote against Kennedy was not a vote on the basis of religion. At the same time Kennedy subtly reminded Catholic voters that he was carrying their cause against bigotry.

In anchoring these appeals Kennedy made subtle use of his heroism in the Pacific.

PT 109 as an Argument Against Religious Intolerance

Kennedy played his heroism in the Pacific against the ministers' contention that his religion disqualified him from the presidency. How could they turn away a bona fide hero, whose exemplary conduct had been mythologized in such secular settings as *Readers' Digest,* which reprinted an article by John Hersey on PT 109, and ABC's "Navy Log" which carried a commercially sponsored, nationally aired, professionally acted, account of Kennedy's heroism when PT 109 sank. To drive these images deep into the public consciousness, hundreds of thousands of copies of the article were distributed by Kennedy campaign workers. Print ads and brochures also carried the saga. Under the picture of a PT boat one of these ads identified Kennedy as a "Decorated War Hero." It said:

In one of World War II's most dramatic stories, the PT boat skippered by Lt. John F. Kennedy (USNR) was rammed by a Japanese destroyer in the 1943 battle for the Solomon Islands. Severely injured and lost nine days in the jungle, Lt. Kennedy called on his remarkable qualities of leadership and endurance to lead his eleven shipmates to safety. He saved one of the men by placing a line from the man's life preserver between his teeth and swimming five miles. For his heroism he was twice decorated. His Navy citation stated that his "courage, endurance and leadership" were "in keeping with high traditions of the United States Naval Service."

Television ads gave the tale visual dimensions denied the medium of print. Both the documentary of Kennedy's life aired in the primaries and the summary of his accomplishments narrated by Henry Fonda and Jackie Kennedy in the general election included pictures of a PT boat; in one the boat churned through the ocean in the fog of night. Another five minute spot featured stock footage of islands, PT boats, and the ocean; in the ad Fonda displayed a coconut "much like the one" on which Kennedy had inscribed the crew's message for help; finally a survivor of PT 109 woodenly recounted Kennedy's heroism. "Everyone who knew Jack, as I did," said his shipmate, "was impressed by his disregard for his own personal safety and his desire to serve his country." The PT boat pins widely distributed in the campaign served as an emblem signifying support for Kennedy's candidacy.

The print ad termed the saga of the rescue "one of World War II's most dramatic stories." It is a story complete with villains—the destroyer, the jungle, the ocean that threatens to end men's lives; a hero who surmounts great odds risking his own life to save his men, and a narrative filled with rising tension. Will all be killed? Will Kennedy save the man held by a strap in his teeth as he swims five miles? Will the men succumb in the jungle? Will the coconut reach the rescuers? Will the tiny crew survive long enough to be rescued?

The setting for all of this is not the morally ambiguous Korean War but the war against an aggressor who forced war on a peaceful people by directly attacking Americans and American ships. So we can glory in Kennedy's triumph without the nagging presence of larger questions about the evil of war. The story functions as a morality play that enables us to relive our survival of Pearl Harbor. Out of the night our ship is destroyed; under the daring leadership of a young lieutenant the crew is saved. His victorious country honors his heroism. Spun into the structure of the story is the whisper that Kennedy personifies the country.

But also underlying this story, as it had underlain other Kennedy campaign material, is a much more important element—rebuttal of the charge that Kennedy had Addison's disease. This charge was leveled on the eve of the convention by those backing Johnson, who viewed Kennedy's claims to "vigor" as an attack on Johnson who had suffered a heart attack in 1955. In carefully worded statements, Kennedy's aides, members of his family, a Kennedy physician, and Kennedy himself denied that he had what is "classically" known as Addison's disease.[28]

Although long kept under wraps by Kennedy family members and intimates, it is now conceded that Kennedy did indeed have Addison's disease, an illness that until quite recently was debilitating and usually fatal. Until cortisone treatment compensated for Kennedy's adrenal insufficiency, the disease and the increased risk of infection that is its trademark threatened his life on a number of occasions. "Addison's disease, like diabetes, is due to a defect in a single hormone, in this case the adrenal hormone," explains Dr. Estelle Ramey, an endocrinologist and professor of physiology and biophysics at Georgetown Medical School. "Monitoring the dose of the cortical steroid Kennedy had to have was an important problem because it's a hormone that's necessary to survive stress. It can in overdose produce emotional changes in the direction of a kind of euphoria. But, in general, if he was well managed it would be difficult to distinguish his behavior problem from the behavior problem of Ronald Reagan who's optimistic all the time while the ceiling is falling in." Ramey adds that the fact that Kennedy had been diagnosed as having Addison's disease was well known in endocrinological circles, which explains the knowledge Johnson's supporters had of it in 1960. Indeed, Ramey mentioned the diagnosis to a *Washington Post* reporter and friend who was having dinner at her home during the 1960 campaign. When the reporter "leapt on it," Ramey, a Kennedy supporter, told him that she would "deny categorically" if he used the information obtained from her.[29]

Had Kennedy's illness and the nature of his medical regimen become public knowledge in the 1960 campaign, it might have changed the outcome of the Democratic convention and, if not, surely would have been a widely discussed and perhaps decisive issue in the fall election, for Eisenhower's heart attack, ileitis, and stroke had raised the public's consciousness of the importance of candidates' health.

The Kennedy campaign chose not to face the problem directly. Indeed, rather than publicly acknowledge that he had the disease but was controlling it by use of medication, Kennedy's campaign material successfully portrayed him as a man of personal vigor and endurance. To questions about a series of painful operations he had undergone and the life-threatening infection that followed one of them, the answer was that these were the legacy of his heroism in the Pacific, a heroism already certified by the article in *Reader's Digest* and the "Navy Log." By explicitly praising his "leadership and endurance," the PT 109 ads facilitated this image building by making it more difficult for anyone who had heard these charges of illness to seriously entertain the possibility that a man who had survived the destruction of his PT boat, had towed another man in the ocean for five miles, and had survived nine days in the jungle could suffer from a supposedly serious disease. While Robert Kennedy and brother-in-law Stephen Smith surely knew of the disease, the admen who worked for them were unaware that their messages were deflecting public attention from the truth about Kennedy's health. So, Kennedy's ads skillfully helped sidetrack public scrutiny of his health.

The Issues of Age and Experience

In the book *The Remarkable Kennedys,* reporter Joe McCarthy defined at least one aspect of the youth problem. "Kennedy's young looks are a big barrier to his path to the White House. Close up, he appears to be forty-three years old, but seen from a distance on the stage of an auditorium, his slim, boyish figure and his collegiate haircut make him seem like a lad of twenty-eight. An often-heard remark about Kennedy, credited to a New York political strategist, is: 'He'll never make it with that haircut.' Another politician in the Midwest had said that Kennedy's youthful appearance is a bigger problem for him than his religion. 'It makes no difference how mature Kennedy may be,' this man says, 'if the bosses and the voters decide that he *looks* immature.' "[30] To avoid discussion of his maturity, Kennedy trimmed "the bushy hair style in which cartoonists had previously delighted."[31] Other changes were made as well. The picture used in his brochures was chosen in part because it made him look older.

The issue of age and experience was complicated because it served as the expression of party regulars' discomfort at Kennedy's headlong rush toward the White House. Just as his brash grab for the 1956 vice-presidency had engendered a certain amount of inner party antagonism, so too his equally brash capture of the presidential nomination in 1960 played into Republican hands when on July 2 at a press conference in Independence, Missouri, Harry Truman declared:

> I have always liked him [Kennedy] personally and I still do—and because of this feeling, I would want to say to him at this time: "Senator, are you certain that you are quite ready for the country, or that the country is ready for you in the role of President in January 1961. I have no doubt about the political heights to which you are destined to rise.
>
> But I am deeply concerned and troubled about the situation we are up against in the world now and in the immediate future. That is why I

would hope that someone with the greatest possible maturity and experience would be available at this time. May I urge you to be patient?"

In a separate assault on Kennedy's candidacy, Truman protested the "prearranged" character of the convention by resigning as a delegate to the convention from Missouri. At the same time, Truman reiterated his endorsement of his fellow Missourian Stuart Symington while also offering for consideration the names of Lyndon Johnson and of a number of other prominent Democrats.

On July 4 in a news conference in New York, covered in its entirety by NBC, Kennedy responded that since he alone had risked "my chances in all the primaries," he did not intend to withdraw his name. Kennedy pledged himself to a convention as open as those that had in every election since 1932 selected their candidate on the first ballot. "But based on my observation of him in 1952, 1956 and last Saturday," Kennedy added, "Mr. Truman regards an open convention as one which studies all the candidates—reviews their records—and then takes his advice."

Responding to Truman's questioning of his maturity and experience, Kennedy declared: "I did not undertake lightly to seek the Presidency. It is not a prize or a normal object of ambition. It is the greatest office in the world. And I came to the conclusion that I could best serve the United States in that office after 18 years in the service of our nation— first as a Naval Officer in World War II—and for the past fourteen years as a member of Congress." This line of argument culminated in the claim that if fourteen years in major elective office was insufficient preparation, then all of the presidents elevated to the office in the twentieth century, including Truman, Wilson, and FDR, should have been disqualified, as should all but three of Truman's preferred candidates.

Among the names of influential statesmen who assumed national leadership at the age of 43 or younger Kennedy included Theodore Roosevelt, William Pitt, Napoleon, and Alexander the Great. And, he added, if 44 were the cutoff age, Washington could not have commanded the Continental Army, Columbus discovered America, or Jefferson written the Declaration of Independence. On the list of young leaders Sorensen also had included Jesus of Nazareth, a name Kennedy wisely deleted.[32] That was reaching too far for an example, he told Sorensen.[33]

Then, once again responding obliquely to the personal health issue while simultaneously confronting the youth issue squarely, Kennedy reminded his audience that it was in youth that the nation could expect to find the vigorous health necessary for an effective presidency. "For, during my lifetime alone, four out of our seven Presidents have suffered major health setbacks that impaired, at least temporarily, their exercise of executive leadership."

Finally, in a passage that would be edited into the campaign documentary, Kennedy offered an argument that he would repeat in the debates "It is true, of course, that almost all of the major world leaders today—on both sides of the Iron Curtain—are men past the age of 65. It is true that the world today is largely in the hands of men whose education was completed before the whole course of international events was altered by two World Wars. But who is to say how successful they have been in improving the fate of the world. . . . The world is changing. The old ways will not do. . . . It is time for a new generation of leadership, to cope with new problems and new opportunities."[34] Young and new had become synonyms. And, as five decades of advertising had insisted, newer is better.

By the time of the general election, therefore, the Kennedy campaign staff was prepared to answer Republican charges on this issue. "Because of Kennedy's youth, which everyone was aware of, we knew that Nixon would make the experience argument," notes Sorensen. "Nixon had been a House member, a member of the Senate and a Vice President so on paper he could claim more experience than Kennedy. So we worried about the experience argument."[35] The advantage Nixon gained from his "experience" galled family patriarch Joseph Kennedy, who on February 24, 1960, wrote Ted Sorensen a letter consisting of a single sentence: "I continually hear about Nixon's experience and I certainly think, for the most part, that experience is a term usually used to describe a lifetime of mistakes."[36]

Since voters were five times more likely to make favorable comments about Nixon's foreign policies than Kennedy's but almost twice as likely to offer favorable comments about Kennedy's domestic policies as about Nixon's,[37] Republican ads reduced questions of domestic policy to questions of foreign policy; Democratic ads did the opposite. Accordingly, in one radio ad Kennedy noted: "I believe if we build a stronger America in this country that the position of the U.S. in the world will rise. I believe if we move ahead here, we will move ahead throughout the world." By contrast, Nixon's broadcast ads translated economic and societal strength at home into an indicator of comparative advantage over the Soviet Union.

Again, in their nationally televised debates, each would lead with his own perceived strong suit in the opening statements. For Kennedy the question of whether the world would exist half-slave and half-free depended "in great measure upon what kind of society that we build, on the kind of strength we maintain."[38] By contrast Nixon built from the premise that "There is no question but that we cannot discuss our internal affairs in the United States without recognizing that they have a tremendous bearing on our international position." The contrast held throughout the election. Nixon opened his election eve telethon by noting that "we are selecting not only the President of the United States but the leader of the free world" and concluded his election eve address by urging the American people to "Vote for the man that you think America and the world needs in this critical period." Alternatively, Kennedy reiterated his promise to get the country moving again.

Kennedy also dealt claims about his comparative experience a sharp blow by reminding audiences that he and Nixon had come to the Congress together fourteen years earlier, a claim Nixon inadvertently substantiated in one of the tenser moments of the Kennedy-Nixon debates. Kennedy further attempted to redefine the terms of the controversy by contending that experience was not enough. Judgment was required.

Republicans Argue that Kennedy Is Inexperienced

The Democrats were forewarned in an October 29 letter by J. William Fulbright of the forthcoming attack on Kennedy's absenteeism. Senators Williams and Hickenlooper had requested an audit of Kennedy's attendance at committee meetings. In response they were informed that Kennedy had attended 24 of 117 committee sessions in 1959 and 3 out of 96 in 1960.[39] Fulbright's radar was accurate. A Republican print ad titled "Young Jack Kennedy's Report Card. 86th Congress" gave him an F for his work on the African Affairs subcommittee for not calling a single meeting, F for his work on the Aging and Disarmament subcommittees for not attending one meeting, and F in Veterans Affairs for not attending one hearing. It also faults him in attendance, reporting that of "171 roll calls, Jack has been absent 129 times." The ad concludes with John Q Public in the role of Principal, failing the young Jack Kennedy.[40] This line of attack had been previewed by Lyndon Johnson in his unsuccessful bid for the presidency at the Democratic Convention. In response Kennedy noted that he had been busy campaigning for president. In the general election Kennedy simply ignored the attack.

The attack was an old wolf in new fur. In 1952 when Henry Cabot Lodge's print ads had indicted Kennedy for absenteeism in Congress, Kennedy had responded that his absence was due to a "war service-connected illness."[41]

"Nothing to fear but Kennedy Folly (according to *his own supporters*)" declared another Republican ad,[42] which then freshened the public's recollection of various comments made by Democratic rivals and party officials, including those made by Humphrey, Stevenson, Eleanor Roosevelt, Lyndon Johnson, and Harry Truman's pre-nomination criticism of

Kennedy's foreign and domestic policy statements and of his campaign tactics and bankroll. James Reston also was quoted calling Kennedy's call for government aid to overthrow Castro his "worst blunder."

The ad reprinted Truman's question: "Senator, are you certain that you are quite ready for the country or that the country is ready for you in the role of president?" Eleanor Roosevelt was quoted as saying that Kennedy had antagonized Negroes who as a result would not vote for him. Humphrey is quoted as claiming that although his opponent may "feel it is possible to buy a state . . . they certainly can't hope to win by such tactics in November." And Johnson declared that he was unprepared to apologize to the Soviet leader, an allusion to Kennedy's recommendation that the U.S. apologize for dissembling over the U2 flights. One of these flights landed Gary Powers in Khrushchev's hands and effectively scuttled the US-USSR summit meeting. So in one fell swoop the ad drew from the mouth of a respected journalist and five influential Democrats indictments of Kennedy's age, fortune, campaign tactics, domestic and foreign policy, and political judgment. Truman's indictment was replayed in small boxed ads that closed with the tag "Don't gamble with peace and freedom, Elect Nixon-Lodge."

Kennedy responded to these Republican resurrections of the indictments of the primaries by airing endorsements by his former indictors. So, for example, radio endorsements by Hubert Humphrey were aired in the farm belt. Truman delivered a televised statement trumpeting Kennedy's case; and in both TV and radio ads Stevenson praised Kennedy's good sense, good judgment, programs, and policies. Muting Mrs. Roosevelt's claim about black disaffection, Harry Belafonte endorsed Kennedy in radio and TV ads. Finally, in radio and TV ads delivered in her characteristically clipped patrician voice, FDR's widow offered her own qualified endorsement, an endorsement that essentially recanted her earlier claim about Kennedy's civil rights' record:

> When you cast your vote for the president of the United States, be sure you have studied the record. I have. I urge you to vote for John F. Kennedy for I have come to believe that as a president he will have the strength and the moral courage to provide the leadership for human rights we need in this time of crisis. He is a man with a sense of history. That I'm well familiar with because my husband had a sense of history. He wanted to leave a good record for the future. I think John F Kennedy wants to leave a good record.

In small boxed ads in black papers, local influentials such as black union leaders and teachers endorsed Kennedy as did such famous blacks as Harry Belafonte and Nat King Cole. The format was constant: a photo of the endorser and a nine to ten line explanation of why that person supported Kennedy. In one, Lena Horne declared: "I'm no politician but it just seems to me that a Democrat like John Kennedy cares more about people. He cares more about all the things that still need to be done in this country—like more jobs and a better chance for everybody. Republicans talk pretty but Kennedy will do something about all the problems. That's what counts. That's why I'm for Senator Kennedy for President."

Ads might not have appeared in black papers at all had it not been for the work of Louis Martin, former head of the Newspaper Publishers Association, who set as a precondition to working for Kennedy that the Democratic National Committee pay the $49,000 debt still owed black papers from the 1956 campaign.

Most important in the campaign to woo black voters were radio ads and pamphlets reminding blacks of JFK's call to Coretta King and RFK's call to a local judge, widely credited with securing King's release from a jail where he was held for charges stemming from a Civil Rights protest. Throughout the ordeal Nixon maintained silence on the grounds that it would be improper for a lawyer to call a judge about a pending case.

Once outside the prison King stated: "I am deeply indebted to Senator Kennedy, who served as a great force in making my release possible. For him to be that courageous shows that he is really acting upon principle and not expediency."[43] That evening Martin Luther King Sr. told the congregation of Ebenezer Baptist Church in Atlanta: "I had expected to vote against Senator Kennedy because of his religion . . . It took courage to call my daughter-in-law at a time like this. He has the moral courage to stand up for what he knows is right. I've got all my votes and I've got a suitcase and I'm going to take them up there and dump them in his lap."[44]

Fearing that white bigots would respond to press accounts of the Kennedys' actions by voting for Nixon, Kennedy's civil rights chief Harris Wofford sought a means of reaching black voters who might switch to Kennedy. As a result, two million pamphlets quoting leading blacks on the Kennedys' actions were distributed in front of black churches throughout the country the Sunday before the election. In Chicago alone half a million were handed out.[45] This tightly targeted message distribution ensured that those unsympathetic to the gesture would be unreminded of it.

The pamphlet differentiated the candidates with the heading " 'No Comment' Nixon versus a Candidate With a Heart, Senator Kennedy," followed by statements by Martin Luther King Jr.; Martin Luther King Sr.; Coretta King; Ralph Abernathy of the Southern Christian Leadership Conference, who promised to return Nixon's silence through King's crisis with his own silence in the voting booth; Gardner Taylor, president of the Protestant Council of New York who praised Kennedy's "moral leadership and direct personal concern," and an editorial in the New York *Post* which noted that Kennedy action "would inflame Southern racists and multiply his difficulties in Dixie."[46]

The Democratic National Committee moved quickly to place comparable ads scripted by Martin on black radio stations as well. "Listen to Dr. Ralph Abernathy" said one. "I honestly and sincerely feel that it is time for all of us to take off our Nixon buttons because Kennedy did something great and wonderful when he personally called Mrs. Coretta King and helped free Dr. Martin Luther King Jr. This is the kind of act I was waiting for. It was not just Dr. King on trial. America was on trial. Mr. Nixon could have helped but he refused to even comment on the case. Since Kennedy showed his great concern for humanity when he acted first without counting the cost, he has my whole hearted support. This is the kind of man we need at this hour."

Just as the pamphlets had been distributed only at black churches, ads catering to the interests of the black voter were aired only on black radio stations—a move designed to minimize the backlash against the Kennedys' actions. In addition, telegrams and phone calls were used to alert influential blacks. "The call [to the judge and Mrs. King] was at the last minute—a few days before the election," Martin recalls. "So we worked the streets through telephone contacts with leaders in the big cities—particularly Chicago, New York, Detroit, Pittsburgh and Los Angeles—and distributed leaflets and aired radio."[47]

The efforts were largely limited to the North because, again in Martin's words, "in those years the Southern Black vote was very limited. Only in a few cities were Blacks free to register. Much of the Black population was effectively disenfranchised in the South."

Here we have an instance in which symbolic action, not legislative performance or promise, swayed voters. Lost in the symbolism was the fact that the Eisenhower administration had approved the first major Civil Rights Bill since reconstruction and backed desegregation with federal troops.

As Martin Luther King Sr.'s statement testifies, the Kennedys' gesture was a powerful means of muting anti-Catholic antagonism among black Baptists. "We were afraid of anti-Catholic sentiment among Blacks in 1960," says Martin. "We went to great lengths to overcome it." Indeed the Kennedy campaign had distributed over 3 million pamphlets containing a statement by the president of National Baptists USA urging tolerance. In addition, the campaign held forums in cities such as Philadelphia at which black churchmen would define the issue as one of "tolerance and fair play."

Had Kennedy simply maintained the black vote won by Stevenson, he would have lost the election. In Illinois, for example, which Kennedy carried by a whisper of 9000 votes, over a quarter of a million blacks voted for him.

Had Nixon Gained the Experience He Claimed?

The one strength Nixon had, however, that no amount of sniping by Kennedy could dispatch was his eight years service in the administration of a man who remained the most highly regarded public figure in America, Dwight Eisenhower. Concomittantly, Eisenhower was the one person who unequivocally could have certified Nixon's competence and ability to perform the job while simultaneously suggesting that such competence and performance were beyond Kennedy's reach. But when invited to do so at the end of a long press conference, for reasons that remain unclear, Eisenhower instead knifed Nixon between the ribs. The Democrats edited Ike's answer into television and radio ads that undercut Nixon's unique selling proposition. The radio ad stated:

> ANNOUNCER: Every Republican politician wants you to believe that Richard Nixon is quote "experienced." They even want you to believe that he has actually been making decisions in the White House. But listen to the man who should know best, the president of the United States. A reporter recently asked President Eisenhower this question about Mr. Nixon's experience.
>
> REPORTER AT PRESS CONFERENCE: I just wondered if you could give us an example of a major idea of his that you had adopted in that role as the decider and final . . . ah . . .
>
> EISENHOWER: If you give me a week I might think of one. I don't remember. (*laughter*)
>
> ANNOUNCER: At the same press conference Eisenhower said
>
> EISENHOWER: No one can make a decision except me.
>
> ANNOUNCER: And as for any major ideas from Mr. Nixon
>
> EISENHOWER: If you give me a week I might think of one. I don't remember.
>
> ANNOUNCER: President Eisenhower could not remember but the voters will remember. For real leadership in the '60's, help elect Senator John F. Kennedy president.

Eisenhower would later explain to Nixon that he had intended the response as a way of ending an already lengthy press conference. Frank Gannon, who reviewed the press conference tape and discussed it with Nixon while working with the former president on his memoirs notes that "It happened at the end of the press conference. It really was 'give me a week and [the implication] we'll talk about it next week.' " The remark was, Gannon concludes, "an unfortunate locution."[48] Still, as Garry Wills argues cogently in *Nixon Agonistes,* that remark is another piece in a puzzle picturing Eisenhower's dislike, distrust, and disinclination to see Nixon as president.[49] Whatever Ike's motive, the remark was damaging, for the only person who could certify Nixon's contributions to the Eisenhower presidency, a person more credible with the public than either of the candidates aspiring to his chair, instead had decertified him.

Since direct rebuttal would call attention to the issue, Finch notes that Ike instead showed his "confidence in and respect for Nixon" in the speeches he delivered on behalf of his vice-president. Kennedy's criticism of Eisenhower's policies, including his campaign accusation of a "missile gap," a gap that would mysteriously disappear once Kennedy got into office, finally propelled Ike to take to the stump on Nixon's behalf. Yet his strong defenses of his administration even when fused to testimony that he was voting for Nixon could not still the echo of his earlier reservation.

The remark haunted Nixon. Before the largest audience of the campaign it was raised in the first debate by Sander Vanocur who quoted Ike's statement and added "Now that was a month ago, sir, and the President hasn't brought it up since, and I'm wondering, sir, if you can clarify which version is correct—the one put out by the Republican campaign leaders ["Experience Counts"] or the one put out by President Eisenhower?"

Looking and sounding cornered Nixon responded: "Well, I would suggest, Mr. Vanocur, that if you know the President, that was probably a facetious remark." The hesitance of the "probably" bespeaks a tenuous relationship between the head of state and his heir apparent and suggests that Nixon feared that if he characterized the statement without that reservation, Ike might retaliate by indicating that the remark was indeed seriously made and seriously meant.

Nixon proceeds to argue that it would be improper for the president to disclose the source of recommendations he has accepted or rejected, notes that the president should in any event make the major decisions himself, says that Ike has asked him for advice and that he has given it, reminds the audience that he has met with legislative leaders, sat in the National Security Council, and been in the cabinet. Throughout, Nixon's syntax is uncharacteristically complex. He says, for example, "I would also suggest that insofar as his statement is concerned, that I think it would be improper for the President of the United States to disclose the instances in which members of his official family had made recommendations, as I have made them through the years to him, which he has accepted or rejected."

Of course, if Nixon had Kennedy's rhetorical reflexes, he never would have attempted to answer Vanocur's question directly. Indeed, later, Kennedy refused to be drawn into commenting on Truman's reported profanity. Instead, he turned the question into a straight line making the point that he would not venture to change Truman's language when even Mrs. Truman had failed. Similarly, at the Democratic Convention he turned aside Lyndon Johnson's lengthy comparison of his and Kennedy's leadership records in Congress by observing that for the exact reasons articulated by Johnson he should remain in the Senate and Kennedy should go to the White House.

But the question here is not simply why Nixon did not deflect Vanocur's question but also why he was without any reasonable response to a question he must have known would arise. Perhaps his aides had failed to warn him that the question was likely to be raised. Perhaps he could not face preparing a response. Perhaps he considered the question to be without substance and hence unlikely to arise in a debate.

Whatever the reason for Ike's statement at the press conference, its existence highlights the complicated relationship between Nixon and Eisenhower that earlier manifest itself in their pas de deux over Nixon's fund in 1952 and over the question of whether Nixon would be the vice-presidential nominee in 1956. Here their troubled ties are of concern first because Ike's statement at the press conference hurt Nixon's candidacy and second because Nixon's decisions on how and when to use Ike in the 1960 campaign may have cost him the election.

Years after both Ike and Mamie's deaths, Nixon revealed in his *Memoirs* that the evening before an October 31 planning meeting with Ike, Mamie called Pat to plead that despite his eagerness to campaign, Ike was not up to the strain. "She begged Pat to have me make him change his mind [about campaigning] without letting him know that she had intervened," wrote Nixon. Nixon also reports that Eisenhower's physician called Nixon to say that "he could not approve a heavy campaign schedule for the president."[50] In 1966 Fred A. Seaton, Eisenhower's Secretary of the Interior confirmed that Eisenhower's physician, Major General Howard Snyder, took Nixon and Seaton aside as they were about to enter the meeting with Ike, told them that Ike had had a restless night that worried both him and Mrs. Eisenhower, and asked that the campaigning demands on Ike's time be cut. "Dick looked like he had been hit by an ax," recalled Seaton. "He turned to me and said, 'I'm going to go in there and knock down any suggestions anybody has except to keep the dates already committed.' " "It was not easy," Seaton added, "The boss was all fired up and steamed up for campaigning and he had his spurs on."[51]

Whether Ike's doctor called Nixon, as his *Memoirs* state, or whether the instructions from Snyder came in the White House, as Seaton's account suggests or whether both occurred is less important than the fact that in the final days of the campaign Nixon limited Ike's activities because he feared for his health.

But the encounters with Mamie and Synder, which occurred on October 30 and 31, do not explain why Nixon failed to draw Ike into the campaign earlier in the general election and why Ike was not asked to appear in television and radio spots endorsing Nixon. Some analysts explain that freed from Eisenhower's leash and sensitive to the liklihood that Kennedy would claim, as he did, that Nixon was unable to campaign on his own merits, Nixon hesitated to appear to rely on Ike. "I would surmise," says Finch, "that Nixon did not want to use Eisenhower as a crutch, he wanted to do this on his own."[52] Nixon himself argues that he "planned to keep Eisenhower in reserve as a political weapon that would be the more powerful for having been sparingly used."[53] In adhering to this strategy, in the final weeks of the campaign, Nixon blitzed the airwaves with a speech by Eisenhower, a joint Nixon-Eisenhower-Lodge program, nightly fifteen minutes speeches by the Republican nominee during the final week, and a four hour telethon the afternoon before the election.

To his death Ike wondered whether, by having done more, he could have saved the White House for his party in 1960. "I did what I thought best, and even more than the Vice President planned for," wrote Ike in his memoirs. "But I participated, on an intensively partisan basis, only in the final week of the campaign. I shall never cease to wonder whether a more extensive program of political speaking on my part might have had a favorable effect on the outcome."[54] Elsewhere in the book, as if to purge himself of responsibility for Nixon's defeat, Eisenhower responds to the comments of "good Republicans" that he did not make as many campaign speeches as he should have by noting the "fact" that he "made far more speeches than the new leaders of the party had originally asked me to."[55]

Those who take literally Ike's post-campaign insistence on his willingness to have done more also might recall that he held the spectre of his own death over those who would have asked for more. His doctors, he says, "had been concerned in the last days that I had temporarily used up all my available cardiac reserves in the closing weeks of the campaign." Not simply his reserves but *all* his reserves. Not simply his strength but his "reserves," a term that assumes added significance when spoken by a former general. Again Ike reports telling Ben Fairless: "I'm going to make eight to ten appearances during the campaign. Motorcades kill me, but I'm going to do them to try to arouse enthusiasm."[56]

The solution to Nixon's dilemma lay in the technology of television. Eisenhower's energy could have been conserved and his health safeguarded had he simply filmed or taped testimonials undercutting the Democratic use of the press conference confession. Since Eisenhower had pioneered the use of televised spot announcements in '52 and both he and Nixon had used them in '56, the thought must have crossed Nixon's mind. So why then did he dismiss it?

If the delay in summoning Eisenhower into the battle simply was a way of ratifying Nixon's political adulthood, then the cost of that rite of passage was high. If Nixon acted from the belief that Ike's involvement should be conserved for maximum impact until the last moment, the belief probably was mistaken. And if he feared that Kennedy would strangle him in Eisenhower's coattails, he could have reciprocated in kind by noting Stevenson's heroic efforts on Kennedy's behalf and Truman's pronounced reservations about Kennedy's maturity.

When Eisenhower did speak to the public on television, his address delivered from 10 to 10:30 on ABC October 28 reached the largest percent of total TV households of any speech or spot aired by either side to that point in the campaign. Capturing a 33.4% share of the audience, Ike's ringing endorsement of Nixon and Lodge reached 17.9% of the TV households in the U.S.[57] On October 31 half page print ads reinforced the message of that speech. Under his picture and over his signature Ike declared: "Only Nixon and Lodge have the experience and special training America needs today. There are no two men in the history of America who have had such careful preparation for carrying out the duties of the Presidency and Vice-Presidency as Nixon and Lodge."

Even as Nixon delayed in summoning Ike into the campaign, he was crafting a campaign in the image of Eisenhower's. Nixon's pledge to campaign in every state recalls a comparable promise made by Ike in '52. Similarly, Nixon's offer to send Ike on a tour of European nations behind the Iron Curtain recalls Ike's pledge to go to Korea. The form of Nixon's spot ads also mimicks Ike's as did Nixon's way of greeting crowds—with arms upstretched in a victory sign.

But unlike Ike, who lodged decisions about advertising with his advisers and media consultants, Nixon reserved those decisions for himself. Nixon's ad firm, Campaign Associates, formulated an innovative use of television and print to bring those ideas alive. Heading Nixon's ad team were Carroll Newton, who coined the campaign's slogan "They Understand What Peace Demands," and Ted Rogers, Nixon's television adviser for the Checkers speech and chief negotiator for the debates. In May, Newton and Rogers recommended a series of half hour programs to underscore public perception of Nixon's character and competence. These were to include a program titled "Khrushchev as I Know Him," a documentary portrait of Nixon and his family, a program showing Nixon's experiences in the first weeks of campaigning, another recapping the campaign, and finally an election eve telethon. They recommended as well a spot showing Kennedy's powerlessness in the summer session of Congress.

For reasons that neither Newton nor Rogers were given, Nixon "pocket vetoed" the ideas. Finch offers two possible explanations for the decision. First the campaign was "concerned about the appearance of lavish expenditures." Second, "it was very difficult to break into the physical schedule of the campaign" to find time for Nixon to participate in such programs. What Nixon settled for instead was the brief speech as spot, a form he had once told Newton he would fire anyone for suggesting.

"You couldn't talk to him," says Newton. "Nixon wouldn't take advice about what to say or how. He said, 'I'll just sit in front of the camera and talk.' And that's what he did. He sat there and winged it. The ads were awful."[58] "He did what he liked to do and was comfortable with," says Finch. "The way he traditionally worked was to talk directly to whoever had control of an area, satisfy himself, accept some suggestions, reject others. We tried to get him to make decisions [about advertising] in advance of going [to the studio] but very often he'd walk in for the hour or two we'd set aside to tape commercials and would just sit down and wing it."

Considering that they were unscripted, Nixon's ads are remarkable for the coherence of his argument and the skill with which he turns questions of domestic policy to answers touting his and Lodge's expertise in foreign affairs. Although by the standards of an entertainment medium the ads were visually bland, their content was salient and Nixon's delivery fluent and reassuring.

Both Newton and Rogers suspect that the real reason their initial proposal was rejected without explanation was the insulation of Nixon by a new guard headed by H. R. Haldeman. "It was an 'iron curtain,' " says Rogers. "After an extremely close personal relationship with Nixon, Haldeman came between me and the candidate and between everyone else, including Rose Mary Woods, and the candidate. That was the beginning of the end of anyone's access to Nixon." Robert Finch, who ran Nixon's vice-presidential office, denies that Nixon's accessibility decreased in '60. "The Nixon of 1960 and in his vice-presidential days was if anything overly accessible. In that sense Haldeman was probably right in husbanding his time [later]," he says. At the same time, Finch agrees that Nixon ran the campaign: "Nixon did everything but sweep out the plane. He even insisted on sitting in the back of the plane and painstakingly writing his own speeches. We had people who were supposed to do that.

They'd leave the plane after a week to ten days because they were not being utilized to the extent they wanted to be." So it seems likely that Nixon himself devised the campaign's advertising strategy, a conclusion bolstered by his discussion of when the campaign should, would, and did peak.

Rogers' and Nixon's disagreement over the advertising strategy in 1960 was not their first. During the 1956 campaign Rogers had scheduled a televised question-and-answer session between a group of editors of college papers and Nixon at Cornell University, Rogers' alma mater. Before the program began, Nixon, who feared "left wing plants," asked how Rogers planned to control the program. Rogers responded that he had no plans to exert any control over the questions or questioners and argued that any hostile questions would discredit the questioner, not Nixon.

The questions were tough. Nixon held his own. The press responded favorably to the performance. But once on the private campaign plane Nixon lunged at Rogers, cursing him for subjecting him to "those liberal sons of bitches" and for "trying to destroy me in front of thirty million people." A reporter for the Baltimore *Sun* restrained Nixon, Rogers recalls.

If Nixon's trust in Rogers had been irrevocably shattered by that experience, it is difficult to understand why he would have dispatched Hall to entice Rogers from California to work on the '60 campaign, why he ultimately vested Rogers with authority to negotiate all the technical arrangements for the four debates, and why he assigned Rogers to produce the election eve telethon, in which Nixon was confronted, as he had been in that traumatic encounter at Cornell, with unscreened questions.

What is clear is that Rogers regained Nixon's confidence after the first debate. Although his request that Nixon rest the day of the debate had been overruled, his suggestion that Nixon be professionally made up rejected, his requests for lighting tests of Nixon ignored, the actual state of Nixon's health and appearance kept from him—Rogers nonetheless bore the brunt of the post-debate criticism about Nixon's appearance, including an attack by Nixon's press secretary, Herb Klein, who blamed Nixon's appearance on the "sloppy job" done by Nixon's TV staff.

Trying to avert a second catastrophe, Nixon's staff followed Rogers' subsequent advice. "Please back off the man-killing schedule," Rogers told Nixon's staff. "For God's sake, no more buffalo burger barbecues in Sullivanville Illinois! Give this man some rest! Doctors . . . please fatten him up. Give him milkshakes, eggs, butter. . . . Please give us time for make-up and lighting tests. It's now a matter of life and death we have these. Does Nixon's knee still hurt him? He favored it during the telecast.

Richard Nixon is not the same man he was June 1. . . . Richard Nixon did not look his usual self because he was not in top shape. Instead of a contrast between experience and youth, the debate became one of health vs. fatigue."[59]

Aware that Rogers publicly had shouldered blame properly resting elsewhere, comfortable in his improved appearance and performance in subsequent debates, apprehensive as the campaign raced toward a photo finish, the day before the election Nixon handed back to the person who had been his media consultant since 1950 some of the authority that he had removed earlier. The telethon was proposed initially by Newton and Rogers, vetoed by Nixon, and reinstated at the urging of wealthy backers of Nixon who feared the election would be lost without it. It was Nixon's best use of television in the 1960 campaign. On it he appeared competent but compassionate, mature, intelligent, articulate, and well informed.

Where Nixon hoarded authority and reserved decisions about advertising to himself, Kennedy delegated such tasks to others, particularly his brother Robert and brother-in-law Stephen Smith. "We were organized in such a way that all the candidate had to do was show up," says Sorensen. "We [those on the road with Kennedy] had almost nothing to do with TV, advertising or campaign decisionmaking."

Thwarted in their plans to showcase Nixon in the half hour documentaries they had proposed, the admen transformed the projected TV specials into a 32-page Sunday newspaper supplement November 6. The supplement included a letter to the American people from Ike endorsing Nixon and Lodge, stills of Nixon and Ike in consultation, a pictoral summary of Nixon's accomplishments including a picture of the kitchen debate with Khruschev and pictures of Nixon and his family at home.

Without mentioning Kennedy or his wealth, the supplement portrayed Nixon as Horatio Alger. "His story," says the ad, "is living proof to the world that America is a land of opportunity for those of humble origin." The future vice-president was born in "a tiny town in southern California" and "grew up in Whittier, California, in the pleasant and wholesome surroundings of typical small-town life in the U.S." A picture of the modest home in which Nixon was born is shown. His family was a "plain family" headed by a farmer who "often perplexed friends when he'd say that the watering and feeding of Dorothy Lamour, Loretta Young and Gary Cooper presented quite a chore." The cows had been named after movie stars.

From his Quaker father, Nixon inherited "his enormous affection for youngsters, an unswerving devotion to the truth, no matter where it led, and intense personal integrity."

Even as a child Nixon embraced the work ethic. " 'He had to work so hard,' his mother said, 'that he missed out on a lot of fun.' " He was always a serious little boy who loved to work, but insisted on pulling down the shades when he helped his mother wash the supper dishes each night. His was "a typical American boyhood: school, sports, music, uniform."

The ad invited comparison between Nixon's youth and Kennedy's. The boy with a golden spoon against the boy who helped his mother do the dishes. The boy whose father was a farmer against the boy whose father was an ambassador. The boy born to a family of modest means against a boy born to luxury. The boy educated at Whittier College against the boy educated at Harvard. There also were points of unspoken comparison. Neither excelled in sports. "Tackle Nixon had a good seat on the fifty-yard line with Whittier College football team. His enthusiasm exceeded his skill on gridiron." Assumed in this detailed description of Nixon's "humble," "typical" origins is the eagerness of the American people to choose one of their own over one of another class.

Eisenhower's cavalier dismissal of the Nixon's vice-presidential credentials forced the Republican nominee to reclaim his own past. So the supplement details both the qualifications that led Eisenhower to choose Nixon as a running mate and his accomplishments as vice-president. He is praised for fighting the Communist conspiracy by "carefully, personally and almost alone" persisting in drawing the evidence against Hiss. "The conviction of Alger Hiss," former President Hoover told Congressman Nixon, "was due to your patience and persistence alone."

In its reconstruction of Nixon's role in the Eisenhower Administration, the ad showed Nixon working with Ike, reporting to Ike, serving as Ike's surrogate as the president recovered from his heart attack, and representing the U.S. in travels throughout the world.

As the supplement suggests, Nixon viewed his experience in foreign affairs as the mark differentiating him and his running mate from Kennedy and Johnson. Accordingly, Nixon's broadcast ads translated questions of domestic policy into questions of foreign policy.

Nixon's spots embraced the form of the Eisenhower Answers America series. A question was posed. The candidate responded. But where the questioners appeared in the Eisenhower spots, their function is here served by a disembodied voice.

To underscore the candidates' competence, the campaign also aired five minute still montage vignettes titled "Meet Richard Nixon" and "Meet Mr. Lodge." Marring the spots featuring Nixon speaking and the still montage spots is the photo that appears at the commercials' end. In it, Lodge, who is substantially taller than Nixon, stands next to the vice-president. Visually, Lodge is the superior, Nixon the subordinate.

This still photo appeared at the end of most of the spot ads aired for the Republican nominee in the general election of 1960.

The role the vice-presidential nominees played in advertising differed drastically in 1960. Unlike Johnson, who was assigned to hold the South for the Democrats, Lodge's appeal transcended any single region of the country. So, where Johnson appeared for a fraction of a second in only two of Kennedy's nationally aired ads, spoke for eight minutes in one nationally aired speech, and briefly from Austin during Kennedy's election eve telecast, the Republicans devoted spot time to Lodge, expanded the concept of the five minute "Meet Mr. Lodge" spot to fifteen minutes by including news footage from trouble spots around the world, featured him in a half hour telecast in which he discussed foreign affairs with a panel of academics, and showcased him in Nixon's telethon.*

Sorensen explains the comparative absence of Johnson in the na-

---

*In answer to a question raised on the telethon, Nixon argued that the Democrats had been playing hide the vice-presidential nominee. A questioner asked: "How do you find time for a four hour telethon when you can't find time for a fifth debate with Senator Kennedy?" Nixon responded that after he suggested and the networks agreed that the vice-presidential candidates should appear in that debate, Kennedy scotched plans for the fifth debate: "I am confident the reason that Senator Kennedy didn't want it was he just didn't want to be seen with Senator Johnson in some of the Northern States. . . . I would like to say, incidentally, I am always proud to be seen with my running mate anywhere in the country, North, South, East, or West."

tional advertising by noting, "our polls showed that voters were making up their minds based on the presidential candidates not the vice-presidential candidates. . . . To the extent that Johnson appeared in local TV in the South which would shore up his natural constituency . . . fine."

One minute and five minute ads produced by Texas adman Jack Valenti featured Johnson speaking directly to the camera. These were aired in the South as was an occasional half hour speech. Valenti recalls that these ads discussed national issues and made no specific appeal to Southern pride.[60]

One of these televised half hour speeches existed specifically because Kennedy felt that not enough had been done for Johnson. Kennedy's time buyer Reggie Schuebel recalls:

> A man called me from the west coast and said, "I will give $30,000 to the campaign if Kennedy'll shake my hand." The next time he was on the west coast, Kennedy shook the man's hand. We collected the check. Afterwards Kennedy said "Let's use it for Johnson." Kennedy thought he hadn't done enough for Johnson. So I hooked up a Southwest network so LBJ could give a speech in the South.[61]

Johnson's insistent demands for more money and more national air time led some on Kennedy's staff "to dig in their heels." "The problem with Johnson," recalls Wilson, "was his personality not the possibility that he would be a political embarrassment.

> He was such a huge carnivorous man who wanted this and that. It was hard to tell Lyndon Johnson to forget it. You had to dodge him. There was a telecast in the Coliseum in New York in which there was a dispute. It was a half hour telecast and Johnson wanted fifteen minutes. The Kennedy people wanted to give him five minutes at the end on the grounds that the presidential candidate deserved twenty or twenty-five minutes. Johnson wouldn't stand for it. But who's going to tell him? I said "I'll do the signals and I'll cut him off and he won't know the difference." One of Kennedy's key advisors said "Don't ever tell anyone you told me this." So after signalling Kennedy, I brought Johnson up. Seven minutes into his fifteen minute speech I gave him a cut signal. I thought he was going to jump me. In such circumstances the speaker doesn't have a real sense of time. Afterwards when he found that he'd only gotten eight minutes he sent Valenti to find me. [The aide told me that Johnson had said] "I'm going to pound that little peckerhead until he dies." I got out of the Coliseum as quickly as I could.[62]

By contrast Lodge was featured in a spot that replayed audio clips from speeches he had delivered at the UN as well as from campaign speeches; forceful, dramatic, still photos recalled the events of which he spoke. Lodge in the UN holding up the U.S. seal that had hidden a Soviet bugging device declares: "The United States has found within its embassies in the Soviet Union and the satellite countries well over one hundred clandestine listening devices." Stills of Russian Ambassador Vishinsky appear. On the audio track we hear angry, menacing Russian words. Lodge points his finger defiantly in response. The spot also showed Lodge and Eisenhower in conversation as Eisenhower is heard praising Lodge's work in the UN. As the spot closed, the announcer intoned: "There is no substitute for the long experience in government and foreign affairs gained by Ambassador Lodge from his years in the Senate, the President's cabinet and in the United Nations. When you vote on November 8, vote for Vice-President Richard Nixon and Ambassador Henry Cabot Lodge. They Understand What Peace Demands."

By recreating the tensions of his term at the UN and his strong response to them, this ad underscored Lodge's competence. The posture toward the Soviets implied by the visual images in this ad argued that Nixon and Lodge's foreign policy would be strong and decisive but measured.*

The spot on Lodge is remarkable also for the skill with which it compensated for Lodge's limits as a scripted television performer. As Gene Wyckoff, one of its creators, observed in his book *The Image Candidates*,[63] Lodge "looked like what you would expect an American statesman to look like. But when he opened his mouth and when he interacted with people on television, there was something not so attractive—something in his demeanor, a touch of hauteur, arrogance, aloofness, or condescension perhaps. His characterization did not ring true."

This sense pervades five direct-to-camera spots of Lodge produced for the campaign. In each, Lodge is obviously uncomfortable. His tone suggests that his endorsement of Nixon's virtues comes not from his heart but from cue cards. His voice lacks conviction. His pose is robotic with only his eyes moving; his posture, arms locked across his chest, is vaguely menacing. By contrast, the exerpts from the UN speeches underscoring the still montage are eloquent and forceful, natural and dynamic. The stills convey competence and conviction obscured in the direct-to-camera spots.

The campaigns' slogans reflected their different assessments of the national strength of the vice-presidential candidates: "Nixon-Lodge: They Understand What Peace Demands" vs. "Kennedy: Leadership for the '60's."

---

*With the Nixon-Lodge tag removed and a bit of internal editing that film was used to make the case for Lodge for president in the 1964 New Hampshire primary. A bit over one-third of the Republicans who cast a ballot in that primary wrote in Lodge's name—to give him the Republican victory over Goldwater, Rockefeller, and another write-in: Richard Nixon.

The Debates as a Test of the Candidates' Experience, Maturity, and Competence

Meanwhile, the debates enabled viewers to judge the issue of competence and experience for themselves. In Converse's judgment the debates in particular—and the mass media in general—also "filled in an image of Kennedy. . . . He was not only a Catholic but was as well . . . quick-witted, energetic, and poised. These are traits valued across religious lines and act at the same time to question some of the more garish anti-Catholic stereotypes. . . . Bit by bit, as religiously innocuous information filled in, the Protestant Democrat could come to accept Kennedy primarily as a Democrat, his unfortunate religion notwithstanding."[64]

In the first debate, Nixon's pale complexion, the byproduct of a recent illness and inadequate make-up and lighting, his dark beard, and the sweat that trickled over his upper lip and down his chin suggested a desperate person crumbling under the stress of the encounter with Kennedy. By replaying one minute and five excerpts of the first debate, the Democrats reminded viewers that Kennedy seemed as experienced and knowledgeable as Nixon in the first debate. At the same time the ads impressed on the public mind the sinister image Nixon projected in the debate. The image—of the small-eyed bearded conspirator—was one that recalled the defamatory images earlier crafted by the Democrats. In the Man on the White Horse ads of 1952, for example, Nixon was identified by his bearded face and the microphone he clutched.

The sweating, bearded, shifty-eyed Nixon of the first debate appeared to be the gutter-dwelling Nixon of Herblock's cartoons given flesh. Ironically, Nixon's verbal demeanor was anything but that satirized by Herblock. Gone was the acerbic style and the strident rhetoric. The words Nixon spoke were not those of Eisenhower's henchman, but a presidential aspirant.

Lost in the cameras' fixation with the stark visual contrast between the two candidates was this verbal message. It was a message radio listeners heard but there were too few of them to give Nixon the public perception of victor in the first debate. What Nixon had inadvertently done before the largest bipartisan audience of the 1960 campaign was visually confirm an image that previously had been painted only by the propagandist's brush.

The tragedy of the first debate for Nixon was that an aggregation of cues irrelevant to the audience's judgment of him as a potential president biased its appraisal of his performance. In part, Nixon was the victim of his genetic heritage. "He has very translucent, almost blue-white skin," notes Rogers. "You can actually see the roots of his beard beneath his skin. TV is just an electronic development that goes beyond x-rays and radar. This x-ray like quality of television made Nixon a bad visual candidate for television."

Additionally, despite application of a specially formulated drying agent, Nixon perspired profusely. Consequently, a guerrilla war over the thermostat occurred in the second debate. Surreptitiously, Rogers turned the thermostat down to the point that when Kennedy arrived he noted that he was cold. "It felt like a meat locker," Kennedy adviser Leonard Reinsch recalls. Reinsch, and another adviser, Bill Wilson, responded by sneaking into the basement to turn the thermostat up as high as they could.

Nixon also suffered when his carefully placed lights were upset by photographers admitted at the last minute by the press secretaries from the two campaigns.

The argument can be made that whether or not a candidate perspires under the hot studio lights should have no bearing on his possible performance as president. Nor should the translucence of his skin. Similarly irrelevant should be whether or not he is adequately made up, lit to advantage, or dressed in a suit that contrasts sharply with its background. That Nixon slouched to one side while standing, giving the impression that he had purchased his suit at a bargain basement sale, meant simply that the injured knee for which he had earlier been hospitalized was causing him pain, pain heightened when he hit it against the car as he alighted from the limousine that carried him to the debate.

These factors appear to have prejudiced viewers' responses. Those who heard the debate on radio—in short, those who relied less on visual image and more on sound and lines of argument—probably made the more seasoned judgment of the actual job-related performance of the two candidates.

The damage this visually disastrous image inflicted was heightened both by the opportunity television provided to directly compare the two candidates and by the size of the audience attracted by the debates. "In the 1960 campaign the average half-hour paid political television network broadcast attracted approximately 30 percent less audience than the program it replaced," CBS president Frank Stanton noted. "The four debates, on the other hand, had audiences averaging 20 percent larger than the entertainment programs they pre-empted."[65]

The five minute Democratic ad clipped from the debates accentuated another of Nixon's problems for it showed him nodding in apparent agreement with one of Kennedy's statements. Republicans promptly charged that such footage had been edited out of context. Robert Finch, Nixon's campaign director, called the scene with Nixon nodding "vicious

political trickery of the most contemptible sort" and added that it, coupled with the UAW "smear sheet," demonstrated "that Kennedy will go
to any length and use any device in his desperate effort to win this
election." Kennedy's press secretary Pierre Salinger replied that the film
was not doctored, noted that Nixon's "partisans wanted no reminders of
the first debate," and concluded that this charge "measures up to the
usual standard for accuracy of Nixon charges, which in recent days seem
to be getting more strident."[66]

Today Maxwell Arnold who produced that ad for Guild, Bascom and
Bonfigli, the agency handling the Democratic National Committee's account, recalls that "we may have taken some poetic license" in that
spot.[67]

Because creation of either a five or a one minute ad from the debate
necessitated editing, covering shots to mask the edits were required.
Democrats argue that the only material available to cover an edit was a
shot of Nixon. Unfortunately for Nixon, not a single reaction shot of him
in the first debate was flattering.

The shot showing Nixon nodding, which covers the two edits in the
five minute Kennedy spot, did occur in the debate but not in the order
shown in the ad. Still, any other reaction shot of Nixon than the one used
would have been more visually damaging. Throughout the debate, cut-
aways of Nixon had uniformly compared unfavorably to those of Kennedy. Kennedy looked intently at Nixon, a posture he deliberately assumed when twice he caught a glimpse of himself in the monitor, and
took occasional notes as if to arm himself in rebuttal; Nixon glanced
furtively to the right of the stage, a nonverbal act suggesting shiftiness,
but probably instead indicating his attention to a side clock; he also licked
sweat from his upper lip, an act that suggested an inability to cope with
pressure, scowled, and once nodded in apparent agreement with Kennedy. In the reaction shots, Kennedy seemed to embody the cliche: he
was calm, cool, and collected. Nixon by contrast seemed tortured—perhaps Rogers speculates, because his knee was causing him actual pain—
and one of those uncomfortable moments was caught in the Democrat's
five minute spot.

Without selecting an even more damaging reaction shot of Nixon,
could Kennedy's producer have covered his edits? "They could have gone
to a reaction shot of the press panel," notes Ted Rogers, Nixon's debate
adviser. "There were two shots and four shots over the shoulder of the
panel. They took the nodding out of context. I don't think something as
important as a presidential debate should be taken out of context." Sorensen notes that "Nixon was nodding in agreement in the first debate
and that embarrassed the Republicans and surprised a good many

people." Yet in response to evidence that the nodding was interpolated out of sequence, Sorensen's reaction is comparable to Rogers. "In that case I regard it as unfortunate. It is too bad that that was done. . . . I can see where the Republicans felt it was misleading."

The controversial ad from the debate was able to be edited and aired because the Democrats were prepared to secure and edit videotape, an art still in its infancy in 1960. Maxwell Arnold, who supervised the account for the Democrat's agency, recalls that the campaign approached its final three weeks with well-placed five minute time commitments in prime time that if canceled would have become available to the Republicans. To fill those spaces with new filmed spots was impossible since processing film required days. By editing the taped debates on tape, the Democrats were able to get ads on the air in time to hold the desirable time commitments.

By lifting radio ads from the debates for airing throughout the country, the Republicans tried to counter the advantage the Democrats gained among viewers of the first debate. Both parties used advertising to try to influence viewers and listeners' recollections of the debates. If, as the academic literature suggests, the debates helped voters choose by reinforcing their existing predispositions, then these uses of advertising probably accelerated those choices. By increasing the electorate's access to the debates, these ads also provided exposure to the debates to those who either missed a debate by chance or advertently missed one or more debates.

Throughout these and the other broadcast and print ads produced on Kennedy's behalf, his identity as a Democrat is stressed. He is "the Democratic candidate," as the announcers note. By contrast, Nixon's party is rarely mentioned. If Kennedy could secure the votes of those identifying themselves as Democrats, he could win: but for Nixon to win, he required conversions. The first debates and debate ads lifted from it helped Kennedy mobilize Democrats without giving Nixon the conversions he needed. Still, had Nixon beaten Kennedy soundly in that decisive first debate, he could easily have won the election for that, if any, was a forum that would have prompted Democrats to abandon their predispositions and support a demonstrably superior Republican candidate.

Evidence of Presidential Aptitude Drawn from Kennedy's Pulitzer Prize

In Kennedy's campaign documentary both *Profiles in Courage* and Kennedy's earlier book *Why England Slept* served as evidence that Kennedy understood what peace demanded. "This book . . . Why England Slept . . . a warning for America . . . a book read by millions, pointing out the folly of unpreparedness" stated the announcer. Later in the film he added: "During his busy days in Washington, John Kennedy found time to write a nation-wide best seller . . . Profiles in Courage . . . [Kennedy is shown in his office with the book in his hands] Translated into Vietnamese, Japanese, Spanish and other languages, *Profiles in Courage* was distributed abroad by the United States Information Agency and called by the head of that agency an important aid to the understanding of American statesmen and American aspirations . . . [the Pulitzer prize certificate is shown] For *Profiles in Courage* John Kennedy was awarded the Pulitzer Prize."

While Nixon could and did recite the number of countries he had visited, the number of leaders he had met, the number of conferences he had attended, none of these statistics demonstrated that he had learned history's lessons. What Kennedy's books provided was the evidence that he had.

By dulling the edge of the religion issue among some and turning it to his use among others, by magnifying public awareness of Ike's reservations about Nixon, by underscoring his televised performance in the first debate, and by creating an image of an heroic, family-oriented, good humored historian, and leader, Kennedy's advertising dispatched the advantage Nixon's eight years of executive service had earned him.

Problems Confronting the Kennedy Campaign

Instead of the well-oiled machine mythologized in the press, the Kennedy campaign seems, from the optic provided by the production of its advertising, to have been an Edsel kept on the road by mechanics frantically redesigning spare parts. Initially, the media operation was located in a city whose labs could not adequately process large quantities of film; then the mobile unit taping on location ads burned to the ground. Additionally, the operation was plagued by terrified mothers, a mortified farmer, listless audience members, a scarcity of stock footage, a candidate prone to expend his voice on a delivery too intense for television, the presence of too many producers governed by too little direction and—the final potentially fatal complication—too little money.

Deciding to headquarter their operations in Washington was a mistake for Kennedy's media advisers. Once in Washington the campaign's media producers found that film that should have been processed in a matter of days was taking weeks, was being lost by the processor, and was not being processed to a high standard of quality. One of those working on the Kennedy account explains this by claiming that the only film lab large enough to handle the Democrat's work was owned by a supporter of Richard Nixon's. Some suspected but were unable to prove sabotage;

others concluded that the labs in Washington were simply unequipped to process the quantity of film being shot by the Kennedy campaign. The problem was solved by relocating to an office in New York owned by Joseph Kennedy.

The second time the film producers suspected but could not prove sabotage occurred when the mobile videotape unit that Kennedy was using to do tape commercials burned down in Paris, Kentucky. Shot on location, these ads and newsclips aired within 24 hours on local television stations. Such mobile units were a major innovation in the history of political advertising; they localized commercials by showing the candidate—framed by recognizable landmarks—speaking to the neighbors and friends of viewers.

Gabriel Bayz, executive assistant in charge of motion picture production, lists some of the possible causes of the fire that destroyed the unit and much of the videotape in it. The wiring might have been taxed by rapid duplication of materials causing an electrical overload. The volatile developing fluid might have accidentally ignited. Or the operation might have been sabotaged. The existence of the unit was causing the Republicans a great deal of distress, comments Bayz, distress eliminated when the unit burned.

Speculation about sabotage was not taken seriously if it was discussed at all in the top levels of the Kennedy campaign. "After what happened in '72 and the true confessions in '73 and '74 by Nixon's entourage saying this was the sort of thing they'd done before, it naturally arouses all kinds of suspicions of what might have been done in 1960 but I didn't know of anything specific," says Sorensen.

But problems in processing film and safeguarding videotape units were not the only ones encountered in production of Kennedy's televised ads. A major innovation of the campaign—use of on location shooting— also caused difficulties not native to studio production. According to Sorensen, the on location spots had the advantage of "getting the candidate in action where he was at his best rather than having him in a more stilted format answering questions or reading a prepared statement in a studio where he was at his worst."

But the tight campaign schedule and the inability of typical voters to relax before the camera caused problems for Jack Denove, Kennedy's film producer. "We were filming a torchlight parade in New York," Denove's brother Richard recalls. "The parade was coming through Times Square. We had lights set on the Lux Theatre. It was pouring rain. We were ready. But the candidate was late—as candidates typically are in campaigns. To save time, Kennedy's car drove through at about 45 miles an hour. We were left with camera swishes instead of good footage."

The voters featured in the spots also posed problems. In one five minute ad, a group of mothers seated in desks in an elementary school classroom ask Kennedy—who is standing in front of the classroom—about his plans to aid education. Their sing-song delivery and expression-less faces suggest that the camera has transformed them into terrified first graders confronting the principal on their first day of school.

In another ad two audience members seated behind Kennedy seemed to be inviting viewers to ignore his speech. As Kennedy's delivery intensi-fied the two men shifted listlessly in their seats. Perhaps soothed by Kennedy's assurances that he would get the country moving again, one finally fixed his gaze vacantly away from the future president while the other half-heartedly warded off sleep.

Yet the on location technique could be rivetting. Speaking convinc-ingly, a West Virginia woman asserts that Kennedy's religion will pose problems for him as president. The tension is palpable. The sense of conviction conveyed in his answer matches hers. A similar sense of drama occurs in an ad shot in a mine in West Virginia, where Kennedy discusses unemployment with miners who seem unaware that they are on camera. The location underscores their concerns.

Kennedy's habits of delivery also posed problems for Denove. Before small groups of miners or teachers he was "charming and soft spoken." But before large audiences "he would bellow and becoming too over-whelming for television. We also worried about his voice which he lost time and again."

To transport a candidate into America's living rooms who would not violate the conversational norms applied to guests, Denove sought out sections of the speeches that Kennedy had delivered with less than usual intensity. He also cut to the audience or to illustrative stock footage every few sentences. Ideally, this alternative footage would have underscored Kennedy's message. Occasionally, it distracted. For example, one five minute ad cuts from Kennedy's statement of his basic political beliefs to shots of the Liberty Bell, a smelting furnace, waving fields of grain, and a factory spewing forth black smoke—then a sign of productivity. The rela-tionship between these images and Kennedy's message is difficult to fathom. A possible explanation for these incongruous scenes appears in a post-election memo from one of the film producers who complained that "supposedly available stock footage" sometimes "failed to materialize."[68]

Kennedy's habit of abandoning his printed texts compounded De-nove's problems. Because the candidate rarely delivered his scripted texts as written, members of the press laughed when Kennedy promised that in delivery of his speech to the Houston ministers he would not be a "tex-tual deviate." To compensate for his inability to forecast the likely location of ad-worthy segments in Kennedy's often extemporaneous remarks, Denove filmed entire speeches and then searched them for usable "chunks." The process was time consuming and costly. To produce an unprecedented 200 ads, over a quarter of a million feet of film was shot during the primaries and general election. "We had five or six labs working at the same time just to process footage from Kennedy's speeches," Richard Denove recalls. "For the ads we took chunks of speeches and build around them graphically or with dialogue from Kennedy or with an [announcer's] voice over." Ideally, of course, Denove would have reduced the cost of film crews, film, lab fees, and editing time by filming only those parts of the speeches that were likely to be included in ads. "We wasted a lot of money by having film crews follow Kennedy all the time and film everything he was saying and then select from that what seemed the best and most useful," Sorensen concludes. It was a mistake that Robert Kennedy's advisers would not repeat in 1968. Still in a campaign that was so short of money that distribution of Kennedy signs and bumper stickers had been curtailed, long distance phone use cut, and some reserved TV time released,[69] here was a way in which money could have been saved.

Cost

In 1960 the Democrats matched the spending of the Republicans by engaging in a level of deficit spending unprecedented in the history of presidential campaigns. Using an index of direct expenditures, Professor Alexander Heard discovered that at the national level in 1952 the Republicans had a 55–45 advantage over the Democrats and in 1956 an advantage of 62–38. Recomputing Heard's figures to account for deficits in 1956, Herbert Alexander[70] concluded that the Republicans had a 59–41 advantage in 1956 while in 1960 the Democrats had a 51–49 edge. In 1956 Stevenson left a debt of over $700,000; the Democratic debt in 1960 was $3,820,000. The Republicans had a post-election debt of $993,000 in 1960.

Before the nomination, Kennedy and the Kennedy family spent $150,000 on his campaign. The family also created a corporation that purchased a $385,000 airplane that it leased to the campaign at $1.75 a mile.[71] In other words, the Kennedy family gave his campaign more money than Humphrey spent in Wisconsin ($116,500) and West Virginia ($23,000)[72] combined.

After outspending Humphrey by over 4–1 in the decisive West Virginia primary, it is ironic that the Kennedy campaign faced financial difficulties in the general election. As I have intimated earlier, some of those problems were self imposed. In direct payments to the advertising firms that produced the majority of their television and radio ads, the Democrats outspent the Republicans. The Republicans paid Campaign Associates, the firm that Newton and Rogers headed, about $2,269,578; the Democrats paid Guild, Bascom and Bonfigli approximately $2,413,227 and paid an additional $377,500 to Kennedy's filmmaking agency Jack Denove Productions.

Because the Democratic National Committee's agency and Denove duplicated each others efforts, the Democrats got less for their money than they would have had they centralized their production under the supervision of a single agency as the Republicans did. The conflict arose because before the party's nominee had been selected, the Democratic National Committee had signed a contract with Guild, Bascom and Bonfigli as they had with Norman Craig and Kummel in '56 and Katz in '52. But where in these earlier races the candidate had bowed—however reluctantly—to the committee's choice, Kennedy had been pleased with the work Denove had done for him in the primaries and wanted to retain his services in the general election as well. "The Kennedy campaign had used Jack Denove in the primaries," says Maxwell Arnold who supervised the account for Guild, Bascom and Bonfigli. "There was a point when they didn't want to work with us but our contract with DNC was binding. . . . The Kennedy campaign didn't see why it should be bound by a decision made by [DNC head] Paul Butler." As the general election began, Jack Denove functioned as the Kennedy's "advertising manager." "In September, we started writing scripts for one minute and five minute spots that Denove was going to film. Anything we wrote we submitted to him. None of them ever cleared. The decision was delayed. Often it simply wasn't made." These unproduced scripts survive in the Kennedy Library. "We had a strange relationship with Guild, Bascom and Bonfigli," recalls Richard Denove. "We were both producers. It was an unenviable position." "A lot of good creative stuff Guild, Bascom and Bonfigli created was thrown out because the Kennedys had their own agency," recalls Sam Brightman. "Denove and the agency were in competition. It was just that simple," reports a campaign insider.

In the final weeks of the campaign, a film lag of uncertain cause occurred and the agency moved into the void, producing the debate spots discussed earlier and scripting the half hour program featuring Jackie Kennedy, Caroline, Jack Kennedy, and Henry Fonda. That program, scripted by Maxwell Arnold, used still photos and family films to capture the highlights of Kennedy's life and showcased Mrs. Kennedy. During the program she reported to her husband on "issues in this election [that are] of the most significance to women." It turns out of course that the issues of concern to women are the issues on which Kennedy has been focusing in the campaign: education, care for the aged, inflation, and peace.

Denove and Arnold were not the only ones writing and producing ads. Bill Wilson, who had been introduced to the Kennedys by friends from the Stevenson campaign of '56, was also taping ads. Wilson, who produced the election eve speeches of Kennedy, Johnson, and Mrs. Kennedy, was added to Guild, Bascom and Bonfigli's payroll.

The cost of the rivalry between the competing producers was high. In a post campaign memo, Bernard Cherin, a volunteer film producer for Kennedy wrote:

> The lack of a clear-cut organizational structure led to continual disputes over authority, and caused much duplication of effort. . . . (the) rivalry within the Films for Kennedy organization was matched by an interagency rivalry which considerably reduced the effectiveness of the operation, and the impact of the final product. For example, the ad agency, the research people and films for Kennedy each worked on different aspects of the distribution problem, but no one ever produced—either separately or in concert—a detailed schedule showing which films were to be shown in which cities. This resulted in such anomalies as a farm film being shown in New York City, and Civil Rights films appearing in the Deep South.
>
> . . . Cameramen were sent to film major speeches without the guidance of a director. This led inevitably to a number of visual "goofs" which rendered otherwise worthwhile footage completely useless. Kennedy's best speech on natural resources could not be used because the most prominent object in the picture was a microphone with the call letters KOOK.[73]

So while the campaign was running short of the money to place ads, make phone calls, and distribute buttons and bumper stickers, money in the form of unusable film and duplicated creative efforts was being tossed to the winds.

The looming deficit meant that some of those who provided the Kennedy campaign with services went unpaid. Alexander reports, for example, that in 1961 pollster Lou Harris was still owed $90,000. And to this day Jack Denove Productions has not been paid for some of the work Denove did for Kennedy.

Jean Kennedy Smith, Kennedy's sister, introduced Denove to the Kennedys after working on the "Christopher Hour," a show Denove produced. Denove worked for Kennedy in both the primaries and the general election. Since campaigns have no credit history to justify their creditworthiness, when money was in short supply Denove rented equipment and contracted for lab space on his own credit. At the campaign's end he was owed $75,000, a sum never paid. The Kennedys argued that, although Jean Kennedy Smith had introduced Denove to the Kennedys and Denove had been asked directly by the Kennedys to produce media, the bill was owed not by them but by the Democratic National Committee. But the official agency of the committee, Guild, Bascom and Bonfigli of San Fransisco, had not subcontracted to Denove so the committee's legal responsibility for the debt was questionable.

To compensate Denove for the personal financial loss, Denove's brother and partner Richard indicates that the Kennedys urged Denove to bid on government filmmaking projects. His bids were not competitive. Says one associate of Denove's, the winners "must have planned to shoot from a taxi in order to maintain bids that low." There was also a tacit understanding that Denove would handle Kennedy's '64 reelection media, an arrangement that would have compensated him for the loss he absorbed in '60. When Kennedy was assassinated, Bayz reports that Johnson's supporters at the Democratic National Committee let the Denove family know that they felt no obligation to pay the debt.

So the wealthiest man to seek the presidency in the age of television, a person whose father had set up a trust fund for him of one million dollars to be available at adulthood, left a film company in Los Angeles with debts unpaid to this day. In partial compensation, Denove retained the masters of the tapes and films he produced for the 1960 campaign, donating them not to the Kennedy Library but to a special collection at UCLA. As a result, the finest collection of televised materials on the Kennedy campaign is not housed in the library honoring Kennedy.

In an article written for *TV GUIDE* in 1959 Kennedy had decried the escalating cost of political television and urged the public to explore means of holding the cost down. Between the convention and the start of the fall campaign in 1960 Kennedy's brother-in-law Steve Smith asked Republican party chief Len Hall if the Republicans would agree to a spending limit in the general election. According to Sorensen, Hall declined. In his first year of office Kennedy recommended federal financing for presidential campaigns.[74] It was an idea whose time had not yet come.

CHAPTER FIVE

1964: Goldwater vs. Goldwater

If ever there was a campaign in which one candidate sought to win the election while the other was more interested in winning the point, the 1964 presidential race between Lyndon Johnson and Barry Goldwater was that contest. The Republican nominee's emergence out of the right wing of his party is less significant than that his final position was no further to the center by the election's end. Indeed, in what was one of the strangest campaigns in modern American history, Barry Goldwater attempted, in the two short months from Labor Day to November 4, to move the vast majority in the middle to where *he* stood rather than attempting to present his philosophy in terms palatable to the moderate middle.

Well before the serious campaign season had begun, turbulence both at home and abroad engulfed the country. Domestically, conflicts over civil rights had reached a series of flash points over the past year; abroad, the U.S. was championing a succession of unstable governments in South Vietnam while gradually escalating toward full-scale war.

On April 3, 1963, the Reverend Martin Luther King had begun leading small groups of blacks to sit at segregated lunch counters in Birmingham, Alabama—a city with a history of cross burnings and bombings and a city whose police force was particularly racist. Those who tried to be seated had been promptly arrested. Store owners had responded to the escalating protests by closing lunch counters; King and his supporters marched in protest. As the protests escalated so too did the arrests. On April 12, 1963, King was arrested.

National television began covering the protests, engendering new support for the movement; forty demonstrators became one thousand and one thousand became five thousand. With the jails threatening to burst and no longer able to contain the mass of demonstrators, the police changed tactics and set dogs and fire hoses on the crowds. Night after night the graphic scenes on the evening news invited viewers to question the legality and morality of police violence against peaceful protestors.

Hostilities continued. The home of King's brother was bombed. Alabama state troopers were sent in to cope with the protestors; U.S. army units were moved into position. Finally, some lunch counters were opened to blacks and the protests subsided. But the protest in Birmingham had functioned as the fuse igniting protests around the country.

On June 19, 1963, in response to the long-overdue need for federal protection of the civil rights of black Americans, President Kennedy placed before the Congress the Civil Rights Act. Despite the public outcry over Birmingham, passage of the act was by no means assured. Five months later, while on a visit to Dallas, Texas, John Kennedy was assassinated. Whether or not and in what form the civil rights bill Kennedy had sent up would get through Congress was now up to the new president.

After Kennedy's death, Lyndon Johnson, his successor, took up the fight, lobbying hard for the bill. In an empassioned, televised speech, Johnson prophesied passage of the bill in the words of the civil rights movement's hymn, "We Shall Overcome." Passage of the Civil Rights Act was complicated by the strong showings of George Wallace who campaigned for "law and order" and against passage of the act in presidential primaries in Indiana, Maryland, and Wisconsin. When the bill came to a vote, Goldwater voted against it.

A year after Kennedy had offered it, the bill as reshaped by Congress passed. The Civil Rights Act of 1964 equalized qualifications for voting, prohibited discrimination in public accommodations, and permitted the suspension of federal aid to communities that discriminated. Its passage represented a personal victory for Johnson.

Although passage of the act marked a highpoint in domestic affairs, foreign affairs were clearly at a low. With disturbing frequency, Buddhist monks immolated themselves in the streets of Saigon to protest the religious and political intolerance of the South Vietnamese regime. Then on August 2, three North Vietnamese patrol boats allegedly attacked the *U.S.S. Maddox* in the Tonkin Gulf. Two days later the *Maddox* and the *C. Turner Joy* were reportedly attacked again. The U.S. responded by bombing North Vietnamese naval bases. Johnson delivered a sober speech to the American people, pledging that we would respond to force with force. Congress passed the Tonkin Gulf Resolution empowering the president to take "necessary measures to repel any armed attack against aggression." Among his supporters on this tough stance was the senior senator from Arizona, Barry Goldwater; since mid-July Goldwater had also become the man against whom Johnson would run in 1964.

A conservative Republican, Barry Goldwater had written a best selling book, *The Conscience of a Conservative,* and was the author of a nationally syndicated column while representing Arizona in the U.S. Senate since 1952. In the Republican primaries Goldwater faced a serious challenge from wealthy New York Governor and moderate Nelson Rockefeller and a short-lived bid by supporters of Ambassador to Vietnam Henry Cabot Lodge, Nixon's running mate in 1960. Rockefeller and Goldwater clashed first in the New Hampshire primary, won by Lodge with a write-in, then in Oregon, won by Rockefeller with Lodge in second place. The polls in California prophesied a Rockefeller victory there as well. Three days before the primary in California, Happy Rockefeller gave birth to a son, news that allowed reporters to remind voters who did not already know that she and Nelson had divorced their spouses to marry and that the new Mrs. Rockefeller had given up the children of her first marriage in a custody agreement with her ex-husband. The impact of the birth on the outcome of the primary is difficult to determine. Nonetheless, Goldwater unexpectedly carried California.

Although he had won only one of three of the major primaries he contested, Goldwater entered the convention held in San Francisco July 13–16 with enough delegates to win nomination on the first ballot, a tribute to a grass roots organization composed of dedicated Conservatives. A last minute challenge by Pennsylvania Governor William Scranton proved futile. As his running mate, Goldwater chose New York Congressman and National Committee Chairman William Miller, prompting college students to shout: "Here's a riddle, it's a killer. Who the hell is William Miller?"

Goldwater entered the convention with the polls showing that Lyndon Johnson would beat him 62–29%. In his acceptance speech Goldwater proclaimed: "Our people have followed false prophets. We must, and we shall, return to proven ways—not because they are old, but because they are true." The speech also detailed the themes he would stress in his campaign, including a condemnation of violence in the streets and corruption in high office. The latter charge attempted to link Johnson to his former protégé Bobby Baker, who was accused of influence peddling. Among the charges against Baker was that he had supplied senators with call girls.

Lyndon Johnson had taken the oath of office on *Air Force One* on November 22, 1963, with John Kennedy's widow looking on. In his first address as president he had implored the country "Let us continue!" and had urged Congress to enact Kennedy's legislative agenda as a means of testifying that Kennedy neither lived nor died in vain. In enacting the Kennedy agenda, Johnson had proven more successful than Kennedy had. Although many of Kennedy's appointees stayed to help Johnson, friction between Johnson's aides and those of the former president was palpable. Increasingly, Johnson's own appointees took control. Increasingly, Johnson stepped from the shadow of his predecessor to act in his own name. By summer 1964, when his party's nomination was his for the asking, Johnson was ready to run on his own for his own term. He entered the convention unopposed.

Johnson named liberal Minnesota Senator Hubert Humphrey as his running mate. Where Goldwater in his acceptance speech looked to the past, in Johnson's, delivered on his birthday, August 27, Johnson looked to the future. "The Founding Fathers dreamed America before it was. The pioneers dreamt of great cities on the wilderness that they had crossed. Our tomorrow is on its way. It can be a shape of darkness or it can be a thing of beauty. The choice is ours." Johnson's address also previewed his campaign. In a section that later would be edited into spot ads he said: "Most Americans want medical care for older citizens. And so do I. Most Americans want fair and stable prices and decent incomes for our farmers. And so do I. Most Americans want a decent home in a decent neighborhood for all. And so do I." The speech also foreshadowed Johnson's use of the nuclear issue against Goldwater. "There is no place in today's world for weakness. But there is also no place in today's world for recklessness. We cannot act rashly with the nuclear weapons that could destroy us all."

Agencies

In the summer before his death John Kennedy had asked his brother-in-law Steve Smith to open discussions with the Madison Avenue agency Doyle Dane Bernbach, whose campaigns for Avis and Volkswagen had impressed the president. No formal agreement had been reached before Kennedy's death. Jack Denove, Kennedy's advertiser in 1960, who in 1963 was still owed money from the 1960 campaign, also was asked to draw up a media plan.

As plans for Johnson's 1964 campaign began to take shape, Johnson's aide Bill Moyers gave his assistant, Lloyd Wright, the task of surveying the major agencies to determine which should be offered the Democratic account. Based on the quality of their work, their total billings, and their personal preference for the Democratic party, Wright recommended Doyle Dane Bernbach. Some in the Democratic National Committee protested that the Madison Avenue agency was too expensive, but Wright, backed by Moyers, won the debate. Confident that Johnson would be his party's nominee, Johnson's representatives signed a contract with Doyle Dane Bernbach on March 19, 1964.

The reason a big name Madison Avenue agency was willing to take the Democratic account was spelled out in a letter from the agency's creative director. "No one knows better than you why we took on the Presidential campaign," Bernbach wrote Moyers on August 17, 1964. "There is only one reason. We are ardent Democrats who are deadly afraid of Goldwater and feel that the world must be handed a Johnson landslide. To play our small part in the achievement of such a victory we risked the possible resentment of some of our giant Republican clients (I personally told one it was none of his business when he phoned me about our action) and we had to turn away companies who wanted to give us their accounts on a long-term basis. Two of the other agencies you were considering withdrew out of fear of their clients. A third agency blithely withdrew and took the Goldwater account."[1] Unspoken was Bernbach's belief that siding with Johnson would put the agency on the winning side.

When Goldwater won the nomination he faced an advertising situation much like that confronting Stevenson in '56 and Kennedy in '60; the Republican National Committee had already contracted with an agency. That agency, whose legacy to the campaign was the slogan "In Your Heart You Know He's Right," was the Leo Burnett Agency of Chicago. But unlike the Democrats who had signed exclusive contracts for the life of the campaign with their agencies in '56 and '60, the Republicans had included in their contract the provision that the contract could be dissolved by either party with reasonable notice.

With Goldwater's nomination, the Goldwater team took over the Republican National Committee, installing Dean Burch as its head. This move eliminated the infighting that had in the past pitted the staff of the committee and that of the nominee against each other. At the direction of its new leaders, the committee then engaged Interpublic, a large consortium of agencies. The advertising in the campaign was handled primarily by Interpublic's subsidiary, Erwin Wasey, Ruthrauff and Ryan, Inc.

In the judgment of Charles Lichenstein, who supervised production of much of Goldwater's advertising, the Democrats made a better choice than the Republicans did. "Johnson's campaign made a brilliant choice. Doyle Dane had made famous the Beetle. They happened to be on the cutting edge of the new media technology. They were brilliant. I'm not so sure our agency had quite the same skills at the same level of polish. . . . At that time I didn't have much experience with TV. I didn't look at it very much. I didn't even like it very much. I was an amateur in the technique of political advertising on TV."[2]

Cost

Of the total money spent on the presidential campaign the Republicans spent 63%[3] and unlike the Democrats, left the campaign without a de-

ficit; obviously the amount of money spent was not decisive in this campaign. Johnson was able to carry his message to the voters, even though it
took three years after the campaign had ended before the full debt to
Doyle Dane was discharged. From the Republican side, no amount of
money seemed able to buy advertising capable of erasing the image of
Goldwater sketched in the primaries by fellow Republicans and filled in
during the general election by Johnson and his advertising.

In 1964, television again was the dominant carrier of political advertising. The Republicans paid $2,000,000 in network charges and $4.4
million in station charges while the Democrats paid $1,925,000 in network
charges and $2.6 million in station charges.[4]

In 1961 Kennedy had set up a bipartisan Commission on Campaign
Costs. In April 1962 the commission recommended incentives for contributors including limited tax credits and tax deductions. It also recommended that Congress provide federal funds to cover presidential and
vice-presidential expenses from election day to the inauguration. The
second proposal passed the Congress and was signed by Lyndon Johnson.
But the proposal for tax breaks languished. Not until his 1966 State of the
Union address did Johnson promise to submit legislation to revise restrictions on contributions, prohibit the multiplication of committees (a problem caused by the requirement that no one committee spend more than 3
million dollars), add strong penalties to the requirement that all contributions be disclosed, and broaden public participation by tax incentives.

In 1964 the Republicans brought the fiscal management of corporate
America to bear on a presidential campaign. The results were mixed. On
the positive side, by appending to the ends of programs and ads a trailer
narrated by Raymond Massey appealing for funds, they elevated to an art
form the process of using media to raise money for media. They also
began fund raising early. Such efforts were well underway in the summer
and fall of 1963 when print ads urged voters to contribute to "retire"
Kennedy to his rocking chair.

On the negative side, Ralph Cordiner, former chair of the board of
General Electric, refused to reserve any ad time unless money was in the
bank or immediately forthcoming to pay for it. "He wanted a balanced
budget at all times," recalls campaign director Denison Kitchel. "That
sounded fine to us at the time [we talked to him about becoming trea-
surer]. It turned out to be totally impractical."[5] Lichenstein agrees. "That
put us behind the curve," he says. "We were off [the air] at some points
in the campaign when suddenly we'd have a big influx of money as we did
after Burch did his show and Reagan did his. Then we'd discover we
couldn't buy good time because none was available. There was no regu-
larity about our advertising on television. It was all very last minute."[6]

The Reagan address to which Lichenstein refers was aired nationally on October 27 and rebroadcast regionally at 5 P.M. on November 1. Although so poorly known among Republican admen that his name was misspelled "Regan" in the Republican ads run in the major newspapers, Reagan's call for a restoration of traditional American values resonated well with party leaders and faithful who foresaw their nominee losing, and hoped that such a loss would not permanently cripple the party. After delivery of that speech, Reagan's political future figured in press speculation. The address was also a financial success, raising over half a million dollars.

By contrast, the Democrats engaged in deficit spending. Despite a clause in their contract that stipulated that the Democrats "agree to pay our invoices on payment dates stated therein, usually within ten days of billing date"[7], in June 1965 the Democratic National Committee still owed Doyle Dane Bernbach $457,000. "The problem is simply there's no water in the well for the bucket to bring up," Moyers wrote to a Doyle Dane executive who was asking for payment in summer 1965. "They just have to keep opening up springs to replenish the well—and that is what they are trying to do . . . but you have priority in their minds as well as ours at the White House."[8]

Minimal financial reporting by the Democrats makes it difficult to determine how much was collected from whom and dispensed when to whom in 1964–65. Not until five months after the election was the Air Force compensated for use of presidential aircraft.[9] From January to June 1965, the official reports suggest that the Democrats spent $1.3 million more than they received.[10] "Where the excess funds came from remains a mystery since 1964 filings did not show large balances or excess income," notes campaign finance scholar Herbert Alexander.[11]

Just as the financial management of their campaigns differed, so too did the philosophy governing the length and content of their paid broadcasts. The Democrats tended to rely on spot ads, the Republicans on half hour programs; the Republicans preempted thirteen half hour shows, the Democrats preempted only eight.

While Goldwater was central to Republican advertising, Johnson was incidental to the Democratic spots, which generally focused on actors delivering scripted messages or on props—such as a plywood model of the U.S., a Social Security card lifted from a wallet and torn apart, and placards showing the faces of Goldwater's Republican primary opponents.

These differences reflect the nature of Johnson's campaign and the fact of his incumbency. As president, he was well known to the country; as a senator from Arizona, Goldwater was comparatively unknown nationally—hence the need to showcase Goldwater in the Republican ads. Additionally, the aggressiveness of Johnson's spot ads dictated that he not be directly associated with them. To minimize a backlash, such attacks are generally disassociated from the candidate on whose behalf the attacks are made. In this case, the ads were designed to imply that it was not Johnson or the Democratic Party attacking Goldwater but other Republicans or, worse for Goldwater, that he was actually engaged in attacking himself. Goldwater's ads showing him delivering calm, rationale speeches attempted to demonstrate that he was not the cavalier, uncaring, unthinking, reckless war monger envisioned in Democratic advertising. Goldwater's reliance on half hour shows had its disadvantages, for in that longer time period he was more likely to attract and hold committed partisans than uncommitted voters or those leaning to Johnson. So his dilemma was this: to reach voters moved by Johnson's short spots, Goldwater needed similar spots of his own but the spot form could not accommodate the demands of the message he needed to communicate, that he was a calm, responsible leader not to be feared.

Johnson and Goldwater also differed in the use they made of their vice-presidential nominees in their advertising. Throughout the five minute Republican spots, Goldwater speaks of a "Goldwater-Miller administration," "Bill Miller and I," "my running mate Bill Miller." By contrast Humphrey is in the Johnson ads the nonentity Johnson was in the Kennedy ads of 1960. Indeed, when Johnson heard an ad using Humphrey as narrator he ordered the spot recut to purge Humphrey from it. Moyers, who conveyed Johnson's directive to the adteam, attributes this to Johnson's "occasional aggravation" when he "thought Hubert achieved parity in terms of the election. He just wanted to make sure that Hubert didn't think he was being elected president."

The general Democratic and Republican strategies also differed. The Democrats began by attacking Goldwater for wanting to wreck Social Security, use the bomb, sell TVA and the like, then shifted to focus on the credits and agenda of Lyndon Johnson and closed with a push to get out the vote. By contrast, the Republicans opened by defending Goldwater against the Democratic charges, and shifted to attack Johnson for sanctioning lawlessness and corruption and diminishing the U.S.'s military preparedness. Phases one and three of the Democratic strategy succeeded; neither of the Republicans' two phases did. Post-election polls suggested that the majority voted not so much for Johnson as out of fear of Goldwater.

To effect the Democratic strategy, Johnson personally OK'd a massive ad campaign. Moyers wrote to Democratic treasurer Richard Maguire on August 31, 1964:

In a meeting Saturday night with Senator Humphrey, the President asked us to proceed with an advertising campaign that would include not only the planned network effort of almost $2 million, but also an additional expenditure of $2 1/2 million for local TV throughout the country, and approximately $1/2 million for local radio. He agreed that as much of this time as possible should be ordered this week and understood that most of the time must be paid for in advance of use.

In addition, the President said he would be willing to add another 15 fund raising dinners if you believe these are necessary—five for him and ten for Humphrey.[12]

"He did not want me to cut back the advertising campaign," Moyers remembers. He "liked Doyle Dane Bernbach's work" and the ads "appealed to his vanity." In addition, Johnson "was determined to roll up the biggest damned plurality ever and he felt that anything that could help—and he believed advertising could help—was worth the price."[13] Johnson, who won by 486 electoral votes to Goldwater's 52, got his money's worth.

Resurrecting the Attacks of Goldwater's Republican Opponents

"We are humbly grateful," said a media executive handling Johnson's advertising, "to the Senator's Republican colleagues for giving us the two big campaign issues—the bomb and Social Security. . . . There is no weapon so effective as the words of one's 'friends.' "[14] Goldwater agreed that he was the victim of fratricide. "LBJ had very little difficulty, with the aid of the Democratic National Committee and his campaign public relations people, in creating a caricature of Goldwater which was so grotesque that, had I personally believed all the allegations, I would have voted against my own candidacy," he wrote in 1970.[15]

Theodore White aptly describes the primaries of 1964 as a "Republican duel," and adds that "when the duel was over, the Republican Party was so desperately wounded that its leaders were fitter candidates for political hospitalization than for governmental responsibility."[16] While a fissioning afterlife enjoyed by intraparty attacks had been part of earlier campaigns, in 1964 such attacks were not simply additional ammunition for the other side, but instead the core of Johnson's case against Goldwater.

Before the primaries had even begun, Goldwater had uttered some of the words that would haunt him in the primaries and in the general election. On October 24, 1963, for example, in Hartford, Connecticut, he endorsed the use of atomic weapons by NATO "commanders." Here, as in subsequent conflicts over what Goldwater really said, or actually meant, there was dispute. Goldwater contended that he had not said "commanders" but "commander" and claimed that since the early Eisenhower years the commander of the NATO forces had had such authority.[17] A week later Goldwater recommended that the TVA be sold.

Soon he had saddled himself or been saddled with other baggage as well. Reporting a speech he had delivered in Concord, New Hampshire, on January 7, a headline in the *Concord Daily Monitor* claimed: "Goldwater Sets Goals: End Social Security, Hit Castro." In contradiction to the headline, the story accurately reported that Goldwater had urged the enlargement of Social Security and an increase in its monetary benefits. Of the headline, Goldwater later wrote, "It was totally unfair; it was totally untrue; it was totally inaccurate."[18] Still, Goldwater's support for Social Security as then constituted was equivocal; in response to a question at a press conference on January 6, 1964, a day before the speech, he had said, "I would like to suggest one change, that Social Security be made voluntary, that if a person can provide better for himself, let him do it."

On May 24, 1964, speaking on "Issues and Answers," Goldwater took another troubling stand. Answering Howard K. Smith's question on how the war in Vietnam might be prosecuted, Goldwater said: "There have been several suggestions made. I don't think we would use any of them. But defoliation of the forests by low-yield atomic weapons could well be done. When you remove the foliage, you remove the cover. The major supply lines, though, I think would have to be interdicted where they leave Red China, which is the Red River Valley above North Vietnam and there, according to my studies of geography, it would be a difficult task to destroy those basic routes."[18] Again the statement is subject to alternative constructions. Was defoliation by low-yield atomic weapons one of the means rejected, or did the discussion constitute approval of it? Goldwater claimed to have been speaking hypothetically about an option his predicating statement had foreclosed. If so, then the statement on defoliation constituted musing on the pros and cons of the decision. Yet enough ambiguity resided in the statement to permit the latter interpretation. Presumably to underscore his original intent, between publication of *The Conscience of a Majority* in 1970 and publication of *With No Apologies* in 1979 Goldwater altered the punctuation of the questionable sentence: "There have been several suggestions made. I don't think we would use any of them, but defoliation of the forest by low-yield atomic devices could well be done."[19] In his own earlier transcription of his televised statement, a period separated "them" from "But," punctuation strengthening the interpretation that defoliation by low-yield atomic weapons was being offered as a feasible option.

Goldwater was not felled by any one statement but by a network of statements that seemed to reinforce one another. "Let's lob one into the men's room of the Kremlin," he said at one point. "Sometimes I think this country would be better off if we could just saw off the Eastern Seaboard and let it float out to sea," he said at another. Theodore White labels such statements "frontier hyperbole," which he calls "the genuine literary expression of the Old West."[20] It was an idiom the American public was not prepared to accept from a presidential aspirant.

Rockefeller's advertising bludgeoned Goldwater with his own rhetoric. To increase public awareness of the headline claiming that Goldwater would destroy Social Security, the Rockefeller campaign mailed a photocopy of it to every Social Security recipient in New Hampshire.[21] Where Goldwater's posters in the California primary read "A Choice not an Echo" and "You Know Where He Stands," Rockefeller's declared "Vote for the Responsible Republican" and "Vote for the Man You Can Trust. Keep America in the Mainstream."[22] A mass mailing sponsored by Rockefeller in that primary asked: "Who Do You Want in the Room with the H Bomb Button?" and then magnified the importance of the question with a series of Goldwater's statements on the possible use of nuclear weapons.

William Scranton's twelfth hour dive for the nomination also exploited fears about Goldwater, exhorting Republicans not to nominate an impulsive person who was not even a true Conservative. "Would Bob Taft destroy Social Security?" Scranton asked.[23] At the convention, Scranton's lieutenants drafted and dispatched over his signature a four-page indictment of Goldwater that demanded a debate between the two.

By underscoring the perception against which it warned, the letter created a self-fulfilling prophesy: "All of us in San Francisco are so close to the hour-by-hour story unfolding here, that there is a danger we may overlook the overall impression being created in the minds of the American people," it said. "Goldwaterism has come to stand for nuclear irresponsibility." Scranton's letter, which Goldwater himself released to the convention's delegates, made other serious claims. Here are some, and Goldwater's recollection of his initial response to them:

> *You have too often casually prescribed nuclear war as a solution to a troubled world.* "I read that sentence twice," Goldwater later wrote. "Never once in all my statements or my writings on foreign policy had I ever advocated nuclear war as a solution to a troubled world."[24]
>
> *You have too often allowed the radical extremists to use you.* "Where? When? Who? How?" Goldwater asked himself.[25]
>
> *You have too often stood for irresponsibility in the serious question of racial holocaust . . . .* "I had voted for every civil rights measure except for the one in June," Goldwater thought, "and my objec-

tions to that piece of legislation were on very solid constitutional ground."[26]

You have too often read Taft and Eisenhower and Lincoln out of the Republican party. "At that point," Goldwater wrote later "I had to wonder if Bill Scranton had taken leave of his senses."[27]

In short, Golderwaterism has come to stand for a whole crazy-quilt collection of absurd and dangerous positions that would be soundly repudiated by the American people in November.[28] After putting the letter down, Goldwater told two of his aides that neither he nor his wife would vote for him had he "done any of the things Scranton charged."[29]

The accusations in that letter fused with Rockefeller's earlier indictments to form a picture of Goldwater unrecognizable to him. Had he accepted the possibility that reasonable persons could and would come to see him as the dangerous extremist Scranton described, Goldwater might have faced the claims head on and blunted them. If he had done so before two ill-starred moments at the convention locked that perception in the public memory, things might have turned out differently. But he did not and those two moments may well have sealed his fate before the general election campaign had even begun.

The first was a startlingly ugly moment that occurred when Nelson Rockefeller tried to speak in defense of one of the draft minority resolutions of the platform committee and was confronted by shouted curses and calumnies from the Goldwater loyalists who drowned him out chanting, "We want Barry!" Taunting them, Rockefeller smiled and nodded. Boiling to the surface in frustration, the crowd's hostility spilled over publicly accepted bounds of partisan dissent. The catcalls, the jeers, the faces contorted in undisguised hatred, the waves of open hostility that washed toward the podium, all suggested that the right to dissent was not held dear by Goldwater's followers. Moreover, this occurred before a national television audience totally unaccustomed to such audience response to political debate.

By its behavior, the audience, composed predominantly of Goldwater supporters, made it possible for Rockefeller to connect its candidate to those unfair campaign tactics that he claimed had been used against him in the California primary. "These things have no place in America," Rockefeller shouted. "But I can personally testify to their existence," he said, referring to his campaign experiences during the California primary. "And so can countless others who have also experienced anonymous midnight and early morning telephone calls, unsigned threatening letters, smear and hate literature, strong arm and goon tactics, bomb threats and bombings . . . infiltration and takeover of established political organizations by Communist and Nazi methods." Understandably, the fury of the crowd mounted. "And as the TV cameras translated their wrath and fury to the national audience," wrote White, "they pressed on the viewers that indelible impression of savagery which no Goldwater leader or wordsmith could later erase."[30]

It must be remembered that this event occurred four years before it became commonplace for Americans to see speakers heckled and hooted down on campuses and at campaign rallies. Although such discourtesy to political speakers was not invented during the 1960s, on that night in 1964 it had not yet occurred within the lifetime of most of those who viewed it on television.

The startling image of intolerance impressed on the public consciousness by the convention's treatment of Rockefeller found reinforcement on the final night of the convention when in his acceptance address Goldwater stated: "Extremism in the defense of liberty is no vice! Moderation in the pursuit of justice is no virtue!"—a declaration that seemed to endorse the audience's intemperate response to Rockefeller and affirm that ends justified means. Fifteen and one tenth million homes witnessed this ostensible embrace of extremism.

A shrewder politician than Goldwater might have seen the potential for disaster and after the Rockefeller incident gone back and rewritten his acceptance speech. Unfortunately for Goldwater, the memorable highlight of the acceptance speech, most likely written in advance of the mistreatment of Rockefeller but following so closely behind that event, appeared by its praise of extremism to endorse the refusal of Goldwater supporters to permit a prominent Republican to exercise his right of free speech before members of his own party. And as if to exacerbate the tension, Goldwater's delivery was harsh, demanding, almost strident—a call to mass the troops for battle.

Some delegates responded to the statement by walking out of the convention. "The first month of the campaign was devoted to healing wounds opened by these two sentences," writes political scientist John H. Kessel.[31] Still, some flaunted the inflammatory sentences on campaign buttons and in print ads.

Such utterances are the stuff that translate conjecture about a candidate into conviction. "The phrase about extremism," wrote Stephen Shadegg, Goldwater's Regional Director for Western States, "which for any other candidate in any other context might have been greeted with loud approval, ripped open old wounds and erected barriers which were never broken."[32]

Confronted with the need to explain the statement to party moder-

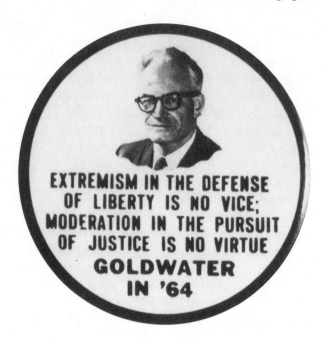

Goldwater button worn by some of his supporters during the general election of 1964. (Reprinted by permission of Senator Barry Goldwater and courtesy Smithsonian Institution, Photo No. 74-11278, Division of Political History)

ates who heard it as an indictment, on August 4, Richard Nixon wrote Barry Goldwater asking him to clarify his intended meaning. Goldwater responded: "One portion of that correct context . . . was the paragraph immediately preceding the two sentences in question. In it I urged that we resist becoming captives of "unthinkable labels. . . . I was urging, in effect, that we understand and view the great problems of the day in their essence and not be diverted by glib political catch words. In that context the sentences that followed were but examples."[33] Indeed, in the sentence before those on extremism and moderation Goldwater had said: "And let our Republicanism so focused and so dedicated not be made fuzzy and futile by unthinking and stupid labels." But in his delivery of the speech Goldwater paused between that first sentence and the others, an occurrence probably related to the fact that on his copy of the manuscript the sentences on extremism and moderation were underlined.

The inability to keep his examples and illustrations moored to their predicating statements, an inability manifest in Goldwater's ill-fated discussion of defoliation and of Social Security, had struck again—this time before the largest audience he would reach during the campaign. This tendency to untether subordinate material from its contexts recast Goldwater's genius at coining memorable phrases—a talent ordinarily prized in politicians—as a curse. Accentuating the damnation wrought by this curse was Goldwater's habit of expressing his illustrations in a more memorable way than the contextualizing sentences, thus inviting audiences to sunder one from the other.

By offering what appeared to be a defense of extremism in the acceptance speech, Goldwater authored his own obituary as a presidential candidate in 1964. Goldwater was aware of the commonly accepted pejorative definition of extremism, but, he later argued, he had used the word in another sense. "I detest extremism in the presently accepted derogatory connotation of that word," he wrote later.[34] "The dictionary gives a number of definitions for extreme—'of a character or kind farthest removed from the ordinary or average—the utmost of highest degree.'" Goldwater says he heard in his statement an echo of what he believed Cicero had said in one of his orations against Catiline: "I must remind you, Lords, Senators, that extreme patriotism in the defense of freedom is no crime and let me respectfully remind you that pusillanimity in the pursuit of justice is no virtue in a Roman." "Perhaps I should have quoted the true author of that statement verbatim," Goldwater mused.[35]

To define himself as the sort of "extremist" we might tolerate in the White House, Goldwater needed first to redefine the meaning of the word, then lodge that new meaning deep in our vocabulary by illustrating it in ways we would welcome. "If it is extreme to stand for a solvent Social Security System," he might have said, "if it is extreme to maintain Eisenhower's policy of permitting the NATO commander to control the use of low-yield nuclear weapons, if it is extreme to demand that a U.S. Senator spurn expensive gifts from the Bobby Bakers of the world, then Eisenhower was an extremist, most Americans are extremists, and I am an extremist." Instead, Goldwater permitted us to read our own pejorative definition into the word "extremism" and to hear him endorse something we abhorred in the name of defense of liberty.

Print ads did try and fail to redeem this new definition of extremism. After quoting Goldwater's convention statement on extremism, "Fighting Aces for Goldwater" declared in a print ad "We were extremists." For seven paragraphs, the ad uses extreme as an adjective before employing it as a noun. In their redefining of terms, moderation means appeasement, while extremism means service, sacrifice, and self-defense.

To defuse attacks on Goldwater's advocacy of extremism, the ad tried to draw American fighting men, JFK, and even Harry Truman into the bull's eye, by associating each with an act the ad defines as extreme. Under a list of their names the aces told why they supported "Barry."

The above were called upon by the Nation to take EXTREME action in time of war. In the service of our country we took the lives of the enemy—the most EXTREME action one man can take against another. And many of our friends gave the most EXTREME sacrifice possible—their lives.

We are airmen and have flown against the enemy in everything from French supplied Nieuports to modern jets. We have seen the face of war—WE DON'T LIKE IT. . . .

Some of us flew in World War II—the product of MODERATION at Munich—and this time over every continent of the globe in a war that was brought on through appeasement and unpreparedness. President Franklin Delano Roosevelt promised that no American soldiers would set foot on foreign shores.

Again the young men of America went to war and many paid the EXTREME price in maimed bodies and death. We witnessed with our own eyes the bitter price paid for appeasement and saw our hard won victory dissipated.

On January 30, 1949, a young veteran of the war in the Pacific—John Fitzgerald Kennedy—spoke for all the EXTREME young men who fought for their Nation when he said ". . . what our young men had saved, our diplomats and our president have frittered away."

For the third time in fifty years, we again took to the air in Korea against the Communist enemy, which drew its strength from our weakness. We were called on to be EXTREMISTS for police action in Korea by Harry S. Truman—a President who knows what EXTREMISM is. It was he—in order to save the lives of hundreds of thousands of Americans and Japanese—who courageously ordered the first and only atomic bombings in history.[37]

What undercuts the ad's pasteurization of "extremism" is its endorsement of the specific sentiments that have caused public concern about a Goldwater presidency. "We have continually been assured that we cannot hope to meet the enemy man for man, but that our technology insures our security. Then why don't we use our technological advantage and win in Vietnam?" it asks. The question combines with the ad's endorsement of Truman's "courageous" decision to drop the atom bomb to suggest that Goldwater might indeed favor use of low-yield atomic weapons to defoliate Vietnam. The same troubling possibility emerges from a section of the ad framed by the question "WAR MONGERS? Who? The boys now fighting in Viet Nam? Or those of us who have fought previous wars? Or those of us who want our Nation to win if we do get into war? Or those of us who want to provide our military with whatever weapons they need to win a war?" Again the echo of Goldwater's claim that the bomb is "merely another weapon." Again the hint that use of the nuclear bomb is a plausible strategic option.

By lacing its claims with the rhetoric of the right, the ad also gratuitously distances its supporters from the population at large. To the authors of the ad, FDR is a villain. To the populace, he is a hero. When the ad drops in an old attack of FDR's broken campaign pledge not to send American soldiers to foreign shores, it converts no one and alienates those who remember FDR fondly. Additionally, the ad's language betrays its ideology by indicting "appeasement and unpreparedness," and "communist slavery," claiming that "We were denied that victory [in Korea] along with the chance to eliminate the Communist cancer in Asia," and condemning as "war mongers" those who "prey on the charitable Godliness of the inexperienced." Instead of minimizing fears about Goldwater, by, for example, pointing out that it was during Democratic administrations that the U.S. became involved in all four of its twentieth century wars, the ad's lines of argument and the style in which they were couched glorified the wars and attacked those who had opposed them.

"The charge of extremism was hung on Goldwater during the primary period and lasted throughout the entire campaign," reported Goldwater's pollster. "Johnson managed to pre-empt the middle of the road in the minds of voters. . . . Far more saw Johnson as moderate or conservative than as liberal, and about 3 people in 10 tagged Goldwater as radical."[38]

In the general election, the legacy of images left by the primaries and the convention was Goldwater's bane and Johnson's blessing. The most difficult attitudes to jar are those formed over a long period of time and reinforced by many discrete pieces of information perceived to be trustworthy. For almost half a year Republicans had battered Goldwater. During that time Goldwater inadvertently had corroborated their claims. A Republican attack on a fellow Republican is more credible than an attack by a Democrat. And the thoroughness with which Rockefeller and Scranton had mined Goldwater's record left few wounds bandaged. Johnson was thus in the enviable position of simply repeating what Republicans had said about the man who would become their party's nominee.

In a futile effort to mend fences that had been splintered during the primaries and smashed at the convention, the Republicans convened a "unity conference" at Scranton's invitation in Hershey, Pennsylvania, on August 12. In attendance were Goldwater, Republican governors and gubernatorial candidates, Nixon, and Eisenhower. Goldwater assured the conferees that "I seek the support of no extremist—of the left or of the right. I have far too much faith in the good sense and stability of my fellow Republicans to be impressed by talk of a so-called 'extremist takeover' of the party."[39]

This conciliatory conference and Goldwater's public moves to disavow extremism led Lyndon Johnson to conclude that Goldwater might manage to march away from his own past. Johnson corroborated that conclusion with intelligence received from friends in Congress including moderate Republicans whom Johnson aide Bill Moyers describes as "alarmed" by the prospect of a Goldwater presidency. As Moyers explains, the prospect that Goldwater might moderate his positions was among the factors that led to the Democratic plan to open the campaign with anti-Goldwater advertising:

> After the Republican convention, the president called me and said "Barry is making a headlong race for respectability. He's trying to shed himself of all of the convictions, beliefs, images and the extremism that had surrounded him all of his career in the Senate and characterized his speeches to the right wing." The president would often get reports of the speeches that Barry Goldwater was making to his right wing groups. He said "He's a nice man but in the political arena he does not represent the respectable element and he's trying to make himself respectable. What we've got to do is remind people of what Barry Goldwater was before he was nominated for president." I passed that word to Lloyd [Wright] and to the Doyle Dane Bernbach people. They came back with the Daisy ad which in one fell swoop seemed to do what it would have taken dozens or hundreds of other ads and speeches and literature to do. That was to remind people that Barry Goldwater had spoken loosely and lightly and recklessly about the overarching issue of nuclear power.[40]

The unity conference also prompted the Democrats to move up the starting date of their advertising. On August 13 Wright wrote to Moyers: "We are convinced that the proposed approach will keep Goldwater from covering up his extremist stands, [his] irresponsibility, etc. That's why the campaign is proposed to start earlier than originally conceived. If we fail to do this, he will have freedom to pursue the course launched yesterday at the Unity Conference—appearing to moderate his stands and assume the offensive in the campaign."[41]

Goldwater's talent for the poetic faux pas was a godsend for Johnson's adteam, which created ads based on Goldwater's statements about lobbing missiles into the men's room of the Kremlin, selling TVA, and sawing off the Eastern Seaboard. Of the three, two aired: those showing the auctioning of TVA and the sawing off of the Eastern Seaboard.

Johnson also exploited the public's revulsion at the convention's treatment of Rockefeller when, speaking to a group of young people in an October 24 telecast, he said that "a great strength of the two-party system is that basically we have been in general agreement on many things and neither party has been the party of extremes or radicals, but temporarily some extreme elements have come into one of the parties

Still from a television ad based on Goldwater's statements produced by Doyle Dane Bernbach for the Johnson campaign and aired during the general election of 1964.

and have driven out or locked out or booed out or heckled out the moderates. . . . I think an overwhelming defeat for them will be the best thing that could happen to the Republican party. . . . Because then you would restore moderation to that once great party of Abraham Lincoln and the leadership then could unite and present a solid front to the world."[42] While revivifying public memories of Republican treatment of Rockefeller, statements such as this also underscored the traditional meanings of "extremism" and "moderation" in ways that recalled Goldwater's controversion of them in his acceptance speech.

Subsequently, a skillfully produced Democratic ad symbolized not only Goldwater's self-destructive talent for poetic but inappropriate imagery but also reminded Rockefeller and his supporters that the Republicanism of Goldwater did not embrace their own. In it, the Eastern Seaboard of a model of the United States was slowly sawed off. As it dropped into the water below and began to float away, the announcer reminded viewers of Goldwater's belief that the country would be better off were the Eastern Seaboard cut off. As president, could such a person serve all the people justly and fairly? the ad asked. By running the ad primarily on the East Coast the Democrats reminded Easterners of the contempt in which Goldwater held them. At the same time the ad set one wing of the party against the other by inviting moderates to recall Goldwater's dismissal of Rockefeller's politics as the "true-to-form eastern seaboard Republican approach."[43] There was a place in Johnson's America for Rockefeller Republicans, implied the ad; there was none in Goldwater's America. President Johnson is president of all the people, the ad said.

In his speech accepting the vice-presidential nomination, Hubert Humphrey drew the contrast between the Democratic and Republican conventions of 1964. "President Johnson has helped to make the Democratic Party the only truly national party," he said. "And this Convention demonstrates our strong and our abiding unity and brotherhood. (*Applause*) What a contrast, what a contrast with the shambles at the Cow Palace in San Francisco. What a contrast with that incredible spectacle of bitterness, of hostility, of personal attack." In Chicago, and during the subsequent campaign four years later, as jeers from anti-war protestors made it impossible on many occasions for Humphrey to be heard by his audiences, these words would take on an ironic echo.

Repeating the Charges of Rockefeller, Romney, and Scranton

"We felt in the initial planning stages of the advertising campaign," recalls Lloyd Wright who, as Moyers' aide, supervised the planning and execution of the Democratic advertising, "that we would need to mount an anti-Goldwater phase built on the trigger-happy image that his votes and conduct had developed."[44] This was the stage at which Democratic treasurer Richard Maguire talked of preparing material that "rips Goldwater."[45] On July 11 representatives of the agency and of the White House agreed to develop a "series of 'rip Goldwater' commercials, both 5-minute and 60-second."

After this first anti-Goldwater phase, says Wright, "we'd move quickly into a pro-Johnson phase. By that point we figured the election would have been decided but we'd be faced with a complacent attitude on the part of voters who might assume it's over and stay at home. So we figured we'd need an intensive get out the vote effort at the end. We diminished the amount of time devoted to the anti-Goldwater phase dramatically when the first phase proved so effective."

Central to the anti-Goldwater phase were dramatic, visual reminders of Republican attacks on Goldwater. "Back in July in San Francisco the Republicans held a Convention," said one ad as the camera panned a confetti-littered floor. "Remember him?" A placard with Rockefeller's picture on it is raised from the litter. "He was there. Governor Rockefeller. Before the convention, he said 'Barry Goldwater's positions can and I quote 'spell disaster for the party and for the country.' " "Or him?" the announcer asks, as a placard showing Scranton's picture is lifted. "Governor Scranton. The day before the convention, he called Gold-

waterism a 'crazy quilt collection of absurd and dangerous positions.' "
"Or this man?" Litter from the convention floor is brushed from a
Romney placard. "Governor Romney? In June he said Goldwater's
nomination would lead to the quote 'suicidal destruction of the Republican party.' So even if you're a Republican with serious doubts about
Barry Goldwater, you're in good company." At the ad's end, the three
salvaged placards stand as sentinels defending the electorate from Barry
Goldwater, the man presumably responsible for dashing them to the
ground. In the judgment of Goldwater's deputy research director and
advertising coordinator Charles Lichenstein, the ad was effective. "Their
floor of the convention ad with all of the broken banners and posters
made it appear as if we had smashed the Republican Party and grabbed
the nomination," he notes.

Newspaper ads also replayed Republican attacks on Goldwater under
the heading "Here's What They Say." Radio too pounded home the
message. A radio ad for Johnson quoted extensively from Scranton's
letter to Goldwater. The announcer concluded: "Now Mr. Scranton isn't
a Democrat. He's the Republican governor of Pennsylvania. But a
Democrat couldn't have said it any better." Although overtures were
made to Goldwater's defeated rivals, only Scranton and Margaret Chase
Smith responded by campaigning with a modicum of enthusiasm for

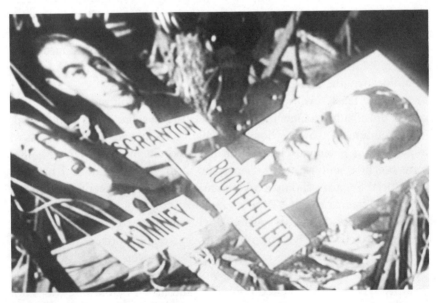

Still from a television ad produced by Doyle Dane Bernbach for the Johnson
campaign and aired in the 1964 general election.

Goldwater. Rockefeller, who had savaged Goldwater in the primaries and in turn had been scorned at the convention, in the words of Goldwater's research director Edward McCabe, "simply sat the election out."[46] The Republicans, McCabe explains, did not ask Scranton to appear in ads countering those using his words against Goldwater because they wanted to keep the campaign focused on Goldwater and Miller and because they did not want to legitimize the charges by "ventilating" them.

By replaying attacks levied by Republicans, Johnson's strategists insulated him from a backlash that could have resulted if the public concluded that the attacks were unfair. The strategy also minimized the evidentiary demands on Johnson. Since the conclusions are those of Scranton, Romney, and Rockefeller, they, not Johnson, are responsible for warranting the claims with evidence.

Goldwater Would Wreck Social Security

Two Democratic broadcast ads charged that Barry Goldwater would destroy Social Security. Since Goldwater had never said "I would destroy Social Security" but had instead argued that it would be strengthened if made voluntary, the Democrats were faced with the need to prompt the inference that a voluntary system would in effect destroy Social Security. Accordingly, one televised ad noted that "on at least seven occasions, Senator Barry Goldwater said he would change the present Social Security system. But even his running mate William Miller admits that Senator Goldwater's voluntary plan would destroy your Social Security. President Johnson is working to strengthen Social Security. Vote for Him on November 3." So in the ad Miller, not Johnson, claims that Goldwater would destroy the Social Security system.

"On at least seven different occasions Barry Goldwater has said he would drastically change the Social Security system," says another ad. The evolution of the storyboard reveals the Democrats in the process of moving from a factual claim to an unsupported inference. In its initial form the first sentence read "Time and again Barry Goldwater has said that Social Security should be voluntary." True. The second version expands the claim to read "Time and again Barry Goldwater has said that the present Social Security system should be changed." Still true. But in its final form the passive voice becomes active and words are imputed to Goldwater that he never said. "On at least seven different occasions Barry Goldwater has said that he would drastically change the Social Security system." In the cited interviews and articles Goldwater does not say that he would drastically change the Social Security system. The

Democratic inference that making it voluntary constitutes a drastic change does not sanction putting that inference in Goldwater's mouth.

The ad then offers what appears to be documentary evidence of its claim that Goldwater said he would drastically change Social Security. "In a Chatanooga Tennessee *Times,* in a "Face the Nation" interview, in the *New York Times* magazine, in a continental classroom TV interview, in the New York *Journal American,* in a speech he made only last January in Concord, New Hampshire, and in the *Congressional Record.* Even his running mate William Miller admits that Barry Goldwater's voluntary plan would wreck your Social Security." The camera cuts from the newspapers, the tapes, and the *Congressional Record* that have been laid one atop the other to Johnson delivering his acceptance speech: "Too many have worked too long and too hard to see this threatened now by policies that promise to undo all that we have done together over all these years." "For over thirty years," adds the announcer, "President Johnson has worked to strengthen Social Security. Vote for him on November 3." By showing such supposed evidence as a newspaper as the *New York Times* interview is cited and a reel filled with 2″ video tape as the continental classroom tape is mentioned, the ad objectifies its claims. In the process it misleads, for the articles laid on the table are props, not actual documents containing Goldwater's claims.

On radio the Democrats filled in the premise missing in the TV ads. The radio ads explained how Goldwater's voluntary plan would wreck Social Security. These radio ads "came about because I and others at the White House charged by the president with making our advertising effective but honest called over a group of Social Security experts and asked how we could deal with this issue in advertising in the most responsible way"[47] says Moyers. One of these radio ads says:

> Barry Goldwater wants to pick your pocket and he's asking you to help him do it. He's after the most valuable thing in your wallet, your Social Security card. Your card represents money that you've already worked for, money that's been put aside for you until you're too old to work. How's Mr. Goldwater going to pick that card right out of your wallet? With his voluntary Social Security plan. You see, employers pay 1/2 of the cost of Social Security. Think you'll get hired if you volunteer for it while the next man in line doesn't? Barry Goldwater's plan means the end of Social Security, the end of widow's pensions, the end of the dignity that comes with being able to take care of yourself without depending on your children. On November 3, vote for keeping Social Security.

What Goldwater had claimed was that he thought Social Security should be voluntary. "My position was clear," he wrote after the campaign. "I said I wanted to make Social Security solvent, to improve it.

The first thing wrong with Social Security is the fact that it is compulsory. Secondly, it is not actuarially sound; it promises more benefits to more people than the income or premiums collected will provide."[48] Assessment of the honesty of the Democratic claim that Goldwater wants to pick the Social Security card from your pocket then hinges on whether a voluntary plan would destroy Social Security. The questions raised by Goldwater's opponents justified the inference that it might well. Wouldn't the young opt for the voluntary plan, thus depriving the system of the funds that support the old? Wouldn't the upper and middle classes abandon Social Security, leaving the poor whose contributions could not sustain it? Wouldn't employers refuse to hire those who opted for the status quo, thus providing an incentive for leaving the present system?

"There was at that time a substantial body, a dominant body of thought that once you opened up Social Security to be voluntary in even the smallest measure you would wreck Social Security," says Moyers. "Before Barry Goldwater even came along, a substantial and distinguished body of opinion had concluded that making it voluntary would wreck Social Security."*

Repeatedly, Goldwater responded that he did not want to wreck Social Security but to strengthen it. In support of this claim, in both print and TV ads he pointed to his record of voting for every Social Security measure that had come before Congress. In a televised ad Senator Margaret Chase Smith, who had herself sought the presidency in 1964, testified that she "knew" that Goldwater supported Social Security. She had been present in the Senate when "time and again" he voted to strengthen it. In closing, Smith noted that Goldwater had voted for the most recent Social Security increase.

Smith marshaled the same defense in the "Brunch with Barry" aired October 23. On that program she displayed Goldwater's votes on Social Security as officially preserved in congressional documents. As an older woman, Smith could speak credibly about an issue of special concern to older Americans, particularly to older women, most of whom outlive their husbands. As a senator, Smith could provide credible testimony about Goldwater's senatorial actions. The ad inoculated. It exposed the audience to the claim that Goldwater would destroy Social Security, rebutted it, and built a base of believable, supportive information to sustain the rebuttal.

---

*Political scientist Benjamin Page disagrees: "It was by no means obvious, for example, that to make Social Security voluntary would 'wreck,' 'destroy,' or 'bankrupt' the system; experts were not all agreed, and the consequences would have depended upon what sort of voluntariness was provided—whether the option of no pension coverage at all was allowed, or merely a choice between public and private plans."[50]

Additionally, as Hess notes, Goldwater issued twenty-two major statements on Social Security and supported Social Security in each of four of five whistle stops per day.[49] On November 1 full page ads on Goldwater's stand on Social Security appeared in major papers. The existence of these defensive claims in the paid programming and stump speeches of the final weeks suggests that the first phase of the Johnson advertising strategy had accomplished its objective. Goldwater's simultaneous assurances that he was not trigger happy indicate that the campaign was being fought on terrain chosen and landscaped by Johnson. At the same time the fact that Johnson refused to dignify charges of corruption and moral decay with discussion suggested that the second phase of Goldwater's advertising strategy had failed to shift the campaign away from attacks on Barry Goldwater to attacks on Lyndon Johnson.

Despite the assurances of Goldwater and Smith, in the words of the Republican pollster, "many millions of voters—particularly the elderly and union families—held to their conviction that Goldwater was a foe of the Social Security system."*[51]

Goldwater Is Not in the Mainstream of His Party

In the campaigns we have studied since the rise of television, the Democratic nominee has capitalized on the numerical advantage his party has in voter registration and party preference by stressing that he is a Democrat. In 1964 Johnson broke with this practice to run a mass media campaign in which his party affiliation was barely whispered. He did this to underscore his claim to be the candidate of all the people, a claim whose corollary was that Goldwater was outside the mainstream of American two-party politics. The theme was previewed in Johnson's acceptance speech at the Convention:

> Most Democrats and most Republicans in the United States Senate . . . voted for the Nuclear Test Ban Treaty. But not Senator Goldwater, the temporary Republican spokesman. (*Applause*)

> Most Democrats and Republicans in the Senate voted for an eleven and a half billion dollar tax cut for the American citizens and American business—but not Senator Goldwater.

> Most Democrats and Republicans in the Senate, in fact four-fifths of the members of his own party, voted for the Civil Rights Act—but not Senator Goldwater.

*Residing in some of the statements on Social Security exploited in the Democratic ads is the same problem that plagued Goldwater's statement on extremism in his acceptance address and his statement on use of low-yield atomic weapons for defoliation of Vietnam. The statements that condition his claims are separated from them.

Most Democrats and Republicans in the Senate voted for the establishment of the United States Arms Control and Disarmament Agency that
seeks to slow down the nuclear arms race among the nations—but not
Senator Goldwater. . . .

Most Democrats and most Republicans in the Senate voted for the
National Defense Education Act—but not Senator Goldwater.

And my fellow Americans, most Democrats and most Republicans in
the Senate voted to help the United Nations in its peace keeping functions when it was in financial difficulty—but not Senator Goldwater.

Yes, my fellow Americans, it is a fact that the temporary Republican
spokesman is not in the mainstream of his party. In fact, he has not even
touched the shore. (*Applause*)

The contention that Goldwater was not really a Republican spawned
print and broadcast ads in which Republicans explained why they were
voting for Johnson. In an ad appearing in the *Los Angeles Times,* the
Chicago Tribune, and the *New York Times* Billy Rose wrote in part:

As for Barry Goldwater, let me make it clear that I think the store-
keeper from Arizona is an attractive, personable gentleman, and some
of the things he advocates are worth pondering. However, on certain
life-and-death matters, I'm uncertain where he stands, and I'm not certain that he's entirely certain himself. He reminds me of a line in one of
Stephen Leacock's "Nonsense Novels"—"Lord Ronald flung himself on
his horse and rode off madly in all directions." . . .

A President who shoots from the hip and lip would involve a bigger risk
than I care to assume. I'd be a lot more comfortable if the man on our
end of the Hot Line were as flexible as he is rigid, as conciliatory as he
is tough, and somewhat more egghead than hot-head . . .

I'M COMFORTABLE WITH LYNDON JOHNSON and so I'm going to vote for
him.[52]

"Republicans for Johnson" invited Republicans to split their tickets
to vote for Johnson. "In Our Heads We Know *He's Wrong*" said one
print ad.[53] Their recommendation was rooted in "loyalty" to their party.
"As loyal Republicans, we can see no reason to support a man who
rejects every tradition of our party . . . Sorry, Senator Goldwater, but
this time we'll have to split the ticket."

An actor, whom the ad identified as a Republican, made the same
case in a five minute televised ad, created by Doyle Dane Bernbach.
Apart from the importance of its appeal to Republicans and the reassurance it offered conservative Democrats, the ad is important for its defiant
break from the conventions of propositional discourse.

Historically, audiences have assessed political argument by standards
applicable both to essays and to public speeches. Among other things we
ask what arguments are being made, what evidence supports them,

whether they are structurally coherent, and what credibility the speaker or author brings to or develops within the rhetorical act. For the same reasons that Joyce's stream-of-consciousness narrative frustrates traditional literary criticism, ads that transport us by associated images frustrate attempts to apply the traditional standards of speech criticism.

The five minute "Confession of a Republican" is a rambling expression of an emotionally arrived at state of mind, not of a set of propositional claims. Structurally, the ad has the coherence of a ball of yarn wound from many multicolored threads.

Looking into the camera, the Republican actor in the ad says:

I don't know just why they wanted to call this a confession. I certainly don't feel guilty about being a Republican. [He has now distanced himself from the ad's ostensible creators and sponsors, an act which hints that this is not a scripted ad.] I've always been a Republican. My father is. His father was. My whole family is a Republican family. I voted for Dwight Eisenhower the first time I ever voted. I voted for Nixon the last time. But when we come to Senator Goldwater, now it seems to me we're up against a very different kind of a man.

This man scares me. Now maybe I'm wrong. A friend of mine has said to me: "Listen. Just because a man sounds a little irresponsible during a campaign doesn't mean he's going to act irresponsibly." You know the theory, the White House makes the man. I don't buy that.

You know what I think makes a president. Aside from his judgment, his experience, are the men behind him. His advisers, the cabinet. So many men with strange ideas are working for Goldwater. You hear a lot about what these guys are against. They seem to be against just about everything but what are they for?

The hardest thing for me about this whole campaign is to sort out one Goldwater statement from another. A reporter'll go to Senator Goldwater and he'll say "Senator on such and such a day you said I quote blah blah blah, whatever it is, end quote." And then Goldwater says "Well, I wouldn't put it that way." I can't follow that. Was he serious when he did put it that way? Is he serious when he says he wouldn't put it that way. I, I, I, just don't get it. A president ought to mean what he says.

President Johnson, now Johnson at least is talking about facts. He says we got the tax cut bill and because of that you get to carry home x number of dollars every paycheck. You got the nuclear test ban and because of that there is x percent less radioactivity in the food. But Goldwater often you can't I can't figure out just what Goldwater means by the things he says. I read now where he says a wave, a craven fear of death is sweeping across America. What is that supposed to mean? If he means that people don't want to fight a nuclear war, he's right, I don't. But I read some of these things Goldwater says about total victory. I get a little worried, you know? I wish, I wish I was as sure that Goldwater is against war as I am that he's against some of these other things. I wish I could believe that he has the imagination to be able to just shut his eyes and picture what this country would look like after a nuclear war.

Sometimes I wish I'd been at that Convention in San Francisco. I mean I wish I'd been a delegate. I really do. Because I would have fought you know I wouldn't have worried so much about party unity because if you unite behind a man you don't believe in—a lie—I tell you those people who got a hold of that Convention—who are they?

I mean when the head of the Ku Klux Klan with all those weird groups come out in favor of the candidate of my party either they're not Republicans or I'm not. I thought about just not voting in this election, just staying home but you can't do that because that's saying you don't care who wins and I do care. I think my party made a bad mistake in San Francisco and I'm going to have to vote against that mistake on the third of November.

ANNOUNCER: Vote for President Johnson on November 3. The stakes are too high for You to Stay Home.

Unlike those accusing him of wanting to sell the TVA and make Social Security voluntary, this Johnson ad does not indict Goldwater for specific stands. Instead it implies that there is an illusive something wrong with Goldwater himself: he is taking contradictory positions; his explanations do not explain; his clarifications do not clarify. If that perception takes hold, then Goldwater's specific attempts to defend his positions will aggravate rather than allay public unease about him.

What such interested citizens as the Republican in the five minute ad and Billy Rose could not argue persuasively was what the presidency actually demanded of a president. Additionally, neither could warrant their support for Johnson in a kind of personal experience denied the electorate at large. When a former member of Eisenhower's cabinet announced his support for Johnson, the Democrats had a person uniquely suited to make claims ordinary citizens could not make both about Johnson and about the burdens and requirements of the presidency. In a print ad that never mentioned Goldwater's name, Robert B. Anderson, who served both as Eisenhower's Secretary of the Navy and Secretary of the Treasury, declared his reasons for voting for Lyndon Johnson.[54] Arguing that he had had "the privilege of knowing and working" with Johnson "(a great part of the time as a member of the opposition) since 1935," Anderson praised Johnson's character and competence. In the process he magnified the difficulty of the job of president. "As the principal arsenal of free men," he wrote, "we have the absolute responsibility of determining whether or not the awesome weapons of destruction should or should not be employed. These are the kinds of responsibility that weigh relentlessly upon the chief executive of our country. There is no burden in all the world that is comparable. The demands are superhuman." In contrast to

Goldwater's appeal to the heart, Anderson appealed to reason. "I cannot bring myself to a denunciation of those who might differ with my judgment, but I can only appeal to the reasoning of every man and woman who must make the same responsible choice that all of us are making now. I have made my choice for President Johnson. In the interest of our country, the community of free nations and the welfare of mankind, I hope that in your heart, in your mind and in your conscience, you will do the same."

The argument that Goldwater was an alien in his own party was also made in a never aired ad that linked him to the Ku Klux Klan. That ad showed Klansmen, played by actors, marching in hooded robes. A burning cross was superimposed over the images as was a picture of the Klan wizard. A quotation from a Klan leader opposing "Judaism," "Catholicism," "Niggerism," and "all the other isms of the world" was read. The Klan's endorsement of Goldwater was noted. Why are these people supporting Goldwater? was the question asked in the ad. Since Goldwater had on two occasions repudiated Klan support, running the ad was freighted with both ethical and political liabilities. On the grounds that it used "guilt by association," the campaign staff finally suppressed it after it had reached final finished form and after preliminarily OK'ing it for regional airing. "It strained the available evidence, it was going too far," explained one Johnson staffer.[55]

The Presidency Is too Important a Job to Entrust It to Someone Like Goldwater

The Democratic ads magnified the importance of the office of president and correlatively belittled Goldwater. In one, a phone buzzes and buzzes. As the camera closes in on it we see that it is the "White House" phone. The announcer intones: "This particular phone only rings in a serious crisis. Keep it in the hands of a man who has proven himself responsible". One might well ask why isn't Johnson answering the phone in this simulated crisis, but the more important point is that the public is being reminded in yet another form that the president answers the red phone and presses the nuclear button.

Magnification of the office would undercut Johnson's candidacy unless he was perceived as up to the job, so other ads made that case. A still montage ad composed of black and white pictures of LBJ in the Oval Office transformed the man who lifted his beagles by their ears into a graceful and dignified president. The announcer says: "The Constitution does not tell us what kind of a man a president must be. It says he must be 35 years old and a natural born citizen. It leaves the rest to the wisdom of the voters. Our presidents have been reasonable men. . . . They have cared about people for the pieces of paper on which they sign their names change peoples lives. Most of all in the final loneliness of this room, they have been prudent."

Like the others, this ad invites enthymematic complicity from an audience primed by Rockefeller, Scranton, and now Johnson to believe that Goldwater is unreasonable, imprudent, and uncaring. "Subliminally," says Moyers, "it was designed to remind people that Johnson was a man of great legislative stature and had held the office for almost a year. By contrast, Barry Goldwater was an interloper."

Print ads carried the same message. Lawyers for Johnson-Humphrey stated that Johnson and Humphrey "have the dedication, the experience, the responsibility and the restraint to assure the integrity of the institutions of our government, to continue our economic well being, to increase justice for all and to advance our efforts toward world peace. Unfortunately, their opponents do not."[56]

Goldwater May Start a Nuclear War

The oblique fashion in which the Democrats argued that Goldwater was more likely than Johnson to start a nuclear war or use nuclear weapons in an existing war whispered their fear that such a claim might be dismissed out of hand as unbelievable or worse as believable but so disquieting that the audience is moved to shoot the messenger who carried it.

The most controversial ad aired in 1964 and arguably the most controversial ad in the history of political broadcasting never mentions either Goldwater's name or any statement he has made about anything. It opens on a female child dressed in a jump suit standing in an open field plucking the petals from a daisy as she counts "1,2,3,4,5,7,6,6,8,9." The authenticity of the child derives in large part from the fact that she counts as children do—with numbers out of proper order. She sounds like a child because she counts like a child, a testiment to the talents of Tony Schwartz who created the conjoined countdowns. When she reaches "9," a Cape Canaveral voice begins a countdown of its own—no longer innocent but ominous. Here is the efficient, straightforward, willful act of an adult: "10,9,8,7,6,5,4,3,2,1, zero." At zero the camera, which throughout this second countdown has been closing on the child's face, dissolves from her eye to a mushroom cloud that expands until it envelops the screen. Lyndon Johnson's voice is heard stating a lesson that could be drawn from the Sermon on the Mount: "These are the stakes. To make a world in which all of God's children can live, or to go into the dark. We must either love each other or we must die."

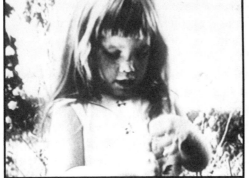

The famous Daisy ad conceived by Tony Schwartz for Doyle Dane Bernbach was aired once by the Johnson campaign in the 1964 general election.

The history of this ad has been amply replayed. Projecting their predispositions into the ad, audiences remembered hearing Goldwater's name and a specific attack on his policies when neither was actually in the ad itself. Tony Schwartz, who conceived the idea for the ad and produced its sound track, explains: "It was comparable to a person going to a psychiatrist and seeing dirty pictures in a Rorschach pattern. The Daisy commercial evoked [as its responsive chord] Goldwater's pro-bomb statements. They were like the dirty pictures in the audience's mind."[57] The ad was aired only once on "Monday Night at the Movies" on September 7.

The idea for the ad grew from Schwartz's fascination with the world of numbers. In keeping with this interest, he had created an ad for Polaroid using a child counting and had plans to create a record on the world of numbers. Prior to the time that Aaron Ehrlich of Doyle Dane Bernbach, who shot the spot, approached Schwartz about creating it, Schwartz had juxtaposed the sound of a child counting to ten with that of a countdown for an atomic explosion. "One symbolized the simplest and the other the most complex use of numbers in the world," Schwartz notes.

The reaction to the spot was immediate. "I was in the office the night it aired," Moyer recalls. "The president called me and said 'Holy shit. I'm getting calls from all over the country.' Most of them said that it was an effective ad. Others said they didn't like it. The White House switchboard lighted up. The president went on for a few minutes in an excited state and then said: 'But I guess it did what we Goddamned set out to do, didn't it.' I said 'I would think so.' " Johnson's special assistant Jack Valenti recalls Johnson telling him that he ordered the ad off the air.[58]

Although the Democrats had originally run the ad on one network, they planned within the next two or three days to air it on all three. Infuriated, the Republicans screamed bloody murder. "The first night it aired," recalls Wright, "it created such a media flap that the next night it was used in its entirety on the newscasts on all three networks. That was time we hadn't budgetted. It exposed the message. We didn't have to run it again."[59] "What is amusing now but wasn't then," says Goldwater's strategist Charles Lichenstein, "is that we gave the daisy ad so much publicity that it was shown over and over on news and commentary programs so a lot of people saw it who wouldn't have ordinarily seen it. We thought it was very damaging so obviously we demanded that it be withdrawn."[60] On behalf of the Goldwater campaign, Dean Burch filed a complaint with the Fair Campaign Practices Committee. "This horror-type commercial is designed to arouse basic emotions and has no place in campaign. I demand you call on the President to halt this smear attack on a United States Senator and the candidate of the Republican party for the Presidency," said Burch.[61] But the Republican protests were rendered moot when the Democrats quickly announced that they would not again air the ad.

The Daisy commercial was not the only ad played a single time but etched into the public consciousness by subsequent discussion and replay. In the second ad, aired on "Saturday Night at the Movies," September 12, a young girl is intently licking an ice cream cone. No exploding bombs will menace her activity. The danger that menaces this child is invisible. Even as it poisons her, she cannot taste the Strontium 90. But as the ad progresses we learn that thanks to the test-ban treaty the child can eat the ice cream without risk. But Goldwater opposed the treaty. So "if he's elected, they might start testing all over again."

The narrative is delivered by a soothing maternal voice, which may be the first use of female voiceover in a political ad. The female announcer reminds the child and us that by voting against the test-ban treaty Goldwater, in effect, endorsed Strontium 90 in the air and food. "Now there's a man who wants to be president of the United States and he doesn't like this treaty. He even voted against it. He voted to go on testing more bombs. His name is Barry Goldwater." But although the female voice is allowed to deliver the voiceover, the ad reverts to the supposedly more authoritative male voice to intone the usual tag.

The fears reflected in the ice cream cone ad mirrored public sentiment. "The big issue in the country was Strontium 90," says Moyers. "Mothers were marching. The dairy industry was greatly concerned. Kennedy had addressed it before his death. That issue played into our hands because Goldwater had called for more nuclear testing."

"They were both brilliantly devised commercials," concludes Lichenstein. "I admire Doyle Dane as skilled professionals for coming up with them. They were much more imaginative than anything we ever did." Goldwater remembers these two ads "with considerable horror".[62] At the time he declared that Americans "are horrified and the intelligence of Americans is insulted by weird television advertising by which this administration threatens the end of the world unless all-wise Lyndon Johnson is given the nation for his very own."[63]

The third ad in this series also used a female voiceover to describe the need for nuclear restraint as a pregnant woman and her daughter are seen strolling idyllically through a lush park. The ad is lyrical. Images of the woman dissolve over the long shots of the two of them. Since no scientific evidence had established that fallout harmed fetuses, Johnson's advisers refused to OK the storyboard. "I remember telling them 'no,' we would never do it." says Wright. "The agency personnel felt so strongly they went out and did it anyway. I saw it in New York and said 'I don't presume to speak for the whole campaign but that will never see the light

Still from a television ad created by Doyle Dane Bernbach but never aired in the election of 1964.

of day.' Bill [Moyers] and the others agreed. There was no body of evidence indicating that fallout would damage a fetus. Bombs do blow up people so the daisy ad was based in reality but this ad was going beyond the realm of accepted reality. It was straining for scare tactics."

The most dramatic of the anti-nuclear ads is a chilling five minute recreation of successive U.S. and Soviet bomb tests. It was, says Wright, "an attempt to visually portray the burgeoning arms race." The ad, whose sound was created by Tony Schwartz, alternates countdowns in English and Russian. At the end of each countdown a bomb explodes and mushrooms onto the screen as the counterpart countdown begins. One countdown follows another in progressively more rapid succession, until they are tumbling over each other simultaneously. The escalating madness stops as John Kennedy's voice announces that negotiations for the test ban treaty have been concluded, a subtle suggestion that a vote for Johnson is a vote to "Let us Continue," as he had promised we would following the assassination of Kennedy. Johnson's voice follows, reminding us that the test ban treaty has led us closer to peace and reduced the overall level of radioactivity. Then, in a veiled reference to Goldwater, Johnson says "those who oppose agreement to lessen the dangers of war curse the only light that can lead us out of the darkness. As long as I am your president I will work to bring peace to this world and the world of our children."

Wright was initially fearful that the "ad wouldn't hold the audience." The ad's continuing power to sustain audience interest suggests that that fear was misplaced.

In a final televised ad, a bomb explodes on the screen as an announcer suggests that Goldwater's attitude toward nuclear weapons is inappropriately casual. "On October 24, 1963, Barry Goldwater said of the nuclear bomb 'merely another weapon.' "Merely another weapon?" repeats the announcer incredulously.

Just as radio carried the details of Scranton's letter while television telegraphed the conclusions Romney, Rockefeller, and Scranton had reached about Goldwater, so too radio assumed the burden of setting in place Goldwater's specific statements on nuclear war and the bomb. Of these statements, used earlier by Rockefeller, the audience could make of the general anti-bomb televised spots specific indictments of a specific candidate. One such radio ad asked: "Is Mr. Goldwater bored with peace?" By imputing a motive to him, the question attempts to silence audience doubts that anyone would willingly precipitate nuclear war. In answer to its question the ad offers a series of statements reportedly made by Goldwater:

> Here are some of the statements he made from April 1959 to September 1963. Barry Goldwater on nuclear testing: "We must not again abandon nuclear testing."
>
> Barry on NATO: "NATO commanders in Europe should have the power to use tactical nuclear weapons on their own initiative."
>
> Barry in the space race: "I don't want to hit the moon. I just want to lob one into the men's room of the Kremlin."
>
> Barry on Vietnam: "I'd drop a low yield atomic bomb on the Chinese supply lines in North Vietnam."
>
> Barry on the bomb: "Merely another weapon."
>
> Barry on nuclear war: "I don't see how it can be avoided."
>
> Is Mr. Goldwater bored with peace? On November 3rd vote for President Johnson. The stakes are too high for you to stay home.

A pseudo-survey, and $100,000 worth of print ads promoting it, also reinforced the perception that Goldwater was dangerous. The magazine *Fact* asked 12,356 psychiatrists and social workers, none of whom had ever examined Goldwater, "Is Barry Goldwater psychologically fit to be President of the United States?" Of the 2,417 who responded, 1,189 said "no," 571 said they had insufficient evidence to form an opinion, and 657 said "yes." Ralph Ginsburg, publisher of *Fact,* promoted the October issue of the magazine, which included the findings, with ads declaring "1,189 Psychiatrists Say Goldwater Is Psychologically Unfit to be President!" The issue sold 160,000 copies.[64] Charging "deliberate character assassination," in September 1965 Goldwater sued Ginsburg. In May 1968, a Federal Court jury awarded Goldwater $75,000 in "punative damages." The AMA and American Psychiatric Association had condemned the survey as had Democratic National Committee Chairman John Bailey, the Republican National Committee, and the Fair Campaign Practices Committee.

The specific claim that Goldwater would use the bomb casually was made neither in radio nor television but in a print ad and a brochure that showed a nuclear explosion with the words "Goldwater's amazing problem solver" impressed over it. Then, like the radio ad, the printed material quoted Goldwater's statements on the use of nuclear weapons.

Efforts to magnify public fear about Goldwater's possible use of nuclear weapons were successful. A Michigan survey team heard 213 unfavorable comments to the effect that Goldwater was too militaristic to 2 about Johnson.[65] Goldwater's pollster found comparable evidence. "Probably most damaging to Goldwater was public acceptance of the idea that he was 'trigger happy.' . . . One of the prominent dimensions of the Goldwater image was 'acts without thinking.' This was most seriously translated—with the help of both his Democratic and Republican opposition—into the notion that he would be likely to involve the country in nuclear war. Even a sizeable number of Republicans and conservatives held this view."[66]

By indicting Goldwater for his inclination to "shoot from the hip" and for being "trigger happy," his opponents identified him with a mythic character from the Old West who invited trouble, whose aim was skewed by his impulsiveness, whose judgment was not trustworthy, who shot first and asked questions later. So, in mid-October, on a swing through the West, Johnson said, "We here in the West know how the West was won. It wasn't won by the man on the horse who thought he could settle every argument with a quick draw and a shot from the hip. We here in the West aren't about to turn in our sterling-silver American heritage for a plastic credit card that reads 'Shoot now, pay later.' "[67] The image of the rampaging cowboy had the advantage of personalizing the decision to use nuclear weaponry.

In an interview in *Der Speigel* published in the U.S. on July 11, Goldwater fueled his trigger-happy image. Asked about his supposed impulsiveness, Goldwater responded: "I possibly do shoot from the hip" but explained that his substantial exposure to problems in the U.S. Senate meant that "I don't have to stop and think in detail about them."[68]

Goldwater's campaign staff could not devise a means of muting the notion that he was trigger happy. "When I went to bed, if ever I could have just a few hours sleep, I would lie awake asking myself at night, how do you get at the bomb issue?" asked Goldwater's campaign director Denison Kitchel. "My candidate had been branded a bomb-dropper—and

I couldn't figure out how to lick it. And the advertising people, people who could sell anything, toothpaste or soap or automobiles—when it came to a political question like this, they couldn't offer anything either."[69]

A look at Goldwater's advertising explains his problem in 1964. Not only did Goldwater fight the campaign on ground that Johnson had chosen but he also magnified rather than downplayed the stands for which Johnson's ads indicted him. In his first paid half hour televised address, aired September 18, Goldwater tried to preempt the charges that he was trigger happy. "No one was happy with the speech." recalls Stephen Shedegg, Goldwater's Regional Director for Western states.[70] "It was defensive, it dealt in generalities, and it opened with Goldwater's repeating the charges his opponents were making, i.e. that he was impulsive, imprudent, and trigger-happy." In the speech Goldwater argued that the Republicans stood for "peace through preparedness. The Republican party is the party of peace—because we understand the requirements of peace, *and because we understand the enemy.*" he noted. The speech embodied the "Republican" posture toward Communism in an analogy in which the enemy was "the schoolyard bully." If he is permitted to push you around, "eventually you'll have to fight." But stand up to him and "he'll back down and there will be no fight."

An eight page advertisement in the October issue of *Reader's Digest* titled "Senator Goldwater Speaks Out On the Issues" also stressed "Peace through Strength." One flaw mars the otherwise effective ad. On page three, a typesetting error placed in bold faced type the claim "There is no greater lie." Also in bold face, the next sentence reads: "I am preoccupied with peace!" The typesetting error created the claim that Goldwater's preoccupation with peace was a great political lie!

On September 22, Eisenhower was called on to certify that Goldwater could be trusted with the presidency. The difficulties of the task were heightened by the fact that during the California primary Eisenhower had written an article for the Republican New York *Herald-Tribune* that seemed to oppose Goldwater's candidacy. The article offered a series of principles describing the ideology of an acceptable nominee. Those principles—support for civil rights and the UN, willingness to probe ways to lower barriers between east and west, avoidance of impulsiveness—seemed point by point to repudiate Goldwater's candidacy. By encouraging Scranton to run, Eisenhower had heaped additional damage on Goldwater's cause.

Consequently, Goldwater's strategists concluded that the public would not find a strong endorsement of Goldwater by Eisenhower convincing, and doubted, moreover, that Eisenhower would deliver a categorical endorsement if one were scripted for him. Accordingly, the Republicans used the forum "to knock down misperceptions about Goldwater" and "to develop a sense that Barry Goldwater was a decent, thoughtful, humane kind of guy." "Everyone knew that Eisenhower was not very enthusiastic about Goldwater," says Lichenstein, who supervised production and editing of the program, "and we felt that it would have been dishonest and not in keeping with Eisenhower's character or image to come on too strong as a pitchman."

In the "Conversation at Gettysburg," filmed at Eisenhower's farm and aired September 22, Ike and Goldwater engaged in a meandering discussion. The film opened with Eisenhower asking, "Well, Barry, you've been campaigning now for two or three weeks, how do you like it? And how does it seem to be going for you?," questions that set the tone of the conversation to follow. Missing was a decisive, unequivocal endorsement by Ike of Goldwater's candidacy. The closest Ike came was in response to Goldwater's assertion that "our" opponents have called us "warmongers." In an answer not only included in the program but edited into a TV ad of its own, Ike said:

> Well, Barry, in my mind this is actual tommyrot. Now, you've known about war, you've been through one. I'm older than you, I've been in more. But, I tell you, no man who knows anything about war is going to be reckless about it. Now, certainly the country recognizes in you a man of integrity, good will, honesty and dedication to his country. You're not going to be doing these things—what do they call it—push the button? I can't imagine anything you would give more careful thought to than the President's responsibility as the Commander-in-Chief of all our armed forces, and as the man conducting our foreign relations. I am sure that with this kind of an approach you will be successful in keeping us on the road to peace.

"The famous 'tommyrot' statement was the climax of the program, the one we were aiming toward," says Lichenstein. "It was a very effective close."

Still, even in that statement, Ike had not explicitly endorsed Goldwater but rather all men who know anything about war—a field that presumably included Lyndon Johnson. Ike had not said that he recognized Goldwater as a man of integrity and dedication but that the country "certainly" recognized in him these virtues; yet the country's doubts were what the Goldwater campaign was trying to allay in this broadcast. Instead of saying that he knew that Goldwater would give careful thought to his responsibilities as Commander-in-Chief, Ike said that he couldn't imagine anything Goldwater would give more thought to, not a strong recommendation for a candidate suspected by many of speaking before thinking. Finally, Ike noted that with "this approach," which he left undefined, Goldwater would be successful in keeping the country on the road to peace. What Ike said was not as damaging as what he left unsaid.

"The most charitable thing I can say about the film is that it wasn't effective," wrote Goldwater later.[71] A post-election questionnaire sent by Shadegg to the Republican convention delegates found only 20 percent expressing approval of the content of the "Conversation at Gettysburg." So pleased was Lyndon Johnson with the low ratings "Conversation" received that a few days after its airing he shared with newspersons the fact that its competitors, "Petticoat Junction" and "Peyton Place," had earned ratings of 27.4 and 25.0 to "Conversation at Gettysburg" 's 8.6.[72]

The "Conversation" was one of two half hour programs Lichenstein places in the first phase of the advertising on Goldwater's behalf. "At the beginning of the campaign we had a problem of beating back what we regarded as very dangerous misperceptions of certain policies and positions of Senator Goldwater. In that phase the advertising followed those themes." In addition to "Conversation" this phase included "a network half hour program using a question-and-answer technique we had used to great effect in the California primary."

But in Lichenstein's judgment this question-and-answer session, broadcast October 6, was less effective than its predecessor. "People in the campaign thought that it [the California format] wasn't slick enough to be used nationally. In slicking up the techniques [with rear screen projection of the questioners and arty camera work] its urgency and potency were greatly diminished." For example, one question was put by a truck driver whom viewers saw not in his truck but reflected in the truck's rearview mirror. Goldwater's delivery also seemed more stilted in the second program. In the earlier film, Goldwater had only seen and answered the questions in a single dry run before the final take. "In the national program we lost our nerve and over-edited it. It lost all spontaneity," says Lichenstein.

The questions asked in this program had an anti-Johnson edge to them. What could be done about the conflict between China and Russia? asked one. Was the war on poverty working? asked another. After indicting Johnson's policies, Goldwater set in place the Goldwater-Miller alternative. Short ads, using the same format, were also produced and aired later in the campaign.

During this first phase of the advertising campaign, Goldwater tried to put into context the charges raised against him. In one ad he argued, for example, that some had distorted his concern with Communism "to make it appear we are preoccupied with war. There is no greater political lie. I am trying to carry to the American people this plain message. This entire nation and entire world risk war in our time unless free men remain strong enough to keep the peace."

Meanwhile, the tidal wave generated by Goldwater's statement about empowering the commander of NATO to use nuclear weapons dissipated when news reporters confirmed that under both Eisenhower and Kennedy the NATO commander had held such power, a point also made by former Vice-President Nixon.[73] Still lingering, however, was the residual impression, whether correct or incorrect, that Goldwater had recommended that such power reside with "commanders" not "the commander."

Recognizing that they were on the defensive about Social Security and use of "the bomb," in early October the Republicans "decided to become more affirmative," says Lichenstein, "to go on the offensive and take the battle to Lyndon Johnson, to make him the issue rather than making Senator Goldwater the issue." The new direction was summarized in a seven-page plan titled "Operation Home Stretch: A Public Relations Strategy" written by Lou Guylay and approved by Goldwater's strategy committee on October 11. In the memo Guylay argued that "we have seen a shocking decline in political morality. . . . This has led to crime and violence on the street—a breakdown of law and order—terrorizing our people. Meanwhile in the world arena we have weakened ourselves and permitted our enemy to make gains all over. Our alliances are failing—the war in Vietnam persists. Cuba is a cancer spreading its poison throughout the Americas."[74] Advertising quickly reflected this new direction.

Morality in Government

A survey conducted by public opinion pollster Samuel Lubell discovered that as the campaign progressed the number of voters disquieted by Johnson's "personal honesty and by how the Bobby Baker case had been handled" was increasing.[75] Bobby Baker, one-time protégé of Lyndon Johnson's, had resigned his position as a Senate staffer after the leadership of the Senate asked him to explain how on a Senate salary of under $20,000 a year he had attained a net worth of over two million dollars. Charges of influence peddling filled the air in fall 1963 and with them the accusation that Lyndon Johnson had accepted a $500 stereo from Baker. The Senate began an investigation. Throughout the spring and summer of 1964 the Republicans hammered away at the Baker-Johnson link. When Billie Sol Estes, a Texas acquaintance of Johnson, was accused of duping the USDA in a complicated con game, his name too was added to the anti-Johnson litany.

Two factors disabled Goldwater's new themes. Since the public did not view Johnson as a direct accomplice in the acts of Bobby Baker or Billy Sol Estes, successful vilification of them did not necessarily redound to Johnson's disadvantage.

Additionally, the importance of a $500 stereo paled when compared with such issues as the abolition of Social Security and the destruction of the world in nuclear war. "We thought that the issues we were mounting were of such significance that the charges [about Baker and Estes] were insignificant by comparison and that the body politic would recognize it," says Wright. The Democratic rationale was sound for another reason. White explains:

> Bobby Baker had never been found guilty of anything—he was, after all, a rabbitlike man with a poor boy's cupidity who had made a lot of deals and some money, and the only thing one might possibly pin on him was the use of "broads." But politicians know that denouncing a man for "broads" is a dangerous matter; at one time or another, too many Americans, Republican and Democratic alike, have sinned with "broads." Billie Sol Estes was too complicated for more than a reference in an occasional speech. And Lyndon Johnson had in no sense ever been guilty of the "hard take."[76]

Equally as important, the five minute ads embodying Goldwater's new strategy were ineptly produced. "They were," explains Lichenstein, "an attempt to hype up and get the attention of the audience and then by contrast show the calm, cool, deliberate, statesmanlike manner of Senator Goldwater. Obviously they failed to convey that view. They were very poor."

In each, dramatic scenes forecast the topic of a brief speech by Goldwater. So, in one, as an announcer melodramatically declared "Crime: Juvenile Delinquency," an obviously staged riot between young men and helmuted police appeared. Their acting resembled that of apprentice stuntmen; punches did not connect with jaws and night sticks beat the air to no effect. The young men, hands over their heads, were then marched to the cattle car of a train. Whether the young men were to be condemned for rioting or the police for brutality, or both, was not clear.

The theme of morality also was embodied in footage of a gum chewing Billy Sol Estes who was paired with a caricature of Bobby Baker with his arm dipping into the Capitol dome. Neither image dramatized the acts of supposed corruption in which each had engaged. Moreover, neither Estes nor Baker looked menacing. Indeed Baker looked a bit like an errant schoolboy. Nothing in the ad justified the pontifical indictment "Corruption!" proclaimed by the announcer as the word pulsated on the screen in a fashion popularized later in the Batman series.

Stills from an ad aired by the Goldwater campaign in the 1964 general election.

Goldwater's theme of immorality in government gained an unexpected assist when, on October 7, presidential assistant Walter Jenkins was arrested on a morals charge. For a number of days, Johnson's associates managed to keep news of the arrest out of the papers arguing that he was a married man with children and had suffered an emotional collapse. Under pressure from Republicans, the story was printed October 14. A local Republican group responded with bumper stickers saying "Johnson is King and Jenkins is Queen." But the Republican advantage was short lived. On October 15, Khrushchev's ouster as Soviet head drove the arrest from the front pages and rendered obsolete a Goldwater ad juxtaposing children pledging allegiance to the flag with Khrushchev's

Stills from an ad aired by the Goldwater campaign in the 1964 general election.

threat to bury them. The following day, China exploded a nuclear device. As a result, the agenda of public and press shifted back to the grounds on which Goldwater was vulnerable—foreign affairs, more specifically, nuclear control and the sort of leadership required to deal with the new Soviet regime.

In a national telecast October 20 arguing that "the moral fiber of the American people is beset by rot and decay,"[77] Goldwater attempted to regain the ground the activities in China and Russia had cost him. Indicting the increase in rioting, juvenile delinquency, corruption in government, the Supreme Court's ruling on prayer in the schools, and the lenient treatment of criminals, the speech claimed that history demonstrated that immorality enters a society "from the top." Is this a time to "ban Almighty God from our schoolrooms?" Goldwater asked. Answering that it was not, he urged Congress to pass a Constitutional amendment to "rectify" the Supreme Court's decision. If elected, Goldwater promised to give every effort "to a reconstruction of reverence and moral strength."

The same themes reappeared in a controversial film. This half hour film called *Choice* was sponsored by a division of Citizens for Goldwater-Miller called Mothers for a Moral America. "Mothers" was, in the words of one Goldwater aide, "a front group" set up to sponsor controversial programming and pamphlets. *Choice* was indeed controversial. The film offered a "choice" between the "Twist," such "pornographic" books as *Call me Nympho, Men for Sale,* and *Jazz Me Baby,* a speeding Lincoln from whose window beer cans were hurled, strippers, riots, a fig-leaf clad male, and a model exhibiting a topless bathing suit—the presumed symbols of Johnson's America—and clean cut youths, the American flag, patriotic music, the Declaration of Independence, the Statue of Liberty, and pictures of the Republican nominee—symbols of Goldwater's America. The difference between the two Americas also manifests itself in the portion of the anatomy on which each focused: Johnson's America displayed itself in closeups of gyrating buttocks and twisting feet; Goldwater's in long shots of masses of white school children reciting the pledge of allegiance. Unlike the people in Goldwater's America, the smiles and laughter of the people in Johnson's America suggested that revelling in the "immoral twist" was fun. Sin is delightful, sanctity dour, was the subtextual message. But, most important, the role of blacks in the two Americas differed. In Goldwater's evocation of the past he wished to conserve, they are shown picking cotton! In Johnson's America, most of the blacks shown are rioters.

The film itself contained indictment after indictment of the status quo, which—whether intentionally or not—was tagged with Stevenson's 1956 slogan "The New America." Without saying it in so many words the film also argued that Johnson had profaned Kennedy's memory by transforming "ask not what your country can do for you, ask what you can do for your country" to "ask what you can take":

> New names hit the headlines. Names connected to the top. The papers call it the age of the fast deal. Angleman. Fixers. Private clubs and private girls. Fortunes made almost overnight in public service. [pictures of Bobby Baker and Billie Sol Estes]. . . . when the people do protest they get only one answer. "Put the lid on it." Turn off the lights at the White House but the lights, your lights, may not now be turned off across America. One very simple reason, it's no longer safe. The New America. Ask not what you can give but what you can take. . . . Demoralization, chaos, this is the changed other America that the people slowly wake up to. In eight short months there are more riots in the United States than in the last eight years. In the streets, the mobs, mobocracy. . . .

Citing scripture for its purpose the film argues that the day of reckoning is at hand. "And I will say to my soul, thou hast much goods laid up for many years. Take they rest. Eat, drink, make good cheer. But God said to him. 'Thou fool. This night do they require thy soul of thee.' This night is here. Now. Two Americas and you, you alone, stand in between them. Which do you really want? Which?" To assist "you" in the process of choosing, John Wayne, a rifle on the wall in back of him, urges "You've got the strongest hand in the world. That's right. Your hand. The hand that marks the ballot. The hand that pulls the voting lever. Use it, will you? Use it."

Mothers for a Moral America focused primarily on the problem of moral decline. In Illinois and Texas, the group distributed over three million copies of a brochure tying Johnson to lawlessness and immorality.[78] Although Mothers for a Moral America, organized at a September meeting in Nashville, had no fund-raising arm, its initial press release about *Choice* indicated that "Mothers" had "conceived" and "financed" the film's production. Later the press learned that Citizens for Goldwater-Miller had provided the funding.[79]

"Mothers" sold 200 copies of the thirty minute film to local groups. A five minute version of it with the topless bathing suit and the book titled *Jazz Me Baby* excised was aired on KTTV in Hollywood. A copy was projected in a Republican headquarters in San Francisco. Finally "Mothers" scheduled the film to air nationally on NBC at 2 P.M. on Thursday October 22, a time likely to reach housewives. NBC agreed to show the film only after the sections showing the bare-breasted model of a topless bathing suit, semi-nude gyrating strippers, and some of the covers of the "pornographic books" that NBC considered "unduly suggestive" were deleted.

As word of the existence of the film spread through the press, Herblock responded with a cartoon showing a man in a rain coat labeled "Goldwater campaign" lurking amid garbage cans in an alley. The man asked a passerby "Pst—Want to See Some Feelthy Pictures?" The Republican National Committee's advertising agency, Erwin Wasey, Ruthrauff and Ryan, Inc., publicly disassociated itself from the film saying it had had no part in its production. "In our professional opinion," said an agency representative, "it had portions that were inflammatory."[80] Lyndon Johnson noted that in addition to the "frontlash" he was gaining as Republicans bolted to the Democrats out of fear of Goldwater's extremism, his candidacy was also benefiting from "smearlash"—the result of people's unwillingness to go along with Republican smear tactics.[81] And Democratic National Committee chief John Bailey called it "the sickest political program to be conceived since television became a factor in

American politics."[82] Meanwhile, Democrats scrambled to secure copies to be used in fund raising and organized a countergroup, "Daddies for a Decent America."

In the transcript of a meeting held in Los Angeles on September 22, Russell Walton, the p.r. director of the *Citizens for Goldwater-Miller* group, defined the film's intent this way:

> The purpose of this film then is to portray and remind the people of something they already know exists, and that is the moral crisis in America, the rising crime rate, rising juvenile delinquency, narcotics, pornography, filthy magazines. . . . We want to just make them mad, make their stomachs turn. . . .
>
> This is what we are going to have to do in this movie: take this latent anger and concern which now exists, build it up, and subtly turn and focus it on the man who drives 90 miles an hour with a beer can in his hands, pulls the ears of beagles, and leave them charged up to the point where they will want to go out and do something about it.[83]

The transcript, made by a shorthand reporting firm, was delivered to the press by "Democratic sources."

The film had apparently been scheduled for network broadcast without the OK of the Goldwater high command. If it was to be removed from the network schedule at this point, Goldwater himself would have to act.

The existence of the film and its scheduled airing created a double bind for Goldwater. If he permitted it to air he would be branded a racist and criticized by his own natural constituency for showcasing strippers, topless bathers, and twisters; if he denounced the film, he would seem to be confessing, in Shadegg's words, that his campaign "had produced a vile, offensive, immoral, racist movie."[84]

The existence of *Choice* harmed Goldwater's candidacy in a second way. By campaigning on morality, Goldwater set a high standard by which his conduct and that of his campaign would be judged. By repudiating *Choice* he passed that test. By creating it, his citizens committee did not. This at a time at which such Democratic ads as "Confessions of a Republican" were magnifying public fears about the persons surrounding Goldwater. Additionally, *Choice*'s reliance on guilt by association blunted the ability of the Goldwater campaign to cry foul over similar tactics in the Daisy spot, the Social Security ads, and the unaired Democratic ads that allied Goldwater with the Klan.

Hess, who was with Goldwater when he saw the film for the first time, reports that Goldwater said: "It can't be used." The reason, says Hess, "was obvious. From start to finish the film was racist provocation. It showed riot after riot, and black hand after black hand raised in violence. It showed Negroes in every bad light it could. The girlie scenes were quite innocuous."[85] Lichenstein who attributes the film to the "hot-heads" in the campaign, agrees with Hess' assessment. "It showed Black rioters and the clear implication was that the Blacks are on the rampage and will take over our society and pull it down off its foundations if LBJ is elected. . . . There are times in a political campaign when you have to ask, In the national interest dare we engage in this sort of character assassination? In that case, most of us and the Senator said it was out of bounds."

On October 22, Goldwater withdrew the film. On October 23 he justified that decision by declaring it "racist."[86] By linking blacks to law-lessness the film threatened to undercut assurances Goldwater had given other Republicans, Johnson, and the American people. In a meeting July 24 both Johnson and Goldwater had agreed to avoid inciting racial tension,[87] a fact announced in a joint statement. Additionally, responding at the unity conference to Romney's fear that the Republican campaign would be racist, Goldwater defended his record on civil rights and prom-ised "with every degree of seriousness and strength that I have that I will never talk about racism. I don't even intend to talk about civil rights. I think it's such an explosive issue."[88] To OK *Choice* after giving such assurances would have opened Goldwater to charges of both racism and hypocrisy.

The film, whose production was supervised by Russ Walton, former executive director of the United Republicans of California, was OK'd by Clifton White, a leader of the Draft Goldwater movement, who claimed that Goldwater had personally approved the original idea.[89] If he did, note members of Goldwater's inner circle, it was as a concept, not in the specific form taken by the film.

The existence and scheduling of the film revealed the need for the inner circle of campaign advisers to tighten its control on the citizens committee. Difficulties in controlling committees was, as McCabe ex-plains, a problem incubated in the finance laws that limited to three million dollars the amount of money one committee could spend. That limit meant that campaigns had to "proliferate committees," which in turn exacerbated problems in controlling the actions each might take on the campaign's behalf.

In the years since the '64 campaign those within the campaign who opposed *Choice* have questioned the political acuity and judgment of those who produced the film and have at the same time sought to disasso-ciate themselves from the producers' views. So, for example, Hess notes that after the campaign, one of those who had worked on *Choice* pro-duced a script that "equated the high instance of veneral disease in Amer-

ica with Democratic monopoly of big-city governments."[90] "I recall,"
adds Hess, "that my mother used to blame dry summers or, alternatively,
wet ones, on the policies of Franklin Roosevelt. She was, however, content to let this intelligence remain Our Secret."

Defining Character as the Key Attribute of the President

To counter Johnson's redefinition of the presidency in his own image, the
Republicans on October 9 aired a half hour on the "Real Job" of the
presidency that featured former Vice-President Nixon and Goldwater.
With its stress on morality in government and the need for peace with
strength abroad, this telecast, like the telecasts on "morality" and foreign
affairs, fits firmly in the second phase of the advertising strategy of the
Goldwater campaign.

Nixon opened the telecast with a message designed to hearten dis-
couraged Goldwater supporters. "There's been an upturn," he noted,
that will produce "the greatest army of volunteer workers in America's
political history on November third." He then introduced Goldwater as a
"reasonable," "calm," and "patriotic man." After reminding viewers of
the immense power of the president, Goldwater argued that our affairs
throughout the world were in shambles. It was a theme he repeated
October 21, in a nationally aired address on the changes in the Kremlin.

The genesis of that second address is a study in the difficulty of
applying the concept of equal time to a president who is also a candidate.
After Khrushchev's ouster and China's explosion of an atomic bomb,
Johnson "speaking as president" took to the air with a calm reassuring
address that in essence justified his foreign policy. Goldwater sought
equal time. Guided by the FCC decision handed down in Stevenson's
appeal in 1956, the networks turned him down. He appealed to the FCC.
The FCC turned him down. Eventually the courts followed suit.

However, one of the networks did give Republican National Committee Chair Dean Burch fifteen minutes. Burch used the time to argue
that Johnson's address had been blatantly political. He also condemned
Johnson for "killing" the investigation of Bobby Baker in the Senate and
castigated him for refusing to debate. Finally, Burch invited those who
believed in fair play to send money to pay for a broadcast by Goldwater.
Over one million dollars poured in enabling Goldwater to purchase a half
hour on ABC three nights after Johnson's address. In that speech he
condemned Johnson for making a false distinction between good and bad
communists and argued that the Democratic foreign policy was a failure.

Where "restraint" and "compassion" were central words in Democratic ads' descriptions of the president, "character" was the key word

offered in Republican ads. The Democrats stressed Johnson's bipartisan credentials, praised his stability and compassion, and argued that the enormous power of the presidency should not be entrusted to someone outside the mainstream who was impulsive and trigger happy. By contrast, Nixon concluded the half hour telecast by arguing "With all the power that a President has, the most important thing to bear in mind is this: you must not give that power to a man unless, above everything else, he has character. Character is the most important qualification the President of the United States can have."[91] And, lest the message be lost for want of a counterpunch, Nixon attacked Johnson for refusing "to disassociate himself from political hanky-panky, from corruption, in his official family, in the Bobby Baker case." Just as in 1964 Humphrey preached a prescient sermon about the Republican convention, so Nixon's words previewed the war cry his opponents would shout as they rocked his administration in 1972 and 1973.

Human Rights

At a July 11 meeting between Johnson's representatives and those working on the Democratic account for Doyle Dane Bernbach, a seven column ad headlined "5 Dead Men . . ." was "killed since civil rights is not to be treated as a separate issue." Parenthetically, the minutes then remind the participants that "Civil rights when used as a part of an ad should be treated in its broadest aspect accenting human rights—equal rights for all, etc." Moyers explains the rationale for that decision this way: "Johnson felt that if you stirred up tempers and passions you'd never be able to do what he wanted to do when elected. . . . He was a builder of consensus and he knew that the big issue he was going to face on the home front was civil rights. He wanted to leave as much room as possible for bringing on board people who would otherwise be opposed to it."

Still when a pamphlet touting Goldwater's commitment to Negro rights and accusing Johnson of being a racist was produced for the Republicans, the Democrats responded with dispatch. The pamphlet, designed for distribution in Washington D.C., noted, among other things, that Goldwater belonged to the National Association for the Advancement of Colored People. The Republican National Committee suppressed the pamphlet on the fear that it might fall "into the wrong hands." Predictably, by distributing it in such Southern states as Georgia, Alabama, Mississippi, and South Carolina, the Democrats ensured that it would fall into exactly what the Republicans considered the wrong hands. Accomplishing this was no small task. Since the light blue ink on the pamphlet did not photocopy well, the Democrats reprinted the pamphlet in the same type and with the same layout, substituting a photo of Goldwater for a line drawing of him and adding to the Republican disclaimer the federally mandated disclosure saying that the pamphlet had been reprinted by the Democrats "as a public service."

The existence of the pamphlet dampened the enthusiasm of conservative Southern whites drawn to Goldwater by his vote against the Civil Rights Act and his defenses of "individualism" and "states rights"—code words for segregation. "As soon as distribution began," writes Bruce Felknor, Executive Director of the Fair Campaign Practices Committee, "newspapers reported it, for here *was* a story indeed. In the South the Goldwaterites were acting as though their Senator had voted against the Emancipation Proclamation. Now in a Northern city, Republicans were draping him in Lincoln's mantle."[92]

Just as the Democrats tried to drive Southern whites from Goldwater, the Republicans attempted to drive blacks from Johnson. Accordingly, a week before the election, a black implying that he was a Republican National Committee representative ordered 1,400,000 simulated telegrams urging blacks to write Martin Luther King in on their presidential ballots. The telegrams, costing $2500, a sum paid in cash, were authorized by "Committee for Negroes in Government, Louisville Kentucky."

The same week, a Louisville man representing the same committee paid a Chicago ad firm to produce and air a radio ad urging the write-in. The $10,000 cost again was paid in cash. The ads were aired in eleven cities with large black populations.[93]

Apart from their acrobatics on civil rights, the two campaigns pivoted on different human rights. While Goldwater concentrated on the right to be free from the fear of crime, Johnson focused on the right to Social Security and the right to a decent standard of living.

As noted earlier, Goldwater's appeal to law and order—an appeal more resonant in 1968 than in 1964—was awkwardly dramatized. By contrast, Johnson's attack on poverty was expressed in the most eloquent political ads created to date in the history of television. Using haunting stills of gaunt raggedly clothed children—some black, some white—saying grace before barely filled plates, in sparsely furnished rooms and make shift houses, the ads argued that America had a special obligation to those whose lives are scarred by poverty. The ads constituted an argument that "people who were poor were poor by accident and not by nature and that there was dignity in these people which poverty should not be allowed to inhibit," says Moyers.

"Poverty is not a trait of character" said one of the televised ads. "It is created by circumstances. Thirty million Americans live in poverty. So will their children unless the cycle is broken. That's the goal of President Johnson's war on poverty. Help win it." Another contrasted the pictures of poverty-ridden children with the voices of other children recounting their good times at summer camp or on jet flights en route to vacations. "This is what poverty looks like," said the announcer. "This is what prosperity sounds like: ". . . for the whole month of July this summer I'm going to Brownie sleep away camp. It's all girls." "The jet flight was actually very terrific and they gave h'ors d'oeuvres and they served dinner which was the following: Southern fried chicken, peas, candied yams, and for dessert there was cheesecake." "An encyclopedia is a series of books that tells things. We have one in our house.' " The ad then cuts to Johnson pledging the nation to "an unconditional war on poverty."

At one level the ads' function was documentary. They established incontrovertibly that there were ill-fed, ill-clothed, and ill-housed children in America. Shooting the ads in black and white rather than color heightened the bleak scenes. By slowly panning the still photos, the camera also increased our attention on the details of each while the camera's movement suggested that poverty crossed geographical boundaries to bond black ghetto children and white Appalachians.

Additionally, by concentrating on children rather than adults, the ads assaulted the defenses of those who argue against governmental aid for the poor on the grounds that poverty is willfully embraced by shiftless adults. The intent gazes and proud carriage of the children suggested that their potential contributions to society were real and redeemable.

Apart from their obvious political purpose, these still montage ads also fulfilled a need felt by agency head Bill Bernbach. "He wanted at least once to show that the aesthetic qualities that he believed advertising should represent could be applied to political advertising," says Moyers. "That ad was one in which our substantive interest met his aesthetic ambitions."

Slogans

The tenor of the 1964 campaign is synopsized in the slogans "In Your Heart You Know He's Right" vs. "Vote for President Johnson on November 3, The Stakes Are Too High For You To Stay Home." Johnson's slogan implied a special urgency about the election. The ads themselves detailed the domestic and foreign reasons for that urgency.

Ad after ad argued that a vote for Goldwater was a high-risk venture. Repeatedly, the voters' anxiety was raised while the structure of the ads assured us that Johnson's election would vanquish fears about abolition of Social Security and nuclear war. By urging a vote for *President* Johnson, the tag also reminded us that as president he had protected the country and safeguarded its social system.

The Johnson tag line not only recapped fears about Goldwater, it also argued that voting was particularly important in this election. Fearful that a projected landslide could lull voters into apathy, and hopeful that an electoral mandate would propel the programs of the Great Society through Congress, Johnson's strategists wrote into the slogan a get out the vote appeal predicated on the whisper that Goldwater might win by default if overconfident Johnson supporters stayed home. Some ads for Johnson specifically made this point. One showed a man, umbrella in hand, plunging through a downpour to vote. "If it rains on November 3, get wet" said the announcer. "Vote November 3, the stakes are too high for you to stay home." Another showed a voter entering the voting booth as an announcer reminded us to remember as we vote that we are at peace. Print ads also urged "Don't let the predictions make you overconfident. Tomorrow get out and vote for Johnson and Humphrey."[94]

As early as October 1, these ads were arguing "No matter how good the prospect for victory on Election Day, every vote will be important and every vote will count. The urgency is not only to win, but to win in a big, decisive way. A huge landslide vote will really show where our nation stands on the great issues of modern times which so deeply affect our people and all mankind. . . . This election . . . will be a chance to eradicate the fanatical right-wing influence in our political life. Possessed by a 19th century mentality, these forces ignore the explosive problems of today and the challenges of tomorrow."[95] In radio ads, a tolling bell reminded voters of the number of hours left to vote.

By contrast, Goldwater's slogan suggested that whatever their stated party preference or public posture, in their hearts voters knew Goldwater was right. The Goldwater tag was an invitation to introspection. The invitation was often obscured by spray painters who rewrote the message of Goldwater's billboards to read "In your heart you know he might," "In your heart you know he's right, extremely right," "In your heart you know he's trite," "In your guts you know he's nuts," and "In your head you know he's wrong." At rallies Goldwater's opponents also transformed the $AuH_2O = 1964$ that his supporters used to signal their support for him to signs of condemnation. AuH_2O in 64 = a mushroom cloud, said some. Others noted $AuH_2O = H_2S$.

On election day voters indicated that in their hearts they still feared Goldwater. The landslide they handed Johnson said that for them the stakes were too high to stay home.

CHAPTER SIX

1968: The Competing Pasts of Nixon and Humphrey

More so than in any other campaign in recent times, the contest in the general election of 1968 turned on the personal pasts of the three men who sought the office. Two of the three, Nixon and Humphrey, seemed so comparable on the issues that it was difficult for most voters to distinguish the promises of one from another.* The outcome of this election hinged not so much on what the candidates promised but on how the electorate came to perceive what each had done and been throughout a lifetime of public service. This, in turn, forced the candidates to reconcile the public's sense of their pasts with the sense the candidates themselves were trying to sculpt and their opponents were trying to destroy. Consequently, the "old" Nixon competed with the "new" Nixon; Humphrey, "the apologist for Johnson's policies in Vietnam," competed with Humphrey, "the veteran social reformer," and the George Wallace who pledged to effect fundamental change in Washington clashed with the George Wallace who as governor seemed to have effected little change in Alabama. Just how successful the candidates would be in molding a vision of the future from selected elements in their pasts was then a decisive question in 1968.

"It was the Vietnam War," wrote Lyndon Johnson's aide Jack Valenti, "that cut the arteries of the LBJ administration."[1] By 1968 the U.S. was spending $82 million dollars a day to wage that war. Even more damaging to the prestige of the Johnson Administration and the continued support it needed to continue to wage the war were the nightly news segments showing American soldiers falling and dying in the Southeast Asian jungle. The weekly body counts were no longer being tallied in tens but in hundreds. Consequently, the perception of 1964 that Democrats were more likely to avoid a war than Republicans reversed in 1968; in that year, among those who perceived a difference in the ability of the

*Benjamin Page notes that Nixon and Humphrey were seen as less than one standard deviation apart on the major issues of Vietnam and urban affairs (p.91).

parties to avoid a larger war, "the Republicans were favored once again by a margin of two to one."[2]

"I was told that if I voted for Barry Goldwater there'd be a land war in Asia," noted one humorist acidly, "I did. They were right." In February, Gallup found 50% disapproving of Johnson's handling of the situation in Vietnam while only 35% approved.

Leading a campaign staffed by student activitists and dubbed a "Children's Crusade," Senator Eugene McCarthy, a Minnesota Democrat, challenged the incumbent president of his own party over his conduct of the war in Vietnam. In the New Hampshire primary, Johnson supporter Governor John W. King responded by branding McCarthy a "spokesman of surrender" and an "appeaser" and by claiming that a large vote for him would "be greeted with cheers in Hanoi."

Full page ads in New Hampshire newspapers proclaimed that the Communists were watching the outcome in New Hampshire "to see if we at home have the same determination as our soldiers in Vietnam." As often as fifteen times daily, radio ads carried the same message.[3] "The North Vietnamese hope to win here what they can't win on the battlefield . . . ." declared one of the radio ads. Another noted: "What do you think would happen to this country if right in the middle of a war, we up and changed our mind? Now he [President Johnson] knows that surrender in Vietnam would be selling the whole country down the river. He knows that turning our backs and running is exactly what every Communist in the world would love to see."[4]

Rather than help extinguish the McCarthy challenge, the Johnson ads produced a backlash. "McCarthy Wins Support as Ad for LBJ Backfires" reported a headline in the *Washington Post* on March 9, three days before the New Hampshire primary.[5] When the dust had settled, Eugene McCarthy had captured a surprising 42.2% of the vote to Johnson's write-in vote of 49.4%. The ads themselves had been condemned in *The Concord Monitor* and the *Portsmouth Herald,* and five delegates pledged to Johnson made a point of publicly disassociating themselves from the ads.[6] This reaction set politicians on notice that the patriotism of those opposing U.S. policies in Vietnam could not be impugned without great risk, a reaction that effectively squelched use of that tack in future primaries and in the general election.

Although Johnson had won in New Hampshire, McCarthy's strong showing exposed the extent of Johnson's political vulnerability. But what McCarthy's unexpected strength in New Hampshire did not establish was that New Hampshire voters favored McCarthy's dovish position on the war. A subsequent poll revealed that by a three to two margin those who voted for McCarthy in New Hampshire favored a harder stance on the war than Johnson's.[7] Anti-Johnson sentiment had crystallized in the primary behind the only serious alternative to the incumbent president.

Reading the message of New Hampshire as a repudiation of Johnson's policies, New York Senator Robert Kennedy announced his candidacy four days later. He declared his dedication "to seek new policies, to close the gaps between black and white, rich and poor, young and old in this country and around the world."

By the time of the Wisconsin primary, Lyndon Johnson's prospects had declined further. After a visit to the state, Johnson's Postmaster General Larry O'Brien predicted that the president would be defeated 60–40 or perhaps even 2 to 1. On the eve of the primary, at the end of a speech announcing a unilateral halt in most of the bombing of North Vietnam, Johnson withdrew from the race. "I shall not seek, and I will not accept, the nomination of my party for another term as your President" he said on March 31. According to Gallup, Johnson subsequently rose 13% in the polls to 49%.

Five days later, on April 4, the nation again was shaken, this time by the news that civil rights leader the Reverend Martin Luther King, Jr., had been assassinated in Memphis. Riots ensued in 125 cities. Over 65,000 troops were called in to contain the violence. When the campaign resumed, its complexion changed. Increasingly, the theme of law and order appeared in the rhetoric of both Republicans and Democrats.

A little more than three weeks later, on April 27, while McCarthy and Kennedy battled it out in the primaries, Hubert Humphrey, Johnson's vice-president, announced his candidacy. Unlike the other two candidates, McCarthy and Kennedy, Humphrey made no attempt to distance himself from Johnson. The perceived link between Humphrey and Johnson persevered even after Humphrey tried to decouple it in the general election. Throughout the general election the public linked Humphrey more tightly to Johnson than to his own running mate Maine Senator Edmund Muskie. In the jargon of political science, their images were "highly assimilated."[8]

In a war and riot torn country, Humphrey's announcement speech voiced a note strikingly out of key. "Here we are, the way politics ought to be in America, the politics of happiness, the politics of purpose, the politics of joy." It was a theme ridiculed by his opponents who saw nothing joyful in the weekly death counts from Vietnam.

As McCarthy and Kennedy battled it out in the primaries, Humphrey quietly moved from state to state gathering delegates not bound to the outcome of primaries. Lost in the crush of images characterizing the Democratic convention is the fact that in late spring Humphrey led Nixon in the polls.

McCarthy swept the Wisconsin primary with 58% of the vote. Next he won Massachusetts 51% to Kennedy's write-in vote of 28%. But in their first head-to-head clash on May 7, Kennedy emerged the victor in Indiana with 42% to McCarthy's 27, then on May 14 in Nebraska 51 to 31. McCarthy's prospects revived in Oregon where he won 45 to Kennedy's 39%.

Throughout the primaries McCarthy was nettled by efforts of an independent group that called itself Citizens for Kennedy. Although Kennedy repeatedly urged the group to abandon its tactics, its members continued to circulate an inaccurate brochure maligning McCarthy's voting record. In a front page story on May 6, 1968, the *New York Times* documented that McCarthy and Kennedy had cast identical votes on most of the measures cited in the brochure, that the brochure confused technical procedural votes with final legislative votes, and that McCarthy had cast a vote on many of the occasions that the brochure reported him absent. The tension between the McCarthy and Kennedy campaigns mounted as one primary after another proved inconclusive.*

With its 172 delegate votes, California was seen by both sides as a crucial test. McCarthy's ads attacked both Robert Kennedy and his deceased brother, a move unlikely to endear McCarthy to the many who still regarded John Kennedy as a martyr and a secular saint. In one ad McCarthy allied Kennedy to his brother's decision to send forces into Vietnam. "There is only one candidate who has no obligations to the present policies in Vietnam and who is under no pressure to defend old mistakes here," declared the ad. Another ad claimed: "Kennedy was part of the original commitment [to Vietnam]. He participated in the decisions that led us to intervene in the affairs of the Dominican Republic. He was directly involved in the disaster of the Bay of Pigs. And as a member of the National Security Council, he must bear part of the responsibility for our original—and fundamentally erroneous—decision to interfere in Vietnam."[9] When Kennedy contended that the ad distorted his involvement in the intervention in the Dominican Republic, McCarthy ordered it withdrawn. In a debate between the two, aired throughout the United States, Kennedy renewed his attack on that ad and elicited from McCarthy the concession that he had in fact withdrawn it.

In the same debate, McCarthy attacked the accuracy and consistency

---

*"A difference, not generally noted by the press, between my campaign and that of Robt. Kennedy's was that I ran against the war," McCarthy recalls, "whereas the thrust of the Kennedy campaign was against Lyndon Johnson and the manner in which he was conducting the war, a fact noted by Henry Kissinger, who in defending his handling of the ending of the war, said that he had followed the steps proposed in the Viet Nam plank proposed by the Kennedy persons at the Chicago Democratic Convention. Henry was nearly correct." (letter to author, December 1, 1983).

of Kennedy's claims. Kennedy's broadcast ads, noted McCarthy, featured former Secretary of Defense Robert McNamara praising Kennedy, a peculiar use of a testimonial since Kennedy's speeches attacked McNamara's policies. When McCarthy challenged Kennedy's use of the "McNamara tapes," Kennedy disingenuously claimed not to know what McCarthy was talking about.

While McCarthy may have exaggerated RFK's responsibility for his brother's decisions, Kennedy clearly sought to erase McCarthy's legislative past. A print ad asked: "Law Enforcement and the Cities. How Do Kennedy and McCarthy Stack Up?" On the left side of the ad were solutions Kennedy had offered. On the right—McCarthy's side—a blank space.

On June 5, Kennedy won the California primary 46–42%. After acknowledging his victory and pledging "on to Chicago, and let's win," Robert Kennedy was assassinated while leaving through a hotel galley.

The 1968 Democratic convention was scheduled to coincide with Johnson's August 27 birthday. Had Johnson continued to be the party's standardbearer, the late summer convention would have posed no problems. As the incumbent, Johnson did not require breathing space in which to formulate strategy and organize a campaign. Once Johnson was out of the running, however, the late convention date disadvantaged the nominee of the party heavily, no matter who that nominee turned out to be.

As a birthday party, this convention was the raw stuff of which nightmares are made. Unwelcome at his own party's party, Johnson did not even appear at the convention. His surrogate, Hubert Humphrey, was enveloped in a scene that gave new meaning to "Virginia Woolf's" game of "Get the Host." Kennedy voters, who might have been expected to transfer their loyalties to the antiwar candidacy of Eugene McCarthy would not do so out of bitterness over the campaign McCarthy had waged in California. With McCarthy too weak and Kennedy no longer a factor, Humphrey was nominated on August 28 on the first ballot.

But unlike Albee's play in which the child was imagined, the children in the streets of Chicago were real, their party favors clubs and night sticks. As the stunned nation watched, the police beat student protestors in the streets of Chicago while inside the convention hall the orchestra played "Happy Days Are Here Again." When Abraham Ribicoff nominated George McGovern, a last-minute Democratic entrant behind whom some of Kennedy's supporters had rallied, he said, "with George McGovern as president of the United States, we wouldn't have these Gestapo police tactics on the streets of Chicago." Although the Gallup poll showed that 56% of the public approved of the police's actions, in an election in which "crime and lawlessness" ranked second only to "Vietnam" as an important issue, the fusion of violence and Humphrey's nomination scarred his candidacy.

In a headline on August 29, the *New York Times* unintentionally identified the two thorns Humphrey had to extricate from his side in order to win the presidency. The headline read: "Humphrey Nominated on the First Ballot After His Plank on Vietnam is Approved; Police Battle Demonstrators in Streets." Under the headline two photos appeared. In one, cheering delegates raise HUMPHREY signs and banners; in the other, helmuted police arrest demonstrators. Not only did the visual images ally Humphrey with the chaos in the streets of Chicago but the actions they depicted also made it more difficult for Eugene McCarthy to endorse the candidacy of his fellow Minnesotan.[10]

As his running mate Humphrey named Senator Ed Muskie from Maine. Although Humphrey's acceptance speech was laced with the language of repentence and reconciliation, in the context that surrounded it few could hear that message. To liberate the meaning of the speech from the message of the streets, Democratic advertising replayed portions of the address including the segment in which the vice-president stated: "Winning the presidency, for me, is not worth the price of silence or evasion on the issue of human rights. . . . I choose not simply to run for President. I seek to lead a great nation." The ads also reminded viewers of the speech's claim that the policies of tomorrow need not be limited by the policies of yesterday. In the speech Humphrey also said:

> I say to America: Put aside recrimination and dissension. Turn away from violence and hatred. Believe—believe in what America can do, and believe in what America can be. . . .

For obvious reasons, the ads did not replay the section of the speech in which Humphrey placed Johnson in the tradition of Roosevelt, Truman, Stevenson, and Kennedy and added, "I truly believe that history will surely record the greatness of his contribution to the people of this land, and tonight to you, Mr. President, I say thank you. Thank you, Mr. President."

In the shadows of Humphrey's public thanksgiving lurked the question, Had the vice president secured the nomination in a Faustian compact that deprived him of his ability to win the election? To redeem his political hopes, Humphrey had to appear to break with Johnson clearly enough to attract those disaffected with Johnson's policies in Vietnam but not so clearly as to alienate those who supported Humphrey because he was Johnson's heir.

During the primary season, Humphrey's advertising had been produced by two agencies: Doyle Dane Bernbach, the agency Humphrey inherited from Lyndon Johnson, and Lennen and Newell, a New York agency. Responsibility for arranging Humphrey's broadcast appearances on talk shows and the like resided with Bob Squier, who had been lured from his post as assistant to the president of Public Broadcasting to serve for what would turn out to be only 48 hours as Johnson's media adviser. When Johnson withdrew, Squier was asked to join the Humphrey campaign.

Humphrey's general election campaign was headed by Larry O'Brien, who had supported Johnson while the president still sought renomination and who worked for the nomination of Robert Kennedy once Johnson withdrew. O'Brien brought into Humphrey's campaign a political consultant, former business partner, and hometown friend named Joseph Napolitan, whom he had known since the late 1940s. Originally a reporter for a Springfield, Massachusetts, newspaper, Napolitan had gone on to attract national attention by managing the upset victory of Milton Shapp in the Democratic gubernatorial primary in Pennsylvania, and by helping defeat Senator Ernest Gruening in Alaska.

In his role as media director of the campaign, Napolitan decided to replace Doyle Dane Bernbach with a team of his own. Napolitan turned to Tony Schwartz, the originator of the Daisy ad, for radio and TV spots; he also invited the assistance of Charles Guggenheim, who had made his political debut in the 1956 Stevenson campaign and had just completed the filmed tribute to RFK aired at the 1968 Democratic convention. When first asked to help, Guggenheim begged off pleading exhaustion from creating the Kennedy documentary but joined the campaign in its final weeks. Napolitan also commissioned a film and some spots from St. Louis documentary maker Shelby Storck. Storck had earlier teamed with Napolitan in the Gravel race against Alaska Senator Ernest Gruening and in Shapp's bid for the governorship. A documentary film on the Democratic Party was produced by Sidney Aronson. Finally, Bill Wilson, who had worked for Stevenson and JFK, produced a number of spots in which Edward Kennedy endorsed Humphrey. In the general election, Bob Squier continued to produce live television including Humphrey's Salt Lake City address, his speech on law and order, and his election eve telethon.

In the 1968 presidential race, a current and former vice-president would face off. But Richard Nixon's road from announcement through acceptance speech would be far less problem pocked than Humphrey's.

On February 1, 1968, the person who had been narrowly defeated for president in 1960 and then decisively defeated for Governor of California in 1962 handed reporters who had assembled in his New York apartment a copy of a letter he had mailed to the voters of New Hampshire. It portrayed Nixon as a phoenix rising from the ashes.

During 14 years in Washington, I learned the awesome nature of the
great decisions a President faces. During the past eight years I have had
a chance to reflect on the lessons of public office, to measure the nation's tasks and its problems from a fresh perspective. I have sought to
apply those lessons to the needs of the present, and to the entire sweep
of this final third of the 20th century.

And I believe I have found some answers.

Six years earlier, in a concession speech following his loss of the California governorship to Pat Brown, Richard Nixon virtually had announced
his retirement from politics, with a parting shot at the press who he noted
would no longer have Dick Nixon "to kick around anymore." Now that
Nixon was back in the political arena, he had to establish that unlike
Goldwater in 1964 and alone among the Republican hopefuls in 1968, he
could return the presidency to Republican control. Like Kennedy in 1960,
by winning he planned to demonstrate that he was a winner.

The Republican competition for the nomination proved to be overcome easily. After the press replayed his admission on a Detroit talk
show that on a trip to Vietnam he had been brainwashed, Michigan
Governor George Romney watched his lead in New Hampshire evapo-
rate. But although his confession to having been brainwashed sealed his
fate, it was not Romney's only error. His billboards proclaimed a slogan
only fellow Mormons and a few dentists could love: "The Way to Stop
Crime Is to Stop Moral Decay." When his own pollster found that he
would win only 10% of the Republican vote in New Hampshire, Romney
withdrew.

Although Nixon won New Hampshire with 79% of the vote,
Romney's absence denied him the image of victor his candidacy required.
In Wisconsin, Nixon faced an absentee campaign by supporters of California Governor Ronald Reagan who pinned their hopes on a half hour
documentary demonstrating that, unlike Nixon, Reagan had beaten California governor Pat Brown. By winning in Wisconsin with 79.4%, Nixon
exceeded his New Hampshire total. Reagan carried only 11% of the
Wisconsin vote. By the end of the primary season, after deferring in
California to Reagan's candidacy as favorite son, Nixon had won primaries in six states; his support never dropped below 70% of the Republican
vote, a record that effectively erased his image as a loser.

On April 30, New York Governor Nelson Rockefeller entered the
race that on March 21 he had promised he would not. That earlier announcement had embarrassed Maryland Governor Spiro Agnew, head of
the draft Rockefeller movement, for Agnew had not been informed of
Rockefeller's decision. Anticipating that Rockefeller would announce his
candidacy—not his noncandidacy—the governor of Maryland had invited

the press to watch the televised statement with him. Recognizing that Agnew had been burned by Rockefeller, the Nixon campaign quickly dispatched lieutenants to invite the Maryland governor to meet with Nixon. Each was impressed by the other. So, indirectly, Rockefeller was responsible for Nixon's selection of Agnew as his running mate.

Rockefeller's last minute start meant that he could not run in the primaries. "He would stage his own national primary," noted his speechwriter Joseph Persico. "Nelson would campaign intensively, make speeches, issue position papers. His bold solutions and personal attractiveness would pull him ahead of Nixon in the polls, and the poll results would be used to persuade convention delegates to latch onto a winner."[11] On May 13 Gallup announced that Rockefeller was more popular than Nixon and could beat any Democrat.

One estimate placed the scope of Rockefeller's advertising between his announcement and the convention at "377 pages in 54 newspapers in 40 cities and 462 television spots a week, on 100 stations in 30 cities; at a cost of $3,000,000."[12]

Fear that he would be ostracized by his party for being a two-time spoiler muted Rockefeller's attacks on Nixon. His campaign focused instead on the claim that Nixon could not win. Just a few days before the convention was to begin, this "strategy was blown up in his face"[13] when on July 29 Gallup found that Nixon, not Rockefeller, was the Republican who could win—over Humphrey 40–38 where Rockefeller could only tie Humphrey 36–36. Although Harris's poll, taken days later, showed Rockefeller beating Humphrey 40–34 and Humphrey beating Nixon 41–36, Rockefeller's prospects vanished with the publication of the Gallup poll. The conflicting polls also propelled the pollsters to gymnastic contortions rivalled only by those brought on by their prediction that Dewey would win in 1948.

On August 8, Nixon was nominated on the first ballot. In a surprise move he selected Maryland Governor Spiro Agnew as his running mate. Unlike Percy or Rockefeller, Agnew was acceptable to both North and South.

Nixon's acceptance speech, a pastiche of his campaign speeches, forecast the themes of his general election campaign and its advertising.

As we look at America, we see cities enveloped in smoke and flame. We hear sirens in the night. We see Americans dying on distant battlefields abroad. We see Americans hating each other; fighting each other, killing each other at home. And as we see and hear these things, millions of Americans cry out in anguish: Did we come all this way for this? Did American boys die in Normandy and Korea and Valley Forge for this?

Listen to the answers to those questions. It is another voice, it is a quiet
voice in the tumult of the shouting. It is the voice of the great majority
of Americans, the forgotten Americans, the non-shouters, the non-dem-
onstrators.

The answer of course is no.

Although the agency, Fuller & Smith & Ross, under the direction of
John S. Poister, was technically in charge of Nixon's advertising, actual
responsibility for the advertising rested not with them but with a troika
consisting of Leonard Garment, Harry Treleaven, and Frank Shakespeare. In fall 1967, Leonard Garment, Nixon's law partner in the New
York firm of Nixon, Mudge, Rose, Guthrie and Alexander, and a self-described Democrat who voted for John Kennedy in 1960,[14] began assem-
bling the adteam for the 1968 campaign. As creative director of advertising, Garment hired Harry Treleaven, who for eighteen years had been
with the J. Walter Thompson agency. Filling out the advertising triad
with Garment and Treleaven was Frank Shakespeare, who on June 21
announced that he was taking a leave of absence from his job as president
of the CBS television Services Division.

Nixon's one hour programs, which formed the core of his regional
advertising strategy, were produced by Roger Ailes, whom Nixon had
met while appearing on the "Mike Douglas Show," which Ailes produced. Ailes, who joined the staff full time in late summer, also produced
Nixon's election eve telethon. Film producer Gene Jones created one and
five minute spot ads that rapidly intercut still photos. These photos underscored Nixon's themes, while Nixon, unseen in all but one of the ads
themselves, delivered the narrative. A half hour biographical interview
with Nixon also was created. Unlike Humphrey's media team, which was
hastily assembled after the convention, Nixon's team was in place long
before. Indeed, key members of the team responsible for the series of
panel shows in the general election pioneered that form in the primaries.
Similarly, the form of Nixon's election eve telethon was forecast by a
telethon held at the end of the Oregon primary.

The wild card in the political deck of 1968 was the leader of the
newly formed American Independent Party, former Alabama Governor
George Wallace. In an impressive logistical feat the Wallace campaign
secured a place for him on the ballots of all fifty states. Arguing that
there was not more than a dime's worth of difference between the Republican and Democratic parties, Wallace promised to champion the interests
of the middle class. In rallies that resembled revival meetings he advocated an end to welfare abuses, an end to federal intervention in states'
affairs, an end to busing to achieve racial quotas, and an assault on crime.
Wallace's early political broadcasts in the general election consisted of

these rallies edited down to thirty minutes. Later these were supplemented with five minute ads arguing that Wallace was a friend of labor, a claim illustrated by Wallace's reminder that both he and his running mate had relatives who were union members. One minute spots opposing busing and favoring law and order were also aired. In one, a brief statement by Wallace against busing is illustrated by a shot of a schoolbus driving away; after Wallace advocates "law and order," the ad shows a street light being broken. Wallace's advertising was produced by the Birmingham firm of Luckie and Forney.

Because he lacked access to the financial resources that normally flow from organized labor to the Democratic nominee and from corporations to the Republican nominee, Wallace was forced to innovate to raise campaign funds. Accordingly, Wallace's supporters sold his buttons, hats, and bumper stickers as a means of raising money. This activity lent itself to profiteering. A person who wished to set up a storefront for Wallace would in theory order a two-hundred-fifty-dollar kit of hats, buttons, ties, bumper stickers, and the like from Montgomery. Ordered at $250 wholesale, the supplies were supposed to sell for $350 in a Wallace storefront, leaving a hundred dollars per order toward the running of the local campaign. But when supporters did not want or could not afford a $250 initial investment, intermediaries arose eager to divide larger shipments into smaller ones in return for a mark-up. As a result, "Hats, six dollar a dozen from Montgomery, supposedly to be sold for a total of nine dollars, were reaching the storefronts priced at a dollar each. The same with buttons: four cents out of Montgomery, eight cents from the middleman, ten cents for the Wallace supporter."[15]

Wallace's supporters also adopted a practice previously used only by product advertisers. For example, C. V. Griffin, a co-owner of the Plaza Park Hotel in Orlando Florida, traded hotel space for radio time for Wallace's ads.[16]

Those inclined to vote for Wallace tended to be nominal Democrats who preferred Nixon over Humphrey in 1968. So Wallace's presence in the race depressed Nixon's total more than Humphrey's, a fact that undoubtedly figured in Humphrey's willingness to purchase time to sponsor a debate among the three and Nixon's refusal to accept such an invitation.

In my judgment, by providing a safety valve in a year characterized by mounting pressure, Wallace's presence benefited Humphrey in a second way. Wallace's rhetoric verbalized the dark side of the national psyche. By giving voice to sentiments that were widely felt (recall the widespread public approval of the police treatment of protestors outside the Democratic convention) but not widely expressed and by implying, for example, that if a protestor lay down in front of his car he'd run him over, Wallace enabled disenchanted Democrats to vent their frustrations. Similarly, his running mate's belief in a victory in Vietnam delivered by nuclear weapons carried to a logical but horrifying conclusion the pent-up need to avenge the nation's honor over the Tet offensive. For a fleeting moment LeMay permitted us to entertain the perversely satisfying realization that, if we so chose, we could nuke 'em back into the Stone Age. Then, having relished the otherwise forbidden thought, we could recoil from it to embrace again the wisdom of restraint.

In short, I suspect that a sizeable proportion of the 21% of those who indicated that they favored Wallace in late September permitted his candidacy to express thoughts they could otherwise only repress. Having expressed them or approved Wallace's expression of them on their behalf, having vented the accumulated fear, hostility, and anger that had percolated from Tet through the assassinations and riots of the spring and early summer and boiled over at the sights and sounds of Chicago in August, these voters could step back and reassess the candidacies of Humphrey and Nixon. Having moved through this period of purgative catharsis, they began their trek back to the two major parties. A five minute ad created by Tony and Reenah Schwartz invited such catharsis. In it, E. G. Marshall, backed by a large picture of Wallace, mused, "When I see this man, I think of feelings of my own which I don't like but I have anyway. They're called prejudices. . . . I think we have to recognize the fact that we have these feelings and that we have the right to conceal them or to express them. . . . Wallace is devoted now to his single strongest prejudice. He would take that prejudice and make it into national law."[17] Without the outlet that Wallace's candidacy provided, Humphrey might have remained a target of anger and resentment for these early Wallace supporters through election day, a factor that would have widened his margin of loss but, more important, a factor that could have made it more difficult for these once and future Democrats to return to their party in subsequent elections.

The philosophy governing the candidates' broadcast ads differed. Humphrey rarely appeared in his spots; Nixon appeared in the spots cut from the acceptance speech and his voice narrated the still montage spots; and Wallace appeared in almost all of his spot ads. The reasons were simple. The least well known of the three required the most direct contact with the voters; the front-runner needed to reassure those already committed to his candidacy that their choice was correct, and the candidate whose party outregistered his opponents' needed to remind Democrats that regardless of how they felt about the nominee, they endorsed the Democratic legislative agenda. This argument focused on freshening the public's commitment to Medicare, the Nuclear Non-Proliferation Treaty, jobs and the like and only then linked them to the nominee who by all accounts was substantially less popular than the programs for which he stood.

Because Republican polls showed that Wallace was draining support from Nixon, in his speeches Nixon argued that Wallace could not win but seldom attacked Wallace or his record. For reasons that his admen cannot explain, this approach did not find its way into broadcast advertising. By contrast, Humphrey needed to win back Wallace supporters, many of whom were inclined toward Nixon as their second choice. Accordingly, Humphrey's ads pointedly differentiated him from both Nixon and Wallace. Since a Wallace supporter was not likely to be won over by a direct attack on Wallace, Humphrey's spot ads generally offered factual data about Alabama under Wallace's governorship, hoping that voters would draw the appropriate inference. In his efforts to lure back blue-collar voters who had defected to Wallace, Humphrey was aided by organized labor, which distributed hundreds of thousands of pamphlets showing the ways in which workers were disadvantaged by low wages, poor working conditions, and inadequate social benefits in Alabama. These too concentrated on laying facts in place. Material distributed by the Committee on Political Education (COPE) of the AFL-CIO noted, for example, that:

> WALLACE'S ALABAMA ranks 48th among states in per-capita annual income and is $900 below the national average.
>
> WALLACE'S ALABAMA meets only one of eight key standards for state child labor laws. . . .

The Campaigns' Liabilities and Assets

From its start, the Humphrey campaign was fettered by three disadvantages: lack of money, lack of time, and its candidate's association with the unpopular presidency of Lyndon Johnson. By contrast, Nixon had a well-funded campaign and ample planning time. But Richard Nixon was no favorite of the press and his choice for vice-president, Spiro Agnew, would prove to be even less popular. Wallace's problems combined those facing Nixon and Humphrey, for he had less money than either of his competitors, little more time than Humphrey, and a running mate whose pronouncements on use of nuclear weapons made Goldwater's seem cautious by comparison.

Money

Nixon outspent Humphrey by almost 2 to 1 on television, by more than 4 to 1 on radio, and by more than 2 to 1 in newspapers. As in 1964 television dominated the media buys, with Humphrey spending $3,525,000 and Nixon $6,270,000 on television. Not until the last week of the campaign did Democratic TV expenditures equal the Republicans'. Despite Nixon's massive ad campaign, his ratings in the polls changed little from May to November. Throughout, his popularity hovered around the 42% mark. This failure to pull up in the polls suggests that his advertising succeeded in reinforcing his supporters' convictions but failed to make converts of undecided voters. Meanwhile, Wallace dropped from 21% in the polls in mid-September to 13% in late October despite an overall expenditure of $3,085,000 for radio, TV, and print advertising.[18] During the same period Humphrey rose from 28% to a neck-and-neck finish with Nixon.

One indicator of the extent to which financial problems plagued the Humphrey campaign may be found in the fact that the architects of the Humphrey campaign, Larry O'Brien, whom Humphrey appointed Democratic National Committee chair, and Joseph Napolitan, media director, both served without salary.

On October 13 Joe Napolitan sent a memo to Humphrey and the staff announcing that "Because of a lack of funds, we have no regional or state television spots this week." At the same time he noted that the TV stations in every state had copies of the Democratic ads and urged supporters to purchase time to air them. Humphrey's friend and fund raiser, Jeno Paulucci, believes that the absence of advertising during that week cost Humphrey the election. The cancellation occurred when a last-minute bid to secure $700,000 from wealthy Texas oilmen failed for want of the promise that Humphrey as president would protect the oil depletion allowance. Paulucci explains:

> Dwayne Andreas, Bob Short, Bob Strauss, and I had lunch at the Petroleum Club with a bunch of high muckedy mucks from the petroleum industry to get an advance of about $700,000 that we needed for the next week's advertising. They asked whether Hubert would promise that he would not touch the oil depletion allowance. My associates tried diplomatically to tell them this was something Humphrey couldn't come right out and affirm verbally or in writing. They said, "No confirmation, no $700,000." So, less than diplomatically, I asked them whether they insure their building? They said "Yes." I said, "My advice to you would be, even though you are for Nixon because you think he's going to save your oil depletion allowance, to spend that $700,000 on insurance." What I said was a little crude. I said "If I was Hubert Humphrey and you didn't give me that money, I not only would take away your depletion allowance, I'd cut off your balls." The others got a little upset with me. But we weren't going to get the $700,000 anyway. When I got downstairs, I called on a pay phone and said "We have to cancel next week's advertising. We don't have the money."[19]

In a staff meeting on October 16, O'Brien noted that Humphrey had learned of Nixon's election eve telethon and "wants us to buy him the same amount of time on a competing network during the same hours." To which treasurer Bob Short responded "This is like a lot of other things. Somebody has got to tell the Vice President at some point that he just can't have everything he asks for."[20]

The task fell to Larry O'Brien. "At one point in the campaign, Humphrey came back from a swing through West Virginia. He was excited. The crowds had been good and there hadn't been the anti-war hecklers who had bedeviled him elsewhere," O'Brien recalled in *No Final Victories*.[21] Humphrey said, "Larry, I don't see any Humphrey signs, any Humphrey literature. I'm out there breaking my butt and I don't see any campaign activity to back me up." "I knew why he hadn't seen any balloons or billboards or brochures," says O'Brien. "We hadn't wanted to worry him, but now we had to tell him the facts of life. 'We're broke, Hubert,' I told him. 'We don't have money and we can't get credit. We're not going to have the materials we wanted, and the television campaign has to be cut to the bone. The money just isn't there.' " The campaign's poverty was the by-product of a long costly primary battle between McCarthy and Kennedy that had drained the resources and the enthusiasm for Humphrey of some Democratic contributors and also of polls showing Humphrey far behind. As long as his victory seemed remote, big contributors sensed no need to hedge their bets by contributing to both major parties.

"On September 1 we started out with a $10,000 account," Short reported on October 18. "Since that time we've generated $5 million in cash. Of this money, $3 [million] in cash has gone to TV and $1.5 million to payroll, advertising, and the various bills that had to be paid in order to stay in business. Of the $5 million cash flow, $1.6 million was in contributions and the balance in loans." Still the staff was encouraged, for despite expenditures of $7 million, Nixon had not risen in the polls. By contrast they had been closing in the polls and had yet to "move in volume on TV."

By October 25, Humphrey's rise in the polls had boosted fund raising. Still, Short reported that "despite some of the money which has been coming in, our debt will be greater than the debt in 1964."

To raise funds, the Democrats added appeals for financial support in print ads and broadcast programs. The idea was Short's. When Short urged that a twenty second appeal for funds appear at the end of the Humphrey biographical film, Napolitan responded that it would destroy the aesthetic of the film. Short "said he thought it would raise $20,000 and asked 'Have you got any other way to raise $20,000?' " "I didn't,"

Napolitan recalls. "It raised $320,000. Sacks of money poured in."[22] While Humphrey's speech from Salt Lake City on Vietnam cost $128,000, the appeal at the end of it raised over $200,000.

Humphrey also used ads to argue that Nixon was buying the election. "Don't let him buy the White House" declared a headline under a smiling picture of Nixon. "No man has ever paid more trying to be President. Richard Nixon has spent more in the last month alone than Hubert Humphrey will spend in his six-month campaign. . . . If you don't do something about it, he will spend at least $5 for every $1 Mr. Humphrey spends. . . . It means we could pick a President, not on what he says, but on how much he spends to say it."[23]

Ironically, the Democrat's ad agency, Lennen and Newell, exacerbated the financial crisis by learning too well the lesson of the 1964 and 1960 Democratic presidential campaigns. By systematically overbilling the Democrats for each purchase of time, the agency hoped to avoid being left with unpaid bills after the election. After election day the agency turned back $318,000 to the campaign. Had the agency followed time buyer Reggie Schuebel's practice of turning over the reserved money in the final crucial days, Napolitan could have placed additional ads in key states. Napolitan remains angry at Lennen and Newell for he believes that "If I'd had $300,000 dollars to spend on key states we could have won. But Lennen and Newell didn't want to gamble on not getting paid."

Although in late March, Nixon's chief fund raiser Maurice Stans tided the financially strapped campaign over with a personal loan of $25,000, multimillionaire W. Clement Stone's willingness to match donations up to one million dollars set the campaign on a firm financial footing. Ultimately, Stone matched not one million dollars but two.[24] By contrast to the Democrats who left the campaign with a $9 million debt, the Republicans were able to set aside $1.6 million for use in the 1972 election.[25]

Time

Because the Democratic convention, originally scheduled to mark the renomination of an incumbent, occurred only days before Labor Day, the traditional starting date of the general election, Napolitan and O'Brien lacked the leisure to conduct polls and do research to help them map their campaign strategy. Napolitan says that he would as soon have had more time as more money. "I like to get involved a year and a half or two years before the election. In 1968 I got involved 9 weeks and one day before the election." More time to research might have provided a clear fix on Nixon's weaknesses. "Nixon had not been vice president for eight years. He was somewhat of an unknown quantity. There weren't a lot of blemishes on his record. In 1968 we had trouble finding handles on which to criticize him. If we had had more time to do research, more time for polling, some of our materials would have been more effective."

The Vice-Presidential Candidates

Although he acknowledged at the convention that his name was not a household word, Spiro Agnew quickly became an expletive deleted for the Republicans and the answer to the Democrat's prayers. He achieved this status with such statements as "when you've seen one slum, you've seen them all" and "Hubert Humphrey is squishy soft on Communism." In a year in which the past of the candidates was particularly germane, Agnew's ignorance of the McCarthyesque overtones in his indictment of Humphrey's "squishy softness on Communism" was of itself a disqualifier. "If Muskie is Humphrey's secret weapon," said Tony Schwartz at the time, "Agnew is Nixon's Achilles' heel."[26]

Agnew's ill-advised remarks made possible the Democratic claims that Nixon's choice of the Maryland governor reflected poorly on his judgment and also that, in the event of Nixon's death or incapacity, Agnew was unqualified to succeed him as president.

To highlight the difference in Agnew and Muskie's qualifications, a print ad noted "Mr. Nixon's first decision" and "Mr. Humphrey's first decision" above pictures of the vice-presidential nominees. Agnew's six-line political biography was followed by half a page of white space; Muskie's filled the page.

In full page ads the Democrats asked "President Agnew?" a question underscored in two controversial TV ads. One often-aired TV ad created by Schwartz showed "Spiro Agnew for Vice President" on a TV screen as a man convulsed in laughter. As he appeared to be about to choke, the print tag said, "This would be funny if it weren't so serious." The spot was criticized for not providing a reason to vote against Agnew, for engaging in an ad hominem attack, and for failing to address an issue. Napolitan justifies it on the grounds that voters can vote for a candidate, for his opponent, against a candidate, or against his opponent. "We felt Agnew was a vulnerability for Nixon. Our job was to give a reason to vote for Humphrey and against Nixon."

On October 25, Napolitan informed the campaign policy committee that he had "ordered off the Agnew-laughter spot. There were some complaints but I feel it had already fulfilled its effect." Its place was taken by another of Schwartz' spots. This ad, which also was frequently aired, showed a monitored heart beat as it asked: "Who is your choice to be a heart beat away from the presidency?" The names of the two vice-presidential candidates appear. The tag then declared: "Humphrey-Muskie: There is no alternative." A radio ad drawn from the TV ad carried the same message. Additionally, a privately sponsored print ad asked "Why vote?" "In the last 50 years, one President out of 3 failed to complete his term."[27]

More serious charges were raised against Agnew in an editorial in the *New York Times,* a newspaper that had endorsed Humphrey-Muskie. Raising indictments that would later prove prescient, the editorial argued that Agnew had accepted payola. The Republicans rebutted the charges in an ad run a week later in the *Times.* The ad relied on statements from other newspapers attesting that these were old charges without foundation. The Republican ad concluded: "In their search for truth, men must rise above the Times!"

The Democrats capitalized on the contrast between the vice-presidential contenders by featuring Muskie in the election eve telethon, in the campaign's filmed biography of Humphrey, and in a half hour biography of his own. In the Humphrey biography produced by Storck, Humphrey, Muskie, and their wives are featured. When the pin setter breaks while they are bowling, both of them in shirt sleeves climb behind the alley to fix it. "Can you just imagine Nixon and Agnew crawling around under a bowling alley?" asks one of Humphrey's advisers.

The luster of George Wallace's candidacy also was tarnished by his selection of former SAC commander retired General Curtis LeMay as his running mate. College students labeled LeMay "bombs away Curtis LeMay," a label spun from his ill-advised statements at the October 3 press conference at which Wallace announced his selection. "We seem to have a phobia about nuclear weapons. I think most military men think it's just another weapon in the arsenal," said LeMay. Later he noted that there was no difference between being killed by a "rusty knife" in Vietnam or by a nuclear weapon and added, "if I had a choice I'd rather be killed by a nuclear weapon."[28]* Using a ratings thermometer to assess the public's favorable response to candidates, two political scientists found that Muskie had a mean score of 61, Agnew, 50, and LeMay 35.[29]

Humphrey's Attempts To Reclaim His Own Past

Until he said otherwise, the public presumption would be that Humphrey's position on Vietnam coincided with Johnson's. "Virtually any statement that differed even a hair from Administration policy would

---

*In one never-aired ad created by Schwartz, after a voter pulls the lever for Wallace-LeMay the voting booth blows up.

have been played as a break with Johnson and could have jeopardized the Paris peace talks," Humphrey wrote in his autobiography.[30] "I could not do that. Now, the chief negotiator, Averell Harriman, no longer raised that objection, having, I suppose, lost heart himself that the negotiations would really succeed. In any case, without his objection my dilemma was solved. . . . I could speak out without damaging negotiations."

The financially strapped campaign scavenged the $128,000 to purchase air time. A debate ensued in the Humphrey campaign on what the speech should say. The key passage in the speech reflected competing viewpoints. In it Humphrey said:

> As President, I would be willing to stop the bombing of North Vietnam as an acceptable risk for peace, because I believe that it could lead to success in the negotiations and a shorter war. This would be the best protection for our troops.
>
> In weighing that risk—and before taking action—I would place key importance on evidence, direct or indirect, by word or deed, of Communist willingness to restore the Demilitarized Zone between North and South Vietnam.
>
> If the Government of North Vietnam were to show bad faith, I would reserve the right to resume the bombing.

The first paragraph bowed to the doves, the second two to Johnson and his supporters. But the symbolism that surrounded the speech's presentation underscored the first rather than the second and third paragraphs. Humphrey was introduced not as the vice-president of the United States but as the Democratic candidate for the presidency. Conspicuous in their absence were the vice-presidential seal and flag.

At the end of the speech Humphrey argued that since 1954 Nixon had "taken a line on Vietnam policy which I believe could lead to a great escalation of the war" a claim that contradicted the Democratic ads' indictment of Nixon's "silence on the issue."

Before the speech was broadcast but after the final version had been taped, Humphrey called Johnson to tell him what he planned to say. Humphrey reports that Johnson responded, "I gather you're not asking my advice." Humphrey responded that that was true but assured Johnson that "there was nothing embarrassing to him in the speech and certainly nothing that would jeopardize peace negotiations."[31] "Johnson said tartly and finally, 'Well, you're going to give the speech anyway. Thanks for calling, Hubert.' And that was that," recalled Humphrey. Bob Squier, the producer of the Salt Lake telecast, overheard Humphrey's end of that conversation. He recalls Humphrey assuring Johnson that the speech did not vary significantly from Johnson's San Antonio formula. After he hung up, Squier recalls, "Humphrey looked not terribly happy. We went back into the room. We screened the speech. When we got to that part [the key part] of the show he turned to me and said wistfully 'I thought I hit that a little harder than I did.' "

The Salt Lake speech marked the turning point in the Humphrey campaign. "The next day," he noted, "I flew to Nashville and there were only two kinds of signs: Wallace signs and those that said, in variations, 'If you mean it, we're for you.' Except for the Wallace signs, the turmoil of pickets, heckling, and hostility diminished and virtually disappeared from that moment on."[32] "The crowds began to swell," noted O'Brien, "the hecklers died out, a little money began to come in, and many of the anti-war liberals began to support us—we began, in short, to move toward a more normal Democratic campaign for the presidency."[33]

Amazingly, all of this was accomplished with a speech that, despite assurances to the press by members of his staff, did not definitely commit Humphrey to a halt in the bombing. "But if that was the fact, it was not borne out by the words of the speech," wrote R. W. Apple Jr. in the *New York Times*.[34] "HHH Bombing Halt Stand Poses More Questions Than It Answers" read a headline in the *Washington Post*.[35]

The speech directly contradicted Johnson only when it predicted that it would be possible to begin withdrawal of American troops from the combat zone in 1969. Johnson had argued, instead, that no one could predict when withdrawals would occur. But the existence of the first of the three key paragraphs, coupled with Humphrey's abandonment of the symbols of his vice-presidential ties to Johnson, enabled those who could join Humphrey's cause only if he seemed to concede something to their own convictions to rationalize their return to the candidate of their preferred party. "Humphrey's speech was shrewd," wrote Nixon in his *Memoirs*.[36] "While it scarcely differed from Johnson's position, he made it sound like a major new departure." "We thought that he [Humphrey] was greatly strengthening his political position," recalls Nixon speechwriter Ray Price.

Print ads used the fact of the speech to invite those who had strayed to Nixon or Wallace back into the fold. The form of the ads was personal testimony that invited the reader into the mind of a prominent American who had publicly opposed Humphrey before the convention and had been inclined to sit the election out or vote for Nixon or Wallace prior to the September 30 speech. So, for example, McCarthy supporter Paul O'Dwyer, a candidate for the Senate from New York, notes: "My decision to endorse the Humphrey-Muskie ticket would not have come without a change in the Vietnam policy for which these men have stood in public. I have been too impressed by the alienation and despair which have overtaken so many of our good young people as a result of this immoral war."[37]

Nixon's Strategy

A week before the New Hampshire primary, Nixon said that "If, in November this war is not over, I say the American people will be justified in electing new leadership, and I pledge to you that new leadership will end the war and win the peace in the Pacific."[38] "A reporter who had just joined the campaign heard the standard stump speech for the first time and thought he was hearing something new," recalls Price. "He raced to his typewriter and put on the wires the claim that Nixon was proposing a plan. Within minutes of the time that hit the wires we were reminding every reporter we could find that they'd heard the same statement before in the stump speech, that there was no plan, and that it would be irresponsible for a candidate to offer a plan because the presidency was such a reactive office."[39] Humphrey quickly pressed Nixon for details saying that "If you know how to end the war and bring peace to the Pacific, Mr. Candidate, let the American people hear your formula now."[39] In his *Memoirs* Nixon elaborates: "As a candidate it would have been foolhardy, and as a prospective President, improper, for me to outline specific plans in detail. I did not have the full range of information or the intelligence resources available to Johnson. And even if I had been able to formulate specific 'plans,' it would have been absurd to make them public. In the field of diplomacy, premature disclosure can often doom even the best laid plans. To some extent, then," he added, "I was asking the voters to take on faith my ability to end the war."[41]

Before moving to this high ground, Nixon rested for a moment on a line of argument based not on morality but expediency. On March 13 he told reporters, " 'I do have some specific ideas on how to end the war. They are primarily in the diplomatic area.' He indicated that he would spell out these thoughts when, or if, he wins the Republican nomination for president, but not in the campaigns in the primaries. 'I'm reserving my big guns against Johnson,' Nixon said. 'I have to adapt my strategy so as to win the primaries with the least expenditure of ammunition.' "[42]

Their appetites whetted by the admitted existence of "specific ideas to end the war" to which they were not privy, reporters probed, with some success, for details about what they but not Nixon labeled Nixon's "plan" to end the war. On March 15, for example, UPI reported that Nixon said that what was needed was the sort of diplomacy Eisenhower used to end the Korean War.[43] Nixon also noted that he had no "gimmick," "no magic formula" and assured the press that if he did he would feel a moral obligation to disclose the plan to Johnson. What the press, in Price and Nixon's judgment, had mischaracterized as a "plan" became, according to Price, a "secret plan" after New York governor Nelson

Rockefeller posed for pictures with his hand in his pocket to dramatize the secrecy of Nixon's "plan." Under increasing pressure to disclose the directions he would pursue in Vietnam, Nixon purchased a block of time on March 31 to make a major speech on Vietnam.

When Nixon's advisers learned that Johnson had notified the networks that he wanted time to deliver a speech on Vietnam the same evening, Nixon cancelled his time buy. That night Johnson changed the complexion of the political year by withdrawing as a candidate in order to pursue peace in Vietnam. Nixon responded by declaring a moratorium on his own comments about the war.

As a result, precisely where Nixon stood on Vietnam or what as president he would do to resolve the war was not revealed. As the preferences of those who voted for McCarthy in the New Hampshire primary suggested, such ambiguity had definite advantages.

To force voters to recognize that they were reading their own predispositions into Nixon's silence, Lennen and Newell created an ad that showed Nixon speaking and gesturing with no sound coming from his mouth. After 12 seconds of silence, the announcer declared: "Mr. Nixon's silence on the issue of Vietnam has become an issue in itself. He talks of an honorable peace but says nothing about how he would attain it. He says the war must be waged more effectively but says nothing about how he would wage it. Even the man who seconded the nomination of Richard Nixon, Senator Mark Hatfield, has said, 'The Paris Peace talks should not become the skirt for timid men to hide behind. Vague promises for quote 'an honorable peace' unquote are not enough. Voters should not be forced to go to the polls with their fingers crossed.' " A ballot then showed a pair of crossed fingers over Nixon and Agnew's names.*

Reclaiming Humphrey's Legislative Past

"All I had ever been as a liberal spokesman seemed lost, all that I had accomplished in significant programs was ignored. I felt robbed of my personal history," wrote Humphrey about the opening of the general election.[44] To recapture that history for the American public, the Democratic ads first minimized Nixon's legislative contributions and then reiterated Humphrey's.

---

*Hatfield's statement had appeared as a signed editorial in the *Ripon Forum*. The editorial did not speak of Nixon by name. Ostensibly, it indicted the evasions of all the candidates. Indeed, in its full context the editorial was an indictment of Johnson-Humphrey: "In 1964 the American people—trusting the campaign promises of the Democratic presidential candidate—thought they were voting for peace, only to have their trust betrayed."

Accordingly, a man looks with puzzlement into the camera as the announcer asks him what Mr. Nixon has ever done for him. Medicare? No. "That was Humphrey's idea. But Nixon . . . Nixon . . . the bomb. No that was Humphrey's idea to stop testing the bomb. But Nixon? What has Richard Nixon ever done for me? Ah, let's see, working people. I'm a worker. Nixon ever do anything. No. Humphrey and the Democrats gave us Social Security. But Nixon? Nothing in education. Housing? Hasn't done anything there." After the announcer tags the ad, the bewildered voter continues to think aloud "That's funny . . . there must be something Nixon's done."

Humphrey repeatedly made this point in his stump speeches by asking: "What has Nixon ever done for the working people of this country?" a question the crowds answered by shouting "Nothing." "And what are you going to do for Mr. Nixon?" asked Humphrey. "Nothing," the crowds responded.

As a counterpart to this message, the Democrats created a TV ad detailing all the things "the Democrats" have done for "you," including aid to education, summer jobs for kids, a higher minimum wage, Social Security, and Medicare.

In a nationally aired radio broadcast October 10, Lyndon Johnson added clauses to Nixon's slogan to argue the potentially damaging claim that Nixon had opposed the popular social legislation for which the Democrats had fought. The people "know" he said "that 'Nixon Is the One' who cast the tie-breaking vote that killed aid to education back when he was Vice-President. They know that 'Nixon Is the One' who said that Medicare 'would do more harm than good.' And they know that 'Nixon Is the One' who speaks for the Republican Party—Mr. Nixon's Republican Party—that always opposes so much vital and progressive legislation."

Courting the Supporters of McCarthy and Kennedy

With the help of McGovern and Edward Kennedy, the Democrats tried to woo back the Kennedy constituency. On October 16, a five minute ad showing Humphrey and Edward Kennedy walking together and talking of the past was aired for the first time. In the ad Kennedy recalled JFK's admiration for Humphrey and noted that President Kennedy "relied on him." The film also was aired during Humphrey's election eve telethon.

The often aired Humphrey biography also showed scenes of Edward Kennedy campaigning on Humphrey's behalf. The film's focus on a scene in which Edward Kennedy is booed while campaigning with Humphrey is a stroke of genius for it invited Robert Kennedy's supporters to identify not with those who booed Humphrey and Kennedy but with Kennedy and by implication with Humphrey. If the filmed sequence succeeded, it invited Robert Kennedy's supporters to see in Humphrey a kindred spirit, one who no longer merited public abuse. At the same time the realization that they were booing one of their own invited them to rethink their decision both to reject the Democratic party and involvement in electing its ticket in 1968.

George McGovern, who briefly raised RFK's standard at the convention, also invited Robert Kennedy's partisans to embrace Humphrey. In the filmed biography McGovern spoke not of Humphrey's links to Johnson but of Humphrey's contribution to the passage of important social legislation.

In his acceptance speech Humphrey explicitly appealed to McCarthy and McGovern "who have given new hope to a new generation of Americans." "I ask your help for our America," Humphrey pleaded. McGovern responded; McCarthy did not. On October 25[45] a full page ad in the *New York Times* signed by over two dozen influential blacks including Martin Luther King Sr. urged McCarthy to endorse Humphrey. "You must know," the ad said, "as we do, that the election of Richard Nixon or George Wallace will produce a new era of social neglect, at best, and repression at worst. Can you honestly believe that the election of Hubert Humphrey will have the same consequences?" At the end of the ad, its signers reconstructed Nixon's slogan "Vote like your whole world depended on it" to read "At this late hour, therefore, we appeal to you with all the force and urgency we command, to give your active help to Hubert Humphrey. Our whole world does depend on it."

When McCarthy's endorsement finally came on October 29 it was equivocal. In it he indicated that he planned to vote for Humphrey but added that Humphrey's position on "ending of the war in Vietnam, the demilitarization of United States government policy, and the reform of the draft laws . . . together with the reform of the political process within the Democratic party—falls far short of what I think it should be."[46] O'Brien notes that defections among liberals "were symbolized by Gene McCarthy's performance that fall. When he finally got around to endorsing Humphrey, his statement was so tepid as to be worthless."[47]

So Republican use of the attacks of McCarthy against Humphrey was politically within bounds. Consequently, a Republican print ad designed to speak to McCarthy's supporters quoted "McCarthy on Humphrey" saying such things as "At the very time when American foreign policy grew most disastrous, Vice-President Humphrey became its most ardent apologist." Each quotation was accompanied by a date and source in which the quotation could be found.[48] On the election eve telethon in a phone conversation McCarthy reiterated his personal support for Humphrey but in a more forceful manner than that suggested by the earlier statement.

Tying Humphrey to Lawlessness, Disorder, and the War

On July 15, 1968, Nixon adman Harry Treleaven wrote in a campaign memo that "It is my belief that the most effective posture for Mr. Nixon is that of *challenger*—which means, of course, that we always regard Mr. Humphrey as a key member of the incumbent administration, sharing responsibility for past and present policies and committed to their continuation in the years ahead. While this may not be entirely true, and will certainly be argued by Mr. Humphrey as he attempts to establish his individuality, it must be the basis for our strategy."[49] There is irony here, for by following this plan Nixon imputed to Humphrey the role that in the Eisenhower administration he himself coveted.

On Monday October 28 the Republicans aired their most controversial ad. In it, scenes depicting the ravages of war and the discord in the streets of Chicago were juxtaposed with a picture of a smiling Hubert Humphrey accepting the nomination of his party. Because the ad aired during "Rowan and Martin's Laugh In," an irreverent and sometimes tasteless television program, some viewers dismissed the ad as part of the show.

The ad opened with a still wide shot of the Democratic convention of 1968, then zoomed in to contentious faces at the convention intercut with stills of Humphrey at the podium. In the ad's background musicians played "Hot Time in the Old Town Tonight." The camera then tightened its focus on stills of rioting in the streets. The music became dissonant. The ad intercut a still of Humphrey looking perplexed, then flags waving at the convention and returned to the photo of Humphrey. Some soldiers in a bunker under attack are shown within a montage of soldiers treating the wounded and a barren Vietnamese landscape littered with exploded armaments. The scene slowly dissolves to a medium closeup of Humphrey as the "Hot Time" music rises on the audio track. In the final sequence, a poor family is shown in Appalachia. First the father, then the mother and the ill-clothed children at a table, then a young girl staring out of the window of the house. Again the music becomes harsh. Slowly the camera closes on Humphrey's face until it fills the whole screen. In the last 10 seconds of the ad the announcer delivers the only verbal message of the ad: "This time vote like your whole world depended on it. Nixon." The tag identifying the ad's sponsor as the Nixon-Agnew Victory Committee appears and the ad ends.

Unlike the other still montage ads, this one, for obvious reasons, did not employ Nixon's voice. An earlier storyboard of the ad called for a well-known and credible entertainment figure to note in the final seconds that "Hubert Humphrey is committed to a continuation of the policies that have brought America to the very brink of disaster. But there's one man who says we can change things, Nixon's the one."[50]

Using television's ability to create associations by juxtaposing otherwise unrelated images, this ad made an argument that if verbalized would evoke disbelief and ridicule. By adjoining a smiling Humphrey to helmeted soldiers crouched behind sand bags waiting to attack or be attacked in Vietnam, the ad implied that Humphrey, at least, was pleased by the U.S. presence in Vietnam, and, at most, joyous at the prospect of American deaths there. "Hot Time in the Old Town Tonight" served in the ad as Humphrey's theme music. Discordant music established the link among the pictures of riots, the war, and the poverty of Appalachia. The bouncy "Hot Time" suggested that Humphrey lived in a world untouched by the realities of war, social unrest, or poverty. "Hot Time" also evoked memories of the "hot time" in Chicago at the convention. This ad's pattern of images challenged Humphrey's ads' claim that he "cares." The ambiguity entailed in the simple association of images opened the ad to differing interpretations. Humphrey could be seen as the cause of the riots, the war, and the poverty or simply as indifferent to them. While Humphrey was striving to disassociate himself from the violence at home and abroad this ad reforged the link.

The Democratic National Committee responded to the ad with telegrams of protest to the network airing it and to the Fair Campaign Practices Committee, a now defunct independent group established to monitor campaign practices. "To distort Hubert Humphrey's record and program by showing scenes of him smiling or laughing against backgrounds of warfare, rioting and starvation—as Republicans did Monday night—is beneath contempt," said the telegram. "It is a smear in keeping with Nixon's below-the-belt reputation in politics and unworthy of a man running for the nation's highest office." Phone calls protesting the ad jammed NBC's switchboard. Unable to get through to the network, frustrated callers phoned major newspapers.[51] Whether, as Republicans charged, this protest was orchestrated by the Democrats is difficult to determine.

Republican campaign manager John Mitchell responded, "It ill behooves the Democratic National Committee to complain about this spot when compared with its media attempts to relate Richard Nixon to the atomic bomb and the vilification the Humphrey campaign has heaped upon Governor Agnew. The Democratic National Committee has suggested a network review of TV commercials. We would welcome this. There has been a growing number of distasteful, distorted spots produced by the Humphrey campaign."[52] Mitchell referred specifically to the spot in which a man convulses in laughter at the prospect of an Agnew vice-presidency and the spot aired during *Dr. Strangelove* October 9. That ad implied that Nixon's opposition to immediate signing of the nonproliferation treaty would lead to nuclear war.

Because Section 315 of the Communications Act prohibits censorship of political commercials, NBC could not refuse to air the Republican ad. Instead, before airing it the network expressed reservations about the spot and asked Nixon's agency to review it a second time. Only after the agency once again OK'd the spot did NBC air it on "Laugh In."

While Mitchell was trying to shift blame from the this ad to the Democratic ads attacking Nixon and Agnew, privately those responsible for the campaign's advertising acknowledged that airing the ad was a mistake. "It was a terrible ad," Garment says. "It was skillfully done but in terrible taste, particularly the scene showing Humphrey smiling after a scene of Vietnam carnage. It got on through bad judgment. I signed off on everything. I don't remember how specifically it got on but however it happened it was our responsibility. We yanked the ad and never put it on again. I said 'pull it as fast as you can.' I have a recollection of calling at night to yank it from some other stations on which it was scheduled to run."[53]

Nixon's ads treat Vietnam, rioting, and increased crime as interconnected facets of the same problem. After urging us to look and listen to America, Nixon declares in one ad: "We see Americans dying on distant battlefields abroad. We see Americans hating each other; fighting each other; killing each other at home. We see cities enveloped in smoke and flame. We hear sirens in the night. As we see and hear these things, millions of Americans cry out in anguish. Did we come all this way for this?"

The ads magnify the effect of the war. In one, almost one of two soldiers is dead, a percentage not representative of the casualty figures from Vietnam. The ads also imply that the demonstrators not the police were responsible for the riot outside the Democratic convention. The scenes of the activities in the streets of Chicago show the demonstrators screaming threats at the police but do not show the police action that might have precipitated such rhetoric. The predominantly white, youthful demonstrators whose photos appear in Nixon's ads bespeak not the urban riots that followed Martin Luther King's assassination but the chaos in the streets outside the Democratic convention. In the viewers who identify these scenes with the convention, the ads invite an anti-Humphrey response.

Stills from ads created by Eugene Jones for the Nixon campaign and aired in the general election of 1968.

The still montage ads, produced by Eugene Jones, a nationally acclaimed filmmaker who earlier had produced the documentary "A Face of War," induced dissonance in audiences by visually and verbally recapping national traumas identified with the Johnson-Humphrey administration. Harsh music gives way to soothing sounds, abrupt intercutting to slow pans and dissolves as Nixon offers his alternative vision of America. The ads forced audiences to confront images they probably would rather have preferred to forget and then offered a means of permanently setting them aside: Nixon's the one. "By portraying the devils in the air and then having Nixon lance them, it is suggested, the Nation may not only choose the right man for President but also engage in a therapeutic exercise which can help people to feel better," wrote *Washington Post* reporter Don Oberdorfer in a perceptive review of the Republican advertising.[54]

In the acceptance speech and the subsequent advertising of the campaign, Nixon differentiated his philosophy from Humphrey's by arguing as Republicans traditionally have that the Democrats see government as the repository of answers whereas Nixon's answers rest in individual initiative. Nixon's acceptance speech notes, for example, that "America is a great nation today, not because of what government did for people, but because of what people did for themselves."

In his acceptance address and in the half hour biographical interview aired repeatedly in the closing week of the campaign, Nixon argues from his own life to the reality of the American dream. At the convention Nixon recounted how as a child "at night he dream[ed] of faraway places where he'd like to go" but it seemed "an impossible dream." He eulogized his father "who had to go to work before he finished the sixth grade" but "sacrificed everything he had so that his sons could go to college," his "gentle Quaker mother" who "wept when he went to war," "a great teacher, a remarkable football coach, an inspirational minister" who encouraged him. Finally he noted that he stands before you, "nominated for President of the United States of America." So, he adds, "You can see why I believe so deeply in the American dream." What he asks of the convention and the listening nation is that "you . . . help me make that [American] dream come true for millions to whom it is an impossible dream."

The filmed biographical interview, the replayed account from Nixon's acceptance speech of the boy listening to trains going by in the night, and the concern Nixon repeatedly expresses in the ads for the country's children are the Republican campaign's equivalent of the Democratic ads' claim that Humphrey cares. But where Humphrey backed his claim with a litany of the social legislation he had championed, Nixon backed his with testimony from his personal past that a poor child could grow up to be president. Since Nixon disputed Humphrey's premise that governmental intervention was the remedy for society's problems, he had available his past and only one other symptomatic warrant to ground his alternative construction of reality. If the riots and the "wave of crime" were manifestations of societal failure, then the Eisenhower-Nixon years which, for the most part, had been free of such turmoil were more socially successful.

The audience Nixon envisions for these appeals is mirrored in the ads. It is an audience Nixon defined as composed of the "forgotten Americans," "the non-shouters." A matronly woman in what the Checkers speech had called a "respectable Republican cloth coat" walks down a street in the night. The message: the middle and upper middle class are being menaced by crime. Nixon's ads also suggest that their intended audience is white, middle-aged and older Americans, not the young. In the still montage ads there are basically two sorts of youths: those rioting and those dying in Vietnam. The people shown in crowd scenes reaching for Nixon's hand are primarily middle-aged. And, as I

The house in Yorba Linda, California, in which Nixon was born in 1913.

Nixon (*right*) with parents Frank and Hannah and brothers Harold (*left*) and Donald.

Nixon at 15.

Julie, her fiance David Eisenhower, Tricia, Nixon, Pat.

In the 1968 general election, Republican campaign literature and the campaign's biographical film *Nixon: A Self-Portrait* included stills such as these to recount the Republican nominee's personal past.

noted earlier, except for black children, most individuals shown in the ads are Caucasian. The spots in effect concede the black vote, of which he will win 97%, to Humphrey, and concentrate on those more inclined to favor a Republican candidate.

In keeping with Treleaven's strategy, while Humphrey's advertising uncoupled him from Johnson's handling of the Vietnam War, from the chaos in the streets of Chicago, and from lawlessness and disorder, Nixon's ads recoupled Humphrey to each. The Republican advertising also contrasted the domestic and foreign turmoil of the Johnson-Humphrey years with the tranquility of the Eisenhower-Nixon administration.

Demythologizing the Eisenhower Years

In his acceptance address Nixon reminded his audience that "we are worse off in every area" than we were "when Eisenhower left office eight years ago." Believing that Nixon was magnifying rose-tinted recollections of the Eisenhower administration, Lyndon Johnson in his October 27 radio address on behalf of Humphrey-Muskie challenged Nixon's reconstruction of the past saying, "I don't believe you, the American people, should let him rewrite the history of his past." The picture of the Eisenhower-Nixon years that Johnson paints is one colored by fear and foreign conquest. Nixon is "a veteran from the time when America's problems were deferred, when America's needs were ignored . . . a man who harks back to the days of 'peace and security' in 1960, though those were the days when he had to be rescued by the Marines from an angry mob in Latin America;—a man who distorts the history of his time when he was in office;—a man who even refuses and neglects to mention that Cuba was lost to communism back in his period of service in the fifties; that in 1960 an ultimatum hung over Berlin; that in Southeast Asia, Laos was disintegrating, and the situation in Vietnam—where he had recommended intervention in 1954, only to be vetoed by his own President— was then growing steadily worse." "Well," Johnson adds, "he doesn't mention those things in the 1960's. That is a pretty long list. But I have cited a part of it lest we forget the shape of the world the last time Richard Nixon held high office."

Although Johnson allies Nixon with his most recent service in elective office, he jumps past Humphrey's recent elective past to recall Humphrey's authorship of Medicare and responsibility for creation of the Peace Corps and for passage of the Nuclear Test Ban Treaty. This leapfrogging characterizes the Humphrey spots and the filmed biography as well. Both Johnson's speech and the biography recall JFK crediting Humphrey with the Test Ban Treaty. "And John Kennedy turned to him at the signing of the Nuclear Test Ban Treaty and he said, 'Hubert, here is this pen; this is your treaty,' " says Johnson.

In one of the few points at which Humphrey's ads clearly differentiate him from Nixon on a pending decision, Democratic spots argued that Nixon's unwillingness to sign the nuclear nonproliferation agreement "now" meant that under his leadership an increasing number of nations would develop nuclear capacity. A five minute ad making that claim was aired in prime time during the showing of *Dr. Strangelove*.

The Democrat's clearest statement of this claim appeared in a spot that showed a nuclear bomb exploding. As assurances about Humphrey's stand were articulated, the film of that explosion was reversed to show the explosion collapsing back into itself. "Do you want Castro to have the bomb?" the announcer asked. "Now?" "Do you want any country that doesn't have the bomb to be able to get it? Of course you don't. Where does Richard Nixon stand on the UN treaty to stop the spread of nuclear weapons? He says he's in no hurry to pass it. Hubert Humphrey wants to stop the spread of nuclear weapons now before it mushrooms. Hubert Humphrey supports the UN treaty now as do the 80 countries that have already signed it."*

So while Nixon tied Humphrey and himself to their respective vice-presidencies, Humphrey tied himself to his senatorial achievements and divorced himself from the Johnson presidency. While Nixon magnified our sense of the turmoil of the Johnson-Humphrey years, Johnson speaking on Humphrey's behalf heightened our sense of the turmoil of the Eisenhower-Nixon years. In this contest over competing pasts Nixon had the upper hand for, by all reasonable measures, the Eisenhower years were more tranquil than the Johnson years. Moreover, to indict the Eisenhower years was to spit on a dying hero.

Nixon's Use of His Own Past

Unlike 1960, when Eisenhower's inability to immediately recall Nixon's contribution to his administration tattered the credibility of one of Nixon's central claims, in 1968, with the marriage of Nixon's daughter Julie and Eisenhower's grandson David in the offing and with his own lingering doubts that he might have cost the Republicans the 1960 elec-

---

*One technical flaw scars the effectiveness of this ad. The bomb is filmed in color, not black and white, transforming it into an almost pleasing rather than a terrifying experience. An airy white bomb explodes gracefully into a placid clear blue sky filled with pillowy white clouds. The scene is the sort one might order on designer sheets. In black and white the same stimuli would have forced us to recoil in horror. Visually, this ad strangles its verbal message. After all, why shouldn't every country have its own lovely, visually lyrical bomb?

Stills from a television ad aired by the Humphrey campaign in the 1968 general election.

tion, Ike's support for Nixon was firm and fast. But unlike 1960, in 1968 Ike was seriously ill, a fact that enabled the Republicans to hint that if the country voted against Nixon it might bear the blame for killing Ike.

In his acceptance speech Nixon says that this time "We're going to win for a number of reasons. First a personal one. General Eisenhower, as you know, lies critically ill in the Walter Reed Hospital tonight. I have talked, however, with Mrs. Eisenhower on the telephone. She tells me that his heart is with us. She says that there is nothing that he lives more for, and there is nothing that would lift him more than for us to win in November. And I say let's win this one for Ike." The 30 minute edited version of the acceptance speech aired as a paid program does not contain this section. None of the advertisers recalls the reason for the deletion but Price supposes that it was not the by-product of conscious strategy but rather of the need to shorten the address without sacrificing its structural core.

By identifying with the policies and practices of the Eisenhower administration, Nixon subtly muted the charge that here was a new Nixon. This argument for fundamental consistency is also made by the recurrent use of clips and words from the acceptance speech in Nixon's advertising. Nixon's identification with the Eisenhower years also transformed his hiatus from governmental service into an asset. Nixon's rhetoric implied that while Johnson and Humphrey were making war and fomenting domestic discord, he had been pondering the meaning of the world in the post-Eisenhower age. The acceptance speech contained evidence of the lessons Nixon had learned.

In his half hour campaign biography "Richard Nixon: A Self-Portrait" Nixon set these lessons in the context of a lifetime. The biography revealed the unsurprising conclusion that the lessons included a respect for hard work, the value of education, the need for discipline, the importance of family, and the value of disappointments. His father was a self-educated man, Nixon reported; he was intelligent "because he worked so hard." Nixon recalled that his brother, who died when he was young, wanted a pony but his parents reluctantly decided against such a purchase. The money was required for clothing, shoes, and groceries. The family was poor but the children did not know that they were poor. On the Fourth of July his was the only family in the neighborhood that did not have fireworks. Instead his mother decorated the table with red, white, and blue bunting, and the family feasted on ice cream. "I remember that Fourth of July more than all the ones I've been through in my whole life," Nixon noted. The film dramatized Nixon's identification with the Protestant ethic.

"Nixon was a very reticent man about his own private life," says Shakespeare, "and we felt it was necessary to let him talk not about public issues in this film but about the fundamental questions of who he was and what formed his character, where he came from, what produced the human being who is Richard Nixon. Nixon was not the sort of man who was ordinarily forthcoming about these matters."

This film is the natural extension of the peroration of his acceptance speech in which he talks of a boy listening to the trains in the distance. In the film, Nixon praises the virtues of small town America and recalls simpler times. There are no riots or controversial wars in this world, no internal dissent. The film implies that a vote for Nixon is a vote for this kind world, a world in which work is rewarded and the traditional values cherished.

While the film offered the public a sense of Nixon's past and the panel shows, which I will discuss in a moment, offered the public a sense of Nixon's present, the radio speeches offered listeners the opportunity to try on the future Nixon presidency. His speech on the presidency show-cased a persona who transcended party for the good of the country. He did not plan to surround himself with "yes-men"; he would draw his administration "from the broadest possible base—an administration made up of Republicans, Democrats and Independents, and drawn from poli-tics, from career government service, from universities, from business, from the professions—one including not only executives and administra-tors, but scholars and thinkers." His would be an "activist" presidency that would "gain mastery over events," an "open presidency," and a presidency that would return to "the states, cities and communities . . . decision-making powers rightfully theirs." Ten radio speeches delivered in late October detailed the principles that would govern foreign and domestic policies and previewed some of these policies.

Democratic Attacks on Nixon's Past

The Old Nixon vs. the New Nixon

The "old Nixon" was a construct lovingly nurtured by the Democrats. It was the image embodied in the bearded, scowling caricature who marched alongside Eisenhower's white horse in the Democratic ads of 1952, the Nixon about whom the "Nervous about Nixon" ads were created in 1956, the haggard, shadowy, sweating, shifty-eyed Nixon whose worst moments in the first Kennedy-Nixon debate were intercut out of sequence into the Kennedy ads of 1960. It was Herblock's sewer-dwelling character assassin who wore a beatific Nixon mask to hide his menacing face. It was Nixon the point man for Eisenhower who lam-basted the Democrats in 1952 and 1956, as Spiro Agnew would do for him in 1970 and 1972.

To accentuate the differences between the old and the new Nixon, Humphrey's strategists considered airing portions of either the Checkers speech or Nixon's valedictory to the press after his gubernatorial defeat in 1962. "I got thirty letters a day saying 'Use that '62 tape," recalls Napoli-tan. "Retrospective memory distorts. When you look at it all you have is sympathy for Nixon. He's not arrogant, not screaming. He's just a tired, beaten guy. We didn't use it because it would have been counterproduc-tive. As for Checkers, that was 1952 and this was 1968. Besides, it was a pretty effective speech. It kept Richard Nixon on the Republican ticket. What could we say about it? Nothing."

Recall that in 1956 the Democratic strategists concluded that there was little usable evidence to sustain the widely held belief that Nixon should not be trusted with the presidency. Nothing that Nixon did in the campaign of 1960 furnished the evidence that was then lacking. In the campaign of 1962 bumper stickers charging "Brown is Pink" and circulars claiming that Brown was manipulated by left wing extremists smacked of the Nixon of the "Pink Lady" sheets, however. But it was difficult to tie the anti-Brown material directly to Nixon. Consequently, branding Nixon with the image perpetuated by Herblock was not feasible in 1968.

So while press and questioners on Nixon's panel shows were pondering whether there was a new Nixon, Democratic ads turned the "old versus new Nixon" into a charge of ideological inconsistency.

In ads tagged "Trust Humphrey," a tag that displaced "Humphrey-Muskie: There is No Alternative" in late October, the Democrats pitted Nixon against Nixon. "Which Nixon is the one?" asked one ad[55] headed by a picture of a smiling Nixon facing a frowning Nixon. "Because Richard Nixon has said no to a national debate, you may never find out. But the more you dig into Mr. Richard M. Nixon, the more he seems to be his own worst enemy. He could practically debate himself. He seems to be for the treaty to stop the spread of nuclear bombs—but he wants to delay it. And delay almost certainly will kill it. He seems to be for outlawing segregation of schools—but he doesn't want to enforce it. . . . Mr. Nixon lists '167 positions.' It's easy to see how he gets so many. He's been taking two or three positions on every issue . . . ." Nixon has "a record of being against minimum wages, against aid to education, against public housing, against consumer protection, against Medicare," said E. G. Marshall in the five minute ad discussed earlier. "When I ask myself what is new about Nixon, I find this answer. His technique is new. In the past, he discussed and debated issues and he lost an election. Now he will not discuss and not debate." Satirists revelled in the debate over the old vs. the new Nixon. Art Buchwald featured a debate between the old and new Nixon, while Russell Baker cast five Nixons onto his political stage.

Ironically, both campaigns saw a major difference between the candidate they championed and that candidate projected on television. Storck saw the challenge of the Humphrey documentary as capturing the real Humphrey. "Media like ours project a totally different, really quite false image of this man," he reported. "He's really a very thoughtful guy, a lot tougher, and not at all as vacuously affable as he appears on camera. It's going to be a real challenge to get the real Hubert Humphrey down on film."[56]

A New Nixon or More Effective Revelation of the Old Nixon?

When asked in the New Hampshire primary whether there was a new Nixon, the Republican candidate answered that "I sometimes think that all these people who keep finding a new Nixon never knew the old Nixon." When the question persisted in the general election, Nixon expanded that answer to account for the change people perceived in him. Responding to a question from Democratic attorney Morris Liebman, a panelist on one of the hour long interview shows the Republicans sponsored in ten regions of the country in the general election, Nixon said "There certainly is a new Nixon. . . . as a man gets older he learns something. If I haven't learned something I am not worth anything in public life. . . . I think my principles are consistent. . . . My answer is, yes, there is a new Nixon, if you are talking in terms of new ideas for the new world and the America we live in."[57]

But new ideas were not the only difference between the Nixon of 1960 and the Nixon of 1968, for one of the lessons Nixon had learned from defeat was that his concept of campaigning would have to change. Where in 1960 he jealously guarded his right to write his own speeches, in 1968 he displayed a greater willingness to delegate a portion of the responsibility. Where in 1960 he moved through the campaign at a frenetic pace symbolized by his pledge to campaign in all 50 states, in 1968 time was built into his schedule for rest, reading, and reflection. Where in 1960 he campaigned part of the day of his most crucial debate with Kennedy, in 1968 he arrived the night before in the city in which panels were to be held and spent a leisurely day preparing for each. Where in 1960 Nixon, in Finch's words, "did everything except sweep out the plane," in 1968, Finch observed: "He's not obsessed now with handling every detail himself."[58] This changed concept of campaigning mirrored a concept of the presidency Nixon detailed in a well-received radio address on the presidency in which he noted that "The President's chief function is to lead, not to administer; it is not to oversee every detail, but to put the right basic guidance and direction, and to let them do the job. This requires surrounding the President with men of stature, including young men, and giving them responsibilities commensurate with that stature."[59]

These changes contributed to the public sense that Nixon was more relaxed and confident in his public appearances in 1968 than he had been in 1960. But the changed public perception was also a function of reliance on substantially less formal, more spontaneous forms of advertising. Where in 1960 Nixon's advertising usually consisted of formal statements spoken directly to the camera, in 1968 the bulk of his purchased televised programming was devoted to showcasing Nixon as "the Man in the Arena." In the arena, Nixon stood alone, without podium or standing mike, responding for an hour to questions from five to seven panelists selected to represent the various important demographic groups in each of the ten regions in which the panel shows appeared.

Evolution of the Panel Shows

Although the panel shows exposed Nixon to substantially less risk than they would have if the studio audience had been impartial and the questioners national journalists, still the risk in such a live, unedited encounter was substantially greater than that posed in any previously used paid format other than the telethon.

None of the individuals who created advertising for Nixon in 1968 had known him personally in 1960. Each reports the experience of finding that their direct perception of Nixon differed markedly from the preconceptions they had formed by watching him on television. "In 1968 we were trying to find ways to get this Nixon we knew to the public," Price recalls.

Contrary to the claim in McGinniss' best selling book *The Selling of the President* that the admen decided what image Nixon should project and then fashioned him in that image, Shakespeare, Price, and Garment argue that they arrived at the "Man in the Arena" concept by asking what formats best revealed the Nixon they knew. "The structure of the book [McGinniss'] was crafted to show that we first decided what image would sell and then contrived to create and sell that image," notes Price. "That was the exact opposite of what we did. Those man in the arena shows grew from a session Len [Garment], Frank [Shakespeare] and I had with a group of others. Frank dug through the archives and got seven hours or so of film of Nixon in action. Early in the campaign we watched these and asked how did he come off well and how did he come off badly. We concluded that he came off best when he was spontaneous. So we tried to create a format that would bring out this spontaneity."

For two mornings at the Hillsboro Town Hall in Hillsboro, New Hampshire, shortly after Nixon officially entered the Republican race, his admen taped him fielding questions from a hand-picked panel of New Hampshire Republicans. "We had seven or eight people seated in chairs and Nixon was seated in a chair," Shakespeare recalls.[60] "It came off so well that we said 'If we go live with this, we'll have something electric in show biz terms and therefore interesting because most political programming is so damned dull.' We wanted something where people would get a sense of excitment and almost of danger because of the liveness of it." The best segments from the Hillsboro taping were edited into five minute ads and a half hour program aired in the primary.

The press had been given no notice of the taping. When reporters learned of it, they were irritated. This was the opening shot of a battle between the admen and the press that, in one form or another, would persist throughout the campaign.

In early July, with his nomination assured but not yet bestowed, Nixon began appearing in half hour shows based on the same format. Called "The Nixon Answer," these panel shows were aired in eight markets in Ohio, and six markets in both Illinois and Michigan—three states whose electoral votes could spell a Nixon victory in November. The press scrutinized the composition of the panels in a search for Nixon partisans. *Broadcasting* reported: "Some of the panelists acknowledged to the press that they were acquainted with Herb Klein, top press and communications aide to Mr. Nixon. Other members of the panel indicated they knew people who either work for Fuller & Smith & Ross Inc., the New York-based advertising agency that's buying time for the campaign, or were aides in the Nixon camp."[61] Unlike the Hillsboro panel and the panels aired in the general election, which were produced on location, the Ohio, Illinois, and Michigan pre-convention panels were taped in New York. Where these panels, like the Hillsboro one, were taped, the panels broadcast in the general election were aired live. These panels also forecast the panels of the general election by including Democratic and Republican questioners. These pre-convention panels are important as well for they indicate that before Humphrey's staff had even devised an advertising plan for the general election, Nixon was on the air in key states.

The first of Nixon's general election panels was set in the studio in Chicago in which his catastropic first debate with Kennedy occurred in 1960. The setting was symbolically important for a second reason. By opening the program with scenes of Nixon's motorcade being greeted by peaceful well-wishers, the Republicans implied that, unlike Humphrey whose nomination occasioned bloodletting, Nixon heralded harmony.

Two local newsmen and six area residents, including a prominent Democratic attorney, constituted the Chicago panel. "Someone [Frank Shakespeare] talked to us before the show went on," Morris Liebman, a partner in the firm of Sidley and Austin, recalls. "He said 'You're on your own and here are the rules of the road about where you sit and that sort of thing.' When we were alone we all said 'Look, we're going to be asking questions of a professional man who's thought about every question we could probably ask so let's ask questions that we're really interested in.' It was straight up like that. I think a lot in the media were disappointed that it was. After the program was over, we were available to talk to the press if the press wanted to talk to us. Afterward Nixon seemed pleased with the show. I was impressed that he really was a new Nixon, listening, outward directed and trying to be affirmative."[62]

The press was housed in a room adjoining the studio in which monitors carrying the question-and-answer show were placed. Shakespeare refused to admit reporters to the studio in which the show was being produced because he wanted them to see it as the viewer at home would. "The press didn't like this. They wanted to be in the studio. We said fairly cold bloodedly, 'If that happens you're going to write about the lights, the cameras and that sort of thing and you're not going to understand what happens in the living rooms of America. Thirty seconds after the program is over the studio doors will open and you can flood in there and meet the questioners, determine for yourselves their legitimacy, talk to the audience," Shakespeare recalls.

Reporters assigned to the campaign acknowledge the accuracy of Shakespeare's statement but add that as a practical matter the need to write the story minimized the likelihood that reporters would spend much time scrutinizing the credentials of panelists. "Because Nixon had few press conferences, many of the news stories that came out of the campaign came from answers to those panel shows," recalls Don Oberdorfer of the *Washington Post*. "As far as we were concerned it was like a press conference although the questions were not being asked by reporters. So as soon as the show was over we had to sit down and write a story about what he said."[63]

"Our primary purpose was to present Nixon as a man of broad competence who didn't need to go to school to be president. At least in our subconscious we were also creating a contrast to Humphrey," says Shakespeare. "Nixon spoke out of a fund of knowledge and he had a pretty definite ideas about what he wanted to do. Those two assets enabled him to speak concisely. Humphrey would go on and on."

Unlike the pre-convention panels, the panelists in the general election were not drawn from the campaign itself or from friends of the campaign staff. Believing that Nixon responded more effectively to tough questions and that tough questions underscored the authenticity of the program, Shakespeare encouraged panelists to ask tough questions and if they did not feel that the question had been adequately answered to follow up. "The toughest thing to do in putting the panels together," says Price, "was to get tough questioners. McGinniss says we were looking for patsies. The opposite was true. We knew the harder the question, the harder the pitch the more chance Nixon would hit a home run. We winced every time we had a soft question that made the questioner look like a patsy."

Although members of the press insisted that their questions would have been tougher than those asked by the citizens, some of the questions were as tough as any the national reporters were asking in press conferences. So, for example, panelists asked if Nixon would ask Republicans in the House to support suspension of section 315 to enable a two-way debate with Humphrey and without Wallace, if Nixon were using the panel shows to avoid professional interviewers, if civil disobedience could ever be justified, what he meant by "an honorable end" to the war, whether "law and order" was a code phrase for racism, should Justice Fortas be confirmed, was there a conspiracy between Nixon and Senator Strom Thurmond to block the confirmation, and whether he favored including the Viet Cong in a coalition government.[64]

The panels also produced revealing moments. When a panelist noted that blacks "are afraid of you," Nixon responded, "I'm not afraid of them." "A Mexican boy in America can only look forward to being a Mexican," said Nixon in Cleveland. "I mean a lemon picker." Some of the answers precipitated controversy. During the North Carolina telecast, for example, Nixon declared that he did not favor the withholding of federal funds from local school districts as a means of enforcing racial integration. In Philadelphia he revealed his opposition to a coalition government in Saigon.

Reporters undoubtedly are more skilled than ordinary citizens in pursuing follow-up questions. Still as Nixon's pirouettes around "Meet the Press" questions about the political motivation of Johnson's bombing halt demonstrate persuasively, long-lived politicians dextrously control what they reveal.[65]

Nixon's advisers justified use of citizen panels by noting that citizens ask questions of greater interest to the viewing audience than reporters. Additionally, the presence of one's neighbors on the panel heightened viewership. However, the questions of local newsmen who were included on the panels did parallel the sort of question asked by the national press.

"Citizens ask questions that are on their minds," notes Oberdorfer. "They are good solid questions. But from a reporter's standpoint they give politicians much more open room to make statements that don't commit them to anything and don't address the burning issues in Washington. They often don't advance the story in journalistic terms but are more comprehensible to most people listening. You can't say one's better than the other. They are different kinds of questions."

Critics of the panel format also charged that the partisan audience applauded with Pavlovian precision at the sound of any answer by Nixon thus enveloping vacuous answers in a favorable context. Additionally, critics argued that the presence of 500 cheering partisans intimidated panelists.

Nixon's admen grant that the audience was perfervidly partisan. "Where we put the integrity and vitality of the show was in the forceful legitimacy of the questioners," says Shakespeare. "The audience was a screened and selected audience."

"If you remember in 1968, there were chanters, people who would shout four letter words and throw eggs. . . . you can't mess around with that on live television. At least we didn't want to. Remember what happened at the Democratic convention."

The View of Nixon in *The Selling of the President*

In 1969, a young journalist named Joe McGinniss published *The Selling of the President,* a book recounting the evolution of Nixon's 1968 advertising campaign. On the book's cover Nixon's face smiles from the jacket of a package of cigarettes. The message of the cover, according to McGinniss, was that Nixon had been packaged and sold just like cigarettes. Although the Surgeon General's report already had detailed the hazards of smoking, McGinniss denies that he was aware that the book's cover seemed also to harbor the warning that Richard Nixon may be hazardous to your health."[66]

The book is a landmark in the history of political advertising, and in the judgment of Don Oberdorfer, the *Washington Post* reporter who covered Nixon in 1968, made "the press become much more conscious of political advertising." McGinniss beat "the world on the best story of the campaign," observes Don Irwin who covered the Nixon campaign in 1968 for the Los Angeles *Times*. "That changed the way everybody covers campaigns to a degree. Political desks are now making that kind of assignment."[67]

McGinniss' book also put political consultants on notice that they too could be subject to press scrutiny. Bob Squier, who produced Humphrey's live television in 1968 and now heads a political consulting firm called The Communication Company, notes that by focusing press attention on the creation of political advertising, McGinniss has helped "keep folks like me honest" because he and his colleagues know that they are answerable to the press for every choice they make.

At the same time, the book polished the damaging public perception that Richard Nixon was not what he appeared to be, a perception that in my judgment coupled with the residual images impressed by Herblock, Democratic advertising, the charges that precipitated the Checkers speech, and the like, to figure importantly in the predisposition of the press to pursue Nixon's possible complicity in Watergate.

The book "prepared the way for the hardening of attitudes for another generation," reports Garment. "I think the book hurt Nixon," notes Price, "simply because so many people assumed it was true."

However, in 1970 *New Republic* correspondent John Osborne held that McGinniss' portrayal humanized Nixon: "The author, Joe McGinniss, has done the President the immense and obviously unintended favor of showing him to be the normal, temperish, profane, vulnerable adult male that his spokesmen at the White House keep insisting he isn't. . . . Whatever we have in the Nixon Presidency, we don't have a potato. Maybe Nixon should hire Joe McGinniss."[68]

The Selling of the President also is noteworthy for creating the mistaken impression that, in a presidential race, advertising is sufficiently powerful to create important public perceptions of candidates that are fundamentally different from the candidates themselves. The book also implied that 1968 was the first year in which persons outside politics engaged in systematic and widespread efforts to transmit a preplanned image of a presidential candidate, a claim that flies in the face of even the history of the 1964 campaign.

Had McGinniss been given access to the Republican campaign of 1952, the Democratic campaign of 1960, or either of the national campaigns of 1964, the undertone of astonishment that pervades *Selling* instead would have been one of ennui. Indeed, had he glanced at the 1968 Humphrey campaign in which questioners interrogated Humphrey for two hours with the resulting tape edited to thirty minutes, he might have concluded that the Nixon panel shows were comparatively nonmanipulative.

Garment approved McGinniss' study of the campaign on the understanding that McGinniss was writing "a post graduate thesis." "We were innocents abroad and let ourselves into it. We thought we would be enshrined in some postdoctoral thesis," he says. But McGinniss contends that he told Garment that he had a contract to write a book. Garment remembers no mention of a contract. Before talking with the Republicans, McGinniss had tried and failed to gain access to the Democrat's inner circle.

"Any Philadelphia journalist, or indeed any reader of McGinniss' column in the *Philadelphia Inquirer,* could have told them how ludicrous" was the notion that McGinniss was writing "a studious, philosophic account of the role of the electronic media in modern Presidential politics" observed John Osborne later.[69] "McGinniss was known in Philadelphia as something of a journalistic prodigy, a sharpshooter with minimal regard for reportorial niceties and a special appeal to young readers." "From a political point of view," McGinniss admits, "I certainly wasn't sympathetic to Nixon."

But these were things Garment, Treleaven, and Shakespeare did not know at the time for none reviewed McGinniss' columns or explored his journalistic reputation. In retrospect they conclude that this ommission was "naive."

McGinniss believes that the central story of his book was that "for the first time on such a large scale professionals from other fields were not simply sprucing up the image of an existing candidate but were creating a whole new person who did not in reality exist. The story was the extent to which the use of television was so effectively controlled by these people. . . . 1968 was the first time an advertising agency was given the task of creating something radically different from what it was with the cooperation of the candidate. The scope, extent and agreement of the candidate and advisors seemed without precedent."

Whether the Republican advertisers created a Nixon who did not exist or a Nixon different from the one that existed I do not know. But what I am sure of is that McGinniss' book does not make the case it claims. Although his book contains such statements as "Into this milieu came Richard Nixon: grumpy, cold, and aloof,"[70] McGinniss did not know Nixon personally. Consequently, McGinniss was in no position to ascertain whether the advertisers had created "something radically different from what it was." Nor does the evidence he amasses support his secondary claim, which is that Nixon's advisers thought that they were creating a "whole new person" who did not exist. To build a case opposite from McGinniss' one simply needs to mine the memoranda he reprints in the appendix to his book. There one finds Price, who as a professional wordsmith should be expected to say what he means, noting:

> We can put together a variety of one or five minute or longer *films of the man in motion,* with the idea of conveying a sense of his *personality*—the personality that most voters have simply not had a chance to see, or, if they have, have lost in the montage of other images that form their total perceptions of the man.

> Another thing we've got to get across is a sense of human warmth. This is vital to the Presidential mystique, and has largely been the "hidden side" of RN, as far as the public is concerned. And it can be gotten across without loss of either dignity or privacy. It shines through in a lot of those spontaneous moments that have been caught on film. . . . It came through at times on the Niven show, and strongly on the Carson show. One of the great plusses of the Carson show was that it hit a lot of people with the *jolt of the unexpected*—it showed people a side of RN *that they didn't know existed and this jarred loose a lot of the old prejudices and preconceptions.*

> I know the whole business of contrived imagemongering is repugnant to RN, with its implication of slick gimmicks and phony merchandising. But it's simply not true that honesty is its own salesman; for example, it takes make-up to make a man look natural on TV. Similarly, it takes art to convey the truth from us to the viewer.[71]

These are very different recommendations than those McGinniss summarized in his interview with David Frost when he said: "And they told him then that what he was going to have to do was develop qualities of personality, or, if not develop them himself, at least allow them to project qualities of personality that the American people wanted in a President. His advertising director listed among these warmth, humor, a sense of compassion, things which I think even Mr. Nixon's friends would not list chief among his virtues. He's in his middle fifties, and it's a little late for a man to change his character. So he allowed them to make it appear as if he had changed his character simply through sophisticated technical uses of television."[72]

Shakespeare, Garment, and Price deny that they were doing anything other than exposing to public view facets of Nixon's character and personality that were not readily apparent in traditional advertising forms. When we turn to McGinniss' book for the evidence for his claim that they thought they were creating a person without basis in reality we find broad inferential leaps from evidence that when taken in context more readily bears an alternative reading. Note, for example, the concluding statement in Price's memo:

> We do want to close the gap between old myths and present realities: we want to remind supporters of the candidate's strengths, and demonstrate to nonsupporters that the Herblock images are fiction. The way to do this is to let more people see the candidate as we see him, remembering that the important thing is not to win debates, but to win the audience; not to persuade them to RN's point of view, but to win their faith in his leadership.[73]

Price is not alone in his conclusion that their job was to let the public see Nixon as he is. John Maddox, a quantitative analyst working for the Nixon campaign, reported that the widest gap between Humphrey and Nixon was on the cold-warm scale of the Semantic Differential, a measurement tool designed to tap affective response. "We believe it highly probable," McGinniss reports Maddox writing, "that if the real personal warmth of Mr. Nixon could be more adequately exposed, it would release a flood of other inhibitions about him—and make him more tangible as a person to large numbers of Humphrey leaners."[74]

Even Treleaven, by profession an advertiser, does not write of creating something that does not exist but of drawing out qualities native to Nixon but not readily projected. "[H]e should make more of a point of displaying his feelings, as well as his knowledge," Treleaven advises.[75]

The one person captured between the pages of McGinniss' book who unequivocally endorses McGinniss' view of the campaign is a minor functionary employed by Eugene Jones. His name is Jim Sage and by McGinniss' own account he is a McCarthy Democrat!

Interpreting the book is complicated by the presence of conversations between key staff members that could have been said jokingly or as humorous castoffs or could have been uttered with deadly seriousness. McGinniss fails to provide the characterizing adverbs that would reveal tone. Consequently, in the following exchange, Treleaven's statement and possibly Garment's are open to conflicting interpretations. They have just viewed a filmed interview featuring Spiro Agnew:

> Frank Shakespeare was up now and pacing the back of the theater. "We can't use any of this," he said. "That picture quality is awful. Just awful. And Agnew himself, my God. He says all the wrong things."
>
> "What we need is a shade less truth and a little more pragmatism," Treleaven said.
>
> "I think Dexedrine is the answer," Garment said.[76]

The central characters in McGinniss' book including Garment, Shakespeare and Ailes acknowledge that in the main they did make the remarks attributed to them but note that McGinniss has selected judiciously from their many conversations. Price who is not featured in the book explains that McGinniss quoted accurately but distorted the context in which the quotes appeared. "I know these people well and I've shared in this black humor with them many times. You make these cracks and laugh. McGinniss left out the laughter. If you engage in this sort of badinage with friends and intimates you say things that would look awful in print but you all know that you are joking. I recognized many of McGinniss' lines from this kind of context."

Roger Ailes explains the problem in interpreting the book this way: "I don't think the quotes were necessarily inaccurate but if I took 3% of your conversation from the last three months would that be misrepresenting you? That's what he did."[77] Ailes also disputes McGinniss' claim that the admen fabricated a new Nixon. "Nixon had been in public life for 30 years," he notes. "George C. Scott can't hold up a performance for more than a few hours. You'd have to be awfully good to pull that off."

Shakespeare and Garment believe that McGinniss entered the project with a bias and selectively sought support for it. He "came at the project," in Garment's judgment, "with a certain point of view: balloon pricking, humorous, pompous, satiric." McGinniss denies this. "I wrote what I saw," he says. "I wrote what happened and there it is for you to make of it what you wish."

Fifteen years after the fact it is difficult to adjudicate these conflicting claims. However, some evidence of selective reading can be gleaned from McGinniss' treatment of the questions and answers between Nixon and a local radio commentator Jack McKinney on the Philadelphia panel show. It is McGinniss' belief that Nixon ducked the tough questions of the national press by instead holding highly orchestrated panel shows using citizen interviewers. "He would not allow himself to be questioned by professional questioners, only under circumstances where his own people would pay for an hour," McGinniss told David Frost. "They would pick the panel themselves, and then they would put him up live and say, 'Here's Nixon answering Americans' questions.' "[78] That is the charge McKinney makes. To McKinney's question McGinniss reports this response from Nixon:

> "I've done those quiz shows, Mr. McKinney. I've done them until they were running out of my ears." There was no question on one point: Richard Nixon was upset.
>
> Staring hard at McKinney, he grumbled something about why there should be more fuss about Hubert Humphrey not having press conferences and less about him and Meet the Press.
>
> It did not seem much of a recovery but in the control room Frank Shakespeare punched the palm of one hand with the fist of the other and said, "That socks it to him, Dickie baby!" The audience cheered.[79]

What McGinniss neglects to report is the substance of Nixon's answer. The *Washington Post's* account of the exchange reads:

> McKinney noted that Humphrey had questioned why Nixon had not appeared on "Meet the Press," "Face the Nation" or "Issues and Answers" for almost two years.
>
> Nixon replied that he had been on those "quiz shows . . . until they were coming out of my ears." He said he was doing something that was much more difficult in holding formal press conferences for the reporters accompanying him on his campaign.
>
> Nixon has held three formal press conferences this month. He asked why Humphrey has held no such press conference on his campaign, except for an informal session during a beach walk in New Jersey last week.[80]

So McGinniss is guilty of dropping from his report of Nixon's answer information that would rebut one of McGinniss' central claims. Newspaper accounts confirm that Nixon was indeed holding press conferences. Additionally, Don Irwin, the *LA Times* reporter assigned to Nixon's campaign confirms that "Nixon would have press conferences at the stops. Usually the announced effort would be to divide the questions between the guys with him and the locals but there was a determined balance going to the locals." Still, the national press was being afforded an opportunity to question the candidate. As McGinniss acknowledges in the book but not on Frost's show, despite his dismissive characterization of them as "quiz shows," in the final week of the campaign Nixon relented and appeared on "Meet the Press" the same day that Humphrey appeared on "Issues and Answers." Theodore White judged both performances "excellent."[81]

I do not wish to suggest that the press enjoyed the level of uncontrolled access to Nixon that it desired or that the access it attained was as easy to come by as it was in other campaigns, but rather that McGinniss' account ignores incontrovertible evidence that runs counter to his case. This curious lapse in information couples with his elliptical report of Nixon's response to McKinney to suggest that McGinniss' inquiry is driven not so much by the evidence as by a preconceived premise.

A second clear instance of argument by omission occurs in McGinniss's guest appearance with Michigan Congressman Gerald Ford on the David Frost Show. From his personal acquaintance with Nixon, Ford contends that "the characteristic [humor] was there [in Nixon], and through the media of the experts they were able to bring it out in the campaign." McGinniss counters that "what I think Richard Nixon did with his television cameras was stage situations which were specifically designed to bring out personality qualities which even his own advisors believed he did not have. The men who worked most closely with him in the image field, I think, would disagree with you, and from listening to their conversations over a period of twelve months they did disagree with you about these qualities of Nixon's. Raymond Price, who was a *New York Herald Tribune* editorial writer, now a White House speech writer, said in 1967, in a memorandum to Mr. Nixon, "It's not what's there that counts, it's what's projected, and we must be very clear on this point, that the response is to the image, not the man, and that this response often depends more on the medium and its use than it does on the candidate himself." Then McGinniss adds: "Now this is Nixon's own man. This is not my accusation."[82]

But it *is* McGinniss' own accusation, for what the author of *The Selling of the President* has done is delete from Price's statement a key sentence that supports Ford's argument. In the memo McGinniss reproduces in his book's appendix, we find Price stating:

> It's not what's *there* that counts, it's what's projected—and, carrying it one step further, it's not what *he* projects but rather what the voter receives. It's not the man we have to change, but rather the *received impression*. And this impression often depends more on the medium and its use than it does on the candidate himself.[83]

In the body of the book itself McGinniss does retain the central sentence: "It's not the man we have to change, but rather the *received impression*." But when Ford challenges McGinniss by making what is in fact Price's claim, McGinniss responds by doing to Price's statement what he had done to Nixon's response to McKinney: excise the sentence that undercuts his case. McGinniss' selective amnesia about parts of memos and answers that contravene his central claims lends credence to the

claims of Nixon's admen about the overall accuracy of the book's portrayal of their efforts on Nixon's behalf. Ironically, McGinniss seems to
be doing to Nixon and Price what he accuses Nixon's admen of doing to
Nixon—creating images that do not comport with reality.

In conclusion, McGinniss was overstepping his evidence when he
claimed that "they [his advisers] shielded him, controlled him, and controlled the atmosphere around him. It was as if they were building not a
President but an Astrodome, where the wind would never blow, the
temperature never rise or fall, and the ball never bounce erratically on
the artificial grass. They could do this, and succeed, because of the special nature of the man. There was, apparently, something in Richard
Nixon's character which sought this shelter. Something which craved
regulation, which flourished best in the darkness, behind cliches, behind
phalanxes of antiseptic advisers."[84]*

The New Nixon Tries on the Presidency

Nixon outspent Humphrey by four to one on radio to deliver a series of
speeches in which he articulated the principles and policies that would
govern his presidency. In ten radio addresses delivered in the closing
weeks of the election Nixon detailed his legislative agenda in such areas
as education, welfare, and crime control. "Those people who said Nixon
was not addressing the issues were not listening to the radio speeches,"
notes Price.

This use of radio conserved Nixon's time. "You can have the candidate in the hotel room, and . . . you can just sit him down with a tape
recorder sitting in his bathrobe and he can knock off four or five radio
speeches in no time," Shakespeare explains.

Radio also reached Nixon's natural rural constituency in a cost efficient manner while inviting press coverage. "The media tend to scoff at
radio," notes Price, "but when it becomes an event they have to report
the speech because a large audience is listening." "We revived radio as a
medium in 1968," he adds. By so doing, the Republican campaign established a model that would be followed by Republican nominees in both
1972 and 1976.

---

*Just as McGinniss magnifies the manipulation he sees and manipulates the magnification,
academics and others have amplified McGinniss' claims. Nowhere does McGinniss assert
that the panelists' questions were prescreened. Yet Watson and Thomas note, for example,
that "the makeup of both the panels and the questions were carefully screened by Nixon's
advisers in order to avoid possible embarrassment or surprise." (p.79)

Johnson's Final Move

On October 31, the Thursday before the election, Johnson threw into the political stew a piece of raw meat of unidentified composition raising the question: Was it steak or possum? He had ordered "all air, naval, and artillery bombardment of North Vietnam" to cease by 8 A.M. the following morning, he said, in anticipation of "prompt, productive, serious and intensive negotiations in an atmosphere that is conducive to progress."

By Saturday morning the world knew that the meat was possum. A headline in the *New York Times* read "Saigon Opposes Paris Talk Plans." Johnson, it turned out, had obtained the agreement of South Vietnamese President Thieu but Thieu had not in turn gained agreement from his national assembly or cabinet. What complicated all of this was the back-door dealings of Nixon supporter Anna Chan Chennault, widow of General Claire Chennault, who, implying that she spoke for Nixon, rallied opposition to the agreement in Vietnam.

Government wiretaps informed Johnson of Chennault's activities before he announced the bombing halt but he dismissed their seriousness. Once aware that she had helped orchestrate the opposition, Johnson relayed that information to Humphrey and Nixon. Nixon denied any knowledge of her activities. Believing him, Humphrey refused to make her dealings a last minute issue in the campaign.

Seeing the Campaigns Through their Election Eve Telethons

On election eve each of the two major parties purchased two hours of time on the East Coast and two on the West to air telethons, tests of endurance in which the candidates fielded questions from the public.

The candidates' previous experience with telethons had been very different. Nixon had successfully used that format on election eve in 1960 and had revived it at the end of the Oregon primary in 1968. Since both of Nixon's telethons went smoothly, it was a format he had no reason to fear. Additionally, the regional panels had refined his skills in dealing with questions from citizens.

By contrast, Humphrey had watched Kennedy use the "Coffee with Kennedy" call-ins successfully against him in the primaries of 1960. But where Nixon's past experience had been positive, Humphrey's own telethon in West Virginia arguably marked the low point of the Humphrey campaign in 1960. During it, a female caller screeched at Humphrey to get out of West Virginia and an operator informed him that he would have to clear the lines because of an emergency.

In the closing weeks of the 1968 campaign, Humphrey adopted a program form in some ways similar to Nixon's panel shows. Questioners sat in a circle around Humphrey who was seated on a stool. The two hour sessions were edited to thirty minutes for broadcast. Napolitan insists that "While we couldn't possibly use all of the material we taped—the sessions usually ran for two hours—we never interfered with the thrust of a question, or edited either the question or the gist of the response."[85] What differentiated these panels from Nixon's was that Nixon's were broadcast live, unedited, and with the press seated in the next room.

The decision to produce a Democratic telethon was made by O'Brien who in a staff meeting October 18 noted that "There is no question in my mind that in 1960 the telethon was Nixon's most effective campaign device. He knows this and wants to do it again." At that meeting, Squier, who would ultimately produce the telethon, observed that "It's possible to lose votes on this kind of program, too." Napolitan argued: "I have a personal feeling on this subject. A telethon would cost about $500,000. I would rather see this money spent on additional spots and advertising in key states."

In a subsequent meeting in his office, O'Brien dismissed Napolitan and Squier's arguments saying, as Squier recalls, "I sat next to John Kennedy on election eve and watched a telethon by Nixon and I'm not going to sit by and hold Hubert Humphrey's hand while he watches a Nixon telethon at the end of this election." Napolitan and Squier then went to Napolitan's office where Squier said, "This is a waste of money." Napolitan agreed. Squier now believes that "We were absolutely wrong. O'Brien was absolutely right."

Had Humphrey realized that there was "no tape delay" protecting him from a revisiting of his experience in West Virginia, he might have been less comfortable in the telethon's environment. As final plans for the telethon were jelling, Squier dropped the tape delay on the assumption that it would be interpreted by the press as a means of censuring questions. Arriving at the last minute before the telethon was to air, Humphrey was not apprised of the change.

The sort of harassment Humphrey experienced in West Virginia did not recur in part because even in the absence of a tape delay the screening mechanism set in place by Squier minimized its ability to recur. Callers initially asked their question of a staff member off stage who determined whether the caller was articulate, the question one that had not been asked, and the questioner from a region of the country different from the preceding caller. Questioners who passed this test were asked to stay on the line until the studio moderator, Jim Dunbar, an on-air personality who hosted a talk show in San Francisco, picked up the phone and relayed their call to Humphrey. Only then did the person ask the question that was broadcast to the nation.

Both Nixon and Humphrey aired separate telethons for the East and

West Coasts, a factor that subjected each candidate to four hours of live television performance. Roger Ailes, formerly producer of the "Mike Douglas Show" produced Nixon's telethon; Bob Squier, formerly of USIA and PBS produced Humphrey's. Nixon's ran on CBS, Humphrey's on ABC, a network with substantially fewer total stations. Consequently, Nixon reached a larger audience and a larger percent of viewing homes. Twenty-two percent of the viewing homes watched the Democratic telethon while twenty-six percent watched the Republican one. Humphrey garnered an audience estimated at fourteen million, Nixon at fifteen million.

The differences between the two telethons were symbolized by their sets. Nixon, looking tired, sat in a swivel chair. Humphrey, a microphone in hand, prowled the set, sometimes sitting, often standing. The Republican set was immaculate, the Democratic littered with empty chairs, exposed television cables, and with an occasional abandoned coffee cup. Humphrey took calls directly from viewers; questions for Nixon were relayed by Bud Wilkinson. "Nixon was better talking to a person than to a camera," Ailes explains.

The contrast between the two telethons was not the by-product of chance. After reviewing the Nixon '60 telethon, the telethon in Oregon, and the announced plans of the Republicans revealed in *TV Guide,* the Democrats "built" in Squier's words "a show against what they were going to do." So calculated was the look of spontaneity that Squier wanted to create that after a crew tidied the studio a half hour before the telethon, Squier littered it up again. "They designed theirs to the style of Humphrey," says Ailes. "We designed ours to the style of Nixon's personality. Nixon is not a casual man." But, he adds, "The coffee cups and exposed wires [on the Humphrey telethon] were simply technical screwups. We didn't make technical mistakes."

The casts of the telethons differed as well. Muskie was central to Humphrey's telecast; although Nixon praised his choice of Agnew and Agnew's qualifications in each telethon, his vice-presidential nominee was nowhere to be seen. Although members of both families were in the telethons' audiences, Nixon's family played a more central role on his telethon than did Humphrey's family on his.

On both telethons important endorsements were given. On Nixon's David Eisenhower testified to his grandfather's support of the Republican ticket. On Humphrey's, prodigal party member Eugene McCarthy phoned in an endorsement.

Fearful that channeling calls directly to the candidate would invite sabotage or obscenity, the Republicans broke from the pattern of direct questioning pioneered in the panel shows and instead created a "Johnny

Carson" like format in which an intermediary relayed questions to Nixon. "You can't sit there with an open mike," says Price, "and let any kook and 10,000 people hired by the opposition make speeches. You've got to have some sort of screening. This format was set up to make sure that Nixon had a chance to answer the questions that were most being asked." Questions directed to Nixon were called in by viewers, rewritten by staff members, and asked of Nixon by football coach Bud Wilkinson. Accounts of the extent to which Nixon's questions were prefabricated differ. McGinniss quotes Ailes saying: "Keyes [a Nixon adviser and "Laugh-In" originator] has a bunch of questions Nixon wants to answer. He's written them in advance to make sure they're properly worded. When someone calls with something similar, they'll use Keyes' question and attribute it to the person who called."[86] Garment says that the questions asked of Nixon originated with actual viewers. If they were altered at all by the staff, he says, it was to make them more concise or more grammatically correct. Ailes now notes that "There was no writing of questions outright. As I understand it they [those fielding calls] took long statements out and condensed the questions for TV time purposes but did not change their sense except to clean them up for grammar."

In retrospect, Shakespeare regards the Republican alternative as a mistake. "If I had to do it over," he says, "I would put Nixon on direct because it would have added to the genuineness and the electricity of the program. You didn't have to worry about Nixon's ability to answer the questions in any event and if you browbeat somebody on the air you arouse sympathies for the underdog so we didn't have to fear harangues."

By contrast, Shakespeare notes, "If I had been advising Humphrey I wouldn't have put him on in too many live situations. He was a decent, kindly man but he was as boring as hell and when he got on a subject he went on and on." "I watched Humphrey give an eleven minute answer to a question once," notes Ailes. "Even the host was looking off camera saying 'What the Hell did I ask this guy, I forgot.' I said, 'We need a format he can't use.' " Squier recognized that Humphrey's "tendency to get carried away" was a problem.

While Nixon answered briefly and concisely without prodding, Humphrey's prolixity was legendary. To minimize this disadvantage Squier designed a format that permitted him to interrupt Humphrey when long-windedness overcame him. In such circumstances, Muskie was asked to break in with a question or a celebrity such as Paul Newman was told to hand Humphrey the phone to take a call. "You can see him [Humphrey] being pulled and jerked around to perform this thing at a much faster pace," Squier recalls.

The producers of both telethons ensured that their candidates would be asked their most critical question early in the program. So, Nixon was asked about Agnew's credentials early in the Republican telethon, and Humphrey asked about his plans to end the war early in the Democratic program. To increase the public's realization that the candidates were taking actual calls, Squier also specifically instructed his staff to put through a tough question on abortion to Humphrey's Catholic running mate.

Humphrey used the telethon as a surrogate debate. After repeatedly urging Nixon to debate him and Wallace, in mid-October Humphrey reserved an hour of TV time for such a debate. Nixon refused on the grounds that he did not want to legitimize Wallace's candidacy. When Humphrey agreed that Wallace would get separate time in return for being excluded from the debate, Nixon ducked again saying even under that arrangement Wallace would be given added exposure. Humphrey then used the time he had purchased for the debate to deliver a speech.

In sections of the telethon Humphrey functioned as if he were debating his Republican opponent by firing questions and answers across the airwaves at Nixon. When Nixon noted that he was disturbed by reports that Vietnamese cities were still being shelled and supplies were still moving down the Ho Chi Minh Trail, Humphrey responded by saying, "Now, Mr. Nixon, I think you know very well that the President's orders did not include the Ho Chi Minh Trail" where bombing continues. In a staff meeting someone had suggested that Humphrey actually phone Nixon's telethon. The idea was rejected. "To phone Nixon would have given him a chance to actually answer," Squier explains. "We assumed the people in Nixon's control room heard Humphrey's questions and asked, 'What are we going to do?' They certainly couldn't tell Nixon. We hoped the questions would generate the feeling that we were open, willing to ask questions. We hoped that people would dial back and forth to create their own debate." Ailes, who was nursing an injured foot in a bucket of ice water as he choreographed the telethon, says that he paid little attention to the control room monitor that displayed Humphrey's telethon.

In an election in which one candidate claimed that there was not a dime's worth of difference between the other two and in which McCarthy and Kennedy's supporters deliberated about sitting the election out entirely, the telethons were an effective means of stimulating voter involvement. The form stresses the candidates' accountability to the voters regardless of their political preferences. At the same time, unlike most political uses of television, it invites active not passive participation by viewers. Finally, in 1968 the telethons enabled voters to compare the two major party candidates in paid formats more comparable than those employed in any previous election in television's history. The format also offered sustained exposure in which the major topics of the campaign—

not simply a pre-chosen few—were addressed. Despite all the criticism of screening and rewriting of questions addressed to Nixon, the questions asked of Humphrey and Nixon were comparable and reflected the concerns of the campaign. Unfortunately, the telethons were scheduled against each other. Ideally, the electorate would have been permitted to watch both without having to change channels to do so, a process that reduced each telethon to fragments.

Slogans

The Nixon campaign opened with the slogan "Nixon's the One," prompting a Democratic prankster to situate in Nixon's audiences obviously pregnant women carrying signs testifying "Nixon's the One." As the campaign progressed that slogan gave way to "Vote Like Your Whole World Depended on It," a slogan that underscored the troubles presumably resulting from Johnson's landslide victory over Goldwater.*

The copy that backed the slogan rendered explicit its implied "You." The headings in one ad argued: "Crime: you can turn the tide"; "Government: you can increase the power of the people"; "Cost of Living: You can bring it under control"; "Vietnam: You can make sure we're not trapped again." You can accomplish all of this by voting for Nixon. In this context the Nixon ads offered power and a sense of control in an environment in which both seemed to be crumbling.

For much of the campaign, Humphrey's advertising foundered in search of a unifying theme and an expressive slogan. "Humphrey-Muskie: There is No Alternative"; "Humphrey-Muskie: Two you can Trust"; "Humphrey has the answers; Let's give him the authority" were all tried before the campaign settled on various versions of "Trust Humphrey."

The alternative slogans reflected what are traditionally viewed as the philosophies of the two parties, with self-reliance identified with the Republicans and trust in a centralized authority with the Democrats.

In the early hours of the day after the election, voters finally concluded by a slim margin—31,770,237 votes to 31,270,533—that Nixon was the one. Wallace garnered 9,906,141 votes.

---

*Richard Whelan, a speechwriter for Nixon during the primaries who left the campaign before the general election, recalls that he, Garment, and Robert Finch "sat for the better part of two hours contemplating a pair of advertising layouts" one claiming "This time, vote as if your whole world depends on it," the other substituting "as if" for "like."

"The weighty subject of our debate was whether Nixon should be sold like a cigarette. I objected to the use of the transparently slick 'like,' but Garment had the advertising agency's market research, showing that a majority of those polled preferred 'like'—they thought 'as if' sounded wishy washy. Finch had the last word. No matter how you said it, the message was true: 'With Agnew on the ticket, this time your whole world damned well *does* depend on Nixon.' " (p. 210)

CHAPTER SEVEN

1972: The President vs. The Prophet

In June 1971, the political deck appeared stacked against Richard Nixon's reelection. The economy was flagging; the war in Vietnam that he had promised to end persisted; and only 48% of the American public approved of his handling of the presidency. The pundits pegged Maine's Senator Edmund Muskie as Nixon's likely opponent in the general election of 1972.

Two factors catapulted Muskie into the position of front-runner for the Democratic nomination. First, as Humphrey's running mate in 1968 Muskie had gained favorable national exposure. Indeed, Humphrey's campaign had spent part of its advertising budget trumpeting the presidential potential of the person they hoped in January 1969 would be a heartbeat away from the presidency. Additionally, in a back-to-back presentation with Richard Nixon on the off-year election eve 1970 Muskie appeared the less partisan, more statesmanlike of the two. How Richard Nixon came to be upstaged by Edmund Muskie is a story in misplaced staff enthusiasm.

Fired up by the crowd's resounding response to an address that he had delivered earlier in an airport hangar in Phoenix, Arizona, Richard Nixon's aides rushed an edited version of the speech onto the air. The afternoon of the telecast, CBS president Frank Stanton called his former colleague Frank Shakespeare, then head of USIA, to tell him that "the technical quality of the tape was not up to broadcast standards." When he relayed that message to a member of Nixon's staff, Shakespeare was told that "we know about this, we've looked at it carefully and we've approved it."[1]

A network official expressed the same concern as Stanton's to Jeb Magruder, who in 1972 would serve as deputy director of the Committee to Re-elect the President, and added that Muskie's tape was first rate and Nixon's terrible, an opinion Magruder relayed to speechwriter William

Safire, chief of staff H. R. Haldeman, and appointments secretary Dwight Chapin.[2] By that point, Nixon had already accepted an invitation to speak elsewhere on election eve and consequently was unavailable to deliver a live address. Nixon's staff also was disinclined to accept the judgment of a network executive over that of Safire and Haldeman. So the edited version of the Phoenix speech was aired.

"It was a fighting, arm-waving, give-'em-hell, law-and-order speech," Magruder writes, "fine for a rally . . . but completely wrong to send into the quiet of people's homes. Moreover, the sound was bad, often inaudible. The tape was in black and white, and some imperfection caused a jagged line to run down the middle of the picture. Finally, because the speech had been edited down to thirteen minutes, it was disjointed to the point of irrationality."[3] "It only cost us a couple of hundred thousand dollars and two or three Senate seats, as all the experts pointed out later," noted Safire who advocated airing the speech. "Nixon's election eve show was 'hot'—hard-driving, angry, and too political—while Muskie's speech was 'cool'—written by Richard Goodwin with a nice sense of place and contrast."[4]

On the assumption that Nixon would deliver a speech from the Oval Office, Bob Squier, who produced Muskie's speech, planned a format and a speech that would be "more personal, more direct and more understandable. Muskie spoke directly to the camera, without a lot of camera shots. The speech was taped in his home, not an office. He was more low key than Nixon could be."[5] The Republican's use of a stump speech heightened the contrast between the two. "Muskie's speech was powerful," notes Squier, "but the contrast to Nixon's heightened its effect. Nixon set the situation up for us." When Muskie wanted to resurrect that format for his 1972 announcement speech, Squier, who feared that the speech could not meet the high expectations set by its predecessor, objected. He was overruled. "My argument was that [to achieve a comparable effect] we needed Nixon to do the intro," Squier recalls.

After the election eve speeches in 1970, the FCC was deluged with calls from incensed Republicans charging that the networks had sabotaged Nixon. But Nixon's poor showing taught the Republicans a lesson. In 1972 Nixon would run not as a candidate but as The President. This strategy, conceived early in the campaign and followed precisely, proved to be both simple and extremely effective. How he accomplished that, with the indirect aid of George McGovern, who violated the public's sense of how a prospective president should look, act, and sound, is the story of this chapter.

The Democratic Primaries

In January 1972 consensus held that Muskie would win the Democratic nomination. He led other Democratic hopefuls in the polls and had amassed endorsements from more members of Congress, senators, governors, and mayors than some candidates who had been their party's nominee. "The endorsement strategy was an unconscious attempt to bring Muskie the nomination rather than forcing him to fight for it," Squier, who served as Muskie's media adviser, now believes. "I always felt that every breath that Humphrey drew fueled his ambition to be president. I always had the feeling that if his country wanted him to serve, Muskie was willing. That's not enough to win."

A number of other Democratic contenders entered the primaries. Those who were listed in the polls as asterisks included New York Congresswoman Shirley Chisholm, Los Angeles Mayor Sam Yorty, Chair of the House Ways and Means Committee Wilbur Mills, and South Dakota Senator George McGovern, whose brief 1968 bid was mentioned in the last chapter.

Those whose candidacies were taken seriously included Hubert Humphrey, who had narrowly lost to Nixon in 1968 and was now seeking a rematch; Senator Henry (Scoop) Jackson of Washington; New York's Mayor John Lindsay, who had resigned from the Republican party to become a Democrat; and Alabama Governor George Wallace, who as leader of a third party movement in 1968 had won five Southern states.

The question mark of the campaign was Senator Edward Kennedy of Massachusetts, whose presidential luster had dimmed when in summer 1969 a car that he was driving plunged off a bridge killing the young woman who was the car's other occupant. Despite Kennedy's disavowals of any intention to run in 1972, the polls conducted for Nixon in January included trial heats between Nixon and Muskie, Nixon and Humphrey, and Nixon and Kennedy.

The New Hampshire primary of March 7 was essentially a contest between Muskie and the high expectations he and the press had set for his candidacy. Facing predictions that he would win 65%, Muskie's candidacy was wounded when he won the primary with 47% of the vote. Many would attribute his loss to his public appearance on February 26 before the offices of the conservative newspaper, the *Manchester Union Leader*.

Standing on a flatbed truck in a moderately heavy snowstorm, Muskie responded to two sallies by *Manchester Union Leader* publisher William Loeb. Two days earlier, on February 24, Loeb had printed a picture of a scrawled letter to him charging that Muskie had approved a slur on Americans of French-Canadian ancestry. The picture ran on the page normally carrying the editorial cartoon. In a front page editorial Loeb called Muskie a hypocrite for tolerating a reference to French-Canadian-Americans as "Canucks." Muskie denied that the reported incident had taken place. The next day Loeb reprinted an item from *Newsweek* that both quoted Muskie's wife telling reporters on the press bus "Let's tell dirty jokes" and claimed that she preferred two drinks before dinner.

Whether the snow was melting on his face or he had begun to cry is impossible to determine from the tapes of the incident, but during his assault on Loeb in which he called the paper's publisher a "gutless coward" for "lying" about him and his wife, Muskie lost composure. The incident raised the question: Could Muskie withstand pressure?

Seven months later, reporters for the *Washington Post* would learn from White House aide and former *Post* reporter Kenneth Clawson that he had written the "Canuck" letter.[6]

The "Canuck" letter was not the only "dirty trick" directed against Muskie's candidacy in New Hampshire. In late February voters began receiving late night or early morning phone calls from persons who said that they had just arrived from Harlem and were calling to solicit votes for Muskie.[7]

Again in Florida Muskie was the victim of sabotage funded by the Republicans. Three days before the vote in the Florida primary, letters written on "Citizens for Muskie" stationery were sent to Democratic party workers charging that Hubert Humphrey had been arrested for drunken driving in 1967. In the car at the time, the letter charged, was a known call girl. What Nixon's chief of staff H. R. Haldeman identifies as other fliers[8] but what their creator Donald Segretti recalls as the same letter[9] charged that Henry Jackson had fathered an illegitimate child in 1929 and that Jackson had been arrested for committing homosexual acts in 1955 and 1957. Another letter on the letterhead of former Senator Eugene McCarthy urged his supporters to vote for Humphrey. Along Florida highways on telephone poles and trees, Segretti posted posters proclaiming "Help Muskie in Busing More Children Now" signed by a nonexistent committee called "Mothers Backing Muskie Committee." An ad in a Miami paper asked: "Senator Muskie, Would you accept a Jewish Running Mate?" Classified ads run in small papers including shoppers' weeklies carried that question as well as the question "Muskie: Would you accept a black running mate?"[10] A Spanish language radio ad which wasn't, in Segretti's words, "anything too derogatory" also was aired on a Cuban radio station in Miami. At a Muskie press conference, Segretti and an accomplice released a handful of white mice with ribbons tied to their tails. The ribbons proclaimed "Muskie is a rat fink."[11]

On October 3, 1973, the Senate Select Committee on Presidential

Campaign Activities learned that these were the works of Donald Segretti, a lawyer paid $16,000 a year plus expenses through White House channels to devise ways to "foster a split between the various Democratic hopefuls."[12] After pleading guilty to conspiracy and illegal campaign activities,* Segretti was sentenced to six months in prison. Muskie's campaign manager testified before the Senate committee that the fraudulent advertising harmed Muskie's candidacy in Florida by forcing him to respond to charges raised against him and by driving away potential backers.[13] But at that point it was all history.

What happened in Florida was that in a field of six, Muskie came in fourth. As predicted, Wallace, who had campaigned on an unequivocal stance against court-ordered busing, won. Considerably behind Wallace, in second place with 18% of the vote to Wallace's 42%, was Hubert Humphrey, followed by Jackson, Muskie, Lindsay, and McGovern.

Had Muskie come in second, the psychological damage would have been minimal, for Wallace had been expected to finish first. By finishing a weak fourth, Muskie lost his status as front-runner, although his prospects revived somewhat when on March 21 he carried the largest number of delegates from Illinois.

Wisconsin, the scene of JFK's 1960 battle with Humphrey, would be for Humphrey what New Hampshire had been for Muskie, a state he should have won and won big. But on April 4, McGovern won, with Wallace second, Humphrey third, Muskie fourth, Jackson fifth, and Lindsay an asterisk. After Wisconsin, Lindsay left the race.

On April 25, Humphrey won Pennsylvania. With less than four days of campaigning McGovern finished second in the delegate race in that state. When McGovern won Massachusetts, Muskie announced that although he would not drop out of the race, release his delegates, or endorse another contender, he would suspend campaigning.

What the press found when it turned to analyze how McGovern had defied its assessments of his prospects was that the former college professor with a Ph.D. in history had organized a grass roots campaign akin to that which had won the nomination for Barry Goldwater in 1964; like the Robert Kennedy and McCarthy campaigns of 1968, McGovern was running a campaign backed by cadres of young volunteers.

In early May, Humphrey carried Indiana, Ohio, and West Virginia; Wallace won North Carolina; and McGovern won Nebraska.

Wallace was the front-runner in the forecasts for the next two primaries, Michigan and Maryland, which were held on May 16. While campaigning in a shopping center in Laurel, Maryland, Wallace was shot. As

*Segretti's posters and letters did not disclose their actual source as required by federal law.

doctors struggled to save his life, both states gave him victories. At that time Wallace had received more total votes than either Humphrey or McGovern, but, paralyzed by the shooting from the waist down, he would withdraw from the race.

After the assassination attempt on Wallace, the contest narrowed to Humphrey and McGovern. In California, Humphrey expanded the attacks he had first launched against McGovern in Nebraska, ridiculing a McGovern plan to pay every adult $1000 and challenging McGovern's plan to cut defense spending by one-third. In a debate between the two in California, Humphrey issued the attack that would find its way into one of the most aired Republican ads of the general election. After criticizing McGovern for halting procurement of the Minute Man and the Poseidon, stopping the BI bomber's prototype, and indicting his phaseout of 230 of our 530 strategic bombers and reduction of our shipbuilding, Humphrey declared that when you "reduce the total number of forces 66,000 below what we had pre-Pearl Harbor . . . you are cutting into the very fiber and the muscle of the defense establishment."[14] An often aired Humphrey TV ad said that these cuts would make the U.S. "a second class power."

Later McGovern would write in his autobiography of the dilemma he faced: "I approached the debate as the virtual nominee of the party needing the support of Humphrey and his followers if I were to defeat Nixon."[15] "I had no interest in attacking Hubert or in embarrassing him. Quite the contrary, I was chiefly concerned about doing nothing that might anger his supporters." But he describes his concern lest these damaging last-minute Humphrey attacks stand without adequate rejoinder. "The fears, anxieties and wounds opened in those debates were sweet music to the Nixon strategists, and from that time on they set the strategy of their campaign: 'Democrats for Nixon'—Democrats who feared the positions of George McGovern as interpreted by Hubert Humphrey."[16] Indeed Magruder did tell a member of the Nixon's advertising team that "Democrats for Nixon" would be set up shortly after the Convention. Once the plan for a separate group called Democrats for Nixon was OK'd, the anti-McGovern spots that the November Group had scripted were tagged Democrats for Nixon instead. While CBS carried the debate between Humphrey and McGovern in the California primary, its rival networks were carrying scenes of Nixon's trip to Moscow.

A second factor minimized the likelihood of reconciliation between Humphrey and McGovern in the general election. "[S]avage leaflets circulated by fake 'peace' committees showed Humphrey as the original architect of the U.S. policy in Vietnam. Some of these had a picture of a large, particularly unpleasant-looking fish, with Humphrey's face superimposed, and the message, 'There's Something Fishy About Hubert

Humphrey.' " "The result," reports McGovern's press secretary Frank Mankiewicz, "was what the Nixon men might have anticipated. By primary day, the possibility of reconciliation between Humphrey and McGovern was far more remote than it would have been had they merely been opponents in a free election."[17] McGovern, too, was the victim of anonymous leaflets distorting his record on Israel, labor, and civil rights. Although Mankiewicz assumed that the leaflets were produced by Nixon supporters, there is no direct evidence to link them to the complex of activities labeled "Watergate." Segretti denies any knowledge of them, noting that the only leaflets he distributed in California were anti-Muskie and appeared months before the primary itself.[18] Bob Woodward, the investigative reporter who with Carl Bernstein broke the Watergate story, does not recall the leaflets.[19]

On June 6 McGovern won California by a narrower margin than pollsters predicted. Humphrey's attacks had taken their toll. Also on June 6 McGovern carried New Mexico, New Jersey, and South Dakota. Two weeks later he won New York.

Prior to the convention, Humphrey supporter and financial backer Jeno Paulucci met with a representative of the November Group to discuss his interest in sponsoring an anti-McGovern advertising campaign. The result was an ad headed "We're Democrats and Independents, and Senator McGovern Has Us Worried" that appeared in the *Washington Post,* the *New York Times,* and six other metropolitan papers. The original copy for the ad was written by November Group creative director, William Taylor, and revised by Paulucci's ad agency in consultation with another member of Nixon's advertising team. Reprints were delivered to delegates to the Democratic Convention. "We ran a print ad at the Democratic Convention signed by a lot of staunch Democrats and Independents who had previously been known to be for Humphrey," Paulucci recalls. "We said it would be a disaster if McGovern were nominated. It was a last ditch attempt for Humphrey but if McGovern got the nomination, we were already putting some nails in his coffin."[20] Paulucci believes that "without a doubt" the anti-Humphrey materials circulating in the California primary exacerbated the tensions between McGovern and Humphrey. He attributes both Humphrey's attacks in the California debate and his own participation in the Nixon campaign to those slurs on Humphrey's reputation and to their belief that McGovern should not be president. As for Paulucci's support of Nixon in the general election, he recalls, "Humphrey tacitly accepted it. Sometimes he offered me a little encouragement. I thought McGovern and his policies were way too liberal. And I was mad. I wanted Humphrey to have the nomination and it was my way of getting back." Later Paulucci would become a leader in Democrats for Nixon and head of Independents for Nixon.

The convention itself opened July 10. After McGovern's forces warded off credentials challenges that would have reduced their number of delegates below the total required for a first ballot nomination, Muskie and Humphrey withdrew. McGovern won nomination on the first ballot.

The Democratic nominee had taught history and political science at Dakota Wesleyan while working for his Ph.D. in history. Twice he was elected to the House of Representatives. In 1960 he lost his first bid for the Senate. JFK named him head of the Food for Peace program in 1961. The next year, McGovern became the first Democrat in 26 years elected to the U.S. Senate from South Dakota. He was reelected in 1968, a year in which he tried and failed to win the presidency. In 1968, he also was named chair of the Democratic National Committee's Commission on Party Structure and Delegate Selection. That group formulated rules to ensure the democratic selection of delegates and to guarantee representation of women and minorities.

In his acceptance address, delivered long after the nation had gone to sleep, McGovern previewed the themes of his general election campaign:

> I make these pledges above all others—the doors of government will be opened, and that brutal war will be closed. . . .
>
> The highest domestic priority of my administration will be to ensure that every American able to work has a job to do. . . .
>
> This year, the people are going to ensure that the tax system is changed so that work is rewarded and so that those who derive the highest benefits will pay their fair share rather than slipping through the loopholes at the expense of the rest of us.

The acceptance address also invited Americans to "Come Home."

In the most critical decision he would make as a candidate that year, McGovern named Thomas Eagleton as his running mate. When asked if there were any skeletons in his closet, Eagleton had neglected to inform McGovern that he had three times been hospitalized for depression and had undergone electroshock therapy. The press revealed the hospitalizations. Although McGovern first claimed to support Eagleton 1000%, he also began hinting through the press that he wanted Eagleton to resign. When Eagleton resigned, McGovern substituted Sargent Shriver, best known as the husband of Eunice Kennedy Shriver and director of the Peace Corps.

The Republican Primaries

Between August 1971 and August 1972 Richard Nixon acted decisively both at home and abroad. At home in August 1971 he imposed a wage price freeze; abroad he mined Haiphong Harbor and traveled to China and Russia.

Nixon entered the election year anticipating a tough race only in the general election. Still, in the primaries he was challenged from the right and from the left. On the left California Congressman Pete McCloskey indicted Nixon's conduct of the war; on the right Ohio Congressman John Ashbrook condemned Nixon's wage price freeze, his family assistance plan, and his overtures to China and Russia. McCloskey dropped out after the New Hampshire primary; Ashbrook stayed the route but drew so few votes that his challenge was not taken seriously after the first primaries.

Throughout the primaries, as the networks showed scenes of Democrats slashing at Democrats, Nixon was depicted in the bipartisan role of The President. Between February 21 and February 27, he presided over what amounted to a national tour of China. On May 8, he ordered the mining of Haiphong Harbor. Between May 22 and 28, he carried the nation with him on a televised mission "of peace" through Russia. On his arrival home, he addressed a joint session of Congress.

After his historic trip to Russia with its summit meeting with Soviet Party leader Leonid Brezhnev, Nixon's approval rating jumped to 61%. The rise was reminiscent of that following his Kitchen Debate with Khrushchev in 1959. Before that Soviet trip, Nixon had trailed Kennedy in the polls 39–61%. After the contest about dishwashers and destinies with Khrushchev, Kennedy led him by a mere 52–48%.[21]

In a televised address on the evening of May 8, Nixon announced that he had ordered the mining of North Vietnamese ports. On May 10, 1972, the *New York Times* editorialized against the mining, arguing that it ran counter to the will of "a large segment of the American people." In the *New York Times* of May 17 a seemingly spontaneous "citizens' ad" endorsed Nixon's mining of Haiphong Harbor. That ad titled "The People vs. *The New York Times*" cited polls showing widespread public support of the action. It was signed by fourteen individuals. A year later, on May 3, 1973, the General Accounting Office (GAO) asked the Justice Department to investigate whether the ad, which was actually paid for by the Committee to Re-elect the President, had violated the campaign disclosure law by not identifying its actual source.

Magruder says that Colson persuaded Haldeman that some sort of ad should be run to rebut the *Times'* editorial. Colson's "hard line" version of the ad was toned down by the November Group before being printed.[22]

The individuals listed on the ad had not written, seen, or paid for it. Half were relatives and friends of persons working for the Nixon advertising team. The other names were provided by the Committee to Re-elect the President. The GAO concluded that the ad seemed to violate the requirement that ads for federal candidates display the name of the committee sponsoring the ad and the committee's officers. In addition, the funding of the ad by the Committee had not been reported as required by law. The ad was found to violate the disclosure law and a fine was assessed.

On April 26, 1973, the *Washington Post* also revealed that the Committee to Re-elect the President (CRP) had sent between two and four thousand ballots to a Washington TV station to influence the outcome of a poll on the popularity of the mining. "We had a dozen people working for several days filling out postcards for the television poll, which eventually announced 5,157 postcards in support of the President (probably half of them from us) and 1,158 in opposition" wrote Jeb Magruder later.[23] "The *Star* [in which the ballots appeared] must have broken all its records for newsstand sales that afternoon, because Rob Odle bought several thousand copies simply for ballots." Barry Sussman of the *Washington Post* offers a different set of figures. "Only 8,000 responses were received in all," he reports, "and the tabulation showed an exact 50–50 split, meaning that without CRP's intervention the poll would have indicated that public sentiment was actually against the mining by at least 2 to 1."[24]

After the majority of the primaries but before the Republican convention in late August, the issue of corruption in government began to surface. International Telephone and Telegraph had put up a subsidy for the Republican convention. Republicans said it was an inducement to build business for an ITT subsidiary, the Sheraton hotels. Democrats argued that it was a payoff for the Justice Department's settlement of a multimillion dollar suit.

On the heels of this discovery came the break-in at the Watergate offices that housed the Democratic National Committee. The men caught on June 17, 1972, while attempting to replace a malfunctioning eavesdropping device were quickly tied by the press to low level White House staff. On June 20, Nixon and his aides began the process that would come to be known as the "cover-up"—a sustained effort to persuade prosecutors, press, and public, initially that the White House, then that Nixon's close associates, and, finally, that Richard Nixon, had neither known of nor approved the Watergate break-in or the payment of "hush" money to the jailed burglars.* At the same time, Nixon hoped to conceal such

*The Democrats responded to the break-in by initiating a one million dollar civil suit against the Committee to Re-elect the President charging invasion of privacy and violation of civil rights. On February 28, 1974, Democratic National Committee Chair Robert Strauss announced that the Committee had agreed to an out-of-court settlement of $775,000.

related activities as the break-in at the office of anti-war protestor Daniel Ellsberg's psychiatrist, alterations in cables from the Kennedy era to establish Kennedy's complicity in the death of the Vietnamese President, the "dirty tricks" of the primaries, and efforts to uncover information that would discredit a possible candidacy of Senator Edward Kennedy. Throughout the general election campaign the cover-up succeeded. Investigative reporters were unable to secure evidence that would tie any of these activities to Richard Nixon.

Shortly after the break-in at Watergate, another potential scandal erupted when evidence surfaced suggesting that a number of major companies had made exorbitant profits on U.S. wheat sales to the USSR. However, none of these scandals seemed to implicate Richard Nixon directly.

Nixon was nominated on the first ballot and once again embraced Spiro Agnew as his running mate, a move that placated conservatives in the Republican party. In his acceptance address on August 23 Nixon forecast the themes on which his campaign would pivot in the general election. Turning McGovern's call to "come home America" back on him, Nixon said, "To those millions who have been driven out of their homes in the Democratic Party, we say come home. We say come home not to another party, but we say come home to the great principles we Americans believe in together."

Nixon also defended his administration's record with its "biggest tax cut in history," increase in jobs, wage price controls, and reduced inflation. Like Lyndon Johnson in 1964, Nixon argued that along with each of his presidential predecessors he favored a strong defense. "[N]ot one of these five men [former presidents], and no President in history, believed that America should ask an enemy for peace on terms that would betray our allies and destroy respect for the United States all over the world."

Nixon then argued that "we" have made progress toward an honorable end to the war in Vietnam. He argued as well that his initiatives toward China and Russia had advanced the cause of peace. In closing, Nixon invited Americans to join "our new majority."

By Labor Day the polls were showing Nixon winning with over 60% of the vote, a percent reflected in the final votes cast on election day.

McGovern's candidacy in 1972 rose on a trajectory set in 1968 when McCarthy, Robert Kennedy, and finally, with Kennedy's death, George McGovern challenged the establishment of the Democratic party over conduct of the war in Vietnam. The absence of widespread campus turmoil in 1972 masks the fact that like the candidacies of McCarthy, Kennedy, and McGovern in 1968, the raison d'etre of McGovern's candidacy in 1972 and the catalyst of support for his candidacy was his conviction that our policies in Vietnam were morally bankrupt and that we should halt all bombing and within 90 days remove our troops. The centrality of Vietnam to McGovern's supporters was demonstrated when a storm of protest arose from them about his fall 1971 plan to spend more time talking about economic matters. It was, writes Page "as if even a decrease in emphasis on Vietnam, let alone a change in position, amounted to heresy."[25] An angrier protest erupted from his supporters in July 1972 when at the Democratic Convention he said that he would maintain some military presence in Thailand and on the seas to demonstrate his resolve that the American POW's be speedily returned. So it is unsurprising that McGovern's advertising telescopes the issues of the election through the issue of Vietnam. From his assumption that the conduct of that war is immoral naturally flows the attendant charge that the Nixon presidency is immoral, a charge fueled by bits of tinder dropped inadvertently by Nixon's aides and their hirelings.

The election of 1972 served as a referendum on whether or not and to what extent the public supported Nixon's program of gradual Vietnamization rather than McGovern's withdrawal within 90 days. Consistent with his claim that Vietnamization is succeeding, Nixon's advertising argues that under his leadership normalcy is returning both at home and abroad after the trauma of the Johnson years.

Advertising Agencies

Both campaigns employed the same admen in the primaries and the general election. From New Hampshire, McGovern's advertising was prepared by Charles Guggenheim, the award-winning filmmaker who made his presidential debut in 1956, created material for Robert Kennedy in 1968, and worked in the Humphrey general election campaign of 1968. His filmed biography of RFK had brought tears to the eyes of delegates to the 1968 convention.

In 1962 Guggenheim had produced the advertising and filmed biography that helped carry McGovern to the U.S. Senate. In 1968 he again created the advertising for McGovern's successful Senate reelection bid. An undisputed master of the documentary film, Guggenheim had pioneered the use of a filmic style known as cinema verité in political advertising.

Guggenheim's television ads placed McGovern in the midst of a group of citizens in a nonstudio environment. The ads generally opened with a wide establishing shot that identified the participants and the setting—a factory, a farmyard, a school. As McGovern responded to the citizens' questions, the handheld camera situated the home viewer as an eavesdropper in the scene—occasionally someone's head would block

part of the view. The questions and answers were spontaneous and unscripted. The cameraman tightened on the candidate as he answered,
then pulled back from him and roamed. Throughout the ad, an announcer provided a running commentary, filling in transitions, underscoring themes. As the commercials drew to a close, the picture froze on the
candidate and the announcer intoned "McGovern—for the People" or,
from mid-September, "McGovern. Democrat. For the People." The
freeze frame suggested that the conversation continued even after the
commercial ended its report of it. In an election in which the Republican
nominee's integrity and openness were issues, the cinema verité style had
the advantage of arguing that McGovern was conducting an open campaign. The same point was made in a dozen half hour telethons aired in
the large industrial states during October and early November.

Endorsement spots featuring Edward Kennedy and Hubert
Humphrey were also aired, as was a five minute spot focusing on McGovern's wife. Guggenheim also developed a half hour filmed biography of
McGovern that stressed the senator's traditional values and rural roots.
The biography, which incorporated some of the material from the campaign biography of 1968, was aired on October 1 and on election eve.
McGovern also narrated a second half hour program that aired in the
final two weeks of the campaign. This program featured voters around
the country. "They weren't for McGovern so much as for the idea that
this country was in serious difficulty," Guggenheim recalls.[26]

McGovern also delivered five major televised speeches including a
speech on Vietnam, October 10; on economics, October 20; on corruption, October 25; and a second speech on Vietnam November 3. Each
speech closed with an appeal for funds. Each raised far more than it cost
to produce and air. For example, the first speech on Vietnam raised
almost a million dollars in a five day period. The telethons also brought in
enough money to pay for themselves. Where Nixon relied on radio addresses to carry his major policy statements to the electorate, McGovern
used television.

In the closing weeks of the campaign, when it was clear that McGovern was making no inroads against Nixon's lead, Gary Hart, McGovern's
campaign manager, called Guggenheim suggesting an advertising strategy
change. "Gary Hart called me," Guggenheim remembers, "and said they
wanted to go negative on television. We were already negative on radio,"
Guggenheim explains. "He said that he knew I didn't want to go negative
on television. I had said that radio is a cool medium. We can attack on
radio and not get a negative response. If we put negative ads on TV we're
going to get a negative response. Gary said 'I'm going to stick with you if
you say no.' I said 'Gary, I haven't moved the polls half a point. What

I'm doing obviously isn't working. If they want to go negative [on television] I respect it but I don't want to do it.' " Larry O'Brien, McGovern's national campaign chairman, favored a shift to "spots that attacked Nixon's record and hammered at the above-the-battle 'presidential' aura with which he had surrounded himself."[27] O'Brien called his friend Tony Schwartz to ask if he would produce some spots. "They came to me eleven days before the end of the campaign," Schwartz recalls. "I did the spots in three days."[28]

Of the six spots that Schwartz produced, two began airing nationally the weekend of October 28. When a state coordinator called asking if Schwartz had any ads he could air, Schwartz sent him a copy of a third ad from the series. This ad was aired at the state level in only one state. Unlike Guggenheim's ads, which featured the candidate, Schwartz's spots were concept spots.

Republican Advertising Agency: The November Group

In 1971, Nixon's staff decided not to contract with an existing ad agency but to form their own in-house agency that they called the November Group.* As a result, the campaign saved the 15% of the amount of television and radio air cost that an agency holds back as the fee for placing an ad. The existence of this charge raises the perpetual question: Has the agency recommended television and radio rather than print, direct mail, or the funding of organizational activities as a means of recouping its costs or increasing its profits? In other words, is the recommendation to increase the use of broadcast ads in the best interest of the candidate and campaign? This question assumes added importance in 1972 for in the general election the head of the November Group did turn back funds originally set for broadcasting to other activities in the campaign. Whether he would have been willing to do so had his agency's profit margin depended on the 15% placement charge is impossible to know.

Peter Dailey took a leave of absence from his Los Angeles advertising agency, Dailey and Associates, to preside over the November Group. Phil Joanou took a leave of absence from Doyle Dane Bernbach's Los Angeles office to assume the role of executive vice-president. As Senior Vice-President and Creative Director, Dailey named William Taylor, who

*For a brief time before this the Nixon campaign engaged the services of Robert Goodman, the Baltimore adman whose ads contributed to the election of Spiro Agnew as Maryland governor. Goodman was commissioned to create a film on the party. In the judgment of Nixon's aides the film contained too little of Richard Nixon to be useable. The film was never aired. Goodman lost the 1972 Nixon account.

held the same posts at Ogilvy & Mather in New York. William Novelli, who had headed the Advertising and Creative Services for Action, functioned as Senior Vice-President and Account Manager.

Those who joined the November Group did so under an understanding with Dailey that "no job opportunities" would be created by the administration for them after their time with the group was up. "There could have been a lot of subverting of what was right if people were looking for jobs," notes Dailey now.[29]

The November Group produced ads for two groups within the campaign: The Committee to Re-elect the President, and Democrats for Nixon. The CRP ads simulated news. Ads on the trips to China and Russia, for example, recap the visual highlights of the trip. The ads for Democrats for Nixon were concept spots that repeated the attacks on McGovern raised by Humphrey in the primaries. The group also created newspaper ads, brochures, and posters. Documentary filmmaker David Wolper produced the two half hour documentaries on Nixon's record. Taylor scripted the Democrats for Nixon ads and the five minute ads on Nixon's trips to China and Russia and on Nixon's record.

To oversee the general strategy and its execution, the November Group set in place an advisory board composed of top level advertising professionals. The Advisory Board was chaired by Richard O'Reilly, executive vice-president of Wells, Rich, Greene, who had proposed the advisory group as a polite way of rejecting the offer to head the November Group. Membership on the board reads like a who's who of advertising. Included on it were Henry Schachte, president of J. Walter Thompson, the agency whose Los Angeles office had once housed H. R. Haldeman, as well as Bart Cummings, executive committee chair of Compton Advertising, John Elliott, Jr., chair of Ogilvy and Mather, John O'Toole, president of Foote, Cone and Belding, and Chester Posey, president of Garmo Inc.[30]

Although the board's ostensible function was to oversee strategy, in actuality it had a second purpose. By securing this group's approval of the November Group's work, Dailey armed himself with weighty evidence to justify his decisions when they clashed with those of persons in the White House or in the Committee to Re-Elect the President. In a letter to *Advertising Age* in May 1973 Posey noted that the November Group's "biggest single problem" was "to fight off efforts of highly placed White House aides to take a 'hard line' in the advertising."[31] As I will argue shortly, some of these efforts, fronted by Charles Colson, may have been ordered by Nixon himself.

On the advice of his lawyers and financial counsel, Dailey engaged

Price Waterhouse, a respected Los Angeles accounting firm, to conduct an ongoing audit of the November Group. He did this not out of prescience about Watergate but rather to protect his own firm from entanglement with the firm that he was setting up for the Nixon campaign. The audits began in January 1972 and concluded that December. "I didn't think much about it," Dailey recalls. "I just threw the statement in the drawer. In about April when all the committees were investigating they came after us. A group of about 100 people who had worked together for ten months. It would have been a disaster to try to recreate the books after the fact. Because I'd had good business advice I could show them the audit statement and say 'If you have any questions ask Price Waterhouse.' " Later when Dailey asked a partner in Price Waterhouse what it would have cost to recreate the audit, which initially cost $50,000, in April 1973, he was told "There wouldn't be enough money in the world to get us to do it."[32]

Cost

In 1972 the Federal Election Campaign Act (FECA), signed into law by Nixon on February 7, set a limit both on the amount candidates for federal office could spend on communication media and a limit on how much they could spend on broadcast advertising. FECA limited the amount a candidate could spend on radio, TV, cable, newspapers, magazines, billboards, and automated telephone systems, but not on direct mail, computers, or polling, to ten cents multiplied by the voting age population in the primary or general election. No more than 60% of this total could be spent on broadcasting. These limits meant in 1972 that Nixon and McGovern could not spend more than 8.4 million on broadcasting after the nomination. By contrast in 1968 the Republicans had spent 12.6 million. An amendment to FECA in 1974 repealed these media spending ceilings.

FECA also increased the value of each dollar spent on broadcast advertising by requiring that within 45 days of a primary or general election, broadcasters not charge political candidates more than the lowest rate charged any advertiser for the same class and amount of time.

For the first time, the act limited the amount of a candidate's personal wealth that could be spent during a campaign. Presidential candidates were limited to personal expenditures of $50,000, a limit that would have crippled Kennedy's candidacy in 1960.

In a provision that proved controversial, FECA required that candidates and committees that received and spent more than $1000 report all contributions of more than $100. Before the disclosure requirement went into effect on April 7, the committees soliciting money to finance Nixon's reelection collected $10.1 million.

Common Cause, a self-described citizens' lobby, charged in June that Nixon's refusal to reveal the names of those who contributed this money "can only lead people to conclude that the office of the Presidency already has been sold to the highest bidders."[33] Common Cause sued to gain disclosure under the reporting requirements of the Federal Corrupt Practices Act of 1925. As a result of an out-of-court settlement, the Finance Committee to Re-elect the President released a partial list of donors in early November. The list confirmed that persons whose firms had been sued by the Justice Department for anti-trust violations were among those giving large amounts.

In the general election McGovern outspent Nixon on both network and regional spot TV, Nixon outspent McGovern on network radio but was outspent on spot radio. McGovern outspent Nixon on newspaper ads. In total TV, radio, and newspaper charges for time and space and production costs Nixon spent $6,912,437, McGovern $6,785,957.[34] Neither campaign approached the $8.4 million limit.

Taken at face value these figures might suggest that money did not help or hinder one campaign disproportionately. Instead, however, the people involved in the November Group report that money was plentiful while those on the Democratic side note that the absence of money circumscribed their creative options. The November Group's Creative Director William Taylor reports, for example, "For us, money was no problem. There was plenty of money." "[O]ur money was coming in literally on a day to day basis," Guggenheim told a Harvard seminar.[35] "So, although you could project what you would like to do in a campaign in terms of production and strategy, it was fairly unreal to say you would go out and produce the material when you didn't have the money to go out and produce it." After the Eagleton affair, people who had pledged about three million dollars either reneged on the promises or adopted a wait and see attitude.[36] To raise funds, the Democrats tagged their ads and half hour broadcasts with appeals for money. Still, unlike any other Democratic campaign we have studied, the McGovern campaign ended in the black.

As in all races against an incumbent, however, the challenger requires higher expenditures in order to attain comparable exposure. By placing the same spending limits on both incumbents and challengers, FECA biased in favor of incumbents.

Reelecting "The President": Nixon's Strategy

On April 18, 1972, the November Group issued a confidential memo to the campaign's strategists blueprinting the remainder of the campaign. The document revealed that Vietnam led the list of issues "most important in deciding a presidential vote," followed by "inflation/economy."[37] The report also noted that the public believed that Nixon was better able than Muskie or Kennedy to handle the issues of Vietnam and inflation. McGovern was not yet figuring in the Republicans' plans.

In general, Nixon's pollsters had found that he was perceived to handle "problems with international scope far more effectively than problems on the domestic scene. Each of the Democratic candidates is perceived in varying degrees as being able to handle the domestic problems in the United States more effectively than the President."

Consistent with the divinations of the polls of earlier campaigns, surveys had again discovered that Nixon was perceived to be experienced, trained, competent, informed, safe, and conservative but not frank, warm, extroverted, or relaxed. Neither was he perceived to have a sense of humor.

Use of Surrogates

The strategy detailed in the November Group's memo became the dogma guiding advertising in the general election. So, for example, the paid broadcast's and campaign's use of surrogates reflected the memo's answer to the question: How should the promises and attacks of the Democrats be countered?

> The President is not good when he becomes the attacker. The President is quite often not his own best spokesman when countering the opposition candidate.

> It is recommended that the opposition candidates' challenges be strongly and immediately repudiated, not by the President, but by key Administration officials. If the opposition attacks the economy, the weakness of his position is pointed out by Connally. If he provides an instant solution to Vietnam, Rogers or Kissinger answers.

> The President never gets down to the level of the opposition, nor does the opposition ever get a chance in the ring on the Presidential level.

The success of this strategic response was evident on the front pages of the nation's newspapers and on the network news. On October 3 the front page of the *Washington Post* had an article headed "McGovern Charges Massive Corruption" that is bracketed by pictures of McGovern and Agnew. The article itself indicates that "Sen. George McGovern yesterday accused the Nixon administration of being 'the most corrupt in history' and charged that the President 'has no constant principle except opportunism and manipulation'. . . . Vice President Spiro Agnew, replying in the same forum five hours later, accused McGovern of 'reckless' charges that Agnew said showed a lack of maturity and self-discipline. . . . Agnew said that 'no amount of verbal pyrotechnics by a desperate opposition' would prevent an overwhelming re-election of the President." The article positions McGovern as Agnew's equal; both assume the posture of candidates. By contrast, Nixon is not a candidate but *The President.* This sort of contrast prompted media critic Ben Bagdikian to write in the *Columbia Journalism Review* " 'Twinning'—equal side-by-side Democratic and Republican daily campaign stories—was the rule in 1972. An uncoerced editor might decide that when George McGovern made a major statement on defense policy which was denounced rhetorically by a Republican campaign official that they were not of equal interest. But twinning made them so in the public eye, demeaning the President's opponent by seeming to accord him the same status as Administration underlings."[38]

Consistent with his role as non candidate, Nixon avoided sustained contact with the press during the 1972 campaign. In other words, he did in 1972 what he was accused of doing in 1968. One of the ironies of the 1972 campaign is that in the two press conferences Nixon held in the general election, the toughest questions were no tougher than the toughest asked in the citizens' panels of 1968 and Nixon's answers were less revealing. For practical purposes, Nixon successfully evaded answering questions about Watergate, disclosure of pre-April 7 donors' names, corruption, and the like.

Paid broadcasts also proffered surrogates when attack was required. In mid-October in prime time on ABC and NBC, John Connally, head of Democrats for Nixon, delivered a broadcast half hour attack on McGovern. Later it was aired on CBS as well. Connally also appeared in ads attacking McGovern's proposals, thus setting McGovern on a par not with *The President* but with a member of Nixon's cabinet.

Nixon appeared only once on paid television in the role of candidate. Without alluding to McGovern or to his plan to end the war, in a nationally televised speech on November 2 Nixon asked "Shall we have peace with honor or peace with surrender?" In the same speech he argued that the "programs proposed by our opponents in this campaign would require a 50-percent increase in Federal taxes." By contrast, Nixon's election eve speech is an almost non partisan get-out-the-vote appeal that specifies the issues he hopes voters will keep in mind as they ballot.

Presenting Nixon as "The President"

The advertising issued by the November Group faithfully characterized The President in the way recommended in the strategy memo. The campaign would:

1. Present the President as an *activist.*

   As a man who takes bold and decisive steps to get things done.

   A man to be judged by his accomplishments, not his words.

Accordingly, the November Group produced radio and television ads detailing the accomplishments of Nixon's trips to Russia and China from file footage purchased from the Department of the Navy. A radio ad noted, for example:

> ANNOUNCER: On Monday, May 22, Richard Nixon arrived in Moscow— the first American president to ever visit the Russian capital. Serious discussions between the President and the Russian leaders were held during the week he was there—and they involved lots of hard bargaining. At the end of the week, the President spoke on Russian television about the results of his discussions.

> NIXON: We have agreed on joint ventures in space; we have agreed on ways of working together to protect the environment, to advance health, to cooperate in science and technology. We have agreed on means of preventing incidents at sea; we have established a commission to expand trade between our two nations. Most important, we have taken an historic first step in the limitation of nuclear strategic arms.

A widely distributed flier documented the consensus of politicians, such world leaders as U Thant and Pope Paul VI, and the press that the trip to China was a "journey of peace." In one of his ads, even McGovern praised the trips to Russia and China.

2. Present the President as a man with *long-range vision.*

   All of the President's accomplishments should be positioned as part of an overall plan being implemented by the President for the betterment of all. Not sudden, expedient or political deeds, but elements of a master plan that *must* be *continued.*

The ads contain such claims as: "Having begun the job of creating the framework for a real and lasting peace in the world, the president is determined to finish it. That's one of the truly important reasons why America needs President Nixon, now more than ever."

As in '68, Nixon chose radio to carry his reflective, philosophical disquisitions on his long-range vision of the presidency. On October 21, in one such little noted nor long remembered address, Nixon spelled-out his political philosophy. The speech indicts the politics of elitism. "Do we want to turn more power over to bureaucrats in Washington in the hope that they will do what is best for all the people?" Nixon asked. "I cannot ally myself with those who habitually scorn the will of the majority, who treat a mature people as children to be ordered about, who treat the popular will as something only to be courted at election time and forgotten between elections" he concluded.

> 3. Present the President as a man who *inherited a mess.*
>
>> Whenever possible, the public should be reminded of the sad state of affairs that existed when the President took office, contrasted with the relatively better situation that now exists.

Consequently, the campaign aired a documentary called "Change without Chaos," in which the problems Nixon had encountered on entering office—the war, environmental pollution, tension between the U.S. and China and Russia, unrest on the campuses—were contrasted with the Republican accomplishments in each area.

The ads both argued that change had occurred and placed Nixon on the side of change, a posture designed to reframe the electorate's dissatisfaction with the direction of the country. "[W]hile people were dissatisfied with the direction of the country, their feeling seemed directed more at intangibles of government, and bureaucracy, than at the President," explains Dailey.[39] "So, very early, we felt that the most important single thing we could do was to have the President take a position on the side of change. He had to be somebody who was identified as being for change, who was operating for change."

"Change Without Chaos" is the by-product of this strategy. According to a memo from William Novelli to Phil Joanou, a test of the impact of the film on over 300 voters found that the film increased approval of the president's handling of his job among all segments of voters, increased the feelings of voters that Nixon had accomplished "quite a lot," contained no claims that voters found hard to believe, and increased the perception of "the President's handling of major vote-determining issues, and is especially effective on the issues of taxes, Vietnam and drugs." In Novelli's judgment the improved perception of the President's handling of taxes was particularly important because it was "possibly the most vulnerable issue facing the President at this time."

> 4. Present the President as a man with *courage, decisiveness, and dedication.*
>
>> The President's personal attributes (not his personality) should be emphasized through his deeds; i.e. the personal committment (*sic*) needed to take the necessary steps.

Accordingly, Nixon is described in the ads as a man of compassion, courage, and conscience," attributes dramatically embodied in an ad's evocation of his speech to the Russian people. In the ad Nixon is seen addressing Russians on television; he is shown laying a wreath at the tomb of the unknown soldier in Leningrad, as he recounts a story suffused with universal appeal.

> Yesterday, I laid a wreath at the cemetery which commemorates the brave people who died during the siege of Leningrad in World War II. At the cemetery, I saw the picture of a twelve year old girl. She was a beautiful child. Her name was Tanya. The pages of her diary tell the terrible story of war. In the simple words of a child, she wrote of the deaths of the members of her family. Zhenya in December. Granney in January. Leka. Then Uncle Vasya. Then Uncle Lyosha. Then mama and then the Savichevs. And then, finally these words, the last words in her diary: "All are dead. Only Tanya is left." As we work toward a more peaceful world, let us think of Tanya and of the other Tanyas and their brothers and sisters everywhere . . .

5. Present *the issues*.

> Radio, TV, and newspaper ads should be developed on specific issues known to be important to prospective voters.

These issues include the economy, world peace, Vietnam, drugs, crime, environment, and older Americans. Five minute ads addressed the concerns of older Americans, the environment, and the young while the documentary spoke of Nixon's actions to ensure world peace, combat drugs and crime, safeguard the environment, and improve the lot of senior citizens.

Earlier campaigns had identified blacks, Hispanics, farmers, older persons, and housewives as audiences that could and should be the object of special broadcast advertising. In 1972 the young were added to this list. Because young people register and vote in proportionately smaller numbers than other age groups, they are not ordinarily the subject of special concern in a general election campaign for the presidency.

However, in 1972, both Democrats and Republicans looked to the twenty-five million voters between the ages of 18 and 24 as an audience worthy of special treatment because this group could account, reckoned Republican strategists in late spring, for between 12 and 17% of all votes cast in November.[40] Among youth, 11.4 million were between the ages of 18 and 20. These young voters had been enfranchised by the Voting Rights Act Amendment of 1970.

Of special interest to the Republicans was a Gallup poll that in February 1972 showed that those under 30 favored Muskie over Nixon 50–37%. The Republicans had also found that "Youth 18–24 are less satisfied than the total electorate with the way President Nixon is handling his job."

Still, the Republicans believed that the mass media's focus both on the number of young who were registering as Democrats and on college students was creating a distorted picture of the likely youth vote. A memo of March 14 concluded that the advertising objectives for this group were:

> 1. Maximize the President's vote among the segment of new voters *who have not attended college and who are employed.* Secondary effort will be directed to the other segments of the 18–24 group.
> 2. Minimize, through the use of copy and media, *general* encouragement to vote among 18–24 year olds, especially among college students. (With estimated registration and voting intentions substantially Democrat-oriented, a wide-spread, highly visible media effort may increase the *total* turnout of this group to the disadvantage of the President.)[41]

The Republicans used posters, print ads, radio, and TV spots to accomplish this objective. On October 26, 1972, Harris reported that by 45–37% those between 18 and 29 felt that Nixon better inspired confidence.[42]

Poster created by the November Group and distributed during the general election on behalf of Richard Nixon's reelection. (Reprinted from the collection of Linda and Jim Cherry)

How much of that improved confidence was the by-product of Republican advertising is difficult to know. However, tests conducted by the Republicans suggested that the materials accomplished their objectives well.

The difference between the Republican and Democratic advertising to youth was that the Democratic material, produced by the Democratic National Committee, took the form of public service announcements urging young voters to register. Three TV spots and a reel of radio appeals were distributed to radio and TV stations in key markets. These stations were then urged to air them as a public service.

The Republican strategy was more sophisticated than the Democratic one. Persuaded by the early polls showing disaffection for Nixon among the young and by the fact that, following in their parents' footsteps, the young registered Democratic more often than Republican, the Democrats believed that a newly registered young voter was substantially more likely to vote for McGovern than Nixon. In fact, approximately half of the newly enfranchised voters voted for Nixon.

Form of Nixon's Ads

The April memo also detailed the form Nixon's ads would take:

> *Use an announcer's voice-over and show film of the President in action.* This technique allows us to show the President as an activist, use excerpts from his speeches, and yet have an announcer tell the basic story. We could not be accused of having the President go into 'hiding' and yet, the effect is of a commercial that is *for* the President, not *by* the President. The difference is important, especially if we are concerned with giving the impression that the President is spending too much time campaigning and not enough time taking care of the country.

To the letter this is the format followed in Nixon's ads. In the same vein the ads' sponsored by The Committee to Re-Elect the President urged voters to "reelect President Nixon." Speechwriter William Safire takes credit for the committee's title. Since the title had to be chosen before Nixon had officially named Agnew as his running mate, "Citizens for Nixon-Agnew" was dismissed. "Citizens for Nixon" would suggest the possibility that Agnew was being dumped. Recalling Nelson Rockefeller's successful use of the slogan "Governor Rockefeller for Governor" in his uphill race in 1966, Safire suggested that the committee be called "The Committee to Re-elect the President."[43]

The memo also forecast that "late in the campaign" Nixon would go "on-camera, talking directly to the public." He did so on election eve, when he delivered an almost nonpartisan appeal to the country to vote. By conserving use of this format, the strategists believed that they would heighten the impact of such an on-camera presentation.

Humanizing "The President"

Just as the admen in the 1968 campaign discussed means of persuading
the public that Nixon had a sense of humor and was a warm, compassionate human being, so too did the staff in 1972. Under the interesting
directive "Humanize the President," the memo recommended:

> The President's personal qualities of compassion, humor and informality
> should *never* be the subject of a commercial. But by careful selection of
> footage, and careful wording of a commercial message, we can emphas-
> ize these characteristics in a subtle yet effective way.

Consequently, we are offered a "glimpse" at "the private man at work
and in his relaxed moments." This is the man, says the announcer, "so
few people know." Here Nixon is shown standing before the audience at
a White House reception honoring Duke Ellington. With the encouragement of the audience he sits down at the piano and plays "Happy Birthday" for Ellington. In the scene captured in the ad, Nixon says:

> Now ladies and gentlemen. (laughter from the audience) Please don't go
> away. (more laughter) Duke was asking earlier if I would play and I said
> I had never done so yet in the White House. But it did occur to me as I
> looked at the magnificent program that's prepared for us that one num-
> ber was missing. You see this is his birthday. Now (audience laughs)
> Now Duke Ellington is ageless, but will you all stand and sing Happy
> Birthday to him, and please—in the key of G. (laughter and the audi-
> ence sings) . . .

At the state dinner in China Nixon also drew laughter and applause
from China's leaders when he turned to his interpreter and, as the ad
reminds us, said:

> I express my appreciation to my Chinese voice, to Mrs. Chung. I list-
> ened to her translation. She got every word right.

Mrs. Chung smiles, blushes, and translates the compliment. The announcer closes the ad by saying: "Richard Nixon, a man of compassion,
courage and conscience, a man America needs, now more than ever."
But warmth would not be shown if it might signal weakness. Accordingly,
White House Chief of Staff H. R. Haldeman ordered that a picture on a
poster that showed Nixon smiling at Mao Tse Tung be replaced with a
sterner pose.[44]

Not only did the ads argue that there was a private, warm side to
Nixon that the public rarely saw but also that what the public perceived as
coldness was actually the more socially acceptable attribute, shyness. "In-
terwoven into the documentaries and into some of the commercials were
little touches of lightness to try to show this shyness," Dailey explains.

"In one, for example, there was a thing with Tricia Nixon talking about the fact that on the night before her wedding, the President wrote her a note and slipped it under the door. It was a very warm, personal note from father to daughter, but he just couldn't tell her his thoughts personally and he felt that he could express them better in a note. Our testing showed that by using things like this we were beginning to create an understanding of the President as a shy man rather than a cold man."[45]

The Tone of the Ads

Finally, the memo advocated that the advertising "maintain a Presidential 'tone' ":

> Throughout the campaign, the tone of our advertising should be honest, direct, underplayed, and believable. The President can only suffer from bombast and exaggeration.
>
> We should admit, in context, that crime and drugs still exist, that inflation is still with us, and that the war is *not* completely over. The American voting public can accept these facts—they know them anyway. They will appreciate the frankness, especially when the great achievements in these areas are pointed out.
>
> A Presidential "tone" also implies a measure of dignity and a quality that is above political rhetoric. Commercials should be tasteful and thoughtful.

The ads argue that "we have taken an historic first step in the limitation of nuclear strategic arms" not "we have limited," "He has opened the door to China and Russia," a comparatively modest claim, and "He is bringing the war to and end."

Democrats for Nixon

A comparable recommendation governed the three TV ads created for Democrats for Nixon. White House aide Jeb Stuart Magruder wrote this about the nature and function of that group:

> Advertising copy must be restrained both in condemnation of McGovern and praise of the President. There is no need to resort to excess emotionalism, distortion, or innuendo to point out the dangers of a McGovern administration. His positions on defense, welfare, taxes, and peace terms are in conflict with the thinking of most Democrats and should simply be exposed as such.
>
> On the other hand, overly lavish praise of the President will probably turn the target audience off faster than you can say Democrats for Nixon.[46]

Cognizant of the difficulty in getting behavioral Democrats to cast a straight Republican vote, the strategy of the Democrats for Nixon presupposed that "No attempt should be made to persuade Democrats to vote the Republican line. It's too tough a sale. It will happen in many cases, anyhow."[47] Presumably to ease voters into casting a presidential vote for an unaccustomed party, Nixon told his Cabinet members in July that when they were campaigning they should refer to "McGovernites" not "Democrats."[48]

The Democrats for Nixon ads argued in a low-key, conversational tone that Democrats had an obligation in 1972 to place country before party; the ads reassured Democrats that Nixon more adequately represented their philosophy than McGovern did. In short, Democrats for Nixon employed the same appeals on Nixon's behalf that Johnson's ads in 1964 had made on his.

Using recognizable leaders from the other party in a committee called "Democrats for . . ." the Republican candidate or "Republicans for . . ." the Democratic candidate is a long-lived tradition in American politics. "Republicans for Roosevelt" existed as did "Democrats for Ike." Such appeals achieve national visibility in elections in which one party believes that massive defections from the opposing party are probable.

But Nixon did not view Democratic defections in 1972 as a transient phenomenon. He saw as the "most exciting aspect of the 1972 election . . . McGovern's perverse treatment of the traditional Democratic power blocs that had been the basis of every Democratic presidential victory for the last forty years and had made possible the creation of a New Republican Majority as an electoral force in American politics." Nixon believed that he "had a much greater affinity with most of them than had their erstwhile Democratic allies."[49]

Tests found that the ads sponsored by the Committee to Re-elect the President were less effective than the same ads credited to the Democrats for Nixon.[50] The credibility of the ads themselves was heightened by the testimony one of them drew from Hubert Humphrey.

Nixon told one of the consultants to the 1972 campaign that he considered the Democrats for Nixon ads the "three best political ads ever made." "I was standing in a receiving line at the White House and since I was the last in line the President talked to me for about five minutes," this consultant reports. "He talked at length about these commercials, that's how familiar he was with them. He said he thought these were the three best commercials ever made."

These three ads were aired more often than any of the other ads produced in the 1972 campaign. The White House liked them so much that CRP and the November Group were told to shelve a dozen and a half or so already produced pro-Nixon spots in favor of the Democrats for Nixon ads. The unaired ads included an endorsement by Mamie Eisenhower, another by Charlton Heston, and a series of short spots detailing Nixon's stands on issues of special interest to youth. The decision not to run these ads was, according to Taylor, "simply a question of air time. The anti-McGovern ads were so popular that the White House and CRP wanted to air them instead."[51]

The first includes a construction worker in hard hat working on scaffolding high above a busy intersection. The worker personifies the blue-collar, ethnic, union tradesmen who, since the New Deal, ordinarily would have supported the Democratic nominee. But this was no ordinary year, for on July 19 the executive council of the AFL-CIO had adjourned without endorsing any candidate for president. Where in 1968 the support of organized labor had propelled Humphrey within a millimeter of the White House, in 1972 just more than half of the American labor movement supported McGovern.[52] Here then is a worker who is less likely in 1972 than he was in 1968 to experience pressure from his union to support the Democratic nominee.

As this worker sits down to eat his brown bagged lunch, the announcer tells him why, in 1972, his vote should go to Nixon:

> Senator George McGovern recently submitted a welfare bill to the Congress. According to an analysis by the Senate Finance Committee, the McGovern bill would make 47% of the people in the United States eligible for welfare. 47%. Almost every other person in the country would be on welfare. The Finance Committee estimated the cost of this incredible proposal at 64 billion dollars the first year. That's six times what we're spending now. And who's going to pay for this? Well, if you're not the one out of two people on welfare, you do.

As the astonished worker, sandwich in mouth, stares in disbelief directly into the camera, his image is frozen on the screen.

The message of this ad and others like it, coupled with McGovern's inability to situate himself within the perceived mainstream of his party, reinforce the perception of traditional Democrats that it was acceptable this year to vote for Nixon. Where in the closing weeks of 1968, messages from their unions and from the Humphrey campaign drew blue-collar workers back to the Democratic party, in 1972, with a major segment of organized labor sitting the election out and McGovern's advertising failing to make strong party-based appeals, these same voters cast their votes for Nixon.

Although the ad, which repeats a charge made by Humphrey in the California primary, is literally true, it invites its audience to draw the mistaken conclusion that the plan it describes is one embraced by

McGovern in the 1972 campaign. McGovern had "submitted" such a bill as the ad claims. He had done so "at the request" of the National Welfare Rights Organization. He had not adopted the bill as his own or pledged that he would press for its enactment were he elected president. Creative Director William Taylor constructed the ad from research he received from CRP. Had Taylor known at the time he scripted the ad that McGovern did not personally favor the bill, he would have "picked another subject." "McGovern was putting his foot in his mouth every time he opened it" so there was no absence of subjects, he says.

One analysis of the impact of this ad concluded that it was "totally ineffective." In political analysts Thomas Patterson and Robert McClure's judgment the impact of the Republican "welfare" spot was neutralized by McGovern's spots' claim that he would get people off welfare and would deny welfare to those who could work but refused. The Democratic ads making this argument were aired more often than the Republican attack ad on the topic, they note.[53] McClure and Patterson's viewers rejected the ad's message. "In response to commercial recall questions, many voters indicated the message was 'unbelieveable'—no presidential candidate, not even George McGovern, would put half the country on welfare."[54] Still, the ad may have achieved effects McClure and Patterson were unable to monitor. By allying McGovern with an extreme claim, the ad may well have fueled the belief that McGovern was more liberal than the viewing voter. In these researchers' report the statement that "no presidential candidate, not even George McGovern would . . ." hints that such reinforcement is lurking in their data.

The Democrats for Nixon ad that attacked McGovern's posture on defense had, according to Patterson and McClure's study, "the clearest impact on voters' beliefs. . . . Of the high television exposure group, 44 percent changed their belief about McGovern between September and November in the direction consistent with the ad's message, while only 15 percent changed in the opposite direction."[55] Nonetheless, the researchers may be overstating the impact of this ad. As they concede, the changes could be attributed to other sources of information. Since exposure to prime time television and to television news do not correlate highly and since there was little treatment of this topic in television news, the researchers downplay this alternative. What falls through the net they cast over the data, however, are the radio ads on the impact of McGovern's defense proposals aired intensively in Syracuse, the site of their panels, during the last week of October[56] and the nationally broadcast speech by Connally attacking McGovern on defense.

Embracing Humphrey's indictment of the "McGovern defense plan" the Democrats for Nixon pitted the Democratic nominee of 1968 against the Democratic nominee of 1972. If, as Magruder argued, "Senator McGovern, in winning the Democratic primary, had been mortally wounded by his old friend Hubert Humphrey,"[57] then here was the autopsy. As a hand swept toy soldiers, ships, and planes from a table the announcer said:

> The McGovern Defense Plan. He would cut the Marines by one third, the Air Force by one third; He'd cut Navy personnel by one fourth; he would cut interceptor planes by one half, the Navy Fleet by one half, and carriers from 16 to 6. Senator Hubert Humphrey had this to say about the McGovern proposal . . . "It isn't just cutting into the fat, it isn't just cutting into manpower, it's cutting into the very security of this country."

As "Hail to The Chief" is played in the background, Nixon is shown reviewing the fleet. Ships are expendable toys to McGovern, to Nixon they are the real thing, the ad implies visually.

The local impact of these proposals was dramatized in radio ads aired heavily in the closing week of the campaign. On October 25, Clark Mac-Gregor, who had replaced John Mitchell as head of the Committee to Re-elect the President, authorized purchase of an additional $85,000 in radio advertising to air in "defense plant and military installation areas in key states." "Except for California and Massachusetts (which have a sufficient number of defense installations in each market to warrant separate commercials)" said the memo, "the copy has been written to cover the potential effects of McGovern's proposal on an entire state."[58]

The ad aired in Rhode Island by the "Radio Committee to Re-elect the President" stated:

> ANNOUNCER: According to a Congressional study, George McGovern's proposed 32 billion dollar slash in the U.S. Defense budget could mean closing down the Davisville Construction Center, the Quonset Point air station and the Newport Naval Base. That's a payroll loss of 88 million dollars and nearly 8 thousand civilians out of work.
>
> The least that could happen to Rhode Island under McGovern would be the firing of nearly 3,000 civilians and an income loss of 30 million dollars. That doesn't include cuts in military personnel and spending.
>
> Hubert Humphrey said of McGovern's defense cuts, "It shocks me, No responsible President would think of cutting back to the level of a second-class power."
>
> Well, George McGovern would. His plan to make America a second-rate power would also turn thousands of Rhode Island workers into second class citizens. That's why we have to re-elect President Nixon.

The word on which the ad hinges is the "could" in the first sentence. The ad is not claiming that this "would" happen but that it "could." What the ads aired in California, New York, Michigan, Wisconsin, Massachusetts, and Rhode Island cloaked under "could" was the fact that the severe impact described in each market "would not" occur under the McGovern proposal. If the cuts were spread across the facilities listed in the ads, none of them would experience the level of projected unemployment detailed in each. If the full impact of the cuts was borne by a few of the facilities, then there would be no impact on employment at the other facilities.

I cannot locate the Congressional report alluded to in this ad. What does exist is a report issued October 7 by Democrats for Nixon. That report was written by James D. Theberge, Humphrey's foreign policy adviser during the 1968 campaign.[59]

Throughout the primaries, the November Group kept track of the positions the Democratic contenders were taking on issues, noting shifts in emphasis as well as position. The request that this be done had come from Chief of Staff H. R. Haldeman who asked for a "recording of our political rivals' *public* speeches to preserve for future use their attacks on each other so we could check the usual inconsistencies." "Hunt and Liddy must have laughed," Haldeman adds. "Compared to their approach, I was in the political—and electronic—dark ages."[60] The ad that grew from this research showed a placard with McGovern's campaign picture on it turning round and round like a weather vane as the announcer said:

> In 1967, Senator George McGovern said he was not an advocate of unilateral withdrawal of our troops from Vietnam. Now of course he is. Last year the Senator suggested regulating marijuana along the same lines as alcohol. Now he's against legalizing it and says he always has been. Last January Senator McGovern suggested a welfare plan that would give a thousand dollar bill to every man, woman and child in the country. Now he says maybe the thousand dollar figure isn't right. Throughout the year he has proposed unconditional amnesty for all draft dodgers; now his running mate claims he proposed no such thing. In Florida he was pro busing; in Oregon he said he would support the anti-busing bill then in Congress. Last year, this year. The question is what about next year?

"These were complex issues but our statements were essentially true," says Taylor. "I have the feeling you could do the same thing with the claims of most candidates. No candidate including Nixon is completely consistent. But McGovern was more inconsistent than most." Ironically, after analyzing McGovern's positions on 12 issues including busing, abortion, amnesty, drugs, and Vietnam, Republican researchers concluded in late spring: "All McGovern commercials (with the exception of the previously noted Nebraska program) were filmed or taped over four months ago and have been used ever since without a single modification. Of all the major candidates, McGovern, in both his advertising and appearances, has sought to provide a clear position and solution on the issues."

The weather-vane ad levied the most damaging attack possible against McGovern's candidacy. In the primaries McGovern's ads had claimed that he was "Right from the Start," a claim predicated on his consistent opposition to the war in Vietnam. If McGovern changed his mind about key issues or, worse, deliberately spoke out of both sides of his mouth, then agreement with any of his stands could as well constitute ultimate disagreement for, as the ad asks: "What about next year?" This attack is more damaging than assaults on specific stands on specific issues, because it calls McGovern's credibility into question. Patterson and McClure find that this ad had some impact.[61]

To argue that a candidate is indecisive or, worse, duplicitous, is to disqualify him as a potential president because "decisiveness" and "honesty" are deeply embedded in our concept of the presidency. A president must command a sense of direction about the country's future and a core political character that makes predictions about future action plausible.

What made the weather vane ad plausible was an act unmentioned in it: McGovern's 1000% support and subsequent replacement of his running mate, Thomas Eagleton. Evidence that that decision eviscerated his candidacy comes from Patrick Caddell, McGovern's pollster, who reported that the most popular politician in the 1972 race was not McGovern, Shriver, Nixon, or Agnew but Thomas Eagleton.[62] Recollection of McGovern's well-publicized contortions over Eagleton's candidacy gave voters reason to suspect McGovern's credibility. The "turn-around" ad built on an existing attitudinal predisposition.

In 1968 many defecting Democrats returned to the fold in the campaign's final weeks; in 1972 they stayed with Nixon in part because the weather vane ad reinforced their convictions at a critical time. Such reinforcement was required because, as Gallup reported on September 25, "half of the vote of Democrats who currently favor Nixon could be described as 'soft.' "

The Republican ads succeeded in embedding a public perception that Nixon's positions on key issues was closer to the average voter's than McGovern's. When asked to plot their own positions on the right, center, or left of an issue scale and then plot the candidates' stands, voters placed McGovern to their left on three of five issues. Only on the issue of urban unrest did McGovern appear closer to the middle of the scale than Nixon. Political scientist Norman Nie and his co-authors conclude that "if we were to take an average of the positions assigned to McGovern and to

Nixon, we would find the former to be perceived by the public to be an outlying candidate with policy positions to the left of the public as a whole, while Nixon would be firmly established in the middle."[63] Political analyst Benjamin Page's comparison of the positions articulated by McGovern in his speeches and the public's sentiment reflected in polls reveals that McGovern was far more of a centrist candidate than people perceived him to be.[64]

Subtlety, rather than hard sell, was the rule in Nixon's 1972 ads; this enhanced their effectiveness as the McGovern seen on the evening news became progressively more strident in language and tone as the campaign evolved.

The low-key approach of the Democrats for Nixon ads marked a departure from the Republican mid-term election advertising of 1970. In that year, under the direction of White House aide Charles Colson, ads had appeared throughout the country accusing those who opposed Nixon of treason. Unlike 1970, the Republicans in 1972 had in place the November Group. The existence of that separate entity made it possible, in Magruder's words, "to keep Colson a good arm's length removed from our advertising program."[65]

When Colson tried to dictate advertising strategy, with the single exception of the ad on the mining of Haiphong Harbor, he was foiled. For example, he wanted to have a Republican plant infiltrate a group of welfare rights demonstrators who were picketing a CRP storefront in Washington. He then planned to call the attention of the media to their action. With the cameras rolling, the plant would hurl a brick through the front window, thus discrediting the picketers and presumably McGovern for lawlessness. To complete the plan Colson ordered that a larger-than-life placard patterned on the one in the weather vane ad be placed in the window of the headquarters. The staff at the November Group thwarted Colson's plan by finding it impossible to meet his request for the placard.

At another point Colson submitted a poster design showing a blue-collar worker in hard hat saying "Hey McGov! Do you still believe in amnesty for all the draft-dodgers? I don't. I fought for my country." "We put it [the Colson poster] behind Joanou's door for eight weeks," one of the members of the November Group told Jules Witcover,[66] "and every-time they [at the White House] asked about it we said we didn't know where it was." Some of those in the November Group who successfully avoided implementing requests from Colson about advertising did at CRP's request sign pledge cards reporting contributions they had not made. These were presumably used to cover illegally gotten funds. "We were political babes in the woods," explained one of the individuals in the November Group who signed such a card.

The Style of Nixon's Ads

The newslike, documentary style of the Republican ads also implied a seeming neutrality. Not only did this style well embody the tone the Republicans wanted their ads to set but it also embraced DeVries and Tarrance's finding that "television news and documentaries and other specials were by far the most important media influences on the split-ticket voter."[67] Presumably, Nixon's ads heightened their credibility with ticket-splitters by using such documentary techniques.

The low-key approach ran counter to the one Nixon outlined to Ehrlichman. In a section of his book *Witness to Power* that corroborates Nixon's close supervision of the advertising campaign, Ehrlichman reports Nixon saying: "The fact sheets we are putting out are too factual and dull. . . . We need more catchy slogans in them like 'get people off the welfare rolls and onto payrolls.' There should be more 'savage attack lines' in our literature."[68] Later, Nixon observed, "McGovern—this is the line—McGovern is left-wing; ADA left-wing. He is a dedicated radical, pacifist left-winger."[69] These were presumably the orders Colson was carrying out with his ad on amnesty.

This was not the only area in which the advertisers held to their own strategy. Nixon apparently opposed exposing McGovern's inconsistency, a lynchpin of the weather vane ad. He told Ehrlichman: "Don't ever let any of our people say, 'McGovern has changed his position.' Rather, say that there is absolutely no question where he stands. The conservative cares about consistency. Look at William Buckley, for example. A conservative would rather lose than change his position. . . . Attack McGovern on his wildest, most radical position."[70] As I've already indicated, members of that group do report that when "wild ideas from Colson and the like" were transmitted, excuses were made to slow their execution and ultimately they were "shelved."

Concept of the Nixon Presidency Embodied by the Ads

In the world created by the Republican advertising in 1972 Nixon was absorbed in being the president and had little time for partisan activities of any sort. He listened to the people, he reflected, he constructed long-range goals and plans, and he acted forthrightly, decisively, and with the well-being of the country and the world uppermost in mind. The image created by the ads exemplified a key defense Nixon used as he insulated himself against the charges that grew from Watergate. He had been too busy running the country to oversee the campaign, he said. Had he been running the campaign none of these things would have happened. The image was a false one.

What Alexander Butterfield's testimony of July 2, 1974,[71] revealed and subsequent evidence from Haldeman and Ehrlichman's books and from the White House transcripts confirmed, was that Nixon was intricately involved with the minutia of the campaign.

The White House transcripts also revealed a Nixon antithetical to the one glorified in the ads. *New York Times* staffer Alden Whitman summarized the contrast well when he wrote: "Transcript readers searched in vain for any discussion by the President of the welfare of the country or the constitutionality of his Watergate actions. Prior to the transcripts he had often been depicted as a tightly controlled, incisive man; but he was now shown letting control over events and persons slip from his grasp, spending hours avoiding any kind of decision. . . . The papers tended to confirm two character traits that many had discerned in Mr. Nixon—that he was a loner, certain of the loyalty of a very few men, and that he could be vindictive against those he saw as his special enemies."[72]

In short, the transcripts confirmed the suspicions about Nixon that McGovern had voiced throughout the campaign. But if McGovern's claims were prescient, why were they unpersuasive in the fall of 1972? We now turn to that question.

The Democratic Strategy: McGovern for the People; Nixon for the Rich

As is customary against an incumbent, the Democrats translated inflation into the increased cost of hamburger and bread. Additionally, they argued that Nixon's wage-price controls had frozen wages but had not actually frozen prices. Missing in these ads until mid-September was a strong identification between McGovern and the Democratic party. In mid-September, the tag on McGovern's ads changed to read: "McGovern. Democrat. For the People."

The decision pitted the judgment of Guggenheim against that of O'Brien. "The legacy of the Democratic party in 1972 was not the legacy of Kennedy or Roosevelt but the legacy of Lyndon Johnson," Guggenheim explains. "McGovern had run against the party candidate. Humphrey was the organization's candidate . . . Also, regulars of the party had been given a hard time at the convention. McGovern had run against the odds in the primaries and most of the organizational people were not for him. The tendency was to run as an independent rather than as a member of the party. When Larry O'Brien came in, his suggestions were traditional. . . . I know that putting "Democrat" in the end [of the ads] was influenced by his suggestion. It may have been a good one. I don't know."[73] By contrast, O'Brien notes: "his slogan on TV and on his literature had been 'McGovern . . . For the People.' We were able in the early weeks of the campaign to get the word 'Democrat' over the door and into the literature, but we were never able to make Democratic Party loyalty basic to the McGovern campaign. . . . McGovern had passionately opposed President Johnson's war policy, and I think that by the time he ran for President, he had distinctly mixed feelings about his own party, or at least significant elements of it."[74]

Only in the final weeks of the campaign did an ad created by Schwartz ask voters leaning toward Nixon to consider their loyalty to their party. Thinking aloud in stream of consciousness narrative, a man in a voting booth ponders whether he should vote for Nixon. As his hand moves to pull down the lever he reminds himself that this is the hand that voted for Kennedy. His father would roll over in his grave if he thought he was voting for a Republican, the man confesses. Finally, he decides to cast his vote for McGovern.

The one economic area in which McGovern edged ahead of Nixon was tax reform. On October 9 the Harris Survey reported that 40% of the voters surveyed thought that McGovern was more likely that Nixon "to put in real tax reform."[75] Thirty-six percent thought Nixon was. The perception was the outgrowth of the public's view that the Nixon administration was too close to big business.

In my judgment, the belief that McGovern was more likely to implement tax reform was in part the by-product of Democratic rhetoric that pervaded the primaries. Practically every one of the Democratic contenders scored Nixon's tax policies. So, for example, Lindsay's broadcast ads argued that "for six years he has had the second toughest job in America. . . . He walked the toughest streets of the toughest city in America summer after summer while most politicians ran for cover. He was the first mayor of New York to tax banks and insurance companies, and he's the one candidate with a plan for immediate property tax relief now, not next year." Wallace's TV ads proclaimed: "The average working man, business man and farmer pays taxes through the nose. About 200 billion dollars of income and wealth is tax exempt in this country. A vote for George Wallace will be a message to the national Democratic Party that we want these tax exemptions removed." Wallace promised to use the money recouped in this way for tax relief for "the average working man." Humphrey also promised redistribution of tax revenues. A commercial taped by actor Lorne Green noted, "Now we know that you're fed up with the Federal Government wasting your tax dollars on unnecessary defense items, when they could be used on health, housing and Social Security." As Humphrey says, "Defense yes. Waste, No." Humphrey's ads tagged him "the peoples' Democrat." McGovern indicted Nixon: "I listen to the president on television when he was talking about inflation, and he blames the working people, and then he says that he is against this excess profits tax because, in his words, high profits are good for everybody. Well, if high profits are good for everybody, why aren't high wages good?"

But when McGovern tried to parlay the public's perception that Nixon was too close to big business into a general charge of corruption, he failed.

Is Nixon Corrupt?

In January 1973 Harvard University sponsored a conference on "Campaign Decision-Making." In attendance were key staff members of the major candidates as well as major newspersons. The following remarks made at that conference verify that Watergate was not a decisive issue in 1972.

> MAGRUDER [representing the Committee to Re-elect the President]: As for the Watergate issue, we saw it as a bothersome problem. We felt very comfortable with our position on it, but it continually harassed us. We felt that it was not an important matter in a Presidential election, and I don't think the public felt it was an important matter in the election.
>
> DAILEY [November Group]: I think there were a few things that kept it from being a major issue. For one, there was no villain in it—there were some guys named Joe—and it was stretched out over a long period of time.
>
> CADDELL [McGovern's pollster]: People got to the point where they were not pleased [about Watergate and the sabotage] and were very concerned; but when they were faced with voting for McGovern, they found themselves unable to do it.[76]

By November 1972 the evidence had simply not emerged to link Nixon to the collective acts of sabotage that became known as Watergate. Additionally, his cover-up of his involvement was unrevealed. In the absence of evidence, McGovern asked questions that he hoped would provoke otherwise unwarranted inferences. So, for example, a radio ad scripted by Guggenheim noted that "President Nixon has received ten million dollars in secret campaign contributions from men and interests whose names Mr. Nixon refuses to reveal to the American people. Who are these men and what do they want?" Another radio ad provided a reason to explain why John Connally had agreed to head Democrats for Nixon: In the ad the announcer said "On April 30th of this year Mr. and Mrs. John B. Connally of Florsville, Texas, invited a few of their friends to dinner to meet Mr. and Mrs. Richard Nixon of Washington. Most of the 200 guests who came had made large fortunes in oil and oil related businesses. . . . At the Connally's that night, Mr. Nixon said, 'I strongly favor, not only the present depreciation rate, but going even further than that.' Perhaps that's why John Connally and some of his friends are supporting Richard Nixon this year."

Faced with the need to preserve McGovern's integrity while puncturing Nixon's, the Democrats broadcast two forms of ads that previously had assumed only print form. The first, which I call a "neutral reporter" ad, is reminiscent of the "Factbook" ad's attack on Ike's health in 1956. In 1972 a "crawl" of words scrolling across the screen invited us to draw inferences about Nixon's presidency from factual comparisons of his promises and performance. One of these Guggenheim ads paired the increased costs of hamburger, bread, and fish with Nixon's optimistic claims about the economy. "Can you afford four more years of Mr. Nixon?" it asked. Another detailed the activities of the Watergate burglars, noted that they reported to a White House assistant, and quoted Nixon's 1968 pledge to "put the right people in charge, provide them with basic guidance and let them do the job." Meanwhile, Tony Schwartz was transforming into broadcast form the strategy found in Al Smith's daughter's print ad in 1960. As Nixon's name changed color on the screen, real people voiced actual sentiments about Nixon:

> WOMAN: He's put a ceiling on wages and has done nothing about controlling prices . . .
> WOMAN: When I think of the White House, I think of it as a syndicate, a crime outfit, as opposed to, you know, a government . . .

This use of the personal testimony occurred when Schwartz' friends and associates opted to deliver their own statements rather than Schwartz' scripted lines. "Personal testimony" and "neutral reporter" ads would prevail over other forms of opposition advertising in the 1976 and 1980 campaign.

Like the persons in Schwartz' ad, McGovern also allied to Nixon words and phrases that function as devil terms. McGovern stands for openness, Nixon for secrecy. Note McGovern's release of the names of his contributors and Nixon's refusal to do so. McGovern stands for the people, Nixon for the privileged. Note Nixon's support of oil depletion allowances and McGovern's opposition. Note that McGovern's campaign is financed by small donations, Nixon's by large ones.

McGovern's case that the Nixon administration was corrupt was laid before the American people in a nationally televised address October 25 where the Democratic nominee replayed the ITT and milk fund scandals, detailed incidents in which regulations affecting large Republican donors were postponed, asked why Nixon was afraid to reveal the names of contributors who donated money before the disclosure date set by the new finance law, and summarized what was then known of the Watergate break-in and of the sabotaging of Muskie in New Hampshire and Florida. McGovern also berated Nixon for nominating inferior candidates to the Supreme Court, for the Cambodian "incursion," and for championing conspiracy laws. In McGovern's judgment the Nixon administration had mounted "a sustained assault" on the country's "most basic institutions."

Nixon's advertising simply ignored McGovern's charges. Yet the Republican ads' focus on Nixon's active presidency did constitute a form of rebuttal to the implication that Nixon was involved in any of the activities McGovern cited. If we accept the premise implicit in the Republican ads, then Nixon lacks the disposition and the time to engage in anything but serious international and domestic pursuits.

The War

In 1968 Nixon had promised to end the war in Vietnam. In 1972 that war continued. Nixon's failure to meet his pledge was a major reason given by the *New York Times* for endorsing McGovern. The endorsement (October 28, 1972) said "Not only has Mr. Nixon failed to carry out his explicit pledge to end the Vietnam conflict, on which he won the election by a hair's breadth four years ago; he has pursued a policy that appears to move in one direction while actually moving in another. Constantly emphasizing the winding down of the war and the withdrawal of American troops, Mr. Nixon has nevertheless enlarged the scope of hostilities, undertaken the biggest bombing campaign in history and committed American prestige to an increasingly authoritarian regime in Saigon."

McGovern wore his early indictment of the Vietnam War as an emblem certifying his morality and farsightedness. His early opposition to the war had the additional advantage of disassociating him from any charge that he was party to the "Democratic" war. In his ads McGovern tried to tie the war around Nixon's neck.

An ad showing McGovern touring a Veterans' Hospital graphically demonstrated the human cost of the war. One of the veterans says, "Believe me, when you lose the control of your bowel, your bladder, your sterility, you'll never father a child, when the possibility of your ever walking again is cut off for the rest of your life, you're 23 years old, you don't want to be a burden on your family, you know where you go from here? To a nursing home. And you stay there till you rot." By way of commentary the announcer observes: "Most of them were still safe in grade school when this man first spoke out against the war, risking political suicide in the hope they might be spared. For them, his early voice has now been heard too late. If the shooting stopped tomorrow, they'd still have to face their long road back, rebuilding shattered lives and broken dreams."

"I'm fed up with old men dreaming up wars for young men to die in," McGovern said in his print advertising. "The war in Indochina is the greatest military, political, economic, and moral blunder in our national history. . . . Now is the time to announce and abide by a timetable for withdrawal of all U.S. armed forces. Until we agree to withdraw, our prisoners will not be returned, the killing will continue, and more billions of dollars will be wasted."

In a McGovern administration, these "wasted dollars" would be used to fund social programs. When "we stop the waste that's going on in this war" McGovern declared in a TV ad, "we can provide a job for every man and woman who wants to work." "Are we going to rebuild the cities of America?" McGovern asks in one spot, "or are we going to destroy the cities in Southeast Asia? You can't do both." "Every single week this war claims $250 million of your taxes" McGovern declared in his televised speech of October 10.[77] "Every week it inflates the cost of everything you buy. Each week it costs $250 million that we need to employ men to rebuild our cities, to fight crime and drugs, to strengthen our schools, and to assist our sick and elderly."

In three televised speeches McGovern indicted Nixon's handling of the war and outlined a plan for withdrawal of fighting forces and return of American prisoners of war. He would, he said in his televised speech of October 10, stop all bombing, terminate shipment of military supplies, begin the "orderly withdrawal of all American forces from Vietnam, from Laos and Cambodia," notify the other side that they should return all prisoners of war within 90 days, and notify all parties that the U.S. would no longer interfere in the internal politics of Vietnam. Once a political solution is in place there, we would, under McGovern's plan, join other countries in "repairing the wreckage left by this war." Additionally, he would expand programs for "our" veterans.

Nixon responded in his televised speech on November 2 by employing a line of argument that had rebounded against Lyndon Johnson when thrown at Eugene McCarthy in the New Hampshire primary in 1968. "The leaders in Hanoi will be watching," Nixon said.[78] "They will be watching for the answer of the American people—for your answer—to this question: Shall we have peace with honor or peace with surrender?" The absence of an outcry akin to that which met comparable attacks on McCarthy in 1968 indicated that McGovern's credibility with press and public was low and that McGovern's extemporaneous identification of Nixon's conduct of the war with Hitler's had expanded the linguistic boundaries within which Nixon could safely tread.

Turning the ongoing war against Nixon required that the war be tied to the Republican president and that Nixon's de-escalation of the war be discounted. To accomplish the first objective Democratic advertising tallied the cost of the war during the Nixon years. In one radio ad an announcer noted:

> Four years ago Mr. Nixon said "I pledged in my campaign to end this war. If I fail to do so I expect the American people to hold me account-able for my failure."
>
> During the Nixon years, more than six million Indochinese have been killed, wounded or made homeless. During the Nixon years, Americans have dropped 3,700,000 tons of bombs. During the Nixon years, 20,000 Americans have been killed, over a hundred thousand wounded and 500 captured or missing. During the Nixon years the Vietnam War has cost American taxpayers 62 billion dollars. Four years ago, Mr. Nixon said, "Those who have had a chance for four years and could not produce peace should not be given another chance."

Print ads made the same point in almost the same words.

Nixon countered by arguing, as he did in his acceptance address, that "We have brought over half a million men home and more will be coming home. We have ended America's ground combat role. No draftees are being sent to Vietnam. We have reduced our casualties by 98 percent." These actions undercut McGovern's ability to credibly make the claims that he did in the televised speech on November 3: "Mr. Nixon will not end the war." "Mr. Nixon . . . has always supported the war." "The more the McGovern side tried to say that the President was in *favor* of the war, the more it worked to our advantage," reported Dailey. "The electorate at that point had pretty well decided that the President had done just about everything he could do, short of crawling, to end it, and they began to support his position."[79]

Faced with the Republican claim that Nixon was ending the war, Democratic ads magnified their audience's awareness of the dangers those still in Vietnam faced and the damage we continued to inflict on innocent civilians in South Vietnam.

McGovern's ads drew from the war's casualties evidence that Nixon's most widely replayed anecdote was offered hypocritically. The story of Tanya appeared first in Nixon's speech to the Soviet people, reappeared in his speech to the joint session, entered its third incarnation in a film shown at the Republican convention, found its fourth form in his accep-tance speech at the Republican convention, and achieved the distinction of being the anecdote unashamedly resurrected most often by a televised campaign when it re-emerged in a Republican ad. Initially, the Tanya narrative dramatized Nixon's compassion; its overuse underscored the truth of Shakespeare's claim that they are as poor who surfeit with too much as they who starve with nothing.

Capitalizing on the fact that Nixon's story of Tanya closed with an appeal to remember the Tanyas of the world as we search for peace, the Democrats tried to pin the Tanya tale on Nixon. The resulting ad implied that even as he was cultivating a perception of compassion Nixon was callously maiming and killing the Tanyas he professed to protect. In the radio ad the announcer said:

> In his speech to the Republican convention, Mr. Nixon spoke of Tanya, a Russian child whose family died in the siege of Leningrad. He quoted the final line in her diary. "All are dead. Only Tanya is left." "Let us think of Tanya," said Mr. Nixon, "and all of the other Tanyas everywhere as we proudly meet our responsibility for leadership."

> Since Mr. Nixon became president, 165,000 South Vietnamese civilians—men, women and children, our allies, people we are fighting to save, have been killed by American bombs. In a recent month, a quarter of the wounded civilians in South Vietnam were children under twelve. As we vote November 7th, let us think of Tanya and all the other defenseless children of the world.

The existence of this radio ad and others that are equally direct gives lie to the claim that Guggenheim fought the use of attack advertising in the 1972 campaign. What Guggenheim opposed, on the assumption that it would create a backlash, was using television as a medium of attack.

McGovern personalized the casualty lists by memorializing the men who died recently in Vietnam. In his televised speech on November 3, for example, McGovern dismissed Kissinger's claim of October 26 that peace was "at hand" by noting that Nixon had rejected the settlement Kissinger had worked out. "So this past week has become another week when the war was not ended." Then McGovern told of a phone call he received the night before from Mr. Charles Stewart of Gladstone, Michigan:

> His son, an Army enlisted man, was killed in Vietnam two days ago. He died on the day the peace was supposed to be signed. He was nineteen. He died on the day Mr. Nixon decided to continue fighting the war, while fighting over what he calls the "details" of peace.

> Charles Stewart, Jr., died for those "details." And he was not alone. This week twenty-two other Americans died for the same "details."

> Charles Stewart, Jr., and all the others are not really dying for details, but for a deception.

> The President may say peace, peace—but there is no peace, and there never was.[80]

To counter Nixon's claim that he had de-escalated the war, McGovern also dramatized the impact of the continuing American involvement on Vietnamese civilians. "The reality of this war is seen in the news photo of the little South Vietnamese girl, Kim, fleeing in terror from her bombed-out school," he said in his televised speech of October 10.[81] "She has torn off her flaming clothes and she is running naked into the lens of the camera. That picture ought to break the heart of every American. How can we rest with the grim knowledge that the burning napalm that splashed over little Kim and countless thousands of other children was dropped in the name of America?"

An unaired TV ad created in three versions by Tony Schwartz laid responsibility for napalming women and children at Nixon's doorstep. Over news footage of a Vietnamese mother clutching her napalm-scarred dead infant to her breast as she runs down a roadway, Henry Kissinger's voice is heard declaring that "We have restricted our bombing, in effect, to the battle area, in order to show our good will." His voice is echoed to accentuate its German accent and to heighten its similarity to the carica-ture, Dr. Strangelove. The footage of the woman is run in slow motion heightening our focus on her agony. A child's voice, the voice of Schwartz' son, then asks the question that the child asked of Schwartz when he first saw the footage: "Does a president know that planes bomb children?" The McGovern high command vetoed the ad. McGovern ex-plains that he feared that it would evoke the kind of response given the Daisy ad.[82] "The top staff agreed that the Vietnam spot should not be used because Nixon had neutralized the war issue with Kissinger's 'peace is at hand' promise" wrote O'Brien.[83]

On October 13, Gallup reported that by 58% to 26% the public perceived that Nixon could do a better job of dealing with the Vietnam situation. The advantage persisted through election day.

McGovern Listens but Can He Lead?

Aware that Nixon was viewed as "cold," Democrats underscored the public perception that McGovern was caring. The argument implied by many of McGovern's ads was "Because McGovern is one of the people, he empathizes with your concerns." In a five minute televised endorse-ment of McGovern, Humphrey differentiated the two presidential candi-dates by stating that "George McGovern and Sargent Shriver are not computers. Like you and me they're human beings with strengths and weaknesses. They've never pretended to be anything else." Humphrey's endorsement, which focused on McGovern's character, could not mute the effectiveness of the "Democrats for Nixon" ads' use of Humphrey's attacks on McGovern. What Humphrey needed to reestablish was McGovern's competence, not his character.

Although his general election ads show McGovern empathizing, they do not indicate how he would solve the problems discussed in the ads. A worker tells McGovern that a man on a job is breathing poison because the company has yet to install a blower system. McGovern responds empathically. "Fifteen thousand people killed in this country on the job. Fifteen thousand. That's as many as we lost in Vietnam in the worst year of the war. Nine million people injured in factories and mills and mines in this country. Some of them permanently disabled. And in some states, if you're disabled for life after working for twenty years, the compensation is so low that you'd be better off never having worked and dumping your family on the welfare rolls. And that's the kind of thing we've got to correct." In another ad older women inform McGovern of the conditions in a nursing home:

WOMAN: We have paraplegics, wheelchairs, crutches—some kind of a facility whereby we wouldn't sit helpless by and watch our neighbors die.

WOMAN: Raise our rent, our food goes up, and we're back in the same position.

WOMAN: We're just being forgotten.

To this, McGovern offers not solutions but sympathy:

MCGOVERN: You know some day, somebody's going to write the history of these times. And I think it's going to be a pretty sad chapter when they write the story on the way we treated our older people. And there isn't anything we ought to want anymore than that those later years can be years of confidence and security and decency and I'm going to do everything I can to see that older people are treated decently. Well I think we're going to make it. I hope you'll help me.

A second ad addressed to older people is even less specific. Its end is empathy not action. In it McGovern says

The thing we all have in common is some day we're all going to be old. We may be lonely. We might be poor. We might be hungry. And we have to somehow understand that every human being no matter what his age is has some obligation to those who are older. I feel that very strongly. I felt it with my parents as they got older. I feel it with other older people that I've seen all over the country. So we want to make that a happy and secure and relaxed time in our lives. Rather than one where we're plagued with anxiety and poverty. I think that's the message we have to get across to the people of the country.

McGovern seems to be running on a platform composed of the Golden Rule. In the Democratic spots McGovern "feels"; in the Republican ads Nixon "acts."

If both candidates were perceived to be competent and safe, then comparative warmth and compassion might have become salient issues, but by October 1972 Nixon was perceived to be both more safe and more competent than McGovern—which meant that, as a practical matter, were McGovern to persuade voters that he was more caring than Nixon, the victory would be pyrrhic, for competence and safety are more important factors in determining voting decisions than warmth. "We were operating under the theory that you don't have to like Nixon to vote for him," recalls Taylor. "We were right. We showed Nixon making decisions and talking strongly and specifically about issues. McGovern seemed to be whining and shaking hands with people." Although McGovern's ads were denying Nixon the label "The President" by referring to him as "Mr. Nixon," Nixon was sounding more presidential than McGovern.

Conventional wisdom about the McGovern campaign suggests that he made the mistake of employing the same sort of advertising in the general election that he had in the primaries. In the primaries, the reasoning goes, the public wants to get a feel for the person behind the persona, but in the general election the voter wants to know specifically which of the two candidates will do the better job, how they see the problems facing the country, and what solutions they offer. This conventional wisdom presupposes that in the general election Guggenheim continued to air the same sorts of spots he used in the primaries. However, although the cinema verité technique persisted, substantively the spots of the general election were less specific than some aired in the primaries. Contrast, for instance, these two ads on tax loopholes, the first a radio ad aired in the New Hampshire primary, the second a televised ad from the general election:

1. *New Hampshire:*

ANNOUNCER: George McGovern has specifically proposed tough new tax laws for the rich, so that they too must pay their fair share.

He has proposed the closing of outrageous loopholes that enable large corporations to shift their tax load to the working man. He has proposed relieving the property tax burden by having the federal government assume the major part of education and welfare costs. And he seeks to phase out oil and gas depletion allowances that cost the New Hampshire home owner an extra hundred and fifty dollars a year in fuel bills.

2. *General Election:*

GEORGE MCGOVERN (*to a group*): Tax shelters, ah, benefit very high income people at the expense of people in the middle. The people in this room are paying a heavier tax burden because we have too many loopholes in the law at the top. I don't mind paying a third of my income in federal taxes until I read where somebody who's making ten times as much as I am pays nothing. And that's what infuriates a lot of these working people that I see in the factories and the shops around this country. They read reports where all the millionaires are paying at a five and six percent rate and they're paying at a 14 to 20% rate as working people. You really can't justify that.

I can locate no radio ads by McGovern detailing his proposals for tax reform in the general election. Similarly, in New Hampshire, one of McGovern's radio ads addressing older persons noted that "He proposes total Social Security benefits to start at age 62 and an increased minimum wage of one hundred and fifty dollars a month with realistic cost of living increases. Also he proposes reforms in tax laws that burden retired people, Medicare benefits to pay for prescription drugs and out of hospital treatment, and expanded housing programs for the elderly." In the ads of the general election these specific proposals were replaced by McGovern's assurance that "there isn't anything we ought to want any more than that those later years can be years of confidence and security and decency and I'm going to do everything I can to see that older people are treated decently." In my judgment, McGovern erred in abandoning the specific action statements embodied in his primary spots.

In the general election McGovern detailed his specific proposals in half hour televised speeches. The difficulty in relying primarily on half hour speeches to carry specific proposals is that, unlike spots that entice the unsuspecting viewer, longer programming tends to attract true believers. So half hour speeches, whether on radio or television, are a good vehicle for a candidate who, in order to win, simply needs to reinforce the convictions of those already inclined to vote for him. This explains the utility of the twelve radio and two radio and television addresses Nixon delivered in the general election.

Since from September through election day almost 60% of the electorate consistently indicated a predisposition to vote for Nixon, the incumbent president simply needed to reinforce this disposition; by contrast, McGovern required a forum in which he could persuade those inclined to vote for Nixon that they should "come home" to the Democratic party. At a time when he required converts, McGovern selected a form of communication that preached to the choir. If a speech was to be the form of the communication, then five minute lengths would have better served McGovern's ends than 30 minute ones. However, in Guggenheim's judgment, the longer speeches were the form most likely to raise the money the campaign desperately needed. Guggenheim doubts that five minute speeches would have raised the money necessary for continuing the campaign.

The need to reach the persuasible was heightened because McGovern had squandered his one opportunity in the campaign to use the full length speech as a form to reach a large national audience. "It was three A.M. in

Miami when I accepted the nomination," he wrote later.[84] "Most of the nation was already asleep. The acceptance speech should have been delivered in prime time. But we were told that it would be complicated and against the spirit of reform and openness to change the order of business or speed the convention along. But it was a mistake. We lost our largest audience of the campaign and our best opportunity to persuade the American people that our reach for fundamental change would help them, not hurt them—that it was rooted in deeply American traditions, and not in some alien radicalism."

The first time that most voters saw or heard a sizeable portion of McGovern's acceptance speech was in the excerpts of it Guggenheim included in his filmed biography of McGovern. In that abbreviated form the power of the address was diminished. So too was the size of the audience and, since the biography was not aired until October, its vulnerability to persuasion.

In short, in the general election the electorate as a whole was not exposed either to McGovern's overarching vision of the country's future or to the specific form that vision would take. Voters were more likely, in other words, to see the specifics of McGovern's proposals refracted from attack ads of Democrats for Nixon than reflected in the Democrat's spot advertising.

The contrast between the images of the candidates presented in the advertising of 1972 is sharp. The cinema verité style through which Guggenheim presented McGovern to the American people meant that we heard extemporaneous statements by the candidate. By contrast, with few exceptions, the Nixon portrayed in the Republican ads was delivering scripted addresses to enthusiastic audiences. Where Nixon sounded firm and decisive, McGovern often did not. Where Nixon was shown performatively—signing into law the 18-year-old vote, dealing with Soviet and Chinese leaders and the like, McGovern was heard promising not that he would act but that he would *try*. Will he actually help older Americans? Not necessarily. He says: "I'm going to do everything I can if I become the President of this country to see that older people are treated decently." Will he produce jobs? Not necessarily. He says: "If the President of the United States can develop a program that will provide decent jobs for every man and woman in the United States, we can have decent schools, we can have good health care for every citizen." Can he? Will he? If so, how? The questions are left unanswered by the spots.

McGovern's difficulty is illustrated in an ad that sets as a criterion for judging a candidate whether he makes more than speeches about crime. Then McGovern proceeds to make a short speech that offers no specific proposals. "If you want to end crime in this country," he says, "it's going to take more than speeches. You're never going to get on top of crime in the United States until you get on top of drugs. Because half of all the crime in this country is caused by the drug addict. They'll kill, they'll steal, they'll do anything to get that money to sustain that drug habit. And we've got to have a program that's better than the one we have now to deal with drugs, if you're going to get on top of the crime problem."

This lack of specificity would be less damaging were it not for the fact that Nixon's ads are offering specific illustrations of the programs he had initiated to reduce the flow of drugs. By indicting McGovern's specific proposals on welfare and defense and by asserting that he has changed his views on the specifics of a number of other key issues, the Democrats for Nixon ads have set in place the notion that when he descends into specifics, McGovern is suspect. Instead of countering that doubt, Democratic ads compound it by defining a problem but not a solution.

The failure was both substantive and stylistic. Scholars of interpersonal communication have noted that persons of low status speak more tentatively than those of high status. Low status individuals couch their opinions in requests for permission to hold them. They do not declare. In some of his ads, McGovern employs a "low status" style. "It seems to me that there ought to be enough employment opportunity in this country so that everybody could have a job" he says. "And we're just going to have to apply tougher standards in these factories" he says when "We will" would have conveyed the same idea with greater conviction. At the same time "just going to have to" suggests that McGovern is the patient not the agent of change. Similarly, McGovern notes that "the President can *help* set a new tone in this country. He can *help* raise the vision and the faith and the hope of the American people, and that's what *I'd like to try to do*" (emphasis mine).

Robert Shrum, one of McGovern's three main speechwriters in 1972, argues that the ads did not capture the McGovern he knew. "He's a tough, strong person," Shrum says. "He came to the Senate in 1963 and one of his first speeches declared that the war in Vietnam was wrong." Shrum also implies that the cinema verité form did not capture McGovern's strength. "There is a distinction between McGovern sitting around talking to people and speaking to a large group. He does have a tentativeness when he's sitting around talking to people. One of the questions of the campaign was, Is he a strong leader? The TV ads didn't leave you thinking that he was."[85]

At one level, the sort of hesitance implied by McGovern in his ads is commendable. After all, presidents do not command the resources or the

power singlehandedly to produce profound social change. But in an election in which "The President," with a large lead in the polls, was arguing
that he had produced important changes, this was not the time to educate
the American people on the limitations of presidential power.

Delivery accentuated McGovern's stylistic and substantive weaknesses as a communicator. Compared to Nixon, McGovern was an inef-
fectual speaker. Nixon's voice is deep and resonant, his tonal range large.
McGovern's higher, occasionally whiney pitch, limited tonal range, and
tendency toward nasalized speech made it difficult to attend to him.
These were impressions not readily dislodged by endorsements such as
that by Senator Mike Mansfield who stated in a Democratic ad that "In
my opinion, he [McGovern] has a spine of steel."

The absence of proposed action coupled with the cues of low status
to underscore the impression created by his delivery. "McGovern is not a
strong, decisive leader" was the resulting message. This conclusion was
reinforced by McGovern's treatment of Eagleton and by the attacks embodied in the Republican advertising. Nixon's stylistic choices and delivery magnified his argument that he engaged in long-range planning and
was decisively responsive to the popular will.

All of this argues that cinema verité ads may not have been an
appropriate means of showcasing McGovern in the general election. Guggenheim explains his decision to use this technique:

> McGovern's victories in the primaries were a tremendous achieve-
> ment . . . There are a number of things that made these things [victo-
> ries] come together. I think the media was considered superior to that of
> his opponents in the primaries. To bring these techniques into the gen-
> eral election was like saying don't change a winning game plan. . . .
> They had worked in 1962 in the most Republican state in the Union. He
> won in '68 using those methods. He won the nomination no one ex-
> pected him to win with those methods. . . . Someone who is down with
> the people and more informal, rubbing shoulders with everyone, is less
> attractive as a presidential candidate in the general election than he
> would be in the primaries. . . . In hindsight, I don't think [carrying the
> technique from the primaries into the general election] was the right
> thing to do.[86]

"I think it is also true that I would not pick McGovern in the first ten
candidates that I've worked for to use that method [cinema verité]. [But]
he was far better in that than he was giving formal speeches," Guggenheim notes. "McGovern would not be my first choice of a person to use
on television period." The choice was not, as some have alleged, a function of Guggenheim's reliance on cinema verité. "We do use cinema
verité," he says, "but there are a lot of elections in which we haven't used
it at all."

Still of cinema verité spot produced by Charles Guggenheim and aired for McGovern in the 1972 general election.

The Prophet vs. "The President"

The view of Nixon as hypocritical was one that pervaded McGovern's rhetoric. As the campaign progressed, McGovern increasingly assumed the role of Old Testament prophet crying in the wilderness, proclaiming to an unhearing people that Nixon's path was one of folly and his one of righteousness. As I will argue, in his role as would-be-president-prophet McGovern carried disabling baggage.

McGovern's embrace of Biblical passages, his use of the language of religion, and his alliance with Isaiah suggest to me that he offered himself to the American people as a prophet. Sections of his acceptance address could comfortably be delivered in a church or at a revival meeting. He stated, for example, "And this is the time. It is the time for this land to become again a witness to the world for what is noble and just in human affairs. It is the time to live more with faith and less with fear—with an abiding confidence that can sweep away the strongest barriers between us and teach us that we truly are brothers and sisters."

Having defined the faith, the speech invites the audience to reject all that he identifies with the Nixon administration. The invitation to reject Nixon mimicks the structure of a litany, a form that bespeaks speechwriter Bob Shrum's Catholic boyhood more so than McGovern's Methodist one:

> From secrecy, and deception in high places, come home, America.
>
> From a conflict in Indochina which maims our ideals as well as our soldiers, come home, America.

From military spending so wasteful that it weakens our nation, come home, America. . . .

He might have added, "from the wages of sin, come home, America." The speech then ends with a prayer:

May God grant us the wisdom to cherish this good land, and to meet the great challenge that beckons us home.

This is the time.

At one point in the campaign McGovern borders on claiming that God is on his side. In what was in effect his second acceptance address, the speech delivered to the National Committee that had ratified McGovern's selection of Shriver to replace Eagleton, McGovern repeated Lincoln's statement that "I know there is a God and that He hates injustice. I see the storm coming, but if he has a place and a part for me, I believe that I am ready." Then he added: "Now, over a century later, when the great issue is restoring peace and justice to our land once again, and we know there is a God and we know He hates injustice, we see the storm coming. But if He has a place for us, let us be ready."

In his nationally televised address of October 10 on Vietnam McGovern again turned to Scripture to close a speech that seems almost Jeremiadic: "This is the choice of a century. But it is also the same choice that human beings have faced from the very beginning. So, let us heed the ancient words: 'I have set before you life and death, blessing and cursing. Therefore, choose life, that thou and thy seed may live.' Thank you. God bless you." Shrum notes that that passage was one McGovern had been using to describe the war in Vietnam for years.

That quote also capped his nationally telecast speech of November 3 that, like the earlier address, focused on Vietnam. The quote identifies McGovern with the forces of life and Nixon with death. Its "thou" and "thy" underscore the Scriptural origin of McGovern's words. The existence of future generations is a function of whether or not voters choose life. The "day of reckoning," as McGovern called it in his speech of November 3, was election day.

Sections of some of McGovern's speeches are explicitly sermonic. In a speech in Los Angeles on September 26, he affirmed that the people of Indochina also "are created in the image of God." Here the struggle over Vietnam was cast as one for the soul of America. "Our children look to us for moral guidance—for America's true ideals. But we protect the prestige of warmongers. And we pay with the soul of our nation." Throughout the campaign McGovern promised "restoration"—not restoration of the kingdom but restoration of ideals, restoration of peace. He spoke in Mosaic fashion of bringing America to the "decent land." So, for example, he closed his speech of September 26 by saying "Come with me, and we will bring America home to the great and good and decent land our people want it to be."

In McGovern's televised address on the economy delivered October 20, his identity as Old Testament prophet was made plain. McGovern ended that address by stating "I want to claim the promise of Isaiah: 'The people shall be righteous and they shall inherit the land.' " Throughout the campaign McGovern's claim to have been among the first to oppose the war implied that his had been a voice crying in the wilderness. Days before the election his speech of November 3 reveals his perception that he remains a prophet without honor in his own country. "Millions are confused and doubtful and suspicious of any candidate who pledges peace" he says. Like the prophet he is willing to speak the truth bluntly, regardless of consequences. "I do not know," he says, "whether the blunt words I have said tonight will help me or hurt me in this election. I do not really care." "After the Eagleton affair, I didn't think we were going to win," says Shrum. "I thought the one thing those of us who worked for McGovern could do for him was help him say some things that were true and right and stood the test of time." He adds: "Nixon's conduct as well as the war brought out the moral religious rhetoric in McGovern. Nixon brought out in you the need for the ethical component in leadership."

One difficulty in assuming the role of prophet is revealed in our language's distinctions between "false prophets" and "prophets." We have no comparable distinction to describe the role Nixon assumed: that of "The President." The Democrats for Nixon ads implied that McGovern was a false prophet. McGovern in effect argued that Nixon was a false president.

A second difficulty comes in the role prophets traditionally are permitted to play. Even when the people heed the warnings of the prophets, they are not the ones summoned to lead the restored nation. Prophets' singlemindedness, their inability to compromise, and their self-righteousness neither suit them well for governing nor endear them to voters.

Finally, expression of political options in the language of "witness," "faith," "brothers and sisters," "restoration," "reckoning," and "image of God" edged dangerously close to the bounds that circumscribe the President's role as head of the country's secular religion. The Constitution reflects its authors' fears of two alternative forms: a theocracy and a monarchy. McGovern seemed to proffer the former while indicting Nixon for the latter. Given such a choice, the electorate, which was dissatisfied with the alternatives it was offered, was disposed to choose the monarch it knew rather than the theocrat it did not know.

Slogans

In the primaries McGovern claimed that he was "Right from the Start," a
theme tied to his early opposition to the Vietnam War. After Eagleton
was replaced by Shriver, McGovern could hardly continue to claim that
he was "Right from the Start."

"McGovern for the People" also appeared in the primaries. That
slogan survived into mid-September when "McGovern. Democrat. For
the People" replaced it. The shift betrayed the need of the McGovern
campaign to "bring home" Democrats leaning toward Nixon.

"President Nixon. Now More Than Ever" was understood by groups
tested by pollster Robert Teeter "to refer to unfinished work in progress." According to Teeter,[87] the tested groups "pictured the President's
past record and looked to the future." The slogan also "embodied the
concept 'help him finish the job.' " "The slogan was not interpreted by
anyone as anti-McGovern." Additionally, the slogan's use of "now" was
found to express a "sense of urgency." Groups mentally added "We
need" to the slogan to form the proposition. "We need President Nixon.
Now More than Ever."

Nixon's slogan encompassed McGovern's. If we needed Nixon "Now
More than Ever," then implicitly he stood for the people. By contrast
McGovern could stand for the people without necessarily making a good
president.

The slogans also betray Nixon's reliance on the shelter of incumbency. We need *President* Nixon not *Richard* Nixon. In the slogan, Nixon
is neither Democrat nor Republican but President. McGovern's slogan
implies no sheltering. He and the people are allied without the trappings
of any office between them.

The irony of the 1972 election, of course, is that Nixon did ultimately
end the war on terms similar to those proposed by McGovern and rejected by Nixon as "surrender"; and McGovern's broadest inferences
about Nixon's involvement in Watergate proved understated. "The President" who in the ads was shown preoccupied with national and international affairs was found to have been preoccupied with covering up his
complicity in Watergate and then in covering up his cover-up of his complicity. The strong decisive president revealed in the ads bore little resemblance to the vacillating, elliptical, profane president exposed by the
White House transcripts. Nixon received 60.7% of the vote. McGovern
carried only Massachusetts and the District of Columbia. As the cover-up
unravelled, drivers in Massachusetts attached bumper stickers to their
cars saying "Don't blame me. I'm from Massachusetts."

CHAPTER EIGHT

1976: Integrity, Incumbency, and the Impact of Watergate

Among the many assumptions shattered by Watergate were the notions that the president does not lie and that, unlike members of Congress, who represent special constituencies, the president represents *all* the people. For both the Republican and Democratic contenders in 1976, and for their advertising teams, the shattering of these assumptions seemed to suggest that 1976 could not be run simply as a typical campaign in which the candidates appealed to the voters' traditional party loyalties and campaigned on the position on the issues that each party took. Rather, in a year in which it was widely perceived that the honesty of a presidential candidate and his commitment to constitutional government were on the line, campaign advertising had to find a way to communicate the trustworthiness of the candidates.

The stress in '76 would thus be on the personal character and integrity of the two candidates, on how atypical as politicians these men were, and on how little each owed party regulars for his candidacy. "[I]t was almost entirely a candidate perception election," reported Ford's pollster. "Almost all of the variants which would account for why people were voting either for Carter or Ford had to do with personal elements . . . not with issues."[1]

As a consequence, although clearly an unintended one, 1976 would be a watershed year in campaign advertising. If there had been any identifiable trend from 1964 through 1972 in presidential campaign advertising, it had been toward the increasing use of carefully scripted, professionally produced ads in which the candidates themselves often neither appeared nor spoke. But such highly polished ads, invoking invisible authority, could not be central in a year in which the prime message of both campaigns was that their candidate was a person of integrity, dependability, leadership, and competence. What we see in 1976, in fact, is a generalized return by both Jimmy Carter and Gerald Ford to direct, old-fashioned, personal appeals and the emergence of persons-in-the-street giving personal testimony and low-key, factual, neutral reporter ads as prime vehicles of attack.

For Gerald Ford, who acceded first to the vice-presidency on the resignation of Spiro Agnew and then to the presidency on the resignation of Richard Nixon, the 1976 race would be a long and ultimately unsuccessful run. The very nature of his ascendancy, as well as the fact that as heir to the Nixon presidency, he had to bear the brunt of the nation's unresolved anger over Watergate, put him in the more difficult position. Still, Ford came to the race with certain strengths—he had put in many years as a highly regarded and extremely well-liked representative from the state of Michigan and later as Minority Leader of the House, where his reputation for personal integrity was unimpeachable. For over two years, he had also handled his presidency-by-succession with more than a degree of competence and with no major scandals. Last, Ford greeted the prospect of running on his own record for his own term of office with a certain gusto.

Gerald Ford had become president on August 9, 1974. As one of his first acts as president, he went on television to assure the American people that the long national nightmare of Watergate was over and that the system worked. Barely a month later, on a Sunday, a day without drive-time radio, afternoon newspapers, or much regularly scheduled evening news, at a time too late to reach the last edition of the Sunday papers, Ford unconditionally pardoned Nixon. In protest over the pardon, Ford's press secretary, former *Detroit News* reporter Jerry Ter-Horst resigned. Ford's decisive, if controversial, decision cost him in public approval. On September 1, Gallup reported that 71% approved of Ford's handling of the presidency. By October 13 that approval had dropped to 50%. A special Gallup survey taken immediately after the pardon showed that the public disapproved of the action by a 2 to 1 margin.

Between Ford's ascension to power and the primary season of 1976, South Vietnam fell, effectively removing an issue that had festered in presidential campaigns since 1964; an American ship, the *Mayaguez,* and its crew were seized by the Khmer Rouge, giving Ford the opportunity to rally the country behind a dramatic rescue mission; and inflation, although not unemployment, began to ease. In his fight against inflation Ford resorted to veto after veto, moves that pitted him (often successfully) against the Democratically controlled Congress. Ford also survived two assassination attempts. Additionally, Nelson Rockefeller, the unelected president's unelected vice-president, bowing reluctantly to the conservatives he could not placate, indicated that he did not want to be considered for the second spot on the ticket in 1976.

In 1974, amendments to the Federal Election Campaign Act (FECA) made federal funding of presidential elections a reality; the presidential election of 1976 was the first such federally funded presidential campaign. What this meant in the primaries was that any candidate who raised at least $5000 in contributions of $250 or less in each of 20 states qualified for matching funds. Individual contributions to candidates could reach as high as $1000 in the primaries, but only the first $250 would be matched. In return for these matching funds, candidates agreed to a spending ceiling in the primaries. In 1976 that ceiling was $10.9 million, a figure that actually became $13.1 million when the 20% allowed for the raising of the money was included.

Under the new law, candidate Ellen McCormack engaged in a publicly funded campaign to define the fetus as a baby and abortion as murder. The Abortion Rights Action League challenged her submissions for matching funds on the grounds that her Pro-Life Action Committee had not made it clear that it was soliciting contributions for a presidential candidate, not an anti-abortion drive. The FEC disagreed and granted McCormack her funds.[2] However, under the law, McCormack's matching funds ceased 30 days after she failed to receive at least 10% of the vote in two consecutive primaries, which occurred in late May.

But more important than looking at how the new law influenced the chances of single-issue candidates is to see how, and in what unforeseen ways, FECA affected the candidacies of those who seriously sought the nominations of the two major parties. In particular, it is interesting to observe how FECA uniquely contributed to the fortunes of both Jimmy Carter and Gerald Ford.

As the incumbent president, Ford was the titular head of his party. Hence the Republican National Committee picked up the tab for $500,000 of his travel in 1975 on the grounds that he was not campaigning for himself but for other candidates. To no avail did the Democratic National Committee and the Citizens for Reagan argue to the Federal Election Commission that this violated the new finance law. In particular, Reagan supporters disputed the classification of Ford as leader of the party. Reagan had raised considerable cash for other candidates, they noted, and had a sizeable following. Consequently, they reasoned, he too was a leader of the party. On November 20, 1975, the FEC responded that as titular head of the Republican party Ford had a right to campaign on behalf of other candidates in his party and the Republican National Committee had the right to pick up the tab. After January 1, 1976, however, these appearances would be counted against Ford's primary spending limit on the assumption that such trips would facilitate his nomination.

But the advantages of incumbency would continue after Ford announced his candidacy. As president, Ford had the option of having the government bill him for Air Force One, while Reagan often was forced to pre-pay for his chartered plane.[3] Ford's opponents also charged that White House aides and administration officials on the federal payroll should have that portion of their salary devoted to Ford's reelection charged against his spending ceiling. When Ford moved his Secretary of Commerce, Rogers C. B. Morton, to a position in the White House where one of his duties included serving as liaison to the Ford campaign, this protest grew louder. But FEC Vice-Chair Thomas Harris dismissed the complaint saying, "It is inconceivable to me that Congress intended, without mentioning it, to confer on this commission responsibility for monitoring political activity by government employees."[4] At the end of March, when Morton moved to the campaign as its manager, the outcry subsided.

The advantages of incumbency would benefit Ford in the general election as well, prompting one Carter aide to complain, "Everything even remotely connected with Carter's campaign must be paid for out of that 21 million, while anything less than total involvement in the Ford campaign gets paid for by the government and is not counted against his 21 million."[5]

Thus, Ford enjoyed a financial advantage that sprang from his incumbency. Carter's edge over his better-known Democratic rivals turned on a provision of FECA limiting the amount an individual might contribute to each candidate. "Without stringent contribution limits," writes Alexander, "better-known candidates who had connections with wealthy contributors could have swamped Carter; and without federal subsidies, Carter would have lacked the money to consolidate his initial lead."[6] Court resolution of a pending suit on FECA also worked, although unintentionally, to Carter's advantage.

On January 30, as the primary season was just getting underway, the Supreme Court ruled on a pending suit, *Buckley* v. *Valeo,* brought by Senator James Buckley and former Senator Eugene McCarthy, among others, challenging the constitutionality of the Federal Election Campaign Act as amended in 1974. Although the court upheld the public financing that resided at the heart of the presidential candidates' plans in 1976,* it also ruled that Congressional appointment of four of the six members of the Federal Election Commission, the law's monitoring body, encroached

---

*The court upheld the $1000 limit on individual contributions and the $5000 limit on a PAC's contributions to a single candidate but struck down the limit on what such committees could spend if they remained independent of the candidate's campaign. Here was the Pandora's box that would let loose a cyclone of PAC advertising in the 1980 presidential race.

on the prerogatives of the executive branch. All six members, it ruled, had to be appointed by the president. Conceding "de facto validity" to the past acts of the Commission, however, the Court provided a thirty-day stay before the Commission, as then constituted, was to cease functioning. In the remaining thirty days, each candidate rushed to document contributions that would garner matching funds. On February 27, the Supreme Court gave Congress an additional three weeks to reconstitute the FEC. This action set March 22 as the new final date on which matching funds could be dispensed.

When the FEC's time ran out, Congressman Morris Udall, who had played a crucial role in passing FECA, was left in the lurch unable to secure the $89,500 to which his campaign was entitled.[7] By May Udall was owed approximately $380,000[8] and Reagan almost a million dollars.[9] As a result, both lost maneuvering room in the crucial Wisconsin primary, where without funds for TV Reagan carried 45% of the vote and Udall, off the air the final Tuesday, Wednesday, and Thursday, lost to Carter by fewer than 5000 votes.

On the final Saturday before the Wisconsin primary, Udall was forced to fly on a commercial plan from Milwaukee to Washington because his campaign could not afford to charter a plane.[10] Strapped for funds, Udall gambled that by spending money, he could raise money. So at the end of April he purchased five minutes on each of the three networks to ask supporters for contributions. The ads raised enough money to pay for themselves and generated some additional funds for the campaign.

The Reagan campaign also suffered. In April the campaign relinquished its chartered jet and high level staff gave up their salaries. Like Udall, Reagan turned to paid programming to raise money. At the end of a nationally aired half hour speech on March 31 Reagan asked viewers for financial support. The program cost approximately $24,000 to produce and $90,000 to air but brought in nearly 1.3 million dollars while reaching 15 million viewers. This infusion of funds kept Reagan on the airwaves until payment of matching funds resumed.[11]

Once Congress sent the law reconstituting the commission to Ford, the incumbent exacerbated the woes of those who sought his job by delaying signing it. The delay prompted Udall to complain, "While Mr. Ford is trying to kill off Reagan, he is shooting me also as an innocent bystander."[12]

What kept Carter ahead of the pack through this period of financial drought was his ability to borrow large sums of money. The freeze "redounded to Carter's advantage,"[13] argues Carter biographer Betty Glad. Under a loophole in the finance law the candidate could spend as much of his own money as he wished. Carter's successes in the early primaries, his willingness to mortgage his personal wealth,* and his close connection to Georgia bankers enabled him and his committee to borrow $775,000 during the freeze. Carter secured these loans by using money owed him in matching funds as collateral, by using receivables owed for transportation from the Secret Service and the press, and by banking on his own personal wealth. His close association with Gerald Rafshoon, who earlier had produced the advertising for his successful bid for the Georgia governorship, also helped Carter. Rafshoon did not press to collect the $500,000 Carter reportedly owed him.

Contrary to the reports filed during the campaign, the 4800-page amended report Carter filed with the FEC three days after the election revealed that his campaign was in debt during most of the primary season. In April, the middle of the cut-off of matching funds, Carter's campaign had reported a balance of $185,795. The audited post-election report revealed that instead the campaign owed $970,045.[15]

The post-election report suggests that contrary to Carter's claim that "to the special interests I owe nothing, to the people I owe everything," he did owe a great deal to a handful of Georgia bankers and Gerald Rafshoon.

The Republican Primaries

Although the issue of Ford's pardon of Nixon would be an important one in the general election and in the media, it did not play a big role in the primaries. Ronald Reagan, Ford's main challenger, had defended Nixon's probable innocence long after most members of Congress, from both parties, had come to the opposite conclusion. Moreover, two weeks after Nixon's resignation, the former California governor noted that "the punishment of resignation certainly is more than adequate for the crime."[16] Consequently, where the pardon became a convenient punching bag among contending Democrats, it was no blot on Ford's escutcheon in the primary contest between Ford and Reagan.

In July 1975, shortly after Ford announced that he would seek his party's nomination, an exploratory committee called Citizens for Reagan was formed. Reagan, who was at the time a retired governor, continued to reach a mass audience with his radio program and newspaper columns. However, two months before he announced his candidacy, Reagan uttered the sentence that probably cost him the nomination. In a speech to the Executive Club of Chicago on September 26, 1975, Reagan pro-

---

*For 1975 Carter reported a gross income of $136,139.[14]

posed to transfer such programs as Food Stamps, Medicaid, and revenue sharing from the federal to the state and local level. Such a transfer, he said, would "reduce the outlay of the federal government by more than $90 billion."

What saved the proposal from the obscurity to which the press had dispatched it was the Ford campaign. Quietly and patiently Ford's strategists detailed the increase in unemployment in the housing industry, the possible bankruptcy of states, and the reductions in services that would follow from Reagan's proposal. With that data in hand, they simply bided their time. On November 20, 1975, the conservative two-term governor from California announced that he would seek his party's nomination.

At the end of that week on ABC's "Issues and Answers" Reagan was informed by Frank Reynolds that the federal government underwrote 62% of the welfare costs in New Hampshire. Reynolds concluded that Reagan's plan would either require a cut in welfare payments or an increase in taxes. Reagan responded that states would be able to pay those costs if the federal government stopped pre-empting "so much of the tax dollar." Since New Hampshire has neither a sales nor an income tax, that meant that Reagan would have to tell the citizens of New Hampshire that one or the other was necessary, did it not, asked ABC's Bob Clark. Reagan responded, "But isn't this a proper decision for the people of the state to make?" Questions about the $90 billion dollar plan plagued Reagan throughout the primaries.

If the $90 billion dollar plan was Reagan's headache, Richard Nixon was Gerald Ford's. Three days before balloting in New Hampshire, Nixon left for a well-publicized visit to the People's Republic of China.

Using advertising that played heavily on images of Ford performing presidential functions, the incumbent president carried New Hampshire by a bit over 1000 votes of the approximately 108,000 votes cast. The following week Ford won Massachusetts and Vermont. Reagan had contested neither. In Florida where Reagan repeatedly attacked Ford over plans to turn control of the Panama Canal over to Panama ("We paid for it, it's ours . . . and we're going to keep it"), Ford won 53% to 47%. Ford also carried Illinois, 59% to 40%. Ford now led Reagan in the delegate count by more than three to one.

Clearly, Reagan's message was not getting across in a way that would win him votes. In North Carolina the campaign changed its strategy. The cinema verité documentary style ads, whose underproduced quality had been intended to convey the Reagan message without underscoring the candidate's background as an actor, were supplemented by a form capitalizing on Reagan's strong suit—his ability to deliver a decisively strong speech to a television audience in a calm, reassuring manner. The strategy worked, and Reagan won in North Carolina. Reagan and his campaign managers began making plans for a nationally televised speech to raise funds to save his foundering, debt-ridden campaign.

Meanwhile, to conserve funds, the Reagan campaign had earlier decided to concede the Wisconsin, New York, and Pennsylvania primaries to Ford and instead concentrate on Texas. In the interim, Reagan's nationally televised speech raised one and a half million dollars, money split between paying off debts and underwriting advertising in Texas.

Reagan overwhelmed Ford in Texas, winning the 96 delegates at stake and catapulting himself back into the race. By winning Alabama, Indiana, and Georgia half a week later, Reagan moved ahead of Ford in the delegate count. What is significant about this for our purposes is that Reagan drew victory from the throat of defeat with two speeches, which reinforced his campaign's decision in 1980 to defy conventional wisdom and rely on ads that had the candidate carry his message directly to the American people.

Ford and Reagan then held each other to a near draw in the remaining primaries with neither emerging with the delegates needed to win the nomination on the first ballot.

Until the California primary Ford's advertising had been handled by Peter Dailey, who had headed the November Group in 1972 and who would coordinate Reagan's advertising in the general election of 1980. "We went to Dailey originally," explains one of Ford's former aides, "because he'd done the '72 campaign for Nixon." But Dailey insisted on supervising the advertising from California, a decision that made it more difficult for him to coordinate with Ford's pollster and harder to maintain day-to-day control of the advertising. More significantly, Ford's senior advisers disagreed with Dailey's use of the still montage ads focusing on Ford in "presidential settings", arguing that these ads were patterned too much on those Dailey had produced for Nixon, and that less "bland" ads were required to fend off Reagan's challenge. Dailey justifies his strategy by arguing that, despite his two years in office, the public still did not associate Gerald Ford with the presidency and that these ads served to make Ford appear more "presidential."

> Before Gerald Ford was made vice-president, if you'd asked any Republicans to name five potential presidential candidates, I would be enormously surprised if Gerald Ford's name came up on any list. He was not perceived as a presidential type. Once in office the strongest asset he had was the office and his stewardship of it.[17]

Dailey believed that the real problem was not the use of still montage but the fact that Ford was being depicted as a president in the advertising but as a candidate in news coverage.

If you are the president, you should be seen in the first ten minutes of news doing the things only a president can do. What happened to Ford is that the advertising showed him doing the things presidents do and TV news showed Henry Kissinger in the Middle East or Paris conferring with world leaders. So at the top of the news you'd see Henry Kissinger and in the bottom of the news, Jimmy Carter in so and so, Ronald Reagan in so and so, and Gerald Ford in so and so. When you show Gerald Ford and Ronald Reagan as candidates and that's the only way you are going to compare them, Gerald Ford loses. That was something we couldn't get across.

Dailey further suggested that Ford himself was simply not committed to a presidential philosophy of campaigning.

President Ford was elected fifteen times over 30 years as a Congressional candidate in a district of only 500,000 people. You reach those people in shopping centers shaking hands. Media aren't that influential. It's hard to go against the guy's instincts.

In Dailey's ads the fluid movement of the camera across stills of President Ford suggests a grace that Ford, who walked into helicopter doors, seemed to lack. Further, by relying on a polished announcer instead of Ford to carry the message, the ads also downplayed Ford's halting delivery.

It is interesting, as a point of comparison, to note that in 1960 and 1964, still montage had been effectively employed for Henry Cabot Lodge and Lyndon Johnson respectively. In both instances, however, the image in the ads was a credible extension, not a contravention, of the image of the candidate captured on the evening news. Moreover, the audiences in those elections were not preoccupied with determining the honesty of the candidates. Unlike Lodge, Ford was not perceived to be personally dynamic and, unlike Johnson, Ford's intelligence had been questioned. Indeed it was Johnson who had put doubts into other people's minds about Ford's intellectual prowess in an often-recycled observation that Ford had played football too long without a helmet. In the context of 1976, the still montage ads seemed manipulative. In the later primaries Dailey had Ford speak directly to the camera.

As Reagan's strength revived, concern in the White House mounted and with it increasing criticism of Dailey's work. David Hume Kennerly, Ford's White House photographer, and Don Penny, formerly a production manager producing a film for the campaign, then a gagwriter, speechwriter, and speech coach for Ford, persuaded Ford to turn to Jim Jordan, head of BBD&O in New York. "The president decided to try Jordan in the California campaign," recalls Ford's aide. "He [Jordan] did the very controversial 'slice of life' ads. In the minds of many of us they weren't very good."

In one of these ads, an actress playing a Ford supporter emerged from a Ford campaign headquarters. There she met her "friend" burdened with bags of groceries. Instead of discussing "ring around the collar," the Ford supporter exclaimed that she was working for Ford's election and asked whether her friend knew that he'd cut inflation in half. "In half?" responded the shopper. "Wow!"

Another slice of life ad portrayed a father lifting his young son to see Ford. But the president the child saw reeked of fakery, for the actors playing father and son were clearly in a studio, and the Ford cavalcade was file footage shot on location. Moreover, by using actors as spokespersons, by adopting the techniques associated with the selling of products, and by artlessly displaying their manipulative intent, these ads undercut Ford's cultivated persona as an open and candid individual and president. Ridiculed by press and party professionals, the slice of life ads championed by Kennerly and Penny, were shelved.

The fact that a production manager turned speechwriter and a still photographer nonetheless had been able to influence a president to change ad strategies not only resulted in this series of unsuccessful ads but also ruffled feathers among Ford's campaign staff. "There was a tendency to walk away from the Nixon presidency's strong chief of staff," complained a person close to the campaign. "The result was an open door. People could walk in who had no idea what they were talking about. Penny and Kennerly were out of their element."

These ads were not the only blunder of Ford's ad hoc adteam in California. Responding to Reagan's statement that as president he would send a small U.S. force to Rhodesia, the Ford campaign aired an ad noting: "Last Wednesday, Ronald Reagan said he would send American troops to Rhodesia. On Thursday he clarified that. He said they would be observers or advisers. What does he think happened in Vietnam?" The ad concluded by asking voters to remember "Governor Reagan couldn't start a war. President Reagan could." When Reagan's pollster learned that half of Ford's supporters and a majority of Independents considered the attack unfair, Reagan used it to illustrate the desperation of Ford's campaign.

At the Republican convention in mid-August Ford squeaked to the nomination on the first ballot 1187 to 1070. In a bow to conservatives, Ford named Kansas Senator Robert Dole as his running mate.

In his acceptance address, delivered August 19, Ford contrasted the state of the country when he took office with its state in August 1976. "Our governmental system was closer to stalemate than at any time since Abraham Lincoln took that same oath of office. Our economy was in the throes of runaway inflation, taking us head-long into the worst recession since Franklin D. Roosevelt took the same oath." Then, adopting the strategy that Truman had parlayed into reelection in 1948, Ford claimed: "For two years I have stood for all the people against a vote-hungry, free spending congressional majority on Capitol Hill. Fifty-five times I vetoed extravagant and unwise legislation; forty-five times I made those vetoes stick."

The contrast was reduced to specific terms without a whisper that it was the record of his Republican predecessor that Ford was assailing. "Two years ago, inflation was twelve percent. Sales were off. Plants were shut down. Thousands were being laid off every week. . . . [Since August 1974] Inflation has been cut in half. Payrolls are up. Profits are up. Since the recession was turned around almost four million of our fellow Americans have found new jobs or got their old jobs back." Ford noted also that "Not a single American is at war anywhere on the face of this earth tonight."

The speech presaged the theme of the advertising of the fall campaign when it declared: "For the next four years I pledge to you that I will hold to the steady course we have begun." It also previewed the ads' attack on Carter: "My record is one of progress, not platitudes. My record is one of specifics, not smiles. My record is one of performance, not promises. It is a record I am proud to run on."

Prior to the convention, the Ford campaign invited the firm of Bailey/Deardourff to handle the general election advertising should Ford be the party's nominee. "We knew we needed a better media operation," recalled a senior member of Ford's staff. "Bailey/Deardourff came highly recommended. They had a lot of experience. We finally reached the point where we had a fairly smooth running campaign. Bailey, Deardourff, Teeter (pollster), and Spencer (strategist) had worked well together before. There was a lot of mutual respect there." In a comment referring to Penny/Kennerly, he then added, "You didn't have people dabbling in things they knew nothing about."

Doug Bailey and John Deardourff met in the Rockefeller campaign of 1964, where Deardourff headed domestic policy research and Bailey functioned as a member of Rockefeller's staff. They formed a consulting firm in 1967. In 1976, theirs was a firm on the rise, for in 1974 it had masterminded William Milliken's reelection in Michigan and boosted John Rhodes to the governorship of Ohio.

Like Napolitan in 1968, Bailey/Deardourff faced immense time pressures. Both campaigns confronted strong challenges in the primaries and at the convention. Neither had found time to plan a fall campaign strategy.

The Democratic Primaries

Traditionally, aspirants to public office have viewed political experience as an asset. In the wake of Watergate, politics became a dirty word, and an experienced politician was presumed to have been soiled. That changed reality is reflected in ads aired in the Democratic primaries. Birch Bayh's ads, for example, tried and failed to bring the discussion back to a more moderate position by arguing: "As president the question isn't whether you're a politician, but what kind of politician you are, because it takes a good politician to be a good president." By contrast, Frank Church's radio campaign pandered to then-current passions by labeling everything he opposed as "politics" and everything he favored as "reality." Setting himself apart from the majority of his opponents, Jimmy Carter complained of the burdensome paperwork and regulations Washington's bureaucracy foisted on governors. In a more illusive reference to Watergate and John Dean's observation that so many of those who had played a part in its cover-up were lawyers, Carter argued that, although he had nothing against lawyers, after all, his son was one, it may now be time for someone trained as "an engineer, a planner, a businessman" to assume the presidency. Establishing a counterpoint to those who defined the presidency by inclusion, Jerry Brown defined it by exclusion: the president, he said, is not a Santa Claus with a bag of tricks.

The Democratic primary ads display their sponsors' preoccupations with certifying their own honesty and decency, traits presupposed in candidates in earlier elections. This fixation on honesty and decency was underscored by commercials calculated to look uncalculating. More so than in previous campaigns, radio and television ads counterfeited the techniques normally associated with news in an effort to appear nonmanipulative. So, for example, cinema verité techniques were employed to permit voters to eavesdrop on interchanges between potential voters and Jerry Brown, Frank Church, Lloyd Bentsen, and Jimmy Carter. In half hour programs in the primaries, George Wallace, seated in a wheelchair, spoke directly to the audience. In most of Carter's primary ads he spoke directly to viewers as well. Bentsen and Reagan were shown responding to questions at press conferences. These spots gained credibility by showing that in face-to-face meetings with actual questioners these candidates were knowledgeable and articulate. They, in short, had nothing to hide. Gone too were ads that argued by visual association rather than with verbal statements about an opponent.

One-term Georgia Governor Jimmy Carter established himself as Democratic front-runner in 1976 with an early win in the Iowa caucus. In Carter's ads he looked just off camera as he promised never to lie to the

American people. Campaigning from a wheelchair, George Wallace won the Mississippi caucus, with Carter coming in second. In 1976 the message Wallace sent was "Trust the People." Carter and former Oklahoma Senator Fred Harris tied in Oklahoma. In New Hampshire, the first real primary, Carter won with almost 30% of the vote, followed by liberal Congressman Morris Udall with 24%.

Carter's hopes for a quick clean-up were muddied by Massachusetts, where labor's candidate, Senator Henry (Scoop) Jackson of Washington, came in first, followed by Udall and Wallace. Carter finished fourth. Meanwhile, Carter won Vermont.

Throughout the early primaries Carter was aided by timebuying and media placement more skillful than any previously seen in presidential primaries. Early advertising in Iowa, for example, reinforced his personal campaigning there, contributing to his victory. In Florida, where Carter faced serious competition from Wallace and Jackson, Carter ads started airing well before the Iowa caucus; his victory in Iowa therefore built on an already established visibility base. Further, when Patrick Caddell's polls told advertising strategist Gerald Rafshoon that Carter's support required ads in one particular part of the state but not another, the advice was followed.

To counter Wallace Carter assured his southern audiences that they could send more than a message this year, they could send a president. Carter won with 34% of the vote to Wallace's 31% and Jackson's 24%. He also carried Illinois and North Carolina and edged by Udall in Wisconsin. Both Jackson and Udall surpassed Carter in New York.

Midway through the primary season, Carter blundered by saying that he saw nothing wrong "with ethnic purity being maintained" in neighborhoods. After being told by the press that the phrase "ethnic purity" summoned memories of Nazi Germany and after being informed by such black supporters as Andrew Young that the remark was a "disaster," Carter, on April 8, apologized for his use of the phrase. On April 13 such prominent blacks as Martin Luther King Sr. publicly forgave Carter and reiterated support for him, thus calming the fears of white liberals and blacks alike. Carter carried Pennsylvania where, despite labor's support, Jackson finished second, followed by Udall. Carter went on to win Texas, Indiana, the District of Columbia, and Georgia, losing Alabama to Wallace.

As Pennsylvanians were balloting, a prominent liberal speechwriter, Robert Shrum, recruited to the Carter campaign only two weeks earlier by Carter's pollster Patrick Caddell, resigned. Caddell and Shrum had become friends in the McGovern campaign of 1972. Four years later, in the 1980 primaries, Shrum would draft the speeches with which Edward Kennedy would blister Carter in the primaries and, with Carey Parker, would write the speech that Kennedy upstaged Carter with at the convention.

In his letter of resignation to Carter, Shrum noted that he was disturbed to discover that "you might favor a substantial increase in the defense budget in spite of your previous pledge to reduce the budget in the range of 5 to 7 percent."[18] Shrum also noted inconsistencies between Carter's public and private positions on benefits for miners with black lung, use of highway monies for mass transit, and legislation for child care. Shrum's resignation and Carter's subsequent public denial that the conversations Shrum reported had taken place raised questions in the press both about Carter's truthfulness and about his actual stands on issues.

Shrum's charges of inconsistency hurt Carter because they added fuel to a fire that was already crackling. Carter's Democratic rivals had previously charged and would continue to charge that Jimmy Carter was saying one thing to one audience and something quite different to another. The most sustained assault on Carter's various and varying stands came from Morris Udall's campaign. In Michigan, Udall's supporters distributed copies of "Udall's Quick Carter Quiz" asking voters to guess Carter's stands on such questions as right to work and reduction or elimination of certain agencies. A thirty second ad featured mirrored cartooned faces of Carter smiling and frowning at each other as his inconsistent stands were recited by actor Cliff Robertson.

In Ohio, Udall's attacks became more pointed. Carter was portrayed as a carnival conman using a shell game to deceive the voters about his stands on the Vietnam War, national health insurance, and tax reform. In a nationally aired telecast during the Ohio primary Udall argued, as he had in ads broadcast in that primary, that no satisfactory answer had been given to the question "Who is Jimmy Carter?"

By pledging that he would never lie to the public, Carter invited sorties such as that made by Udall. "I'll never tell a lie, I'll never avoid a controversial issue," Carter pledged in his ads in the primaries. "If I ever do any of those things, don't support me." "The lines played like someone had taped a 'kick me' sign to the seat of Carter's pants," observed reporter Martin Schram.[19] "Carter's critics seized gleefully on the challenge and sought to unearth anti-Carter evidence. Eventually, documented reports showed that Carter, like most politicians, had at times at least misled and evaded."

Caddell's polls in Pennsylvania before the April 27 primary revealed that voters were beginning to perceive that Carter was not specific enough, that he was "too wishy washy." "I said 'We don't have time to do much. He's on the road,' "[20] Carter's media adviser Gerald Rafshoon recalls. Two cosmetic changes were made in the existing TV ads. A still saying "Jimmy Carter on the issue of . . ." now introduced Carter's ads as the announcer declared "Jimmy Carter on the issue of . . ." A reminder of the "issue" on which Carter had spoken was tagged to the announcer's closing lines. If you "see this critical issue" as Jimmy Carter does, the announcer urged you to vote for him. After the changes were made, Rafshoon says, the public concern "went away." It would return in the general election.

California Governor Jerry Brown and Idaho Senator Frank Church entered the last set of primaries hoping to deadlock the convention but despite winning more than they lost, their efforts were too late to deprive Carter of a first ballot nomination.

As his running mate, Carter named a candidate who had dropped out of the primaries before the first votes had been cast, Hubert Humphrey's liberal protégé, Senator Walter Mondale of Minnesota.

In his acceptance address, Carter promised to "give the government of this country back to the people of this country." The speech was filled with rhetoric uniquely Carter's. "I have never met a Democratic President," he said "but I have always been a Democrat." "I have spoken many times about love," he noted, "but love must be aggressively translated into simple justice."

His ads in the primaries had promised that what he had done in Georgia he would do for America. The speech reiterated that idea. "As governor I had to deal each day with the complicated, confused, overlapping and wasteful federal government bureaucracy. As president, I want you to help me evolve an efficient, economical, purposeful and manageable government for our nation."

His ads had claimed that the tax system was a "disgrace to the human race," a phrase repeated in the speech.

His ads had promised a government as good as its people. His speech foresaw an America that lives up to "the simple decency of our people."

Both his ads and his speech promised a "president who is not isolated from our people, but who feels your pain and shares your dreams, and takes his strength and wisdom and courage from you."

The speech also featured an oblique reference to Gerald Ford's pardon of Nixon: "It is time for our government leaders to respect the law no less than the humblest citizen, so that we can end the double standard of justice in America. I see no reason why big-shot crooks should go free while the poor ones go to jail." Later when confronted with a question about the pardon in his first debate with Ford, Carter opted to pass by merely noting that "it's very difficult for President Ford to explain the difference between the pardon of President Nixon" and his refusal to pardon those who "violated the draft laws."

The speech also previewed the attacks Carter's ads would levy against Ford in the final weeks of the fall campaign. "We have been a nation adrift too long. We have been without leadership too long. We have had divided, deadlocked government too long. We have been governed by veto too long. We have suffered enough at the hands of a tired, worn out administration without new ideas, without youth or vitality, without vision, and without the confidence of the American people."

In 1976 Carter retained the media services of Gerald Rafshoon, who had helped him in the last five weeks of his unsuccessful gubernatorial race against Lester Maddox and had produced the advertising for his winning run for the governorship of Georgia in 1970.

Rafshoon is a self-described "army brat," born in New York, but educated at the University of Texas. After a stint in the Navy, he worked as Southeastern advertising publicity representative for Twentieth Century Fox Film Corporation in Atlanta. It was after leaving Fox that Rafshoon opened his own ad agency in Atlanta. Having gone to school in the South, having spent most of his adult years in the South, having married two Southern women and raised "Southern children," Rafshoon considers himself a Southerner.[21] In 1966 a mutual friend introduced him to Jimmy Carter.

When Carter decided to run for president, Rafshoon said to him, "You know I've never done a Presidential campaign like this although I've done national advertising. If you want I'd be glad to find us a national media type and I'll step aside." Carter replied, "You know I've never run for president before. If I can run for president, you can do the advertising." "So I said ok." Rafshoon then notes, "Frankly, in 1972 when Hamilton [Jordan] and I were walking away from the Democratic Convention in Miami, we were saying 'If Scoop Jackson and Birch Bayh, Fred Harris, George McGovern, Ted Kennedy and all these characters could run for president why couldn't Jimmy? More so, if all these jerks around them could run a campaign why can't we?' "[22]

In 1976 Rafshoon brought an unprecedented number of women into a presidential campaign in managerial positions. In earlier campaigns, one could count the number of women in high positions on one hand. These included time buyers Reggie Schuebel and Ruth Jones and Reenah Schwartz, who writes copy for political ads produced by her husband. Of course, an occasional female copywriter tied to an agency under contract to a candidate might end up doing important work but, overall, presidential advertising has been dominated by males. In 1976 Rafshoon's agency included a female creative director, media director, comptroller, assistant media director, and a staff of timebuyers primarily composed of women. In 1980, the pattern continued. Rafshoon's Washington office manager was Becky Hendrix, and Beverly Ingram had moved up from assistant media director to become Media Director. At one point, Ingram reports, Rafshoon joked that "it sure would be nice to see a male face around here." So, says Ingram, "I hired some men."[23] Additionally, the print production manager was black and there were a number of black timebuyers.

Cost

Under the provisions of FECA, in the 1976 general election, Ford and Carter were each given 21.8 million dollars. The national parties were permitted to raise and spend an additional two cents for each person of voting age or 3.2 million dollars. These amounts functioned as ceilings that could not be exceeded through direct expenditures by candidates or parties. Consequently, the difference between Republican and Democratic campaigns in 1976 was not in how much each spent but in how each spent it.

Both campaigns devoted the majority of their media budgets to TV. Ford spent $2,500,000 on network TV, $3,885,000 on local TV, $1,490,000 on radio, and $1,290,000 on print advertising for a total of $9,165,000.[24] Carter budgeted $7,553,166 for TV, $1,086,728 for radio, and spent $348,909 for newspaper ads and $190,604 for magazine ads. So Carter outspent Ford on TV, while Ford outspent Carter on radio and print advertising.

The times at which the two campaigns purchased access to the voting public also differed. Faced with a new adteam and a decision not to advertise in the period in which the voters suspended political decision making before the first debate, the Republicans conserved their funds for a final week and a half blitz in six key states—a wise decision for their candidate, for as things turned out, Ford would be coming from behind in the race but closing in the polls. As a result, in the last ten days of the campaign, Ford spent four million dollars on radio and television. Trying to sustain his lead in the polls, Carter began advertising before the debate and purchased time steadily from then until election eve. This meant that in the final ten days, when Ford's advertising was saturating the key states, Carter no longer had the revenue to match him dollar for dollar. In this respect the ceiling worked to Ford's advantage and Carter's disadvantage in the general election.

One result of the imposed spending ceiling was a decrease in total campaign spending. In 1972, McGovern spent a total of $30 million to

Nixon's $60 million.[25] Faced with a choice between funding field opera-
tions and mass media, in 1976 both campaigns chose to concentrate their
funds on mass media advertising. As a result the number of bumper
stickers, buttons, and the like distributed by the two campaigns dropped
dramatically from the number distributed in previous years.

The Interplay of Advertising in the 1976 Campaign

Because the Republican and Democratic advertising shared many objectives in 1976, it makes sense to integrate the analysis of the two campaigns. In their preliminary media plan, drawn up after the convention,
Bailey/Deardourff identified eight objectives for their advertising:

1. Strengthen the human dimension of President Ford.
2. Strengthen the leadership dimension of President Ford.
3. More clearly portray President Ford's compassion for less fortunate
   Americans.
4. Portray his accomplishments in office in a believable way.
5. Present his program for the future.
6. Portray the important differences between the two men.
7. Cut Jimmy Carter down to size.
8. Help boost momentum when we need it.[26]

In phase one, which would last until October 7, their ads would
concentrate on the first four objectives. From October 8 to October 21
they would focus on presenting Ford's program and establishing differences with Carter. The final phase would continue to attack Carter as it
built momentum for Ford. Although Carter did not directly attack Ford
in his ads until Ford's attack ads had begun to narrow their gap in the
polls, Carter's overall media plan is comparable.

The Look of Innocence in 1976

Translating the post-Watergate focus on character into acceptable yet
effective ads dictated that two questions be asked of every piece of paid
and unpaid broadcast material: (1) Did this particular ad in any way
contradict the image of the candidate projected across the various news
media? (2) Was this ad unacceptably manipulative? The manipulative
aspect was important because it bore on the larger issues of honesty and
trust. The *topos* controlling both questions was, of course, that of public
versus private self. Was the private self, which would control the power
of the presidency, consistent with the public self? Since the private self
revealed in a campaign always is, to some extent, masked, clues to the

real private self were sought by the public and the press in examining to what extent a particular candidate's ads had changed in style or substance during the campaign. Both Rafshoon, who produced most of Carter's material, and Michael Kaye, who produced Jerry Brown's broadcast material, took pride in the fact that the same ads, with only minor modifications, were used across the primaries. Ford's strategists, on the other hand, were embarrassed by the need to produce and reject two very different broadcast campaigns before turning to Bailey and Deardourff after the convention.

Overall, the congruity in 1976 between radio and television campaigns was high. Unlike 1972, when the radio campaigns produced for Nixon and McGovern carried attacks not found in the televised campaigns, radio ads in 1976 consisted primarily of modified audio tracks of the televised commercials. Radio and television functioned to reinforce each other.

The speech played an important role in the broadcast commercials of Reagan, Ford, and Carter because by clipping sections into ads, the candidates produced evidence that they were communicating the same message to all audiences. In addition, Reagan, Ford, and Brown purchased half hour blocks of time to deliver speeches to a national audience. Reagan's nationally televised speech testified that consistency was so paramount a virtue in 1976 that one could surfeit in it without penalty, when, with the polish of an actor, he delivered almost pause for pause, his stock campaign address. Brown's half hour address was equally faithful to the content and manner of his campaign rhetoric. The imprecise diction, casual grammar, tangential construction, and stock themes of his campaign permeated the speech. Only Ford's rebroadcast of an edited version of his address accepting the Republican nomination was dissonant with his stock rhetoric.

Building and Reinforcing the Electorate's Sense of the Candidate

Some acceptance speeches have been the low points of campaigns. Humphrey's meaning could not be heard by an electorate mesmerized by the turmoil in the Chicago streets outside the convention hall. McGovern's address was delivered so late that it went unheard by the audience whose votes he required. In his acceptance address, Goldwater's seeming commitment to extremism scarred his candidacy. By contrast, Ford's acceptance speech at the convention was the highpoint of his campaign. His staff had "hounded and hectored him with a videotape recorder until after a dozen rehearsals he could say every word right and, over again, *with* feeling."[27]

A newfound dynamism replaced Ford's customary indifferent delivery. He neither stumbled over sentences nor stepped on his applause lines. "Our judgment tells us that as he comes away from Kansas City, people may now have new feelings about the president," Ford's media team proclaimed. "They may see him as a tougher leader, as a stronger President, as a man who is standing up to Congress, as a man who is sure of himself. We believe that his performance in Kansas City is a tremendous plus to the campaign. Our advertising should try to build on the momentum of Kansas City."[28] Bailey/Deardourff quickly edited the speech to thirty minutes for rebroadcast.

In the acceptance speech Ford took the offensive by challenging Carter to debate. The challenge had three advantages. First, it preempted a move Carter planned to make the following day. Second, it muted criticism of Ford's use of the "Rose Garden Strategy," for Ford's retreat to the symbolic action of incumbency could not be convincingly allied to Nixon's retreat in 1972 once Ford showed that he was eager to debate his opponent. Finally, because the public suspended the process of decision making as it awaited the first debate, the challenge purchased breathing space in which Ford's new adteam could create and execute an advertising strategy. Accordingly, Ford's spot ads did not begin to air until after the first debate, September 23.

When these ads did begin to run, they concentrated, as Bailey/Deardourff had planned, on showing Ford's "human dimension." The ads revealed him as his wife and children saw him, as he was seen by others, and as he saw himself. The announcer previewed a five minute ad about Ford's family by saying, "Sometimes a man's family can tell a lot about the man. That's why we want you to meet the Fords." One by one the Ford children speak about their father. Steve tells a North Dakota audience that he asked his father what he could tell them and was told to assure them that there would be no embargo. Mike is the Republican's answer to Carter's appeal to born again Christians. "The religious feelings within our family are very strong," he says. "My mom and dad are very devout and serious believers in their lord and they practice that in their daily lives. I received a great deal of affirmation and encouragement as I expressed and explained to them my interest in the ministry, Christian ministry." Ford notes that it gives him "a great deal of satisfaction to see a son who wants to give of himself through religion."

In response to Susan's testimony that she and her father are "very very close," Ford observes that he assumed a protective attitude toward her "when she was growing up and had three pretty rugged brothers." An uninitiated observer might conclude that Ford is running not for president but for father of the year.

In the closing sequence of the ad, Ford, with his wife at his side, demonstrates why in the ads created in the primaries Dailey relied on still montage with little use of Ford speaking. Ford introduces his wife by saying "my greatest source of strength, one person who I love, respect and am darn proud to have." Betty Ford thanks the audience for their support for "the president" and adds "I sort of like him too." Then in a spontaneous expression of affection, she reaches up and kisses him. "Sometimes a man's family can say a lot about the man," intones the announcer. As their dog romps at their side, Betty and Gerald Ford walk stiffly across the lawn toward the White House.

"People want to know where this person comes from who makes the decisions about nuclear weapons and the budget," explains Bailey/Deardourff Vice-President Paul Wilson. "This sort of ad tells them."[29]

Rafshoon too would use a member of his candidate's family to flesh out the public's sense of the Democratic nominee. In the battle over family image, Ford had the advantage of having more attractive children, where Carter's advantage was a mother who seemed to have stepped from the Great American novel. Miz Lillian had joined the Peace Corps long after most her age would have retired. Of the cast in the drama of 1976 she was the most suited to television. Her face, which would have served a character actress well, hinted devilishly that she might just tell something about her son that he would prefer untold.

The ad opens by describing Carter as a "man whose roots are founded in the American tradition." After Carter observes that his folks "have been farmers for more than 200 years," his mother recalls that "He had to work every afternoon. He didn't have a chance to run around. We didn't have a car for him." "We had to work together," comments Carter. "We didn't recognize hardships. We thought we were having a great life and I think we probably were and ah there was a tight knit family life ah bound together with love." His mother notes that she never really spanked him and then, as he apparently disagrees, adds, "I might have given you a little lick in passing but a real whipping I never gave him. I left that with his father." Their moment of differing recollections dulls the glare of Carter's public piety by permitting the inference that as a child Carter merited an occasional spanking from his father and a "lick in passing" from his mother.

The ad tells of a child who worked his way up. His generation was the first in his family to finish high school. "I know I've had a good chance to get an education as an engineer, a scientist."

After Carter declares that "we've always worked for a living. We know what it means to work," the announcer ties Carter's biography back to the central themes of his campaign. "And it was the working people not the special interests that Jimmy Carter represented as governor of the largest state east of the Mississippi. He gave them an administration responsive to their needs and proved that an efficient and well-managed government can be achieved."

In a single ad Rafshoon has leapt beyond the comparable Republican ad to draw the case for Carter's competence from the humanizing claims he and his mother make. Like all of Rafshoon's 1976 ads this one affirms a traditional value, in this case the value of hard work. The work is of a special sort. It is not simply manual labor but work with the land, a fact underscored in scenes showing Carter dressed in work clothes scooping peanuts from a large bin and walking through peanut fields. These scenes are central to the political identity of the engineer, businessman, farmer who bridges the country's agrarian past and its technological future without sacrificing either in the process. The candidate whose "roots are founded in the American tradition," who pledges to "root out discrimination," visually roots himself in the land in his ads and in the process establishes that unlike his opponents in the primaries and general election he is not a politician by profession.

This ad had the additional advantage of repeating the message of an often-aired ad from the primaries in which Carter said, "I think it is time to have a non-lawyer in the White House for a change, somebody that had to work with his hands. Somebody who's had to run a complicated business."

The value of hard work is a theme interlaced throughout the ads. Carter's wife, Rosalynn, says in one ad, "When people say how does Jimmy Carter come from nowhere to where he is today? I tell them it's hard work." She also indicates that one of the things that she has learned while campaigning is that "There are good, honest, hard-working people all over our country."

Although his ads promise a government as good as its people, what they are actually advocating is a president as good as the people. Just as the people are "good, honest and hard working" so too claim the ads is Carter. In the same ad that notes that the campaign has been hard work, Rosalynn Carter concludes, "Jimmy is honest, unselfish and truly concerned about the country. I think he'll be a great president." Only in 1976 can a claim that a candidate is honest, unselfish, hard-working and concerned about the country warrant the conclusion that he will be a great president.

The continuous affirmation of the value of work is then rolled into an indictment of Ford's administration when in an ad Carter declares: "It's very bad on the father or mother who's been employed fifteen or twenty years to go on unemployment compensation and then when that unemployment compensation runs out to draw the first welfare check. It hurts human dignity. This has become a welfare administration and not a work administration. We're going to change that next year." In another ad he specified that he favors welfare only for those unable to work. Correlatively, his administration will make it possible for those who want to work and are able to work to find a job. From his commitment to the value of work, Carter spins conclusions about his character, his opposition to special interests, his commitment to employment, and his opposition to welfare (except for those who can't work). He differentiates himself from his opponents by citing the hard work he put into early campaigning. Finally, Carter's commitment to the value of work spawns an indictment of the Ford Administration.

This focus on work was sound strategy. The Michigan Center for Political Studies' post-election study found that among those identifying a "single most important problem" confronting the country, 31% named unemployment.[30] An NBC poll revealed that 75% "of those whose primary economic concern was over jobs and unemployment voted for the Georgian."[31]

Carter's Use of his Identity as a Southerner

Before the convention, Hamilton Jordan handed Jimmy Carter a memo outlining the strategy for the general election.[32] The memo was predicated on the assumption that Carter would carry ten Southern states (Alabama, Arkansas, Georgia, Kentucky, Louisiana, Mississippi, North Carolina, South Carolina, Tennessee, and Virginia) with a total of 96 electoral votes. Jordan also expected Carter to win four traditionally Democratic states—Massachusetts, Wisconsin, Minnesota, and the District of Columbia with their 38 votes for a total base of 134 electoral votes or 49% of the 270 votes needed to win the election. "The Southern states provide us with a base of support that cannot be taken for granted or jeopardized," Jordan told Carter. Since the Republicans "cannot win if they write off the South," Jordan predicted challenges in the border states of Maryland and Missouri and the Southern states of Texas and Florida.

But the natural support for Carter in the South had to be mined judiciously. "Although the Southern states provide us with a rich base of support," Jordan noted, "it would be a mistake to appear to be overly dependent on the South for victory in November. It would be harmful nationally if we were perceived as having a 'Southern strategy.' " Still, Jordan prophesied, "Southern regional pride can be used to great advantage without unnecessarily alienating potential anti-Southern voters."

Jordan's projections proved prescient. Carter pieced together a total electoral vote of 297 to Ford's 241 by following the strategy laid out by his top aide. Of the ten Southern states Jordan pegged as likely, Carter won all but Virginia. Carter also carried the two border states—Maryland and Missouri—and the two Southern states—Texas and Florida—that Jordan had viewed as winnable. Finally, Carter picked up all four of the states Jordan isolated as likely to vote Democratic and carried three of the large industrial states—New York, Pennsylvania, and Ohio, proving that his appeal to the South had not fatally alienated voters in key Northern states.

Because the almost solid support of the South guaranteed Carter's election, we might well ask how Carter managed in Jordan's words to use Southern regional pride "to great advantage" without "alienating potential anti-Southern voters" and in the process how Carter translated what Ford's pollsters considered a "negative"—being a Southerner—into an asset. At the same time we might ask how Carter salvaged South Carolina, Mississippi, and Kentucky, where he held only a precarious margin in mid-October,[33] how he overcame Ford's mid-October lead in Louisiana, and how he stopped his slide in Texas.

The answer lies in part in nationally aired and reported speeches that kneaded his Southern background into his image as an outsider and simultaneously depicted Carter as the victim of anti-Southern discrimination and as a symbol of the New South.

Custom dictates that the Democratic candidate for president open the general election campaign in Detroit's Cadillac Square, a location that identifies the candidate with the party's blue-collar constituency, with the unions that infuse the party with votes and in kind contributions, and with the voters of a state with 21 electoral votes. In 1976 Carter defied this political precedent by launching his fall campaign not in the home state of the incumbent president but in his own home state of Georgia.

As a candidate whose sculpted image as an outsider had served him well both in his successful campaign for governor and in the presidential primaries, Carter sought symbolic gestures to distinguish himself from incumbent Ford. Accordingly, Carter's opening speech of the 1976 general election campaign was delivered from the front porch of FDR's summer rest spot at Warm Springs, Georgia, a setting that identified Carter with the New Deal and the New Deal with the South without, at the same time, casting Carter as a typical politician. The presence of FDR's sons, James and FDR Jr., lent the Roosevelt family's blessing to this amalgamation of identities. Also present was the black accordianist whose anguish at FDR's death had been captured in a photo transmitted by presses throughout the world to symbolize the nation's grief. By playing Roosevelt's favorite rendition of "Happy Days are Here Again," he telegraphed to viewers the unspoken promise that Carter would pick up where FDR left off. All "that is missing," wrote Schram, "is Jim Farley and Fala."[34]

In the nationally televised speech itself Carter allied himself with FDR and Ford with Herbert Hoover. FDR's opponent in 1932, recalled Carter, "was an incumbent president, a decent and well-intentioned man who sincerely believed that our government could not or should not with bold action attack the terrible economic and social ills of our nation." Quoting Truman's "The Buck Stops Here," Carter noted: "No one seems to be in charge. No one is responsible."

The speech at Warm Springs fused the symbol of Carter as Southerner and Carter as outsider. "As a political candidate, I owe the special interests nothing. I owe the people everything," he declared.

An earlier speech Carter delivered at the Martin Luther King Jr. Hospital in Los Angeles on June 1, 1976, had argued that a Southerner could bring unique insight to the White House. "I sometimes think that a Southerner of my generation can most fully understand the meaning and the impact of Martin Luther King's life" he said. "He and I grew up in the same South, he the son of a clergyman, I the son of a farmer. We both knew, from opposite sides, the invisible wall of racial segregation." The speech proceeded to argue that King, Kennedy, and Johnson ("a man who many black people distrusted") advanced "the dream of equality." By passing the voting rights bill they "made it possible for the South to come out of the past and into the mainstream of American politics . . . and made it possible for a Southerner to stand before you this evening as a serious candidate for the President of the United States."

In Carter's construction of reality, Southerners only recently have entered the mainstream of American politics. Indeed, his serious candidacy is a mark of achievement both for the nation and for the South. And if blacks distrust him because he is a Southerner, he will allay their fears by invoking their experience with Lyndon Johnson and by trading on the endorsements of such influential blacks as Andrew Young and Martin Luther King Sr. To the nation at large Carter argued that acceptance of his candidacy was a sign of the nation's maturity and insinuated his belief that a Southerner brought special insights to the presidency.

These speeches suggest that the candidate who wrote in his autobiography "I am a Southerner and an American" saw political advantages in his regional heritage. But as the pollsters for both candidates recognized, liabilities lurked in this regional identification as well.

Those who assume that Lyndon Johnson had broken the Civil-War-erected barrier blocking the election of a Southerner find it difficult to understand Carter's perception that the country might be reluctant to entrust its highest office to a Southerner. But just as Eskimos see more varieties of snow than the rest of us, those schooled in the nuances of regional identification see Johnson as a Southwesterner and view Carter as a true Southerner. And to a person born and bred in the deep South the presidency might well seem elusive since the last person elected president from the deep South was Louisianan Zachary Taylor, sent to the White House in 1848. "The possibility that the nation would actually choose as a leader someone from the Deep South meant that the bitterness of the past could be overcome," wrote Carter in *Keeping Faith.*[35]

In the early plans of many of the Democratic hopefuls, Carter was to serve as the candidate who would block Wallace in the South while they mopped up the delegates in the other regions of the country. In the Florida primary in particular, Carter was to play Gabriel to Wallace's Lucifer. Until the Iowa caucuses propelled Carter ahead of the pack, the other contenders gave little thought to the possibility that Carter would daunt their own plans as well as Wallace's.

Carter embraced the role of Southern savior in early fund-raising appeals to Northern liberals. In a fund-raising letter seeking contributions to stop Wallace, Carter wrote: "The enclosed envelope, addressed to Atlanta, Georgia, might cause you some hesitation if you're not from the South. You may have reservations about helping a Southerner become president. Please look at it as an opportunity to give a progressive new area of national leadership a chance."[36] Carter's letters reminded prospective donors that he had never "stood in a school house door to bar the entrance to a school child and never passed [out] ax handles with his name on them." Having disassociated himself from the blatant segregationism of George Wallace and Lester Maddox, Carter reminded readers that a Southerner "doesn't have to be a redneck or a bigot."

Once Wallace had been dispatched, Carter discarded the Lucifer-Gabriel scenario as needlessly divisive. "With the passing of the Florida primary and Wallace's hopes for the nomination," Glad observed, "Carter deemphasized the 'good'/'bad' Southerner dichotomy, accentuating instead a motif that would solidify the entire South behind his candidacy—the new South as a political force and as the source of a new morality for the nation."[37]

In Massachusetts and Rhode Island, states with large Catholic populations, Carter's advertising urged tolerance to match that shown by Georgia to John Kennedy in '60. "Some people say the nation will never vote for a Southerner for President," stated Carter, "but they said in 1960 that the South would never vote for a liberal Irish Catholic senator from Boston." When the returns came in, John Kennedy got the biggest margin of victory not in Massachusetts but in Georgia. "And I believe that the people in New England will be just as open-minded in 1976." Indeed, Georgia had given Kennedy 62.6% of its vote while Massachusetts had given its favorite son 60.2%.

But to the South, Carter carried not a message of tolerance but an opportunity to avenge intolerance. His message there was that his election symbolized Southern legitimacy and Southern power. So, for example, a radio ad aired in the South in the last weeks of the campaign declared that "On November 2, the South is being readmitted to the Union. If that sounds strange, maybe a Southerner can understand. Only a Southerner can understand years of coarse, anti-Southern jokes and unfair comparison." Op-eds, editorials, and letters to the editor in Southern papers reinforced this theme and united in a chorus that argued that at least some of the attacks on Carter were blatant manifestations of hostility toward the South. Jim Merriner wrote, for example, in the Atlanta *Constitution* that "After all these years, since the Civil War, it is still there, that condescending, patronizing air from the North."[38] Lurking beneath the surface of these accounts is the echo of John Wilkes Booth's cry as he leapt from the balcony of Ford's Theatre, "The South is avenged!"

Carter's ad continued: "Only a Southerner can understand what it means to be a political whipping-boy. But then only a Southerner can understand what Jimmy Carter as President can mean." Historically, a whipping-boy has been the undeserving recipient of the punishment merited by one, such as a king or a cardinal, whose high rank insulated him from physical chastisement. The phrase invites the question, In whose stead is the South being whipped?

The phrase also functions as an indictment of the North. The recollection of how the word "boy" denied black male slaves their manhood couples here with memories of the savage whippings inflicted by the slavemaster. The New South, the ad implies, should not be made to expiate the guilt of the Old South. The Old South kept slaves; the new South, embodied in Jimmy Carter, sings "We shall overcome," honors the memory of Martin Luther King Jr., embraces the Voting Rights Act, and condemns the segregationist acts of Wallace and Maddox. Why then is she being whipped? The phrase "whipping-boy" indicates that the North stands condemned in the very docket she constructed to convict the Old South—for she has used the South as a whipping-boy. If the whipping is deserved, it is owed the North for treating the South as the South once treated the slaves. The act of voting for Carter removes the whip from the control of the North. And that is the meaning in Carter's election "only a Southerner can understand."

The announcer then defines November 2 as "the most important day in our region's history" and interlaces Carter's identity as an outsider and a Southerner with the audience's swelling regional pride by asking, "Are you going to let it pass without having your say? Are you going to let the Washington politicians keep one of our own out of the White House?" The determination to vote is cast as a test of the individual and collective masculinity of Southerners. Will you let this opportunity pass? "Not if this man can help it," declares the announcer.

What we know with hindsight is that, without the support of black voters, Carter would not have carried enough of the Southern states to ensure his electoral victory. To mobilize the black vote, Carter, as did Johnson and Kennedy before him, relied heavily on print advertising and on black radio. So a 45-rpm record of Martin Luther King Sr.'s endorsement of Carter was distributed to black churches to be played the Sunday before key primaries and a tape of the endorsement aired on black radio.[39]

Andrew Young's apologia on Carter's behalf also was widely distributed. In January 1976, Andrew Young, at first a cautious suporter of Carter, responded to an attack on Carter in the *Village Voice* with a strongly worded rebuttal asserting: "Carter is one of the finest products of the most misunderstood region of our nation."[40] Carter's forces distributed 50,000 copies of the essay to voters in the New York primary.

Ads on black radio also recalled Governor Carter's inaugural declaration that the "time for racial discrimination is over," and noted that Amy attends a school where about 60% of her classmates are black. Carter also called passage of the civil rights acts "The best thing that happened in the South in my lifetime." The form of this ad rings with echoes of the practice of religious witnessing. Throughout the primaries, ads on black radio carried the claim that more blacks had voted for Carter than any other candidate. "Let's keep it going." These were themes unarticulated in the TV ads or "non-black" radio ads aired in the South.

When Carter stumbled into an endorsement of "ethnic purity" in neighborhoods and when the press learned that his church in Plains would not admit blacks, influential black supporters such as King and Young staunched the resulting hemorrhaging in Carter's campaign with their public statements of confidence. Either of these events could otherwise have cost him sufficient numbers of black votes to swing key Southern and industrial states. Ford's supporters attempted to capitalize on the controversy over integration of Carter's church by sending telegrams to some 400 black ministers asking how if Carter could not influence his own church he expected to influence Congress. The speed with which Ford's operatives acted to publicize the integration attempt underscored Carter's claim that the attempt itself was politically motivated.

So, in the process of rethinking the characteristics required of the president, the electorate was asked to judge whether being a Southerner was a blessing or a bane, and black Southerners and blacks in larger industrial states were asked, in part, to assess whether a Southern Baptist was more attuned to their needs than Ford. Meanwhile, Southerners were encouraged to see regional vindication in Carter's election, not simply because he was a Southerner, but because as a Southerner he could only secure election through their votes. "We can do it [assure the South its rightful place]," said Carter in a TV ad aired in the South, "but I need your help because when it comes right down to it, I'm depending on you more than anyone else."

Can This Person Lead the Country?

To meet their second objective—showing Ford as a leader—Bailey/Deardourff shifted to a value more directly relevant than work to being president. Where Carter worked, Ford lead. In a masterful ad, the perception that Ford is an unintelligent bumbler is put in context by specific claims about his past and present leadership. Where Carter's ads are trying to enable the electorate to see Carter, Ford's ads face the more difficult task of getting the electorate to see Ford in a new light. The need for a new context was reiterated each Saturday night as Chevy Chase's incarnation of Ford on the program *Saturday Night Live* stumbles down stairs, knocks over his podium, or strangles himself with his own phone chord. By walking into helicopter doors, confusing the names and locations of cities, states, and universities, and liberating Poland in his second debate with Carter, Ford freshened Chase's repertoire.

The ad designed to recreate our sense of Ford opens on Ford asking the nation in his first speech as President to confirm him with its prayers. The announcer notes that "In this new leadership, honesty and moral integrity are essential." Ford met these standards, says the ad, in the "exhaustive" confirmation investigation by both Republicans and Democrats in both houses.

"Without seeking the presidency, Gerald Ford had been preparing for it for a lifetime," says the announcer, articulating the ad's thesis. "His was an American ethic, an obligation to serve, to reach for the highest possible in personal achievement." As still photos underscore its narrative, the ad notes that Ford was an Eagle Scout, a member of the National Honor Society, captain of the high school football team, and lettered for three years at Michigan where he was voted most valuable player. The claims about football are enveloped in information about his academic abilities. At Yale he helped coach the football team, a job that took time from his studies. Then in a section that appears to be rationalizing Ford's academic performance, a surprising bit of information appears: "Besides Governor Scranton this extraordinary class at Yale Law School was to produce Supreme Court Justices Stewart and White. Of the 120, 99 were Phi Beta Kappa. Gerald Ford graduated in the top third."

His service in the "decisive Pacific campaign" is recounted by one of those who served there with him. "On this particular occasion we were attacked by Japanese torpedo bombers; two of them penetrated the destroyer screen and launched torpedoes. The torpedos missed. Gerald Ford didn't miss. He fired and they both went down." (When the ad was screened for Ford he commented that the person telling the story "had a vivid imagination.")

Ford's twelve terms in Congress are noted as is the fact that his colleagues elected him "leader of his party in the House of Representatives." Then when there is "a failure of trust in the presidency," high inflation, and a tense nation, Ford, who brings "a lifetime of leadership" to the presidency, "goes to work." "He opens the presidency to public view. A war is ended. Inflation is beaten back."

In a statement that invites misinterpretation, the announcer then says, "Had we known him better we could not have expected less." The ad concludes: "Gerald Ford has always been best when the going was toughest. A tough road still lies ahead. The recovery must be completed. The nation must remain secure. We know what President Ford can do. Let's keep to that steady course." The closing lines hint at the claim the later ads will employ to differentiate Ford from Carter. Ford, the known, safe alternative vs. Carter the unknown. Ford the performer vs. Carter the promiser.

Where Ford's ad implicitly divorces his administration from Nixon's by stressing Ford's certified integrity and Ford's role as the president who successfully combated the inflation and lack of trust in government that were Nixon's legacy, Carter's ads indict Ford and Nixon's record, and by implication their presidencies, as if the administrations of Carter's two immediate predecessors were indistinguishable. "It took 70 years to build up home ownership in the United States," said Carter, in an extemporaneous speech edited into an ad by Rafshoon. "Up through 1969 we had had over 50% of all the homes in America owned by the families that lived in them. It only took eight years under Nixon and Ford to tear that down. In only eight years we now have only 32%, less than 1/3 of the homes in this country owned by families. That shows what a terrible change took place when the Democrats went out of office. What we took

70 years to do, the Republicans have destroyed in eight years. We have an administration now with no direct concern for the people of this country." Apart from displaying one of Carter's indictments of Ford, the ad previews Carter's sometimes disabling fondness for statistical detail.

Does the Candidate Care?

Because Ford had to carry such "largely Democratic states" as New York, Pennsylvania, and Illinois, Wilson notes, "there was a need to appeal to voters on the compassion dimension which traditionally is a difficult thing for a Republican to do." "In many of the target states," said the advertising plan, "where Democrats and Independents are needed to win, the most serious problem a Republican candidate has is the perception of Republicans in general as hard-nosed, big-business types—against the working people, against the poor people, against minorities. President Ford has to break the Republican stereotype. . . . One way to show compassion is in his treatment of the issues. When he talks about economic issues, he must do so from the viewpoint of those who suffer most. He must talk about people rather than statistics."[41]

To meet the advertising plan's third objective, Ford's ads portrayed his "compassion for" such groups as farmers, blue-collar workers, and older persons. The watchword of these ads was empathy. "I say frequently and I mean it," said Ford to a group of senior citizens seated around him in the White House, "there's no reason why someone should go broke just to get well." Then, in a summary not surfeiting in subtlety, the announcer adds: "A sensitive man: President Ford." Still, by showing essentially unresponsive older people who have sat lifelessly as Ford spoke to them, the ads undercut the ability of the typical older American, who contrary to stereotypes is neither senile nor comatose, to identify with Ford's message.

To demonstrate his own compassion and Ford's insensitivity, Carter focused on unemployment, a problem that Ford could not claim to have conquered. "We've seen the devastating blows that have been hit on the American people by the Nixon-Ford Administration," Carter stated in an ad. "Two and a half million more people on the unemployed rolls in the last two years alone. A fourteen percent increase in the cost of living in the last two years alone. These kinds of personal impacts of bad management in Washington have human meanings." Here we see the second of Carter's central themes turned against Ford. Carter, the scientist, engineer, businessman who claims to have managed both his business and his state efficiently, indicts not just the Ford administration but Washington, the city of which he conspicuously is not a part.

What the Candidates Have Done; What They Will Do

Because Bailey/Deardourff believed that "*Vision* [goals, where we're going, where we want to be] is one characteristic most voters seek in a
President: it is part of their perception of leadership," they set out to
present Ford's "program for the future" as their next objective.

Here cinema verité ads showed Ford juggling the roles of challenger
and incumbent as, in shirt sleeves, he tells small groups of voters in
factories and on farms of his plans to fight crime, reduce the unfair tax
burden, and make it possible for young persons to own a home.

In another similar ad, a person in the group asks Ford what "the
situation on crime [is] in this country today?" Ford responds that 75 to
80% of crime in committed by "professional career criminals" and goes
on to defend a plan of his already implemented in twelve cities to "really
go after the career criminals."

Rather than articulate a vision of the future, Ford's ads offer a
series of specific proposals. The specificity provides a useful contrast to
Carter's calculated vagueness but does not create a clear sense of what a
full-term Ford presidency would aspire to accomplish beyond keeping to
his steady course. According to Deardourff, that vision was simply hard
to elicit from the Ford White House. "I was never sure" he told Witcover, "that the President or anybody else that he had around him had
a clear sense of what you did for an encore after you got things back on
an even keel."[42] "The ads failed to convey the vision our fifth objective
envisioned," says Bailey/Deardourff's vice-president. "We felt that it
was critically important that there be a sense of what a Ford presidency
for the next four years would be. There wasn't a major effort in the
Ford White House to develop a Ford program. Carter was at least
articulating a sense of hope and bringing with him a sense of vision of a
different kind of presidency." A senior official in the Ford White House
responds that "We used to have debates over what the vision of the
future would be but certainly I didn't see it more difficult to identify in
that campaign than in others. It's always hard to articulate that kind of
thing. If you're Ronald Reagan against Jimmy Carter your vision is that
you are going to get rid of the person you're running against. An incumbent is going to offer more of the same so you wind up with themes like
'Stay the course.' "

In an election that focused on defining what is expected of a president, Carter's ads not only claimed to define his vision of the future but
also his vision of the presidency and of the people. Carter's advertising
differed from Ford's in that he specifically used the phrase "vision of

America." Like "Jimmy Carter speaking on the issue of . . .," the use of the phrase serves as a marker contending that a vision does indeed follow. "I have a vision of America, a vision that has grown and ripened as I've travelled and talked and listened and learned and gotten to know the people of this country," said Carter. "I see an America poised not only at the beginning of a new century but at the brink of a long new era of more effective and efficient, and sensitive and competent government.

I see an America that has turned away from scandals and corruption. I see an American president who governs with vigor and with vision and affirmative leadership, a president who is not isolated from our people but a president who feels your pain and who shares your dreams. . . . This is my vision of America. I hope you share it and I hope that you will help me fight for it."

These ads are articulating premises so obvious until Watergate that to voice them in an earlier election year would have invited ridicule. However, in 1976 candidates were required to demonstrate that they understood and embraced the presuppositions on which the compact between the people and the president was based.

The specifics of Carter's vision of America reside not in the ads but in the audience. Just as the Democrats invited the audience to read its own anxieties about Goldwater into the Daisy ad, just as Nixon tacitly encouraged audiences to invest his plan to end the war with their own preferred meanings, so too in 1976 Carter invited the audience to shape his vision of the next four years in their own image. "If there are things you don't like in your own government," he said in a number of TV ads, "if we've made mistakes that you don't want to see made again or if there are hopes or dreams in your own lives or in the lives of your children that you'd like to see realized, I hope that you will join me in a personal commitment to change our government for the better."

So where Ford offered specific programs in place of a vision, Carter rehearsed the public's sense of itself, the presidency, and its hopes for the future and then invited voters to see his presidency as the realization of their dreams and aspirations—whatever they might be. The liability of this strategy is that it may purchase election with the currency of unrealizable, conflicting expectations.

Just as the Democrats created an ad provoking viewers to ask specifically how Nixon would end the war, so too the Republicans produced ads that wondered where Carter really did stand on the issues. Until election eve Carter's answers came not in advertising but in the debates where, for example, he spelled out specific deadlines by which he would balance the budget and lower unemployment.

Carter Lusts and Says LBJ Lies

In late September the public learned through the news media that Carter had said in an interview done for *Playboy* that he lusted in his heart and that LBJ was a liar. The interview was to be published in the November issue, available in mid-October.

By pledging that he would never lie to the American people, by proclaiming to the masses that he loved them, and by responding to reporters' questions about his born again Baptist beliefs, Carter had telegraphed his religious commitments to a public preoccupied with morality in government. His closing remarks to interviewers from *Playboy* cultivated among voters a wariness about the form those religious beliefs assumed.

"I've committed adultery in my heart many times," Carter told *Playboy*. "This is something that God recognizes I will do—and I have done it—and God forgives me for it. But that doesn't mean that I condemn someone who not only looks on a woman with lust but leaves his wife and shacks up with somebody out of wedlock." The pastor of the nation's largest Baptist church responded that Carter was "mixed up in his moral values."[43]

The interview not only raised questions among Carter's co-religionists, to use a term favored by Kennedy in 1960, but also weakened some of the bonds Carter's plain talk and symbolic action had forged with voters. After all, words such as "wedlock" and phrases such as "look on a woman with lust" are, for most Americans, linguistic relics. By using them Carter introduced doubts into the minds of a large portion of his audience about just what they were getting into by supporting a born again Southern Baptist. And to compound Carter's difficulties, the audience whose language he was speaking was likely to be offended by publication of the interview in what a past president of the pastors' conference of the Southern Baptist Convention called a magazine "known for its gutter approach to life."[44] The same audience was likely to condemn Carter's nonjudgmental posture toward "shacking up" and "lusting" and to question the advisability of bridging his world and *Playboy*'s by placing the word "screw" in Christ's mouth, for as Carter supporter Reverend Bailey Smith noted, " 'screw' is just not a good Baptist word."[45] ("Christ says don't consider yourself better than someone else because one guy screws a whole bunch of women while the other guy is loyal to his wife," Carter had told the interviewers.)

Carter's revelation that he had lusted was not the only self-inflicted wound in the interview; he also declared "I don't think I would ever take on the same frame of mind that Nixon or Johnson did, lying, cheating, and distorting the truth. Not taking into consideration my hope for strength of character, I think that my religious beliefs alone would prevent that from happening to me." By allying Nixon and Johnson in this statement, Carter committed political heresy. Although he phoned Lady Bird in an effort to mend his political fences in Texas, the remark, kept alive by Texas Republicans, remained a prominent issue. The day after the first debate, while traveling through Texas—a state he hoped to win in November—Carter, the candidate who swore that his religious beliefs would prevent him from lying and distorting the truth, claimed that the statement about LBJ in *Playboy* was a "summary" of what he had said and that the reference to lying and cheating referred only to Nixon.

Republican strategists, naturally, had a party with the *Playboy* interview and mercilessly milked it for all it was worth, and then some. First they mailed two million copies of a tabloid called *Heartland* to rural America. The front page visually contrasted Betty Ford, shown feeding a deer as the family watched, with reactions from prominent religious spokespersons to the *Playboy* interview. Inside, exerpts from the interview appeared, as did a photo of *Playboy's* cover. The tabloid's lead story was an account of Ford's meeting with religious broadcasters.[46] Meanwhile, a print ad for Ford run in "350 small-town newspapers in 32 states" displayed the covers of *Playboy* and of *Newsweek,* while enjoining readers to read the cover story about Ford to learn about him and to read *Playboy* to learn more about Carter. Despite the ad's request that its audience read *Newsweek, Newsweek* representatives objected that permission to reproduce the cover had not been secured. The Republican ads magnified the damage Carter had done his candidacy in the interview and provided a telling contrast between the two candidates. That damage was great. Carter's pollster told Elizabeth Drew that "the *Playboy* incident was devastating. . . . The numbers just started diving."[48]

The revelations about lust and LBJ injured Carter's candidacy by reinforcing negative perceptions of him to which the public already subscribed. A memo given to Ford by his strategists shortly before the convention identified the following negative perceptions of Carter:

An arrogant man.

A man who wears his religion on his sleeve; he is self-righteous. Lacks humility.

A man who tries to be all things to all men; we don't know where he stands on the issues.

A man about whom we don't know enough; we really don't know who he is as a person.

A Southerner.

May not be experienced enough to be President. . . .[49]

The *Playboy* interview and the Republican's subsequent replays of it underscored the first four of these perceptions.

To "defuse 'lust in your heart,' " Rafshoon ran "in soap operas" an ad in which Rosalynn Carter says, "People ask me every day, 'How can you stand for your husband to be in politics and everybody know everything you do?' And I just tell 'em that we were born and raised and still live in Plains Georgia. It has a population of 683 and everybody has always known everything I did. (*laughter from audience*) And Jimmy's never had any hint of scandal in his personal or in his public life. I really believe he can restore that honesty and integrity, openness, competence in government that we so sorely need in our country today. I think he'll be a great president." In his final debate with Ford, Carter noted that "from hindsight, I would not have given that interview, had I to do it over again. If I should ever decide in the future to discuss my deep Christian beliefs and condemnation and sinfulness, I'll use another forum besides *Playboy*."

Additionally, to quiet the convulsion in Texas in the end of October, as anti-Carter ads saturated the airwaves, Rafshoon aired a five minute evocation of the country's past that restored Johnson to the pantheon of presidents. As upbeat patriotic music plays, the camera shows the Constitution, then famous Indians, then pictures of Woodrow Wilson, FDR, Truman, JFK, and LBJ. "If there is one thing that can bind our country together, that can make us have hope again and faith in the future" says the announcer, "it's a president who's in touch with the American people." Carter speaks of walls, of dreams, and of "one person in this country who can set a standard of ethics and morality." The ad closes on a bridge and a sunset.

Georgians Indict the Georgian

Recognizing that attack ads treaded on thin ice in an election year in which the conduct of the candidate was being scrutinized for clues about character, Ford's ads replayed the doubts of others and then moved to a straightforward reporting of "facts." In ads that began airing in mid-October persons testified "I feel uneasy about Carter." Other comments ranged from the repeated claim that Carter is "wishy-washy" to assertions that he wasn't much of a governor.

These ads encouraged public scrutiny of the details of the Carter dream, a scrutiny largely absent in the primaries, where voters tended to perceive Carter in their own likeness. So, for example, the *New York Times* found that conservatives saw Carter as a conservative, while liberals and moderates also viewed him as one of their ideological kin.[50]

The Republicans also hoped that these ads would provoke a counter-productive counter-attack by Rafshoon. Since their candidate was behind in the polls, his ads could attack, provided the attack was perceived as fair. As front-runner, Carter attacked Ford at the risk of being perceived as mean spirited. After the election, Bailey called Rafshoon's restrained response his "wisest" decision.[51]

In the Georgian in the street ads, one man notes that he and all his friends have tried to remember what Carter accomplished as governor and can't come up with a thing. "He was just your average . . . run of the mill governor." It would be nice to have a governor from Georgia, says another "but not Carter." He "didn't so much as do anything" gripes another disgruntled Georgian. These ads had the advantage of reinforcing the charges of Carter's Democratic primary opponents and of his short-term liberal speechwriter; both sides agree that they proved successful in narrowing the gap in the polls.

When Carter failed to reply in kind, low key factual "neutral reporter" ads escalated the confrontation by adding evidence to back the Georgians' assertions.

In the final weeks of the campaign, the Republicans aired an ad that opened with a still of Carter shown on a television set. The announcer declared: "What he did as governor, he will do as president." A map of Georgia appeared as the announcer recited Carter's record. "Government spending increased 58%. . . . government employees up to 28%. . . . bonded indebtedness up 20%." As a map of the U.S. rose on the screen the announcer pleaded not to let Carter do as president what he did as governor. In the final days of the campaign the Republicans also argued that "Those who know Jimmy Carter best are from Georgia. That's why we thought you'd like to know." What followed was a crawl—white letters over a picture of Ford—listing all the newspapers in Georgia that had endorsed Ford. Its message was clear: Those who knew Carter best trusted him least. Although the announcer's voice trailed off at the end of the ad to suggest that the list of endorsing papers was endless, the ad, in fact, had exhausted its list. The ad was misleading on a second count for it invited the inference that an overwhelming number of newspapers in Georgia had endorsed Ford. Instead, twelve of Georgia's twenty-two newspapers with a total circulation of 306,347 supported Ford while ten papers, including the Sunday *Atlanta Constitution,* had endorsed Carter. These papers reached an audience of 956,700.[52]

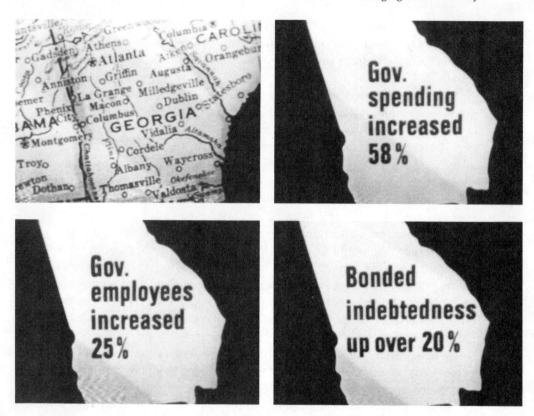

Stills from an anti-Carter ad run during the general election illustrating Carter's record as governor of Georgia.

Carter Indicts Ford

Rafshoon responded to the assault with ads produced by Tony Schwartz showing Carter "speaking about where he wanted to move the country and speaking about Ford's drifting economy." In these ads, aired in the closing weeks of the campaign, Carter abandoned the plaid shirt and rural setting of earlier ads. Instead of looking just off camera, as he did in previous ads, Carter now addressed the camera directly. In one of the ads, scripted by Reenah Schwartz, Carter combines the language of competence and the language of compassion to state that "7.8% unemployment is what you arrive at when incompetent leaders follow outdated, insensitive, unjust, wasteful, economic policies." Carter also criticizes Ford for voting "against Medicare, against food stamps for the elderly, against adequate housing."

Heartbeat Away Dole

To differentiate the campaigns, Schwartz also refurbished the heartbeat-away ad he created for Humphrey in 1968. Still photos of Dole and Mondale replaced the monitored heartbeat of 1968. As the audience focused on the pictures, the announcer asked: "Have you thought about the vice-presidential candidates? What do you think of Mondale . . . of Dole? What kind of men are they? When you know that four out of the last six vice-presidents have wound up being president, who would you like to see a heartbeat away from the presidency?" But where the 1968 ad permitted the audience to answer without prompting, this ad minimized participation by drawing its own conclusion. "Well," stated the announcer, "this is why many people will be voting for Jimmy Carter and Walter Mondale." Visually, the ad emphasized this answer by dissolving the pictures of Dole and Mondale into a campaign photo of Carter and Mondale. Because Carter's advisers feared that Mondale's liberalism would hurt the Democratic ticket in the South, this ad was downplayed in that region.[53]

The ad's invitation to choose between the vice-presidential contenders was the by-product of Caddell's reports that nearly half of his respondents thought Dole was unqualified to be president. By contrast, Ford's pollster reported little negative effect.[54] Gallup's findings more closely paralleled Caddell's. According to Gallup, one of twenty who switched from Ford to Carter during the campaign gave as a reason their dislike of Dole; by contrast only one in a hundred of those who switched from Carter to Ford cited Mondale's candidacy as a reason.

Although Dole, like Ford, was a conservative Midwesterner, he was selected because he satisfied the ideological requirements of Reagan's natural constituency and because the Kansan could help Ford secure the farm states from the challenge of the farmer who headed the Democratic ticket. Similarly, Carter's choice of Mondale represented a gesture of good will toward the Democratic party's liberals and at the same time provided a geographical balance and gave the ticket headed by the Washington outsider the expertise that comes from being a Washington insider.

But in an electorate fixated on the candidates' personal characters, Dole's penchant for verbal stillettos was a liability. In the vice-presidential debate, for instance, Dole suggested that AFL-CIO president George Meany "was probably Senator Mondale's make-up man," identified the two world wars, the Korean War, and the Vietnam War as "Democrat wars" and claimed that there were three presidential debates because Carter has "three positions on everything." Mondale responded, "I think that Senator Dole has richly earned his reputation as a hatchet man tonight."

Reaction to Dole's strident style was disapproving. Conservative columnist George Will noted that "Until Dole took wing in his debate with Walter Mondale, it was unclear when this campaign would hit bottom." *Washington Post* reporter Jules Witcover wrote in *Marathon,* "There was a nervous, erratic quality about Dole, a carelessness. He spun off snide remarks almost as if he were unaware of the huge television audience or, perhaps more accurately, as if he were intentionally disdainful of it."[55]

If the Republicans considered Dole an advantage nationally, their advertising did not reflect it. Dole is a nonperson in the national Republican advertising. By contrast, after the vice-presidential debate, Carter regularly mentioned Mondale in his speeches—citing his selection as evidence that an outsider could appoint a strong cabinet and asserting that Mondale would make a great president. Rafshoon also considered featuring Mondale in television ads. "We started to do some Mondale," he says. "Fritz was terrible on camera. He hated television." Mondale is prominently featured in the print ads placed by the Democrats in the final weeks of the campaign.

Ford's Vision of the Future

As Ford's attacks and Carter's missteps closed the distance between the two in the polls, the question voters asked shifted from "Why or why not Carter?" to "Which? Carter or Ford?" The latter placed a burden on Ford to define his vision of the country. Indeed the very success of which his ads bragged when they credited him with healing the country and putting it on a steady course necessitated that now he reveal what he wanted to do as president.

In the last week and a half of the campaign, Ford attempted to define his vision for the future. He did so in a series of nationally broadcast radio programs and telecasts. Following a strategy refined by Nixon in 1968, in the final ten days of the campaign Ford appeared in carefully crafted half hour programs in six key states: Illinois, Pennsylvania, California, New York, Ohio, and Texas. Hosting the programs was baseball player turned sportscaster Joe Garagiola. In the telecasts, which cost about $60,000 apiece, Garagiola played "everyman"—the undecided voter leaning toward Ford. His face mirrored the words scripted for him by Ford's advisers and immortalized on cue cards. When asking the questions he was bewildered but quizzical, then intent, as Ford began his answers, finally nodding his commitment to Ford's answers.

The telecasts opened with Garagiola introducing clips of the president and his family arriving in the state. In Ohio, for example, Betty Ford was shown receiving a bouquet from a child as she disembarked from the plane. Mike Ford followed eating a hamburger. As President Ford shook hands with the crowd the band played the Michigan fight song.

In the studio setting reminiscent of the *Today* show, Ford responded to slow ball questions from Garagiola. Why should voters believe Ford rather than Carter, Garagiola wondered aloud. What happened to Ford's hands—don't they get "pretty banged up shaking all those hands?" Is the economy going to improve?[56] The program's message was straightforward: Ford was a capable decent person who deserved a full term of his own. What the telecasts did not clearly indicate was precisely what Ford hoped to do in that term.

Between October 25 and election day November 2, Ford also delivered seven nationwide radio addresses. Speaking on inflation, taxes, the concern of senior citizens, peace, crime, law enforcement, his vision of America, and leadership and the presidency, Ford summarized the accomplishments of his administration, and attempted to lay out the philosophy of government that would guide his next term.

In the broadcasts Ford became his own commercial by intrusively insinuating his campaign slogans in a way that could only remind the listener that these are not the messages of a president but the messages of a presidential candidate. Of inflation he said, "We've been on a steady and stable course for 2 years now—and it's working." After noting that we are at peace, honor has been restored to the White House, and inflation is down, he added. "Things are getting better. That's why we're feeling good about America." Unlike the spot ads, a chorus did not swell with the Ford theme song "I'm feelin' good about America. I'm feelin' good about me" but the fact that we expected it suggested the problem in Ford's invocation of his own slogans.

By heightening our consciousness of their identity as paid broadcasts, these repetitions of the slogans raised our guard against Ford's message, a guard that would have remained down had the messages preserved the nonpartisan illusion of reports to the nation, as Nixon's successfully had in 1972. At the same time, Ford's invocation of his own ad slogans demeaned him by reducing him to the level of his own pitchman.

In the broadcast on the day before the election Ford phrased the question on voters' minds. People have told him, Ford said, that they support his stand on jobs, inflation, and foreign policy but "are not quite sure what it all adds up to . . . are not quite clear where you are aiming to lead America." What followed were platitudes that could as easily have been uttered by Carter as Ford. His vision, Ford says, is of "a nation that is strong and good. . . . in which basic human rights are respected and maintained." These include the right to worship, to stand equal before the law, to bargain freely in the economic marketplace.

Ford ultimately defined his vision by what he had not done: He had not overpromised. Finally, in a statement that failed to differentiate him from Carter, Ford embraced "a vision of limited government and unlimited opportunity."

In a final radio address delivered over the Mutual Radio Network on election day, Ford broke with the pattern of his previous radio speeches to specifically compare his candidacy to Carter's:

> I believe I offer experienced leadership; you will have to decide whether my opponent can make the same claim.
>
> I think my approach could properly be called steady and dependable; it is my opinion, that even as I speak to you, his claims are unclear and untested.
>
> To single out just one issue, my course promises a lid on spending and a tax cut for every American family; Mr. Carter's approach shifts with the wind, leaving me with the feeling that we, the American people, could be left high and dry.
>
> To stay on our steady and dependable course I need your help; I need your vote. To me it is more than a choice between different approaches to government. It is the test of our political system. A test of the qualities we Americans seek in our leadership.
>
> For these past two years, I have been careful never to promise what I could not deliver. It has been my goal to inspire your confidence in America through solid performance rather than through mere words. . . . We're at peace in our world; we have peace of mind here at home; inflation has been cut in half; we've set a peacetime record of 4 million new jobs in 17 months; and honor has been restored to the White House. I'm proud of that extraordinary comeback.

Consistent with this summary, on November 1, Ford's print ads offered voters "one final thought." The thought was Ford's. Its linguistic form was reminiscent of *Love Story*'s "Love means never having to say you're sorry." In white letters against a black background Ford declared: "It is not enough for anyone to say 'trust me.' Trust is not having to guess what a candidate means. Trust is not being all things to all people, but being the same thing to all people. Trust is leveling with the people before the election about what you're going to do after the election. Trust is saying plainly and simply what you mean—and meaning what you say. Trust must be earned."[57] An ad in the *Detroit News* carried a comparable message. It argued that Ford stood for "Progress—not Platitude. Performance—not Promises."

As if to rebut visually Ford's large type and simple message, Carter's final print ads were visually dense discussions of his stands on various issues.

By contrast to his earlier advertising in the closing weeks of the election, Carter's TV ads allied him with a reassuring tradition of Democratic presidents. In an ad created by Tony Schwartz, the actor E. G. Marshall narrated a stream-of-consciousness recollection of great presidents that placed Carter squarely in the Democratic tradition. Without identifying the "I" who was speaking, Marshall's resonant voice informed us that "I'd always felt that when Franklin Roosevelt died that was the end of the good and great presidents, and then after Harry Truman, I thought well, that's the last of them. And then we had Jack Kennedy. For such a short time, too. I learned something from them. I learned that in the proper time the man and the moment can meet, so to speak. A good man can become a great man. A person of vision can become a president of vision. Take up a country and lead it into a more secure future. Where the goal truly is justice for all. I look forward to voting for Jimmy Carter. That's the truth of it. I feel it's in the air that we're going to have a new Democratic president. In the tradition of the best Democratic presidents."

Conspicuously absent from Marshall's list of great presidents are Ford, whom the ad supposed suffers by comparison to FDR, Truman, and Kennedy, and Lyndon Johnson. The absence of Johnson in this pantheon of "good and great" presidents is highlighted by the dissolves that blend the image of FDR into Truman's, Truman's into JFK's, and JFK's into Carter's. Omission of Johnson undoubtedly would have rankled Texans who could easily have pieced it together with Carter's indictment of LBJ in the *Playboy* interview into a picture of a Southerner who urged the South to unite behind his candidacy while knifing another native son in the back. But the ad went unaired in Texas.

Identification of Johnson as a great president could have been fatal in liberal states, for his presence would have reminded viewers that Carter had broken with Johnson's policies on the war fashionably late. By sanctifying Johnson, the ad would have muted the effectiveness of Carter and Mondale's efforts to tie Ford to Nixon. After all, as Carter noted in the *Playboy* interview, both former presidents had lied to the American people. It was acceptable in 1976 to include LBJ's picture as the five minute ad did but claiming that he was either good or great went too far.

By bonding Carter to his party, this spot capitalized on the predisposition of the majority of the electorate to vote Democratic. Party allegiance was an important factor in Carter's victory since the rate of party defection in 1976 was unusually low. Eighty-five percent of the voters with an expressed party loyalty voted with their party.[58]

In an election in which the public perceived the major issues to be economic, specifically unemployment and inflation, Carter's link to the party traditionally perceived as the party of prosperity was a plus. An election survey corroborated this. By a 2 to 1 margin, the electorate believed that the Democratic party was better able to keep the nation prosperous.[59]

Election Eve

On election eve the Democrats moved to mute the attacks levied against Carter in the "map" ad, the "newspaper endorsement" ad, the Georgians in the street ads and Ford's radio speeches. For the election eve broadcast, Rafshoon turned to the producer of Humphrey's election eve telethon, Bob Squier. Recognizing the "residual" impact of the "wishy-washy" and "he wasn't much of a governor" attacks, Rafshoon told Squier "to make a half hour [broadcast] and answer every question."

In his introduction to the program, Carter described it as being "untarnished and direct and unrehearsed: a good presentation of the proper relationship between the future president and the people he hopes to serve."

Squier went around the country filming "a cross section of Americans asking questions." The questions recapped every charge made in a Ford ad. The form, with people in their home environments raising questions, evoked the form of Ford's ads as well. Carter's answers served as rebuttal. Meanwhile, Ford's election eve broadcast was offering voters little that would resurrect their doubts about Carter. Instead, it was reviving doubts about Ford.

The contest on election eve was more critical than in most other elections because in 1976 an unusually large percent of the electorate decided how to vote at the last minute. In mid-September 1976, according to Gallup, two out of three Americans were pretty sure about how they would vote. Still 27% thought they might switch allegiance before election day and 9% had not decided how to vote. These figures proved prophetic. One out of five of the persons who entered a voting booth in 1976 had at some time thought they would vote for a candidate other than their final choice. Unlike the other elections we have studied, about half (48%) of the voters did not decide who to vote for until the period between the conventions and election day. A full 12% decided at the last minute or on election day. Carter's polls found and an NBC poll confirmed that about 60% of those who were undecided the weekend before the election voted for Carter.

On election eve Ford's campaign offered the viewer a structurally fragmented program that failed to underscore even the steadiness that was Ford's great asset. "[I]f I had a segment of film I would want to take back and was never happy putting on the air," said Bailey, "it was the last two minutes of advertising . . . when he spoke from the plane into the camera."[60]

Ford, who spoke to the American people over the roar of the engines of Air Force One, did not look or sound like the safe, known Jerry Ford who toasted his own English muffins and vetoed 55 congressional bills. His voice almost gone, his face shouting his exhaustion, the Ford who rasped his appeal for votes into the camera neither looked nor sounded presidential. Rather than sounding like someone who had kept to a steady course, Ford sounded desperate.

Inexplicably, the broadcast also included singer Pearl Bailey, whom some in the audience identified as the saleswoman for Oursman Dodge. Bailey was not on the plane but was intercut into a sequence that suggested that she should have been. Her endorsement was hardly ringing. "He's made some mistakes, honey, you'd better believe he has," she said. Joe Garagiola also testified to Ford's competence and compassion. Those not in the six states in which the Joe and Jerry show had aired would be at a loss to explain what Joe Garagiola was doing on the plane. And those in the six states might wonder as well. Use of Garagiola and Bailey exaggerated Ford's weaknesses rather than his strength. Neither was articulate. Neither could deliver a constituency. Both could testify to Ford's popular appeal but what was needed in this broadcast was not further evidence of Ford's ability to relate to the common folk but instead evidence that Ford was up to the job he had inherited.

Sandwiched between Garagiola and Bailey and the rasping president, Bailey/Deardourff had layered every patriotic symbol except the lone bald eagle and Thomas Jefferson's pen: Ford ringing the bell on the *USS Forrestal;* Ford on the Fourth of July with the tall ships; potatoes, grain, streams, mountains, and fields.

While replaying material from a five minute biographical ad aired earlier in the campaign, the program showed Ford as the all-American kid who made good: an eagle scout, a football player, a law student who graduated in the upper third of his class, and Ford taking the oath of office. Throughout the ad, associates and his family, whose self-interest in Ford's election was plain, testified to his character and conscience.

The ad also portrayed Betty and Gerald Ford as characters in a "love story," a tactic that enabled the producers to remind viewers of their empathy for her and her family as she underwent a mastectomy.

Throughout, pictures of Air Force One were used to cover edits. The plane was shown soaring and banking. Oddly, although the program was airing in the evening, the shots were of a plane flying in daylight. What the footage of and in the plane meant in practical terms was that on election eve the incumbent president sacrificed the most potent symbol at his disposal, a symbol his opponent could not replicate—the White House. At the same time the footage from inside the plane raised the question: who was minding the store? Where was the red phone? Were it to ring, would Ford be able to hear it over the roar of the engines? How steady was Ford's course when his plane kept banking?

Doug Bailey agrees that the election eve program is flawed. "It made the one mistake we warned against [in the media plan]; it overstated the case," he says. "The rest of our material understated the case, relaxed it and did not confront people with a heavy imperial presidency, which is what Ford had gotten rid of. The music, the announcer's voice, the picture of all the weapons going off was a hard sell in a campaign that to that point had been calm and easy going and reassuring about a stable presidency and hadn't sold him as the biggest thing since sliced bread. The line was that he's making America great again not that America's the greatest thing ever and Gerald Ford is the greatest president we've ever had. [The other advertising in the campaign] was understated. That film overstated."[61]

By election eve the roles of the contenders had reversed. Ford, rasping from the plane, epitomized the candidate; Carter, composed and dignified, speaking from Plains, better embodied the presidency than the president. The campaigns' final spot ads previewed the reversal. Here, Carter, dressed in a conservative suit, spoke quietly, directly into the camera. In these spots, the first in the campaign scripted for Carter, the awkward pauses that fractured subject from verb and verb from object in his extemporaneous delivery, vanished as did the misplaced emphasis on syllables that led him in earlier ads to pledge to banish "Miss Management" from Washington. Carter had evolved from the candidate of the plaid workshirt walking in the peanut fields or leaning against a farm fence to the calm, dignified, suited presidential aspirant reassuring the country. Where in his primary and early general election ads Carter had either spoken to crowds in his ads or just off camera to an unseen interviewer or listener, as election day neared Carter assumed the right to address the entire nation directly.

By contrast, in his final spot ads, Ford appeared in open collar shirts speaking to groups of voters. Where Carter's most polished delivery occurred in his last ads, Ford's occurred in his acceptance address. In the final wave of spots, Ford's delivery of one promise was so mangled by misplaced pauses that his message appeared to be that he too had once had a friend. What he meant to say was that, like his audience, he had had friends who had faced the staggering costs of long-term illness. So

These stills contrast the early primary ads (in which Ford is seen as presidential and Carter shown as an outsider who is not a politician but a farmer, engineer, and businessman) and later, general election ads (in which Carter is shown in a conservative suit and Ford is depicted informally).

Ford, who had opened his bid for the nomination with the visual and verbal rhetoric of incumbency, closed his general election campaign looking and sounding like a candidate.

Symbolically, Carter gradually invested himself with the presidency while Ford progressively stripped himself of it. On election day the electorate ratified the symbolic transformations the candidates had already accomplished. Ironically, in 1980 Reagan would follow the model set by Carter in 1976 while Carter embraced the pattern of transformation adopted by Ford.

As Johnny Carson joked, the contest between Carter and Ford pitted fear of the known against fear of the known. On election eve, Carter allayed fears while Ford aggravated them.

Slogans

In 1976 Ford's first general election slogan was "President Ford: Let's Keep to his Steady Course." In the final weeks of the election that evolved into "President Ford: He's Making Us Proud Again." Both statements stress continuity. By contrast, the Democrats stressed change. Carter's TV ads embraced the tag "Leadership for a Change." In a variant on the same theme, print ads featuring Carter and Mondale said, "Leaders for a Change." In 1980 Reagan's slogan "The time Is Now for Leadership" would hang Carter with a variant of his own earlier slogan.

By establishing that he too could make us proud and plot an acceptably steady course for the future, Carter narrowly won the election. Neither Ford's speeches nor his ads quieted the uneasy sense on the part of a small but decisive portion of the electorate that the pardon of Nixon had not made us proud and was a course that ought not to have been taken. The most often noted negative comments about Ford by voters explaining their votes in 1976 concerned the pardon. "Ford's pardon of Nixon clearly rankled many voters in 1976," concludes Burnham,[62] "and it is quite possible that this act in the end cost him the election." That is a view shared by Ford.[63]

Although his nationally aired acceptance speech spoke obliquely of it, Carter's ads did not breathe a word of the pardon. However, since the pardon was the only scar on Ford's openness and honesty, Carter's reiteration of those themes kept the question alive. Even though both Carter and Mondale had alluded to it in stump speeches, when the issue was raised in the debates both Democratic candidates sidestepped it. The choice was a wise one. Had Carter stressed the issue he might have been seen as petty and vindictive. Additionally, he would have risked such questions as, What punishment would you have exacted from Nixon? It was to Carter's advantage to keep the issue alive without being perceived to be keeping it alive. Accordingly, in the ads he spoke only of the Nixon-Ford Administration, never of the pardon. Rafshoon avoided addressing the pardon for fear that overt use of it by Carter would make Carter seem like a typical politician, hurt his reputation as the candidate of honesty and integrity, and destabilize the election. He was unsure whether it would precipitate a landslide victory or a loss.[64]

In keeping the issue smoldering, Carter had the assistance both of Nixon and of the press. Nixon's trip to China on the eve of the New Hampshire primary bespoke vindication of Nixon that the pardon alone made possible. The press also raised the heat under this simmering issue by asking about the pardon in the first Carter-Ford debate and in the Mondale-Dole debate.

Ironically, Ford's own advertising slogan "He's making us proud again" increased the salience of the pardon. That difficulty was underscored by the ads themselves. By airing an ad in which he promised that criminals would go to jail, Ford seemed to taunt those disquieted by the pardon to see inconsistency in his actions. In answer to the question of a young girl seated on the floor in front of him in a group of children at the Oval Office, Ford says in another ad that his greatest accomplishment has been healing America. His theme song reminds us that we're feeling good about America. His ads and his slogans are contextualized by the traumas we experienced before he took office. If Ford's major accomplishment is healing America, or its corollary, making us proud again, how can he take credit for that accomplishment without summoning memories of the major decision made in the name of healing? That is a dilemma neither the Ford campaign nor Ford's ads address for there is no good way to address it.

Building from his secure Southern base, Carter won the election, 297–241 electoral votes.

CHAPTER NINE

1980: "I'm Qualified To Be President and You're Not"

Massachusetts Senator Edward Kennedy, youngest brother of John and Robert Kennedy, had every reason to believe in late 1979 that the Democratic nomination was his for the asking. After all, during every presidential contest since the death of his brother Robert, the press had proposed Teddy as prospective nominee, if not heir apparent. As important, in early October 1979, when party regulars were asking themselves the key question about the upcoming election—can this candidate win?—Gallup polls showed that Jimmy Carter's approval rating had reached an all-time low of 29%. Gallup also reported that polled Democrats favored Teddy two to one as the party's nominee.

Still, the spectre of assassination must surely have shadowed any discussion of Edward Kennedy's presidential candidacy, and the horror of such a possibility must have given pause to those who might otherwise have freely encouraged Kennedy to run. But one other event from Kennedy's past may also have played a part in his decision-making calculus. For the question remained whether or not—and to what extent—the public had forgotten or at least forgiven Kennedy for his actions of nearly ten years ago, when late on the night of July 18, 1969, a car he was driving plunged off a bridge on Chappaquiddick Island, resulting in the death of a young political aide, Mary Jo Kopechne, who was with him in the car.

Kennedy had been on Chappaquiddick Island for a party he had helped arrange for political aides and staff. Ms. Kopechne, a former aide to his brother Robert, had been invited. According to Kennedy's later testimony, he lost his way, and thinking he was on the main road back to the ferry slip, he ended up on an unpaved road that eventually took him over a narrow wooden bridge. What is known is that his car went off this narrow bridge. When the car plunged into the water, he was able to swim free but, not seeing Ms. Kopechne surface, he dove into "the strong and murky current" repeatedly in efforts to save her.

When these efforts failed, however, Kennedy did not seek the nearest available help. Nor did he promptly report the accident. Indeed, in one version of what happened, he went back to the scene of the party, climbed into one of the other autos, and, exhausted, fell asleep. Ms. Kopechne's death and Kennedy's subsequent actions raised doubts at the time that were not fully resolved, not only about his ability to act sensibly under pressure, but about his personal integrity.

Seven days later, on July 25, 1969, the day on which he entered a guilty plea to the charge of leaving the scene of an accident, Edward Kennedy delivered a televised address telling his "fellow citizens" "what happened and . . . what it means to me." In the address Kennedy conceded "as indefensible the fact that [he] did not report the accident to the police immediately," and even went so far as to admit that he had entertained "all kinds of scrambled thoughts—all of them confused, some of them irrational." He also confessed to panicking. "I was overcome, I'm frank to say, by a jumble of emotions—grief, fear, doubt, exhaustion, panic, confusion and shock." But he also stated that there was "no truth, no truth whatever, to the widely circulated suspicions of immoral conduct that have been leveled at my behavior and hers regarding that evening." He also declared that he was not "driving under the influence of liquor."

In the speech, Kennedy portrayed himself as the victim of forces he did not control. The "car that I was driving on an unlit road went off a narrow bridge," not "I drove the car off a narrow bridge." After the accident he wondered "whether some awful curse actually did hang over all the Kennedys."

Although some believed that his behavior at Chappaquiddick should have been sufficient cause to disqualify him from ever running for the presidency (and would have been had it been anybody else), three years later, in 1972, and then again in 1976, Kennedy's name was being widely touted for his party's nomination. Both times Kennedy declined, saying this was not to be the year. Kennedy's popularity, however, did not decline. Once again, in September 1978 an ABC-Harris poll showed Kennedy in a strong position, this time leading incumbent Jimmy Carter 40% to 21% among Independents and Democrats.

Kennedy's speech at the party's mid-term convention in Memphis in December 1978, with its strong attack on Carter's cuts in social welfare programs, its championing of national health insurance, and its appeal to his party to sail against the wind, was the first real hint that this time Kennedy might not reject the party's nomination out of hand. Carter's return sally would not come until nearly a year later, in mid-October 1979, when Carter upstaged Kennedy at the dedication of the John F. Kennedy Library. In a gracious speech that nonetheless made its points,

Carter situated himself as heir to the legacy of John Kennedy and argued in the same breath that times had changed. A few weeks later the challenge would be accepted, but not before intervening events had decidedly changed the presidential prospects of Ted Kennedy and Jimmy Carter.

Because with politics, particularly election year politics, one day can make an enormous difference, it is interesting to recall how quickly fortunes changed on the night of November 4. On that Sunday evening, CBS ran a one-hour special called "Teddy," narrated by its top political reporter, Roger Mudd, long considered a Kennedy family friend. The special managed, in its brief sixty minutes, to produce what may be remembered as two of the most politically damaging segments ever to air on national television. In one, Kennedy offered a rambling, pause pocked, incoherent answer to Roger Mudd's query about why he wanted to be president. Even Mudd was taken aback by Kennedy's total collapse. "After the interview," Mudd later noted, "I felt like I had an 800-pound rock on my chest. I had been and am still an admirer of Kennedy as a Senator, a politician and a man of considerable intelligence and skill. [But] I felt that I had been in a room where no one else had ever been. It was for me a process of original discovery, simply because I didn't know how poorly collected he was. . . . The whole problem was that he [Kennedy] ran before he was ready."[1] The press would later dub this disastrous segment of the interview the "Mudd Slide."

In the other damaging segment, the viewer is taken back by a car-mounted camera to the road that leads to the bridge at Chappaquiddick. The car retraces Kennedy's ride. At first, the camera monitoring the road is steady. Then, as the car takes a discernible right turn off the main road and onto the side road that led to the bridge from which Kennedy's car ultimately plunged, the camera shots jump erratically on the screen. The side road seems, in Mudd's description, like a "washboard." The footage suggests two things: first, that Kennedy had to deliberately turn the car to get off the main road onto the side road, meaning that he could not easily have mistaken the two, as he claimed, and, second, that the change in the surface of the road is marked, and should have alerted him to the fact that he had left the main road. In answer to Mudd's question about how, when all signs, including the surface of the road, direct the driver to the left, Kennedy could have managed to take a right turn, Kennedy responds that only one sign suggested that the paved road veered left. Coming after this dramatic contradictory camera-eye tour, the answer seems feeble, if not dishonest. Nearly a year later, at a seminar at the University of Maryland, Roger Mudd would comment, "If you're a journalist and you go up to Martha's Vineyard and you take that trip you come back knowing that he's lied, and when you have somebody who wants to be president of the United States and you know he's lying, you go for the Holy Grail."[2]

The second event that dramatically tipped the presidential popularity scales in Carter's behalf took place, by sheer accident, that same day but thousands of miles away. On November 4, in the city of Teheran, young militant followers of Ayatollah Ruhollah Khomeini seized the U.S. embassy in Iran, taking fifty-three American diplomats hostage. The militants sought the return of the deposed Shah of Iran, whom Carter had agreed to admit the week before to the U.S. for medical treatment for cancer.

The seizure of the embassy and the taking of the hostages presented Carter with a "crisis" around which to rally the country. Suddenly Carter could act decisively yet with restraint. He halted oil imports from Iran and asked the UN Security Council to condemn the Iranian action. He also cancelled all immediately scheduled political trips. Despite the "Mudd Slide," despite the good press Carter began to receive for his handling of Iran, despite Chappaquiddick, and despite the wrenching fate that had taken the lives of his two brothers, three days later, Edward Kennedy threw his hat into the ring, announcing on November 7 that he was a candidate for the presidency. By late November, for whatever combination of reasons, Jimmy Carter had pulled ahead of Kennedy in the polls.

The Democratic Primaries

Through the early primaries, Jimmy Carter used the hostage situation and the Russian's Christmas-time invasion of Afghanistan as the rationale for not campaigning. Accordingly, he withdrew from a debate in Iowa with California Governor Jerry Brown and Kennedy, thus effectively quashing Brown's best chance to attain the legitimacy he needed to be taken seriously as a national candidate. Carter's focus on the Russians in Afghanistan and the hostages also overshadowed the 18% inflation and 18% interest rates, which Kennedy tried and failed to make a central part of the public's agenda. Carter's symbolic response to the hostage-taking—which included not lighting the national Christmas tree—was less unpopular than his response to the Russian invasion (Carter embargoed grain sales to Russia and withdrew the U.S. from the Moscow Olympics). Meanwhile Kennedy's personal affairs continued to top the tabloids, which frequently treated their readers to "new" and "shocking" revelations about Kennedy's faltering marriage or to "inside information" about his extramarital romances. These underscored the sense that Kennedy was not, in the venerable phrase, "a good family man."

In the Iowa caucuses January 21, whose importance was established in 1976 when Carter's win there crowned him front-runner, Kennedy was beaten almost two to one. Kennedy's failure to establish a focus for his campaign in the early primaries demonstrated that his foundering answer to Roger Mudd's question about why he sought the presidency had revealed not just momentary inarticulateness on Kennedy's part. Tony Schwartz, for example, who was hired to produce radio spots, complained that he could not obtain a clear sense of what the campaign was trying to communicate. Herb Schmertz, vice-president of Mobil Oil and a friend of the Kennedy family, who had taken a leave of absence from Mobil to coordinate the advertising, asked Schwartz, "What do you need research for?" Schwartz recalls. Finally persuaded of the value of research, Kennedy's campaign did then engage pollster Peter Hart, but Schwartz decided, nonetheless, to resign.

Schwartz explains his resignation by saying that he would have loved to see Kennedy win but couldn't "help him the way I was forced to work. I'd do a spot," notes Schwartz, "and it would be gone over by 20 people. You can't run a campaign that way. You need a general or a knowledgeable dictator."[3] "Schwartz's ads were too slick, too sophisticated and too negative for Iowa," responded Kennedy's press secretary Bob Shrum.[4] Charles Guggenheim, who had worked for Robert Kennedy in 1968 and had produced advertising for Kennedy's Senate races, also created ads that the Kennedy staff judged ineffective. Guggenheim was ultimately eased aside for New York producer David Sawyer.

The commercials televised for Kennedy in the early primaries were poor. One half hour juxtaposed Kennedy delivering a speech with an ineptly produced fifteen minute discussion featuring persons from Iowa. In another ad, Robert Kennedy's widow, Ethel, appeared in a tennis dress talking about Edward Kennedy's dedication to her children and praising him for "holding the family together." In another, Kennedy and his family were shown walking along the beach as an announcer said, "The kinds of things he has suffered have made him a strong, more mature man." "They tried to make out that he was a happily married man," says Schwartz. "I call that image re-touching. You can't tell people something when they know the opposite."

By contrast, Carter's half hour documentary, produced by Bob Squier and aired nationally before the caucus, showed a decisive president. The idea for the documentary grew from Squier's presence at Camp David, where he had assisted Gerald Rafshoon while Carter was negotiating the accords with Sadat and Begin. Although people perceived that Carter was "a warm and cuddly human being" recalls Squier, "they also thought that he was absolutely and totally incompetent. I got a very different view at Camp David."[5]

Still photo drawn from the half hour documentary produced by Bob Squier and aired before the Iowa caucuses. The same scene reappeared in Democratic spot ads televised in the general election campaign.

Footage for the documentary was gathered during three "morning until night" days of shooting at the White House. Wireless mikes were attached to Carter and his aides. "With three cameras running simultaneously" Squier captured three working days in the life of the incumbent president. The documentary shows Carter confronting complex problems decisively, a message underscored by the documentary's stress on the Camp David Accords. The message is capsulized when Carter responds to a problem by saying "I'll make a decision on it today."

Parts of the documentary are narrated by Carter himself. "We showed him at work and let him tell his own story," says Squier.

By design, the days selected for shooting included the day on which the Pope visited the White House. Throughout the film we see Carter practicing the line of Polish that he will deliver to the Pope. Carter's actual delivery of the statement to the pleased pontiff caps the film. When facing a Catholic opponent, implied papal approval of the Southern Baptist was a useful message to telegraph to the heavily Catholic primary states in the Northeastern corridor. In addition, by demonstrating Carter's work schedule, the documentary underscored Carter's claim that, with the Iranian "crisis" added to his normal responsibilities, he could neither campaign nor debate.

Shorter ads stressed the area in which Carter was perceived to be strong and Kennedy weak: character. One of the sections of the documentary was edited to a spot ad that showed Carter helping his daughter Amy with her homework. In his own voice Carter provides the narrative, "I don't think there's any way you can separate the responsibilities of a husband and father and a basic human being from that of the president. What I do in the White House is to maintain a good family life, which I consider to be crucial to being a good president." Then to underscore the contrast between Carter's good family life and Kennedy's troubled one, the announcer adds: "Husband. Father. President. He's done these three jobs with distinction."

Since such great presidents as FDR led troubled family lives, the argument is on the face of it an odd one. Were the ad simply reminding viewers that Kennedy had separated from his wife, that she may have been an alcoholic or even that he was believed to have been involved with other women, it would have risked a sympathetic backlash for Kennedy. Instead, veiled by "Husband, Father," and "basic human being," is an indictment of the personal morality that led Kennedy to the bridge at Chappaquiddick and governed his unwillingness to promptly report the accident and to provide a candid, coherent, cogent account of it.

While Carter's ads attacked Kennedy, both Kennedy's and the Republicans' ads attacked Carter. Republican candidate George Bush's tag in the early primaries was "George Bush: A President we won't have to train." Lest its intent be unclear, one version of one of the ads added "this time." In the Southern primaries one Bush radio ad would encompass both Carter and Reagan in the question: "Can we afford the same mistake twice?" In the later primaries Bush's media consultant, Robert Goodman, substituted "George Bush is the one candidate Jimmy Carter hopes he never has to run against."

It was not until January 28, 1980, in a speech at Georgetown University that Kennedy finally answered cogently the question Mudd had asked him in the fall. The speech blamed the Russian invasion and the taking of the hostages on Carter. It identified the questions voters should ask: can America "risk four more years of uncertain policy and certain crisis—of an administration that tells us to rally around their failures—of an inconsistent nonpolicy that may confront us with a stark choice between retreat and war?" Kennedy taped an edited version of the Georgetown speech for broadcast in New England. In an introduction tacked onto the speech he acknowledged what pollsters knew—that his actions at Chappaquiddick were still at issue.

Just as there had really been two Watergates—first the break-in itself and then the attempt to cover it up—so too were there two Chappaquiddicks—the first involving why Kennedy was driving with Mary Jo Ko-pechne in the middle of the night to a ferry that would not have been there to take them to the main island had they reached it; the second, what he had said and done once the tragedy of the accident had occurred. Carter's ads were implying that about one or both, Kennedy had not told the whole truth.

Clearly, Kennedy had a real problem. At the inquest, during his tele-vised address to the nation following the inquest, in interviews on the anni-versary of the accident, in response to reporters' queries, and in response to Roger Mudd, Kennedy had contended that he had told all the truth there was to tell. If he now introduced a more detailed account, he, in ef-fect, admitted that those previous statements had been incomplete at best. If he raised the issue himself, in order to repeat that he had told all there was to tell, he risked magnifying the issue and at the same time reminding people that they did not believe his explanation. Last, since Carter's ads were not airing nationally but primary by primary, it was unlikely that the issue would dissipate once familiarity with it bred boredom.

Kennedy tried in New Hampshire to transform the issue from one of his truth telling to one of American fair play. In his televised speech there he said, "While I know many will never believe the facts of the tragic events at Chappaquiddick, those facts are the only truth I can tell because that is the way it happened, and I ask only that I be judged on the basic American standards of fairness." The attempt in New Hampshire failed; in my judgment, it could not have done otherwise. What the primary campaign itself could, and, I believe, did do, was enable Kennedy to expiate for Chappaquiddick, not absolve himself for responsibility for his actions of that night. A woman's life had been lost. Despite his claims to the contrary about the ongoing sense of tragedy with which he would have to live for the rest of his life, Kennedy seemed to have escaped punishment for his admitted responsibility and admitted guilt. He was not jailed. He retained his Senate seat. And now he sought the presidency.

By denying him that office, voters publicly inflicted on Kennedy the punishment the court had foresworn. By accepting the public flagellation in humiliating defeat after defeat and by continuing to ask the public to believe that he would undergo that process for the ideals they shared, Kennedy did the one thing in his power to purge himself of the disqualifi-cation of Chappaquiddick. Hence the ingenuity in the ad first run heavily in the New York primary [which Kennedy won] that noted that "This man *has endured personal attacks* in order to lead the fight for specific solutions to our problems, like mandatory wage and price controls to stop inflation, and programs to help the poor and the elderly on fixed in-comes" (emphasis added). Helpful in this process of expiation was word from Mary Jo Kopechne's mother that she planned to cast her vote for Kennedy in the Pennsylvania primary.

In Maine Kennedy finished a close second to Carter.

When Kennedy pressed his attack on Carter's foreign policy in a speech at Harvard, Carter responded by claiming at a press conference that the thrust of Kennedy's statements damaged "the achievement of our goals to keep the peace and get our hostages released." In New Hampshire, Carter won 49% to 38%. As expected, Kennedy won the Massachusetts primary, and the Georgian carried South Carolina, Florida, Georgia, and Alabama. Illinois posed the first real test after New Hampshire and there on March 18 Carter defeated Kennedy by over two to one. In Illinois, Kennedy tried to come to grips with the character issue in an ad that described him as the survivor of four brothers.

Kennedy had to win New York on March 25 to remain a viable candidate. He had two major advantages in his efforts to do so. First, through what Carter described as a communications failure, the U.S. had cast a vote for a UN Security Council resolution calling for Israel to disassemble her settlements in Arab territories including Jerusalem.* Second, a set of ads featuring Carroll O'Connor, of Archie Bunker fame, tried to link Jimmy Carter and the double-digit inflation and high interest rates of 1979 with Herbert Hoover, the Great Depression president who kept telling a nation in its worst depression that prosperity was "just around the corner." In another spot O'Connor noted that Carter may "give us a Depression which may make Hoover's look like prosperity. . . . We're looking at industrial layoffs and unemployment in all parts of the country . . . and Jimmy stays in Washington making warm-hearted speeches." Playing on Carter's theme, a solid man in a sensitive job, the ad labeled Kennedy "a strong leader with a strong record in the Senate." And to counter Carter's claims on Chappaquiddick, O'Connor noted, "I trust Ted Kennedy. I believe him in every way, folks."

David Sawyer, Kennedy's media adviser, drove home the economic issues in a spot that showed Carter smiling as the announcer recited: "This man has led our country into the worst economic crisis since the Depression. His broken promises cost New York a billion dollars a year. He betrayed Israel at the U.N., his latest foreign policy blunder." Capitalizing on anti-Carter sentiment, the ad closed with the appeal: "Let's join Ted Kennedy and fight back against four years of failure." Kennedy pressed the UN vote aggressively in New York. Kennedy also played on fears in New York that in his efforts to balance the budget Carter would

---

*That vote may have harmed Carter in the general election as well, where it contributed to erosion of his support among Jewish voters. In 1976 Carter received 67% of the Jewish vote, in 1980 only 47%.[6]

cut aid to New York. Carter responded with thirty and sixty second ads showing him signing New York's loan guarantee and a thirty second endorsement ad in which Mayor Koch explained the UN vote and tried to refocus the election on Kennedy by claiming that Carter was a "responsible" man who "admits rather than covering up" when he makes a mistake. Kennedy won New York decisively and carried Connecticut as well.

The next major primary occurred in Wisconsin and was viewed by the press as a test of whether Kennedy's victory in New York was serendipitous. At 7:13 on the morning of the Wisconsin primary Carter appeared on national television live from the Oval Office hinting that the release of the hostages was imminent. Whether as a result of this false hope or not, Carter carried Wisconsin. The early morning press conference that seemed to promise what was not later delivered created a skepticism about Carter that damaged his credibility and circumscribed his ability to issue a comparable statement in the closing hours of the general election.

In Pennsylvania Sawyer's Kennedy spots stressed a new theme: Carter, the president with his fingers crossed. The announcer noted, "Today we have twenty percent inflation. On housing, interest rates, even foreign affairs, his attitude was 'I'll keep my fingers crossed.' " The new television spots showed Carter watching as a softball moved by home plate. By contrast, the ads argue, Kennedy is a man of action. The announcer says at the spots' end, "We have a choice. We can choose a man who'll do the job. Or we can keep our fingers crossed. Take a stand. Kennedy for President." Without saying so explicitly, one of Kennedy's ads evoked the presidency of his brother by allying the space program, which JFK championed, to a kind of leadership Carter lacked. As a rocket lifts from the launch pad, the announcer bemoans the fact that we have lost the spirit that "put man on the moon, the spirit that enabled us to solve the toughest problems and meet the greatest challenges." The announcer then asks if we believe the spirit is still in us and closes "Ted Kennedy, because we've got to do better."

Throughout, Kennedy's ads make modest claims. He can do better than Carter. Carter countered with ads reminiscent of those run against him by Ford in '76. In these, local residents expressed concern about Kennedy's character.

"If he won big in Pennsylvania," recalls Rafshoon, "then we thought he'd stay in." Thus the person in the street spots were born. These spots, which helped close a thirty point lead Kennedy had over Carter in Pennsylvania, reflected voters' sentiments about Kennedy, notes Carter's media creator.[7]

Kennedy won the Pennsylvania primary by less than half a percent and won the Michigan caucuses, as well. In Carter's ads the key question had been character; in Kennedy's it was competence. In the primaries "we started out by showing Carter's strengths as they related to Kennedy's weaknesses," Rafshoon notes. "Later when Kennedy started to give us trouble, even though we knew we were going to win the nomination we tried to knock him out [with the stronger ads] hoping that he'd get out eventually because it was draining us. The Kennedy challenge hurt us in the general election."

On April 11, Carter ordered the joint Chiefs of Staff to go ahead with a military rescue of the fifty-three Americans still being held hostage in Iran. Thirteen days later, on April 24, U.S. planes and helicopters set off from the Gulf to an uninhabited desert rendezvous area in Iran. But when it was apparent that mechanical damage to three of the helicopters threatened the success of the mission, it was terminated before a rescue attempt had ever been made. As the assembled volunteers left the desert to return home, a helicopter and a plane collided. Eight men were killed. The dead were abandoned in the flaming planes. National television would shortly show an Ayatollah ghoulishly poking at their bodies.

On national television the next morning Carter reported the existence and failure of the rescue mission. Secretary of State Vance, who had opposed the mission, resigned before its outcome was known. Carter replaced him with Maine Senator Edmund Muskie. Five days after the aborted raid, Carter declared the "challenges" of Afghanistan and Iran "manageable enough now for me to leave the White House." Kennedy quickly began asking whether 18% interest rates and an 18% rate of inflation were indeed manageable.

Kennedy defeated Carter in five of the last eight primaries, including California. In California, the Carroll O'Connor ads declared: "Carter equals Reagan equals Hoover equals depression." Carter carried Ohio, on which he had concentrated his efforts. Despite the fact that Kennedy was clearly gaining in popularity and Carter declining, Carter had won enough delegates to ensure his nomination on the first ballot.

In retrospect, some would wonder whether Carter's persistent use of the person in the street ads, even after his nomination was assured, fueled the smoldering perception that he was "mean." "We couldn't take the chance of continuing to lose primaries against him even though mathematically he wouldn't be able to take the nomination," Rafshoon explains. "There was that drive for a so called open convention [one in which bound delegates would be unbound] . . . and these were states that were important to us in the general election." Additionally, Rafshoon notes, Kennedy was perceived as "being more negative than Carter."

I have treated Kennedy's advertising at length because it set in place themes that Reagan would polish in the general election. Additionally, by securing a majority of the Democratic votes cast in key states with a campaign that argued that Carter was incompetent, Kennedy secured a behavioral commitment on which Reagan could build. Using the folk hero of the working class as their vehicle, the "Archie Bunker" ads invited blue collar workers and members of unions to vote against Carter, a move many repeated in the general election.

In the primaries Kennedy had not argued that Carter was less competent than he but that Carter was incompetent. Unless Carter could establish in the general election that he was more competent than Reagan, that argument would yield a second vote against Carter in the general election. So it is not surprising that in the key states Kennedy won, the Republicans in the general election aired clips from Kennedy's speeches that indicted Carter's handling of the presidency. Rafshoon countered with endorsement spots by Kennedy shot not by Rafshoon but by Sawyer, Kennedy's advertising strategist, at a $35,000 to $40,000 cost to Carter. With evident bitterness, Carter's media adviser notes that he could have produced the same spots at a cost of $1500 to $2000. Some in the Carter campaign suspect that their money was used to pay off Kennedy's production debt to Sawyer, a charge Kennedy's press secretary categorically denies.

Rafshoon got little for his money. In Kennedy vs. Kennedy, the Kennedy of primaries past was more convincing. One of the Republican ads captured Kennedy in a stump speech shouting "I say it's time to say no more hostages. (cheers) No more high interest rates, no more high inflation and no more Jimmy Carter." By contrast in a tepid Democratic spot Kennedy says, "Jimmy Carter and the Democratic party are fighting for the things in this election that really matter: for the rights of working people and for health and safety on the job, for farmers, for small businesses, for middle income families, for equal rights of women, for a halt in the nuclear arms race. During the Democratic Convention I spoke about my deep belief in the ideals of the Democratic party and that is why I'm working for the re-election of President Carter." "If I had scripted an ad that said Carter has brought interest rates down and done a terrific job with the economy," says Shrum, "Kennedy would have said 'I'm not going to say that. Not only is it not true but I've said the opposite.'" But Shrum adds that the ads fulfilled the objective set for them. "What we were told by the Carter people including [pollster] Caddell was they wanted the ads to say 'Democratic Party, Democratic party, Democratic Party.'"

Rafshoon summarizes the damage Kennedy's candidacy inflicted on Carter's hopes for reelection this way: "He kept us in a political mode all the way through the convention. Carter was having to fight for his life the whole time so anything he did looked like reactive politics. . . . He also convinced the blue collar working person that Carter was not a good Democrat. When we finally went up against Reagan, the economic ills were being blamed on Carter's insensitivity. . . . Kennedy spawned the Anderson challenge.* If Carter hadn't been hit on the left so long, Anderson wouldn't have been able to run. So Kennedy and Khomeini are responsible for Ronald Reagan being president. Both of them should have to pay for it some day." As his parting shot in the battle of the advertising strategists, Shrum responds, "Carter defeated Carter."

At the Democratic Convention, Kennedy's supporters tried and failed to release delegates to vote their preference on the first ballot. Carter was nominated on the first ballot. Again he named Walter Mondale as his vice-presidential running-mate.

The great irony of the Democratic convention was that its finest address was delivered not by its party's nominee but by the person who had tried and failed to win the nomination. In his speech, more clearly than at any time in the campaign, Kennedy defined and defended the Democratic credo.

Carter's acceptance address, on August 14, paled by comparison. In one of the opening paragraphs, Carter pleaded for Kennedy's support. "I reach out to you tonight," Carter said, "and I reach out to all those who supported you in your valiant and passionate campaign. Ted, your party needs and I need you." At the end of Carter's speech, the person whose character Carter's ads had impugned throughout the primaries suggested to his supporters that he was not eager to reconcile by avoiding Carter's attempts to entrap him in the uplifted arm clasp that traditionally signals the commitment of the also rans to the candidacy of the party's nominee. "Twice Kennedy came up to the podium where the President and Vice-President stood," recalls Carter's press secretary Jody Powell. "Twice he turned aside, studiously avoiding the signal that their bitter fight had ended and the party would face the Republicans united. It looked awful, and it was."[8] The absence of that key symbolic act coupled with Carter's mauling of Hubert Humphrey's name—Hubert Horatio Hornblower Humphrey he called him—dampened the effect of Carter's speech.

In addition to establishing Carter's desire to reunify his bloodied party, the acceptance speech set down the lines of argument on which his fall campaign would pivot. Carter detailed at length what he had learned from the presidency. What he had learned presumably disqualified Reagan: It is a job with no easy questions and no easy answers, a job in which experience is the best guide, a job requiring compassion.

*John Anderson would run as a third party candidate.

Carter envisioned the election as "a stark choice between two men, two parties, two sharply different pictures of what America is and what the world is, but it's more than that—it's a choice between two futures." Later in this chapter I note that in the general election campaign as Carter particularized this theme he overstepped the bounds of acceptable campaign discourse.

Unlike Reagan, Carter argued, he was a person of "forceful but peaceful" action. "When Soviet troops invaded Afghanistan, we moved quickly to take action. I suspended some grain sales to the Soviet Union; I called for draft registration; and I joined wholeheartedly with the Congress and with the U.S. Olympic Committee and led more than 60 other nations in boycotting the big propaganda show in Russia—the Moscow Olympics. The Republican leader opposed two of these forceful but peaceful actions, and he waffled on the third."

The speech's qualified treatment of the economy pointed to a major weakness in his presidency. "[L]ast year's skyrocketing OPEC price increases have helped trigger a worldwide inflation crisis. We took forceful action, and interest rates have now fallen, the dollar is stable and, although we still have a battle on our hands, we're struggling to bring inflation under control."

The specific indictments Carter would levy against Reagan in the advertising of the general election also were forecast. Bush's charge during the Republican primary campaign that the Kemp-Roth bill, which Reagan supported, would cause greater than 30% inflation and his labeling of it as "voodoo economics" were noted. The Republicans also were charged with wanting to make Social Security voluntary, "reversing our progress on the minimum wage, full employment laws, safety in the work place, and a healthy environment."

The Republican Primaries

Ronald Reagan had tried and failed to secure the presidency in 1968 and 1976. In his first attempt to secure elective office, the California governorship, Reagan defeated incumbent California governor Pat Brown in 1966. Brown made the mistake of underrating Reagan's vote-getting appeal. One ad run on Brown's behalf included scenes from Reagan's movies and commercials. "Ronald Reagan has played many roles. This year he wants to play governor. Are you willing to pay the price of admission?" In one scene of a documentary, Brown asks a small child if she knew who killed President Lincoln. When she fails to answer he comes to her rescue by noting that it was an actor.

Reagan's victory over Brown should have set his future opponents on notice that here was a candidate who should be taken seriously. Before serving two terms as the governor of California, Reagan had starred in "B" movies, headed the Screen Actors Guild, hosted "Death Valley Days" on television, and toured the country as a spokesperson for General Electric. In the process he had refined his skills as a communicator. In fact, Reagan had burst onto the national scene with a half hour speech on behalf of the candidacy of Barry Goldwater in 1964. In addition to increasing Reagan's national visibility, the speech had raised a large amount of money. The print ad promoting the speech in the *New York Times* misspelled Reagan's name.

After narrowly losing the nomination to Ford in 1976, 1070 to 1187, Reagan delivered a gracious, moving speech thanking his supporters and whispering that he would return. "[R]ecognize," he told them, "that there are millions and millions of Americans out there that want what you want, that want it to be that way, that want it to be a shining city on the hill." With the '76 campaign over, Reagan resumed writing his nationally syndicated newspaper column and delivering weekly radio commentaries. With his one million dollars in leftover campaign funds, he organized a political action committee, Citizens for The Republic (CFTR). "Throughout 1977," writes *Washington Post* reporter Lou Cannon, "CFTR newsletters stoked the conservative fires with periodic attacks on the Panama Canal treaty, the Russians, Cuba, government 'destruction' of the work ethic and the supposed duplicity of the Carter administration. It was an insufficient platform for winning a national election, but it kept the conservative activists waiting in the wings."[9]

Just as JFK would redefine the age at which a person could be elected president, so too would Reagan, who turned 69 during the 1980 primaries. Reagan was caught by age and profession in a double bind. When he delivered speeches perfectly, his performance was dismissed as that of an actor; when he fumbled words, it was taken as a sign of incipient senility. So, for example, Haynes Johnson of the *Washington Post* juxtaposed a paragraph noting that "in the pitiless eye of the TV camera his age shows through" with one noting "There's a certain hesitance, a stumble here and there, that one doesn't recall from other Reagan campaigns. He blows his lines now and then."[10] Time was on Reagan's side in one respect. In 1980 Reagan was the beneficiary of the Aging Rights Movement that since 1977 had been hammering into the national consciousness the notion that competence was not age bound.

In a field of candidates that included Tennessee Senator Howard Baker, former Texas governor and Nixon cabinet member John Connally, Illinois member of Congress John Anderson, former member of Congress and Ambassador George Bush, Kansas Senator and former vice-presidential nominee Robert Dole, and Illinois member of Congress Philip Crane, the race narrowed rapidly to a contest among three candidates: Reagan, Bush, and Anderson. Anderson, who won no primaries, gained sufficient support in the media and the public to launch an independent bid in the general election. Reagan refused to debate the other six Republicans in Iowa. On January 21, Bush won in the Iowa caucuses. Deprived of the posture of nominee-apparent by Bush's victory, Reagan began functioning as a campaigning candidate. In Manchester, New Hampshire, on February 20, he debated the other Republicans. His pollster, Richard Wirthlin, found that Republican voters in New Hampshire perceived Reagan as the winner in that debate.

Between the balloting in Iowa and New Hampshire, three other significant events occurred. First, by heralding Reagan's sixty-ninth birthday on February 6 with parties throughout the East Coast, his advisers defied his opponents to make it an issue and in their defiance defused the age issue. In the second, Reagan demonstrated that unlike Bush he could think and act sensibly under pressure. Finally, Reagan changed advertisers and advertising.

In the New Hampshire primary, a single symbolic act dramatized the debut of Reagan's new image as candidate and the demise of Bush's presidential hopes. It occurred during what was scheduled to be a two person debate between Bush and Reagan in Nashua, New Hampshire, on February 23, the Saturday before balloting. As it turned out, Bush crumbled under pressure orchestrated by Reagan's camp.

Initially, both Reagan and Bush had seen advantages in a two person debate sponsored by a local newspaper. When the FEC ruled that newspaper sponsorship of the debate amounted to an illegal campaign contribution and when Bush refused to pay half of the debate's cost, Reagan agreed to underwrite it himself. Reagan then moved to include the other five contenders—a move that identified him both as a candidate and a unifier. When the other candidates showed up on stage, Bush froze.

As Reagan made his case for inclusion of the other candidates, the moderator ordered Reagan's mike turned off. Reagan responded, "I'm paying for this microphone, Mr. Green." The fact that the moderator's name was Breen seemed to matter little. The crowd cheered. When neither the newspaper hosting the debate nor Bush would accede to the inclusion of the others, the other candidates left the stage. Reagan's prospects had been boosted, Bush's buried. Reagan carried New Hampshire 50% to Bush's 23%.

The day of the New Hampshire primary, Reagan fired his campaign director John Sears, who was rumored to have been unable to work harmoniously with other members of Reagan's inner circle. Sears' legacy to the campaign was advertiser Elliott Curson, head of his own agency in Philadelphia. Reagan's first ads, produced by the C.T. Clyne Company of New York, placed Reagan in settings that recalled his early career as a product pitchman for soaps and shirts. In a schoolroom with children he spoke of the $75,000 their college educations would cost if inflation continued at its existing rate. Clutching a handful of heating bills he blamed the increased cost of fuel on "blackmail" by foreign countries. Although the ads closed by saying, "Only one man has the proven experience we need," they did little to detail that experience. Incubating in the ads, however, was a central theme of Reagan's campaign. In each ad, Reagan noted that this great country was not "being run" like a great country.

Unimpressed by these ads, and willing to deflect blame for the bad news from Iowa, Sears sought out Curson, whose work he had seen when the Philadelphian ran Jeffrey Bell's successful primary ad campaign against New Jersey Senator Clifford Case and his losing campaign against Democrat Bill Bradley. Since Bell was an apostle of supply side economics, Curson was an experienced proponent of Reagan's economic gospel.

In a single day Curson shot the ads that would run from New Hampshire through the remainder of the primaries. At Reagan's suggestion, radio was lifted from them. The TV ads featured Reagan talking directly into the camera. As Curson recalls, "I had a feeling that he should have very simple commercials explaining his programs himself not on film but on videotape, close-up so voters would have a chance to examine him, because all they knew was that he was a governor, an actor and a conservative."

The ads offered concise nuggets of political philosophy. "We're taxing work, savings, and investment like never before," said one. "As a result, we have less work, less savings, and less invested." Reagan then praised the economic impact of JFK's tax cut. When Kennedy's "30% federal tax cut became law, the economy did so well that every group in the country came out ahead. Even the government gained 54 million dollars in unexpected revenues." So Reagan's controversial 30% tax cut was wrapped as a tribute to the wisdom of Jack Kennedy, rather than Jack Kemp.

On March 16 on "Issues and Answers" John Laurence disputed the rate of the cut Reagan in his ad attributed to Kennedy. The actual rate of Kennedy's cut had been closer to 19% than to 30%. Reagan responded, "I honestly don't know what the rate of tax cut was" and later in the exchange, "I don't even remember reading that." These responses prompted Laurence to wonder aloud whether Reagan knew what he was saying in his ads. The observation previewed the charges that would plague Reagan throughout the early weeks of his general election campaign and throughout the press reports of his press conferences during his first two years as president.

Another ad signaled Democrats that Reagan would not sacrifice the programs on which the needy depend. "We're got to move ahead," Reagan said, "but we can't leave anyone behind."

Reagan's commitment to a strong defense was telegraphed not in specific statements such as his indictment in '76 of the Panama Canal "give-away" but in a set of premises few would dispute. After a clip of Soviet regiments marching through Red Square on May Day, Reagan observed that strength, not weakness keeps the peace. "Our foreign policy has been based on the fear of not being liked," said Reagan. "Well, it's nice to be liked. But it's more important to be respected." If viewers felt inclined to hear a commitment to the B1 bomber or the MX missile in the ad that, of course, was their prerogative. Reagan would not make the mistake Goldwater had. His ads would not try to answer Democratic arguments framed from a Democratic perspective.

Another ad highlighting Reagan's record as governor included the false claim, later embraced in the ads of the National Conservative Political Action Committee, that in California Reagan cut welfare program costs while increasing benefits "for the truly needy forty three percent." An examination of Reagan's record by the *Los Angeles Times* revealed instead that "Welfare grants were increased an average of about 12% in the first year after the reforms and 23.6% over the four-year period from 1971 to 1975—not 43% as indicated by Reagan."[12]

Unlike the earlier ads, Curson's placed Reagan in a presidential setting. Wearing a dark suit, he spoke from an office set. By showing Reagan, wrinkles and all, unsoftened by film, filters, or flattering lighting, Curson brought the Reagan of the commercials into visual congruity with the Reagan captured on the news.

Curson's ads had another major advantage. The Reagan campaign, which had pegged its plans on the presumption that it would knock out the other contenders in the early primaries, now faced Bush's win in Iowa with most of its allowable spending behind it. By providing eleven TV spots and accompanying radio lifts for a total cost of $18,000 and, additionally, by offering assurances that "those are all the ads you need," Curson was a gift from the gods.

Curson's ads had been airing for weeks when the Reagan high command decided that Curson's patron, John Sears, had to go. After Sears' fall from favor, Curson had no further contact with Reagan or his lieutenants. "I was brought in by John Sears," he notes, "and I think they viewed me as being Sears' person. Sears was on [the] outs so I guess I was on [the] outs." Curson played no role in Reagan's general election advertising.

Bush carried only four states, Massachusetts, Connecticut, Pennsylvania (where he won the popular vote but lost the majority of the delegates), Michigan, and Puerto Rico, to Reagan's twenty nine. By the time Bush had won Michigan, Reagan had come close enough to cinching the nomination to give Bush's aides pause. Bush's staff announced shortly thereafter that it was closing shop in California. An absence of money made it impossible to continue, they said. Bush withdrew before the final primaries on June 3.

Unlike Carter, Reagan survived the primaries neither bloodied nor bowed. Only in his indictment of Reagan's economic program had Bush done some damage. There he had called the package "voodoo economics" and predicted that it would spawn high inflation. But that strong language had not pervaded either his advertising or his campaign. After Pennsylvania, Bush's gloved rhetoric suggested that he was running for 1984 or for vice-president in 1980, or for both.

By comparison to Carter, who had been gored by Kennedy's central claims, Reagan had been barely scratched by Bush's attacks. As important was the fact that the states that Bush had carried were not central to Reagan's victory. Nonetheless, when negotiations over a Ford vice-presidency broke down, Reagan named Bush his running-mate, enabling those who had once chosen Bush over Reagan the chance to vote Bush again, this time over Jimmy Carter and Walter Mondale.

In his acceptance address, July 17, 1980, Reagan indicted the Democratic party for "a disintegrating economy, a weakened defense and an energy policy based on the sharing of scarcity." Embracing what had been a central theme of Ted Kennedy's candidacy, Reagan declared, "I will not stand by and watch this great country destroy itself under mediocre leadership that drifts from one crisis to the next, eroding our national will and purpose."

Reagan promised a restoration of "sanity to our economic system," including a 30% reduction in income tax over three years. He also stated that it was time to put America back to work and promised new job opportunities to make that possible.

Aware that Carter would paint him as a menace to peace, Reagan included a long paragraph establishing that his first objective was the "establishment of lasting world peace." As befits a man of peace, Reagan closed his acceptance address with a moment of silent prayer.

The Adteams

Gerald Rafshoon advised Carter in his unsuccessful run for the governorship in 1966 and in his successful race in 1970, and in both the 1976 primaries and general election. In May 1978 Rafshoon put his assets in Rafshoon Advertising of Atlanta in a blind trust when he entered the White House as a special assistant to the President. His subsequent attempts to improve Carter's presidential image prompted Doonesbury's Garry Trudeau to coin the term "Rafshoonery." In 1979 Rafshoon sold his Atlanta agency.

In September of that year, Rafshoon left the White House and returned to Rafshoon Communications, an agency he had founded in Washington in anticipation of a 1980 campaign by Carter. With the exception of the documentary created in fall 1979 but not aired until early 1980 (which was produced by Bob Squier), the ads created for Carter were Rafshoon's. Rafshoon was assisted in 1980 by Rebecca Hendrix, Greg Schneiders, and Harry Muheim, among others.

As noted earlier Reagan began the primary season with ads produced by C. T. Clyne Co. After Iowa, Reagan switched to Elliott Curson. For the general election, Peter Dailey of Dailey and Associates, Los Angeles, was asked to form an independent campaign group to handle communications. Dailey had headed the November Group in 1972 and produced Ford's advertising in the early primaries of 1976.

In 1980, Dailey's group was called "Campaign '80." Initially, its executive vice-president and general manager was to be Jack Savage, former president of Norman, Kummel and Craig, who prior to being tapped for the Reagan job had been working as a consultant to the Federal Trade Commission.

The appointment was short-lived. In early August, Savage resigned and was replaced by Richard O'Reilly, who in 1972 had headed the advisory group to the November Group and had briefly performed the same function for Dailey in 1976. Prior to joining Campaign '80, O'Reilly had headed his own consulting company, Richard T O'Reilly Inc. O'Reilly was named president of "Campaign '80." Another veteran of 1972, Phil Joanou, was appointed vice-chairman.

What differentiated Reagan's advertising effort most significantly from Carter's was the Republican's willingness to test their advertising on select markets (market testing) or on small groups of voters (focus group testing) and the practical absence of such testing by the Democrats. With the notable exception of 1960, when the Kennedy campaign relied on pollster Lou Harris to tell it what issues should be addressed in what states and where advertising should be concentrated, and in 1964 when ideology, not effects governed the Goldwater campaign, the Republicans in modern general elections have been more willing to do polling and have placed greater reliance on information obtained through polls and market and focus group tests.

The first full-scale testing of political advertising had occurred eight years earlier in 1972 in Dailey's "November Group," where alternative slogans, alternative designs for posters and concepts for ads, as well as completed ads were pretested before airing. In 1980, Dailey and pollster Richard Wirthlin brought the same philosophy to the Reagan campaign.

Consequently, when a survey of top advertising executives by *Advertising Age* concluded that Reagan's ads were "kind of dull,"[13] when journalist Bill Moyers and author Ron Powers expressed astonishment at the poor quality of Reagan's primary commercials,[14] when at cocktail parties their professional colleagues chided the adteam for their "boring, repetitious" ads[15], Reagan's media team sloughed off the criticism, confident that their message was getting through to the audience that mattered. Without the assurance and guidance provided by the research, they instead might have been steamrolled into a more "Madison Avenueish," less effective, ad campaign. When groups within the campaign pressured the adteam to create tougher, more strident anti-Carter ads, Campaign '80 could rebut them with data from tests of such ads in focus groups and in a test media market. And when a group within the campaign wrested control from Campaign '80 long enough to tape a set of ads showing Reagan bemoaning the high cost of such items as a pound of hamburger as he lifted each from his supermarket cart, tests quickly verified that the ads were poorly received. The life expectancy of those ads, that had aired for a few days in Ohio, dropped dramatically as a result. Moreover, although all in the campaign who will speak about it report that they had seen the documentary on Reagan's record more often than they would have liked, that ad stayed on the air until the research showed that its message had reached the undecided voter.

By contrast, the Democrats employed no focus group tests of their ads and conducted only small-scale market testing in Cedar Rapids, Iowa, and Roanoke, Virginia. They also gleaned what information they could about the impact of their ads from their polls. A poll can indicate the voters' attitudes at a given point in time but, without surveying a comparable control market in which the tested ads do not air, it is difficult for a pollster to determine whether ads are producing the effects the data report. Audiences' self reports of what influences them are notoriously unreliable. After the election the Democrats were surprised to learn of the extent to which the Republicans had tested their own and the Democratic ads. "We just didn't have the money to do more," explains Rafshoon's Washington office manager, Becky Hendrix.[16] The Republicans were "astonished," to repeat O'Reilly's word, at the practical absence of testing by the Democrats.[17]

Indeed, the Republicans had paid a firm to take from the air all of

Carter's ads so that they would be able to test them against their own. The Democrats engaged no comparable service.

Cost

Under the rules of the Federal Election Commission the Carter and Reagan campaigns were allotted $29,440,000 for the general election. Since Anderson was not the nominee of either of the major parties he qualified for no direct federal financing in 1980. One result was that an "Anderson difference" was the airing of too little advertising to warrant extended treatment in this chapter. The Federal Election Commission did rule, however, that if Anderson secured 5% or more of the November vote he would be eligible for campaign funds on a retroactive basis. Anderson borrowed money from people who believed he would meet that percent. With 6.6% of the vote, he exceeded the FEC's threshold.

The 1980 campaign's increase in federal funding and in the spending cap on the primaries had not kept pace with inflation. In 1976, candidates were permitted to spend $13,092,000 in the prenomination period. In 1980 that amount had increased to $17,664,000. By contrast, as Adam Clymer documented in the *New York Times,* "In 1976, a 60-second political spot on a top-rated, prime-time television program in Boston cost $4,800. This year [1980] it costs $7,400. A one-page campaign flier then cost 3.8 cents. Now it costs 6.2 cents. A pollster's in-person interview that cost $8 now costs $16."[18]

Hoping to destroy Reagan's credibility and establish Carter's early in the general election, the Democrats concentrated their spending in the first two-thirds of the general election. By mid-October Carter had spent nearly $24 million of his allotted $29.4. By mid-October Reagan had spent less than $17 million of his total funds. Reagan's advisers had learned the lesson of the primaries, where heavy early spending meant that they rubbed up against the ceiling long before Bush did and as a result were forced to curtail advertising in the last set of contested primaries. Fortunately for Reagan, Bush's inability to raise money—even though he had not yet approached the spending ceiling—meant that he dropped out before the final primaries on June 3. Had Bush been able to secure the money to stay in the race, he would have been able to monopolize the airwaves, for Reagan could no longer legally spend as much as Bush. That lesson played a role in the Republican's decision to conserve money for a last minute blitz of the airwaves. The Republican campaign spent nearly $6 million on media in the last ten days of the campaign. Consequently, at the time at which Carter most needed advertising, to counter the effect of the daily stories of the anniversary of the taking of the hostages, Reagan was able to outspend him two and a half to one on the networks. Carter's media director, time buyer Beverly Ingram notes, however, that Carter was able to match Reagan in spot market buying in the final weeks.[19]

Campaign Themes

If one may venture to take a moment to comment, with the benefit of hindsight, on the unspoken dynamics of the 1980 campaign, it is important to remember that Jimmy Carter had come to Washington four years earlier proud of the fact that he was, and would continue to be—at least by Washington's standards—an "outsider." During his four years in office, Carter was remarkably true to his word, so much so that during his first term he may well not have made enough new friends among political insiders who would be seriously enough committed to his reelection to make a difference. Could such a president, who was unsuccessful by choice in his relationships with the two most important opinion-making elements in the country—the politicians, including senators, members of congress, governors, and mayors, and the press—ever be able to reach the public with his message? It was certainly a hard task Jimmy Carter set out for himself.

Looking back on the campaign, one may also wonder if Ronald Reagan's campaign staff did not identify Carter's problem early on and design their strategy to take advantage of it. Repeatedly in the campaign, and then, to be sure no one missed it, in the closing statement of the debate, Reagan said to the American public: "Ask yourself, are you better off now than you were four years ago?" Of course the question did have a certain validity independent of political overtones but what Reagan may also have been asking the American public to consider was the fact that so few people in the press or in influential political positions seemed to have a good word for the Carter presidency. Certainly suggestive of the fact that Reagan understood and did not wish to reproduce the Carter policy in this regard is the fact that as one of his first acts as president-elect Ronald Reagan, who also campaigned against big government and the Washington bureaucracy, made it his business to make an early and highly visible courtesy call on Congress.

The Democratic Strategy

In the general election Reagan was not vulnerable, as Kennedy had been, to assaults on his personal character. Still Carter had to make Reagan the issue for, if he did not, the nation's attention would focus on the hostages, still captive in Iran, the Soviets, still fighting in Afghanistan, and the economy, still not in as good shape as it had been when Ford transmitted it to Carter. Carter attempted to do to Reagan what Johnson had done to Goldwater—make him appear unsafe. Conversely, given the ongoing economic problems and the ongoing crises in Afghanistan and Iran, if Reagan could simply establish that he was a safe alternative to Carter, he would appear the better alternative, for the public was clearly dissatisfied with the status quo. In the process of making his case against Reagan, Carter made the mistake of sacrificing the advantage his own "character" had given him against Kennedy.

By contrast, Reagan's willingness to debate Anderson, his masterful treatment of Carter in their one debate, and his advertising, whose genius was its calculated dullness undercut Carter's ability to make Reagan appear unsafe. Throughout the campaign, Reagan played gentleman although not scholar. The dirty work of attacking Carter was done only gently in Reagan's ads. Strong anti-Carter ads did air but when they did they were disassociated from Reagan and did not count against his spending ceiling. These ads were generated by independent political action committees, permitted because of a loophole in the election law. Most important, Reagan did not seek, as Goldwater had, to win ideological battles. His advertising, his demeanor, his response to challenge were all designed to lead to one goal: victory at the polls.

Contrasting Definitions of the Presidency

In 1980 Reagan and Carter engaged in a struggle to define each other out of the presidency. Reagan's campaign argued that a president must preserve the American dream and create for the electorate a confidence that they are better off under his leadership than they were before. In Reagan's judgment, he will succeed at both and Carter has failed. Carter defined the president as one who must be stable, well-informed, intelligent, and vigorous, a circle within which he placed himself and from which he attempted to exclude Reagan.

In a memo dated July 3, 1980, Rafshoon outlined a general election media plan predicated on the assumption that "The public is now convinced that Jimmy Carter is an inept man. He has tried hard but he has failed. He is weak and indecisive—in over his head. *We have to change peoples' minds.*"

The Democratic gameplan called for two or three weeks of positive spots beginning near Labor Day, followed by spots underscoring Reagan's shortcomings. Not explicit in the plan but understood by the campaign was that the ads would close on a positive note in the final weeks of the campaign.

The Republicans predicted loudly after their convention that Carter would run an attack campaign against Reagan because they claimed he could not stand on his record and win. Like their well-publicized prediction of an unspecified "October Surprise," this claim created public expectations with which the Democrats had to deal. The Democrats defied that expectation by airing a first wave of positive spots. "We didn't start the negative material right away because we were battling the impression that we were going to run an exclusively negative campaign," recalls Rafshoon's lieutenant Greg Schneiders. "It was assumed that the President would not run on his record but would focus on the vulnerabilities of Ronald Reagan. We showed the positive ads to the press and quite honestly assured them that there were no negative spots in production."[20]

The first phase of advertising was designed to make two points. First, it told voters "We know you think Carter has not done much as President. But give us your attention—and an open mind—for a few minutes and we think you may be surprised by what you learn." These spots will have to be long, said the memo, "(probably five minutes) and packed with hard and surprising facts." Second, the opening phase would offer the "positive message" that "CARTER IS SMARTER THAN REAGAN. The President is a man who grasps what is going on. We must show Carter as a man who comprehends the facts."

In the primaries, Carter's ads had argued that his three prime functions were being a good father, a good husband, and a good president. In the general election, his functional definition of the presidency shifted from character toward competence. The Democrats believed that Reagan had not reached the threshold of acceptability as president required to secure the office. Additionally, as Rafshoon's deputy Greg Schneiders noted, they felt that the press's focus on confrontation and failure had obscured Carter's successes. Accordingly, the first wave of spots "showed President Carter doing the sorts of things that a president does that do not involve confrontation or failure." At the same time these ads identified intelligence, a command of information, stamina, and stability as defining elements of the presidency. These were attributes the public believed Carter but not necessarily Reagan possessed. What the ads failed to show was what Carter's intelligence, information, stamina, and stability had done to make the country or the world a better, safer, more economically secure place to be in 1980 than it was in 1976. In short, Carter's ads failed to provide a clear, cogent answer to the central question Reagan successfully framed for the electorate.

The opening Democratic spots of the general election defined four key responsibilities for the president, being chief of state, commander in chief, planner of the nation's future, and educator. To each of the first three Rafshoon devoted five minute spots ads that began to air in early September.

In this first wave, chief of state Carter is shown meeting with foreign leaders and shepherding the Camp David accords, which produced a settlement between Egypt and Israel. In the encomium to Carter as commander in chief, he is shown reviewing the troops. His background at Annapolis is praised.

In the universe projected by the ads, a president must be knowledgeable—an indirect jab at Reagan who couldn't seem to get his facts straight in either the primaries or the general election.

The ads also imply that unlike Reagan, Carter has the stamina to conduct the presidency.

In addition to showing the president in authoritative roles, the first wave of ads also featured Carter speaking with groups of housewives, workers, and older persons. These spots were shot on location rather than in the White House. They had the advantage of reminding voters that Carter had initiated town meetings and had conducted an open presidency. "They reinforced Carter's strong suit," says Schneiders, "his honesty, his compassion, and his identification with the people." They had the disadvantage of diminishing his status as incumbent.

In my judgment, this set of spots is poorly produced. A plane is heard overhead in a spot shot in the backyard of an Arlington, Virginia, home where Carter is talking with a group of housewives. The differing amounts of background noise picked up by Carter's mike and the single mike capturing the women's questions and comments draws attention to each edit. The setting itself lacks credibility. The women dressed in their Sunday best are seated on folding chairs. It is difficult to believe that the president of the United States has simply dropped by to chat. If the tasks of the Oval Office are as taxing as the commander-in-chief, chief of state spots suggest, the flow of information so constant and pressing, why is Carter standing in a backyard explaining the intricacies of inflation and interest rates to a handful of people? If these spots embody his role as educator, that task might be more efficiently accomplished with larger groups in a town meeting or in the White House where Ford was shown meeting with groups in the closing ads of the 1976 campaign.

In the spot in Arlington, Carter argues that his first term has prepared him for a better second term. "I think I'll be a better president in the next four years just continuing what we're doing." "The theme we were developing throughout," explains Schneiders, "when he said 'he'd be a better president' was a roundabout *mea culpa*. It was probably as close as we would get Jimmy Carter to a *mea culpa* too. We wanted him to be seen saying 'I recognize that we've had some problems in this first term. This is natural in any new president who is learning. As a result of this learning I expect to be a better president.' " The disadvantage of this admission was that it was too roundabout to enable forgiveness but yet invited voters to recall that they had elected the Washington outsider on the promise that Carter's background as a farmer, engineer, businessman, and "nuclear physicist" adequately prepared him for the White House.

When the Republicans tested the first wave of Carter ads in focus groups they found that "the Carter commercials appear to be quite ineffective. Elements of them reinforce his weaknesses even while they are trying to portray his strengths. The negative feelings about him are so strong among the uncommitted that when panelists viewed one of his commercials in a forced viewing situation, they tended to tune out the accomplishments portrayed by the commercials." The general response to the ads, according to O'Reilly, was "Well, so what. A president is supposed to work long and hard. He's supposed to be a leader. Why doesn't he do something."

Attack Reagan

In the second phase of their advertising, the Democrats moved onto the attack. Rafshoon's July memo forecast the areas of contrast this way:

CARTER	REAGAN
Safe/sound	Untested
Young	Old
Vigorous	Old
Smart	Dumb
Comprehensive mind	Simplistic
Engineer	Actor
Experienced president	Naive/inexperienced
Compassionate	Republican
Moderate	Right/wing

Ads shot in the Oval Office (at an angle that inexplicably makes it appear to be a den) focus on the president's desk and empty chair, as an announcer reads a script that simultaneously crawls up the screen. Each of these ads opens with the question: "When you come right down to it, what kind of a person should occupy the Oval Office? Should it be a person who, like Ronald Reagan, who . . ." Each closes with the needless enjoinder "Figure it out for yourself."

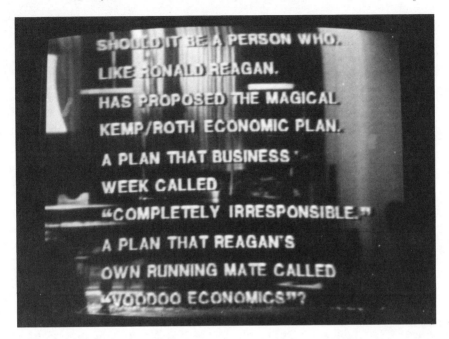

Still photo drawn from anti-Reagan spot ad produced by Gerald Rafshoon and aired during the general election campaign of 1980.

The bodies of these ads juxtapose Reagan's proposals with Carter's achievements. Bush's indictment of Reagan's economic program as "voodoo economics" is recalled in one. Another listed instances in which Reagan had recommended the use of military force, including his statement that a destroyer should be sent to Equador to deal with a "fishing controversy."

This second set of ads also, inadvertently, creates a contradiction, although few voters were likely to catch it. The message of the first wave was that Carter was a president who worked "night and day." But where the first wave showed him climbing the stairs to the Oval Office and a light appearing in its window at night, the second set shows the office empty, with the light burning. After the election, Bob Squier, who had spent three days in the White House filming Carter's documentary, revealed that the second set of ads was more accurate than the first. "All of that stuff about his walking back to the Oval Office to work till 9:00, which Ronald Reagan couldn't do, is nonsense," said Squier. "He left at 4:30 every day."[21]

As another part of the attack-Reagan phase, the Carter campaign ran a series of ads about Reagan's governorship of California. By comparing

Reagan's claims about what he had accomplished as governor with their own facts about his governorship, one ad in this series attempts to do to Reagan what in the closing days of 1976 Ford had done to Carter. But where Ford's ads had, in effect, argued that Carter was lying about having reduced the size of Georgia's government and cut its number of state employees, Carter's ad merely notes omissions in what Reagan was revealing. Carter aide Dick O'Reilly observes that the facts in the Carter ad attacking Reagan and the facts in Reagan's own ads about his governorship are both essentially correct.

With a picture of the California seal on screen, the Democratic ad said "When Ronald Reagan speaks of the good old days when he was governor of California, there are some things he does not mention. For example, he increased state spending by 120%; he brought three tax increases to the state; he added 34,000 employees to the state payroll. The Reagan campaign is reluctant to acknowledge the accuracy of these facts today but can we trust the nation's future to a man who refuses to remember his own past?"

Finally, in this second wave, people from California speak out for Carter, as individuals from Georgia had in 1976 for Ford. So again Carter did unto Reagan what Ford had done unto him. In 1980, for reasons I will note in a moment, the attack from the home state was less effective than it had been in 1976.

The Carter personal witness spots that aired in phase two of the Democratic campaign depicted Reagan as dangerous and lacking in compassion. The difficulty in getting this perception to take hold with the voters is commented on by Schneiders. "Reagan is superb at not looking like what his record indicates that he may be." In his debate with Anderson, September 21, and his subsequent debate with Carter, October 28, Reagan sounded caring and looked calm. Additionally, his willingness to include the other Republican candidates in the debate at Nashua, New Hampshire, his willingness to debate Anderson, and his willingness to debate Carter suggested that his was the politics of inclusion, not, as Carter charged, the exclusionary politics of the ultra-right.

Moreover, his willingness to defend his views in the supposedly adversarial format of the debates suggested that he had confidence in their defensibility and, if he appeared to hold his own in the exchanges, as he did, that these views in fact were defensible. He simply did not fit the image sculpted by the Democratic ads. Since the debates of the general election were confrontational, held on neutral ground, and sponsored by disinterested third parties, the impression candidates created during them was highly credible. The credibility of Reagan's image was enhanced by the consistency between it and the sense of Reagan conveyed in his own ads, in which he played a central role, and in his election eve speech, in which he tried on the presidency.

After the election, a producer in Hollywood told Rafshoon that he should have known better than to try to portray Reagan as dangerous and insensitive. "Let me tell you something," said the producer. "Ronald Reagan is not a good actor. I've known him for years and he's not a good actor. But he played in 59 movies and in all but one he played the same role and that was of a sincere guy. Now, as I say, he is not a great actor but he knows how to play sincere people. And you should have known better. If you play sincere people in 59 roles, it's got to rub off."

The person-in-the-street ads underscoring the danger of a Reagan presidency attempt to ally Reagan's widely reported misstatements of fact with the idea, argued in the second wave of spots, that he is dangerous:

> "It certainly is risky."
> "I think it's very risky."
> "I just don't think he's well enough informed."
> "It's different I guess being governor than being president. There's no foreign policy when you're governor."
>
> ANNOUNCER: One of the most important questions the people ask about a potential president is how he would respond in a time of great turmoil.
>
> "I think Governor Reagan in a crisis situation would be very fast to use military force."
>
> "I think Reagan might cause us an international incident. He's very strong willed it seems to me. He states his points like the old Western movies: you know. Go out and shoot 'em dead type attitude and I think that could really get us into a lot of trouble."
>
> "To lead this country today you've really got to you've gotta have your wits totally about you."
>
> "We really have to keep our heads cool and I don't think that ah Reagan is cool."
>
> "Reagan doesn't stop to think of things before he does it."
>
> "That scares me about Ronald Reagan. It really does."
>
> "My decision is made. I'm going to stick with President Carter. . . ."

Early in the fall campaign Reagan's repeated misstatements of facts had fueled public fears that were being fanned by this ad. In mid-September an ABC-Harris poll reported 82% agreeing that Reagan makes too many remarks requiring explanations or apologies. But in the debate with Carter, Reagan demonstrated that he was "cool," had his wits about him, and was "informed." His repeated assertions that he stood for peace complemented his non verbal messages to suggest that he was not "risky."

The Carter campaign moved quickly to counter that impression by airing an ad demonstrating that Reagan had lied in the debate when he denied ever saying that "nonproliferation of the control of nuclear weapons is none of our business." Pirating news footage from ABC, Rafshoon assembled an ad that adjoined Carter's charge, Reagan's denial, and a clip of Reagan making the denied statement in a speech in January. Two barriers blocked the Carter campaign's ability to drive its point home. First, when Carter is shown saying "Ronald Reagan has made the disturbing comment that nonproliferation of the control of nuclear weapons is none of our business," Carter has not quoted Reagan precisely and, to add to his problems, is himself hard to follow. Had he omitted "of the control" to say "nonproliferation of nuclear weapons is none of our business" or, better still, dropped the double negative and said "proliferation of nuclear weapons is none of our business," his meaning would have been clear. When the ad shows Reagan saying "I have never made the statement he suggested about nuclear proliferation," those viewers, of whom, one suspects, there were many, who were unable to untangle Carter's claim, will agree that clear-spoken Reagan probably did not say what Carter says he said. If the ad could then cut to Reagan saying "nonproliferation of the control of nuclear weapons is none of our business," Carter's claim that Reagan had lied would still be home free, regardless of whether the audience knew what that meant. Instead, the clip shows Reagan saying "I just don't think it's any of our business. Unilaterally the United States seems to be the only nation on earth . . ." Since the clip seems to both open and close mid sentence, raising the suspicion that it has been sundered from its context, since it does not indicate what is "none of our business," since it fails to mention nonproliferation, control, or nuclear weapons, and since it is phrased in the standard straightforward simple Reagan style bearing no resemblance to Carter's stylistically dense rephrasing of it, the ad is readily dismissed as another instance of what Reagan in the debate good-naturedly characterized as "There you go again . . ." Carter's claim was correct. But the ad simply couldn't prove it. The final flaw in the ad is strategic. By asking "Which Ronald Reagan should we believe?" the ad impugned Reagan's honesty when it should have dramatized the risk in the position Reagan had espoused in January.

Again and again, as Johnson had so successfully done in his campaign against Goldwater, Carter attempted to polarize Reagan's position on the issues. In a radio speech delivered in mid-October, Carter charged that Reagan wanted to abandon SALT for an all-out nuclear race to "frighten the Soviets into negotiating a new agreement based on American nuclear superiority." Reagan avoided the temptation to answer the argument, and instead responded with reassurances that he favored negotiation and reducing nuclear arsenals. Then he contextualized Carter's claims by saying "My own views have been distorted in an effort to scare people through innuendos and misstatements of my positions. Possibly Mr. Carter is gambling that his long litany of fear will influence enough voters to save him from the inevitable consequences of his policies, which have brought so much human misery."

In a moment of self-destructive honesty uncharacteristic of political advertising, one of the Carter ads defensively concedes the very point the Reagan campaign had been making with its five minute documentary on Reagan's two terms as governor. In the Carter ad the announcer says "A lot of Californians feel pretty good about Ronald Reagan but others feel a sense of continuing concern." By contrast to the 1976 Carter ads, in which Carter himself was shown extolling his past achievements as governor of Georgia, the Reagan documentary was offering more credible testimony about Reagan's gubernatorial accomplishments in the form of specific praise from unexpected sources, such as a major labor leader in the state and an editorial in a San Francisco paper. In short, "a lot of Californians feel pretty good about Ronald Reagan" reminded viewers of something Reagan's people had been telling them.

Finally, these person-in-the-street ads suffer from a creative flaw. The line drawing of Carter that closes each is created by a rapid explosion of dots and lines, creating the impression that the president is being attacked by a particularly virulent strain of smallpox!

Republican tests of Carter's person-in-the-street ads revealed that they had, in O'Reilly's words, "no believability." Persons in focus groups said "You can get people to say anything." Some thought " 'these must be paid actors,' which we knew" O'Reilly adds, "they were not."

Still Reagan's pollsters found that through October the " 'dangerous' label," a label reinforced by these ads, "adhered to Ronald Reagan." This is consistent with what the Democrats were finding. "Until the debate," says Rafshoon, "we had come up to pretty well even. The anti-Reagan stuff was working. The man on the street [ads] were working. We were running [first phase ads also] and were coming up."

But in the process of tying "dangerous" around Reagan's neck, Carter had blundered. Convinced that the message carried by such surrogates as Mondale was not making its way into the nation's headlines, in his opening trip to California in the general election Carter noted that the election would decide "whether we have war or peace." That attack marked the beginning of public erosion of the one electoral asset that could have carried Carter to the White House despite the general perception that Carter was incompetent. "It was almost as if the campaign decided to pick the president up and bash Ronald Reagan with him," says Squier. "More of that could have been done with paid media and surrogates. That might have saved some of the warm feeling people had for Carter."[22] Until Carter's Manichaean attack on Reagan the public had conceived the incumbent president as a decent, fair, honorable, religious man of goodwill. "In time," wrote journalists Jules Witcover and Jack Germond, " 'the war-and-peace issue' led to what came to be called 'the meanness issue'—to the very great detriment of the President's reelection prospects."[23]

On October 6 at a fund raiser in Chicago, Carter magnified the perception that he was mean-spirited by noting that his loss of the election would mean "Americans might be separated, Black from White, Jew from Christian, North from South, rural from urban." "When Carter started doing these things [attacking Reagan] personally and, I guess, overspoke himself, [the perception that he was mean] started hurting," says Rafshoon. Carter had fulfilled a prophecy Rafshoon had made in his memo of July 3. The memo noted that "People would feel more comfortable if they could get their thoughts and perceptions about Jimmy Carter straight. Either: 'Yes, he is a good man *and* a good President,' or 'He's a lousy President and he's not a particularly nice man either. He tricked us.' " But where Rafshoon had planned, through advertising, to "make it easy for people to change their minds about the competence issue," Carter's strident attacks made it easy for people to change their minds about Carter's fundamental decency and fairness. The change was facilitated by a dormant backlog of supportive information: Carter's claim that he would whip Kennedy's ass, his ads questioning Kennedy's character, his seemingly callous forecasting on the morning of the Wisconsin primary of the good news that the hostages would be transferred to the control of the Iranian government, a possibility that subsequently failed to materialize. "The President's overblown attack rhetoric stuck him with the tag, 'dirty campaigner,' for the remainder of the election," Reagan's pollsters found. "As a result, the President lost credibility. . . . By election day, Ronald Reagan was viewed as more 'presidential' than the President."[24]

Testimonials for Carter

The third wave of Carter ads was positive. In this wave Henry Fonda and Mary Tyler Moore, a farmer, a working woman, a steelworker, and an Hispanic among others, and Democratic governors and other party influentials, including Edward Kennedy, explained why they were supporting Carter. Against lush farm scenery that exuded prosperity, a farmer noted that we had produced more grain in the last four years than "we have in history" and concluded that "I can't help but be optimistic about the next four years." The farmer also defended the grain embargo on the grounds that "it was a very cheap price to pay for freedom" and that "we didn't get into a war over it."

In another ad from this wave a worker in a tire plant praises Carter for bailing Chrysler out. "That wasn't a move to save big business," he says. "That was a move to save jobs. But it also saved a lot of undue hardship to families especially. That in itself clues me into the fact that he is concerned." The worker concludes: "The president has done more for labor in this country than any president since Roosevelt. That's a matter of record." In another ad a steelworker states that he thinks "that the president is more aware of the problems that the workingman faces than either Reagan or Anderson." Ads featuring Hispanics and working women make comparable claims.

In an ad addressed specifically to women "but men are more than welcome to listen, too" actress Mary Tyler Moore reminded viewers that Carter has "appointed more women to high level jobs than any president in history. He's been consistently in favor of any legislation that would give women equal rights." The not so subtle reminder that Reagan opposed the Equal Rights Amendment is an attempt to widen what later would come to be called the gender gap.

Additionally, governors William Winter, Bob Graham, and Dick Riley appealed to regional Southern pride and testified that Carter had been good for their states.

Appeals to Southern Pride

Since by losing his Southern base in 1980, Carter lost all chance of winning the election, let's turn for a moment to analyze an eloquent, positive ad seen only in the South. The ad capsulized the themes of the Southern ads of 1976. Its genius lay in the way in which it communicated Carter's most notable achievement—the Camp David Accords—through a Southern optic.

The five minute ad shows Carter delivering a speech to a large audience in Tuscumbia, Alabama, a location Reagan would misidentify as the birthplace of the Ku Klux Klan. In the speech he recalls that "Two years ago I was at Camp David with President Sadat and Prime Minister Begin. After several days of hard negotiating there was a deadlock. We weren't getting anywhere. So I said, 'Let's take a day off.' And I took them across the border, the Maryland-Pennsylvania border, to Gettysburg. I wanted to show these two men that we Americans know something about war and we know about neighbors fighting against neighbors. The three of us walked through the valleys and hills where more than forty thousand young Americans fell in battle. As we looked across the fields, standing on the same place where General Robert E. Lee stood, I remembered that in all of our nation's wars, every war, young men from the South have led the rolls of volunteers and also led the rolls of casualties. We Southerners believe in the nobility of courage on the battlefield and because we understand the cost of war, we also believe in the nobility of peace." As Carter recounts this odyssey, Rafshoon pans the battlefields of Gettysburg, pausing intermittently on the statues that define its meaning. The ad is a commentary on the futility of war. By underplaying Carter's Camp David accomplishment, and putting it roots in the Southern experience, the ad invites the audience to compensate for the ad's modesty, forging a powerful identification with the people of his region. They are ennobled by his deed. At the same time the ad demonstrates Carter's sensitivity and humanity in a way ads shouting "Husband. Father. President" or "Carter: Peacemaker" could not, and the radio ad in which Carter declared "You people here have the same background, the same families, the same upbringing that I have" did not. In my judgment, had the nation been shown this Carter response to the Gettysburg battlefield as the charge of "meanness" was building, the charge might have been blunted.

But what the television ad giveth, the radio ad taketh away. The image nurtured in the television ad is contradicted by the arrogance that comes through in a radio ad in which Carter agrees to share his heritage with the South. "You share my past and my values, yes," says Carter. "And I pray to God that we in the South, and the people of this nation, will never get away from those values which do not change. But you also share my love of this country. It was you who put me on the road to the greatest honor that any American can possibly have—to serve as your President." In reality, it is not *his* past, *his* values, and *his* love of this country that the South shares. He and they share a common past, common values, and a common love of country. Carter, not the people, is at the center of this speech. Even the credit he gives them for his election is miserly. "You put me on the road," he says.

If, as Rafshoon believes, Carter lost his Southern base in 1980 because he had proven more liberal than white Southerners had expected him to be, then no appeals to Southern values could have saved him. Advertising, whether brilliant or banal, is powerless to dislodge deeply held convictions anchored in an ample amount of credible information.

Appeals to Blacks

Carter's strongest, most effective radio ads were those addressing blacks, the one group in the Democratic coalition that remained loyal to him in 1980. In one, the Reverend Jesse Jackson is heard saying "Jobs are important. But in slavery, everybody had a job. But we had no justice, no protection under the law, no housing, no health care, no right to public education. When Reagan speaks of the good ol' days, he is serious. Reagan made 3,709 appointments in his first term as governor, nine were Blacks." In another radio ad Jackson declares: "When Reagan went to Philadelphia, Mississippi, where three civil rights workers had been killed, he gave a speech for state's rights. State's rights really means the opposite of civil rights. It is consistent with Reagan's statements against minimum wage, against food stamps, against CETA, his nonsupport of women—he is insensitive."

Edward Kennedy's strongest endorsement of Carter also comes in the ad aired on black radio. "President Carter has appointed blacks to senior government positions in the Cabinet, in every agency, and on the White House staff" said Kennedy. "In the areas of education, civil rights, economic justice, there's a clear choice for black America between Jimmy Carter and Ronald Reagan." But, with Carter paying the bill, the ad also underscores *Kennedy's* claim to black loyalty should he again seek the presidency. "As Chairman of the Senate Judiciary Committee, I've worked with President Carter to achieve a federal judiciary that represents the diversity of our people. The number of black federal judges has nearly doubled in the last four years."

Election Eve

In an election eve telecast that, unlike the Republican's national broadcast of Reagan's election eve speech, was run only in key states, the Democrats strongly appealed to Democrats to vote for their party and its nominee. Henry Fonda narrated the program, which consisted of statements by Fonda, one of Sawyer's spots of Kennedy endorsing Carter, the convention film, and a closing speech by Carter.

Fonda set the context for the appeals to party by noting that "every four years" the Republicans "suddenly become the friends of working people and the friends of old people and the friends of poor people. They need the votes."

The film, aired originally at the convention, displayed such party notables as Tip O'Neill verifying that Carter had worked effectively with Congress and that Carter had done what the country needed even when such action was unpopular. After a recapitulation of some of the ridicule to which such presidents as Lincoln had been subjected, the announcer notes that "no president has been entirely beloved in his own time. Putting them [presidents] down is one of the favorite pastimes of American politics."

By the standards he set in his presidency, Carter's closing speech is well delivered. But where Reagan's speech is a classic exercise in the rhetoric of the presidency, the speech of the incumbent president is bothersome both in what it says and in what it does not say.

The speech's opening attempts to establish common ground, but is sabotaged by Carter's presumption that it is he who has the right to judge whether or not the political system is working. What he says is that "In this long campaign I've talked to many people in many states and I've listened too and it's particularly pleasing to me as I fly South to vote tomorrow to know that the American political system set up so long ago in our Constitution is working. You've listened. You've agreed or disagreed. You've thought about how you should cast your vote and through all of this it has become quite clear that the people of this country really care about the future of this country."

The speech then reintroduces the suggestion that Carter's second term will be more successful than his first. However, Carter's reference to an improved second term presumes that he will be given this second term, thus tempting the viewer to think: "Wait. I still have a voice in that." Carter goes on: "Over the last four years I've had a great experience and I've gained experience too. I've grown and I've learned for the presidency is a great teacher. Because I've learned I'll be even a better president in my second term." The word "even" muffles Carter's faint *mea culpa,* under an assumption the audience may be unwilling to grant.

The speech winds down with a peroration that is Carter at his worst. In the first wave of advertising, Carter's ads had argued that a prime function of the president was that of educator. Here Carter, the educator, delivers a schoolmarmish civics lecture that assumes a patronizing "I-you" relationship with its audience. Consistent with this posture, the simplified syntactic structure of the sentences and the diluted vocabulary beckon an audience of schoolchildren. Carter said:

> A few hours from now the sun will rise up out of the Atlantic to shine on the state of Maine. In coastal towns and mountain villages and bustling cities, people will get up to go to work and sometime during the day to vote. As the light of day moves West, millions more of you all across the land will get up to go to work and to vote. Eighteen hours after the polls open in Maine, they'll close in Hawaii and Alaska and the job will be done. You the people will have spoken and in America what the people say goes.

It's terribly important for you to participate in this great national decision tomorrow. Our whole country, our whole future will actually go in the direction that you steer it. If you don't vote you give your voice to someone else, perhaps to those with whom you completely disagree about the future. So tomorrow, wherever you are, vote, participate, make your voice heard.

Finally, it is difficult to divine precisely what Carter is trying to say in the final sentences of the speech. "There's much to do." he said. "We've just begun and we will go on (pause) searching to fulfill the vision, working for ourselves but also reaching out hopefully and helpfully to the other 4 billion people who are riding on this planet with us. In the words of Franklin D. Roosevelt, 'Let us move forward with a strong and active faith.' Thank-you and God Bless You and good night."

Rafshoon's Washington Office manager Becky Hendrix notes that the speech was not shot in the Oval Office but was instead taped in a motel room in Cleveland at 5 A.M. the morning after the Reagan-Carter debate. "That was the only time we could get on the schedule," she says. "We had to get curtains and all the props and lighting to match the Oval Office. It was the morning after the disastrous debate and everybody was in the most foul mood and it was awful. I guess we matched it pretty well."[25] Carter had reviewed the speech before delivering it and had made some changes. On an hour's sleep, Hendrix typed the speech into the TelePrompTer. Carter delivered his election eve speech in a single take.

The RNC and NRCC

In 1974 the Republicans vowed to rise from the ashes of Watergate. A poll by Market Opinion Research found that when asked what came to mind when "Republican" was mentioned, people said Nixon and Hoover. The poll also revealed that when a Republican faced a Democrat in a congressional race with the electorate knowing nothing about either, the Democrat started with a fifteen point advantage.

In 1978 the Republicans spent two million dollars airing a series of five minute ads to try to repair the image of their party. The televised ads featuring Republican members of Congress appeared on 57 stations in 18 markets. The ads were not highly partisan. In one, for example, Congressperson Ralph Regula offered tips on how to save money on vacation travel by making use of Amtrak passes and by buying plane tickets early. Viewers were urged to write in for a free pocket atlas. These tips, said Regula, were brought to the public by "147 men and women working to improve the government and the quality of life for the people of this nation. On behalf of all the Republicans in Congress," said Regula at the ad's close, "drive safely and have a great vacation." Approximately 35,000 people requested a free atlas. A subsequent survey concluded that the ads had indeed improved the image of the Republican party but to the Republicans' dismay the ads had also polished the image of everybody in Congress, Democrat and Republican alike.

In 1979 a poll jointly commissioned by the Republican National Committee (RNC) and the National Republican Congressional Committee (NRCC) found that, for the first time since 1974, respondents were ready to admit that Republicans had some good ideas and could be trusted to manage the country. The poll also revealed that 80% thought that the country was headed in the wrong direction. Inflation, lack of an energy policy, wasteful government spending, and taxes were among the areas of dissatisfaction identified by the poll. Congress was viewed as a cause of the problems. Additionally, the Republicans learned, the electorate was unaware that the Democrats had controlled Congress for the past 25 years. A three-wave ad campaign was created to drive that fact into the public consciousness.

Wave one began February 1, 1980. In this wave an actor who looked like Democratic House Leader Tip O'Neill is seen driving down the road, as a young aide at his side warns him that they are running out of gas. Because the O'Neill look-alike ignores the warning, the car runs out of gas in the middle of nowhere. "The Democrats are out of gas. We need some new ideas. Vote Republican for a Change" advised the ad.

A second ad chronicles the aging of five-year old Mike from the time the Democrats took control of Congress to the present, to dramatize the large increases in governmental spending and taxes that have occurred over the twenty-five years the Democrats had control of Congress. A third identifies Democrats as million-dollar-a-minute spenders.

Another ad foreshadows one of Reagan's central attacks on Carter. "Here are some hard facts about the U.S. and Russia" it says. "The Soviets are outproducing us in missiles, outproducing us in warships, in tanks, combat planes, helicopters, attack subs. They're growing stronger than we are because the Democrats who controlled Congress voted down defense program after defense program defeating all Republican opposition. But it's not too late to make America strong again." All of the ads close with an appeal to "Vote Republican for a Change."

The second phase of ads began airing in April. Here the Republicans pin inflation on the Democrats. In one of the two ads in this wave a truck driver learns that if inflation continues at the current rate, he will soon have to double his paycheck just to maintain the standard of living he now enjoys.

The final wave of spots tied unemployment and inflation to the Democrats. In one an older woman thinks aloud as she walks through a supermarket: "Some of my friends just can't live with the inflation. My son and his family. It's so hard for them. Why doesn't somebody in Washington do something about prices?" Since the woman is seen wandering about the store without a cart while picking up items, the spot had to be reshot. In the first version, recalls NRCC's media director Ed Blakely, she appears to be shoplifting![26]

In a second ad an unemployed Baltimore worker tours his closed factory. "I used to work here," he says. The ad asks, if Democrats are so good for working people how come so many people are out of work? When the ad's star obtained employment shortly before the ad was to be taped, the script was rewritten to accommodate that fact.*

These professionally produced ads gave the voters a reason to vote Republican and at the same time tried out key themes that would be used against Carter in the fall. "I was delighted when I saw the NRCC and RNC ads," noted O'Reilly. "They did part of what might have been our job and did it so well that we said 'Let's not do it.' "[27]

In September 1980, the NRCC and RNC projected that they would spend eight million dollars on spots in 1980.[28] According to Blakely, they finally spent seven million dollars. The Democratic National Committee broadcast no paid party advertising in 1980. Since the money the Republicans spent was not spent on the presidential campaign, it was not governed by the 4.6 million dollar ceiling on money each party was permitted to raise and spend on behalf of its presidential candidate. In addition to monies spent on nonpresidential advertising, the Republicans raised and spent the full 4.6 million dollars they were allowed; the Democrats raised and spent about a million dollars less.

Independent Political Action Committees (PACs)

Although spending by Carter and Reagan was capped and underwritten by federal law, additional expenditures by independent committees were permitted by a 1976 Supreme Court ruling. Approximately 12 million dollars was spent by independent groups for Reagan; less than $50,000 was spent for Carter.[29] By contrast, in 1976, PACs had spent altogether, for both candidates, almost two million dollars. What this meant was that in 1980 Reagan spent $18,476,000 of his federal allocation on advertising[30]

---

*In 1982 the same worker, Bruzzy Willders, starred in a Democratic ad in which he said "I'm a Democrat but I voted Republican once, and it's a mistake I'll never make again. And I didn't get paid to say this." The Republicans had paid Willders union scale to appear in their ad.

but garnered benefits from over $30,000,000. Meanwhile, the absence of substantial support from both PACs and the Democratic National Committee meant that Carter's ability to reach a mass audience with advertising was tightly leashed to his federal funds.

In 1980, the Democratic incumbent did have three compensating advantages: greater access to news coverage and free air time, an ability to channel the perquisites of incumbency toward his reelection, and the support of organized labor. As president, he had had automatic access to the news media for three years and during that time was able to take his case to the American people in nationally telecast news conferences and speeches. Indeed, a correlation had been demonstrated to exist between the number of national broadcasts a president delivers and the level of his public support.[31]

Additionally, those significant actions he took as president were reported as a matter of routine in newspapers and on television. Although the press tries to distinguish between presidential and political statements, once an incumbent announces his candidacy, in reality, most of the advantage remains.

Moreover, the power of incumbency meant in 1980 that Carter could do to Kennedy and Reagan what in 1976 Ford had done to him. He could award grant monies to key states at key times and secure a certain amount of campaign work at governmental rather than campaign expense, as aides planned the campaign from the White House.

In 1980 Kennedy's supporters brought suit against Carter on precisely these grounds. The appellants charged that "federal power and federal funds" had been misused "to purchase the renomination of Jimmy Carter." In *Winpisinger* v. *Watson* (628 F. 2nd 133 [D.C. Cir. 1980]; cert. den. 446 U.S. 929, 1980) the appellants complained that invitations to travel on Air Force One were revoked when the invitees announced support for Kennedy; that discretionary federal grants had been awarded in New York City, Detroit, Los Angeles, Newark, San Francisco, Florida, and Iowa in support of elected officials there while monies had been withdrawn from Chicago and Philadelphia, whose majors had supported Kennedy; and that federal officials not barred by the Hatch Act from doing so had been required by Carter to support his nomination.

Kennedy's supporters were no more successful in pressing such charges against Carter than Ford's opponents had been in lodging them against him in 1976. The U.S. Court of Appeals for the District of Columbia held that Kennedy's supporters lacked standing to sue the incumbent unless they charged a distinct and palpable injury to themselves and proved a relationship between the incumbent's supposed conduct and their supposed inability to influence the electoral process.

Assuming that in 1984 the Republicans again gain greater financial support from PACs and party than the Democrats, the inequity in resources will tilt dramatically toward their cause, for the incumbent Republican will benefit as well from greater total access to news channels and from the discretionary powers of incumbency.

In regard to the third Democratic advantage, the support of organized labor, political scientists have noted that the influence of labor leaders on its membership has been diminishing as voters give increasing weight to candidates' stands on issues and to the candidates themselves. As Nie et al. observe: "The individual voter evaluates candidates on the basis of information and impressions conveyed by the mass media, and then votes on that basis. He or she acts as an individual, not as a member of a collectivity."[32] Accordingly, union workers defected to Nixon in large numbers in 1972 and in 1980 Carter led Reagan among union workers by only 4%.

Consistent with this conclusion regarding the support of labor, Rafshoon dismisses the notion that labor's reported expenditure of 15 million dollars in 1980[33] equalized the advantage the Republicans gained in spending by PACs. "Hell, I'd have been glad to have taken a check for $500,000 and asked labor not to do anything," he notes. "All labor could do was run their little ads in their newspapers. They gave us some volunteers and some phone banks but as far as public education, as far as strong advertising, they never have done a very good job at that. Print doesn't move even labor's constituency the way mass media does."

Even when labor's get-out-the vote and voter-registration drives are included, campaign finance expert Herbert Alexander places total funding for Reagan in 1980 at over 10 million dollars above total funding for Carter, with Reagan benefiting from $64.6 million dollars and Carter from $53.93.[34]

PAC Spending Doubled Reagan's Exposure in Some Markets

In some of the media markets the independent committees outspent Reagan. "In Harris County Texas in September, Carter and Reagan were dead even," recalls Brad O'Leary of Americans for Change. "The Reagan campaign spent approximately $50 per precinct nationwide but in Houston (Harris County), from what we could find out from the radio and TV stations and newspapers, they spent $107,000. The independent committees spent $157,000 in that media market."[35]

In July 1980 Common Cause unsuccessfully challenged the existence of the independent committees in a suit brought against Americans for Change, a group headed by Senator Harrison Schmitt and formed to aid

Reagan's election.[36] Four other major conservative PACs supporting Reagan (NCPAC, Americans for an Effective Presidency, Fund for a Conservative Majority, and The Congressional Club) were named as codefendents in the suit. The Carter campaign also brought suit.

Common Cause argued that the committee had violated the Internal Revenue Code's ban on the spending of more than $1,000 by an organized committee for a candidate receiving federal funds. When Congress had rewritten FECA, to bring it into line with *Buckley* v. *Valeo,* it had not amended that provision. Nor had the court ruled on that provision. Common Cause also charged that Americans for Change had collaborated with the Reagan campaign. The Carter campaign argued that the PACs weren't truly independent. The lower court, which ruled for the independent committees, suggested that the issue of collusion be taken to the FEC. There it remained, unresolved on election day 1980.

Although the challenges were unsuccessful, their existence dampened the abilities of the committees to raise funds. The Democrats encouraged the perception that contributing to these committees and their ads might prove illegal. Carter's legal counsel, Tim Smith, sent letters to radio stations informing them that the legality of the committees was under question in the courts:

> We had a pending case before the Court of Appeals and the FEC arguing that the Reagan independent committees weren't independent. Common Cause filed a separate case. We had 300 pages of specific factual indications that there wasn't independence. The one that I remember is that Jesse Helms was interviewed on the floor of the Republican Convention and when asked about independent expenditures said [something to the effect of] "That's right and that's why I don't co-ordinate what we do with Reagan directly. I talk to Paul Laxalt." To us whether that is what Congress meant by independent expenditures was an important legal question. So we thought it was fair game to say to the stations: (1) Don't be confused that you have equal time obligations; (2) there is pending legal action against these committees about whether their expenditures involve violation of the law. We wrote pretty tough communications to that effect.[37]

As a result, some radio stations refused to sell Americans for Change air time until an attorney for the committee informed the stations' attorneys of the resolution of the suit in the lower court. "It cost us $150,000 in legal fees just to stay alive," reported the group's director Brad O'Leary.

When Common Cause lost in the lower court on its PAC challenge, Carter's forces petitioned the FCC for an expedited ruling giving free time to Carter on stations airing independent advertising for Reagan. The FCC voted against that idea.

"All of this created an atmosphere of fear," reported O'Leary. "We would go out to place an ad on radio and be told by the station 'we can't take your ads'. Also contributors were fearful of contributing to a group that might be illegal." Doug Bailey of Americans for an Effective Presidency reports no comparable problem in placing ads.

Americans for Change had hoped to spend 10 to 20 million dollars and instead spent $711,856. Americans for an Effective Presidency had hoped to spend 8 to 10 million and instead spent $1,270,208.

In order to get a sense of the mix of ideas the independent committees added to the political cauldron in 1980, I will briefly sample from their ads.

Americans for Change

The change Americans for Change advocated was the election of Ronald Reagan. The founders of the group believed that, as the incumbent, Carter enjoyed the power to dominate the mass media. By running newspaper and radio ads, the group hoped to help neutralize that advantage.

Americans for Change's ads were placed in media markets that met two criteria. First, Carter and Reagan had to be neck and neck in the polls or separated by one or two percentage points. Second, Reagan had to be expected to benefit from increased turn-out in that market. Consequently, the group concentrated on areas in which polls revealed that voters would vote for a Republican if motivated to vote. The areas on which Americans for Change concentrated included Ohio, Illinois, New York, Florida, New Jersey, Louisiana, Arkansas, Connecticut, Maryland, and the District of Columbia. Reagan carried all but Maryland and the District of Columbia.

The print ads that appeared in September detailed reasons to vote for Reagan. The radio ads, which began airing after the Anderson-Reagan debate, were anti-Carter. These ads highlighted the chasm between Carter's promises in 1976 and his performance in the White House. "We simply reinforced Carter's negatives," says O'Leary.

One ad asked the listener to try to remember one promise that Jimmy Carter had kept. The theme of this ad had come out of a poll in which that very question had been asked. Only one voter in ten had been able to supply an answer.

To raise funds the group sent audio cassettes to 6,000 prospective donors, with the unexpected result that twenty or so of the persons receiving the tapes "went down to the radio station and bought radio time. Then they called the committee saying 'I've bought $340 worth of radio ads. I've appointed myself treasurer and changed the disclaimer.' We said 'Oh, my God,' " recalls O'Leary, "and got our lawyer on the phone."

Approximately 20,000 contributors gave an average of $45 each to Americans for Change. Direct mail was used to raise funds.

National Conservative Political Action Committee (NCPAC)

In "an attempt to set strong national defense, tax cuts, budget cuts, and less government on the national issue agenda," in 1980 NCPAC aired both pro-Reagan and anti-Carter ads.[38] In the primaries it also sponsored anti-Kennedy materials including full page ads in the *Washington Post* and *Boston Globe* greeting Kennedy's announcement of candidacy with six questions that the ad dared reporters to ask the Massachusetts senator. These questions included:

> Senator Kennedy, when you were Majority Whip for the Democratic Party you were unceremoniously deposed by a former member of the KKK [Ku Klux Klan]. You have been in the United States Senate for 18 years, yet not one major piece of legislation bears your name. You haven't even been able to get a national health insurance bill out of your own subcommittee. Your personal background shows very little to be proud of in leadership qualities, particularly under pressure. With this type of record, what makes you think you have the leadership ability to be a president? . . . *On Chappaquiddick:* . . . will you assist in getting all legal records on the matter made public? Will you encourage everyone associated with the affair to speak out publicly? . . .
>
> Andrew Young was forced to resign because he lied to the president and the American people. Do you think he should have been forced to resign? If not, would you be willing to bring back John Ehrlichman and Bob Haldeman since they resigned for the same reason?

NCPAC spent $247,918 against Kennedy's candidacy.

NCPAC's pro-Reagan spots were concentrated in Louisiana, Mississippi, and Alabama. The choice of states was skillful. Reagan won Mississippi and Alabama by less than 1% of the votes cast. One set of pro-Reagan ads showed Reagan speaking to large crowds. What differentiates these ads from those actually produced for the Reagan campaign is production quality: NCPAC's ads have a less finished look. In a number of them Reagan is wearing a white suit, making him appear to be a waiter or an ice cream vendor as he speaks to the Utah Republican Convention. "Because we were legally required to remain independent of the Reagan campaign," NCPAC's director Terry Dolan told a University of Maryland seminar, "we couldn't say 'Hey Ron, wear a nice dark suit.' We decided to film that speech and he showed up in a white jacket. Presidents don't wear white jackets. They usually meet people who wear white jackets."[39]

The pro-Reagan spots also featured Ronald Reagan's Congressman who informed viewers "about his record": "When Ronald Reagan was governor, he gave Californians almost six billion dollars in tax relief. He cut welfare rolls by 400,000 people yet increased payments to the needy by 43%. He turned a $194 million dollar deficit into a $554 surplus. When he had the second toughest job in America, Reagan delivered." The NCPAC ads closed with the tag "Ronald Reagan for President. He'll Make America Great Again." As I note elsewhere, these statistics, drawn from those used by Reagan in his speeches are both inaccurate and misleading. Welfare payments increased by 23.6%, not 43%. The turnaround of the deficit and the tax rebate were the by-products of tax increases, not tax cuts or fiscal restraint, and the drop in the number of persons on welfare was accelerated by an improving national economy and a liberalized abortion bill that Reagan signed but later disavowed.

In Rafshoon's judgment, NCPAC's anti-Carter ads hurt Carter in the South. He singles out an ad that showed still photos of Carter's appointees as the announcer said: "In 1976 Jimmy Carter said 'Why not the Best?' Let's look at what he gave us. Andrew Young, Carter's U.N. Ambassador who called Iran's Ayatollah Khomeini a saint, forced to resign after lying to the president. Bert Lance also forced to resign. Dr. Peter Bourne, the Carter drug expert, forced to resign after supplying drugs to a White House staffer. And the list goes on. If you want a president whose judgment you can trust, then vote for Ronald Reagan for President." Rafshoon believes that the widespread use of this ad in the South was an attempt to marshal racist resentment over Carter's close association with Andrew Young.

In my judgment the most damaging NCPAC ads are those that replay promises Carter made in the 1976 debates with Ford and then contrast those promises with Carter's record. In one of these, Carter says, "by the end of the first four years of the next term we can have the unemployment rate down to 3% and adult unemployment which is about 4 1/2% overall." As the data crawl up the screen, the announcer notes: "The current national unemployment rate is 8%. During the four years of Jimmy Carter's term one million more Americans were put out of work." A magnified closeup of Carter is shown asserting: "I keep my promises to the American people." The pledge is then replayed in an echo chamber giving it an ominous, otherworldly quality: "I keep my promises," "I keep my promises, promises, promises." "We trusted Jimmy Carter once," says the announcer, "can we afford to trust him again?" The contrast between Carter's promises and performance on tax reduction and balancing the budget also are highlighted in ads that employ the same structure.

Additionally, NCPAC responded to Carter's claim in the 1980 debate that he was respected by world leaders with a TV ad that quoted

Still photo from NCPAC anti-Carter ad televised in the general election of 1980. (Reprinted with the permission of the National Conservative Political Action Committee)

disparaging statements by foreign leaders about Carter. The spot aired in Illinois.

Reagan could not have sponsored ads of this type without damaging his image as a decent, sensitive, positive leader. NCPAC provided this valuable service besides increasing access to the electorate beyond that permitted by the candidate's spending ceiling. According to its director of communication, NCPAC spent almost two million dollars ($1,935,000) in support of Reagan's candidacy and $109,000 against Carter in swing states in which neither Carter nor Reagan concentrated resources. These states included Alabama, Louisiana, Mississippi, and the Florida Panhandle. "We read in the newspaper that the Reagan strategy was to go North," says Craig Shirley, "so we went South."[40]

The Fund for a Conservative Majority

In late August anti-Carter ads sponsored by The Fund for a Conservative Majority were previewed.[41] In one a woman removes pieces of a puzzle showing Carter's face and replaces them with pieces showing Reagan's face as Carter's foreign and domestic policy failures are recounted.

Another showed a balloon with Carter's face on it. As the rising cost of consumer goods is detailed the balloon slowly is inflated until, at the ad's end, the balloon explodes. A third displayed portraits of Washington, Lincoln, John Kennedy, and finally Carter. "Being President used to mean something," says the ad, "but during the past four years it has meant only one thing: failure." The most unusual of the ads shows actors portraying a Russian general, an Arab oil shiek, Fidel Castro, and the Ayatollah Khomeini pushing Uncle Sam around. The ad asserts that under Carter we have lost military strength and international prestige.

Reagan responded disapprovingly to this ad. Instead of airing the set, FCM recast uncopyrighted 1976 Carter ads. In one, Carter condemns Ford's 6.5% rate of inflation. His image freezes as an announcer notes: "He did do something about the inflation rate. He more than doubled it. Are you satisfied with what you have or are you going to change it?" "We hoped they'd sue to take their own 1976 ads off," recalls FCM treasurer Ken Boehm. "Instead they said they were effective ads."

The Fund for a Conservative Majority spent just over two million dollars for Reagan ($2,062,456), targeting ads to New York, Pennsylvania, Florida, and Connecticut. Ads in Spanish were written for Cubans in Miami. Blue-collar union workers were a special focus as were Catholics opposed to abortion. In a mass mailing to Republicans, FCM offered to sell its ads at cost.

Americans for an Effective Presidency

Bailey-Deardourff and Associates, the agency that handled Ford's general election advertising, created pro-Reagan and anti-Carter ads for Americans for an Effective Presidency. This group spent nearly 1.3 million dollars ($1,270,208) aiding Reagan's cause. The group concentrated on televised advertising in swing states such as Ohio, Texas, Florida, New Jersey, Illinois, and Missouri. Like Americans for Change, this PAC was formed specifically for the 1980 general election. The individuals forming it believed, says Doug Bailey, "that the single most important thing they could do for America was to defeat Jimmy Carter. . . . There were some people who looked at Americans for an Effective Presidency and saw people who had been active with Ford who were active in this effort and had not been active in the campaign for the 1980 nomination and obviously had not been active after Reagan's nomination. Some saw this as Ford people who wanted to do something where they felt comfortable but not a total embrace of Reagan," Bailey says. "Perhaps psychologically to some degree that was true."[42]

Although Bailey says that the group was not formed to vindicate

Ford, it did film Ford noting that if the misery index was high enough in 1976 to oust one president the substantially higher misery index now justified ousting Carter.

The committee's ads on inflation, unemployment, and defense "pointed out firmly, aggressively but politely, with respect for the office, Carter's failures to perform."[43] One, played heavily in Ohio, was tailored market by market to show pictures of plants that either had closed or suffered major layoffs during Carter's term. The argument on inflation was carried by showing basic food products shrinking in size as the rate of inflation was noted. Weapons systems approved by Ford but eliminated by Carter disappeared from the screen in the defense ad. The ad also included footage of the Soviet invasion of Afghanistan and of rioters in the streets of Teheran. "There is the suggestion that everything has gone to hell in a handbasket," says Bailey, "although it isn't said in quite that way."

Other Independent Ads

Individuals also aired and printed ads. A wealthy Fort Worth business-man, for example, bought radio spots on 700 stations in 18 states to declare his displeasure with high prices, flag burnings, deficit spending, high taxes, and the liberal Congress.[44]

In the final week of the campaign a Washington-based political action committee called Christian Voice Moral Government Fund purchased $50,000 of TV time in swing states in the South to air spots charging Carter with "advocating acceptance of homosexuality." By contrast, the ads claimed Reagan "stands for the traditional American family." The committee spent a total of $406,199 on the presidential campaign.

These ads were created by Long Advertising of Miami, the agency that had assisted in the anti-gay rights campaign run by Anita Bryant in 1977 in Dade County. In one of the spots a self-identified "Christian mother" states that she opposes those who teach children "that abortion and homosexuality are perfectly all right." Carter disagrees, she adds. Consequently, it is her duty to vote for Reagan, who "will protect my family values."[45]

"They were making people think that Jimmy Carter was not a good Christian," recalls Rafshoon. "I'm from Atlanta and I'd go down South and I would hear about these spots run during Church time on Sunday talking about Carter meeting in the White House with homosexuals, Carter being anti-Christ. Rosalynn Carter came down and said she had this bizarre thing happen. A bunch of Church women coming up and saying 'Jimmy's anti-Christ.' "[46]

Before the rise of PAC advertising, candidates were held accountable by the electorate for the content of ads benefiting them. This fact functioned as a check on the fairness and facticity of campaign advertising. Consequently, Reagan would never sponsor advertising suggesting that Carter endorsed the teaching of homosexuality and abortion in the schools for, in fact, Carter had not. Yet a PAC can make such a claim with impunity. Of course, the possibility always existed that Reagan might absorb the blame for these ads if voters could be persuaded that by saying nothing he was, in part, responsible for these "dirty" attacks. But it was just as likely that viewers would not see through these ads that played on their baser emotions. In short, PAC ads can act as loose cannons careening across the political deck and in the process impede the public's ability to rationally assess political claims.

This fact was dramatically illustrated by an ad sponsored by North Carolina Senator Jesse Helms' National Congressional Club in the final weeks of the campaign. The Congressional Club, originally formed in 1972 to pay off Helms' campaign debt, was the first conservative PAC to engage in widespread advertising to influence a presidential race. In 1976 it had sponsored television ads featuring Helms explaining the importance of adopting a conservative platform at the Republican convention.

In 1980 the Club proffered an ad in which pictures of Ted Kennedy and John Anderson appeared on the screen. In a sneering tone, an announcer said, "Ted Kennedy. John Anderson. Ted Kennedy. John Anderson. Both voted against building the strategic B-1 bomber. Both voted for useless busing. Both voted billions of dollars for wasteful foreign aid. Both voted to give away our canal in Panama. And both voted to use federal funds for abortions. Ted Kennedy. John Anderson. Ted Kennedy. John Anderson. We defeated one. Now we must defeat the other." Because Carter, not Reagan, had defeated Kennedy, irate voters, assuming that the ad had been sponsored by Carter's campaign, called his headquarters to protest. In fact, the ad had been an attempt by a Republican PAC to bring Anderson voters back to Reagan. If one viewed it thinking it was a Democratic ad, it seemed to be one more manifestation of Carter's "meanness." So the ad achieves a second effect, creating a backlash against Carter, its presumed, but not actual sponsor.

"We were very frustrated and angry about that ad," says the Carter campaign's legal counsel, Tim Smith. "I think it was one whose authorization flashed in tiny print and you couldn't tell who authorized it. We looked into whether that was the way to attack it, because it didn't seem to adequately identify its source, as required by FCC, which specifies a specific size [for the authorization] and the number of seconds it has to be shown. We decided against an FCC filing, I believe, because it seemed futile. By the time you do all the paperwork and file the thing and get an answer, [it can] be a long time and what would they say? Don't do it again. Also the damage had been done. If we went to the stations we'd be subject to criticism [as we were the first time for warning them about the lawsuit against the PACs]. The emotion I associate with that ad is frustration, because there didn't seem to be anything effective we could do about it."[47]

In sum, the independent PACs carried the case that Carter had broken his promises. The PAC ads highlighted high inflation, interest rates, and unemployment and, to a lesser extent, a weakened U.S. defense. At the same time they contended that Reagan had kept his promises to the people of California and, unlike Carter, would keep the promises he was making in 1980. Moreover, they reiterated, a Reagan presidency would be an effective presidency, a presidency that would lead the country in constructive change. Some of the PAC ads, such as those on homosexuality and on Kennedy and Anderson, nibbled away at the public perception that Carter was a decent person.

The PACs magnified the impact of their efforts by concentrating on states in which the swing of a small percent of the electorate would turn the state's electors from Carter to Reagan. With few exceptions they focused on the same core group of states and with few exceptions their efforts dovetailed with those of the Reagan campaign. Doug Bailey explains how in a "totally legal, totally allowed by the law and totally up and up" way this consistency emerged:

> There was sufficient political sophistication involved that the right hand did in fact know what the left hand was doing. It wasn't that anyone was trying to communicate to us what the target states for Reagan were but: first, we all had the same political education so we approached the process in the same way and felt confident that everyone would come to the same conclusions; and secondly we didn't shy away from stating in the press what our own goals were and neither did they. In that sense there was communication. If they ever did want to communicate with us all they had to do was hold a press conference and say "Gee we hope none of these independent expenditure committees will ever run a spot that includes the B-1 bomber." That's communication although no one picked up a phone. I never thought any communication was ever directed at us but nonetheless we knew where they were going.[48]

The Reagan Campaign

After nearly four years of observing his actions as president, voters approached the general election confident that they knew that Jimmy Carter was a well-intentioned, fundamentally decent person but an incompetent president. Here was a situation ripe for the appeal used by the Republicans in 1952: it's time for a change. Unsurprisingly, that was the chief reason 38% of those who voted for Reagan gave the *New York Times* as the rationale for their vote.[49]

By contrast, voters knew comparatively little about Ronald Reagan, a situation that gave him latitude in sculpting the public's sense of himself. At the same time however, this relative anonymity allowed the Democrats to do to Reagan what the Republicans had done to the newcomer McGovern in 1972—nurture perceptions of him as an unsafe, unacceptable alternative to the status quo. Predictably, Republicans would underscore the public's existing perception that Carter was a poor leader and Democrats would discredit Reagan as a poorer alternative. Reagan's task was to exceed what the Democrats came to call the threshold of presidential acceptability, while the Democrat's task was to prop Carter above it and hold Reagan below it.

The Republicans faced the easier of the two tasks. Attitudes formed over a long period of time and supported by a deep informational base are extremely difficult to change. Attitudes formed over a short period of time and supported by minimal information are easier to shape or reshape. In the general election, Reagan's ads told voters things about his record they had not before known where Carter's ads revealed sides of the presidency with which Carter's strategists felt the electorate was unfamiliar. By seeing the job in a new light, Rafshoon hoped that voters would see its occupant and potential occupant in a new light. Still, Carter's strategists faced the difficult task of changing strongly held attitudes where Reagan's faced the easier one of filling in the broad outline of existing attitudes with fresh information or drawing new attitudes on a tabula rasa.

The Pro-Reagan Campaign

In June 1979 Reagan's polling firm Decision/Making/Information (D/M/I) headed by Richard Wirthlin conducted a national study of "six scenarios for the future." Given a choice from among options ranging from "less is better" to "America can do," the majority preferred the "America can do" theme.[50]

The "can do" theme pervaded Reagan's advertising. "Don't let anyone tell you that inflation can't be controlled. It can be, by making some tough decisions to control federal spending," Reagan declared in a thirty second TV ad. "As president, I'm ready to make those decisions."

Allied to the "can do" theme were strong assertions about Reagan's past and potential leadership, the by-product of the pollsters' finding that

Leadership, Competence, Strength and Decisiveness are "the presidential values a majority of Americans think are important."[51] "We did it in California. And we can do it for America," says Reagan in the ads. "What he inherited was a state of crisis," says the announcer in the five minute documentary. "California was faced with a $194 million dollar deficit and was spending a million dollars a day more than it was taking in. The State was on the brink of bankruptcy. Working with teams of volunteers from all sectors, Governor Reagan got things back on track." Many of the ads aired in October and November close with the declaration "The time is now for strong leadership. Reagan for President."

Another factor decisively shaped the Republican presidential advertising. Reagan's strategists were unswervingly confident in his abilities as a communicator. Since their data showed that voters did not want "slick" ads but rather "wanted to see the candidate addressing them directly, describing what he would do if elected,"[52] the ads had Reagan talking about what America *could do* under his *leadership* and, at the same time, documented what the Californian *had done* as governor.

As a result of this strategy, in 1980 voters saw more ads showing Reagan speaking directly to the camera than they had seen of any presidential candidate since the 1960 race. Of the 254 Reagan commercials run on network television in the general election, 41% were documentary spots focusing on Reagan's record and plans for the future, 33% were talking head spots featuring Bush, Ford, Nancy Reagan, or Ronald Reagan, with Reagan the star of most; and 26% were anti-Carter concept spots, such as the ad that used a bar graph to demonstrate the effects of inflation.[53]

By adopting a talking head format, the Republicans defied the conventional wisdom dictating that talking heads are dull and dispose the audience to disinterest. Reagan's successful use of that format justifies the strategists' confidence in his skill as a communicator and at the same time lends credence to the results of a study by the NRCC that found that this format communicates information and personality well, is particularly well received by conservatives, and, if used skillfully, promotes high recall.[54]

Moreover, extensive use of five minute ads to carry Reagan's message—74 of the 254 ads aired nationally were five minutes long—had the advantage of increasing the redundancy of the message and the audience absorption time thus increasing the likelihood that Reagan's message would be remembered and positively evaluated.[55]

Another advantage that accrued from the use of Reagan speaking in his own behalf is that voters were being familiarized with the candidate. "Forty percent of the population didn't know enough about Reagan to vote for him," recalls O'Reilly. "They knew his name, but his record as governor was largely unknown. Voters were leery about him in the foreign affairs area. There was a sense that he might be trigger happy. Voters had a sense that he would cut taxes, increase defense spending, get tough with the Russians, get tough on welfare and cut down big government. Each of these perceptions had a downside. To cut taxes they thought he might cut education and aid to senior citizens; by increasing defense spending he might trigger an arms race; by getting tough with Russia he might risk war; being tough on welfare might mean that he lacked compassion. Governor Reagan did have considerable hard core support among Republicans but Republicans are only 20% of the electorate and he didn't have all of them."[56] By letting Reagan speak for himself in his ads, his strategists could expose the electorate to his reassuring manner, get across his record and proposals, and at the same time mute the fears evoked by the downside of his perceived proposals and magnified by the Democratic campaign.

The cornerstone of the Republican advertising was a five minute documentary on Reagan's life and record. Sixty and thirty second "lifts" were also drawn from it. Of the 73 purchases of five minute time in network television, 60 were used to air the documentary; of the 41 purchases of 60 seconds of time, 35 were devoted to the documentary.[57] The documentary was designed to fill the information gap about Reagan. "Campaign 80's television ads focusing on Ronald Reagan's California record served that end well," one of Reagan's pollsters told a seminar at the University of Maryland after the election.[58] "Through September and the first weeks of October, the California record ads were run so often that all of us were sick of them. But they were doing the job. More and more voters were beginning to know Ronald Reagan better," O'Reilly recalls. At one point early in the fall campaign the documentary "constituted 75% of the weight of the ads being run for Reagan. One governor called Reagan to say that if he saw the documentary again he was going to throw up." In the last two weeks of the campaign the documentary gave way to a second generation documentary called "This Is a Man."

The documentary on Reagan's record is a case study in the art of identification. Reagan was raised "in America's heartland, small town Illinois. From a close knit family a sense for the values of family, even though luxuries were few and hard to come by." As a star his "appeal came from his roots, his character" and then in a statement whose lack of subtlety undermines it: "he appealed to audiences because he was so clearly one of them." He was "a peacetime volunteer army officer and with the outbreak of World War II he signed on for active duty. Four years later Air Force Captain Reagan returned to Warner Brothers and

A still photo of Captain Ronald Reagan from the five minute documentary ad aired frequently by Campaign 80 in the general election.

to the most challenging period of his life. A dedicated union man, he was elected president of the Screen Actors Guild six times." His swearing-in ceremony as governor is shown. We see him pledging to "support and defend the Constitution of the United States and the Constitution of the State of California." He takes a state in "crisis" and puts it "back on the track," said the ad.

Reagan is reelected as governor. Into this account are woven key identifying phrases: "creative leadership," "greatest tax reformer," "property tax relief," "tax reforms totalling nearly $3 billion dollars." Juxtaposed with these claims is a quote from *The San Francisco Examiner*. The ad originally credited the quote to the *San Francisco Chronicle*. The two papers merge on Sunday and the statement appeared in a Sunday paper. But the section from which the quote had been taken was the *Examiner*. The Republicans tore the ad apart, made the change, and substituted the new credit for the old. The paper said that he "has saved the state from bankruptcy."

The ad neglects to specify how he saved the state from "bankruptcy." By allying tax reform and tax relief with the credit for saving the state from bankruptcy it implies that Reagan's record in California proves that his proposal to cut taxes at the federal level will not sacrifice essential social services and will revive the economy. That conclusion is rendered explicit when the announcer sums up Reagan's California record by saying "When Governor Reagan left office, the $194 million dollar deficit had been transformed into a $554 million surplus. And while saving the taxpayers hundreds of millions of dollars, he improved the quality of life for the people of California."

Yet the way Reagan saved the state from bankruptcy was by increasing not decreasing taxes! Comparing Reagan's claims with his record, *Los Angeles Times'* reporters Bill Stall and William Endicott noted that "Reagan omits the fact that the tax refunds he boasts of were made possible only because his administration imposed three large tax increases that raised billions of dollars more than any of the experts imagined they would."[59] So in the documentary the credibility of a newspaper's claim that he saved the state from bankruptcy is used to prompt the false inference that the kind of tax cutting he was proposing at the federal level had been tried and had succeeded at the state level. Carter's person in the street and Oval Office ads fill in this blank with reminders that Reagan raised taxes. However, both use forms of evidence—assertion by strangers and by a paid announcer—less credible than that of a newspaper. To pinpoint the false inference being prompted by the Reagan documentary, Carter's ads might instead have shown headlines from California newspapers reporting the tax boosts.

More so than in previous campaigns, in 1980 the press acted as a watchdog over the nationally telecast advertising. The ads most likely to be scrutinized were those run nationally or in such media centers as New

A still photo of Reagan being sworn in as governor of California. This scene was included in the five minute Republican documentary on Reagan aired during the general election of 1980.

York, Washington, or Los Angeles. If an ad by a prominent candidate was aired repeatedly and made questionable claims, it was likely to attract scrutiny. So, for example, when an often aired ad for Baker juxtaposed an applauding audience with his rejoinder to an attack by an irate Iranian student, television and print reporters alerted their audience that the applause had not closely followed Baker's statement. Similarly, the sins of omission and commission in Reagan's documentary were probed by the *New York Times*. Additionally, *The Los Angeles Times* and CBS Evening News' Bill Plante documented the falsity of many claims in the documentary indirectly in their analysis of the factual base for the Reagan stump speech. To determine the effectiveness of the political ads on the air, both during the primaries and in the general election, the *Washington Post* conducted and reported on the results of a focus group analysis of them.

Reagan's assertions about tax reform and rebated surpluses overcame attitudinal inertia by repetition. Meanwhile, the comforting familiarity of Reagan's past—small town, to officer, to union leader, to governor—repeated night after night, complete with pictures documenting each, insinuates Reagan into our lives. There is a calming predictability about seeing the same spot again and again. And the story of how he came to be what he is today is not one scripted to end "and then the small town boy who grew up to be an officer, a union leader, a successful governor blew up the world." Nor is the Reagan of the talking head spots, of the debates, or of the election eve speech the sort who seems likely to separate North from South, black from white, or lead us into war.

Since the documentary had reassured us about Reagan's past, in the final weeks the "This Is a Man" five minute spot summarized Reagan's philosophy and spelled out his program for the future. This is a man, says the announcer, "whose principles have been familiar to Americans for thirty years . . . who rejects the concept of lowered expectations because he believes in the boundless opportunities of the American idea."

Then Reagan spells out what he will do to control inflation. He will freeze all federal hiring, eliminate "every example of waste and inefficiency in government," enlist the best minds from labor and industry to help find waste, balance the budget, "think pricetag whenever we think program," and elicit recommendations from private sector and labor about how to curb inflation. Included in this spot is the characteristic assurance that the unspecified "programs that meet the needs of the American people" will not be "sacrificed." Like Carter in 1976 Reagan is offering the country enthymemes. Fill in what you would like to hear; hear the assurances that you require to vote for me.

It is interesting here to look at two ads that never aired. These were ads answering the Carter charge that Reagan was trigger happy. Both were written late in the campaign, probably between October 15 and 23. In both, Reagan was to speak directly into the camera. Both are thirty seconds long. In one the announcer opens by saying, "Ronald Reagan talks about peace." Reagan then says, "Peace requires that we be strong, *and* always willing to negotiate. President Eisenhower believed in peace through strength, as well as negotiation. So do I. That's why if elected President, I will go to Moscow, sit down with President Brezhnev, and finally negotiate a fair, sensible arms limitation treaty. However long it takes, a Reagan Administration will work to achieve the strong *lasting* peace every American wants." The second is more specific. This ad opens on Reagan who says, "War versus Peace. That is just one area where we need strong leadership. I pledge to you, that, within the first 100 days of my Administration I will go to Moscow. I will sit with President Brezhnev and negotiate a fair arms reduction treaty. However long it takes, we will achieve a strong, secure peace."

By setting a specific expectation of action within 100 days this ad would have established a clear test by which the success or failure of Reagan's first 100 days would be judged. Such a promise would have opened Reagan to the charge levied implicitly in the first wave of Carter ads and explicitly in the second wave: that he did not understand the complexity of the presidency. In the past it has taken substantially longer than 100 days for American diplomats to break the ground and secure the agreements that enabled American and Russian heads of state to meet at the summit to negotiate agreements. Since Reagan had roundly criticized Ford's foreign policy in 1976, he could not now simply pick up its pieces either.

The proposal carried a second liability, for the only president who in recent memory had, in head-to-head negotiations with other heads of state, hammered out a previously unlikely agreement was Carter at Camp David. If the ability to engage heads of state on a one-to-one basis in a comparatively short period of time and reach an acceptable agreement is a central criterion by which one's fitness for the presidency should be assessed, then Carter not Reagan should be president.

Moreover, this claim sunders Reagan from the moorings he repeatedly tied to his gubernatorial past as he did, for example, when he educed his economic solutions for national problems from the solutions he employed in California. Having done so, he sets a strong economy as a centerpiece in his plans for a strong defense. But nothing in his gubernatorial past warrants the conclusion that he could negotiate an arms reduction treaty within 100 days of assuming the White House.

Ford's Endorsement of Reagan

Reagan's candidacy in 1976 had done to Ford what Kennedy's candidacy
did to Carter in 1980. The endorsement ads Reagan delivered for Ford
also parallel those Kennedy delivered for Carter. In them Reagan indicates his support for the platform directly and for Ford obliquely, just as
Kennedy insinuates his commitment to Carter within the context of the
vision of the party Kennedy delivered at the convention. Both Kennedy's
and Reagan's endorsement ads clearly speak the message: there is no love
lost between them and their party's nominee.

But Reagan's efforts to make Ford his vice-president and Ford's hostility toward the person who defeated him in 1976 coupled to add unscharac-
teristic passion to the ads in which Ford endorsed Reagan in 1980. In one,
Ford praised Reagan's record of accomplishment in California. In the
other, Ford noted that people come up to him and tell him how much they
wished they'd voted for him. The ad goes on to compare things in 1976 and
1980 and clearly and unequivocally urge a vote for Reagan.

The Anti-Carter Campaign

The Republicans' data told them that they enjoyed an advantage identified by Carter's pollster four years earlier. The Republican Black Book
quotes Patrick Caddell saying in 1976: "It must be kept in mind that it is
likely that a voter who is unenthusiastic about an incumbent is *more likely*
to actually turn out and vote for his choice than is a voter who is unenthusiastic about a challenger."[60] In 1976 this fact increased Carter's chances,
in 1980 Reagan's.

Still the Republicans recognized that dissatisfaction with Carter
would not automatically translate into support for Reagan. "Unless we
develop confidence in Governor Reagan," notes the Black Book, "independents and moderate Democrats will display their dissatisfaction with
Carter by not voting in the presidential race, voting for John Anderson,
or not voting at all."[61] To this point I have indicated how the campaign
bolstered confidence in Reagan. Here we examine the ways in which it
magnified dissatisfaction with Carter.

Attacking Carter's Record

Because Carter was perceived to be an "honest, moral man," more
"compassionate" than Reagan but nonetheless a "well-intentioned amateur," the Republicans decided to "attack his record and his performance, but *not* the man."[62] When they did attack Carter as a person it

was Nancy Reagan who carried the message and that message assumed the form of a rebuttal to the charges Carter had made about her husband. In that ad, which aired twice on network television in the last weeks of October, Nancy Reagan said that she was offended by Carter trying "to portray him [my husband] as a war-monger, or a man who would throw the elderly out on the street and cut off their Social Security, when in fact he never said anything of the kind, at any time, and the elderly people have enough to worry about now. They are scared to death of how they are going to live, without this thrown on top of them. That's a cruel thing to do. It is cruel to the people; it is cruel to my husband. I deeply, deeply resent it, as a wife and a mother, and woman." This use of Reagan's wife is a radical departure from the tradition of presidential advertising. In the past, wives have been featured in ads with their husbands, as were Jackie Kennedy and Mamie Eisenhower, or speaking about what they had learned in the campaign and what their husbands would do for America, as did both Muriel Humphrey and Eleanor McGovern. But here Nancy Reagan assumes the role of her husband's champion.

The campaign's other attacks on Carter were handled more indirectly.

Attacks on Carter's Foreign Policy

The Republicans' focus on Carter's record governed what the advertisers did and what they did not do. They drafted but did not produce an ad that would have had influential Republicans such as Donald Rumsfeld, Alexander Haig, and a former admiral such as Moorer or Zumwalt label Carter's various claims about his defense record "a lie." "Jimmy Carter has said that the Nixon and Ford Administrations cut defenses. That is a lie." The facts, the ad would have said, are that despite Democratic cuts in the Senate "there was real growth and modernization during those years. Jimmy Carter has said that he has pursued 'a steady rebuilding of our defenses.' That is a lie," someone such as Haig would have added. The facts are that Carter cut $6 billion from Ford's budget in 77, $8.4 billion the next year and a total of more than $38 billion "from the defense program that he inherited from President Ford." The ad also would have dismissed as lies the claims that Carter "had improved the life of our military personnel" and "has strengthened the United States Navy."

Instead, a five minute ad titled "Peace" made the point that Reagan would reiterate in both his debate with Anderson and his debate with Carter and would repeat on election eve: "Of all the objectives we seek, first and foremost is the establishment of lasting world peace." The ad also included a warning that spoke words comforting to the political right in language whose echoes of JFK's inaugural soothed the political center. "But let our friends and those who may wish us ill take note: The United States has an obligation to its citizens and to the people of the world never to let those who would destroy freedom dictate the future course of life on this planet."

Reagan's indictment of Carter is indirect. Here, as in other ads, Reagan tries to translate dissatisfaction with domestic affairs into dissatisfaction with foreign affairs. "With our economy in a shambles," he says, "the enemies of freedom gain strength. With our allies respect for America at an all-time low, the enemies of freedom gain confidence. With our military strength becoming weaker by the day, the enemies of freedom gain courage. This must stop. To enjoy the strong peace we all yearn for, we must maintain our margin of safety." "Margin of safety" functions as the phrase that synthesizes Reagan's philosophy of defense. Unlike such alternatives as "unquestionable superiority," the phrase has a benign sound. The five minute ad titled "Peace" aired nationwide three times between August 28 and September 14, its 30 second offspring nine times between October 28 and September 28.

"The peace issue was a hard one," recalls O'Reilly. "Research showed that Governor Reagan was believed to be more likely to start a war than Jimmy Carter. We felt the way to defuse that was to have him stand up and say he is a man of peace. We didn't know of any other way to do it. We didn't think that an aggressive attack on Carter's foreign affairs was a good strategy. What helped us more than anything else was the debate and the turmoil on Iran. At the end of the campaign we were almost even on the subject of who would be more likely to start a war."

In the last weeks of the campaign the Republicans did broadcast a two minute and a thirty second version of an attack ad that showed pictures from war zones culminating in a still of Carter. "Very slowly, a step at a time, the hope for world peace erodes," said the announcer. "Slowly we once slid into Korea. Slowly into Vietnam. And now the Persian Gulf beckons. Jimmy Carter's weak indecisive leadership has vascillated before events in Angola, Ethiopia and Afghanistan. Jimmy Carter still doesn't know that it takes *strong* leadership to keep the peace—weak leadership will lose it." Notably missing from this list is Iran. Here, as in the other Republican ads, the most damning indictments are invited from but not forced on the audience.

Before airing this ad, the Republicans market tested it. "We got a good response," O'Reilly reports. "Eighteen percent thought it was terrible, eighteen percent thought it was right and the rest said we need a stronger defense." This ad was run exclusively in the South where defense is a key issue and the desire for a strong national defense intense.

So outside the blinders of the national audience, the battle in paid television in the South pitted the Camp David Accords, seen through the optic of Gettysburg, against the suffering created by current conflicts, viewed through the optic of Carter's "weak indecisive leadership."

The strongest of Reagan's attack advertising was held in reserve to be used only if the "October surprise" the Republicans had so universally forecast brought the hostages home in the closing days of the election. The Black Book had made what its authors called the reasonable assumption that "the hostages will be home before election day."[63] But the existence of advertising readied for release in the event of their return marked a deviation from the Black Book's recommendation that "We must not be surprised by Carter's 'October Surprises,' nor should we design specific commercials in response." The original plan recommended that Reagan "praise their return. And say nothing about the fact that it took 10 long, painful months. Governor Reagan must take the high road. Let Senate Republicans and the press raise the doubts."[64]

If Carter was to be attacked, in effect, for bringing the hostages home, an event that Rafshoon believes would have won him the election, any responsive Republican advertising would have to disassociate itself from Reagan. So a produced but never aired television ad sponsored by "Democrats for Reagan" repeats an indictment raised by *New York Times* columnist William Safire. "In a copyrighted story in the *New York Times* on October 27," said the ad, "William Safire wrote, 'the smoothest of Iran's diplomatic criminals was shown on American TV this weekend warning American voters that they had better not elect Ronald Reagan. Ayatollah Khomeini and his men prefer a weak and manageable U.S. president and have decided to do everything in their power to determine our election results.' A reminder from Democrats for Reagan."

By the Sunday noon before the election, Reagan's strategists had concluded that the return of the hostages would not help Carter enough to necessitate responsive advertising. "On Sunday morning, November 2," wrote Reagan pollsters Richard Wirthlin, Vincent Breglio, and Richard Beall after the election, "the hostage situation came back into the headlines. Through a national sample, we confirmed that even if the hostage dilemma were resolved prior to the election, it would provide Carter only slight benefit—nothing approaching the 10% shift we envisioned earlier."[65]

Attacks on Carter's Domestic Record

In keeping with their plan to forego attacks on Carter for attacks on his record, Reagan's advertisers quashed a scripted ad in which grinning and sour-faced pictures of Carter were shown as the announcer said, "In 1976, Jimmy Carter promised the American people that he would turn things around, that he would make Americans proud, that he would deliver a better America. Three and a half years later, this same man, the most inept president in our nation's history, blames us, the American people, for his failure, for his record of broken promises. He calls it a malaise. In 1980, Jimmy's running scared. Again promising more, but with only a promise of more of the same."

By contrast, the economic flip-flop that did air focused not on "the most inept president in American history" but on Carter's specific promises. As pictures of a frowning and smiling Carter alternated, the announcer asked: "Can we afford four more years of broken promises? In 1976, Jimmy Carter promised to hold inflation to 4%. Today it is 14%. He promised to fight unemployment. But today there are 8 1/2 million Americans out of work. He promised to balance the budget. What he gave us was a $61 billion deficit. Can we afford four more years?" That ad began airing nationally the week of October 20 and continued to air through the week of the election.

By changing the visual form and adding new inflation-soaked items to each run of these neutral reporter ads, strategists kept inflation before the public without deflating attention to their message. In an initial wave of person-in-the-street ads, in talking head ads featuring Reagan, in a bar chart, in an ad delivered by Bush, in a spot about Carter's refusal to debate, in an ad about increases in the price of groceries, and in ads featuring Edward Kennedy week after week the same question was hammered home: Can we afford four more years of high inflation? High interest rates and joblessness played supporting roles in some of these ads.

The first set of Reagan ads that aired in early September were personal witness ads attacking Carter's economic failures. A carpenter noted, for example, that although he voted for Carter in 1976 he wanted to go back to work and so was voting for Reagan. Another man observed that he had been out of work since April and was still looking for a job. A third averred that he couldn't afford to buy a home. These ads aired from August 28 through the week of September 14 and were then discontinued. Dailey told reporters that he was unhappy with them. They appeared to be staged. "They just didn't work," says O'Reilly. Subsequent tests by Wirthlin would suggest that Carter's person-in-the-street ads lacked credibility as well.

The economic indictment was reinforced in a thirty second TV spot called "Everything Up" that aired nationally from the week of September 29 through election week. In it a bar graph shows the increases in food, auto, home, clothing, and transportation prices. The 50% in transportation costs drives the final bar off the screen. "The new Carter economics

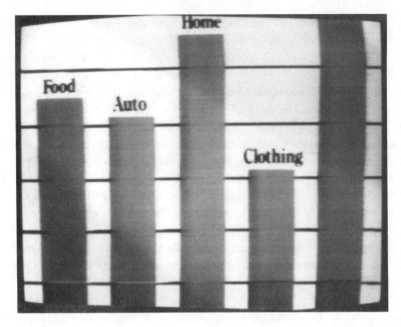

Anti-Carter ad televised from late September through election week by the Republicans.

will give us more of the same. That adds up to less for everyone. The Carter record speaks for itself," intoned the announcer at the ad's end.

From the week of September 15 into the week of September 29, the Republicans linked these same economic indictments to Carter's unwillingness to participate in the Reagan-Anderson debate. The spot, which aired intensively the evening of the debate, focused on an empty podium and was narrated by a woman whose precise diction and low-keyed, authoritative tone invited viewers to conclude that she was a spokesperson for the League of Women Voters. The ad's message: Carter was unwilling to debate because he could not defend his economic record. "The League of Women Voters invited President Carter to join in the 1980 debates," noted the announcer. "He refused the invitation. Maybe it's because, during his administration, inflation has gone as high as 18%. . . . the number of Americans out of work has reached 8 1/2 million . . . housing starts have hit a new low . . . while interest rates have hit a new high . . . maybe he won't debate because he knows the real question is: Can we afford 4 more years of this?"

The week of October 27, the same argument was refreshened with a TV ad that contrasted Carter's 1976 promise to stabilize food prices with the cost of bread "up over 74%. Hamburger, up over 114%. Milk, up over 86%. Sugar, up over 156%. Thanks to Carter's runaway inflation," says the announcer, "we pay more and more and the farmer makes less. Can we afford four more years of this?"

Just as the strongest foreign policy attacks on Carter would have been carried in an ad sponsored by Democrats for Reagan, insulating Reagan from any negative feedback, so too the strongest economic ads simply rebroadcast a section of a stump speech delivered by Kennedy in the primaries. In the speech, Kennedy criticized Carter's handling of the hostage crisis, Carter's high interest rates, and Carter's inflation. Like the ad indicting Carter's indecisive foreign policy, these ads were aired selectively. But where the ad on foreign policy was broadcast in the South, the Kennedy ads were aired in states in which Kennedy had defeated Carter in the primaries.

The use of the "Kennedy ads" was not part of the original Republican strategy. "We tested them," O'Reilly recalls. "I was so amazed by the results I had them tested again. The reaction was 'That's what Senator Kennedy feels about Jimmy Carter. It's not dirty.' "

Rebroadcasting the attacks of the primaries had been a practice Rafshoon used against Ford in 1976. When the Republicans had countered with ads showing Reagan now endorsing Ford, Rafshoon responded with ads replaying Reagan's earlier indictments of Ford and Kissinger. In '76 the Republicans had made no efforts that I know of to remove the Democratic attacks from the air.

In 1980, however, the use of the "Kennedy ads" spawned a legal fight between the two campaigns. Cyrus Gardner, counsel to the Carter-Mondale campaign in California, sent a wire to television stations demanding that they refrain from airing the ads. He was acting, he says, on the personal authorization of Edward Kennedy,[66] obtained by Carter California campaign manager Mickey Kantor. The wire said:

> SENATOR KENNEDY UNEQUIVOCALLY SUPPORTS PRESIDENT CARTER'S RE-ELECTION, AND BROADCAST SAID COMMERCIAL KNOWINGLY AND MALICIOUSLY PLACES THE SENATOR IN A FALSE LIGHT BY SUGGESTING OTHERWISE. FURTHER, THE FEDERAL ELECTION COMMISSION CONFIRMED TODAY THAT DEMOCRATS FOR REAGAN IS NOT, REPEAT NOT, A CAMPAIGN COMMITTEE AUTHORIZED BY GOVERNOR REAGAN. THIS BROADCAST IS THEREFORE DECEPTIVELY LABELED IN VIOLATION OF FCC AND FCC (sic) REGULATIONS AND FEDERAL STATUTES, AND CONTAINS MATERIAL DEFAMATORY AS TO OUR CLIENT. DEMAND IS HEREBY MADE THAT YOU REFRAIN FROM PUBLISHING, UTTERING OR BROADCASTING IN ANY MANNER THE FOREGOING COMMERCIAL. YOU ARE HEREBY NOTIFIED THAT YOUR FAILURE TO HONOR SAID DEMAND WILL RESULT IN OUR CLIENT PURSUING ALL APPLICABLE LEGAL REMEDIES AS AGAINST YOU.

Kennedy confirms authorizing the action. In fact, Democrats for Reagan was a committee authorized by Reagan. Gardner says that the FEC could find no confirmation of that fact at the time his contacts in Washington checked with it. Neither Kennedy nor the Carter campaign took any subsequent legal action against the stations. Indeed they could not. The law explicitly forbids stations to censor political ads by bona fide candidates and in return protects stations from libel suits resulting from the airing of such ads.

At the advice of their attorney Mark Fowler, the Republicans sent a wire to each of the stations airing the "Kennedy" ads that said: "Reference telex you may have received from C. J. Gardner, purported representative of Senator Edward Kennedy. That telex is a malicious attempt to discourage broadcast of spots purchased by Democrats for Reagan. Please be advised as follows: 1. Democrats for Reagan is an authorized committee. . . .; 2. Under Section 315(a) of the Communications Act of 1934, as amended, a station may not censor or refuse to broadcast spots authorized by Governor Reagan and authorized committees because of content. The Supreme Court has ruled that in light of the no-censorship provision, a station is immune from law suits for libel, as threatened by Gardner. 3. The sponsorship ID on all spots comports with all FEC and FCC requirements. The Gardner telex contains false information and is an effort to frighten broadcasters. . . ."

Some stations then contended that they would not air the ads because they were "banding," that is, lines were running through the spots. "I called our attorney," notes O'Reilly, "and said they [the stations] were taking off the spots because of banding. 'The law says they can't be taken off because of banding' he said. Their next response was to say that they'd lost the spots. We responded that we wanted to see their logs. We also said that we're delivering another commercial and we intend to pursue this matter with the FCC. If you have problems call the FCC. Then we decided, if they're [the Carter campaign] so upset about this, let's increase the allocations. We were only running them 20% of the time. We upped that to 40%."

This series of economic ads set in place the evidence to be used by voters to answer the question Reagan phrased both at the end of the debate with Carter and in his election eve speech. "Are you better off now than you were four years ago?"

Reagan's Election Eve Speech

Reagan's nationally telecast election eve speech is a memorable condensation of his campaign. In its opening and closing sections it recaps the vision embedded in his positive ads. When he asks the country to vote for Carter if it is better off now than four years ago he frames the central question raised by his campaign's anti-Carter ads.

Reagan's speech countered what he projected to be Carter's vision of

America and celebrated his own. Reagan's was a vision that reassured conservatives that he was one of them at the same time as it signaled moderates and liberals that they had nothing to fear from a Reagan presidency. Reagan envisioned "a society that frees the energies and ingenuity of our people while it extends compassion to the lonely, the desperate, and the forgotten."

"Does history still have a place for America, for her people, for her great ideals?" Reagan asked. Some, presumably Carter, say no, "that our energy is spent, our days of greatness at an end, that a great national malaise is upon us." By contrast, Reagan found "nothing wrong with the American people." He then added: "Last year I lost a friend who was more than a symbol of the Hollywood dream industry. To millions he was a symbol of our country itself. Duke Wayne did not believe our country was ready for the dustbin of history. Just before his death, he said in his own blunt way, 'Just give the American people a good cause and there's nothing they can't lick.' "

The fact that Reagan battles the supposed vision of Carter with the convictions of John Wayne, it should be noted, does not provoke sniggers from the press, who instead hold that this was a fine speech. This suggests the extent to which Reagan has managed to accomplish his ends. First, he has surmounted any barriers his acting career imposed on his presidential chances. Second, he has managed to hold onto his conservative base. Wayne was a spokesman for the political right. He had previously appeared in the Goldwater film "Choice" and in ads advocating the election of conservative James Buckley to the U.S. Senate from New York. On election eve, the Democrats offered as their representative American, their symbol of the American people, Henry Fonda/"Mr. Roberts," while Reagan offered John Wayne/"Rooster Cogburn."

Third, he has managed to belie the worst fears premised by the Carter campaign. Reagan closes with an appeal that whispers peace and posterity, hardly the message of a mad bomber. "Let us resolve tonight [not the I and you of the Carter speech but a mutual covenant] that young Americans will always . . . find there a city of hope in a country that is free. . . . And let us resolve they will say of our day and of our generation, we did keep the faith with our God, that we did act worthy of ourselves, that we did protect and pass on lovingly that shining city on a hill. Thank you and good night."

In the speech, which was taped in a single take in Peoria, Illinois, Reagan tried on the role of president. This speech was for him what John Kennedy's taking of the oath in the address to the Houston ministers was in the 1960 campaign—the dress rehearsal. In it Reagan established that he understood the nature of presidential rhetoric better than did the incumbent president. Reagan demonstrated not simply that he met his definition of a president—he could preserve the American dream and instill confidence that the country would be better off under his leadership than Carter's—but he also tacitly reminded viewers that he had drawn himself into Carter's circle, for he too was well-informed, vigorous, stable, and intelligent enough to be president.

Slogans

"The Time Is Now," "The Time Is Now for Leadership," and "The Time is Now for Reagan" digested meaning comparable to Eisenhower's "It's Time for a Change." Meanwhile, the ads reminded voters that change was overdue and detailed the kind of leadership Reagan had provided in California and would provide the nation if elected. The slogan also whispered that the electorate had waited four years too long for Carter's promises to be kept.

"A Solid Man in a Sensitive Job" justified a vote for Carter only if Carter's opponent was not solid or not able to handle a sensitive job. With Chappaquiddick shadowing him, the slogan defined Carter's comparative advantage over Kennedy. It was less effective against an opponent who was successfully arguing his competence and Carter's incompetence. So the Democrats fell back on "Re-Elect President Carter on November 4," a slogan suggesting a need to mobilize apathetic or disenchanted voters who might opt to stay home on November 4 but a slogan that provided no reason to vote for Carter. This absence of a compelling reason to vote for Carter was not a weakness for which the advertising or its slogan should be indicted, however. It is instead an indictment of the Carter presidency. As political analyst Walter Dean Burnham writes, "In the most fundamental sense, the 1980 election was a *landslide vote of no confidence in an incumbent administration.*"[67] Reagan won 489 electoral votes to Carter's 49. Reagan carried 50.75% of the vote, Carter 41.02%, and Anderson 6.61%.

Conclusion

Political advertising is now the major means by which candidates for the presidency communicate their messages to voters. As a conduit of this advertising, television attracts both more candidate dollars and more audience attention than radio or print. Unsurprisingly, the spot ad is the most used and the most viewed of the available forms of advertising. By 1980 the half hour broadcast speech—the norm in 1952—had been replaced by the 60 second spot.

Ads enable candidates to build name recognition, frame the questions they view as central to the election, and expose their temperaments, talents, and agendas for the future in a favorable light. In part because more voters attend to spot ads than to network news and in part because reporters are fixated with who's winning and losing instead of what the candidates are proposing, some scholars believe that ads provide the electorate with more information than network news. Still, ads more often successfully reinforce existing dispositions than create new ones.

Ads also argue the relevance of issues to our lives. In the 1950s the public at large did not find political matters salient to it.[1] From the late 1950s to the early 1970s the perception of the relevance of political matters to one's day-to-day life increased[2] at all educational levels. Citizens saw a greater connection between what occurred in the political world and what occurred in their lives.[3]

TV ads' ability to personalize and the tendency of TV news to reduce issues to personal impact have, in my judgment, facilitated that change. Ads argued, for example, that a vote against nonproliferation could increase the Strontium 90 in children's ice cream. As the salience of political issues increased so too did the consistency of the beliefs of individual voters. Dissonant views are less likely to be simultaneously held now than before. This tendency is also reinforced by political advertising, for politicians have increasingly argued the interconnection of issues of importance to them. In 1980 Reagan predicated a strong defense on a strong economy. In 1968 Nixon tied crime, lawlessness, and the war in Vietnam into a single bundle and laid it on Humphrey's doorstep.

Ads also define the nature of the presidency by stipulating the attributes a president should have. In the process they legitimize certain occupations. Ike polished the assumption that being a general was a suitable qualification. Carter argued that being an outsider plus an engineer, a farmer, a businessman but not a lawyer qualified him. Reagan contended that being the governor of a large state as well as a union leader were stronger qualifications than being an incumbent president. Eisenhower, Nixon, Johnson, Ford, and Carter argued that being the incumbent qualified one for the presidency.

This book was premised on the assumption that advertising provides an optic through which presidential campaigns can be productively viewed. In the eight campaigns I have focused on we have seen, for example, various styles of leadership reflected in the candidates' treatment of their advertisers and advertising. Where Nixon maintained tight control over advertising decisions in 1960, Kennedy delegated all responsibility for advertising to others. At the same time, ad campaigns that lurched uncertainly from one message form to another, from one set of strategists to another, as Ford's did in the Republican primaries of 1976, suggested perhaps that the candidate and his advisers were unable to provide a clear sense of the direction in which they wanted to take the country, an observation consistent with that of Ford's admen in the general election who tried and failed to divine the administration's vision of the future under Ford.

Occasionally, a candidate's response to the requirements of advertising raises troublesome questions about his suitability for the office or, perhaps, about the intensity of his desire to hold it. Adlai Stevenson's perpetual quest for the perfect word or perfectly phrased argument and his apparent need to continue to perfect texts even as he was walking to the stage invite doubts about his ability to act decisively.

When the acceptance speech and the election eve telecasts are taken as the brackets bounding advertising, a focus on paid messages can reveal a campaign's fundamental coherence or incoherence. In a coherent campaign, the acceptance speech at the convention synopsizes and polishes the message the candidate has communicated in the primaries as a means of forecasting both the themes of the general election campaign and of this person's presidency. The message is then systematically developed in the advertising of the general election and placed in its final form on election eve where the candidate tries on the presidency by indicating for the country his vision of the next four years under his leadership. When from the first campaign advertising of January through the last on election eve in November, candidates offer consistent, coherent messages about themselves and the future as they envision it, they minimize the likelihood that their record or plans will be distorted effectively by opponents, and create a clear set of expectations to govern their conduct in office, expectations that may haunt them when they seek reelection.

Viewing campaign advertising as an extended message rather than a series of discrete message units also enables us to see how a candidate's response to attacks in the primaries can either strengthen or strangle the candidate's chances in the general election. When attacks are raised in the primaries and effectively neutralized, as were questions about Kennedy's age and religion in 1960, the issues can be effectively dispatched in the general election. Kennedy's widely aired speech to the Houston ministers builds on a structure of belief first cemented in Kennedy's speeches and ads in the West Virginia primary. Accordingly, those including NCPAC, Glenn, and Hart, whose ads in 1984 exploited Mondale's vulnerability to the charge that he was the captive of special interests, may have done Mondale a favor since the charges forced him to demonstrate that he had called and would continue to call for sacrifices from every segment of the electorate including those whose endorsements fueled his candidacy. At the same time, these charges against Mondale forced his natural constituencies to accept a fact they might otherwise have rejected—that if they demanded Mondale's public and total embrace of their agendas, that embrace would enfeeble his candidacy and the credibility of their endorsements.

Preventing candidates from using advertising to create a sense of themselves discrepant from who they are and what they have done is the vigilant presence of opponents and the increasingly vigilant presence of the press. Throughout this book we have seen instances in which candidate's words and actions in settings they did not control undermined the crafted images of their ads. So, for example, the image of the sweating, gaunt, pale Nixon of the first debate in 1960 clashed with the polished presence in his ads. Although ads can and have lied, the vigilance of press and opponents makes that increasingly unlikely.

In many ways televised political advertising is the direct descendant of the advertised messages carried in song and on banners, torches, bandannas, and broadsides. Ads continue to ally the candidate with the people, only now that takes the form of showing the candidate pressing the flesh or answering questions from groups of citizens. Candidates continue to digest their messages into slogans, yet these now appear at the end of broadcast ads rather than on banners and torches. Candidates continue to overstate their accomplishments and understate their failures. So, for example, as governor, despite his claims to the contrary, Ronald

Reagan did not increase welfare benefits 43%, although he did increase them just as, contrary to his advertising, Andy Jackson had served in one, not two wars.

What differentiates the claims of Jackson's time from those aired today is the role the press has now assumed as monitor of presidential advertising. While the partisan papers controlled by his opponent revealed Jackson's actual war record and noted that his was not the hand that guided the plow, those papers were not a credible source of information for Jackson's likely supporters. By contrast, in the 1980 campaign, credible newspaper articles and network news stories—bearing the imprint of neither party—publicly scrutinized the adequacy of Reagan's claims. The difficulty in relying on news to correct distortions in advertising is, of course, that comparatively few people consume news while many are exposed to ads.

One of the argumentative ploys born in the political and product advertising of the nineteenth century was refined by politicians in the age of television and then shunted aside by Watergate. By visually associating the favored candidate with pictures of well-fed cattle, happy families, large bundles of grain, and bulging factories, banners and broadsides argued to literate and illiterate alike that this candidate stood for prosperity. The opponent, on the other hand, was visually tied to drawings of starving cattle, poverty-ravished families, empty grain bins, and fireless factories. Some of the associations seemed to have no direct bearing on what sort of president the candidate would make.

Political argument by visual association flowered for the same reason it appeared in product advertising. Initially, advertising for products simply identified the existence, cost, function, and way to obtain the product. As success bred success, products performing the same function proliferated. Distinguishing attributes—some real, some fictional—were sought to persuade customers that one product rather than its twin should be purchased. Van Buren and Harrison were parity products, differentiated by the associations sculpted by their respective campaigns. Since the advertising of the early nineteenth century relied on drawings rather than photographs the range of possible associations was limited only by the artist's imagination.

The wizardry of videotape and film editing did not change the nature of argument from visual association—it simply increased its subtlety. In the process, the evidentiary burden that candidates should assume dropped. So, for example, Goldwater's ads juxtaposed a picture of Billie Sol Estes with scenes of street riots and then intercut a picture of Bobby Baker. Goldwater then appeared on screen to indict the Democrats for their disregard of law, order, and morality. Estes' relation to Baker, the relation of either to the street riots, or the relation among the three and Lyndon Johnson are not explicitly argued.

In 1968 this type of argument reached a new level of complexity in the Republican ad that intercut scenes from the Vietnam War and from the riots outside the Democratic convention with pictures of Hubert Humphrey, including one in which he appears to be smiling. The juxtaposition of highly evocative images invites the audience to impute causality.

The form of argument embodied in this ad is as powerful as it is irrational. It solicits a visceral and not an intellectual response. As a vehicle of attack, this type of ad was vanquished by Watergate because Watergate forced politicians and public to consider what is and is not fair attack in a political campaign. Lurking in McGovern's campaign are the forms of attack ad that will replace it: the personal witness ad and the neutral reporter ad. Both of these mimic some of the features of news. The personal testimony ads consist of actual individuals reporting their opinions of the opposing candidate's performance. They resembled person-in-the-street interviews and are almost a survey; the opinions expressed are not scripted—indeed, their ungrammatical nature underscores their spontaneity. They do not appear to be unfair because, first, we are taught that everyone is entitled to express his or her opinion and, second, these people are voicing opinions that the electorate presumably is disposed to share. In 1976 Ford used this form against Carter; in 1980 Reagan briefly used it against Carter; in both the primaries and general election of 1980 Carter employed it against his rivals. In the early primaries of 1984 Glenn used it against Mondale.

In the neutral reporter spot, an announcer whose delivery is deliberately low key details facts about the opponent. The ad itself rarely draws any conclusion from the data. That task is left to the audience. Ford did this in a 1976 ad comparing Carter's statements in the campaign with his actual record as governor of Georgia. An ad by Carter did the same to Reagan in 1980.

As strange as it may seem since the independent PACS have been roundly criticized for their advertising against Democratic senators, the PAC presidential ads also fall, in the main, in 1980, into the neutral reporter category. A typical one simply quotes a promise by Carter and demonstrates that he had not kept it. The most cogent are those by the National Conservative Political Action Committee that edit from the Carter-Ford debates specific promises by Carter, show him making them, freeze the frame, and print across the screen the evidence establishing that the promise has been broken.

By replacing attack ads that use visual not verbal means to prompt sweeping inferences with attack ads that verbally and visually invite judgments based on verifiable facts, Watergate temporarily transformed a form of presidential attack advertising from an exercise in the prompting of false inferences to an exercise in traditional argument.

Just as political attack advertising survives, but in a circumscribed form, so too the political speech survives, albeit in shortened form, in televised advertising. Contrary to popular belief, the speech remains the staple of paid political broadcasting. There is not a presidential general election campaign in the televised age in which each candidate did not deliver at least two nationally broadcast speeches. In most campaigns far more are given and the candidates deliver short speeches in spot ads as well. Speeches and segments of speeches also recur in telecast campaign biographies.

The reason we mistakenly think the broadcast speech is an object of antiquity is that half hour speeches tend to draw smaller, more highly partisan audiences than spots. Additionally, when a candidate such as Nixon or Ford delivers addresses by radio, he is speaking on a medium to which many of us do not routinely attend. Moreover, we tend not to think of five minute or 60 second statements by the candidate as speeches. Finally, a televised speech by a presidential candidate was more novel in the 1950s than it is now and so we are more likely to have noted and to long remember its occurrence then than now. Still, if judged by number of minutes on the air in which the candidate is speaking directly to the audience, Reagan's total exceeds Eisenhower's from either 1952 or 1956. If judged by the total number of televised appearances each made speaking directly to the audience, Reagan leads by a substantial margin.

The widespread perception that being able to present broadcast messages persuasively to a mass public would emerge as a criterion governing selection of presidential candidates is not convincingly confirmed from 1952 to 1980. Of the candidates to receive their party's nomination since 1952, Kennedy was an adequate speaker, Goldwater and Nixon often excellent, and only Reagan a master. In short, the ability to deliver televised messages artfully, while certainly an asset for those who possess it, has not become so central a qualification for the presidency that it has exiled candidates who lack it.

Another misconception about political advertising holds that spots and paid programming are somehow alien to the political speech, a thing apart, a bad dream, an aberration. An analysis of both the stock campaign speeches and the acceptance addresses of the presidential candidates suggests instead that the advertising is rarely anything but a digest of the speeches being delivered throughout the country. Occasionally, but not often, the candidate will say something important in a stump speech that does not appear in the paid broadcasting. But these things are usually strategic blunders such as Carter's assertion that Reagan will rend the country North from South.

As I have noted in each chapter, the convention acceptance speeches are a highly reliable predictor of the content of the candidate's ads in the general election. For those who read the campaign's position papers, examine its brochures, and listen to its stump speeches, the ads function as reinforcement. Those who ignore the other campaign-produced materials receive a digest of them in the ads. This is true both of the advertising against the opponent and the advertising supporting the candidate.

The cost of reaching voters through broadcast advertising poses other problems. Since spot advertising is both costly and often the most cost efficient means of reaching a mass of voters, the contemporary reliance on spots means that those who cannot afford to purchase them, with rare exceptions, are denied the ability to have their ideas either heard or taken seriously in presidential primaries.

For these and related reasons, as I noted in the Introduction, public concern over the nature and influence of political advertising has been rising. Responding to this escalating public concern, legislators drafted or considered drafting bills that can be grouped into three broad categories. The first would have either the public or the radio and TV stations assume the burden of financing some or all of candidate advertising; the second would give candidates attacked by PACs free response time or— regardless of the origin of attack—would give the attacked candidate free response time; the third, still in the talking stage as this book goes to press, would promote changes in the form by offering free time to those agreeing to certain formats (e.g., mandate talking head ads) or lengths (e.g., specify a minimum length or make available free time in no less than five minute and half hour blocks).

Underlying the debate over these and like proposals is widening consensus that the electoral process would benefit if the candidates' cost of reaching a mass audience could be reduced; if all bona-fide candidates could be provided with sufficient access to communicate their basic ideas; if politicians made greater use of longer forms of communication and the electorate as a whole attended more readily to such forms; if candidates assumed or could be enticed to assume the obligation of being viewed by the public in forms such as debates that they do not control; if the advantage PACs can bring to a presidential candidate could be countered or muted.

Still, if political advertising did not exist we would have to invent it. Political advertising legitimizes our political institutions by affirming that change is possible within the political system, that the president can effect change, that votes can make a difference. As a result, advertising channels discontent into the avenues provided by the government and acts as a safety valve for pressures that might otherwise turn against the system to demand its substantial modification or overthrow.

Political advertising does this, in part, by underscoring the power of the ballot. Your vote makes a difference, it says, at the same time as its carefully targeted messages imply that the votes that would go to the opponent are best left uncast.

Political ads affirm that the country is great, has a future, is respected. The contest they reflect is over who should be elected, not over whether there should be an election. The very existence of the contest suggests that there is a choice, that the voters' selection of one candidate over the other will make a difference. Ads also define the problems we face and assure us that there are solutions. If there are no solutions, a candidate would speak that truth at great risk.

Notes

CHAPTER ONE

1. Reprinted in *American Heritage* (October, 1976), 5.
2. Porter, 4.
3. *Ibid.,* 7–8.
4. Lurie, 27.
5. Richard P. McCormick, "New Perspectives on Jacksonian Politics," in Bonadio, 552.
6. For discussion see Burnham, *The Current Crisis in American Politics.*
7. Weisberger, 63–64.
8. Smith, *John Adams II: 1784–1826,* 898.
9. *Ibid.,* 901–2.
10. Quoted by Smith, *ibid.,* 900.
11. Ward, *Andrew Jackson: Symbol for an Age,* 55.
12. *Ibid.,* 57.
13. Ward, *Society, Manners, and Politics in the United States: Letters on North America,* 306.
14. William Graham Sumner, *Andrew Jackson as a Public Man,* 115.
15. These handbills can be found in the Rare Books Room of the Library of Congress.
16. Lorant, *The Presidency,* 108.
17. See Schlesinger, *The Age of Jackson,* 25–26.
18. Chambers, 45.
19. Rossiter, *Parties and Politics in America,* 47.
20. Fitzpatrick, XXXI, 47–48.
21. Boyd, XIV, 650.
22. Cf. Chambers, *Political Parties in a New Nation,* 32–33.
23. McCormick, in Bonadio, 551.
24. Bryce, II, 74, 77, 72.
25. Nevins, 472.
26. *Ibid.,* I, 486.
27. Washburn, "Campaign Banners," 181.
28. Richard J. Oglesby, *Century Magazine* (June 1900), n.p.
29. Harrison to Gen. Solomon Van Rensselaer, August 25, 1836, in Bonney, II, 56–57.

30. Cleaves, 308.
31. *Ibid.,* 316.
32. *Ibid.,* 327.
33. Gunderson, 167.
34. *Ibid.,* 171.
35. *Ibid.,* 171.
36. *Ibid.,* 174.
37. *Ohio State Journal* (September 23, 1852), n.p.
38. Nicolay, 134ff.
39. Baringer, 3ff.
40. *New York Times,* October 4, 1936, 8.
41. "Character of Democracy in the United States," in Woodrow Wilson, III, 113.
42. Bryan, 618.
43. Samuel L. Becker, "Presidential Power: The Influence of Broadcasting," in *Quarterly Journal of Speech,* XLVII (February, 1961), 12.
44. *New York Times,* November 4, 1928, 16.
45. *The Public Papers and Addresses of Franklin D. Roosevelt: The Genesis of the New Deal: 1928–1932,* 659.
46. *New York Times,* November 4, 1928, 16.
47. Stevenson, xxiv–xxv.
48. *New York Times,* November 4, 1928, 16.
49. *New York Times,* November 4, 1928, 2.
50. *New York Times,* October 4, 1936, 8.
51. Smith, *Campaign Addresses,* 310.
52. *New York Times,* October 4, 1936, 16.
53. *Ibid.*
54. Mott, 216.
55. *Ibid.,* 720.
56. Redding, 255–59.
57. *Ibid.*
58. *New York Times,* December 7, 1923, 3.
59. *Ibid.*
60. David G. Clark, 231.
61. Samuel L. Becker and Elmer W. Lower, 27.
62. David G. Clark, 231.
63. *New York Times,* November 4, 1928, 16.
64. *Ibid.*
65. David G. Clark, 232.
66. Coolidge, 219.
67. *New York Times,* October 28, 1928, 1.
68. Becker, *op. cit.,* 10.
69. *New York Times,* October 28, 1928, 1.
70. David G. Clark, 234.
71. Farley, 319.
72. *Ibid.*
73. Barnouw, *The Golden Web,* 208.
74. *Ibid.,* 209.
75. Personal interview with the author.

76. Redding, 239–41.
77. See Bormann, 121.
78. Quoted by Schlesinger in *The Coming of the New Deal*, 558–59.
79. See *FDR: The Intimate Presidency*, 51.
80. See Tompkins, 139.
81. See Barnouw, *The Golden Web*, 51–52.
82. Schlesinger, *The Politics of Upheaval*, 617.
83. Fielding, 50.
84. *Ibid.*, 49.
85. *Ibid.*
86. Redding, 253. See also *New York Times*, October 19, 1948, 22.
87. Personal interview with the author (Brightman).
88. Redding, 254.
89. Personal interview with the author. (Brightman).
90. Barnouw, *The Golden Web*, 257.
91. *New York Times*, July 18, 1948, 7.
92. Raymond Carroll, 178.
93. *New York Times*, December 31, 1948, 3.
94. *Broadcasting* (September 10, 1951), 26.
95. Rosenbloom, 50.

CHAPTER TWO

1. John Bartlow Martin, 392.
2. Halberstam, *The Powers That Be*, 328.
3. *Ibid.*, 237.
4. *New York Times Magazine*, November 2, 1952, 12.
5. *Tide* (May 19, 1956), 27.
6. See Report of Senate Rules Subcommittee on Privileges and Elections; Kelly, *Professional Public Relations*, 190–91; Shaffer, 620.
7. Personal interview with the author (McGowan).
8. Campbell et al., *The American Voter*, 25.
9. Sellers, 22.
10. In Campbell et al., *Elections and the Political Order*, 294.
11. Churchill, 56–60.
12. Morin, 113.
13. Speech reprinted in *New York Times*, October 25, 1952.
14. Barton J. Bernstein, "Election of 1952," in Schlesinger, *History of American Presidential Elections 1789–1968*, 3225.
15. Chester, *Radio, Television and American Politics*, 83.
16. Campbell et al., *Elections and the Political Order*, 302.
17. *New York Times*, October 30, 1952, 35.
18. Thomson, 200. Unless otherwise indicated, all polling data cited are drawn from *The Gallup Poll*.
19. Hughes, 33.
20. See Table 2-12 in Campbell et al., *The American Voter*, 25.
21. *New York Times*, October 28, 1952, 35.
22. *New York Times*, October 30, 1952, 38.
23. *New York Times*, October 24, 1952, 15.

24. *New York Times,* October 28, 1952, 22.
25. *New York Times,* October 24, 1952, 15.
26. *New York Times,* October 28, 1952, 35.
27. *New York Times,* October 28, 1952, 40.
28. Personal interview with the author (McGowan).
29. Personal interview with the author (Wirtz).
30. Copy obtained from Judge Carl McGowan.
31. A copy of the telecast survives in the audiovisual collection of the JFK Library.
32. September 18, 1952, 1.
33. In Doyle, 174.
34. Personal interview with the author (Tubby).
35. Personal interview with the author (Guggenheim).
36. Quoted by William McCormick Blair Jr. in Doyle, 237.
37. Personal interview with the author (Wirtz).
38. In Doyle, 149–50.
39. Personal interview with the author (McGowan).
40. *Ibid.*
41. Cf. Kenneth Davis, *The Politics of Honor,* 289.
42. In Doyle, 125.
43. Personal interview with the author (Wilson).
44. Eric Sevareid quoted by Fawn Brodie, *Richard Nixon,* 309.
45. *Ibid.,* 308.
46. August 25, 1952, in Schlesinger, ed., *History of American Presidential Elections,* 3297.
47. Margaret Truman, 569.
48. Quoted by McGrory in Doyle, 177.
49. *New York Times,* October 16, 1952, 21.
50. *New York Times,* October 16, 1952, 21.
51. *The Oregonian,* September 21, 1952, 42.
52. Nixon, *Memoirs,* 88.
53. Eisenhower, *Mandate for Change,* 65.
54. *Ibid.,* 97.
55. *Ibid.,* 68.
56. Los Angeles, *The Mirror,* September 22, 1952, 2.
57. Personal interview with the author (Rogers).
58. Thomson, 57.
59. *Los Angeles Times,* September 25, 1952, 5.
60. *Los Angeles Times,* September 25, 1952, 1.
61. John Bartlow Martin, *Adlai Stevenson of Illinois,* 703.
62. Wills, 108–9.
63. Nixon, *Six Crises,* 86.
64. *Ibid.,* 110.
65. *Los Angeles Times,* September 25, 1952, 1.
66. Information obtained from Ted Rogers who served as Nixon's media adviser in that campaign.
67. *Washington Post,* September 29, 1952, 2.
68. *Los Angeles Times,* September 24, 1952, 1.
69. *Los Angeles Times,* September 25, 1952, 6.

70. Robert W. O'Brien and Elizabeth Jones, 35.
71. September 24, 1952, 1.
72. Eisenhower, *Mandate for Change,* 69.
73. *Ibid.*
74. Personal interview with the author (Rogers).
75. Halberstam, *The Powers That Be,* 330.
76. Nixon, *Six Crises,* 129.
77. *The Baltimore Sun,* November 3, 1952.
78. Campbell et al., *The American Voter,* 46–47.
79. Thomson, 7.
80. Gordon Cotler, "That Plague of Spots from Madison Avenue," *The Reporter,* November 25, 1952, 7–8; see also Griese, 34–38.
81. Mayer, 294–95. Much of the factual information on the 1952 spot strategy is drawn from Mayer's book and from articles by Bradford, Griese, Hollitz, and Wood.
82. *New York Times,* October 16, 1952, 21.
83. These spots are housed in the audiovisual collection of the Wisconsin Historical Society.
84. Levin's memo can be found at the Wisconsin Historical Society.
85. Hughes, 27.
86. *New York Times Magazine,* November 2, 1952, 70.
87. Campbell et al., *The American Voter,* 50.
88. Personal interview with the author (Brightman).
89. Ball, 143–144.
90. *Ibid.,* 143.
91. Eisenhower, *Mandate for Change,* 73.

CHAPTER THREE

1. Chester, *Radio, Television and American Politics,* 76.
2. Campbell et al., *The American Voter,* 49.
3. Personal interview with the author (Fritchey).
4. *Ibid.*
5. Democratic National Committee files, John F. Kennedy Library.
6. *The Reporter,* September 6, 1956, 20.
7. Personal interview with the author (Wilson).
8. Harris, xxiv–xxv.
9. *Ibid.,* 206.
10. *Ibid.,* 242.
11. *Ibid.,* 249.
12. *Ibid.,* 5.
13. Personal interview with the author (Brightman).
14. *The Reporter,* September 6, 1956, 16.
15. Personal interview with the author (Ball).
16. See data in Runyan.
17. Chester, *Radio, Television and American Politics,* 99.
18. Democratic National Committee files, John F. Kennedy Library.
19. *Tide,* May 19, 1956, 29.

20. Personal interview with the author (Schuebel Ballard).
21. *Ibid.*
22. Eisenhower, *Mandate for Change,* 569.
23. The speech is reprinted in Schlesinger, *History of American Presidential Elections.*
24. *New York Times,* November 5, 1956, 12.
25. *New York Times,* November 4, 1956, 79.
26. *New York Times,* October 29, 1956, 17.
27. Nixon, *Memoirs,* 167.
28. *Ibid.,* 170.
29. *Ibid.,* 170.
30. Brodie, 353.
31. Nixon, *Memoirs,* 173.
32. *Ibid.*
33. *New York Times,* October 9, 1956, 12.
34. *New York Times,* October 24, 1956, 8.
35. *New York Times,* October 31, 1956, 10.
36. Personal interview with the author (Wirtz).
37. Personal interview with the author (Tubby).
38. Personal interview with the author (Wirtz).
39. Democratic National Committee files, John F. Kennedy Library.
40. Personal interview with the author (Ball).
41. Personal interview with the author (Stern).
42. Personal interview with the author (Newton).
43. Personal interview with the author (Stern).
44. *New York Times,* August 28, 1956, 16.
45. Gallup, October 7, 1955.
46. Personal interview with the author (Wilson).
47. Minow et al., 36.
48. *Ibid.*
49. *New York Times,* October 28, 1956, 13.
50. *New York Times,* October 19, 1956, 6E.
51. *Ibid.*
52. Democratic National Committee files, John F. Kennedy Library.
53. Campbell, *The American Voter,* 25.
54. Lorant, *The Glorious Burden,* 808.
55. *New York Times,* November 3, 1956, 12.
56. Martin, *Adlai Stevenson and the World,* 392.
57. Personal interview with the author (Ball).
58. *New York Times,* November 2, 1956, 17.
59. Ball, 145–46.
60. Eisenhower, *Waging Peace,* 18.
61. Campbell, *The American Voter,* 47.
62. *New York Times,* October 3, 1956, 1.
63. *New York Times,* September 30, 1956, 63.
64. *Ibid.*
65. *New York Times,* July 8, 1956, 42.
66. These storyboards survive in the Democratic National Committee files of John F. Kennedy Library.

CHAPTER FOUR

1. Chisholm, 2.
2. O'Donnell and Powers, 146.
3. Sorensen files, John F. Kennedy Library.
4. *Ibid.*
5. Parmet, 242–43.
6. White, *Making . . . 1960,* 289.
7. *Ibid.,* 127.
8. These ads and the others cited in this chapter survive in the Schuck Collection at John F. Kennedy Library and/or in the Denove Collection at UCLA.
9. O'Brien, 73.
10. Sorensen, *Kennedy,* 139.
11. Personal interview with the author (Finch).
12. *New York Times,* November 4, 1960, 18.
13. See *New York Times,* September 18, 1960, 50.
14. Democratic National Committee files, John F. Kennedy Library.
15. *Ibid.*
16. A videotape of the meeting survives in the John F. Kennedy Library.
17. Halberstam, *The Powers That Be,* 325–26.
18. Personal interview with the author (Wilson).
19. Personal interview with the author (Denove).
20. Personal interview with the author (Schuebel Ballard).
21. Personal interview with the author (Reinsch).
22. The time-buying information survives in John F. Kennedy Library.
23. Sorensen files, John F. Kennedy Library.
24. Personal interview with the author (Sorensen).
25. "Religion and Politics: The 1960 Election," in Campbell et al., *Elections and the Political Order,* 123.
26. *New York Times,* October 16, 1960, 56.
27. Personal interview with the author (Reinsch).
28. Blair and Blair, 588–608.
29. Personal interview with the author (Ramey).
30. McCarthy, *The Remarkable Kennedys,* 136.
31. Sorensen, *The Kennedy Legacy,* 108.
32. Sorensen, *Kennedy,* 152.
33. Personal interview with the author (Sorensen).
34. The texts of Truman's statement and of JFK's response are preserved in Sorensen's files in the John F. Kennedy Library.
35. Nixon argued specifically from the types of experience only the vice-presidency could provide.
36. Sorensen files, John F. Kennedy Library.
37. SRC survey data.
38. The text of the debates is included in Kraus ed., *The Great Debates.*
39. Sorensen files, John F. Kennedy Library.
40. *New York Times,* November 3, 1960, 43.
41. Parmet, 241.
42. *New York Times,* October 27, 1960, 12.
43. Wofford, 22.

44. *Ibid.*, 23.
45. White, *The Making of the President 1960,* 387.
46. Wofford, 24.
47. Personal interview with the author (Martin).
48. Personal interview with the author (Gannon).
49. Wills, 124ff.
50. See Nixon, *Memoirs,* 219–22.
51. Seaton files, Dwight David Eisenhower Library.
52. Personal interview with the author (Finch).
53. Nixon, *Memoirs,* 221.
54. Eisenhower, *Waging Peace,* 652–53.
55. *Ibid.*
56. Eisenhower, *Waging Peace,* 597.
57. Runyon, 247.
58. Personal interview with the author (Newton).
59. At Nixon's request, Rogers summarized his recollections of the Fund speech and the debates in a memo to be used as background by Nixon in writing his memoirs.
60. Personal interview with the author (Valenti).
61. Personal interview with the author (Schuebel Ballard).
62. Personal interview with the author (Wilson).
63. Wyckoff, 49.
64. Campbell et al., *Elections and the Political Order,* 124.
65. Speech to Sigma Delta Chi Luncheon, New York, December 3, 1960, in Sorensen files, John F. Kennedy Library.
66. *New York Times,* October 22, 1960, 12.
67. Personal interview with the author (Arnold).
68. Democratic National Committee files, John F. Kennedy Library; Bernard Cherin, "The Constant Campaign," November 15, 1960.
69. Sorensen, *Kennedy,* 209.
70. "Financing the 1960 Election," in Alexander, *Studies in Money in Politics,* 10–14.
71. *Ibid.*, 16–17.
72. *Ibid.*, 19.
73. Cherin, "The Constant Campaign," *op. cit.*
74. *New York Times,* May 6, 1961, 14.

CHAPTER FIVE

1. Moyers' files, Lyndon B. Johnson Library.
2. Personal interview with the author (Lichenstein).
3. "Financing the 1964 Election," in Alexander, *Studies in Money in Politics,* 8.
4. *Ibid.*, 54.
5. Personal interview with the author (Kitchel).
6. Personal interview with the author (Lichenstein).
7. The contract survives in the Lyndon B. Johnson Library.
8. June 16, 1965, Moyers to Graham; see also Carter from Moyers June 24, 1965, in Lyndon B. Johnson Library.
9. Alexander, *op. cit.*, 113.

10. Alexander, *op. cit.,* 115.
11. *Ibid.*
12. Moyers files, Lyndon B. Johnson Library.
13. Personal interview with the author (Moyers).
14. James Graham, quoted by Karl Hess, 90.
15. Goldwater, *The Conscience of a Majority,* 40–41.
16. White, *The Making of a President 1964,* 98.
17. Goldwater, *With No Apologies,* 168.
18. Goldwater, *The Conscience of a Majority,* 184.
19. Goldwater, *With No Apologies,* 178.
20. White, *op. cit.,* 104.
21. Goldwater, *With No Apologies,* 170.
22. White, *op. cit.,* 117–18.
23. *Ibid.,* 160.
24. Goldwater, *With No Apologies,* 188.
25. *Ibid.,* 189.
26. *Ibid.*
27. *Ibid.*
28. White, *op. cit.,* 197–98.
29. Goldwater, *With No Apologies,* 190.
30. White, *op. cit.,* 201.
31. Kessel, 184.
32. Shadegg, 167.
33. Quoted by Kessel, 186–87.
34. Goldwater, *With No Apologies,* 194.
35. *Ibid.*
36. Cicero, in Bovie, 125–26.
37. *New York Times,* October 28, 1964, 10.
38. Benham, 190.
39. Transcript of conference is in an appendix of Hess.
40. Personal interview with the author (Moyers).
41. All correspondence and memos on the campaign cited in this chapter are housed in the Lyndon B. Johnson Library in the Democratic National Committee, Moyers, or Wright files. Johnson's TV and radio ads are in the Lyndon B. Johnson Library; some of Goldwater's TV ads and Johnson's radio and TV ads are in the Schuck collection at the John F. Kennedy Library.
42. Johnson, *The Vantage Point,* 13.
43. Goldwater, *With No Apologies,* 93.
44. Personal interview with the author (Wright).
45. Undated memo from Wright to Graham in Wright's files at the Lyndon B. Johnson Library.
46. Personal interview with the author (McCabe).
47. Personal interview with the author (Moyers).
48. Goldwater, *With No Apologies,* 200.
49. Hess, 99.
50. Page, 127–28.
51. Benham, 191.
52. *New York Times,* October 23, 1964, 54.
53. *Washington Post,* October 26, 1964, A 20.

54. *New York Times,* October 22, 1964, 23.
55. I can find no evidence to support Spero's claim that this ad aired.
56. *New York Times,* October 28, 1964, 32.
57. Personal interview with the author (Schwartz).
58. Personal interview with the author (Valenti).
59. Personal interview with the author (Wright).
60. Personal interview with the author (Lichenstein).
61. In Faber, 168.
62. Goldwater, *With No Apologies,* 201.
63. Barnouw, *Tube of Plenty,* 361.
64. *New York Times,* May 25, 1968, 1.
65. Angus Campbell, "Interpreting the Presidential Victory," in Cummings, 262.
66. Benham, 191.
67. Faber, 245.
68. *Ibid.,* 168.
69. White, *op. cit.,* 330.
70. Shadegg, 247.
71. Goldwater, *With No Apologies,* 204.
72. White, *op. cit.,* 330.
73. See *Time,* September 25, 1964, 15–19.
74. Kessel, 204.
75. Faber, 206.
76. White, *op. cit.,* 333.
77. *New York Times,* October 21, 1964, A5.
78. *Washington Post,* October 26, 1964, A8.
79. *Ibid.*
80. *Washington Post,* October 23, 1964, A2.
81. *Ibid.*
82. *Washington Post,* October 21, 1964, A13.
83. *Washington Post,* October 20, 1964.
84. Shadegg, 255.
85. Karl Hess, 140.
86. *Los Angeles Times,* October 24, 1964.
87. Faber, 146.
88. Hess, *op. cit.,* 206.
89. Bloom, 147.
90. Hess, *op. cit.,* 140.
91. Kessel, 207.
92. Felknor, 153.
93. Felknor, 152–53.
94. *New York Times,* November 2, 1964, 47.
95. *New York Times,* October 1, 1964, 6; October 3, 1964, 8.

CHAPTER SIX

1. Valenti, 367.
2. Converse et al., "Continuity and Change in American Politics: Parties and Issues in the 1968 Election," in *The American Political Science Review* (1969), 1086.

3. *New York Times,* March 7, 1968, 20.
4. *Washington Post,* March 9, 1968, A2.
5. *Ibid.,* 1.
6. *Ibid.*
7. Converse et al., *op. cit.,* 1092.
8. *Ibid.,* 1090.
9. Witcover, *85 Days: The Last Campaign of Robert F. Kennedy,* 238.
10. In his poem "Grant Park, Chicago," McCarthy expressed the traumas engendered by the students' confrontation with the police:

> The guitar is smashed
> the tongue gone from the bell
> all kites have fallen, to the ground
> or caught in trees
> and telephone wires
> like St. Andrew, crucified
> hand upside down.
> the balloons are broken
> flowers faded in the night
> fountains have been drained
> no hair blows in the wind
> no one sings.

(p. 116. Eugene J McCarthy, *The Hard Years* [New York: The Viking Press, 1975.] Reprinted with permission of Eugene McCarthy.)
11. Persico, 64.
12. Witcover, *The Resurrection of Richard Nixon,* 307.
13. Persico, 74.
14. *New York Times Magazine,* September 29, 1968, 127.
15. Chester et al., *An American Melodrama,* 664–65.
16. *Broadcasting,* September 16, 1968, 5.
17. In Napolitan's judgment this is the best five minute ad produced in the history of political television.
18. Alexander, *Financing the 1968 Election,* 89, 92.
19. Personal interview with the author (Paulucci).
20. The stenographic transcripts of these meetings survive in the Democratic National Committee files at John F. Kennedy Library. I have confirmed their accuracy with key participants.
21. O'Brien, 261.
22. Personal interview with the author (Napolitan).
23. *New York Times,* October 25, 1968, 51.
24. Stans, 136.
25. *Ibid.,* 140.
26. *New York Times Magazine,* October 13, 1968.
27. *New York Times,* November 5, 1968, 37.
28. Witcover, *The Resurrection of Richard Nixon,* 412–13.
29. Weisberg et al., 1169.
30. Humphrey, *Education,* 401.
31. *Ibid.,* 403.
32. *Ibid.*
33. O'Brien, 265.

34. October 1, 1968, 1.
35. *Ibid.*
36. Nixon, *Memoirs,* 318.
37. *New York Times,* November 3, 1968, 7e.
38. Whalen, 91.
39. Personal interview with the author (Price).
40. *Washington Post,* March 9, 1968, A2.
41. Nixon, *Memoirs,* 298.
42. *Washington Post,* March 14, 1968, A2.
43. *Washington Post,* March 15, 1968, A2.
44. Humphrey, *The Education of a Public Man,* 395.
45. *New York Times,* October 25, 1968, 24.
46. McCarthy, *The Year of the People,* 241.
47. O'Brien, 265.
48. *New York Times,* November 4, 1968, 68. I break with the conventional explanations of McCarthy as a spoiler who withheld his endorsement of Humphrey
until it was too late to matter. Instead, I would suggest that, like Wallace,
McCarthy performed an indispensable function in 1968 that served to help
rather than hurt Humphrey's candidacy. As McCarthy's print ads argued, he
had made it possible for America's children to come home. Although the
children shown in those ads were not children but college-age adults, by
conceiving them as children redeemed by the surrogate parent, McCarthy
appealed to parents through their children. The children whom McCarthy
brought home were "clean for Gene"—shaven, well dressed, visibly transformed under his influence from symbols of a culture their parents dreaded to
symbols of constructive change within a value structure their parents could
embrace.

    In Chicago the powerlessness of the "children" had been dramatically dem-
onstrated both by the convention's dismissal of McCarthy's candidacy and by
the actions of the Chicago police. By withholding his endorsement, McCarthy
regained power for them and for him. By refusing to endorse Humphrey after
the Salt Lake City speech, McCarthy increased his credibility, not with
Democrats as a whole but with his still disaffected followers for he was saying
what many of them continued to believe: that on the issue of the war the
nominee had no clothes. By continuing to withhold his endorsement he increased his own power and that of his supporters; only with the endorsement
withheld could they and he continue to pressure Humphrey to liberalize his
stand on the war. By specifying in his tepid endorsement that Humphrey's
stand on the war did not meet his expectations, McCarthy retained the credibility of his followers, a credibility he required if on election eve he was, as he
did, to issue a statement of support. So, in my judgment, McCarthy retained
his credibility and rebuilt the perceived sense of the power of his constituency
in ways that increased rather than decreased the potency of his last minute
appeal for support for Humphrey.
49. McGinniss, 252.
50. *Washington Post,* September 22, 1968, A1.
51. *New York Times,* October 29, 1968, 35.
52. *Broadcasting,* November 4, 1968, 38.
53. Personal interview with the author (Garment).

54. *Washington Post,* September 22, 1968, A4.
55. *New York Times,* October 23, 1968, 33.
56. *New York Times Magazine,* October 13, 1968.
57. McGinniss, 67.
58. *New York Times Magazine,* September 29, 1968, 128.
59. *Newsweek,* September 30, 1968, 25.
60. Personal interview with the author (Shakespeare).
61. July 22, 1968, 53.
62. Personal interview with the author (Liebman).
63. Personal interview with the author (Oberdorfer).
64. See *Chicago Tribune,* September 5, 1968, 2; *The Plain Dealer,* September 14, 1968, 1; *Philadelphia Inquirer,* September 21, 1968, 1.
65. November 3, 1968, Volume 12, No. 43. Transcript provided by NBC.
66. Personal interview with the author (McGinniss).
67. Personal interview with the author (Irwin).
68. Osborne, *The Nixon Watch,* 105; 108.
69. *Ibid.,* 106.
70. McGinniss, 24.
71. *Ibid.,* 206, 207, 208–9. Reprinted with permission of Ray Price.
72. Frost, *The Americans,* 210.
73. McGinniss, 210.
74. *Ibid.,* 78.
75. *Ibid.,* 189.
76. *Ibid.,* 52.
77. Personal interview with the author (Ailes).
78. Frost, *The Americans,* 213.
79. McGinniss, 109–10.
80. *Washington Post,* September 21, 1968, A5.
81. White, *op. cit.,* 477.
82. Frost, *The Americans,* 212.
83. McGinniss, 204.
84. McGinniss, 33.
85. Napolitan, 59.
86. McGinniss, 154.
87. Whalen, 210.

CHAPTER SEVEN

1. Personal interview with the author (Shakespeare).
2. Magruder, 131.
3. *Ibid.*
4. Safire, 336.
5. Personal interview with the author (Squier).
6. Sussman, 33.
7. *Washington Post,* March 1, 1972, A6.
8. Haldeman, 237.
9. Personal interview with the author (Segretti).
10. *Ibid.*
11. *Ibid.*

12. Sobel, 108.
13. *Ibid.,* 110.
14. White, *The Making of the President 1968,* 168.
15. McGovern, *Grassroots,* 185.
16. *Ibid.*
17. Mankiewicz, 13.
18. Personal interview with the author (Segretti).
19. Personal interview with the author (Woodward).
20. Personal interview with the author (Paulucci).
21. *Washington Post,* June 4, 1972, A8.
22. Magruder, 208.
23. *Ibid.*
24. Sussman, 202.
25. Page, 141.
26. Personal interview with the author (Guggenheim).
27. Lawrence O'Brien, 337.
28. Personal interview with the author (Schwartz).
29. Personal interview with the author (Dailey).
30. *Advertising Age,* May 14, 1973, 3.
31. *Ibid.*
32. Personal interview with the author (Dailey).
33. Sobel, 14.
34. Alexander, *Financing the 1972 Election,* 316.
35. May and Fraser, 202.
36. *Ibid.,* 208.
37. The November Group's planning documents were made available to me by a member of the group.
38. Bagdikian, 10.
39. May and Fraser, 196.
40. Memo from Novelli to Joanou, March 14, 1972.
41. *Ibid.*
42. "On Assessing Poll Results for '72 Election," 2.
43. Safire, 646.
44. Information obtained from a diary kept by a member of the November Group.
45. May and Fraser, 198.
46. Magruder, 267.
47. *Ibid.,* 266.
48. Safire, 652.
49. Nixon, *Memoirs,* 669–70.
50. May and Fraser, 198.
51. Personal interview with the author (Taylor).
52. Gary Hart, 309.
53. Patterson and McClure, *Political Advertising,* 21.
54. *Ibid.,* 22.
55. *Ibid.,* 20.
56. Memo from Novelli to Strachen, October 24, 1972.
57. Magruder, 210.
58. Memo from Joanou through Magruder for MacGregor, October 25, 1972.

59. *Washington Post,* October 8, 1972, A12.
60. Haldeman, 118.
61. Patterson and McClure, *op. cit.,* 21.
62. May and Fraser, 211.
63. Nie et al., 311.
64. Page, 55.
65. Magruder, 208.
66. *Washington Post,* June 24, 1973, E6.
67. DeVries et al., 78.
68. Ehrlichman, 327.
69. *Ibid.,* 328. I tried unsuccessfully to obtain interviews with Colson and Ehrlichman.
70. *Ibid.,* 327.
71. Sussman, 90.
72. *New York Times, End of a Presidency,* 10–11.
73. Personal interview with the author (Guggenheim).
74. Lawrence O'Brien, 330–31.
75. *Washington Post,* A11.
76. May and Fraser, 216–17.
77. McGovern, *An American Journey,* 111.
78. Nixon, *The Public Papers of Presidents,* Washington, D.C.: USGPO, 1973, 1086.
79. May and Fraser, 229.
80. McGovern, *An American Journey,* 129.
81. *Ibid.,* 112.
82. Letter to author.
83. Lawrence O'Brien, 338.
84. McGovern, *An American Journey,* 17.
85. Personal interview with the author (Shrum).
86. Personal interview with the author (Guggenheim).
87. Memo from Teeter to Haldeman, June 20, 1972.

CHAPTER EIGHT

 1. Moore and Fraser, 119–20.
 2. Alexander, *Financing the 1976 Election,* 268.
 3. Witcover, *Marathon,* 386.
 4. Alexander, *op. cit.,* 400.
 5. *Ibid.*
 6. *Ibid.,* 232.
 7. Witcover, *op. cit.,* 413.
 8. Alexander, *op. cit.,* 388.
 9. Witcover, *op. cit.,* 413.
10. *Ibid.,* 281.
11. Alexander, *op. cit.,* 321–22.
12. *Ibid.,* 289.
13. Glad, 263.
14. *New York Times,* June 17, 1977, 13.

15. Alexander, *op. cit.,* 392–93.
16. Cannon, 188.
17. Personal interview with the author (Dailey).
18. Witcover, *op. cit.,* 319.
19. Schram, 26.
20. Personal interview with the author (Rafshoon).
21. *Ibid.*
22. *Ibid.*
23. Personal interview with the author (Ingram).
24. Alexander, *op. cit.,* 411.
25. *Ibid.,* 6.
26. "Preliminary Media Plan for President Ford Campaign," p. 8. A copy of the plan was obtained from Bailey/Deardourff.
27. Hartmann, 403.
28. Media Plan, 4–5.
29. Presentation to a seminar at the University of Maryland's Department of Communication Arts, November 1983.
30. Burnham, *The Current Crisis in American Politics,* 234.
31. *Ibid.,* 237.
32. Schram, 239ff.
33. See Caddell memo, October 16, 1976, in Schram, 329.
34. Schram, 274.
35. Carter, *Keeping Faith,* 22.
36. Glad, 341.
37. *Ibid.*
38. *Ibid.,* 343.
39. *Ibid.,* 326.
40. *Ibid.*
41. Media Plan, 10.
42. Witcover, *op. cit.,* 538.
43. *Ibid.,* 567.
44. *Ibid.,* 568.
45. Glad, 384.
46. Drew, 490.
47. *New York Times,* October 22, 1976.
48. Drew, *American Journal,* 475.
49. In Schram, 256–57.
50. June 11, 1976.
51. Devlin, 243.
52. Spero, 164–65.
53. Moore and Fraser, 141.
54. Witcover, *op. cit.,* 616.
55. *Ibid.,* 615.
56. Stroud, 394–95.
57. *New York Times,* November 1, 1976, 49.
58. Asher, 205.
59. The Inter-University Consortium for Political Research.
60. Devlin, "Contrasts in Presidential Campaign Commercials of 1976," 242.
61. Personal interview with the author (Bailey).

62. Burnham, *op. cit.*, 235.
63. Witcover, *op. cit.*, 643.
64. *Broadcasting,* January 3, 1977, 75.

CHAPTER NINE

1. Presentation to University of Maryland, Department of Communication's Election Debriefing, November 1980.
2. *Ibid.*
3. Personal interview with the author (Schwartz).
4. Personal interview with the author (Shrum).
5. Personal interview with the author (Squier).
6. *New York Times,* November 9, 1980, 36.
7. Personal interview with the author (Rafshoon).
8. Powell, 250.
9. Cannon, 230.
10. *Washington Post,* February 4, 1980, 1.
11. Personal interview with the author (Curson).
12. *Los Angeles Times,* April 12, 1980, Part 1, 24.
13. *Advertising Age,* September 29, 1980, 2.
14. "Bill Moyers' Journal," February 21, 1980.
15. Personal interview with the author (O'Reilly).
16. Personal interview with the author (Hendrix).
17. Personal interview with the author (O'Reilly).
18. *New York Times.* February 4, 1980, A14.
19. Personal interview with the author (Ingram).
20. Maryland Debriefing, *op. cit.*
21. *Ibid.*
22. *Ibid.*
23. Germond, 245.
24. Richard Wirthlin, Vincent Breglio, and Richard Beal, "Campaign Chronicle," *Public Opinion,* February/March 1981, 48.
25. Personal interview with the author (Hendrix).
26. Maryland Debriefing, *op. cit.*
27. Personal interview with the author (O'Reilly).
28. *Advertising Age,* September 1, 1980, 3.
29. Drew, *Politics and Money,* 134.
30. Reagan Campaign '80 Inc. "Financial Statements and Supplementary Data," March 9, 1981.
31. Haight, 41–60.
32. Nie et al., 347.
33. See table one, p. 54, in Alexander, "The Regulation and Funding of Presidential Elections."
34. *Ibid.*
35. Maryland Debriefing, *op. cit.*
36. *Common Cause* v. *Schmitt,* 512 F. Supp. 489 (D.C.D.C. 1980); 455 US 129 (1982).
37. Personal interview with the author (Smith).
38. Personal interview with the author (Craig Shirley).

39. Maryland Debriefing, *op. cit.*
40. Personal interview with the author (Shirley).
41. *Advertising Age,* August 18, 1980, 58.
42. Personal interview with the author (Bailey).
43. *Ibid.*
44. *Broadcasting,* March 10, 1980, 29.
45. *Advertising Age,* November 3, 1980, 1, 98.
46. Personal interview with the author (Rafshoon).
47. Personal interview with the author (Smith).
48. Personal interview with the author (Bailey).
49. Cited by Burnham in *The Hidden Election,* 19.
50. Wirthlin et al., 47.
51. "Seven Conditions of Victory," October 9, 1980, memo.
52. Wirthlin et al., p. 47.
53. "Summary-Commercial Allocation."
54. "Political Advertising on Television," 11.
55. Cf. Sanders, "Political Television Commercials: An Experimental Study of Time and Length," *Communication Research,* 5 (1978): 57–70.
56. Personal interview with the author (O'Reilly).
57. "Summary-Commercial Allocation."
58. Vincent Breglio, Maryland Debriefing, *op. cit.*
59. *Los Angeles Times,* April 12, 1980, 1.
60. Black Book, 6–7.
61. *Ibid.,* 27.
62. *Ibid.,* 25.
63. *Ibid.,* 5.
64. *Ibid.,* 31.
65. Wirthlin et al., 49.
66. Personal interview with the author (Gardner).
67. In Burnham, *The Hidden Election,* 127.

CONCLUSION

1. Samuel Stouffer, *Communism, Conformity and Civil Liberties.* New York: Wiley, 1955.
2. Nie et al., 152.
3. *Ibid.,* 153.

Bibliography

Abels, Jules. *The Degeneration of Our Presidential Election.* New York: Macmillan, 1968.

Abrams, Burton A. and Russell F. Settle. "Broadcasting and the Political Campaign Spending 'Arms Race.' " *J. of Broadcasting,* 21(Spring 1977): 153–62.

———. "The Effect of Broadcasting on Political Campaign Spending." *J. of Political Economy,* 84(October 1976): 1095–1108.

Adams, Sherman. *Firsthand Report.* New York: Popular Library, 1961.

Adamany, David. "The Media in Campaigning," *League of Women Voters Quarterly,* 47(Autumn 1972): 46–47.

Agranoff, Robert., ed. *The New Style in Election Campaigns.* Boston: Holbrook Press, 1972.

Alexander, Herbert E. "Broadcasting and Politics," in *The Electoral Process,* Jennings, M. Kent and L. Harmon Ziegler, eds. Englewood Cliffs, N.J.: Prentice-Hall, 1966.

Alexander, Herbert E. "Communication and Politics: The Media and the Message." *Law and Contemporary Problems,* 34(Spring 1969): 255–77.

———. *Financing the 1960 Election,* in *Studies in Money in Politics.* Princeton, N.J.: Citizens' Research Foundation, 1965.

———. *Financing the 1964 Election,* in *Studies in Money in Politics,* II. Princeton, N.J.: Citizens' Research Foundation, 1970.

———. *Financing the 1968 Election.* Lexington, Mass.: Lexington Books, 1971.

———. *Financing the 1972 Election.* Toronto: Lexington Books, 1976.

———. *Financing the 1976 Election.* Washington, D.C.: Congressional Quarterly Inc., 1979.

———. *Political Broadcasting: What's Its Impact on Elections?* Center for Information on America, 1964.

———. *Political Financing.* Minneapolis: Burgess Publishing Co., 1972.

———. "The Regulation and Funding of Presidential Elections." *The Journal of Law and Politics* (Fall, 1983): 43–63.

Allport, G. W. and Hadley Cantril. *The Psychology of Radio.* New York: Harper, 1935.

The American Institute for Political Communication. *Evolution of Public Attitudes Toward the Mass Media During an Election Year.* Washington, D.C.: American Institute for Political Communication, November 1969.

The American Institute for Political Communication. *Media and Non-Media Ef-*

fects on the Formation of Public Opinion. Washington, D.C.: American Institute for Political Communication, 1969.

Anderson, Patrick. "Issues vs. Image." *New Republic,* 158(April 27, 1968): 32–35.

Anderson, Totton J. and Charles G. Bell. "The 1970 Election in California." *West. Polit. Quarterly* (June 1971): 252–73.

Arons, L. and M. A. May. *Television and Human Behavior.* New York: Appleton-Century-Crofts, 1963.

Asher, Herbert B. *Presidential Elections and American Politics.* Homewood, Ill.: The Dorsey Press, 1976.

Atkin, C. K. and G. Heald. "Effects of Political Advertising." *Public Opinion Quarterly,* 40(1976): 216–28.

Atkin, Charles K., Lawrence Bowen, Oyuz B. Nayman, and Kenneth G. Sheinkopf. "Quality versus Quantity in Televised Political Ads." *Public Opinion Quarterly,* 37(1973): 209–24.

Atwood, L. Erwin, Adrian Combs, and JoAnne Young. "Multiple Facets of Candidate Image Structure: Effects of the McGovern Television Biography." Presented at convention of the Association for Education in Journalism, Fort Collins, Colo., August, 1973.

Bagdikian, Ben H. "The Fruits of Agnewism." *Columbia Journalism Review,* 11 (January/February '73): 9–23.

Bailey, Robert Lee. "Network Television Prime-Time Special Political Programs." *J. of Broadcasting,* 12(Summer 1968): 287–88.

Bailey, Thomas A. *Presidential Greatness: Image and the Man.* Englewood Cliffs, N.J.: Prentice-Hall, 1966.

Baker, Samm Sinclair. *The Permissible Lie: The Inside Truth About Advertising.* Cleveland: World, 1968.

Ball, George W. *The Past Has Another Pattern.* New York: W. W. Norton, 1982.

Barber, James David, ed. *Choosing the President.* Englewood Cliffs, N.J.: Prentice-Hall, 1974.

Baringer, William E. *House Dividing: Lincoln as President Elect.* Illinois: Abraham Lincoln Assoc., 1945.

Barnouw, Erik. *The Golden Web: A History of Broadcasting in the United States, 1933–1953.* New York: Oxford University Press, 1968.

———. *The Image Empire: A History of Broadcasting in The United States from 1953.* New York: Oxford University Press, 1970.

———. *Mass Communication: Television, Radio, Film, Press.* New York: Holt, Rinehart and Winston, 1956.

———. *A Tower in Babel: A History of Broadcasting in the United States—to 1933,* New York: Oxford University Press, 1966.

———. *Tube of Plenty: The Evolution of American Television,* London: Oxford University Press, 1977.

"The Battle of the Fences." *American Heritage,* XIX, October 6, 1968: 49–64.

Barone, Michael. "Nonlessons of the Campaign." *New York Times Magazine* (November 28, 1976): 36–37, 101–4.

Becker, Jerome D. and Ivan L. Preston. "Media Usage and Political Activity." *Journalism Q.,* 46(Spring 1969): 129–34.

Becker, John F. and Eugene E. Heaton, Jr. "The Election of Senator Edward W. Brooke." *Public Opinion Quarterly,* 31(Fall 1967): 346–58.

Becker, L. B. and J. C. Doolittle. "How Repetition Affects Evaluations of and Information Seeking About Candidates." *Journalism Q.,* 52(1975):611–617.

Becker, L. B., E. McCombs, and J. M. McLeod. "The Development of Political Cognitions," in S. Chaffee, ed. *Political Communication.* Beverly Hills, Calif.: Sage, 1975.

Becker, L. B. and D. C. Whitney "Effects of Media Dependencies on Audience Assessment of Government." *Communication Research, 7(1980): 95–120.*

Becker, Samuel L. "Presidential Power: The Influence of Broadcasting." QJS, XLVII(1961): 10–18.

Becker, Samuel L. and Elmer W. Lower. "Broadcasting in Presidential Campaigns," in Sidney Kraus, ed. *The Great Debates.* Bloomington: Indiana University Press, 1962, 25–55.

––––––. "Broadcasting Presidential Campaigns, 1960–1976," in Sidney Kraus, ed., *The Great Debates: Carter vs. Ford, 1976.* Bloomington: Indiana University Press, 1979, 11–40.

Bennett, Ralph K. "Television and the Candidates." *National Observor,* May 20, 1968: 1 + .

Benham, Thomas W. "Polling for a Presidential Candidate: Some observations on the 1964 campaign." *Public Opinion Quarterly,* 29(Summer 1965): 185–99.

Berelson, Bernard, Paul F. Lazarsfeld, and William McPhee. *Voting: A Study of Opinion Formation in a Presidential Campaign.* Chicago: University of Chicago Press, 1954.

Bernays, Edward L. *Biography of an Idea: Memoirs of a Public Relations Counsel.* New York: Simon and Schuster, 1965.

Billington, Ray Allen. "The Know-Nothing Uproar." *American Heritage, X,* (February 1959): 58–61, 94–97.

Binkley, Wilfred. *American Political Parties: Their Natural History.* New York: Knopf, 1966.

Biow, Milton H. *Butting In: An Adman Speaks Out.* Garden City, N.Y.: Doubleday, 1964.

Bitzer, Lloyd and Theodore Rueter. *Carter vs. Ford: The Counterfeit Debates of 1976.* Madison: The University of Wisconsin Press, 1980.

Blair, Joan and Clay Blair, Jr. *The Search for JFK.* New York: Berkley Publishing, 1976.

Bliven, Bruce. "Politics and TV." *Harper's Magazine,* 205(November 1952): 27–33.

Bloom, Melvyn H. *Public Relations and Presidential Campaigns.* New York: Crowell, 1973.

Bluem, A. William. *Documentary in American Television: Form, Function, Method.* New York: Hastings House, 1965.

Blum, Daniel C. *Pictorial History of TV.* Philadelphia: Chilton, 1958.

Blumenthal, Sidney. "Marketing the President." *New York Times Magazine* (September 13, 1981): 42–43; 110, 112, 114, 116, 118.

––––––. *The Permanent Campaign: Inside the World of Elite Political Operatives.* Boston: Beacon Press, 1980.

Blumler, Jay G. and Denis McQuail. "Television and Politics." *New Society,* 12(December 5, 1968): 834–35.

––––––. *Television in Politics: Its Uses and Influence.* Chicago: University of Chicago Press, 1969.

Bogart, Leo. *The Age of Television.* New York: Ungar, 1958.

Bogart, Leo, B. Stuart Tolley, and Frank Orenstein. "What One Little Ad Can Do." *J. Advert. Res.,* 10(August 1970): 3–14.

Bonadio, Felice A., ed. *Political Parties in American History.* New York: G. P. Putnam's, 1974.

Bonafede, Dom. "As Pollster to the President, Wirthlin Is Where the Action Is." *National Journal,* 13(December 1981): 2184–88.

Bone, Hugh A. "The 1970 Election in Washington." *Western Polit. Quarterly* (June 1971): 350–61.

Bonney, Catharina. V. R. *A Legacy of Historical Gleanings.* 1875.

Boorstin, Daniel J. *The Americans: The Democratic Experience.* New York: Random House, 1973.

———. *The Image: A Guide to Pseudo-Events in America.* New York: Harper & Row, 1961.

Bormann, Ernest G. "This is Huey P. Long Talking." *J. of Broadcasting,* 2(Winter 1957–58): 111–22.

Bovie, Palmer, trans. *Cicero: Nine Orations and the Dream of Scipio.* New York: New American Library, 1967.

Bowers, Thomas A. "Issues and Personality Information in Newspaper Political Advertising." *Journalism Q.,* 49(Autumn 1972): 446–53.

———. "Newspaper Political Advertising and the Agenda-Setting Function." *Journalism Q.,* 50(Autumn 1973): 543–48.

Boyd, Julian P., ed. *Papers of Thomas Jefferson.* XIV. Princeton, N.J.: Princeton University Press, 1958.

Bradford, Robert F. "Republicans and Sinners." *Harvard Business Review,* 34(July-August 1956): 125–32.

Bradlee, Benjamin C. *Conversations with Kennedy.* New York: W. W. Norton Co., 1975.

Broadcast Advertisements: Hearings Before a Subcommittee of the Committee on Interstate and Foreign Commerce. House of Representatives, 88th Congr, 1st Sess. Washington, D.C.: Government Printing Office, 1963.

Broder, David S. *Changing of the Guard.* New York: Penguin Books, 1980.

Brodie, Fawn M. "The Great Jefferson Taboo." *American Heritage,* XXIII, 4(June 1972): 48–57, 97–100.

———. *Richard Nixon: The Shaping of His Character.* Cambridge, Mass.: Harvard University Press, 1983.

Brogan, D. W. *Politics in America.* New York: Harper & Row, 1954.

Brooks, John. "The Businessman and the Government: Corruption, Yesterday and Today." *American Heritage,* XXVIII, 4(June 1977): 66–73.

Brown, Michael. *The Politics and Anti-Politics of the Young.* Beverly Hills, Calif.: Glencoe Press, 1969.

Bryan, William Jennings. *The First Battle.* Chicago: W. B. Conkey Co., 1898.

Bryce, James. *American Commonwealth.* Chicago: Charles Sergel, 1891.

Buchanan, Lamont. *Ballot for Americans.* New York: E. P. Dutton, 1956.

Buchwald, Art. *Son of the Great Society.* New York: G. P. Putnam's, 1965.

Burnham, Walter Dean. *The Current Crisis in American Politics.* New York: Oxford University Press, 1982.

———. "The Great Earthquake: Realignment, Reaction or What," in *The Hidden Election: Politics and Economics in the 1980 Presidential Campaign.* Thomas Ferguson and Joel Rogers, eds. New York: Pantheon Books, 1981, 98–140.

Butterfield, Roger. "Pictures in the Papers." *American Heritage,* XIII, 4(June 1962): 32–55.

Buzzi, Giancarlo. *Advertising: Its Cultural and Political Effects.* Minneapolis: University of Minnesota Press, 1968.

The Campaign Broadcast Reform Act of 1969: Hearings Before the Communications Subcommittee of the Senate Committee on Commerce. Washington, D.C.: Government Printing Office, 1969.

Campaign Finance Reform Hearings held before the Task Force on Elections of the Committee on House Administration. 98th Congr. Washington, D.C.: Government Printing Office, 1984.

"Campaign '72: Political Advertising: Making It Look Like News." *Congressional Q. Weekly Rep.,* 30(November 4, 1972): 2900–2904.

Campbell, Angus. "A Classification of the Presidential Elections," in Angus Campbell et al., *Elections and the Political Order.* New York: Wiley, 1966, 63–77.

———. "Has Television Reshaped Politics?" *Columbia Journalism Review* (Fall 1962): 10–13.

———. "Voters and Elections: Past and Present." *J. Polit.,* 26(November 1964): 745–57.

Campbell, Angus, Philip E. Converse, Warren E. Miller, and Donald E. Stokes. *The American Voter.* New York: Wiley, 1960.

———. *Elections and the Political Order.* New York: Wiley, 1966.

Campbell, Angus, Gerald Gurin, and Warren E. Miller. "Television and the Election." *Scientific American,* 188(May 1953): 46–48.

Cannon, Lou. *Reagan.* New York: G. P. Putnam's, 1982.

Carey, John. "How Media Shape Campaigns." *J. of Communication,* 26(Spring 1976): 50–57.

Carney, Francis M. and H. Frank Way, Jr., eds. *Politics 1968.* Belmont Calif.: Wadsworth, 1967.

———. *Politics 1972.* Belmont, Calif.: Wadsworth, 1971.

Carpenter, F. B. *Six Months at the White House with Abraham Lincoln.* New York: Hurd and Houghton, 1867.

Carroll, Maurice. "TV Ads Voting Studied in New Jersey." *New York Times,* January 28, 1973: 50.

Carroll, Raymond. "The 1948 Truman Campaign: The Threshold of a Modern Era." *J. of Broadcasting,* 24(1980): 173–88.

Carson, Gerald. "The Speech That Toppled a President." *American Heritage,* XV(August 1964): 108–11.

Carter, Jimmy. *A Government as Good As Its People.* New York: Simon and Schuster, 1977.

———. *Keeping Faith: Memoirs of a President.* Toronto: Bantam Books, 1982.

Cater, Douglass. "A Strategy for Political Broadcasting." *J. of Communication,* 26(Spring 1976): 58–64.

Chaffee, Steven H., ed. *American Politics Quarterly,* 3(October 1975): 355–473.

———. *Political Communication, Issues and Strategies for Research.* Beverly Hills, Calif.: Sage, 1975.

Chaffee, Steven H. and S. Y. Choe. "Time of Decision and Media Use During the Ford-Carter Campaign." *Public Opinion Quarterly,* 44(1980): 53–69.

Chaffee, Steven H. and Jack M. McLeod. "Individual Vs. Social Predictors of Information-Seeking." *Journalism Q.,* 50(Summer 1973): 237–45.

Chagall, David. *The New Kingmakers.* New York: Harcourt Brace Jovanovich, 1981.

Chambers, John Whiteclay II. "Presidents Emeritus." *American Heritage,* XXX, 4(June/July 1979): 16–25.

Chambers, William Nisbet. *Political Parties in a New Nation.* New York: Oxford University Press, 1963.

Chambers, William Nisbet and Walter Dean Burnham. *The American Party Systems.* New York: Oxford University Press, 1975.

Chester, Edward W. *A Guide to Political Platforms.* Hamden, Conn.: Archon Books, 1977.

———. *Radio, Television and American Politics.* New York: Sheed and Ward, 1969.

Chester, Giraud, Garnet R. Garrison, and Edgar E. Willis. *Television and Radio.* New York: Appleton-Century-Crofts, 1963.

Chester, Louis, Godfrey Hodgson, and Bruce Page. *An American Melodrama: The Presidential Campaign of 1968.* New York: The Viking Press, 1969.

Chisholm, Shirley. *The Good Fight.* New York: Bantam Books, 1973.

Christian, George. *The President Steps Down.* New York: Macmillan, 1970.

Churchill, Winston S. *Triumph and Tragedy* New York: Bantam Books, 1962.

Clark, David G. "Radio in Presidential Campaigns: The Early Years (1924–1932)." *J. of Broadcasting,* 6(Summer 1962): 229–38.

Clark, Raymond B. "Historical Handkerchiefs." *New York State History* (April 1955): 189–96.

Cleary, Robert E. "Elections and Image Building." *Today's Education,* 60(December 1971): 30–32, 58–59.

Cleaves, Freeman. *Old Tippecanoe: William Henry Harrison and His Time.* Port Washington, N.Y.: Kennikat Press, 1969.

Cohen, A. "Radio vs. TV: The Effect of Medium." *J. of Communication,* 26(1976): 29–35.

Collins, Herbert R. "Political Campaign Torches." *United States National Museum Bulletin* 241. Washington, D.C.: Smithsonian, 1964.

———. *Threads of History: Americana Recorded on Cloth 1775 to the Present.* Washington, D.C.: Smithsonian, 1979.

Commager, Henry Steele. "The Search for a Usable Past." *American Heritage,* XVI, 2(February 1965): 4–9, 90–96.

Common Cause v. *Schmitt,* 512 F.Supp. 489(D.C.D.C. 1980); 455 U.S. 129 (1982).

Cone, Fairfax M. *With All Its Faults: A Candid Account of Forty Years in Advertising.* Boston: Little, Brown, 1969.

Congressional Quarterly, Inc. *National Party Conventions 1831–1972.* Washington, D.C.: Congressional Quarterly, 1976.

Converse, P. E., W. E. Miller, J. G. Rusk, and A. Wolfe. "Continuity and Change in American Politics: Parties and Issues in the 1968 Election." *American Pol. Sci. Rev.,* 63(1969): 1083–1105.

Coolidge, Calvin. *The Autobiography of Calvin Coolidge.* New York: Cosmopolitan Book Co., 1929.

Cooper, Eunice and Marie Jahoda. "The Evasion of Propaganda: How Prejudiced People Respond to Antiprejudice Propaganda." *J. of Psych.*, 23(January 1947): 15–25.

Crockett, Davý. "How to Win an Election." *American Heritage.* IX, 5(August 1958): 112.

Cronin, Thomas E., ed. *Rethinking the Presidency.* Boston: Little, Brown, 1982.

Crouse, Timothy. *The Boys on the Bus.* New York: Ballantine, 1972.

Cummings, Milton C., ed. *The National Election of 1964.* Washington, D.C.: The Brookings Institution, 1966.

Cunliffe, Marcus. *The American Heritage History of the Presidency.* New York: Simon and Schuster, 1968.

Damon, Allan L. "Presidential Accessibility." *American Heritage,* XXV, 3(April 1974): 60–63, 97.

Davis, James W. *Presidential Primaries: Road to the White House.* Westport, Conn.: Greenwood Press, 1980.

Davis, Kenneth. *The Politics of Honor: A Biography of Adlai E. Stevenson.* New York: G. P. Putnam's, 1957.

Davis, Kenneth S. "The Sage of Emporia." *American Heritage,* XXX, 6 (October/November 1979): 81–96.

Davison, W. P. *International Political Communication.* New York: Praeger, 1965.

Dennis, J. and S. H. Chaffee. "Legitimation in the 1976 U.S. Election Campaign." *Communication Research,* 5(1978): 371–94.

Devlin, L. Patrick. "Contrasts in Presidential Campaign Commercials of 1972." *J. of Broadcasting,* 18, 1(Winter 1973/74): 17–26.

———. "Contrasts in Presidential Campaign Commercials of 1976." *Central States Speech Journal, 28, 4(Winter 1977): 238–49.*

———. "Contrasts in Presidential Campaign Commercials of 1980." *Political Communications Review.* 7(1982): 1–38.

———. "Reagan's and Carter's Ad Men Review the 1980 Television Campaigns." *Communication Q., 30(Winter 1981): 3–12.*

DeVries, Walter and Lance Tarrance. *The Ticket-Splitters.* Grand Rapids, Mich.: Eerdmanns, 1972.

Diamond, Edwin. "The Ford & Carter Commercials They Didn't Dare Run." *More, 6(December 1976): 12–17.*

Diamond, Robert A., ed. *Congressional Quarterly's Guide to U.S. Elections.* Washington, D.C.: Government Printing Office, 1975.

Dizard, Wilson P. "The Political Impact of Television Abroad." *J. of Broadcasting, 9(Summer, 1965): 195–214.*

Donohue, Thomas R. "The Impact of Viewer Predispositions on Political Television Commercials." *J. of Broadcasting,* 18(Winter 1973): 3–17.

Donohue, Thomas R. and Timothy P. Meyer. "Perceptions and Misperceptions of Political Advertising." *J. Bus. Comm.,* 10(Spring 1973): 29–40.

Doyle, Edward P. ed. *As We Knew Adlai.* New York: Harper & Row, 1966.

Drew, Elizabeth. *American Journal: The Events of 1976.* New York: Random House, 1976.

———. *Politics and Money.* New York: Macmillan, 1983.

———. *Portrait of an Election: The 1980 Presidential Campaign.* New York: Simon and Schuster, 1981.

Dreyer, Edward C. "Media Use and Electoral Choices: Some Political Consequences of Information Exposure." *Public Opinion Quarterly,* 35(Winter 1971–72): 544–53.

———. "Political Party Use of Radio and TV in the 1960 Campaign." *J. of Broadcasting,* 8(Summer 1964): 211–17.

Driberg, Tom. "The First Television Election." *New Statesman,* 61(March 10, 1961): 374–76.

Duckett, Kenneth W. "The Harding Papers: How Some Were Burned." *American Heritage,* XVI, 2(February 1965): 24–31, 102–109.

Duncan, Hugh Dalziel. *Symbols in Society.* New York: Oxford University Press, 1968.

Duncombe, Herbert S. and Boyd A. Martin. "The 1970 Election in Idaho." *West. Polit. Quarterly,* 24(June 1971): 292–300.

Dunlap, Orrin E. Jr. *Radio Advertising.* New York: Harper, 1931.

Dunn, S. Watson. *Advertising: Its Role in Modern Marketing.* New York: Holt, Rinehart and Winston, 1969.

Durant, John and Alice Durant. *Pictorial History of American Presidents.* New York: A. S. Barnes and Co., 1955.

Dutton, Frederick G. *Changing Sources of Power: American Politics in the 1970's.* New York: McGraw-Hill, 1971.

Dygert, Warren. *Radio as an Advertising Medium.* New York: McGraw-Hill, 1939.

Edelman, Murray. *The Symbolic Uses of Politics.* Urbana: University of Illinois Press, 1967.

Ehrlichman, John. *Witness to Power.* New York: Simon and Schuster, 1982.

Eisenhower, Dwight D. *The White House Years: Mandate for Change 1953–1956.* Garden City, N.Y.: Doubleday, 1963.

———. *Waging Peace, 1956–1961,* New York: Doubleday, 1965.

Eldersveld, Samuel J. "Experimental Propaganda Techniques and Voting Behavior." *American Polit. Sci. Rev.,* 50(March 1956): 154–65.

Ernst, Harry W. *The Primary That Made a President: West Virginia 1960.* Eagleton Institute Cases in Practical Politics. New York: McGraw-Hill, 1962.

Eulau, Heinz and Peter Schneider. "Dimensions of Political Involvement." *Public Opinion Quarterly,* 20(Spring 1956): 128–42.

Faber, Harold, ed. *The Road to the White House.* New York: New York Times, 1965.

"Face Off: A Conversation with the Presidents' Pollsters Patrick Caddell and Richard Wirthlin." *Public Opinion,* 3(December/January 80/81): 2–12, 63–64.

Fagen, Richard R. *Politics and Communication: An Analytic Study.* Boston: Little, Brown, 1966.

Farley, James A. *Behind the Ballots.* New York: Harcourt Brace, 1938.

FCC. *Public Service Responsibility of Broadcast Licensees.* Washington, D.C.: FCC, 1946.

———. *Pacifica Foundation.* 36 FCC 147 (1964).

———. *WCBS-TV.* 8 FCC 2nd 381 (1967).

———. *Network Coverage of the Democratic National Convention.* 16 FCC 2nd 650 (1969).

———. *Use of Broadcast Facilities by Candidates for Public Office.* 24 FCC 2nd 832 (1970).

———. *Democratic National Committee.* 25 FCC 2nd 216 (1970).

FDR: The Intimate Presidency. Washington, D.C.: Smithsonian Institution, 1982.

Federal Register. Use of Broadcast and Cablecast Facilities by Candidates for Public Office 37 FR 5796 (1972).

Felknor, Bruce L. *Dirty Politics.* New York: W. W. Norton and Co., 1966.

Fielding, Raymond. *The March of Time 1935–1951.* New York: Oxford University Press, 1978.

Fitzpatrick, John C., ed. *The Writings of George Washington.* Washington, D.C.: Government Printing Office, 1940.

Fixx, James, ed. *The Mass Media and Politics.* New York: Arno Press, 1972.

Fleming, Thomas J. " 'A Scandalous, Malicious and Seditious Libel.' " *American Heritage,* XIX, 1(December 1967): 22–27, 100–106.

Frank Leslie's Illustrated Newspaper. October 4, 1884: 163.

Freed, Fred. "The Rise and Fall of the Television Documentary." *Television Quarterly,* 10(Fall 1972): 55–62.

Friendly, Fred W. "The Campaign to Politicize Broadcasting." *Columbia Journalism Review* (March/April 1973): 9–18.

———. "What's Fair On The Air." *New York Times Magazine.* March 30, 1975: 11–12, 37–48.

Froman, Lewis A., Jr. "A Realistic Approach to Campaign Strategies and Tactics," in *The Electoral Process.* Jennings, M. Kent and L. Harmon Ziegler, eds. Englewood Cliffs, N.J.: Prentice-Hall, 1966, 1–20.

Frost, David. *The Americans.* New York: Stein and Day, 1970.

Frost, S. E., Jr. *Is American Radio Democratic?* Chicago: University of Chicago Press, 1937.

Funt, Peter. "How TV Producers Sneak in a Few Extra Commercials." *New York Times.* August 11, 1974: 1B.

Furguson, Thomas and Joel Rogers, eds. *The Hidden Election: Politics and Economics in the 1980 Presidential Campaign.* New York: Pantheon Books, 1981.

Gallagher, Robert S. " 'Me for Ma and I Ain't Got a Dern Thing Against Pa' " *American Heritage,* XVII, 6(October 1966): 46–47, 104–105.

Gallup, George H. *The Gallup Poll: Public Opinion 1935–1971.* New York: Random House, 1972.

———. "Six Political Reforms Most Americans Want." *Reader's Digest,* 113 (August 1978): 59–62.

Gallup, George, Jr., et al. *Politics and the Press.* Washington, D.C.: Acropolis, 1970.

Galanoy, Terry. *Down the Tube: Or, Making Television Commercials Is Such a Dog-Eat-Dog Business It's No Wonder They're Called Spots.* Chicago: Regnery, 1970.

Gardner, Allan D. "Political Ads: Do They Work?" *Wall Street Journal,* 179(February 1, 1972): 10.

Garramone, Gina M. "Issue versus Image Orientation and Effects of Political Advertising." *Communication Research,* 10(1983): 59–76.

Garraty, John A. "La Follette: The Promise Unfulfilled." *American Heritage,* XIII, 3(April 1962): 76–79, 84–88.

Geller, Henry. *The Fairness Doctrine In Broadcasting: Problems and Suggested Courses of Action.* Santa Monica, Calif.: Rand Corporation, 1973.

Gelman, Morris J. "Television and Politics: '62" *Television Magazine,* 19(October 1962): 64–67, 82–87.

Germond, Jack W. and Jules Witcover. *Blue Smoke and Mirrors: How Reagan Won and Carter Lost the Election of 1980.* New York: The Viking Press, 1981.

Gilbert, Robert E. *Television and Presidential Politics.* North Quincy, Mass.: Christopher Publishing House, 1972.

Glad, Betty. *Jimmy Carter: In Search of the Great White House.* New York: W. W. Norton and Co., 1980.

Glaser, William A. "Television and Voting Turnout." *Public Opinion Quarterly,* XXIX, I(1965): 71–86.

Goldman, Eric F. "Just Plain Folks." *American Heritage,* XXIII, 4(June 1972): 4–8, 90–91.

Goldwater, Barry. *The Conscience of a Conservative.* Sheperdsville, Ky: Victor Publishing Co., 1960.

———. *The Conscience of a Majority.* Englewood Cliffs, N.J.: Prentice-Hall, 1970.

———. *With No Apologies.* New York: Berkeley Books, 1979.

Gordon, Leonard V. "The Image of Political Candidates: Values and Voter Preference." *J. Appl. Psych.,* 56(October 1972): 382–87.

Gould, Jack. "Television Techniques on the Political Stage," *New York Times Magazine* (April 25, 1954): 12–13, 42, 44.

Graber, Doris A. *Mass Media and American Politics.* Washington, D.C.: Congressional Quarterly Press, 1980.

———. "Personal Qualities in Presidential Images: The Contribution of the Press." *Midwest J. Polit. Sci.,* 16(February 1972): 46–76.

———, ed. *The President & The Public.* Philadelphia: Institute for the Study of Human Issues, 1982.

Graham, Irving, ed. *Encyclopedia of Advertising.* 2nd ed. New York: Fairchild, 1969.

Graff, Henry F. "The Wealth of Presidents." *American Heritage,* XVII, 6(October 1966): 4–5, 106–11.

Greene, Bob. *Running—A Nixon-McGovern Journal.* Chicago: Regnery, 1973.

Greenfield, Jeff. *Playing to Win: An Insider's Guide to Politics.* New York: Simon and Schuster, 1980.

———. *The Real Campaign: How the Media Missed the Story of the 1980 Campaign.* New York: Summit Books, 1982.

Gregory, Dick. *Write Me In.* New York: Bantam, 1968.

Griese, Noel L. "Rosser Reeves and the 1952 Eisenhower TV Spot Blitz." *J. of Advertising* (1975): 34–38.

Guback, Thomas H. "Political Broadcasting and Public Policy." *J. of Broadcasting,* 12(1968): 191–211.

Guide to U.S. Elections. Washington, D.C.: Congressional Quarterly, 1975.

Gunderson, Robert. *The Log-Cabin Campaign.* Lexington: University of Kentucky Press, 1957.

Haight, Timothy and Richard Brody. "The Mass Media and Presidential Popularity: Presidential Broadcasting and News in the Nixon Administration." *Communication Research,* 4(1977): 41–60.

Halberstam, David. *The Best and the Brightest.* New York: Random House, 1972.

———. *The Powers That Be.* New York: Alfred A. Knopf, 1979.

Haldeman, H. R. *The Ends of Power.* New York: New York Times Books, 1978.

Hamill, Pete. "When the Client Is a Candidate." *New York Times Magazine* (October 25, 1964): 30–31, 128, 130–131.

Hamilton, Charles and Lloyd Ostendorf. *Lincoln in Photographs: An Album of Every Known Pose.* Norman: University of Oklahoma Press, 1963.

Hanser, Richard. "Of Deathless Remarks." *American Heritage,* XXI, 4(June 1970): 54–59.

Harper's Weekly. October 8, 1892: 971; October 11, 1884: 669; October 13, 1860: 650.

Harris, Seymour and Arthur Schlesinger, Jr., eds. *The New America.* New York: Harper & Row, 1957.

"The Harrison Bandwagon." *American Heritage,* XXVI, 6(October 1975): 18–27.

Hart, Gary Warren. *Right From the Start: A Chronicle of the McGovern Campaign.* New York: Quadrangle Books, 1973.

Hart, James D. "They All Were Born in Log Cabins." *American Heritage,* VII, 5(August 1956): 32–33, 102–105.

Hartmann, Robert T. *Palace Politics: An Insider's Account of the Ford Years.* New York: McGraw-Hill, 1980.

Herring, E. Pendleton. "Politics and Radio Regulation." *Harvard Business Review,* 13(January 1935): 167–78.

Hersh, Burton. *The Education of Edward Kennedy: A Family Biography.* New York: William Morrow and Co., 1972.

Hess, Karl. *In A Cause that Will Triumph.* Garden City, N.Y.: Doubleday, 1967.

Hess, Stephen. "The Long, Long Trail." *American Heritage,* XVII, 5(August 1966): 41–45, 69–78.

———. *The Presidential Campaign: The Leadership Selection Process After Watergate.* Washington, D.C.: The Brookings Institution, 1974.

Hess, Stephen and Milton Kaplan. *The Ungentlemanly Art.* New York: Macmillan, 1975.

Hettinger, Herman S. *A Decade of Radio Advertising.* Chicago: University of Chicago Press, 1933.

Hiebert, Ray, Robert Jones, Ernest Lotito, and John Lorenz, eds. *The Political Image Merchants: Strategies in the New Politics.* Washington, D.C.: Acropolis, 1971.

Hinson, Dolores. "Presidential Quilts." *The Antiques Journal* (July 1971): 17–19.

Hoff, Syd. *Editorial and Political Cartooning.* New York: Stravon Educational Press, 1976.

Hofstadter, Richard. *The American Political Tradition.* New York: Random House (Vintage Books), 1974.

Hofstetter, C. R. and C. Zukin. "TV Network News and Advertising in the Nixon and McGovern Campaigns." *Journalism Q.,* 56(1979): 106–15; 152.

Hollitz, John E. "Eisenhower and the Admen." *Wisconsin Magazine of History,* 66(Autumn 1982): 25–39.

Hoover, Herbert. "The Ordeal of Woodrow Wilson." *American Heritage,* IX, 4(June 1958): 65–85.

Hoyt, Edwin. *Jumbos and Jackasses: A Popular History of the Political Wars.* Garden City, N.Y.: Doubleday, 1960.

Hughes, Emmet John. *The Ordeal of Power: A Political Memoir of the Eisenhower Years.* New York: Atheneum, 1963.

Humphrey, Hubert H. *The Education of a Public Man.* Garden City, N.Y.: Doubleday, 1976.

Hy, Ronn. "Mass Media in Election Campaigns (Extent to Which Voters Are Affected by Political Advertisement in the Mass Media)." *Pub. Admin. Surv.,* 20(January 1973): 1–6.

Hyatt, Richard. *The Carters of Plains.* Huntsville, Ala.: Strode, 1977.

The Illustrated London News. October 15, 1864.

Innis, Harold A. *The Bias of Communication.* Toronto: University of Toronto Press, 1951.

———. *Empire and Communication.* Oxford: Clarendon Press, 1950.

Jacobson, Gary C. "The Impact of Broadcast Campaigning on Electoral Outcomes." *J. of Politics,* 37(1975): 769–93.

Jamieson, Kathleen Hall and Karlyn Kohrs Campbell. *Interplay of Influence: Media and Their Publics in News, Advertising, Politics.* Belmont, Calif.: Wadsworth, 1983.

Jennings, M. Kent and L. Harmon Ziegler, eds. *The Electoral Process.* Englewood Cliffs, N.J.: Prentice-Hall, 1966.

Johnson, Gerald W. "Political Correlatives of Voter Participation: A Deviant Case Analysis." *American Polit. Sci. Rev.,* 65(September 1971): 768–76.

Johnson, Lyndon Baines. *The Vantage Point.* New York: Holt, Rinehart and Winston, 1971.

Jordan, Hamilton. *Crisis: The True Story of an Unforgettable Year in the White House.* New York: Berkley Books, 1982.

Josephson, Matthew. *1896–1919 The President Makers: The Culture of Politics and Leadership in an Age of Enlightenment.* New York: G. P. Putnam's, 1940.

Joslyn, R. A. "The Content of Political Spot Ads." *Journalism Q.,* 57(1980): 92–98.

Kahler, James G. *Hail to the Chief.* Princeton, N.J.: Pyne Press, 1972.

Kaid, Linda L., Keith R. Sanders, and Robert O. Hirsch. *Political Campaign Communication: A Bibliography and Guide to the Literature.* Metuchen, N.J.: Scarecrow Press, 1974.

Kaid, Linda L. and Keith R. Sanders. "Political Television Commercials: An Experimental Study of Type and Length." *Communication Research,* 5 (1978): 57–70.

Kane, Joseph Nathan. *Facts About the Presidents.* New York: H. W. Wilson Co., 1974.

Katz, Elihu. "Platforms and Windows: Broadcasting's Role in Election Campaigns." *Journalism Q.,* 48(Summer 1971): 304–14.

Katz, Elihu and Samuel Eldersveld. "The Impact of Local Party Activity Upon the Electorate." *Public Opinion Quarterly,* 1961: 1–24.

Katz, Elihu and Paul F. Lazarsfeld. *Personal Influence: The Part Played by People in the Flow of Mass Communications.* Glencoe, Ill.: The Free Press, 1955.

Kearns, Doris. *Lyndon Johnson and the American Dream.* New York: New American Library, 1976.

Kelley, S., Jr. "Policy Discussion in Political Campaigning," in James D. Barber ed. *Readings in Citizen Politics.* Chicago: Markham, 1969.

Kelley, Stanley, Jr. *Political Campaigning: Problems in Creating an Informed Electorate*. Washington, D.C.: The Brookings Institute, 1960.

———. *Professional Public Relations and Political Power*. Baltimore, Md.: Johns Hopkins University Press, 1956.

Kendrick, Alexander. *Prime Time*. Boston: Little, Brown, 1969.

Kennamer, D. and S. H. Chaffee. "Communication of Political Information During Early Presidential Primaries: Cognition, Affect and Uncertainty," in M. Burgoon, ed. *Communication Yearbook,* 6(1982).

Kenski, Henry. "The Impact of Economic Conditions on Presidential Popularity," *J. of Politics,* 39(1977): 764–73.

Kessel, John H. *The Goldwater Coalition: Republican Strategies in 1964*. Indianapolis and New York: The Bobbs-Merrill Co. Inc., 1968.

Key, V. O., Jr. *The Responsible Electorate*. Cambridge, Mass.: Harvard University Press, 1966.

Kiester, Edwin, Jr. "That 'News' Item May Be A Commercial." *TV Guide* (October 5, 1974): 10–13.

Kimsey, W. D. and L. E. Atwood. "A Path Model of Political Cognitions and Attitudes: Communication and Voting in a Congressional Campaign." *Communication Monographs,* 46(1979): 219–30.

Kinder, D. R. "Political Person Perception: The Asymmetrical Influence of Sentiment and Choice on Perceptions of Presidential Candidates." *J. of Personality and Social Psych.,* 36(1978): 859–71.

Kinter, Robert E. "Television and the World of Politics." *Harper's,* 230(May 1965): 121–33.

Kirkpatrick, Samuel A. "Political Attitude Structure and Component Change." *Public Opinion Quarterly,* 34(Fall 1970): 403–407.

Kjeldahl, Bill O., Carl W. Carmichael, and Robert J. Mertz. "Factors in a Presidential Candidate's Image." *Speech Monographs,* 38(June 1971): 129–31.

Koenig, Louis W. "Consensus Politics, 1800–1805." *American Heritage,* XVIII, 2(February 1967): 4–7, 74–80.

———. "The Election That Got Away." *American Heritage,* XI, 6(October 1960): 4–7, 99–104.

Kraus, Sidney, "The Political Use of TV." *J. of Broadcasting,* 8(Summer 1964): 219–28.

Kraus, Sidney and Raymond G. Smith. "Issues and Images," in Sidney Kraus, ed. *The Great Debates*. Bloomington: Indiana University Press, 1962, 289–312.

Kraus, Sidney, Timothy Meyer, and Maurice Shelby, Jr., "Sixteen Months After Chappaquiddick: Effects of the Kennedy Broadcast." *Journalism Q.,* 51 (Autumn 1974): 431–40.

Krugman, Herbert E. "A Comparison of Physical and Verbal Responses to Television Commercials." *Public Opinion Quarterly,* XXIX, 2(1965): 323–25.

———. "The Impact of Television Advertising: Learning Without Involvement." *Public Opinion Quarterly,* XXVI(1962): 349–56.

Ladd, Everett. *American Political Parties*. New York: W. W. Norton, 1971.

Lader, Lawrence. " 'To Serve the World—Not To Dominate It.' " *American Heritage,* XXVIII, 1(December 1976): 42–51.

Lang, Kurt and Gladys Engel Lang. "The Mass Media and Voting," in *American Voting Behavior*. Burdick, Eugene J. and Arthur J. Brodbeck, eds. Glencoe, Ill: The Free Press, 1959.

————. *Politics and Television*. Chicago: Quadrangle Books, 1968.

————. "The Unique Perspective of Television." *American Soc. Rev.*, XVIII, I(1953): 103–12.

Lang, Serge. *The Scheer Campaign*. New York: Benjamin, 1968.

Lau, R. R., D. O. Sears, and R. Centers. "The 'Positivity Bias' in Evaluations of Public Figures: Evidence Against Instrument Artifacts." *Public Opinion Quarterly*, 43(1979): 347–58.

Lawhorne, Clifton O. *Defamation and Public Officials: The Evolving Law of Libel*. Carbondale: Southern Illinois University Press, 1971.

Lazarsfeld, Paul F. *Radio and the Printed Page*. New York: Duell, Sloan and Pearce, 1940.

Lazarsfeld, Paul F., Bernard Berelson, and Hazel Gaudet. *The People's Choice*. New York: Duell, Sloan, and Pearce, 1944.

————. "Radio and the Printed Page as Factors in Political Opinion and Voting," in Wilbur Schramm, ed. *Mass Communications*. Urbana: University of Illinois Press, 1960, 513–26.

Lazarfeld, Paul F., and Harry Field. *The People Look at Radio*. Chapel Hill: University of North Carolina Press, 1946.

Lazarsfeld, Paul F. and Patricia L. Kendall. *Radio Listening in America: The People Look at Radio Again*. Englewood Cliffs, N.J.: Prentice-Hall, 1948.

Lee, James Melvin. *History of American Journalism*. Boston and New York: Houghton Mifflin Co., 1917; 1923.

Lee, Jong R. "Rallying Around the Flag: Foreign Policy Events and Presidential Popularity." *Pres. Studies Q. (1977)*: 252–56.

Leech, Margaret. "The Front Porch Campaign." *American Heritage*, XI, 1(December 1959): 33–45.

Lefevre, Edwin. "Washington Historical Kerchiefs." *Antiques* (July 1939): 14–17.

Levin, Murray B. and Murray Eden. "Political Strategy for the Alienated Voter." *Public Opinion Quarterly*, 26(Spring 1962): 47–57.

Lewis, Chester, Godfrey Hodgson, and Bruce Page. *An American Melodrama: The Presidential Campaign of 1968*. New York: Viking, 1969.

Lichty, Lawrence W., Joseph M. Ripley, and Harrison B. Summers. "Political Programs on National Television Networks: 1960 and 1964." *J. of Broadcasting*, 9(Summer 1965): 217–29.

Liston, R. A. *Politics from Precinct to Presidency*. New York: Delacourte Press, 1968.

Lorant, Stefan. *The Glorious Burden*. New York: Harper & Row, 1968.

————. *The Presidency: A Pictoral History of Presidential Elections from Washington to Truman*. New York: Macmillan, 1952.

Lorenz, Lawrence. "Truman and the Broadcaster." *J. of Broadcasting*, 13(Winter 1968–1969): 17–22.

Lucas, Darrel B. and Stewart H. Britt. *Measuring Advertising Effectiveness*. New York: McGraw-Hill, 1963.

Lurie, Leonard. *Party Politics: Why We Have Poor Presidents*. New York: Stein and Day, 1980.

Lyon, Peter. "The Honest Man." *American Heritage*, X, 2(February 1959): 4–11, 104–106.

MacDougall, Malcolm D. *We Almost Made It*. New York: Crown, 1977.

MacNeil, Robert. "Marketing the Candidates—The Use of Television in the American Election." *Listener,* 80(November 14, 1968): 631–32.

———. *The People Machine: The Influence of Television on American Politics.* New York: Harper & Row, 1968.

McCarthy, Eugene J. *The Hard Years.* New York: The Viking Press, 1975.

———. *Dictionary of American Politics.* Baltimore Md.: Penguin Books, Inc., 1968.

———. *The Year of the People.* Garden City, N.Y.: Doubleday and Co., 1969.

McCarthy, Joseph W. *The Remarkable Kennedys.* New York: Dial Press, 1960.

McCombs, Maxwell E. "Mass Communication in Political Campaigns and Information, Gratification, and Persuasion," in P. J. Tichenor and F. Gerald Kline, eds. *Current Perspectives in Mass Communication Research.* Beverly Hills, Calif.: Sage, 1972, 169–94.

McCombs, Maxwell E. and L. E. Mullins. "Consequences of Education: Media Exposure, Political Interest, and Information-Seeking Orientations." *Mass Comm. Rev.,* 1(August 1973): 27–31.

McGinniss, Joe. *The Selling of the President, 1968.* New York: Trident, 1969.

McGovern, George. *An American Journey: The Presidential Campaign Speeches of George McGovern.* New York: Random House, 1974.

———. *Grassroots.* New York: Random House, 1977.

McLoughlin, William G. "Trade Cards." *American Heritage,* XVIII, 2(February 1967): 48–63.

McLeod, Jack, Scott Ward, and Karen Tancill. "Alienation and Uses of the Mass Media." *Public Opinion Quarterly,* 29(Winter 1965): 584–94.

Magruder, Jeb Stuart. *An American Life: One Man's Road to Watergate.* New York: Atheneum, 1974.

Mankiewicz, Frank. *Perfectly Clear.* New York: Quadrangle, 1973.

Martin, John Bartlow. *Adlai Stevenson and the World.* Garden City, N.Y.: Doubleday, 1977.

———. *Adlai Stevenson of Illinois.* Garden City, N.Y.: Doubleday, 1976.

Martin, Ralph G. *Ballots and Bandwagons.* New York: New American Library, 1964.

Max, Nicholas, *President McGovern's First Term.* Garden City, N.Y.: Doubleday and Co., 1973.

May, Ernest R. and Janet Fraser. *Campaign '72: The Managers Speak.* Cambridge, Mass.: Harvard University Press, 1973.

Mayer, Martin. *Madison Avenue, U.S.A.* New York: Harper & Row, 1958.

Mazo, Earl. *Richard Nixon: A Political and Personal Portrait.* New York: Avon Book Division of the Hearst Corporation, 1959.

Melder, Keith. *Bryan The Campaigner, United States National Museum Bulletin.* 241. Washington, D.C.: Smithsonian, 1965.

Mendelsohn, Harold and Irving Crespi. *Polls, Television and the New Politics.* Scranton, Pa.: Chandler, 1970.

Mendelsohn, Harold and G. J. O'Keefe. *The People Choose a President: Influences on Voter Decision Making.* New York: Praeger, 1976.

Merton, Robert K. *Mass Persuasion: The Social Psychology of a War Bond Drive.* New York: Harper, 1946.

Meyer, Peter. *James Earl Carter: The Man and the Myth.* Mission Kans.: Sheed, Andrews and McMeel, 1978.

Mickelson, Sig. *The Electric Mirror: Politics in an Age of Television*. New York: Dodd, Mead, 1972.

———. "TV and the Candidate." *Saturday Review,* 43(April 16, 1960): 13–15, 51.

Midgley, Ned. *The Advertising and Business Side of Radio*. Englewood Cliffs, N.J.: Prentice-Hall, 1948.

Milburn, M. "A Longitudinal Test of the Selective Exposure Hypothesis." *Public Opinion Quarterly,* 43(1979) 507–17.

Milhollen, Hirst D. and Milton Kaplan. *Presidents on Parade*. New York: Macmillan, 1948.

Miller, A. H., E. N. Goldenberg, and L. Erbring. "Type-Set Politics: Impact of Newspapers on Public Confidence." *American Pol. Sci. Rev.,* 73(1979): 67–78.

Miller, Lillian B. et al. *If Elected . . . Unsuccessful Candidates For the Presidency*. Washington, D.C.: Smithsonian, 1972.

Miller, Merle. *Plain Speaking: An Oral Biography of Harry S. Truman*. New York: G. P. Putnam's, 1973.

Miller, Warren E. and Teresa E. Levit: *Leadership and Change: Presidential Elections from 1952 to 1976*. Cambridge, Mass.: Winthrop Publishers Inc., 1976.

Minow, Newton N. *Equal Time*. New York: Atheneum, 1969.

Minow, Newton N., John Bartlow Martin, and Lee M. Mitchell. *Presidential Television*. New York: Basic Books, 1973.

Monroe, Kristen R. "Economic Influences on Presidential Popularity." *Public Opinion Quarterly,* 42(1978): 360–69.

Moore, Jonathan, ed. *The Campaign for President: 1980 in Retrospect*. Cambridge, Mass.: Ballinger, 1981.

Moore, Jonathan and Janet Fraser, eds. *Campaign for President: The Managers Look at '76*. Cambridge, Mass.: Ballinger, 1977.

"A Moral in the Mail." *American Heritage,* X, 6(October 1959): 90–91.

Morin, Relman. *Dwight D. Eisenhower*. New York: Simon and Schuster, 1969.

Morison, John R. and Donald K. McNeil. "State Supreme Court Rules Political Programming May Not Be Restricted." *Educational Broadcasting Review,* 4(August 1970): 7–14.

Morris, Dan and Inez Morris. *Who Was Who in American Politics*. New York: Hawthorn Books, 1974.

Morrison, Matthew C. "The Role of the Political Cartoonist in Image-Making." *Central States Speech Journal,* 20(Winter 1969): 252–60.

Mott, Frank Luther. *American Journalism*. New York: Macmillan, 1962.

Mueller, John E. "Presidential Popularity from Truman to Johnson." *American Polit. Sci. Rev.,* 64(March 1970): 18–34.

Murphy, Paul L. *Political Parties in American History,* vol. 3. New York: G. P. Putnam, 1974.

National Association of Broadcasters. "Political Broadcast Catechism." Washington, D.C.: NAB, 1968.

Napolitan, Joseph. *The Election Game and How to Win It*. Garden City, N.Y.: Doubleday, 1972.

Neustadt, Richard E. *Presidential Power, the Politics of Leadership*. New York: Wiley, 1961.

Nevins, Allan, ed. *The Diary of Philip Hone: 1828–1851.* I. New York: Dodd, Mead, 1927; reprinted New York: Kraus Reprint Co, 1969.

New York Times. The End of a Presidency. Toronto, New York, London: Bantam Books, 1974.

Newman, Joseph, ed. *Guide to the '72 Elections.* Washington, D.C.: U.S. News and World Report, 1972.

Nicolay, Helen. *Personal Traits of Abraham Lincoln.* New York: Century Co., 1912.

Nichols, David. *Financing Elections.* New York: New Viewpoint, 1974.

Nichols, Roy F. "It Happens Every Four Years." *American Heritage,* VII, 4(June 1956): 20–33.

Nicholas, William, *The Bobby Kennedy Nobody Knows.* Greenwich, Conn.: Fawcett Publications Inc., 1967.

Nie, Norman H., Sidney Verba, and John R. Petrocik. *The Changing American Voter.* Cambridge, Mass.: Harvard University Press, 1979.

Nimmo, Dan. *The Political Persuaders: The Techniques of Modern Election Campaigns.* Englewood Cliffs, N.J.: Prentice-Hall, 1970.

Nimmo, Dan and Thomas Ungs. *American Political Patterns: Conflict and Consensus.* Boston: Little, Brown, 1969.

Nixon. Richard. *Memoirs of Richard Nixon.* New York: Grosset and Dunlap, 1978.

———. *Six Crises.* Garden City, N.Y.: Doubleday, 1962.

Noggle, Burl. *Teapot Dome: Oil and Politics in the 1920's.* Baton Rouge: Louisiana State University Press, 1962.

O'Brien, Lawrence F. *No Final Victories.* New York: Ballantine Books, 1974.

O'Brien, Robert W. and Elizabeth Jones. *The Night Nixon Spoke.* Los Alamitos, Calif.: Hwong Publications, 1976.

O'Donnell, Kenneth P. "TV in the Political Campaign." *Television Quarterly,* 5(Winter 1966): 20–23.

O'Donnell, Kenneth P. and David F. Powers with Joe McCarthy. *"Johnny We Hardly Knew Ye."* New York: Pocket Books, 1973.

O'Keefe, G. J. and L. E. Atwood. "Communication and Election Campaigns," in D. D. Nimmo and K. R. Sanders, eds. *Handbook of Political Communication.* Beverly Hills, Calif.: Sage, 1981.

Office of Social Research, Columbia Broadcasting System. *Bandwagon: A Review of the Literature.* New York: Office of Social Research, 1964.

Osborne, John. *The Nixon Watch.* New York: Liveright, 1970.

———. *The Second Year of the Nixon Watch.* New York: Liveright, 1971.

———. *The Fifth Year of the Nixon Watch.* New York: Liveright, 1974.

Oxford Research Associates, Inc. *Influence of Television on the Election of 1952.* Oxford, Ohio: Miami University Press, 1954.

Page, Benjamin I. *Choices and Echoes in Presidential Elections: Rational Man and Electoral Democracy.* Chicago: University of Chicago Press, 1978.

Parmet, Herbert S. *Jack: The Struggles of John F. Kennedy.* New York: Dial Press, 1980.

Patterson, Thomas. *The Mass Media Election: How Americans Choose Their President.* New York: Praeger, 1980.

Patterson, Thomas E. and Robert D. McClure. *Political Advertising: Voter Reac-*

tion to Televised Political Commercials. Study no. 23. Princeton, N.J.: Citizens' Research Foundation, n.d.

———. "Television News and Political Advertising." *Communication Research,* 1:(January 1974): 3–31.

———. *The Unseeing Eye: The Myth of Television Power in National Politics.* New York: G. P. Putnam's, 1976.

Pearce, Michael, M. Cunningham Scott, and Avon Miller. *Appraising the Economic and Social Effects of Advertising: A Review of Issues and Evidence.* Cambridge, Mass.: Marketing Science Institute, 1971.

Pease, Otis. *The Responsibility of American Advertisers: Private Control and Public Influence, 1920–1940*. New Haven, Conn.: Yale University Press, 1958.

Perkins, Frances. *The Roosevelt I Knew*. New York: Harper, 1946.

Persico, Joseph. *The Imperial Rockefeller*. New York: Washington Square Press, 1982.

"Political Puffery." *American Heritage,* XXX, 5(August/September 1979): 110.

Polsby, Nelson W. and Aaron B. Wildavsky. *Presidential Elections: Strategies of American Electoral Politics*. New York: Charles Scribner's Sons, 1971.

Pomper, Gerald. *The Election of 1980*. Chatham, N.J.: Chatham Publishers, 1981.

Porter, Kirk Harold. *History of Suffrage in the United States*. Chicago: University of Chicago Press, 1918.

Porter, Kirk H. and Donald Bruce Johnson. *National Party Platforms 1840–1964*. Urbana and London: University of Illinois Press, 1966.

Post, Robert C., ed. *Every Four Years*. Smithsonian Exposition Books; Distributor: New York: W. W. Norton, 1980.

Powell, Jody. *The Other Side of the Story*. New York: William Morrow and Co., 1984.

Presbrey, Frank. *The History and Development of Advertising*. Garden City, N.Y.: Doubleday, 1929.

Price, Raymond. *With Nixon*. New York: The Viking Press, 1977.

Priest, Robert F. and Joel Abrahams. "Candidate Preference and Hostile Humor in the 1968 Elections." *Psych. Rep.,* 26(June 1970): 779–83.

Pusateri, C. Joseph. "FDR, Huey Long, and the Politics of Radio Regulation." *J. of Broadcasting,* 21(Winter 1977): 85–95.

Rarick, Galen R. "Political Persuasion: The Newspaper and the Sexes." *Journalism Q.,* 47(June 1973): 167–73.

Rather, Dan and Gary Paul Gates. *The Palace Guard*. New York: Warner, 1975.

Redding, Jack. *Inside the Democratic Party*. New York: The Bobbs-Merrill Co., 1958.

Reeves, Rosser. *Reality in Advertising*. New York: Knopf, 1961.

Riggs, Frank L. "The Changing Role of Radio." *J. Broadcasting,* 8(Fall 1964): 321–39.

The Ripon Society. *The Lessons of Victory*. New York: The Dial Press, 1969.

Robinson, Michael J. and Margaret A. Sheehan. *Over the Wire and on TV*. New York: Russell Sage Foundation, 1980.

Robinson, Michael J. and Clifford Zukin. "Television and the Wallace Vote." *J. of Communication,* 26(Spring 1976): 79–83.

Robinson, Patrick J., Homer M. Dalbey, Irwin Gross, and Yoram Wind. *Advertising Measurement and Decision Making*. Boston: Allyn and Bacon, 1968.

Roman, Kenneth, and Jane Maas. *How to Advertise*. New York: St. Martin's, 1976.

Roosevelt, Franklin Delano. *The Public Papers and Addresses of Franklin D. Roosevelt*. New York: Russell and Russell, 1969.

Rose, Richard. *Influencing Voters: A Study of Campaign Rationality*. London: Faber and Faber, 1967.

Roseboom, Eugene H. *A History of Presidential Elections*. New York: Macmillan, 1970.

Rosenberg, Marvin and Dorothy Rosenberg. "The Dirtiest Election." *American Heritage*, XIII, 5(August 1962): 4–9, 97–100.

Rosenbloom, David Lee. *The Election Men: Professional Campaign Managers and American Democracy*. New York: Quadrangle Books, 1973.

Ross, Irwin. *The Lonliest Campaign: The Truman Victory of 1948*. New York: The New American Library, 1969.

Rossiter, Clinton. "Our Two Greatest Presidents." *American Heritage*, X, 2(February 1959): 12–15, 100–101.

———. *Parties and Politics in America*. Ithaca, N.Y.: Cornell University Press, 1960; New York: New American Library, 1967.

———. "The Presidents and the Presidency." *American Heritage*, VII, 3(April 1956): 28–33, 94–95.

Roucek, Joseph S. *Influence of Television on American Politics*. Bridgeport, Conn.: University of Bridgeport, 1963.

Royko, Mike. *Boss: Richard J. Daley of Chicago*. New York: New American Library, 1971.

Rubin, Bernard. *Political Television*. Belmont, Calif.: Wadsworth, 1967.

Runyon, John H., Jennefer Verdini, and Sally S. Runyon, eds. *Source Book of American Presidential Campaign and Election Statistics 1948–1968*. New York: Frederick Ungar Publishing Co., 1970.

Rushford, Edward. "Electioneering without Electricity." *Antiques* (November 1939): 236–39.

Russell, Francis. "The Four Mysteries of Warren Harding." *American Heritage*, XIV, 3(April 1963): 5–9, 81–86.

———. "The Harding Papers . . . and Some Were Saved." *American Heritage*, XVI, 2(February 1965): 24–31, 102–10.

———. "As Warm A Heart As Ever Beat." *American Heritage*, XXVI, 5(August 1975): 4–9, 77–81.

Rutkus, Denis S. "Presidential Television." *J. of Communication*, 26(Spring 1976): 73–78.

Rutland, Robert Allen. *The Newsmongers: Journalism in the Life of the Nation, 1690–1972*. New York: Dial Press, 1973.

Sabato, Larry J. *The Rise of Political Consultants*. New York: Basic Books, 1981.

Saerchinger, Cesar. "Radio as a Political Instrument." *Foreign Affairs*, 16(January 1938): 244–59.

Safire, William. *Before the Fall*. Garden City, N.Y.: Doubleday, 1975.

Sandage, C. G. and Vernon Fryberger. *Advertising Theory and Practice*, 18th ed. Homewood, Ill.: Irwin, 1971.

Saunders, Frances W. "Love and Guilt: Woodrow Wilson and Mary Hulbert." *American Heritage,* XXX, 3(April/May 1979): 68–77.

Scammon, Richard and Ben Wattenberg. *The Real Majority.* New York: Coward-McCann, 1970.

Schandler, Herbert Y. *The Unmaking of a President.* Princeton, N.J.: Princeton University Press, 1977.

Schlesinger, Arthur M., Jr. *The Age of Jackson.* New York: New American Library, 1953.

———. *A Thousand Days.* Boston: Houghton Mifflin, 1965.

———. *The Coming of the New Deal.* Boston: Houghton Mifflin, 1959.

———. *The Coming to Power: Critical Presidential Elections in American History.* New York: McGraw-Hill, 1972.

———. *The Crisis of the Old Order.* Boston: Houghton Mifflin, 1957.

———. *The Politics of Upheaval.* Boston: Houghton Mifflin, 1960.

———, ed. *History of American Presidential Elections: 1789–1968.* New York: McGraw-Hill, 1971.

Schomp, Gerald. *The Political Assassination of Robert A. Taft.* Plantation, Fla.: Allegiance Books, 1967.

Schram, Martin. *Running for President, 1976: The Carter Campaign.* New York: Stein and Day, 1977.

Schwartz, Tony. *The Responsive Chord.* Garden City, N.Y.: Doubleday, 1974.

Seagull, Louis M. "The Youth Vote and Change in American Politics." *Annals of the American Academy of Political and Social Sci.,* 397(September 1971), 88–96.

Sears, David O. and Jonathon L. Freedman. "Selective Exposure to Information: A Critical Review." *Public Opinion Q.,* XXXI, 2(1967): 194–213.

Sears, D. O. and R. E. Whitney. "Political Persuasion," in I. de Sola Pool et al., eds. *The Handbook of Communication.* Chicago: Rand McNally, 1973.

"Secession's Mailbag." *American Heritage,* XIII, 3(April 1962): 66–67.

Sellers, Charles. "The Equilibrium Cycle in Two-Party Politics," *Public Opinion Quarterly,* XXIX(1965): 16–38.

Settel, Irving. *A Pictorial History of Radio.* New York: Grosset & Dunlap, 1967.

Settel, Irving and William Laas. *A Pictorial History of Television.* New York: Grosset & Dunlap, 1969.

Seymour-Ure, Colin. *The Political Impact of Mass Media.* London: Constable; Beverly Hills, Calif.: Sage, 1974.

Shadegg, Stephen. *What Happened to Goldwater?* New York: Holt, Rinehart and Winston, 1965.

Shaffer, Helen B. "Television and the 1956 Campaign." *Edit. Res. Rpts.* (1955): 613–32.

Shannon, Jasper B. *Money and Politics.* New York: Random House, 1959.

Shannon, William V. "The Age of the Bosses." *American Heritage,* XX, 4(June 1969): 26–31.

———. *The Heir Apparent: Robert Kennedy and the Struggle for Power.* New York: Macmillan, 1967.

Sheinkopf, Kenneth G., Charles K. Atkin, and Lawrence Bowen. "How Political Party Workers Respond to Political Advertising." *Journalism Q.,* 50(Summer 1973): 334–39.

Sherrill, Robert. *The Last Kennedy.* New York: The Dial Press, 1976.

Sherrod, Drury R. "Selective Perception of Political Candidates." *Public Opinion Quarterly,* 35(Winter 1971–72): 554–62.

Sherwood, Robert E. *Roosevelt and Hopkins: An Intimate History.* New York: Harper, 1950.

Shogan, Robert. "1948 Election." *American Heritage,* XIX, 4(June 1968): 22–31, 104–11.

Shurick, E. P. J. *The First Quarter-Century of American Broadcasting.* Kansas City: Midland, 1946.

Shyles, Leonard. "Defining 'Images' of Presidential Candidates from Televised Political Spot Advertisements." *Political Behavior,* 6, 1(1984): 53–63.

––––––. "Defining the Issues of a Presidential Election from Televised Political Spot Advertisements." *J. of Broadcasting,* 27, 4(Fall 1983): 333–43.

Siepmann, Charles. *Radio, Television and American Society.* New York: Oxford University Press, 1950.

Silber, Irwin. *Songs America Voted By.* Harrisburg, Pa.: Stackpole Books, 1971.

Simon, Herbert A. and Frederick Stern. "The Effect of Television Upon Voting Behavior in Iowa in the 1952 Presidential Election." *American Polit. Sci. Rev.,* 49(June 1955): 470–77.

Sinclair, Upton. *I, Candidate For Governor, and How I Got Licked.* New York: Farrar & Rinehart, 1935.

Smallwood, Frank. *The Other Candidates: Third Parties in Presidential Elections.* Hanover and London: University Press of New England, 1983.

Smith, Al. *Campaign Addresses.* Washington, D.C.: The Democratic National Committee, 1929.

Smith, Page. *John Adams II: 1784–1829.* Westport, Conn.: Greenwood Press, 1963.

Sobel, Lester A., ed. *Money and Politics.* New York: Facts on File Inc., 1974.

Sorensen, Theodore. *Kennedy.* New York: Harper & Row, 1965.

––––––. *The Kennedy Legacy.* New York: Macmillan, 1969.

Sorensen, Thomas C. *The World War: The Story of American Propaganda.* New York: Harper & Row, 1968.

Spalding, John W. "1928: Radio Becomes a Mass Advertising Medium." *J. of Broadcasting,* 8(Winter 1964): 31–44.

Spero, Robert. *The Duping of the American Voter.* New York: Lippincott and Crowell, 1980.

Stans, Maurice. *The Terrors of Justice.* New York: Everest House, 1978.

Stein, Robert. *Media Power: Who is Shaping Your Picture of the World?* Boston: Houghton Mifflin, 1972.

Stempel, Guido H., III. "Selectivity in Readership of Political News." *Public Opinion Quarterly,* 25(Fall 1961): 400–404.

Stevenson, Adlai. *Major Campaign Speeches of Adlai E. Stevenson.* New York: Random House, 1953.

Stimpson, George. *A Book About American Politics.* New York: Harper and Brothers, 1952.

"The Storytelling Cigar." *American Heritage,* XXX, 1(December 1978): 80–91.

Stouffer, Samuel. *Communism, Conformity and Civil Liberties.* New York: Wiley, 1955.

Stroud, Kandy. *How Jimmy Won.* New York: William Morrow and Co., 1977.

Summers, Harrison B. ed. *A Thirty-Year History of Programs Carried on National Radio Networks in the United States 1926–1956.* Columbus: Ohio State University, 1958.

Sumner, William Graham. *Andrew Jackson as a Public Man.* Boston: Houghton Mifflin Co., 1893.

Sussman, Barry. *The Great Cover-Up.* New York: New American Library, 1974.

Swanson, David L. "Political Information, Influence, and Judgement in the 1972 Presidential Campaign." *Quarterly J. of Speech,* 59(April 1973): 130–42.

Tannenbaum, Percy H., Bradley S. Greenberg, and Fred R. Silverman. "Candidate Images," in Sidney Kraus, ed. *The Great Debates.* Bloomington: Indiana University Press, 1962, 271–88.

Thompson, B. F. "The Wide Awakes of 1860." *Magazine of History With Notes and Queries.* (November 10, 1909): 293–96.

Thompson, Dr. Hunter S. *Fear and Loathing on the Campaign Trail.* New York: Popular Library, 1973.

Thomson, Charles A. H. *Television and Presidential Politics.* Washington, D.C.: The Brookings Institution, 1956.

Time. "The Reselling of the President?" (July 9, 1973): 20–21.

Tompkins, C. David. *Senator Arthur H. Vandenberg: The Evolution of a Modern Republican, 1884–1945.* Ann Arbor: Michigan University Press, 1970.

Topping, Malachi C. and Lawrence W. Lichty. "Political Programs on National Television Networks: 1968." *J. of Broadcasting,* 15(Spring 1971): 161–79.

Trenaman, J. and Denis McQuail. *Television and the Political Image.* London: Methuen and Co., Ltd., 1961.

Truman, Harry S. *Memoirs: Year of Decisions.* Garden City, N.Y.: Doubleday, 1955.

———. *Memoirs: Years of Trial and Hope 1946–1952.* Garden City, N.Y.: Doubleday, 1956.

Truman, Margaret. *Harry S. Truman.* New York: William Morrow and Co., 1973.

Tucker, Duane E. "Broadcasting in the 1956 Oregon Senatorial Campaign." *J. of Broadcasting,* 3(Summer 1959): 225–43.

Tull, Charles J. *Father Coughlin and the New Deal.* Syracuse, N.Y.: Syracuse University Press, 1965.

Turner, Ernest S. *The Shocking History of Advertising.* New York: Dutton, 1953.

Turner, Robert W. *"I'll Never Lie to You": Jimmy Carter in His Own Words.* New York: Ballantine Books, 1976.

U.S. Bureau of the Census. *Historical Statistics of the United States: Colonial Times to 1957.* Washington, D.C.: Government Printing Office, 1960.

———. *Long-Term Economic Growth, 1860–1965.* Washington, D.C.: Government Printing Office, 1966.

University of Michigan. *Television and the Political Candidate.* New York: Cunningham and Walsh, 1959.

Valenti, Jack. *A Very Human President.* New York: W. W. Norton Co., 1975.

Van Doren, Ronald. *Charting the Candidates '72.* New York: Pinnacle Books, 1972.

Vinson, J. Chal. *Thomas Nast, Political Cartoonist.* Athens: University of Georgia Press, 1967.

Wanat, John. "Political Broadcast Advertising and Primary Election Voting." *J. of Broadcasting,* 18(Fall 1974): 413–22.

Ward, John William. *Andrew Jackson: Symbol for an Age.* New York: Oxford University Press, 1953, 1971.

Ward, John William, ed., of Michael Chevalier. *Society, Manners, and Politics in the United States: Letters on North America.* Trans. after T. G. Bradford edition. Garden City, N.Y.: Doubleday, 1961.

Warshaw, P. R. "Application of Selective Attention Theory to Television Advertising Displays." *J. of Applied Psychology,* 63(1978): 366–72.

Washburn, Wilcomb E. "Campaign Banners." *American Heritage,* XXIII, 6(October 1972): 8–13.

———. "The Great Autumnal Madness: Political Symbolism in Mid-Ninteenth-Century America." *Quarterly J. of Speech,* XLIX(December 1963): 417–31.

Watson, Richard A. and Norman C. Thomas. *The Politics of the Presidency.* New York: Wiley, 1983.

Wayne, Stephen J. *The Road to the White House: The Politics of Presidential Elections.* New York: St. Martin's Press, 1984.

Weaver, D. H., D. A. Graber, M. E. McCombs, and C. H. Eyal. *Media Agenda-Setting in a Presidential Election: Issues, Images, and Interest.* New York: Praeger, 1981.

Weinberg, Meyer. *TV in America: The Morality of Hard Cash.* New York: Ballantine, 1962.

Weingast, David E. *We Elect a President.* New York: Julian Messner Inc., 1962.

Weisberg, Herbert F. and Jerrold G. Rusk. "Dimensions of Candidate Evaluation." *American Pol. Sci. Rev.,* 64(1970): 1167–85.

Weisbord, Marvin R. *Campaigning for President.* Washington, D.C.: Public Affairs Press, 1964.

Weisberger, Bernard A. "How to Get Elected." *American Heritage,* XV, 5(August 1964): 62–77.

Whale, John. *Half-Shut Eye: Television and Politics in Britain and America.* New York: St. Martin's Press, 1969.

Whalen, Richard J. *Catch the Falling Flag: A Republican's Challenge to His Party.* Boston: Houghton Mifflin, 1972.

"When Everything Hung By a Thread." *American Heritage,* VIII, 6(October 1957): 40–41.

"Which Way Are the Political Winds Blowing?" *Public Opinion,* 5(August/September 1982): 2–7.

White, F. Clifton. *Suite 3505: The Story of the Draft Goldwater Movement.* New Rochelle, N.Y.: Arlington House, 1967.

White, Theodore H. *America In Search of Itself: The Making of the President 1956–1980.* New York: Warner Books, 1982.

———. *Breach of Faith: The Fall of Richard Nixon.* New York: Dell, 1975.

———. *The Making of the President 1960.* New York: Atheneum, 1961.

———. *The Making of the President 1964.* New York: Atheneum, 1965.

———. *The Making of the President 1968.* New York: Atheneum, 1969.

———. *The Making of the President 1972.* New York: Atheneum, 1973.

White, William S. *The Professional: Lyndon B. Johnson.* New York: Houghton Mifflin, 1964.

Whiteside, Thomas. "Annals of Television: The Man from Iron City." *The New Yorker,* 45(September 27, 1969): 47–92.

Wicker, Tom, Kenneth P. O'Donnell, and Rowland Evans. "Television in the Political Campaign." *Television Quarterly,* 5(Winter 1966): 13–26.

Willis, Edgar E. *Foundations in Broadcasting.* New York: Oxford University Press, 1951.

———. "Radio and Presidential Campaigning." *Central States Speech Journal,* 20(Fall 1969): 187–93.

Wills, Garry. *Nixon Agonistes: The Crisis of the Self-Made Man.* Boston: Houghton Mifflin, 1970.

Wilson, Rufus Rockwell. *Lincoln in Caricature.* Elmira, N.Y.: The Primavera Press, 1945.

Wilson, Woodrow. *Selected Literary and Political Papers and Addresses of Woodrow Wilson.* III. New York: Grosset and Dunlap, 1921.

Winpisinger v. *Watson.* (628 F. 2nd. 133 [D.C. Cir. 1980]; cert. den. 446 U.S. 929, 1980).

Wirthlin, Richard, Vincent Breglio, and Richard Beal. "Campaign Chronicle." *Public Opinion,* 4(February/March 1981): 43–49.

Witcover, Jules. *85 Days: The Last Campaign of Robert F. Kennedy.* New York: Ace, 1969.

———. *Marathon: The Pursuit of the Presidency, 1972–1976.* New York: Viking, 1977.

———. *The Resurrection of Richard Nixon.* New York: G. P. Putnam's, 1970.

Wofford, Harris. *Of Kennedys and Kings.* New York: Farrar, Straus and Giroux, 1980.

Wolfe, Charles H., ed. *Modern Radio Advertising.* New York: Funk & Wagnalls, 1949.

Wood, Stephen. "Eisenhower Answers America: A Critical History." Seminar paper. University of Maryland, 1982.

Woodward, Bob, and Carl Bernstein. *All the President's Men.* New York: Warner Books, 1975.

Wooten, James. *Dasher: The Roots and the Rising of Jimmy Carter.* New York: Summit Books, 1978.

Worsnop, Richard L. "Television and Politics," *Ed. Res. Rep.,* 19, 1(1968): 363–84.

Wright, Charles R. "Evaluating Mass Media Campaigns," *Int. Soc. Sci. Bull.,* 7, 3(1955): 417–30.

Wyckoff, Gene. *The Image Candidates: American Politics in the Age of Television.* New York: Macmillan, 1968.

Zajonc, R. B. "Attitudinal Effects of Mere Exposure." *J. of Personality and Social Psychology Monograph Supplement,* 9(1968): 1–27.

Zeigler, Henry A. *Lyndon B. Johnson: Man and President.* New York: Popular Library, 1963.

Zerbe, Farran. "Bryan Money. Tokens of the Presidential Campaigns of 1896 and 1900—Comparative and Satirical." *The Numismatist,* 39(July 1926): 313–76.

Zimmerman, Fred L. "Contrary to Theory, More than Just a Pretty Ad is Needed to Win in Politics, The Candidates Find." *Wall Street Journal,* 179(May 10, 1972): 34.

Index